More Praise for
THE PRICE OF INEQUALITY
by Joseph E. Stiglitz

"Joseph E. Stiglitz's new book, *The Price of Inequality*, is the single most comprehensive counterargument to both Democratic neoliberalism and Republican laissez-faire theories. While credible economists running the gamut from center right to center left describe our bleak present as the result of seemingly unstoppable developments—globalization and automation, a self-replicating establishment built on 'meritocratic' competition, the debt-driven collapse of 2008—Stiglitz stands apart in his defiant rejection of such notions of inevitability. He seeks to shift the terms of the debate."
—Thomas B. Edsall, *New York Times Book Review*

"Sweeping. . . . Passionate about the need for political reform."
—Jacob Hacker and Paul Pierson, *New York Review of Books*

"[Stiglitz] does liberal thinkers everywhere an immensely important service: He gives them a trenchant, engaging tool for arguing economics from the left in 2012. . . . Stiglitz writes clearly and provocatively. . . . A thoughtful, step-back analysis of what's driving inequality and why it is dangerous."
—Dante Chinni, *Washington Post*

"In *The Price of Inequality*, Joseph E. Stiglitz passionately describes how unrestrained power and rampant greed are writing an epitaph for the American dream. . . . In the process, Stiglitz methodically and lyrically (almost joyously) exposes the myths that provide justification for 'deficit fetishism' and the rule of austerity. . . . *The Price of Inequality* is a powerful plea for the implementation of what Alexis de Tocqueville termed 'self-interest properly understood.' "
—Yvonne Roberts, *Guardian* (UK)

"An impassioned argument backed by rigorous economic analysis."
—*Kirkus Reviews*, starred review

"A definitive examination of inequality's effects not only on the economy, but on democracy and globalization. Here is the account of one of the world's greatest problems." —*Daily Beast*

"Stiglitz's ideas in this book will prompt wide discussion and debate." —Mary Whaley, *Booklist*

"Stiglitz . . . makes a powerful case for the damaging consequences of inequality." —*Christian Century*

"Stiglitz's recent book, *The Price of Inequality*, rips off America's rose-colored glasses and shows us exactly where we stand in the world of industrialized countries on the gap between rich and poor."
—Lynn Stuart Parramore,
Institute for New Economic Thinking Blog

"Stiglitz's cogently argued indictment of American inequality is an important work. Paired with fellow Nobel laureate Paul Krugman's *End This Depression Now!*, they provide an accessible picture of current liberal economic thought. Essential reading for all Americans."
—Lawrence Maxted, *Library Journal*, starred review

"Offering creative solutions and recommendations as well as an expert's analysis of the problem, *The Price of Inequality* is an absolute 'must-read' for any concerned about the precarious state of America, and is worthy of the highest recommendation."
—*Midwest Book Review*

"Stiglitz offers his plan for changing our current fiscal and budgetary policies [to create] a more just and prosperous future."
—The Commonwealth Club of California

"Stiglitz incisively details the policies and practices underpinning the extreme levels of inequality in the United States today. In doing so, he provides a rationalist foothold for progressive politics."
—Boone Shear and Stephen Healy, Truth-out.org

"Stiglitz is a powerful rhetorician, but he doesn't shy away from pragmatism." —Worth.com

THE PRICE OF
INEQUALITY

ALSO BY JOSEPH E. STIGLITZ

*Freefall: America, Free Markets,
and the Sinking of the World Economy*

*The Three Trillion Dollar War:
The True Cost of the Iraq Conflict*
(with Linda J. Bilmes)

Making Globalization Work

The Roaring Nineties

Globalization and Its Discontents

THE PRICE OF INEQUALITY

JOSEPH E. STIGLITZ

W. W. NORTON & COMPANY

NEW YORK · LONDON

For information about permission to reproduce selections from this book,
write to Permissions, W. W. Norton & Company, Inc.,
500 Fifth Avenue, New York, NY 10110

For information about special discounts for bulk purchases, please contact
W. W. Norton Special Sales at specialsales@wwnorton.com or 800-233-4830

Manufacturing by Courier Westford
Production manager: Devon Zahn

The Library of Congress has catalogued the hardcover edition as follows:

Stiglitz, Joseph E.
The price of inequality : how today's divided society
endangers our future / Joseph E. Stiglitz. — 1st ed.
p. cm.
Includes bibliographical references and index.
ISBN 978-0-393-08869-4 (hbk.)
1. Income distribution—Social aspects—United States.
2. Equality—United States. 3. United States—Economic conditions—
21st century. 4. United States—Social conditions—21st century. I. Title.
HC110.I5S867 2012
305.50973—dc23
2012014811

ISBN: 978-0-393-34506-3 (pbk.)

W. W. Norton & Company, Inc.
500 Fifth Avenue, New York, N.Y. 10110
www.wwnorton.com

W. W. Norton & Company Ltd.
Castle House, 75/76 Wells Street, London W1T 3QT

1 2 3 4 5 6 7 8 9 0

To Siobhan and Michael and Edward and Julia,
In the hopes that they will inherit
a world and a country that are less divided

Contents

PREFACE TO THE PAPERBACK EDITION   ix

PREFACE   xxxvii

ACKNOWLEDGMENTS   lix

Chapter One
AMERICA'S 1 PERCENT PROBLEM   1

Chapter Two
RENT SEEKING AND THE MAKING
   OF AN UNEQUAL SOCIETY   35

Chapter Three
MARKETS AND INEQUALITY   65

Chapter Four
WHY IT MATTERS 104

Chapter Five
A DEMOCRACY IN PERIL 148

Chapter Six
1984 IS UPON US 183

Chapter Seven
JUSTICE FOR ALL? HOW INEQUALITY
IS ERODING THE RULE OF LAW 234

Chapter Eight
THE BATTLE OF THE BUDGET 259

Chapter Nine
A MACROECONOMIC POLICY AND A CENTRAL
BANK BY AND FOR THE 1 PERCENT 298

Chapter Ten
THE WAY FORWARD: ANOTHER
WORLD IS POSSIBLE 332

NOTES 365

INDEX 503

PREFACE TO THE
PAPERBACK EDITION

———

I T WAS CLEAR FROM THE RECEPTION OF *THE PRICE*
of Inequality that it had hit a chord. Not just in the United
States but around the world as well, there is mounting concern about the increase in inequality and about the lack of
opportunity, and how these twin trends are changing our
economies, our democratic politics, and our societies. As I
traveled around the United States and through Europe discussing inequality, its causes and consequences and what
could be done about it, many people shared with me their
personal stories of how what was going on was affecting them,
their families, and their friends. Behind these stories, though,
was a raft of new data that also has a bearing on the arguments of the book. In this preface to the paperback edition, I
want to share some of the more telling moments from these
discussions of inequality, provide some of the new data that
reinforce my original conclusions, and examine other changes
to the political and economic landscape. In the United States,

the most important development was the bruising presidential contest of 2012 and the eventual reelection of Barack Obama; in Europe it was the continuation of the euro crisis, with its profound effects on inequality.

Early on in my book tour, in Washington, DC, I realized the magnitude of the student loan crisis. Student after student described the dilemma that they confronted: there were no jobs; the best use of their time—and the best way to enhance their prospects—was to go to graduate school. But unlike the child of a well-to-do parent, they would have to pay for the graduate school themselves, with student loans. They were already frightened by their current indebtedness, knowing the near impossibility of discharging these debts even in the worst of circumstances.[2] They didn't want to take on even more loans, and their sense of disillusionment, of hopelessness, was sobering and sad. Their bitterness increased as they looked around at peers with wealthy parents, who could take unpaid internships to beef up their resumes. The children of ordinary Americans can't afford that. They have to accept whatever temporary job they can get, no matter how dead-end. Data subsequently released would only have confirmed those impressions. While tuition and fees in public colleges and universities increased, on average, by a sixth between 2005 and 2010[3]—understandable given the cutbacks in government budgets[4]—median income continued to shrink.[5] (In some states, like California, matters were even worse: inflation-adjusted tuition increased by 104 percent in public two-year schools, by some 72 percent in public four-year schools, between 2007–08 and 2012–13.)[6] Getting ahead seemed almost impossible.

Perhaps the statistics that most resonated as I met with groups from coast to coast—and the ones that most surprised foreign audiences—were those relating to lack of opportunity in America. Both those in America and those abroad had simply assumed that America was the land of opportunity. A Pew poll showed that the vast majority of Americans—some 87 percent—agree that "our society should do what is necessary to make sure that everyone has an equal opportunity to succeed."[7] But it was obvious that we weren't.

The crisis continues to hurt those in the middle and at the bottom

It has been more than half a decade since the recession began. The jobs deficit—the difference between the actual number of jobs and what employment would be if the economy were functioning normally—keeps growing. And the incomes of ordinary Americans keep shrinking. As the economic slump grinds on—as this book goes to press, more than five years after the beginning of the Great Recession—the combined consequences of persistent inequality, of a deficient safety net, and of growing austerity are increasingly felt.

Those at the top, of course, have continued to be helped by the Federal Reserve. Its low-interest rates were designed to help bolster stock prices. Those prices have now returned to their precrisis level (though, adjusted for inflation, they are still lower). Anyone who had the wherewithal and gumption to stay in the market has fully recuperated. The wealthiest 5 percent of Americans, who own more than two-thirds of all household stock wealth, are back on track.[8] Those at the top continued to garner for themselves an enormous share of the nation's income. As even the typically "free market"–oriented *Economist* observed, "In America the share of national income going to the top .01% (some 16,000 families) has risen from just over 1% in 1980 to almost 5% now—an even bigger slice than the top .01% got in the Gilded Age."[9] Warren Buffett, himself a member of the superrich who has recognized the harm of America's egregious inequality, took to the pages of the *New York Times* in the fall of 2012 to underline the divergence by a different measure: the 400 wealthiest Americans took home an hourly "wage" of $97,000 in 2009 (the last year for which the IRS has provided data)[10]—a rate that has more than doubled since 1992.[11]

Those in the middle and at the bottom, who have much of their wealth in housing, have not fared so well. Recently released data show that in the period of the recession, from 2007 to 2010, median wealth—the wealth of those in the middle—fell by almost 40 percent,[12] back to levels last seen in the early 1990s. All of the wealth accumulation in this country has gone to the top. If the bottom had shared equally in America's increase in wealth, its wealth over the past two decades would have gone up by some 75 percent. Newly released data also show that those at the bottom suffered even worse than those in the middle. Before the crisis, the average wealth of the bottom fourth was a *negative* $2,300. After the crisis, it had fallen sixfold, to a negative $12,800.[13]

Not surprisingly, the persistent economic slump has led to a continuing weakening of wages: real wages have declined, by nearly 1 percent for men and more than 3 percent for women from 2010 to 2011 alone.[14] So have incomes of the typical American. Adjusted for inflation, median household income in 2011 (the most recent year for which we have data) was $50,054, lower that it was in 1996 ($50,661).[15]

The text (chapter 1) describes how households with those of limited education are faring even worse, and have seen marked decreases in their standards of living.[16]

These disturbing trends in income and wealth inequality were outdone by even more disturbing evidence about inequalities in health. As medical care has improved, life expectancy has increased—on average, in the United States, by some two years between 1990 and 2000. But for the poorest group of Americans there has been no progress, and for poor women life expectancy has actually been declining.[17]

Today, women in the United States, on average, have the lowest life expectancy of women in any of the advanced countries.[18] Educational attainment, which is often tied in with income and race, is a large and growing predictor of life span. Non-Hispanic white women with a college degree have a life expectancy that is some ten years greater than the life expectation of black or white women without a high school diploma. Non-Hispanic white women without a high school diploma lost about five years of life expectancy between 1990 and 2008.[19] The three-year decline in life expectancy of white males without a high school diploma over the same period was only slightly less dramatic.[20]

Decreases in income and decline in standards of living are often accompanied by a multitude of social manifestations—malnutrition, drug abuse, and deterioration in family life, all of which take a toll on health and life expectancy. Indeed, these declines in life expectancy are often considered more telling than income numbers themselves. In the years after the fall of the Iron Curtain, incomes in Russia fell, but perhaps a more reliable indicator of how bad things were was provided by data showing a dramatic fall in life expectancy. Not surprisingly, health care experts have drawn parallels between recent declines in the United States and what happened in Russia. Michael Marmot, director of the Institute of Health Equity in London and a leading expert on the relationship between incomes and health, observed that "the five-year decline for white women rivals the catastrophic seven-year drop for Russian men in the years after the collapse of the Soviet Union."[21]

While there is no agreement about the causes of these large changes, one important factor (not adequately reflected in income statistics) is the growing lack of access to health insurance among the groups at the bottom of the population.[22] One of the main objectives of Obamacare (the Affordable Health Care Act) was to remedy this, but the recent Supreme Court decision[23] giving states the right to opt out of Medicaid expansion without losing funding makes it likely that a significant fraction of the population will remain uncovered.

THE INEQUALITY "DEBATE"

As I traveled around the world and as reviews of the book came in over the last year, I was heartened at how little challenge there was to the book's central theses.[24] The magnitude of the inequality and the lack of opportunity was hard to deny. As usual, academics quibble: levels of inequality might look a little better depending on how we value the benefits supplied by Medicare, Medicaid, and employer-provided health insurance.[25] While spending on these has gone up, much of this increase can be attributed to rising medical costs. It's not that the benefits themselves have increased.[26] On the other hand, the numbers would look considerably worse if we took into account the increased economic insecurity. It was equally hard to deny that the United States was no longer the land of opportunity portrayed by Horatio Alger stories of "rags to riches." Nor was there any attempt to deny that much of America's concentration of wealth at the top was a result of rent seeking—including monopoly profits and the excessive compensation of some CEOs and, especially, that of the financial sector. As expected, a few critics (including a former head of the Confederation of British Industry)[27] suggested that I paid less attention to market forces than I should have and, correspondingly, gave too much weight to rent seeking. As I explain in the text, it is essentially impossible to single out any one factor's relative contribution, given how intertwined the various forces shaping inequality are; there can be honest differences of opinion. But as I emphasize in chapter 2, markets don't exist in a vacuum. They are shaped by our politics, often in ways that benefit those at the top. Moreover, while we may be able to do only a little to change the direction of market forces, we can circumscribe rent seeking. Or at least we could, if we managed to get our politics right.

Most heartening to me was the fact that even more conservative publications joined the discussion. In an excellent special report, the *Economist* highlighted the extent of the increase in inequality and the reduction in opportunity, and agreed with most of our diagnosis and many of our prescriptions.[28] Noting, as I had, that much of America's inequality, especially at the top, was due to rent seeking,[29] the *Economist* concluded, in particular, that "inequality has reached a stage where it can be inefficient and bad for growth."[30] Sharing our concern about the lack of opportunity in the United States, the report cites results obtained by Sean Reardon of Stanford[31] that the "gap in test scores between rich and poor American children is roughly 30–40% wider than it was 25 years ago."[32] Not surprisingly, the *Economist*'s recommendations began with an "attack on monopolies and vested interests" and then moved on to ways of improving economic mobility, where the "target should be pre-school education, as well as more retraining for the jobless."[33] It even recognized the need for more progressive taxation, including "narrowing the gap between tax rates on wages and capital income; and relying more on efficient taxes that are paid disproportionately by the rich, such as some property taxes."

The debate was more intense, though, around an argument (made explicitly in a book published shortly after mine)[34] that was based on another variant of trickle-down economics. In this new version of an old myth, the rich are the job creators; give more money to the rich, and there will be more jobs. The irony was that the author of this book, like the presidential candidate whom he supported, was from a private-equity firm with a well-established business model that involved taking over companies, piling on debt, "restructuring" by firing large number of workers, and selling out one's stake (it was hoped) before the firm subsequently went bankrupt. There were, of course, real innovators in the economy, and they did create jobs; but even the firm that had become iconic of America's success, Apple, whose market value in 2012 was larger than that of General Motors at its peak, had only 47,000 employees in the United States.[35] In a world of globalization, creating market value had become entirely separated from creating employment. There was no reason to believe that giving more money to America's wealthy would lead to more investment in the United States: money goes to where returns are highest, and with America's downturn, returns often look higher for investments in the emerging markets. And even when there is investment in the United States, it's not necessarily investment related to job creation: much of the investment is in machines designed to replace labor, to destroy jobs.

Remarkably, in the heyday of unbridled capitalism, the early years of this century, a period in which inequality at the top increased at historic rates, there was *no* private-sector job creation. And if we exclude construction—based on a real estate bubble—the record looks even worse.

Not only doesn't the money given to the top not necessarily go into "job creation" and innovation; some of it goes into distorting our politics, especially in this new era of unbridled campaign contributions ushered in by *Citizens United*. What we have seen quite clearly is that a common use of wealth is to gain advantage in rent seeking, perpetuating inequalities through the political process. Later in this preface I'll describe some of the telling examples of rent seeking that have come to light just in the past year.

The same old "myth" that we should celebrate the wealth of those at the top because we all benefit from it has been used to justify the maintenance of low taxes on capital gains. But most capital gains accrue not from job creation but from one form of speculation or another. Some of this speculation is destabilizing, and played a role in the economic crisis that has cost so many jobs.

The presidential campaign

In the campaign, the word "inequality" wasn't heard often—indeed, given the attention focused on the 1 percent by the Occupy Wall Street movement, the absence of attention to the issue might seem surprising, until one remembers that much of the more than $2 billion spent on the campaign was raised (by both parties) from persons in the 1 percent—and one wouldn't want to offend them. But the wound of America's growing inequality festered not far beneath the surface. When the Democrats talked about protecting the middle class, they were really saying that the American economy has not been delivering for most Americans, that only those at the top have benefited from the increase in GDP. Any economic agenda focusing on the middle class is, by its nature, an agenda centered on shared prosperity; and that means halting and reversing the trend of growing inequality.

Perhaps the moment when inequality moved closest to being front and center in the campaign was when Mitt Romney suggested that 47 percent of Americans were paying no income tax, living off of government handouts.[36] The statement, made at a $50,000-a-plate fund-raiser in lavish settings in Boca Raton, Florida, stirred up its own hurricane. The irony, of course, was that people like Romney are the true freeloaders: the taxes that he has said he is paying (as a percentage of his *reported* income) are (at 14 percent in 2011) far less than those of people with substantially less income.

What Romney said reflects views held by many Americans, and not just those in the 1 percent. Many of those who are working hard feel that they are being taken advantage of, that their taxes are being used either to bail out rich bankers or to provide welfare payments for people who refuse to work. They see themselves as "victims," and this perception has played a role in the rise of the Tea Party, which seeks to downsize government. Nothing perhaps gave more impetus to this movement than the huge gifts to the banks and the bankers; government stepped in to help those who had caused the crisis, and did little to help those who suffered. The Tea Partyers and others sympathetic to them were right to be outraged, but their diagnosis was wrong: without government, they would have suffered even more; without government, the banks would have abused them even more. The government didn't do what it should have done to prevent the crisis and banks' exploitive behavior—or to resuscitate the economy or to help those that were suffering from the economic downturn—but, given the imbalances in American politics, it is perhaps more remarkable what *was* done.

In his remarks, Romney articulated a set of widespread misunderstandings. First, even those who don't pay income taxes pay a host of other taxes, including payroll, sales, excise, and property taxes.[37] Second, many of those receiving "benefits" paid for them—through Social Security and Medicare contributions funded out of payroll taxes. They're not free riders. We should remember why those programs were started: before the arrival of Medicare and Social Security, the private sector left most elderly bereft of support, the market for annuities essentially didn't exist, and the elderly couldn't get health insurance. Even today, the private sector doesn't provide the kind of security that Social Security provides—including protection against market volatility and inflation. And the transactions costs of the Social Security Administration are markedly lower than those in the private sector. In addition, many of the people who receive government benefits without paying for them are our young, obviously unable to pay, say, for their own education. But spending on them is an investment in the country's future.

An efficient system of social protection is an important part of any modern society. The market failed to provide adequate insurance, for instance, for unemployment or disability. So the government stepped in. But people receiving those benefits typically paid for them, either directly or indirectly, through contributions they or their employer made on their behalf to these insurance funds. Aside from a person's right to draw benefits from programs they helped fund, social protection can make for a more productive society. Individuals can take on more high-return, high-risk activities if they know there is a safety net that will protect them if things don't work out. It's one of the reasons that some economies with better social protection have been growing much more rapidly than that of the United States, even during the recent recession.

Many of the persons at the bottom—who have become so dependent on government benefits—are there partly because government has failed in one way or the other. It has failed to provide them with skills that would make them productive, so they could earn an adequate living. It has failed to stop banks from taking advantage of them through predatory lending and abusive credit card practices. It has failed to stop for-profit schools from taking advantage of their aspirations to move up in the world through education. And it has failed to manage the overall economy in a way that sustains full employment.

Finally, those at the top have tried to sell the idea that discussions about inequality are just about "redistribution," taking from some to give to others—or, as Romney would put it, taking from the job creators to give to the freeloaders. But it's not. Part of America's problem today is that too many of those at the top don't want to contribute their fair share to the "public goods" that are necessary if our society, and our economy, are going to function. While there may be some disagreement about what "fair" means, when those at the top pay a smaller percentage of their income than those with much less income, it is clearly unfair.[38]

While a few on the right tried to contest the now widely accepted view that inequality is bad for the economy, I received, on the other hand, criticisms that the book overemphasized an *economic* perspective on inequality (perhaps not surprising, given my background). I had suggested not only that the economy as a whole would be better-off if there were less inequality but also that even those in the 1 percent would be better-off. It was in their "enlightened" self-interest[39] that there be less inequality. But, especially during the discussion following a talk I gave at the Union Theological Seminary, it was forcefully argued to me that this was too narrow a perspective. After I spoke, Cornel West, who was in attendance, rose to say the following:

The great movements in America—abolitionism, civil rights movement, feminist movement, anti-homophobic movement—they didn't argue we need self-interest properly understood. If that was the slogan, black folks would still be in Jim Crow. Something else was going on. Strong moral forces, strong spiritual forces, linked to stories—about a nation, in terms of national identity, in terms of what it means to be human, our connection to other countries. . . . There's not going to be a matter of even "self-interest properly understood" if it's not informed by very rich stories of the art of living, loving, serving others.

What West was hinting at, I think, is that the real solution to the inequality crisis lies in focusing on *community* rather than simply on self-interest—both community as a means to prosperity and as a goal in its own right. And I agree. Indeed, we are a community, and all communities help those who are less fortunate among them. If our economic system leads to so many people without jobs, or with jobs that do not pay a livable wage, dependent on the government for food, it means that our economic system has not worked in the way it should, and then government has to step in.

We do have a divided society. But the division is not, as Romney has suggested, between freeloaders and the rest. Rather, it is between those (including many members of the 1 percent) who see America as a community and recognize that the only way to achieve sustained prosperity is to have shared prosperity, and those who don't; between those who have some empathy for those who are less fortunate than themselves, and those who don't.

Even if it were true that 47 percent of the population are freeloaders, it would mean that something is wrong with our society. Every society will have some rotten apples, but most individuals intrinsically want to make a contribution to their communities, to have a meaningful job; they want "decent work."[40] But if a country doesn't give a large proportion of the population the education that they need to earn a decent living, if employers don't pay workers a decent wage, if a society provides so little opportunity that many people become alienated and demotivated, then that society and its economy won't work well.

It shouldn't, of course, come as a big surprise that some of the wealthiest Americans are promoting an economic fantasy in which their further enrichment benefits everyone. It is, perhaps, a surprise that they've done such a good job of selling these fantasies to so many Americans.

The presidential campaign reinforced the concerns I had raised about the nexus between economic inequality and political inequality, as the consequences of recent Court decisions giving increased scope for money in politics became manifest, with the unbridled spending of the super PACs—80 percent of their money coming from two hundred very rich donors.[41] The campaign also saw concerted efforts at disenfranchisement in a large number of states.[42] But the outcome of the election reinforced the glimmer of hope that I expressed at the end of the book: there was a backlash, as those who would be disenfranchised rose up and voted in unprecedented numbers for President Obama and the Democrats. The failure of money to buy the election provided further hope that we might break the money-inequality political/economic nexus.

GLOBAL PERSPECTIVES

In the short time since the book first came out in the United States, it has been published in the United Kingdom and translated into French, German, Spanish, Japanese, and Greek. Almost everywhere, there is a concern about growing inequality, and especially at the top. Almost everywhere, the economic downturn has made matters worse, particularly in the middle and at the bottom. But in each country the debates centered on somewhat different issues. The UK, for instance, had the dubious distinction of being the best "emulator" of the American model. Thirty years ago, inequality in Britain was just average for the advanced industrial countries. But now it is second only to the United States. Finance played perhaps an even more important role in British inequality than it did in the United States.

Indeed, the global scandals that have surrounded the financial markets since the beginning of the current century only continue to grow, and in some ways London is at their center. Libor, the London Interbank Offered Rate, is a number that plays a pivotal role in a multitude of contracts—some $300 to $350 trillion of derivatives, and hundreds of billions of dollars of mortgages. By linking interest payments to the Libor rate, one allowed automatic adjustments to occur as interest rates rose and fell. Such automatic adjustments, it was believed, led to more-efficient financial markets. And that might have been the case if Libor were, as people thought, an objective, real number that reflected the interest rates at which banks actually lent to each other. But it wasn't. That should have been obvious when, in 2007, banks stopped lending to each other. They all knew that they were in trouble; they knew that they couldn't really ascertain their own financial state, let alone the financial state of any other bank. But if no banks were lending, what could the "London Interbank Lending Rate" possibly mean? It was, to put it bluntly, a fiction—a made-up number—on which much of Western financial markets rested.

As investigators looked more closely into Libor, they realized that it had been phony for long before the market officially disappeared. The banks had been manipulating the number—sometimes to garner more profits from unsuspecting parties, sometimes to convince the market that they were sounder than they really were, so sound that they could borrow from others at very low interest rates. More remarkable still is the fact that even after the scandal became public, Libor continues to be used and to be manipulated. Even as the "market" shows that a bank's risk of bankruptcy has soared, a bank will claim that it can continue to borrow from others at an essentially unchanged interest rate, a claim that is almost surely fiction.

If London has become the capital of the global financial rent seekers, the focus in Spain is at the other end. During the decade before the crisis, Spain was one of the countries to buck global trends; wage inequality actually fell. But Spain has been especially hard hit by the global slump. In fact, with overall unemployment reaching 25 percent and youth unemployment exceeding 50 percent, Spain can now be safely said to be in depression.

Spain illustrates two themes. The first is the nexus between inequality and recession/depression. As Spain's downturn has persisted, unemployment has increased. But as unemployment increases, wages (adjusted for inflation) decrease. This weakens demand—the vicious circle we describe in chapter 3.

But one more ingredient is added to this toxic mixture. Inevitably, as GDP decreases (as this book went to press, Spanish GDP was still below the level of 2007) and unemployment increases, tax revenues fall, and expenditures on social programs rise. The deficit increases. Ordinarily, countries could lower their exchange rate and interest rates to make their economy more competitive; the resulting increase in exports would help boost the economy. Spain gave up these important tools when it joined the eurozone, but remarkably the eurozone didn't offer new policy instruments to take the place of these traditional adjustment mechanisms.

Though the problems in the eurozone first became apparent in Greece, other countries such as Ireland, Portugal, Spain, Cyprus, and Italy soon joined the list of countries facing difficulties. The length of the list should have made it clear that it was not a matter of one country's going "astray." There was something systemically wrong. But the diagnosis of Europe's leaders was fundamentally flawed, the prescriptions that followed were misguided, and in the end they actually made matters worse. All of this illustrates the central theme of chapters 3 and 9, that macroeconomic policies—including monetary policies—have to too large an extent been circumscribed by ideology, and it's the market fundamentalist ideology that serves the interests of the top, often at the expense of the rest of society.

The diagnosis of the European leaders focused on fiscal profligacy—ignoring the fact that two of the crisis countries, Spain and Ireland, had been running surpluses before the crisis. The downturn caused the deficits, not the other way around. But the prescription that followed from the diagnosis of fiscal profligacy was austerity—never mind that there have been almost no instances of countries that have recovered from a crisis through austerity. Unless export growth can compensate for contracting government expenditures, austerity will lead to higher unemployment. But the crisis countries couldn't adjust their exchange rate, and amid a global slowdown, expansion of exports would, in any case, have been difficult. The result was as predicted: the countries that followed austerity—whether voluntarily, as in the case of UK, or involuntarily, as in the case of most of the other eurozone countries—went into deeper downturns, and as the downturns deepened, the hoped-for improvements in the fiscal position were disappointing.

The bankers, and the political leaders who seemed to have served them so well, had figured out how to design a financial system that could engage in excessive risk taking, market manipulation, and predatory practices. But they had far fewer insights into how to make a financial system that actually did what a financial system is supposed to. "Free market" principles had led to a Europe that made it easy for capital to move across borders. It was argued that doing so would improve economic performance; but the bankers and the political leaders hadn't realized that details matter. Banks have always received implicit subsidies from governments—made very evident in the crisis of 2008, when government after government engaged in massive bailouts. Confidence in a country's banking system depends on confidence in the ability and willingness of governments to bail out the country's banks. But when a country is weakened by an economic downturn, its ability to come to the rescue of its banks is weakened, just at the time when assistance is most needed. Confidence in the country's banking system inevitably diminishes; but Europe's framework then made it easy for money to leave the country—exacerbating the downturn, further eroding confidence in the banking system, and accelerating the decline of the economy. Spain provides a perfect illustration: in the aftermath of the bursting of its property bubble and the adoption of austerity programs, it was just a matter of time before confidence in the country's banking system would start to erode. The problems increased as talk of Spain's leaving the euro increased. To many, good risk management meant switching money out of Spanish banks into German institutions; one could feel more confident about getting one's money back—and getting it back in euros, not some new, devalued currency. The puzzle was more how long it took money to start leaving Spain, not that money left. But as money left the banking system, the banks grew weaker, they lent less, the credit squeeze got tighter, and the combined effects of austerity and the credit squeeze amplified the downturn, another vicious circle. The founders of the euro had created a dynamically unstable system, but their successors failed to grasp the gravity of the situation. They talked about the need for a common banking system, but they focused on a common regulatory framework, not, say, a common deposit insurance system that would have stemmed the outflow of money.

As this book goes to press, turmoil in the eurozone continues—more than three years after the problems came to the fore. Europe has had dozens of meetings and a multitude of initiatives, some dramatic, some small. One or two have managed to calm markets and bring down interest rates for a few weeks; some have worked for even a shorter period of time. This book is not about what Europe could or should have done to address crises in Spain and elsewhere. It is about inequality, and about how flawed economic policies—based on flawed economic theories and ideology—have managed to exacerbate inequality on both sides of the Atlantic. Earlier we saw how this played out in the United States. But things are even worse in many parts of Europe, where austerity has led not only to skyrocketing unemployment and declining wages[43] but also to massive cutbacks in public services at a time when the services are needed most. In Greece, for instance, there is a shortage of life-saving medicines, a condition that one encounters only in the poorest of developing countries. Those who can get work take any job offered, even if it is not what they trained for and aspired to. Many who can't get a job, especially among the young, are emigrating; families are being torn apart. Countries are being hollowed out of their most talented people.

Many of the 1 percent are unscathed—at least for now. And Europe's political framework is providing a challenge, made apparent in late 2012 as France discussed raising taxes on its highest-income individuals. Bernard Arnault, the country's richest man, decided to seek Belgian citizenship in what was widely interpreted as an attempt to reduce his tax obligation. With movements within Europe so easy, and with no tax harmonization, it is relatively easy for rich individuals to relocate to low-tax jurisdictions. Thus, free mobility of labor without tax harmonization is an invitation to a race to the bottom— for jurisdictions to compete to attract high-income individuals and profitable corporations by offering them lower taxes. Tax competition thus weakens the ability to engage in progressive tax policies, and limits the ability to "correct" an increasingly unequal market distribution.

While market forces are at play in all countries, how they play out differs markedly. Japan provides an instance of a country that managed to grow rapidly for a long time with a high degree of equality. Since its 1989 bubble broke, its growth has been very slow (the Japanese "malaise"), but the country has nonetheless managed to avoid the high levels of unemployment and to limit the increases in inequality that have marked other advanced countries.

While other advanced countries can claim some satisfaction in performing better than the United States—at least in this dimension—there is a risk of smugness. Success at one moment of time does not guarantee success at later dates. While inequality in Japan is still markedly less than that in the United States, and Europe's inequality is somewhat smaller than that of the United States, it has been increasing in both Japan and most of the European countries—just as it has been in the United States. Could these countries wind up with divided societies, the kinds of divisions that marked them in the years before World War II? This book thus provides an important set of warnings and lessons even for less unequal countries like Japan: it should not take for granted its past successes in creating a more equal and fair society and economy. It should worry about increasing inequality and its social, political, and economic consequences.

Even more than the United States, Japan and many of the European countries face large debts and aging societies. They may be tempted to cut back investments in the common good or undermine the existing systems of social protections. But such policies would put at risk basic values and future economic prospects.

Policies are available that would simultaneously increase growth and equality—creating a shared prosperity. For Japan and Europe, as for the United States, the question is more one of politics than of economics. Will they be able to curb rent seekers and their pursuit of their own narrow interests, which inevitably harms the economy as a whole? Will they be able to construct a social contract for the twenty-first century, ensuring that the benefits of such growth as occurs will be fairly shared?

The answers to these questions are crucial to the future of Japan and Europe.

The challenges facing the developing countries are, if any-thing, even greater. Historically, early stages of growth are often marked by large increases in inequality, as some parts of the country grow faster than others, and as some individuals are better equipped to cope with modernization than others.[44] This growth of inequality is certainly apparent in China, but it is far from inevitable: Brazil has seen a reduction of inequal-ity, as a result of investments in education and programs to protect the poor, especially poor children.

In these and other developing countries, changes in inequality are related to international rules of the game that are beyond the control of individual countries. And here, too, it is politics, not just economics, that matters; it is the inter-national rules that govern globalization. When those rules allow rich countries to subsidize their rich farmers, global agricultural prices are depressed, and many of the poorest in the poor countries, those working in agriculture, suffer. When countries in the advanced industrial countries fail to regulate their banks adequately and to manage their mac-roeconomies well, the developing countries and emerging markets often suffer from the collateral damage. And it is typically the poorest in these countries who suffer the most. As this book goes to press, it appears that this is once again happening, with the global slowdown, which began with America's 2008 financial crisis, now being worsened by the euro crisis.

SOME CONCLUDING REFLECTIONS

When did we go astray?

One of the questions I have been repeatedly asked is, when did we go astray? If I had to locate a time when we started down the path toward widening inequality, when would that moment be?

There's no easy answer to such a question, but clearly the election of President Ronald Reagan represented a turning point in the United States. Among the precipitating events were the beginning of the deregulation of the financial sector and the reduction in the progressivity of the tax system. Deregulation led to the excessive financialization of the economy—to the point that before the 2008 crisis 40 percent of all corporate profits went to the financial sector. The path of deregulation upon which Reagan set the country was, unfortunately, followed by his successors. So was the policy of lowering taxes at the top. First the top rate was lowered from 70 percent to 28 percent (under Reagan), and then (after Bill Clinton had raised the top rate to 39.6 percent in 1993) they were lowered under George W. Bush to 35 percent. But then the taxes on forms of income received disproportionately by the rich (capital gains, more than half of which are earned by the top 0.1 percent) were lowered further, under Clinton to 20 percent in 1997 and then under Bush to 15 percent.[45] Interest on municipal bonds, another favorite of the rich, is not even taxed. The result is that the top 400 income earners in the United States paid an average tax rate of just 19.9 percent in 2009.[46] Overall, the richest 1 percent of Americans pay effective income tax rates in the low twenties, lower than those of Americans with more moderate incomes.

Reagan's breaking of the air controllers' strike in 1981 is often cited as a critical juncture in the weakening of unions, one of the factors explaining why workers have done so badly in recent decades. But there are other factors as well. Reagan promoted trade liberalization, but even if he and his successors hadn't explicitly pushed the opening up of markets, lower transportation and communications costs would have led to more competition from abroad. Some of the growth in inequality can be attributed to globalization and the replacement of semiskilled jobs with new technologies and outsourced labor.

What's different about America, however, is the remarkable growth in incomes of the very top—the 1 percent and top 0.1 percent—and the greater poverty at the bottom. This trend is far greater in America than in most of Europe and comes out of the distinctively American policies, ranging from tax systems that are less progressive, safety nets and social protections systems that are weaker, an education system where a child's educational, economic, and social attainments are more linked to that of his parents than in other countries, to a smaller role for unions and a larger role for banks, especially after Reagan's deregulatory fervor.

Throughout its history, America has struggled with inequality. But with the tax policies and regulations that existed in the post–World War II war period—and the heavy investments in education, like the GI Bill—matters were improving. The tax cuts at the top and deregulation that began in the Reagan years reversed that trend.

There is, as a participant in one of my seminars pointed out, a two-way relationship between before-tax and after-tax inequality. The fact that the United States has the least progressive tax system and the most inequality in "market" incomes may not be an accident. It shows up systemically in the data: on average, countries with less progressive taxation have more inequality. This could be partly because societies with more economic inequality tend to have more political inequality, especially when it reaches the outsize levels found in the United States and a few other countries. And with a political system that allows the rich to exercise so much influence, it's perhaps no surprise that taxes on the rich are as low as they are. But there is another explanation: in chapter 2, I explain how much of the inequality, especially at the top, is related to rent seeking. Rent seeking is, on average, destructive, because the rent seekers gain for themselves less than they take away from others, so evident in the destruction wrought by the rent seekers in the financial sector. The more those gains are taxed, the fewer the resources that get devoted to rent seeking, and the more the efforts that get devoted to activities that may not pay as well, but that increase the size of the nation's income and are satisfying in their own right.

Is there hope?

I want to end with a discussion of a question I raised briefly in the last chapter of this book, but which has come up again and again: Is there hope? Americans are an optimistic people and want to believe that there is a way out. As a two-handed economist, I have to admit there are a few rays of hope, although the reasons for despair are obvious: the low levels of inequality of opportunity suggest that inequality in the future may be even worse than it is today. That there are economic policies that could bring down the high levels of inequality is clear: but the nexus between economic and political inequality raises the question—what are the prospects that these policies will be adopted?

On the other hand, I describe in the text other countries that have even managed to reduce inequality. It is not inevitable either that it remain so large, or that it continue to grow. One of the main messages of this book is that our economy, our democracy, and our society would all benefit from reducing inequality and increasing equality of opportunity. Some countries seem to have grasped this. The question is, will America?

Two periods in America's history were marked by high levels of income and wealth disparities: the Gilded Age of the late nineteenth century and the boom times of the Roaring Twenties. Both were marked by high levels of inequality and corruption, including in the political process. In fact, until the middle part of the past decade, income inequality had never reached the levels of the 1920s. Of course, some of those who amassed their fortunes in both periods made great contributions to our society—the robber barons in building the railroads that transformed the country. But both periods were also marked by speculation, instability, and excesses. Although some were doing very well, it was not a shared prosperity.

In both of these instances, the country pulled back from the brink. Our democratic processes worked. The Gilded Age was followed by the Progressive Era, which curbed monopoly power. The Roaring Twenties was followed by the important social and economic legislation of the New Deal, which strengthened the rights of workers, provided greater social protection for all Americans, and introduced Social Security, which almost completely eliminated poverty among the elderly.

The question is, will the political inequalities of the twenty-first century allow what happened in those earlier instances to happen *now*? The voters' rejection of Romney gives a glimmer of hope: with the exception of Franklin Delano Roosevelt's reelection in 1936, no incumbent has been reelected with a level of unemployment anywhere near that prevailing in November 2012. As I suggested earlier, the stance of Romney and many Republicans on inequality, and the policies that would affect it, played an important role in this outcome. But fully addressing a problem of the magnitude, depth, and duration of inequality in the United States will take comprehensive actions, of a kind that will require bipartisan support. Traditionally, persons in both parties have understood that a nation divided cannot stand—and the divisions today are greater than they have been in generations, threatening basic values, including our conception of ourselves as a land of opportunity.

Will we once again pull back from the brink? This book is written in the hope that we can and that we will—if only we grasp what has been happening to our economy and our society.

PREFACE

—

T HERE ARE MOMENTS IN HISTORY WHEN PEOPLE all over the world seem to rise up, to say that *something is wrong*, to ask for change. This is what happened in the tumultuous years 1848 and 1968. Each of these years of upheaval marked the beginning of a new era. The year 2011 may prove to be another such moment.

A youth uprising that began in Tunisia, a little country on the coast of North Africa, spread to nearby Egypt, then to other countries of the Middle East. In some cases, the spark of protest seemed at least temporarily doused. In others, though, small protests precipitated cataclysmic societal change, taking down long-established dictators such as Egypt's Hosni Mubarak and Libya's Muammar Qaddafi. Soon the people of Spain and Greece, the United Kingdom, and the United States, and other countries around the world, had their own reasons to be in the streets.

Throughout 2011, I gladly accepted invitations to Egypt, Spain, and Tunisia and met with protesters in Madrid's Buen

Retiro Park, at Zuccotti Park in New York, and in Cairo, where I spoke with young men and women who had been at Tahrir Square.

As we talked, it was clear to me that while specific grievances varied from country to country and, in particular, that the political grievances in the Middle East were very different from those in the West, there were some shared themes. There was a common understanding that in many ways the economic and political system had failed and that both were fundamentally unfair.

The protesters were right that something was wrong. The gap between what our economic and political systems are supposed to do—what we were told they did do—and what they actually do became too large to be ignored. Governments around the world were not addressing key economic problems, including that of persistent unemployment; and as universal values of fairness became sacrificed to the greed of a few, in spite of rhetoric to the contrary, the feeling of unfairness became a feeling of betrayal.

That the young would rise up against the dictatorships of Tunisia and Egypt was understandable. The youth were tired of aging, sclerotic leaders who protected their own interests at the expense of the rest of society. They had no opportunities to call for change through democratic processes. But electoral politics had also failed in Western democracies. U.S. president Barack Obama had promised "change you can believe in," but he subsequently delivered economic policies that, to many Americans, seemed like more of the same.

And yet in the United States and elsewhere, there were signs of hope in these youthful protesters, joined by their parents, grandparents, and teachers. They were not revolutionaries or anarchists. They were not trying to overthrow the system. They still believed that the electoral process *might* work, if only governments remembered that they are accountable to the people. The protesters took to the streets in order to push the system to change.

The name chosen by the young Spanish protesters in their movement that began on May 15 was "los indignados," the indignant or outraged. They were outraged that so many would suffer so much—exemplified by a youth unemployment rate in excess of 40 percent since the beginning of the crisis in 2008—as a result of the misdeeds of those in the financial sector. In the United States the "Occupy Wall Street" movement echoed the same refrain. The unfairness of a situation in which so many lost their homes and their jobs while the bankers enjoyed large bonuses was grating.

But the U.S. protests soon went beyond a focus on Wall Street to the broader inequities in American society. Their slogan became "the 99 percent." The protesters who took this slogan echoed the title of an article I wrote for the magazine *Vanity Fair*, "Of the 1%, for the 1%, by the 1%,"[1] which described the enormous increase in inequality in the United States and a political system that seemed to give disproportionate voice to those at the top.[2]

Three themes resonated around the world: that markets weren't working the way they were supposed to, for they were obviously neither efficient nor stable;[3] that the political system hadn't corrected the market failures; and that the economic and political systems are fundamentally unfair. While this book focuses on the excessive inequality that marks the United States and some other advanced industrial countries today, it explains how the three themes are intimately interlinked: the inequality is cause and consequence of the failure of the political system, and it contributes to the instability of our economic system, which in turn contributes to increased inequality—a vicious downward spiral into which we have descended, and from which we can emerge only through concerted policies that I describe below.

Before centering our attention on inequality, I want to set the scene, by describing the broader failures of our economic system.

The failure of markets

Markets have clearly not been working in the way that their boosters claim. Markets are supposed to be stable, but the global financial crisis showed that they could be very unstable, with devastating consequences. The bankers had taken bets that, without government assistance, would have brought them and the entire economy down. But a closer look at the *system* showed that this was not an accident; the bankers had incentives to behave this way.

The virtue of the market is supposed to be its efficiency. But the market obviously is *not* efficient. The most basic law of economics—necessary if the economy is to be efficient—is that demand equals supply. But we have a world in which there are huge unmet needs—investments to bring the poor out of poverty, to promote development in less developed countries in Africa and other continents around the world, to retrofit the global economy to face the challenges of global warming. At the same time, we have vast underutilized resources—workers and machines that are idle or are not producing up to their potential. Unemployment—the inability of the market to generate jobs for so many citizens—is the worst failure of the market, the greatest source of inefficiency, and a major cause of inequality.

As of March 2012, some 24 million Americans who would have liked a full-time job couldn't get one.[4]

In the United States, we are throwing millions out of their homes. We have empty homes and homeless people.

But even before the crisis, the American economy had not been delivering what had been promised: although there was growth in GDP, *most citizens were seeing their standards of living erode*. As chapter 1 shows, for most American families, even before the onset of recession, incomes adjusted for inflation were lower than they had been a decade earlier. America had created a marvelous economic machine, but evidently one that worked only for those at the top.

So much at stake

This book is about why our economic system is failing for most Americans, why inequality is growing to the extent it is, and what the consequences are. The underlying thesis is that we are paying a high price for our inequality—an economic system that is less stable and less efficient, with less growth, and a democracy that has been put into peril. But even more is at stake: as our economic system is seen to fail for most citizens, and as our political system seems to be captured by moneyed interests, confidence in our democracy and in our market economy will erode along with our global influence. As the reality sinks in that we are no longer a country of opportunity and that even our long-vaunted rule of law and system of justice have been compromised, even our sense of national identity may be put into jeopardy.

In some countries the Occupy Wall Street movement has become closely allied with the antiglobalization movement.

They do have some things in common: a belief not only that something is wrong but also that change is possible. The problem, however, is not that globalization is bad or wrong but that governments are managing it so poorly—largely for the benefit of special interests. The interconnectedness of peoples, countries, and economies around the globe is a development that can be used as effectively to promote prosperity as to spread greed and misery. The same is true for the market economy: the power of markets is enormous, but they have no inherent moral character. We have to decide how to manage them. At their best, markets have played a central role in the stunning increases in productivity and standards of living in the past two hundred years—increases that far exceeded those of the previous two millennia. But government has also played a major role in these advances, a fact that free-market advocates typically fail to acknowledge. On the other hand, markets can also concentrate wealth, pass environmental costs on to society, and abuse workers and consumers. For all these reasons, it is plain that markets must be tamed and tempered to make sure they work to the benefit of most citizens. And that has to be done repeatedly, to ensure that they continue to do so. That happened in the United States in the Progressive Era, when competition laws were passed for the first time. It happened in the New Deal, when Social Security, employment, and minimum-wage laws were passed. The message of Occupy Wall Street—and of so many other protesters around the world—is that markets once again must be tamed and tempered. The consequences of not doing so are serious: within a meaningful democracy, where the voices of ordinary citizens are heard, we cannot maintain an open and globalized market system, at least not in the form that we know it, if that system year after year makes those citizens worse-off.

One or the other will have to give—either our politics or our economics.

Inequality and unfairness

Markets, by themselves, even when they are stable, often lead to high levels of inequality, outcomes that are widely viewed as unfair. Recent research in economics and psychology (described in chapter 6) has shown the importance that individuals attach to fairness. More than anything else, a sense that the economic and political systems were unfair is what motivates the protests around the world. In Tunisia and Egypt and other parts of the Middle East, it wasn't merely that jobs were hard to come by but that those jobs that were available went to those with connections.

In the United States and Europe, things seemed more fair, but only superficially so. Those who graduated from the best schools with the best grades had a better chance at the good jobs. But the system was stacked because wealthy parents sent their children to the best kindergartens, grade schools, and high schools, and those students had a far better chance of getting into the elite universities.

Americans grasped that the Occupy Wall Street protesters were speaking to *their* values, which was why, while the numbers protesting may have been relatively small, two-thirds of Americans said that they supported the protesters. If there was any doubt of this support, the ability of the protesters to gather 300,000 signatures to keep their protests alive, almost overnight, when Mayor Michael Bloomberg of New York first suggested that he would shut down the camp at Zuccotti Park, near Wall Street, showed otherwise.[5] And support came not just among the poor and the disaffected. While the police may have been excessively rough with protesters in Oakland—and the thirty thousand who joined the protests the day after the downtown encampment was violently disbanded seemed to think so—it was noteworthy that some of the police themselves expressed support for the protesters.

The financial crisis unleashed a new realization that our economic system was not only inefficient and unstable but also fundamentally unfair. Indeed, in the aftermath of the crisis (and the response of the Bush and the Obama administrations), almost half thought so, according to a poll at the time.[6] It was rightly perceived to be grossly unfair that many in the financial sector (which, for shorthand, I will often refer to as "the bankers") walked off with outsize bonuses, while those who suffered from the crisis brought on by these bankers went without a job; or that government bailed out the banks, but was reluctant to even extend unemployment insurance for those who, through no fault of their own, could not get employment after searching for months and months;[7] or that government failed to provide anything except token help to the millions who were losing their homes. What happened in the midst of the crisis made clear that it was *not* contribution to society that determined relative pay, but something else: bankers received large rewards, though their contribution to society—and even to their firms—had been *negative*. The wealth given to the elites and to the bankers seemed to arise out of their ability and willingness to take advantage of others.

One aspect of fairness that is deeply ingrained in American values is opportunity. America has always thought of itself as a land of *equal opportunity*. Horatio Alger stories, of individuals who made it from the bottom to the top, are part of American folklore. But, as we'll explain in chapter 1, increasingly, the American dream that saw the country as a land of opportunity

began to seem just that: a dream, a myth reinforced by anec-
dotes and stories, but not supported by the data. The chances
of an American citizen making his way from the bottom to the
top are less than those of citizens in other advanced industrial
countries.

There is a corresponding myth—rags to riches in three generations—suggesting that those at the top have to work hard
to stay there; if they don't, they (or their descendants) quickly
move down. But as chapter 1 will detail, this too is largely
a myth, for the children of those at the top will, more likely
than not, remain there.

In a way, in America and throughout the world, the youthful
protesters took what they heard from their parents and politicians at face value—just as America's youth did fifty years ago
during the civil rights movement. Back then they scrutinized
the values *equality*, *fairness*, and *justice* in the context of the
nation's treatment of African Americans, and they found the
nation's policies wanting. Now they scrutinize the same values
in terms of how our economic and judicial system works, and
they have found the system wanting for poor and middle-class
Americans—not just for minorities but for *most* Americans of
all backgrounds.

If President Obama and our court system had found those
who brought the economy to the brink of ruin "guilty" of some
malfeasance, then perhaps it would have been possible to say
that the system was functioning. There would have been at
least some sense of accountability. In fact, however, those
who should have been so convicted were often not charged;
and when they were charged, they were typically found innocent or at least not convicted. A few in the hedge fund industry have been convicted subsequently of insider trading, but
this is a sideshow, almost a distraction. The hedge fund indus-

try did not cause the crisis. It was the banks. And it is the bankers who have gone, almost to a person, free.

If no one is accountable, if no individual can be *blamed* for what has happened, it means that the problem lies in the economic and political system.

From social cohesion to class warfare

The slogan "we are the 99 percent" may have marked an important turning point in the debate about inequality in the United States. Americans have always shied away from class analysis; America, we liked to believe, is a middle-class country, and that belief helps bind us together. There should be no divisions between the upper and the lower classes, between the bourgeoisie and the workers.[8] But if by a class-based society we mean one in which the prospects of those at the bottom to move up are low, America may have become even more class-based than old Europe, and our divisions have now become even greater than those there.[9] Those in the 99 percent are continuing with the "we're all middle class" tradition, with one slight modification: they recognize that we're actually not all moving up together. The vast majority is suffering together, and the very top—the 1 percent—is living a different life. The "99 percent" marks an attempt to forge a new coalition—a new sense of national identity, based not on the fiction of a universal middle class but on the reality of the economic divides within our economy and our society.

For years there was a deal between the top and the rest of our society that went something like this: we will provide you jobs and prosperity, and you will let us walk away with the bonuses. You all get a share, even if we get a bigger share. But now that tacit agreement between the rich and the rest, which was always fragile, has come apart. Those in the 1 percent are walking off with the riches, but in doing so they have provided nothing but anxiety and insecurity to the 99 percent. The majority of Americans have simply not been benefiting from the country's growth.

Is our market system eroding fundamental values?

While this book focuses on equality and fairness, there is another fundamental value that our system seems to be undermining—a sense of *fair play*. A basic sense of values should, for instance, have led to guilt feelings on the part of those who were engaged in predatory lending, who provided mortgages to poor people that were ticking time bombs, or who were designing the "programs" that led to excessive charges for overdrafts in the billions of dollars. What is remarkable is how few seemed—and still seem—to feel guilty, and how few were the whistleblowers. Something has happened to our sense of values, when the end of making more money justifies the means, which in the U.S. subprime crisis meant exploiting the poorest and least-educated among us.[10]

Much of what has gone on can only be described by the words "moral deprivation." Something wrong happened to the moral compass of so many of the people working in the financial sector and elsewhere. When the norms of a society change in a way that so many have lost their moral compass, it says something significant about the society.

Capitalism seems to have changed the people who were ensnared by it. The brightest of the bright who went to work on Wall Street were like most other Americans except that they did better in their schools. They put on hold their dreams of making a lifesaving discovery, of building a new industry, of helping the poorest out of poverty, as they reached out for salaries that seemed beyond belief, often in return for work that (in its number of hours) seemed beyond belief. But then, too often, something happened: it wasn't that the dreams were put on hold; they were forgotten.[11]

It is thus not surprising that the list of grievances against corporations (and not just financial institutions) is long and of long standing. For instance, cigarette companies stealthily made their dangerous products more addictive, and as they tried to persuade Americans that there was no "scientific evidence" of their products' dangers, their files were filled with evidence to the contrary. Exxon similarly used its money to try to persuade Americans that the evidence on global warming was weak, though the National Academy of Sciences had joined every other scientific body in saying that the evidence was strong. And while the economy was still reeling from the misdeeds of the financial sector, the BP oil spill showed another aspect of corporate recklessness: lack of care in drilling had endangered the environment and threatened jobs of thousands of those depending on fishing and tourism in the Gulf of Mexico.

If markets had actually delivered on the promises of improving the standards of living of most citizens, then all of the sins of corporations, all the seeming social injustices, the insults to our environment, the exploitation of the poor, might have been forgiven. But to the young *indignados* and protesters elsewhere in the world, capitalism is failing to produce what was promised, but is delivering on what was not promised— inequality, pollution, unemployment, and, *most important of all*, the degradation of values to the point where everything is acceptable and no one is accountable.

Failure of political system

The political system seems to be failing as much as the economic system. Given the high level of youth unemployment around the world—50 percent in Spain and 17 percent in the United States[12]—it was perhaps more surprising that it took so long for the protest movements to begin than that protests eventually broke out. The unemployed, including young people who had studied hard and done everything that they were supposed to do ("played by the rules," as some politicians are wont to say), faced a stark choice: remaining unemployed or accepting a job far below that for which they were qualified. In many cases there was not even a choice: there simply were no jobs, and hadn't been for years.

One interpretation of the long delay in the arrival of mass protests was that, in the aftermath of the crisis, there was hope in democracy, faith that the political system would work, that it would hold accountable those who had brought on the crisis and quickly repair the economic system. But years after the breaking of the bubble, it became clear that our political system had failed, just as it had failed to prevent the crisis, to check the growing inequality, to protect those at the bottom, to prevent the corporate abuses. It was only then that protesters turned to the streets.

Americans, Europeans, and people in other democracies around the world take great pride in their democratic institutions. But the protesters have called into question whether there is a *real* democracy. Real democracy is more than the right to vote once every two or four years. The choices have to be meaningful. The politicians have to listen to the voices of the citizens. But increasingly, and especially in the United States, it seems that the political system is more akin to "one dollar one vote" than to "one person one vote." Rather than correcting the market's failures, the political system was reinforcing them.

Politicians give speeches about what is happening to our values and our society, but then they appoint to high office the CEOs and other corporate officials who were at the helm in the financial sector as the system was failing so badly. We shouldn't have expected the architects of the system that has not been working to rebuild the system to make it work, and especially work for most citizens—and they didn't.

The failures in politics and economics are related, and they reinforce each other. A political system that amplifies the voice of the wealthy provides ample opportunity for laws and regulations—and the administration of them—to be designed in ways that not only fail to protect the ordinary citizens against the wealthy but also further enrich the wealthy at the expense of the rest of society.

This brings me to one of the central theses of this book: while there may be underlying economic forces at play, politics have shaped the market, and shaped it in ways that advantage the top at the expense of the rest. Any economic system has to have rules and regulations; it has to operate within a legal framework. There are many different such frameworks, and each has consequences for distribution as well as growth, efficiency, and stability. The economic elite have pushed for a framework that benefits them at the expense of the rest, but it is an economic system that is neither efficient nor fair. I explain how our inequality gets reflected in every important decision that we make as a nation—from our budget to our monetary policy, even to our system of justice—and show how these decisions themselves help perpetuate and exacerbate this inequality.[13]

Given a political system that is so sensitive to moneyed interests, growing economic inequality leads to a growing imbalance of political power, a vicious nexus between politics and economics. And the two together shape, and are shaped by, societal forces—social mores and institutions—that help reinforce this growing inequality.

What the protesters are asking for, and what they are accomplishing

The protesters, perhaps more than most politicians, grasped what was going on. At one level, they were asking for so little: for a chance to use their skills, for the right to decent work at decent pay, for a fairer economy and society, one that treats them with dignity. In Europe and the United States, their requests were not revolutionary, but evolutionary. At another level, though, they were asking for a great deal: for a democracy where people, not dollars, matter; and for a market economy that delivers on what it is supposed to do. The two demands are related: unfettered markets do not work well, as we have seen. For markets to work the way markets are supposed to, there has to be appropriate government regulation. But for that to occur, we have to have a democracy that reflects the general interests—not the special interests or just those at the top.

The protesters have been criticized for not having an agenda, but such criticism misses the point of protest movements. They are an expression of frustration with the political system and even, in those countries where there are elections, with the electoral process. They sound an alarm.

In some ways the protesters have already accomplished a great deal: think tanks, government agencies, and the media have confirmed their allegations, the failures not just of the market system but of the high and *unjustifiable* level of inequality. The expression "we are the 99 percent" has entered into popular consciousness. No one can be sure where the movements will lead. But of this we can be sure: these young protesters have already altered public discourse and the consciousness of ordinary citizens and politicians alike.

CONCLUDING COMMENTS

In the weeks following the protest movements in Tunisia and Egypt, I wrote (in an early draft of my *Vanity Fair* article),

> As we gaze out at the popular fervor in the streets, one question to ask ourselves is this: when will it come to America? In important ways, our own country has become like one of these distant, troubled places. In particular, there is the stranglehold exercised on almost everything by that tiny sliver of people at the top—the wealthiest 1 percent of the population.

It was to be but a few months before those protests reached the shores of this country.

This book attempts to fathom the depths of one aspect of what has happened in the United States—how we became a society that was so unequal, with opportunity so diminished, and what the consequences are likely to be.

The picture I paint today is bleak: we are only just beginning to grasp how far our country has deviated from our aspirations. But there is also a message of hope. There are alternative frameworks that will work better for the economy as a whole and, most importantly, for the vast majority of citizens. Part of this alternative framework entails a better balance between markets and the state—a perspective that is supported, as I shall explain, both by modern economic theory and by historical evidence.[14] In these alternative frameworks, one of the roles that the government undertakes is to redistribute income, especially if the outcomes of market processes are too disparate.

Critics of redistribution sometimes suggest that the cost of redistribution is too high. The disincentives, they claim, are too great, and the gains to the poor and those in the middle are more than offset by the losses to the top. It is often argued on the right that we could have more equality, but only at the steep price of slower growth and lower GDP. The reality (as I will show) is just the opposite: we have a system that has been working overtime to move money from the bottom and middle to the top, but the system is so inefficient that the gains to the top are far less than the losses to the middle and bottom. We are, in fact, paying a high price for our growing and outsize inequality: not only slower growth and lower GDP but even more instability. And this is not to say anything about the other prices we are paying: a weakened democracy, a diminished sense of fairness and justice, and even, as I have suggested, a questioning of our sense of identity.

A few words of caution

A few other prefatory remarks: I often use the term "the 1 percent" loosely, to refer to the economic and political power of those at the top. In some cases, what I really have in mind is a much smaller group—the top one-tenth of 1 percent; in other cases, in discussing access to elite education, for instance, there is a somewhat larger group, perhaps the top 5 percent or 10 percent.

It may seem to readers that I talk too much about the bankers and corporate CEOs, too much about the financial crisis of 2008 and its aftermath, especially (as I'll explain) since the problems of inequality in America are of longer standing. It is not just that they have become the whipping boys of popular opinion. They are emblematic of what has gone wrong. Much of the inequality at the top is associated with finance and corporate CEOs. But it's more than that: these leaders have helped shape our views about what is good economic policy, and unless and until we understand what is wrong with those views—and how, to too large an extent, they serve *their* interests at the expense of the rest—we won't be able to reformulate policies to ensure a more equitable, more efficient, more dynamic economy.

Any popular book like this entails more sweeping generalizations than would be appropriate in more academic writing, which would be replete with qualifications and footnotes. For this, I apologize in advance and refer the reader to some of the academic writing cited in the more limited number of footnotes that my publisher has allowed me. So too, I should emphasize that in castigating "bankers" I oversimplify: many, many of the financiers that I know would agree with much that I have said. Some fought against the abusive practices and predatory lending. Some wanted to curb the banks' excessive risk taking. Some believed that the banks should focus on their core businesses. There are even several banks that did just that. But it should be obvious that most important decision makers did not: both before the crisis and after it, the largest and most influential financial institutions did behave in ways that can rightly be criticized, and someone has to take responsibility. When I castigate the "bankers," it is *those* who decided, for instance, to engage in fraudulent and unethical behavior, and who created the culture within the institutions that facilitated it.

Intellectual debts

A book such as this rests on the scholarship, theoretical and empirical, of hundreds of researchers. It is not easy to put together the data that describe what is happening to inequality, or to provide an interpretation of why what has been occurring has happened. Why is it that the rich are getting so much richer, that the middle is being hollowed out, and that the numbers in poverty are increasing?

While footnotes in subsequent chapters will provide some acknowledgments, I would be remiss if I did not mention the painstaking work of Emmanuel Saez and Thomas Piketty, or the work over more than four decades of one of my early coauthors, Sir Anthony B. Atkinson. Because a central part of my thesis is the intertwining of politics and economics, I have to stretch beyond economics, narrowly defined. My colleague at the Roosevelt Institute Thomas Ferguson, in his 1995 book *Golden Rule: The Investment Theory of Party Competition and the Logic of Money-Driven Political Systems*, was among the first to explore with some rigor the fundamental puzzle of why, in democracies based on one person one vote, money seems to matter so much.

The link between politics and inequality has, not surprisingly, become a focus of much recent writing. This book, in some sense, picks up where the excellent book by Jacob S. Hacker and Paul Pierson, *Winner-Take-All Politics: How Washington Made the Rich Richer—And Turned Its Back on the Middle Class*,[15] leaves off. They are political scientists. I am an economist. We all grapple with the question of how the high and growing inequality in the United States can be explained. I ask, How can we reconcile what has happened with standard economic theory? And though we approach the question through the lens of two different disciplines, we come to the same answer: to paraphrase President Clinton, "It's the politics, stupid!" Money speaks in politics, as it does in the marketplace. That that is so has long been evident, and brought forth a bevy of books, such as Lawrence Lessig's *Republic, Lost: How Money Corrupts Congress—And a Plan to Stop It*.[16] It has also become increasingly clear that growing inequality is having a major effect on our democracy, as reflected in books such as Larry Bartels's *Unequal Democracy: The Political Economy of the New Gilded Age*[17] and Nolan McCarty, Keith T. Poole, and Howard Rosenthal's *Polarized America: The Dance of Ideology and Unequal Riches*.[18]

But how and why money should be so powerful in a democracy where each person has a vote—and most voters, by definition, are not in the 1 percent—has remained a mystery, on which I hope this book will shed a little light.[19] Most importantly, I try to illuminate the nexus between economics and politics. While it has become evident that this growing inequality has been bad for our politics (as evidenced by the pack of books just mentioned), I explain how it is also *very* bad for our economy.

A few personal notes

I return in this book to a subject that drew me into the study of economics a half century ago. I was initially a physics major at Amherst College. I loved the elegance of the mathematical theories that described our world. But my heart lay elsewhere, in the social and economic upheaval of the time, the civil rights movement in the United States, and the fight for development and against colonialism in what was called then the Third World. Part of this yearning was rooted in my experience growing up in the heartland of industrial America, in Gary, Indiana. There I saw at first hand inequality, discrimination, unemployment, and recessions. As a ten-year-old, I wondered why the kindly woman who took care of me much of the day had only a sixth-grade education, in this country that seemed so affluent, and I wondered why she was taking care of me, rather than her own children. In an era when most Americans saw economics as the science of money, I was, in some ways, an unlikely candidate to become an economist. My family was politically engaged, and I was told that money wasn't important; that money would never buy happiness; that what was important was service to others and the life of the mind. In the tumult of the 1960s, though, as I became exposed to new ideas at Amherst College, I saw that economics was much more than the study of money; it was actually a form of inquiry that could address the fundamental causes of inequity, and to which I could effectively devote my proclivity for mathematical theories.

The major subject of my doctoral dissertation at MIT was inequality, its evolution over time, and its consequences for macroeconomic behavior and especially growth. I took some of the standard assumptions (of what is called the neoclassical model) and showed that under those assumptions there should be a convergence to equality among individuals.[20] It was clear that something was wrong with the standard model, just as it was clear to me, having grown up in Gary, that something was wrong with a standard model that said the economy

was efficient and there was no unemployment or discrimination. It was the realization that the standard model didn't
describe well the world we lived in that set me off on a quest
for alternative models in which market imperfections, and
especially imperfections of information and "irrationalities,"
would play such an important role.[21] Ironically, as these ideas
developed and gained currency within some parts of the economics profession, the opposite notion—that markets worked
well, or would, if only the government kept out of the way—
took hold within much of the public discourse. This book,
like several of those that preceded it, is an attempt to set the
record straight.

ACKNOWLEDGMENTS

═════

I HAVE BEEN WORKING, AS I NOTED, ON THE ORI-
gins and consequences of inequality since my days as a
graduate student, and in the almost fifty years since beginning
my studies, I have accumulated enormous intellectual debts,
too many to enumerate. Robert Solow, one of my thesis advisers, and with whom I wrote an early paper on distribution
and macroeconomic behavior, had written his own thesis on
inequality. The influence of Paul Samuelson, another of my
thesis advisers, will be apparent in the discussion of globalization in chapter 3. My first published papers on the subject
were written with my fellow graduate student George Akerlof,
with whom I shared the 2001 Nobel Prize.

At the time I went to Cambridge University, as a Fulbright
scholar in 1965–66, the distribution of income was a major
focus of debate, and I owe debts to the late Nicholas Kaldor,
David Champernowne, and Michael Farrell, and especially to
Sir James Meade and Frank Hahn. It was there that I first
began my work with Tony Atkinson, who subsequently has

become one of the world's leading authorities on inequality. At the time, it was still thought that there were major trade-offs between inequality and growth, and Jim Mirrlees was just then beginning his work on how one could design optimal redistributive taxes (work for which he would later receive the Nobel Prize).

Another of my teachers at MIT (and then a fellow visitor at Cambridge in 1969–70) was Kenneth Arrow, whose work on information greatly influenced my thinking. Later, his work, paralleling my own, would focus on the impact of discrimination; how information, say about relative abilities, affects inequality; and the role of education in the whole process.

A key issue that I touch upon in this book is the measurement of inequality. This turns out to raise theoretical issues that are closely akin to the measurement of risk, and my early work, four decades ago, was done jointly with Michael Rothschild. Subsequently, I began work with a former student, Ravi Kanbur, on the measurement of socioeconomic mobility.

The influence of behavioral economics on my thinking should be evident, especially in chapter 6. I was first introduced to these ideas some forty years ago by the late Amos Tversky, a pioneer in this field, and subsequently Richard Thaler and Danny Kahneman have greatly influenced my thinking. (When I founded the *Journal of Economic Perspectives* in the mid-1980s, I asked Richard to do a regular column on the subject.)

I benefited enormously from the discussions with Edward Stiglitz of some of the legal issues treated in chapter 7, and with Robert Perkinson on the issues related to America's high incarceration rate.

I have always benefited a great deal from discussing ideas as I formulate them with my students, and I want to single out Miguel Morin, a current student, and Anton Korinek, a recent one.

I had the good fortune to be able to serve in the Clinton administration. Concerns about inequality and poverty were central to our discussions. We debated how we could best deal with poverty, for instance, with welfare reform (discussions in which David Ellwood of Harvard played a central role), and what we could do about the extremes of inequality at the top, through tax reform. (As I note later, not everything we did was a move in the right direction.) The influence of the insights of Alan Krueger (now chairman of the Council of Economic Advisers) into labor markets, including the role of the minimum wage, should be apparent. Later in the book I refer to work with Jason Furman, and with Peter Orszag. Alicia Munnell, who served with me on the Council, helped me better understand the role of social insurance programs and CRA (the Community Reinvestment Act, which imposed requirements on banks to lend to underserved communities) requirements in reducing poverty. (For the many others who greatly influenced my thinking in this period, please see the acknowledgments in *The Roaring Nineties* [New York: W. W. Norton, 2003].)

I also was fortunate to be able to serve as chief economist of the World Bank, an institution that sees one of its central missions as the reduction of poverty. With poverty and inequality the focus of our attention, every day was a learning experience, every encounter an opportunity to get new insights and to shape and reshape views about the causes and consequences of inequality, to better understand why it differed across countries. While I hesitate to single out anyone, I should mention my three successors as chief economist, Nick

Stern (whom I first met in Kenya in 1969), François Bourguignon, and Kaushik Basu.

In chapter 1 and elsewhere, I emphasize that GDP per capita—or even other measures of income—do not provide an adequate measure of well-being. My thinking in this area was greatly influenced by the work of the Commission on the Measurement of Economic Performance and Social Progress, which I chaired, and which was also led by Amartya Sen and Jean-Paul Fitoussi. I should also acknowledge the influence of all the twenty-one other members of the commission.

In chapter 4, I explain the link between instability and growth, my understanding of which was greatly influenced by another commission I chaired, the Commission of Experts of the President of the United Nations General Assembly on Reforms of the International Monetary and Financial System.

I especially want to thank my colleagues at the Roosevelt Institute, including Bo Cutter, Mike Konczal, Arjun Jayadev, and Jeff Madrick. (Others who have worked with Roosevelt Institute events, including Robert Kuttner and Jamie Galbraith, are also deserving of thanks.) Paul Krugman has been an inspiring voice for all of us who would like to see a more equitable society and a better-functioning economy.

In recent years, the economics profession hasn't, unfortunately, paid sufficient attention to inequality—just as it didn't pay sufficient attention to the other problems that could give rise to the kind of instability that the country has experienced. The Institute for New Economic Thinking has been created to try to rectify these and other deficiencies, and I want to acknowledge my indebtedness to INET, and especially to its head, Rob Johnson (also a colleague at the Roosevelt Institute and a member of the UN commission), for extensive discussions of the topics of this book.

As always, I want to acknowledge my indebtedness to Columbia University, for providing an intellectual environment in which ideas can flourish, be challenged, and be refined. I must especially extend my gratitude to José Antonio Ocampo and my longtime colleague and collaborator, Bruce Greenwald.

While these are my broad intellectual debts, I owe an especial set of debts to those who helped in one way or another in this book.

This book grew out of an article in *Vanity Fair*, "Of the 1%, for the 1%, by the 1%." Cullen Murphy solicited the article and did a marvelous job of editing. Graydon Carter suggested the title. Drake McFeely, president of Norton, and my longtime friend and editor, then asked me to expand the ideas into a book. Brendan Curry, once again, did a superb job in editing the book.

Stuart Proffitt, my editor from Penguin/Allen Lane also again did an impressive job combining "big think" ideas on how to strengthen the arguments and making them clearer with detailed comments on the writing.

Karla Hoff read the book cover to cover, improving both the language and the argument. But even before I began to write the book, discussions with her on the ideas that are central to the book helped shape my own thinking.

For the paperback, I must extend a special thanks to those readers, editors, and scholars who made suggestions for revisions and improvements to the book. In particular, I am indebted to several readers who took the time to write to me to alert me of errors in the hardcover, some of which would likely not have been caught otherwise. They will see their diligence reflected in this paperback edition. Among those in academia who provided me with important suggestions were

Stephen Jenkins of the London School of Economics and Teresa Ghilarducci, director of the New School's Schwartz Center for Economic Policy Analysis; the additional data she provided on inequalities in life expectancy was invaluable for the new preface. I additionally benefited from conversations both informal and formal with economists, policymakers, and activists at conferences in several different countries since the publication of the hardcover.

A team of research assistants, headed by Laurence Wilse-Samson and including An Li and Ritam Chaurey went well beyond the task of fact-checking. They suggested where the analysis could be extended, argued about where it needed to be more qualified, and seemed as excited about the project as I was. Julia Cunico and Hannah Assadi also provided invaluable comments and support throughout the writing process.

Eamon Kircher-Allen not only managed the whole process of producing the manuscript but served as editor and critic as well. I owe him an enormous debt.

As always, my biggest debt is to Anya, who encouraged me to do the book, repeatedly discussed the ideas behind it, and helped shape and reshape it.

To all of them—and to the enthusiasm for the book that they continually shared with me—I am deeply indebted. None of them should be held responsible for any errors and omissions that remain in the book.

THE PRICE OF INEQUALITY

CHAPTER ONE

AMERICA'S 1 PERCENT PROBLEM

THE 2007–08 FINANCIAL CRISIS AND THE GREAT Recession that followed cast vast numbers of Americans adrift amid the flotsam and jetsam of an increasingly dysfunctional form of capitalism. A half decade later, one out of six Americans who would like a full-time job still couldn't find one; some eight million families had been told to leave their homes, and millions more anticipate seeing foreclosure notices in the not-too-distant future;[1] still more saw their lifetime savings seemingly evaporate. Even if some of the green shoots that the optimists kept seeing were, in fact, the harbinger of a real recovery, it would be years—2018 at the earliest—before the economy returned to full employment. By 2012 many, however, had already given up hope: the savings of those who had lost their jobs in 2008 or 2009 had been spent. Unemployment checks had run out. Middle-aged people, once confident of a swift return to the workforce, came to realize they were in fact forcibly retired. Young people, fresh out of college with tens of thousands of dollars in debt, couldn't find any work at all. People who had moved in with friends and relatives at the start of the crisis had become homeless. Houses bought during the property boom were still on the market or sold at a loss; many more stood empty. The grim underpinnings of the financial boom of the preceding decade lay exposed at last.

One of the darkest sides to the market economy that came to light was the large and growing inequality that has left the American social fabric, and the country's economic sustainability, fraying at the edges: the rich were getting richer, while the rest were facing hardships that seemed inconsonant with the American dream. The fact that there were rich and poor in America was well known; and even though this inequality was not caused solely by the subprime crisis and the downturn that followed—it had been building up over the past three decades—the crisis made matters worse, to the point where it could no longer be ignored. The middle class was being badly squeezed in ways we'll see later in this chapter; the suffering of the bottom was palpable, as weaknesses in America's safety net grew obvious and as public support programs, inadequate at best, were cut back further; but throughout all this, the top 1 percent managed to hang on to a huge piece of the national income—a fifth—although some of their investments took a hit.[2]

There was greater inequality wherever one sliced the income distribution; even within the top 1 percent, the top 0.1 percent of income earners was getting a larger share of the money. By 2007, the year *before* the crisis, the top 0.1 percent of America's households had an income that was 220 times larger than the *average* of the bottom 90 percent.[3] Wealth was even more unequally distributed than income, with the wealthiest 1 percent owning more than a third of the nation's wealth.[4] Income inequality data offer only a snapshot of an economy at a single moment in time. But this is precisely why the data on wealth inequality are so troubling—wealth inequality goes beyond the variations seen in year-to-year income. Moreover, wealth gives a better picture of differences in access to resources.

America has been growing apart, at an increasingly rapid rate. In the first post-recession years of the new millennium (2002 to 2007), the top 1 percent seized more than 65 percent of the gain in total national income.[5] While the top 1 percent was doing fantastically, most Americans were actually growing worse-off.[6]

If the rich were growing richer and if those in the middle and at the bottom were also doing better, that would be one thing, especially if the efforts of those at the top were central to the successes of the rest. We could celebrate the successes of those at the top and be thankful for their contributions. But that's not what's been happening.

Members of America's middle class have felt that they were long-suffering, and they were right. For three decades before the crisis, their incomes had barely budged.[7] Indeed, the income of a typical full-time male worker has stagnated for well over a third of a century.[8]

The crisis made these inequalities worse in innumerable ways, beyond the higher unemployment, lost homes, stagnating wages. The wealthy had more to lose in stock market values, but those recovered reasonably well and relatively fast.[9] In fact, the gains of the "recovery" since the recession have accrued overwhelmingly to the wealthiest Americans: the top 1 percent of Americans gained 93 percent of the additional income created in the country in 2010, as compared with 2009.[10] The poor and middle had most of their wealth in housing. As average house prices fell more than a third between the second quarter of 2006 and the end of 2011,[11] a large proportion of Americans—those with large mortgages—saw their wealth essentially wiped out. At the top, CEOs were remarkably successful in maintaining their high pay; after a slight dip in 2008, the ratio of CEO annual compensation to that of the typical worker by 2010 was back to what it had been before the crisis, to 243 to 1.[12]

Countries around the world provide frightening examples of what happens to societies when they reach the level of inequality toward which we are moving. It is not a pretty picture: countries where the rich live in gated communities, waited upon by hordes of low-income workers; unstable political systems where populists promise the masses a better life, only to disappoint. Perhaps most importantly, there is an absence of hope. In these countries, the poor know that their prospects of emerging from poverty, let along making it to the top, are minuscule. This is *not* something we should be striving for.

In this chapter, I lay out the scope of inequality in the United States and how it affects the lives of millions in different ways. I describe not only how we are becoming a more divided society but also how we are no longer the land of opportunity that we once were. I discuss the low chances that a person born at the bottom can rise to the top, or even the middle. The level of inequality and the absence of opportunity that we see in the United States today is not inevitable, nor is its recent rise simply the product of inexorable market forces. Later chapters will describe the causes of this inequality, the costs to our society, our democracy, and our economy of this high and growing inequality, and what can be done to reduce it.

THE RISING TIDE THAT
DIDN'T LIFT ALL BOATS

Although the United States has always been a capitalist country, our inequality—or at least its current high level—is new.
Some thirty years ago, the top 1 percent of income earners
received *only* 12 percent of the nation's income.[13] That level
of inequality should itself have been unacceptable; but since
then the disparity has grown dramatically,[14] so that by 2007
the average after-tax income of the top 1 percent had reached
$1.3 million, but that of the bottom 20 percent amounted to
only $17,800.[15] The top 1 percent get in one week 40 per-
cent more than the bottom fifth receive in a year; the top 0.1
percent received in a day and a half about what the bottom
90 percent received in a year; and the richest 20 percent of
income earners earn in total *after tax* more than the bottom 80
percent combined.[16]

For thirty years after World War II, America grew together—
with growth in income in every segment, but with those at
the bottom growing faster than those at the top. The country's
fight for survival brought a new sense of unity, and that led to
policies, like the GI Bill, that helped bring the country even
closer together.

But for the past thirty years, we've become increasingly a
nation divided; not only has the top been growing the fastest,
but the bottom has actually been declining. (It hasn't been
a relentless pattern—in the 1990s, for a while, those at the
bottom and in the middle did better. But then, as we've seen,
beginning around 2000, inequality grew at an even more rapid
pace.)

The last time inequality approached the alarming level we

see today was in the years before the Great Depression. The economic instability we saw then and the instability we have seen more recently are closely related to this growing inequality, as I'll explain in chapter 4.

How we explain these patterns, the ebb and flow of inequality, is the subject of chapters 2 and 3. For now, we simply note that the marked reduction in inequality in the period between 1950 and 1970, was due partly to developments in the markets but even more to government policies, such as the increased access to higher education provided by the GI Bill and the highly progressive tax system enacted during World War II. In the years after the "Reagan revolution," by contrast, the divide in market incomes increased and, ironically, at the same time government initiatives designed to temper the inequities of the marketplace were dismantled, taxes at the top were lowered and social programs were cut back.

Market forces—the laws of supply and demand—of course inevitably play some role in determining the extent of economic inequality. But those forces are at play in other advanced industrial countries as well. Even before the burst in inequality that marked the first decade of this century, the United States already had more inequality and less income mobility than practically every country in Europe, as well as Australia and Canada.

The trends in inequality can be reversed. A few other countries have managed to do so. Brazil has had one of the highest levels of inequality in the world—but in the 1990s, it realized the perils, in terms both of social and political divisiveness and of long-term economic growth. The result was a political consensus across society that something had to be done. Under President Fernando Henrique Cardoso, there were massive increases in education expenditures, including for the poor.

Under President Luiz Inácio Lula da Silva, there were social expenditures to reduce hunger and poverty.[17] Inequality was reduced, growth increased,[18] and society became more stable. Brazil still has more inequality than the United States, but while Brazil has been striving, rather successfully, to improve the plight of the poor and reduce gaps in income between rich and poor, America has allowed inequality to grow and poverty to increase.

Worse still, as we will show, government policies have been central to the creation of inequality in the United States. If we are to reverse these trends in inequality, we will have to reverse some of the policies that have helped make America the most economically divided developed country and, beyond that, to take further actions to lessen the inequalities that arise on their own from market forces.

Some defenders of the current level of inequality claim that although it's not inevitable, doing anything about it would be just too costly. They believe that for capitalism to work its wonders, high inequality is an inevitable, even necessary feature of the economy. After all, those who work hard should be rewarded, and have to be, if they are to make the efforts and the investments from which all benefit. Some inequality is indeed inevitable. Some individuals will work harder and longer than others, and any well-functioning economic system has to reward them for these efforts. But this book shows that both the magnitude of America's inequality today and the way it is generated actually undermine growth and impair efficiency. Part of the reason for this is that much of America's inequality is the result of market distortions, with incentives directed not at creating new wealth but at taking it from others. It is thus not surprising that our growth has been stronger in periods in which inequality has been lower and in which we have been growing together.[19] This was true not only in the decades after World War II but, even in more recent times, in the 1990s.[20]

Trickle-down economics

Inequality's apologists—and they are many—argue to the contrary that giving more money to the top will benefit *everyone*, partly because it would lead to more growth. This is an idea called trickle-down economics. It has a long pedigree—and has long been discredited. As we've seen, higher inequality has not led to more growth, and most Americans have actually seen their incomes sink or stagnate. What America has been experiencing in recent years is the opposite of trickle-down economics: the riches accruing to the top have come at the *expense* of those down below.[21]

One can think of what's been happening in terms of slices of a pie. If the pie were equally divided, everyone would get a slice of the same size, so the top 1 percent would get 1 percent of the pie. In fact, they get a very big slice, about a fifth of the entire pie. But that means everyone else gets a smaller slice.

Now, those who believe in trickle-down economics call this the politics of envy. One should look not at the relative size of the slices but at the absolute size. Giving more to the rich leads to a larger pie, so though the poor and middle get a smaller *share* of the pie, the piece of pie they get is enlarged. I wish that were so, but it's not. In fact, it's the opposite: as we noted, in the period of increasing inequality, growth has been slower—and the size of the slice given to most Americans has been diminishing.[22]

Young men (aged twenty-five to thirty-four) who are less

educated have an even harder time; those who have only graduated from high school have seen their real incomes decline
by more than a quarter in the last twenty-five years.[23] But even
households of individuals with a bachelor's degree or higher
have not done well—their median income (adjusted for inflation) fell by a tenth from 2000 to 2010.[24] (Median income is
the income such that half have an income greater than that
number, half less.)

We'll show later that whereas trickle-down economics
doesn't work, trickle-up economics may: all—even those at
the top—could benefit by giving more to those at the bottom
and the middle.

A snapshot of America's inequality

The simple story of America is this: the rich are getting richer,
the richest of the rich are getting still richer, [25] the poor are
becoming poorer and more numerous, and the middle class is
being hollowed out. The incomes of the middle class are stagnating or falling, and the difference between them and the
truly rich is increasing.

Disparities in household income are related to disparities in wages and in wealth and income from capital—and
inequality in both is increasing.[26] Just as overall inequality has
been growing, so have inequalities in wages and salaries. For
instance, over the last three decades those with low wages (in
the bottom 90 percent) have seen a growth of only around 15
percent in their wages, while those in the top 1 percent have
seen an increase of almost 150 percent and the top 0.1 percent of more than 300 percent.[27]

Meanwhile, changes in the wealth picture are even more
dramatic. For the quarter century before the crisis, while

everyone was getting wealthier, the rich were getting wealthier at a more rapid pace. As we noted, however, much of the wealth of the bottom and the middle, resting on the value of their homes, was phantom wealth—based on bubble housing prices—and while everyone lost out in the midst of the crisis, those at the top quickly recovered, but the bottom and middle did not. Even after the wealthy lost some of their wealth as stock prices declined in the Great Recession, the wealthiest 1 percent of households had 225 times the wealth of the typical American, almost double the ratio in 1962 or 1983.[28]

Given the inequality in wealth, it's not surprising that those at the top get the lion's share of the income from capital—before the crisis, in 2007, some 57 percent went to the top 1 percent.[29] Nor is it surprising that those in the top 1 percent have received an even larger share of the *increase* in capital income in the period after 1979—some seven-eighths—while those in the bottom 95 percent have gotten less than 3 percent of the increment.[30]

These broad-spectrum numbers, while alarming, can fail to capture the current disparities with sufficient force. For an even more striking illustration of the state of inequality in America, consider the Walton family: the six heirs to the Wal-Mart empire command wealth of $69.7 billion, which is equivalent to the wealth of the entire bottom 30 percent of U.S. society. The numbers may not be as surprising as they seem, simply because those at the bottom have so little wealth.[31]

Polarization

America has always thought of itself as a middle-class country. No one wants to think of himself as privileged, and no one wants to think of his family as among the poor. But in recent years, America's middle class has become eviscerated, as the "good" middle-class jobs—requiring a moderate level of skills, like autoworkers' jobs—seemed to be disappearing relative to those at the bottom, requiring few skills, and those at the top, requiring greater skill levels. Economists refer to this as the "polarization" of the labor force.[32] We'll discuss some of the theories explaining why this is happening, and what can be done about it, in chapter 3.

The collapse of the good jobs has happened during the last quarter century, and, not surprisingly, wages for such jobs have gone down and the disparity between wages at the top and those in the middle has increased.[33] The polarization of the labor force has meant that while more of the money is going to the top, more of the people are going toward the bottom.[34]

THE GREAT RECESSION MAKES HARD LIVES EVEN HARDER

America's economic divide has grown so large that it's hard for those in the 1 percent to imagine what life at the bottom—and increasingly in the middle—is like. Consider for a moment a household with a single earner and two children. Assume that the earner is in good health and manages to work a full 40 hours a week (the average workweek of American workers is only 34 hours)[35] at a wage somewhat above the minimum: say, around $8.50 per hour, so that after paying his Social Security tax, he gets $8 per hour, and thus receives $16,640 for his 2,080 hours. Assume he pays no income tax, but his employer charges him $200 a month for health insurance for his entire family and picks up the rest of the $550 per month cost of insurance. This brings his take-home pay to $14,240 a year. If he is lucky, he might be able to find a two-bedroom apartment (with utilities included) for $700 a month. This leaves him with $5,840 to cover all other family expenses for the year. Like most Americans, he may consider a car a basic necessity; insurance, gas, maintenance, and depreciation on the vehicle could easily take up some $3,000. The family's remaining funds are $2,840—under $3 a day per person—to cover basic expenses like food and clothing, not to mention things that make life worth living, like entertainment. If something goes wrong, there is simply no buffer.

As America went into the Great Recession, something did go wrong, for our hypothetical family and millions of real Americans nationwide. Jobs were lost, the value of their homes—their major asset—plummeted, and, as government revenues fell, safety nets were cut back just when they were needed most.

Even before the crisis, America's poor lived on the precipice; but with the Great Recession, that became increasingly true even of the middle class. The human stories of this crisis are replete with tragedies: one missed mortgage payment escalates into a lost house; homelessness escalates into lost jobs and the eventual destruction of families.[36] For these families, one shock may be manageable; the second is not. As some fifty million Americans lack health insurance, an illness can push the entire family close to edge;[37] a second illness, the loss of a job, or an auto accident can then push them over. Indeed, recent research has shown that by far the largest fraction of personal bankruptcies involve the illness of a family member.[38]

To see how even little changes in programs of social protection can have big effects on poor families, let's return to our family, which had $2,840 a year to spend. As the recession continued, many states cut back on assistance for child care. In Washington State, for instance, the average monthly cost of childcare for two children is $1,433.[39] Even if our family has a second parent who could get a job with a similar salary, without public assistance child care would still be impossible to afford.

A *labor market without a safety net*

But the hardship faced by those who lost their jobs and couldn't find another was even greater. Full-time employment declined by 8.7 million from November 2007 to November 2011,[40] a period during which *normally* almost 7 million new persons would have entered the labor force—an increase in the true jobs deficit of more than 15 million. Millions of those who couldn't find a job after searching and searching gave up and dropped out of the labor force; young people decided to stay in school, as employment prospects even for college graduates seemed bleak. The "missing" workers meant that the official unemployment statistics (which by early 2012 suggested that the unemployment rate was "only" 8.3 percent) presented an overly rosy picture of the state of the labor market.

Our unemployment insurance system, one of the least generous in the advanced industrial world, simply wasn't up to the task of providing adequate support for those losing their jobs.[41] Normally, insurance extends for only six months. Before the crisis, a dynamic labor market at full employment meant that most of those who wanted a job could find one within a short time, even if the job wasn't up to their expectations or skills. But in the Great Recession that was no longer true. Almost half of the jobless were long-term unemployed.

The term of eligibility for unemployment insurance was extended (typically after a very hard congressional debate),[42] but, even so, millions are finding that they are still unemployed when the benefits expire.[43] As the recession and the weak job market continued into 2010, a new segment of our society emerged, the "99ers"—those who had been unemployed for more than 99 weeks—and even in the best states, even with federal assistance, they were left out in the cold. They looked for work, but there just weren't enough jobs to be had. There were four job seekers for every job.[44] And given how much political capital had to be spent to extend unemployment insurance to 52, 72, or 99 weeks, few politicians even proposed to do anything about the 99ers.[45]

A poll by the *New York Times* late in 2011 revealed the extent of the inadequacies in our unemployment insurance system.[46] Only 38 percent of the unemployed were then receiving unemployment benefits, and some 44 percent had never received any. Of those receiving assistance, 70 percent thought that it was very or somewhat likely that the benefits would run out before they got a job. For three-quarters of those on assistance, the benefits fell far short of their previous income. Not surprisingly, more than half of the unemployed had experienced emotional or health problems as a result of being jobless but could not get treatment, since more than half of the unemployed had no health insurance coverage.

Many of the unemployed who were middle-aged saw no prospect of ever finding another job. For those over forty-five, the *average* duration of unemployment is already approaching one year.[47] The only positive note in the survey was the optimistic response that, *overall*, 70 percent thought it was very or somewhat likely that they would get a job in the next twelve months. American optimism, it seemed, still survived.

Before the recession, the United States appeared in some ways to be performing better than other countries. While wages, say, in the middle might not be growing, at least everyone who wanted a job could get one. This was the long-vaunted advantage of "flexible labor markets." But the crisis showed that even this advantage seemed to be disappearing, as America's labor markets increasingly resembled those of Europe, with not merely high but long-lasting unemployment. The young are frustrated—but I suspect that upon learning what the current trend portends, they would be even more so: those who remain unemployed for an extended period of time have lower lifetime employment prospects than those with similar qualifications who have been luckier in the job market. Even when they get a job, it will be at a lower wage than that of persons with similar qualifications. Indeed, the bad luck of entering the labor force in a year of high unemployment shows up in the lifelong earnings of these individuals.[48]

Economic insecurity

It is easy to understand the growing insecurity that so many Americans feel. Even the employed know that their jobs are at risk, and that with the high level of unemployment and the low level of social protection, their lives could suddenly take a turn for the worse. The loss of a job meant the loss of health insurance and perhaps even the loss of their home.

Those with seemingly secure jobs faced an insecure retirement, because in recent years, the United States has changed how it manages pensions. Most retirement benefits used to be provided through defined-benefit retirement schemes—where individuals could be sure of what they would get when they retired, with corporations bearing the risk of stock market fluctuations. But now most workers have defined-contribution schemes, where the individual is left with the responsibility of managing his retirement accounts—and bearing the risk of stock market fluctuations and inflation. There's the obvious danger: if the individual had listened to financial analysts and put her money into the stock markets, she took a beating in 2008.

The Great Recession thus represented a triple whammy for many Americans: their jobs, their retirement incomes, and their homes were all at risk. The housing bubble had provided a temporary reprieve from the consequences that would have followed from falling incomes. They could, and did, spend beyond their income as they struggled to maintain their standard of living. Indeed, in the mid-2000s, before the onset of the Great Recession, people in the bottom 80 percent were spending around 110 percent of their incomes.[49] Now that the bubble has broken, not only will these Americans have to live *within* their income; many will have to live *below* their income to pay back a mountain of debt. More than a fifth of those with mortgages are underwater, owing more on their house than it's worth.[50] The house, instead of being the piggy bank to pay for retirement or a child's college education, has become a burden. And many persons are at risk of losing their homes—and many have done so already. The millions of families that we noted lost their homes since the crashing of the housing bubble lost not only the roof over their heads but also much of their life savings.[51]

Between the loss on retirement accounts and the $6.5 trillion loss in housing valuations,[52] ordinary Americans have been hard hit by the crisis, and poorer Americans, who were just beginning to glimpse the American dream—or so they thought, as they bought a home and saw the value of their houses rise in the bubble—have done particularly badly. Between 2005 and 2009, the typical African American household has lost 53 percent of its wealth—putting its assets at a mere 5 percent of the average white American's, and the average Hispanic household has lost 66 percent of its wealth. And even the net worth of the typical white American household was down substantially, to $113,149 in 2009, a 16 percent loss of wealth from 2005.[53]

A *standard of living in decline*

The income measures on which we have focused so far, dismal as they are, do not fully capture the decline in the standard of living of *most* Americans. Most face not only economic insecurity but also health insecurity and, in some cases, even physical insecurity. President Obama's health care program was designed to extend coverage, but the Great Recession and the budget stringency that followed have led to a move in the opposite direction. Medicaid programs, on which the poor depend, have been scaled back.

Lack of health insurance is one factor contributing to poorer health, especially among the poor. Life expectancy in the United States is 78 years, lower than Japan's 83 years, or Australia's or Israel's 82 years. According to the World Bank, in 2009 the United States ranked fortieth overall, just below Cuba.[54] Infant and maternal mortality in the United States is little better than in some developing countries; for infant mortality, it is worse than Cuba, Belarus, and Malaysia, to name a few.[55] And these poor health indicators are largely a reflection of the dismal statistics for America's poor. For instance, America's poor have a life expectancy that is almost 10 percent lower than that of those at the top.[56]

We noted earlier that the income of a typical full-time male worker has stagnated for a third of a century, and that of those who have not gone to college has declined. To keep incomes from declining even more than they have, work hours per family have increased, mostly because more women are joining the workforce alongside their husbands. Our income statistics do not take into account either the loss of leisure or what this does to the quality of family life.

The decline in living standards is also manifested in changing social patterns as well as hard economic facts. An increasing fraction of young adults are living with their parents: some 19 percent of men between twenty-five and thirty-four, up from 14 percent as recently as 2005. For women in this age group, the increase was from 8 percent to 10 percent.[57] Sometimes called the "boomerang generation," these young people are forced to stay at home, or return home after graduation, because they cannot afford to live independently. Even customs like marriage are being affected, at least for the moment, by the lack of income and security. In just one year (2010), the number of couples who were living together without being married jumped by 13 percent.[58]

The consequences of pervasive and persistent poverty and long-term underinvestment in public education and other social expenditures are also manifest in other indicators that our society is not functioning as it should: a high level of crime, and a large fraction of the population in prison.[59] While violent-crime statistics are better than they were at their nadir (in 1991),[60] they remain high, far worse than in other advanced industrial countries, and they impose large economic and social costs on our society. Residents of many poor (and not so poor) neighborhoods still feel the risk of physical assault. It's expensive to keep 2.3 million people in prison. The U.S. incarceration rate is the world's highest and some nine to ten times that of many European countries. Almost 1 in 100 American adults is behind bars.[61] Some U.S. states spend as much on their prisons as they do on their universities.[62]

Such expenditures are not the hallmarks of a well-performing economy and society. Money that is spent on "security"— protecting lives and property—doesn't add to well-being; it simply prevents things from getting worse. Yet we consider these outlays part of the country's gross domestic product (GDP) as much as any other expenditure. If America's growing inequality leads to more spending to prevent crime, it will show up as an increase in GDP, but no one should confuse that with an increase in well-being.[63]

Incarceration even distorts our unemployment statistics. Individuals in prison are disproportionately poorly educated and come from groups that otherwise face high unemployment. It is highly likely that, if they weren't incarcerated, they would join the already swollen ranks of the unemployed. Viewed in this light, America's true unemployment rate would be worse: if the entire prison population of nearly 2.3 million was counted, the unemployment rate would be well above 9 percent.[64]

Poverty

The Great Recession made life for America's diminishing middle class harder. But it was especially hard for those at the bottom, as illustrated by the data presented earlier in this chapter for the family trying to survive on a wage slightly above the minimum wage.

An increasingly large number of Americans can barely meet the necessities of life. These individuals are said to be in poverty. The fraction of those in poverty[65] was 15.0 percent in 2011, up from 12.5 percent in 2007, the last year for which data is available. And our discussion above should have made clear how low the standard of living is of those at that threshold. At the very bottom, by 2011 the number of American families in *extreme poverty*—living at least one month of the year on two dollars a day per person or less, the measure of poverty used by the World Bank for developing countries—had doubled since 1996, to 1.5 million.[66] The "poverty gap," which is the percentage by which the mean income of a country's poor falls below the official poverty line, is another telling statistic. At 37 percent, the United States is one of the worst-ranking countries in the Organization for Economic Cooperation and Development (OECD), the "club" of the more developed countries, in the same league as Mexico (38.5 percent).[67]

The extent of poverty is illustrated by the fraction of Americans depending on government to meet their basic food needs (one in seven); and even then, large numbers of Americans go to bed at least once a month hungry, not because they are on a diet but because they can't afford food.[68]

The measurement of poverty—like the measurement of income—is difficult and far from uncontroversial. Until 2011, standard poverty measures focused on income before the effects of government programs are taken into account, and those are the numbers that are given above. This is what life would be like in the absence of government safety nets. Not surprisingly, government programs *do matter*. And they matter especially in economic downturns. Many of the programs, like unemployment insurance, provide only short-term assistance. They are directed at those facing temporary hardship. With the reform of the welfare system in 1996 (Personal Responsibility and Work Opportunity Reconciliation Act), welfare payments, too, became time limited (federal funds are generally limited to at most five years).

Looking at these programs, and simultaneously examining more carefully the different needs of various groups in society—those in the rural sector face lower housing costs; the elderly face higher medical costs—yields a more nuanced picture of poverty, one in which there are fewer rural poor, more urban poor, fewer poor children, and more poor elderly than in the older measures, which didn't take into account the different circumstances of different groups of the poor. Under this new measure (as well as by the old), the numbers in poverty have been increasing rapidly, by some 6 percent just from 2009 to 2010 alone, and the numbers in poverty under the new measure are even higher than under the old, so that almost one out of six Americans is now in poverty.[69]

It may be true that "the poor always ye have with you," but that doesn't mean that there have to be *so many* poor, or that they should suffer so much. We have the wealth and resources to eliminate poverty: Social Security and Medicare have almost eliminated poverty among the elderly.[70] And other countries, not as rich as the United States, have done a better job of reducing poverty and inequality.

It is particularly disturbing that today almost a quarter of all children live in poverty.[71] Not doing anything about their plight is a political choice that will have long-lasting consequences for our country.

OPPORTUNITY

Belief in America's essential fairness, that we live in a land of *equal opportunity*, helps bind us together. That, at least, is the American myth, powerful and enduring. Increasingly, it is just that—a myth. Of course, there are exceptions, but for economists and sociologists what matters are not the few success stories but what happens to *most* of those at the bottom and in the middle. What are their chances of making it, say, to the top? What is the likelihood that their children will be no better-off than they? If America were really a land of opportunity, the life chances of success—of, say, winding up in the top 10 percent—of someone born to a poor or less-educated family would be the same as those of someone born to a rich, well-educated, and well-connected family. But that's simply not the case, and there is some evidence that it's getting less so.[72] Indeed, according to the Economic Mobility Project, "there is a stronger link between parental education and children's economic, educational, and socio-emotional outcomes" in the United States than in any other country investigated, including those of "old Europe" (the UK, France, Germany, and Italy), other English speaking countries (Canada and Australia), and the Nordic countries Sweden, Finland, and Denmark, where the results were more expected.[73] A variety of other studies have corroborated these findings.[74]

This decline in opportunity has gone hand in hand with our growing inequality. In fact, that pattern has been observed across countries—countries with more inequality systematically have less equality of opportunity. Inequality persists.[75] But what's particularly disturbing about this relationship is what it bodes for the country's future: the growing inequality over recent years suggests that the level of opportunity in the future will be diminished and the level of inequality will be increased—unless we do something. It means that the America of 2053 will be a much more divided society than even the America of 2013. All the social, political, and economic problems arising out of inequality that we discuss in subsequent chapters will be that much worse.

It is at the bottom and the top where the United States performs especially badly: those at the bottom have a good chance of staying there, as do those at the top, and much more so than in other countries. With full equality of opportunity, 20 percent of those in the bottom fifth would see their children in the bottom fifth. Denmark almost achieves that— 25 percent are stuck there. Britain, supposedly notorious for its class divisions, does only a little worse (30 percent). That means they have a 70 percent chance of moving up. The chances of moving up in America, though, are markedly smaller (only 58 percent of children born to the bottom group make it out),[76] and when they do move up, they tend to move up only a little. Almost two-thirds of those in the bottom 20 percent have children who are in the bottom 40 percent—50 percent more than would be the case with full equality of opportunity.[77] So too, with full equality of opportunity, 20 percent of the bottom would make it all the way to the top fifth. No country comes close to achieving that goal, but again both Denmark (with 14 percent) and the UK (with 12 percent) do much better than the United States, with a mere 8 percent. By the same token, once one makes it to the top in the United States, one is more likely to remain there.[78]

There are many other ways of summarizing the disadvantageous position of the poor. The journalist Jonathan Chait has drawn attention to two of the most telling statistics from the

Economic Mobility Project and research from the Economic Policy Institute.[79]

- Poor kids who succeed academically are less likely to graduate from college than richer kids who do worse in school.[80]
- Even if they graduate from college, the children of the poor are still worse-off than low-achieving children of the rich.[81]

None of this comes as a surprise: education is one of the keys to success; at the top, the country gives its elite an education that is the best in the world. But the average American gets just an average education—and in mathematics, key to success in many areas of modern life, it's subpar. This is in contrast to China (Shanghai and Hong Kong), Korea, Finland, Singapore, Canada, New Zealand, Japan, Australia, Netherlands, and Belgium, which perform significantly above average on *all* tests (reading and mathematics).[82]

A stark reflection of the inequality of educational opportunity in our society is the composition of students in America's highly selective colleges. Only around 9 percent come from the bottom half of the population, while 74 percent come from the top quarter.[83]

So far, we have constructed a picture of an economy and a society that is increasingly divided. It shows up not only in income data but also in health, education, crime—indeed, in every metric of performance. While inequalities in parental income and education translate directly into inequalities of educational opportunity, inequalities of opportunity begin even before school—in the conditions that poor people face immediately before and after birth, differences in nutrition and the exposure to environmental pollutants that can have lifelong effects.[84] So difficult is it for those born into poverty to escape that economists refer to the situation as a "poverty trap."[85]

Even as the data show otherwise, Americans still believe in the myth of opportunity. A public opinion poll by the Pew Foundation found that "nearly 7 in 10 Americans had already achieved, or expected to achieve, the American Dream at some point in their lives."[86] Even as a myth, the belief that everyone had a fair chance had its uses: it motivated people to work hard. It seemed we were all in the same boat; even if some were, for the moment, traveling first-class while others stayed in steerage. On the next cruise positions might be reversed. The belief enabled the United States to avoid some of the class divisions and tensions that marked some European countries. By the same token, as the reality sinks in, as most Americans finally grasp that the economic game is stacked against them, all of this is at risk. Alienation has begun to replace motivation. Instead of social cohesion we have a new divisiveness.

A CLOSER LOOK AT THE TOP: GRABBING A BIGGER SLICE OF THE PIE

As we've noted, the growing inequality in our society is visible at the top, the middle, and the bottom. We've already observed what's happening at the bottom and in the middle. Here we take a closer look at the top.

If struggling poor families get our sympathy today, those at the top increasingly draw our ire. At one time, when there was a broad social consensus that those at the top earned what they got, they received our admiration. In the recent crisis, however, bank executives received outsize bonuses for outsize losses, and firms fired workers, claiming they couldn't afford them, only to use the savings to increase executive bonuses still more. The result was that admiration at their cleverness turned to anger at their insensitivities.

Numbers on compensation of corporate executives—including those who brought on the crisis—tell the story. We described earlier the huge gap between CEO pay and that of the typical worker—more than 200 times greater—a number markedly higher than in other countries (in Japan, for instance, the corresponding ratio is 16 to 1)[87] and even markedly higher than it was in the United States a quarter century ago.[88] The old U.S. ratio of 30 to 1 now seems quaint by comparison. It strains credulity to think that over the intervening years CEOs as a group have increased their productivity so much, relative to the average worker, that a multiple of more than 200 could be justified. Indeed, the available data on the success of U.S. companies provide no support for such a view.[89] What's worse, we have provided a bad example, as executives in other countries around the world emulate their American counterparts. The UK's High Pay Commission reported that the executive pay at its large companies is heading toward Victorian levels of inequality, vis-à-vis the rest of society (though currently the disparity is only as egregious as it was in the 1920s).[90] As the report puts it, "Fair pay within companies matters; it affects productivity, employee engagement and trust in our businesses. Moreover pay in publicly listed companies sets a precedent, and when it is patently not linked to performance, or rewards failure, it sends out the wrong message and is a clear symptom of market failure."[91]

INTERNATIONAL COMPARISONS

As we look out at the world, the United States not only has the highest level of inequality among the advanced industrial countries, but the level of its inequality is increasing in absolute terms relative to that in other countries. The United States was the most unequal of the advanced industrial countries in the mid-1980s, and it has maintained that position.[92] In fact, the gap between it and many other countries has increased: from the mid-1980s France, Hungary, and Belgium have seen no significant increase in inequality, while Turkey and Greece have actually seen a decrease in inequality. We are now approaching the level of inequality that marks dysfunctional societies—it is a club that we would distinctly not want to join, including Iran, Jamaica, Uganda, and the Philippines.[93]

Because we have so much inequality, and because it is on the rise, what's happening to *income (or GDP) per capita* doesn't tell us much about what the typical American is experiencing. If Bill Gates and Warren Buffett's incomes go up, the *average* income for America goes up. More meaningful is what's happening to the *median* income, the income of the family in the middle, which, as we saw, has been stagnating, or even falling, in recent years.

The UNDP (the UN Development Program) has developed a standard measure of "human development," which aggregates measures of income, health, and education. It then adjusts those numbers to reflect inequality. Before adjustment for inequality, the United States looked reasonably good in 2011—fourth, behind Norway, Australia, and Netherlands. But once account is taken of inequality, the United States is ranked twenty-third, behind all of the European countries. The difference between the rankings with and without inequality was the largest of any of the advanced industrial countries.[94] All of the Scandinavian countries rank much higher than the United States, and each provides not only universal education but also health care to its citizens. The standard mantra in the United States claims that the taxes required to finance these benefits stifle growth. Far from it. Over the period 2000 to 2010, high-taxing Sweden, for example, grew far faster than the United States—the country's average growth rates have exceeded those of the United States—2.31 percent a year versus 1.85 percent.[95]

As a former finance minister of one of these countries told me, "We have grown so fast and done so well because we had high taxes." Of course, what he meant was not that the taxes themselves led to higher growth but that the taxes financed public expenditures—investments in education, technology, and infrastructure—and the public expenditures were what had sustained the high growth—more than offsetting any adverse effects from the higher taxation.

Gini coefficient

One standard measure of inequality is the Gini coefficient. If income were shared in proportion to the population—the bottom 10 percent getting roughly 10 percent of the income, the bottom 20 percent getting 20 percent, and so forth— then the Gini coefficient would be zero. There would be no inequality. On the other hand, if all the income went to the top person, the Gini coefficient would be one, in some sense "perfect" inequality. More-equal societies have Gini coefficients of .3 or below. These include Sweden, Norway, and

Germany.[96] The most unequal societies have Gini coefficients of .5 or above. These include some countries in Africa (notably South Africa with its history of grotesque racial inequality) and Latin America—long recognized for their divided (and often dysfunctional) societies and polities.[97] America hasn't made it *yet* into this "elite" company, but it's well on the way. In 1980 our Gini coefficient was just touching .4; today it's .48.[98] According to UN data, we are slightly more unequal than Iran and Turkey,[99] and much less equal than any country in the European Union.[100]

We end this international comparison by coming back to a theme we raised earlier: measures of income inequality don't fully capture critical aspects of inequality. America's inequality may, in fact, be far worse than those numbers suggest. In other advanced industrial countries, families don't have to worry about how they will pay the doctor's bill, or whether they can afford to pay for their parent's health care. Access to decent health care is taken as a basic human right. In other countries, the loss of a job is serious, but at least there is a better safety net. In no other country are so many persons worried about the loss of their home. For Americans at the bottom and in the middle, economic insecurity has become a fact of life. It is real, it is important, but it's not captured in these metrics. If it were, the international comparisons would cast what's been happening in America in an even worse light.

CONCLUDING COMMENTS

In the years before the crisis, many Europeans looked to America as a model and asked how they could reform their economy to make it perform as well as that of the United States. Europe has its problems, too, caused mainly by countries' joining together to form a currency union without making the necessary political and institutional arrangements to make it work, and they will pay a high price for that failure. But setting that aside, they (and people in countries around the world) now know that GDP per capita does not provide a good picture of what is happening to most citizens in society—and in a fundamental sense, then, of how well the economy is doing. They were misled by the GDP per capita data to thinking the United States was performing well. Today that is no longer the case. Of course, economists who looked beneath the surface knew back in 2008 that America's debt-driven growth was not sustainable; and even when all appeared to be going well, the income of most Americans was declining, even as the outsize gains of those at the top were distorting the overall picture.

The success of an economy can be assessed only by looking at what is happening to the living standards—broadly defined—of most citizens over a sustained period of time. In those terms, America's economy has not been performing well, and it hasn't been for at least a third of a century. Although it has managed to increase GDP per capita, from 1980 to 2010 by three-fourths,[101] most full-time male workers have, as we've noted, seen their incomes go down. For these workers, the American economy is failing to bring the increases in living standards that they had come to expect. It is not that the American economic engine has lost its ability to produce. It is that the way the American economic engine has been run has given the benefits of that growth to an increasingly small sliver at the top—and even taken away some of what had previously gone to the bottom.

This chapter has illuminated certain stark and uncomfortable facts about the U.S. economy:

(a) Recent U.S. income growth primarily occurs at the top 1 percent of the income distribution.

(b) As a result there is growing inequality.

(c) And those at the bottom and in the middle are actually worse-off today than they were at the beginning of the century.

(d) Inequalities in wealth are even greater than inequalities in income.

(e) Inequalities are apparent not just in income but in a variety of other variables that reflect standards of living, such as insecurity and health.

(f) Life is particularly harsh at the bottom—and the recession made it much worse.

(g) There has been a hollowing out of the middle class.

(h) There is little income mobility—the notion of America as a land of opportunity is a myth.

(i) And America has more inequality than any other advanced industrialized country, it does less to correct these inequities, and inequality is growing more than in many other countries.

The American Right finds the facts described in this chapter inconvenient. The analysis runs counter to some cherished myths that it would like to propagate: that America is a land of opportunity, that most people have been benefiting from the market economy, especially in the era since Reagan deregulated the economy and downsized government. Members of the Right would like to deny the facts, but the accumulation of data makes it hard to do so. They especially can't deny that those at the bottom *and in the middle* are doing poorly and that those at the top are grabbing an increasing fraction of the nation's income—so much of a larger share that what's left over for the rest is diminished; and that the chances that those at the bottom or in the middle will make it to the top are far lower than the chances that those at the top will remain there. Nor can the Right really deny the fact that government can help ameliorate poverty—it has done so especially effectively among the elderly. And that means that cutbacks in government programs, including Social Security, unless they are very carefully designed, are likely to increase poverty.

In response, the Right offers four retorts. The first is that in any year someone will be down and out and someone else will enjoy a bonanza. What really matters is lifetime inequality. Those with the lowest incomes will, by and large, have higher incomes in later years, so lifetime inequality is less than these data suggest. Economists have taken a hard look at differences in lifetime income—and, unfortunately, the wish of the Right doesn't conform to today's reality: lifetime inequality is very large, almost as great as income at each moment of time, and has increased enormously in recent years.[102]

The Right also sometimes claims that poverty in America is not real poverty. After all, most of those in poverty have amenities that are not available to the poor in other countries. They should be grateful for living in America. They have TVs, indoor plumbing, heating (most of the time), and access to free schools. But as a National Academy of Sciences panel found,[103] one cannot ignore relative deprivation. Basic standards of sanitation in America's cities lead naturally to indoor plumbing. Cheap Chinese TVs mean that even the poor can afford them—and indeed, even in poor Indian and Chinese villages, there is in general access to TV. In today's world, this is not a mark of affluence. But the fact that people may be enjoying a small TV doesn't really mean that they aren't facing stark poverty—nor does it mean that they are participating in the American dream.[104]

The third response is to quibble about the statistics. Some might claim that inflation may be overestimated, so growth in incomes may be underestimated. But, if anything, I suspect that the numbers underestimate the travails facing the typical American family. As family members work longer hours to maintain their standard of living—"for the family"—family life often suffers. Earlier in this chapter, we described the increasing level of insecurity that the poor and the middle class in America face—and this, too, is not reflected in the income statistics. Plausibly, true inequality may be far larger than the measures of inequality of income would suggest. Indeed, as we noted earlier, when the Census Bureau recently took a more careful look at the poverty statistics, it found that the poverty rate for 2010 went up from 15.2 percent to 16 percent.[105]

The final retort by the Right makes reference to an economic and moral justification of inequality, accompanied by a claim that attempting to do anything about it will simply "kill the golden goose," and so weaken America's economy that even the poor will suffer.[106] As Mitt Romney put it, inequality is the kind of thing that should be discussed quietly and privately.[107] The poor, in this land of opportunity, have only themselves to blame. In later chapters we'll address these arguments. We'll show that, for the most part, not only should we not blame the poor for their plight but also that the claim of those at the top, that they earned their money "on their own," doesn't have much merit. We'll see that the 1 percent are by and large not those who earned their incomes by great social contributions—they are not the great thinkers who have transformed our understanding of the world or the great innovators who have transformed our economy. We'll also explain why creating a more equal society can create a more dynamic economy.

The trauma of the Great Recession—with large numbers of people losing their jobs and homes—has triggered a chain reaction, affecting not just the lives of the individuals concerned but also society as a whole. We now see that, for most Americans, the economy wasn't really performing as it should even before the recession. We can no longer ignore America's growing inequality and its grave economic, political, and social consequences. But if we are to understand what to do about it, we have to understand the economic, political, and social forces that give rise to it.

CHAPTER TWO

RENT SEEKING AND THE MAKING OF AN UNEQUAL SOCIETY

AMERICAN INEQUALITY DIDN'T JUST HAPPEN. IT was created. Market forces played a role, but it was not market forces alone. In a sense, that should be obvious: economic laws are universal, but our growing inequality—especially the amounts seized by the upper 1 percent—is a distinctly American "achievement." That outsize inequality is not predestined offers reason for hope, but in reality it is likely to get worse. The forces that have been at play in creating these outcomes are self-reinforcing.

By understanding the origins of inequality, we can better grasp the costs and benefits of reducing it. The simple thesis of this chapter is that even though market forces help shape the degree of inequality, government policies shape those market forces. Much of the inequality that exists today is a result of government policy, both what the government does and what it does not do. Government has the power to move money from the top to the bottom and the middle, or vice versa.

We noted in the last chapter that America's current level of inequality is unusual. Compared with other countries and compared with what it was in the past even in the United States, it's unusually large, and it has been increasing unusually fast. It used to be said that watching for changes in inequality was like watching grass grow: it's hard to see the changes in any short span of time. But that's not true now.

Even what's been happening in this recession is unusual. Typically, when the economy weakens, wages and employment adjust slowly, so as sales fall, profits fall more than proportionately. But in this recession the share of wages has actually fallen, and many firms are making good profits.[1]

Addressing inequality is of necessity multifaceted—we have to rein in the excesses at the top, strengthen the middle, and help those at the bottom. Each goal requires a program of its own. But to construct such programs, we have to have a better understanding of what has given rise to each facet of this unusual inequality.

Distinct as the inequality we face today is, inequality itself is not something new. The concentration of economic and political power was in many ways more extreme in the precapitalist societies of the West. At that time, religion both explained and justified the inequality: those at the top of society were there because of divine right. To question that was to question the social order, or even to question God's will.

However, for modern economists and political scientists, as also for the ancient Greeks, this inequality was not a matter of a preordained social order. Power—often military power— was at the origin of these inequities. Militarism was about economics: the conquerors had the right to extract as much as they could from the conquered. In antiquity, natural philosophy in general saw no wrong in treating other humans as means for the ends of others. As the ancient Greek historian Thucydides famously said, "right, as the world goes, is only in question between equals in power, while the strong do what they can and the weak suffer what they must."[2]

Those with power used that power to strengthen their economic and political positions, or at the very least to maintain them.[3] They also attempted to shape thinking, to make acceptable differences in income that would otherwise be odious.

As the notion of divine right became rejected in the early nation-states, those with power sought other bases for defending their positions. With the Renaissance and the Enlightenment, which emphasized the dignity of the individual, and with the Industrial Revolution, which led to the emergence of a vast urban underclass, it became imperative to find new justifications for inequality, especially as critics of the system, like Marx, talked about exploitation.[4]

The theory that came to dominate, beginning in the second half of the nineteenth century—and still does—was called "marginal productivity theory"; those with higher productivities earned higher incomes that reflected their greater contribution to society. Competitive markets, working through the laws of supply and demand, determine the value of each individual's contributions. If someone has a scarce and valuable skill, the market will reward him amply, because of his greater contribution to output. If he has no skills, his income will be low. Technology, of course, determines the productivity of different skills: in a primitive agriculture economy, physical strength and endurance is what mattered; in a modern hi-tech economy, brainpower is more relevant.

Technology and scarcity, working through the ordinary laws of supply and demand, play a role in shaping today's inequality, but something else is at work, and that something else is government. Inequality is the result of political forces as much as of economic ones. In a modern economy government sets and enforces the rules of the game—what is fair competition, and what actions are deemed anticompetitive and illegal, who gets what in the event of bankruptcy, when a debtor can't pay all that he owes, what are fraudulent practices and forbidden. Government also gives away resources (both openly and less transparently) and, through taxes and social expenditures, modifies the distribution of income that emerges from the market, shaped as it is by technology and politics.

Finally, government alters the dynamics of wealth by, for instance, taxing inheritances and providing free public education. Inequality is determined not just by how much the market pays a skilled worker relative to an unskilled worker, but also by the level of skills that an individual has acquired. In the absence of government support, many children of the poor would not be able to get basic health care and nutrition, let alone the education required to acquire the skills necessary for enhanced productivity and high wages. Government can affect the extent to which an individual's education and inherited wealth depends on that of his parents. More formally, economists say that inequality depends on the distribution of "endowments," of financial and human capital.

The way the American government performs these functions determines the extent of inequality in our society. In each of these arenas there are subtle decisions that benefit some group at the expense of others. The effect of each decision may be small, but the cumulative effect of large numbers of decisions, made to benefit those at the top, can be very significanat.

Competitive forces should limit outsize profits, but if governments do not ensure that markets are competitive, there can be large monopoly profits. Competitive forces should also limit disproportionate executive compensation, but in modern corporations, the CEO has enormous power—including the power to set his own compensation, subject, of course, to his board—but in many corporations, he even has considerable power to appoint the board, and with a stacked board, there is little check. Shareholders have minimal say. Some countries have better "corporate governance laws," the laws that circumscribe the power of the CEO, for instance, by insisting that there be independent members in the board or that shareholders have a say in pay. If the country does not have good corporate governance laws that are effectively enforced, CEOs can pay themselves outsize bonuses.

Progressive tax and expenditure policies (which tax the rich more than the poor and provide systems of good social protection) can limit the extent of inequality. By contrast, programs that give away a country's resources to the rich and well connected can increase inequality.

Our political system has increasingly been working in ways that increase the inequality of outcomes and reduce equality of opportunity. This should not come as a surprise: we have a political system that gives inordinate power to those at the top, and they have used that power not only to limit the extent of redistribution but also to shape the rules of the game in their favor, and to extract from the public what can only be called large "gifts." Economists have a name for these activities: they call them rent seeking, getting income not as a reward to creating wealth but by grabbing a larger share of the wealth that would otherwise have been produced without their effort. (We'll give a fuller definition of the concept of rent seeking later in the chapter.) Those at the top have learned how to suck out money from the rest in ways that the rest are hardly aware of—that is their true innovation.

Jean-Baptiste Colbert, the adviser to King Louis XIV of France, reportedly said, "The art of taxation consists in so plucking the goose as to obtain the largest amount of feathers with the least possible amount of hissing." So, too, for the art of rent seeking.

To put it baldly, there are two ways to become wealthy: to create wealth or to take wealth away from others. The former adds to society. The latter typically subtracts from it, for in the process of taking it away, wealth gets destroyed. A monopolist who overcharges for his product takes money from those whom he is overcharging and at the same time destroys value. To get his monopoly price, he has to restrict production.

Unfortunately, even genuine wealth creators often are not satisfied with the wealth that their innovation or entrepreneurship has reaped. Some eventually turn to abusive practices like monopoly pricing or other forms of rent extraction to garner even more riches. To take just one example, the railroad barons of the nineteenth century provided an important service in constructing the railroads, but much of their wealth was the result of their political influence—getting large government land grants on either side of the railway. Today, over a century after the railroad barons dominated the economy, much of the wealth at the top in the United States—and some of the suffering at the bottom—stems from wealth transfers instead of wealth creation.

Of course, not all the inequality in our society is a result of rent seeking, or of government's tilting the rules of the game in favor of those at the top. Markets matter, as do social forces (like discrimination). This chapter focuses on the myriad forms that rent seeking takes in our society, and the next turns to the other determinants of inequality.

GENERAL PRINCIPLES

Adam Smith's invisible hand and inequality

Adam Smith, the father of modern economics, argued that the private pursuit of self-interest would lead, as if by an invisible hand, to the well-being of all. [5] In the aftermath of the financial crisis, no one today would argue that the bankers' pursuit of their self-interest has led to the well-being of all. At most, it led to *the bankers'* well-being, with the rest of society bearing the cost. It wasn't even what economists call a zero-sum game, where what one person gains exactly equals what the others lose. It was a negative-sum game, where the gains to winners are less than the losses to the losers. What the rest of society lost was far, far greater than the bankers' payoff.

There is a simple reason for why financiers' pursuit of *their* interests turned out to be disastrous for the rest of society: the bankers' incentives were not well aligned with social returns. When markets work well—in the way that Adam Smith hypothesized—it is because private returns and social benefits are well aligned, that is, because private rewards and social contributions are equal, as had been assumed by marginal productivity theory. In that theory, the social contribution of each worker is exactly equal to the private compensation. People with higher productivity—a larger social contribution—get higher pay.

Adam Smith himself was aware of one of the circumstances in which private and social returns differ. As he explained, "People of the same trade seldom meet together, even for merriment and diversion, but the conversation ends in a conspiracy against the public, or in some contrivance to raise prices."[6] Markets by themselves often fail to produce efficient and desirable outcomes, and there is a role for government in correcting these market failures, that is, designing policies (taxes and regulations) that bring private incentives and social returns into alignment. (Of course, there are often disagreements about the best way of doing it. But few today believe in unfettered financial markets—their failures impose too great a cost on the rest of society—or that firms should be allowed to despoil the environment without restriction.) When government does its job well, the returns received by, say, a worker or an investor are in fact equal to the benefits to society that his actions contribute. When these are not aligned, we say there is a market failure, that is, markets fail to produce efficient outcomes. Private rewards and social returns are not well aligned when competition is imperfect; when there are "externalities" (where one party's actions can have large negative or positive effects on others for which he does not pay or reap the benefit); when there exist imperfections or asymmetries of information (where someone knows something relevant to a market trade that someone else doesn't know); or where risk markets or other markets are absent (one can't, for instance, buy insurance against many of the most important risks that one faces). Since one or more of these conditions exist in virtually every market, there is in fact little presumption that markets are in general efficient. This means that there is an enormous potential role for government to correct these market failures.

Government never corrects market failures perfectly, but it does a better job in some countries than in others. Only if the government does a reasonably good job of correcting the most important market failures will the economy prosper. Good financial regulation helped the United States—and the world—avoid a major crisis for four decades after the Great Depression. Deregulation in the 1980s led to scores of financial crises in the succeeding three decades, of which America's crisis in 2008–09 was only the worst.[7] But those governmental failures were no accident: the financial sector used its political muscle to make sure that the market failures were *not* corrected, and that the sector's private rewards remained well in excess of their social contributions—one of the factors contributing to the bloated financial sector and to the high levels of inequality at the top.

Shaping markets

We'll describe below some of the ways that private financial firms act to ensure that markets *don't work well*. For instance, as Smith noted, there are incentives for firms to work to reduce market competition. Moreover, firms also strive to make sure that there are no strong laws prohibiting them from engaging in anticompetitive behavior or, when there are such laws, that they are not effectively enforced. The focus of businesspeople is, of course, not to enhance societal well-being broadly understood, or even to make markets more competitive: their objective is simply to make markets work *for them*, to make them more profitable. But the consequence is often a less efficient economy marked by greater inequality. For now, one example will suffice. When markets are competitive, profits above the normal return to capital cannot be sustained. That is so because if a firm makes greater profits than that on a sale, rivals will attempt to steal the customer by lowering prices. As firms compete vigorously, prices fall to the point that profits (above the normal return to capital) are driven down to zero, a disaster for those seeking big profits. In business school we teach students how to recognize, and create, barriers to competition—including barriers to entry—that help ensure that profits won't be eroded. Indeed, as we shall shortly see, some of the most important innovations in business in the last three decades have centered not on making the economy more efficient but on how better to ensure monopoly power or how better to circumvent government regulations intended to align social returns and private rewards.

Making markets less transparent is a favorite tool. The more transparent markets are, the more competitive they are likely to be. Bankers know this. That's why banks have been fighting to keep their business in writing derivatives, the risky products that were at the center of AIG's collapse,[8] in the shadows of the "over the counter" market. In that market, it's difficult for customers to know whether they're getting a good deal. Everything is negotiated, as opposed to how things work in more open and transparent modern markets. And since the sellers are trading constantly, and buyers enter only episodically, sellers have more information than buyers, and they use that information to their advantage. This means that on average, sellers (the writers of the derivatives, the banks) can extract more money out of their customers. Well-designed open auctions, by contrast, ensure that goods go to those who value them the most, a hallmark of efficiency. There are publicly available prices for guiding decisions.

While lack of transparency results in more profits for the bankers, it leads to lower economic performance. Without good information, capital markets can't exercise any discipline. Money won't go to where returns are highest, or to the bank that does the best job of managing money. No one can know the true financial position of a bank or other financial institution today—and shadowy derivative transactions are part of the reason. One would have hoped that the recent crisis might have forced change, but the bankers resisted. They resisted demands, for instance, for more transparency in derivatives and for regulations that would restrict anticompetitive practices. These rent-seeking activities were worth tens of billions of dollars in profits. Although they didn't win every battle, they won often enough that the problems are still with us. In late October 2011, for instance, a major American financial firm[9] went bankrupt (the eighth-largest bankruptcy on record), partly because of complex derivatives. Evidently the market hadn't seen through these transactions, at least not in a timely way.

Moving money from the bottom of the pyramid to the top

One of the ways that those at the top make money is by taking advantage of their market and political power to favor themselves, to increase their own income, at the expense of the rest.

The financial sector has developed expertise in a wide variety of forms of rent seeking. We've already mentioned some, but there are many others: taking advantage of asymmetries of information (for instance, selling securities that they had designed to fail, but knowing that buyers didn't know that);[10] taking excessive risk—with the government holding a lifeline, bailing them out and assuming the losses, the knowledge of which, incidentally, allows them to borrow at a lower interest rate than they otherwise could; and getting money from the Federal Reserve at low interest rates, now almost zero.

But the form of rent seeking that is most egregious—and that has been most perfected in recent years—has been the ability of those in the financial sector to take advantage of the poor and uninformed, as they made enormous amounts of money by preying upon these groups with predatory lending and abusive credit card practices.[11] Each poor person might have only a little, but there are so many poor that a little from each amounts to a great deal. Any sense of social justice—or any concern about overall efficiency—would have led government to prohibit these activities. After all, considerable amounts of resources were used up in the process of moving money from the poor to the rich, which is why it's a negative-sum game. But government didn't put an end to these kind of activities, not even when, around 2007, it became increasingly apparent what was going on. The reason was obvious. The financial sector had invested heavily in lobbying and campaign contributions, and the investments paid off.

I mention the financial sector partly because it has contributed so powerfully to our society's current level of inequality.[12] Much of what I have said about the financial sector, though, could be said about other players in the economy that have had a hand in creating current inequities.

Modern capitalism has become a complex game, and those who win at it have to have more than a little smarts. But those who win at it often possess less admirable characteristics as well: the ability to skirt the law, or to shape the law in their own favor; the willingness to take advantage of

others, even the poor; and to play *unfair* when nece
As one of the successful players in this game put it, t...
adage "Win or lose, what matters is how you play the game"
is rubbish. *All that matters is whether you win or lose.* The
market provides a simple way of showing that—the amount
of money that you have.

Winning in the game of rent seeking has made fortunes
for many of those at the top, but it is not the only means by
which they obtain and preserve their wealth. The tax system
also plays a key role, as we'll see later. Those at the top have
managed to design a tax system in which they pay less than
their fair share—they pay a lower fraction of their income
than do those who are much poorer. We call such tax systems
regressive.

And while regressive taxes and rent seeking (which takes
money from the rest of society and redistributes it to the
top) are at the core of growing inequality, especially at the
top, broader forces exert particular influence on two other
aspects of American inequality—the hollowing out of the
middle class and the increase in poverty. Laws governing corporations interact with the norms of behavior that guide the
leaders of those corporations and determine how returns are
shared among top management and other stakeholders (workers, shareholders, and bondholders). Macroeconomic policies determine the tightness of the labor market—the level
of unemployment, and thus how market forces operate to
change the share of workers. If monetary authorities act to
keep unemployment high (even if because of fear of inflation),
then wages will be restrained. Strong unions have helped to
reduce inequality, whereas weaker unions have made it easier
for CEOs, sometimes working with market forces that they

have helped shape, to increase it. In each arena—the strength of unions, the effectiveness of corporate governance, the conduct of monetary policy—politics is central.

Of course, market forces, the balancing of, say, the demand and supply for skilled workers, affected as it is by changes in technology and education, play an important role as well, even if those forces are partially shaped by politics. But instead of these market forces and politics balancing each other out, with the political process dampening the increase in inequality in periods when market forces might have led to growing disparities, instead of government *tempering* the excesses of the market, in America today the two have been working together to increase income and wealth disparities.

RENT SEEKING

Earlier, we labeled as *rent seeking* many of the ways by which our current political process helps the rich at the expense of the rest of us. Rent seeking takes many forms: hidden and open transfers and subsidies from the government, laws that make the marketplace less competitive, lax enforcement of existing competition laws, and statutes that allow corporations to take advantage of others or to pass costs on to the rest of society. The term "rent" was originally used to describe the returns to land, since the owner of land receives these payments by virtue of his ownership and not because of anything he *does*. This stands in contrast to the situation of workers, for example, whose wages are compensation for the *effort* they provide. The term "rent" then was extended to include monopoly profits, or monopoly rents, the income that one receives simply from the control of a monopoly. Eventually the term was expanded still further to include the returns on similar ownership claims. If the government gave a company the exclusive right to import a limited amount (a quota) of a good, such as sugar, then the extra return generated as a result of the ownership of those rights was called a "quota-rent."

Countries rich in natural resource are infamous for rent-seeking activities. It's far easier to get rich in these countries by gaining access to resources at favorable terms than by producing wealth. This is often a negative-sum game, which is one of the reasons why, on average, such countries have grown more slowly than comparable countries without the bounty of such resources.[14]

Even more disturbing, one might have thought that an abundance of resources could be used to help the poor, to ensure access to education and health care for all. Taxing work and savings can weaken incentives; in contrast, taxing the "rents" on land, oil, or other natural resources won't make them disappear. The resources will still be there to be taken out, if not today, then tomorrow. There are no adverse incentive effects. That means that, in principle, there should be ample revenues to finance both social expenditures and public investments—in, say, health and education. Yet, among the countries with the greatest inequality are those with the most natural resources. Evidently, a few within these countries are better at rent seeking than others (usually those with political power), and they ensure that the benefits of the resources accrue largely to themselves. In Venezuela, the richest oil producer in Latin America, half of the country lived in poverty prior to the rise of Hugo Chavez—and it is precisely this type of poverty in the midst of riches that gives rise to leaders like him.[15]

Rent-seeking behavior is not just endemic in the resource-rich countries of the Middle East, Africa, and Latin America. It has also become endemic in modern economies, including our own. In those economies, it takes many forms, some of which are closely akin to those in the oil-rich countries: getting state assets (such as oil or minerals) at below fair-market prices.

Another form of rent seeking is the flip side: selling to government products at *above* market prices (noncompetitive procurement). The drug companies and military contractors excel in this form of rent seeking. Open government subsidies (as in agriculture) or hidden subsidies (trade restrictions that reduce competition or subsidies hidden in the tax system) are other ways of getting rents from the public.

Not all rent seeking uses government to extract money from ordinary citizens. The private sector can excel on its own, extracting rents from the public, for instance, through monopolistic practices and exploiting those who are less informed and educated, exemplified by the banks' predatory lending. CEOs can use their control of the corporation to garner for themselves a larger fraction of the firms' revenues. Here, though, the government too plays a role, by not doing what it should: by not stopping these activities, by not making them illegal, or by not enforcing laws that exist. Effective enforcement of competition laws can circumscribe monopoly profits; effective laws on predatory lending and credit card abuses can limit the extent of bank exploitation; well-designed corporate governance laws can limit the extent to which corporate officials appropriate for themselves firm revenues.

By looking at those at the top of the wealth distribution, we can get a feel for the nature of this aspect of America's inequality. Few are inventors who have reshaped technology, or scientists who have reshaped our understandings of the laws of nature. Think of Alan Turing, whose genius provided the mathematics underlying the modern computer. Or of Einstein. Or of the discoverers of the laser (in which Charles Townes played a central role)[16] or John Bardeen, Walter Brattain, and William Shockley, the inventors of transistors.[17] Or of Watson and Crick, who unraveled the mysteries of DNA, upon which rests so much of modern medicine. None of them, who made such large contributions to our well-being, are among those most rewarded by our economic system.

Instead, many of the individuals at the top of the wealth distribution are, in one way or another, geniuses at business. Some might claim, for instance, that Steve Jobs or the innovators of search engines or social media were, in their way, geniuses. Jobs was number 110 on the *Forbes* list of the world's wealthiest billionaires before his death, and Mark Zuckerberg was 52. But many of these "geniuses" built their business empires on the shoulders of giants, such as Tim Berners-Lee, the inventor of the World Wide Web, who has never appeared on the *Forbes* list. Berners-Lee could have become a billionaire but chose not to—he made his idea available freely, which greatly speeded up the development of the Internet.[18]

A closer look at the successes of those at the top of the wealth distribution shows that more than a small part of their genius resides in devising better ways of exploiting market power and other market imperfections—and, in many cases, finding better ways of ensuring that politics works for them rather than for society more generally.

We've already commented on financiers, who make up a significant portion of the top 1 or 0.1 percent. While some gained their wealth by producing value, others did so in no small part by one of the myriad forms of rent seeking that we described earlier. At the top, in addition to the financiers, whom we have already discussed,[19] are the monopolists and their descendants who, through one mechanism or another, have succeeded in achieving and sustaining market dominance. After the railroad barons of the nineteenth century came John D. Rockefeller and Standard Oil. The end of the twentieth century saw Bill Gates and Microsoft's domination of the PC software industry.

Internationally, there is the case of Carlos Slim, a Mexican businessman who was ranked by *Forbes* as the wealthiest person in the world in 2011.[20] Thanks to his dominance of the telephone industry in Mexico, Slim is able to charge prices that are a multiple of those in more competitive markets. He made his breakthrough when he was able to acquire a large share in Mexico's telecommunications system after the country privatized it,[21] a strategy that lies behind many of the world's great fortunes. As we've seen, it's easy to get rich by getting a state asset at a deep discount. Many of Russia's current oligarchs, for example, obtained their initial wealth by buying state assets at below-market prices and then ensuring continuing profits through monopoly power. (In America most of our government giveaways tend to be more subtle. We design rules for, say, selling government assets that are in effect partial giveaways, but less transparently so than what Russia did.)[22]

In the preceding chapter, we identified another important group of the very wealthy—corporate CEOs, such as Stephen Hemsley from UnitedHealth Group, who received $102 million in 2010, and Edward Mueller from Qwest Communications (now CenturyLink, after a merger in 2011), who made $65.8 million.[23] CEOs have successfully garnered a larger and larger fraction of corporate revenues.[24] As we'll explain later, it is not a sudden increase in their productivity that allowed these CEOs to amass such riches in the last couple of decades but rather an enhanced ability to take more from the corporation that they are supposed to be serving, and weaker qualms about, and enhanced public toleration of, doing so.

A final large group of rent seekers consists of the top-flight lawyers, including those who became wealthy by helping others engage in their rent seeking in ways that skirt the law but do not (usually) land them in prison. They help write the complex tax laws in which loopholes are put, so their clients can avoid taxes, and they then design the complex deals to take advantage of these loopholes. They helped design the complex and nontransparent derivatives market. They help design the contractual arrangements that generate monopoly power, seemingly within the law. And for all this assistance in making our markets work not the way markets should but as instruments for the benefit of those at the top, they get amply rewarded.[25]

Monopoly rents: creating sustainable monopolies

To economists large fortunes pose a problem. The laws of competition, as I have noted, say that profits (beyond the normal return to capital) are supposed to be driven to zero, and quickly. But if profits are zero, how can fortunes be built? Niches in which there isn't competition, for one reason or another, offer one avenue.[26] But that goes only a little way to explaining sustainable excessive profits (beyond the competitive level). Success will attract entry, and profits will quickly disappear. The real key to success is to make sure that there won't ever be competition—or at least there won't be competition for a long enough time that one can make a monopoly killing in the meanwhile. The simplest way to a sustainable monopoly is getting the government to give you one. From the seventeenth century to the nineteenth, the British granted the East India Company a monopoly on trade with India.

There are other ways to get government-sanctioned monopolies. Patents typically give an inventor a monopoly over that innovation for a temporary period, but the details of patent law can extend the length of the patent, reduce entry of new firms, and enhance monopoly power. America's patent laws have been doing exactly that. They are designed not to maximize the pace of innovation but rather to maximize rents.[27]

Even without a government grant of monopoly, firms can create entry barriers. A variety of practices discourage entry, such as maintaining excess capacity, so that an entrant knows that, should he enter, the incumbent firm can increase production, lowering prices to the point that entry would be unprofitable.[28] In the Middle Ages, guilds successfully restricted competition. Many professions have continued that tradition. Although they argue that they are simply trying to maintain standards, restrictions on entry (limiting the number of places at medical school or restricting migration of trained personnel from abroad) help keep incomes high.[29]

At the turn of the previous century, concern about the monopolies that formed the basis of many of the fortunes of that period, including Rockefeller's, grew so great that under the trust-busting president Theodore Roosevelt, America passed a slew of laws to break up monopolies and prevent some of these practices. In the years that followed, numerous monopolies were broken up—in oil, cigarettes, and many other industries.[30] And yet today, as we look around the

American economy, we can see many sectors, including some that are central to its functioning, where one or a few firms dominate—such as Microsoft in PC operating systems, or AT&T, Verizon, T-Mobile, and Sprint in telecommunications.

Three factors contributed to this increased monopolization of markets. First, there was a battle over ideas about the role that government should take in ensuring competition. Chicago school economists (like Milton Friedman and George Stigler) who believe in free and unfettered markets[31] argued that markets are naturally competitive[32] and that seemingly anticompetitive practices really enhance efficiency. A massive program to "educate"[33] people, and especially judges, regarding these new doctrines of law and economics, partly sponsored by right-wing foundations like the Olin Foundation, was successful. The timing was ironic: American courts were buying into notions that markets were "naturally" competitive and placing a high burden of proof on anyone claiming otherwise just as the economics discipline was exploring theories that explain why markets often were *not* competitive, even when there were seemingly many firms. For instance, a new and powerful branch of economics called game theory explained how collusive behavior could be maintained tacitly over extended periods of time. Meanwhile, new theories of imperfect and asymmetric information showed how information imperfections impaired competition, and new evidence substantiated the relevance and importance of these theories.

The influence of the Chicago school should not be underestimated. Even when there are blatant infractions— like predatory pricing, where a firm lowers its price to force out a competitor and then uses its monopoly power to raise prices—they've been hard to prosecute.[34] Chicago school

economics argues that markets are presumptively competitive and efficient. If entry were easy, the dominant firm
would gain nothing from driving out a rival, because the
firm that is forced out would be quickly replaced by another
firm. But in reality entry is not so easy, and predatory behavior does occur.

A second factor giving rise to increased monopoly is related
to changes in our economy. The creation of monopoly power
was easier in some of the new growth industries. Many
of these sectors were marked by what are called network
externalities. An obvious example is the computer operating
system: just as it's very convenient for everyone to speak the
same language, it's very convenient for everyone to use the
same operating system. Increasing interconnectivity across
the world naturally leads to standardization. Those with a
monopoly over the standard that is chosen benefit.

As we have noted, competition naturally works against the
accumulation of market power. When there are large monopoly profits, competitors work to get a share. That's where the
third factor that has increased monopoly power in the United
States comes in: businesses found new ways of resisting entry,
of reducing competitive pressures. Microsoft provides the
example par excellence. Because it enjoyed a near-monopoly
on PC operating systems, it stood to lose a lot if alternative
technologies undermined its monopoly. The development of
the Internet and the web browser to access it represented just
such a threat. Netscape brought the browser to the market,
building on government-funded research.[35] Microsoft decided
to squelch this potential competitor. It offered its own product, Internet Explorer, but the product couldn't compete in
the open market. The company decided to use its monopoly

power in PC operating systems to make sure that the playing field was not level. It deployed a strategy known as FUD (fear, uncertainty, and doubt), creating anxiety about compatibility among users by programming error messages that would randomly appear if Netscape was installed on a Windows computer. The company also did not provide the disclosures necessary for full compatibility as new versions of Windows were developed. And most cleverly, it offered Internet Explorer at a zero price—free, bundled in as part of its operating system. It's hard to compete with a zero price. Netscape was doomed.[36]

It was obvious that selling something at a zero price was not a profit-maximizing strategy—in the short run. But Microsoft had a vision for the long run: the maintenance of its monopoly. For that, it was willing to make short-run sacrifices. It succeeded, but so blatant were its methods that courts and tribunals throughout the world charged it with engaging in anticompetitive practices. And yet, in the end, Microsoft won—for it realized that in a network economy, a monopoly position, once attained, is hard to break. Given Microsoft's dominance of the operating system market, it had the incentives and capabilities to dominate in a host of other applications.[37]

No wonder, then, that Microsoft's profits have been so enormous—an average of $7 billion per year over the last quarter century, $14 billion over the past ten years, increasing in 2011 to $23 billion[38]—and reaping wealth for those who bought shares early enough. The conventional wisdom has it that in spite of its dominant position and huge resources, Microsoft has not been a real innovator. It did not develop the first widely used word processor, the first spreadsheet, the first browser, the first media player, or the first dominant search engine. Innovation lay elsewhere. This is consistent with theory and historical evidence: monopolists are not good innovators.[39]

Looking at the U.S. economy, we see in many sectors large numbers of firms, and therefore infer that there must be competition. But that's not always the case. Take the example of banks. While there are hundreds of banks, the big four share between them almost half of the country's banking assets,[40] a marked increase from the degree of concentration fifteen years ago. In most smaller communities, there are at most one or two. When competition is so limited, prices are likely to be far in excess of competitive levels.[41] That's why the sector enjoys profits estimated to be more than $115 billion a year, much of which is passed along to its top officials and other bankers—helping create one of the major sources of inequality at the top.[42] In some products, such as over-the-counter credit default swaps (CDSes), four or five very large banks totally dominate, and such market concentration always gives rise to the worry that they collude, albeit tacitly. (But sometimes the collusion is not even tacit—it is explicit. The banks set a critical rate, called the London Interbank Offered Rate, or Libor. Mortgages and many financial products are linked to Libor. It appears that the banks worked to rig the rate, enabling them to make still more money from others who were unaware of these shenanigans.)

Of course, even when laws that prohibit monopolistic practices are on the books, these have to be enforced. Particularly given the narrative created by the Chicago school of economics, there is a tendency not to interfere with the "free" workings of the market, even when the outcome is anticompetitive. And there are good political reasons not to take too strong a position: after all, it's antibusiness—and not good for campaign contributions—to be too tough on, say, Microsoft.[43]

Politics: getting to set the rules and pick the referee

It's one thing to win in a "fair" game. It's quite another to be able to write the rules of the game—and to write them in ways that enhance one's prospects of winning. And it's even worse if you can choose your own referees. In many areas today, regulatory agencies are responsible for oversight of a sector (writing and enforcing rules and regulations)—the Federal Communications Commission (FCC) in telecom; the Securities and Exchange Commission (SEC) in securities; and the Federal Reserve in many areas of banking. The problem is that leaders in these sectors use their political influence to get people appointed to the regulatory agencies who are sympathetic to their perspectives.

Economists refer to this as "regulatory capture."[44] Sometimes the capture is associated with pecuniary incentives: those on the regulatory commission come from and return to the sector that they are supposed to regulate. Their incentives and those of the industry are well aligned, even if their incentives are not well aligned with those of the rest of society. If those on the regulatory commission serve the sector well, they get well rewarded in their post-government career.

Sometimes, however, the capture is not just motivated by money. Instead, the mindset of regulators is captured by those whom they regulate. This is called "cognitive capture," and it is more of a sociological phenomenon. While neither Alan Greenspan nor Tim Geithner actually worked for a big bank before coming to the Federal Reserve, there was a natural affinity, and they may have come to share the same mindset. In the bankers' mindset—despite the mess that the bankers had made—there was no need to impose stringent conditions on the banks in the bailout.

The bankers have unleashed enormous numbers of lobbyists to persuade any and all who play a role in regulation that they should not be regulated—an estimated 2.5 for every U.S. representative.[45] But persuasion is easier if the target of your efforts begins from a sympathetic position. That is why banks and their lobbyists work so strenuously to ensure that the government appoints regulators who have already been "captured" in one way or another. The bankers try to veto anyone who does not share their belief. I saw this firsthand during the Clinton administration, when potential names for the Fed were floated, some even from the banking community. If any of the potential nominees deviated from the party line that markets are self-regulating and that the banks could manage their own risk there arose a hue and cry so great that the name wouldn't be put forward or, if it was put forward, that it wouldn't be approved.[46]

Government munificence

We've seen how monopolies—whether government granted or government "sanctioned," through inadequate enforcement of competition laws—have built the fortunes of many of the world's wealthiest people. But there is another way to get rich. You can simply arrange for the government to hand you cash. This can happen in myriad ways. A little-noticed change in legislation, for example, can reap billions of dollars. This was the case when the government extended a much-needed

Medicare drug benefit in 2003.[47] A provision in the law that prohibited government from bargaining for prices on drugs was, in effect, a gift of some $50 billion or more per year to the pharmaceutical companies.[48] More generally, government procurement—paying prices well above costs—is a standard form of government munificence.

Sometimes gifts are hidden in obscure provisions of legislation. A provision of one of the key bills deregulating the financial derivative market—ensuring that no regulator could touch it, no matter how great the peril to which it exposed the economy—also gave derivatives claims "seniority" in the event of bankruptcy. If a bank went under, the claims on the derivatives would be paid off before workers, suppliers, or other creditors saw any money—even if the derivatives had pushed the firm into bankruptcy in the first place.[49] (The derivatives market played a central role in the 2008–09 crisis and was responsible for the $182 billion bailout of AIG.)

There are other ways that the banking sector has benefited from government munificence, evident most clearly in the aftermath of the Great Recession. When the Federal Reserve (which can be thought of as one branch of the government) lends unlimited amounts of money to banks at near-zero interest rates, and allows them to lend the money back to the government (or to foreign governments) at much higher interest rates, it is simply giving them a hidden gift worth billions and billions of dollars.

These are not the only ways that governments spur the creation of enormous personal wealth. Many countries, including the United States, control vast amounts of natural resources like oil, gas, and mining concessions. If the government grants you the right to extract these resources for free, it doesn't take a genius to make a fortune. That is, of course, what the U.S.

government did in the nineteenth century, when anyone could stake a claim to natural resources. Today, the government doesn't typically give away its resources; more often it requires a payment, but a payment that is far less than it should be. This is just a less transparent way of giving away money. If the value of the oil under a particular piece of land is $100 million after paying the extraction costs, and the government requires a payment of only $50 million, the government has, in effect, given away $50 million.

It doesn't have to be this way, but powerful interests ensure that it is. In the Clinton administration, we tried to make the mining companies pay more for the resources they take out of public lands than the nominal amounts that they do. Not surprisingly, the mining companies—and the congressmen to whom they make generous contributions—opposed these measures, and successfully so. They argued that the policy would impede growth. But the fact of the matter is that, with an auction, companies will bid to get the mining rights so long as the value of the resources is greater than the cost of extraction, and if they win the bid, they will extract the resources. Auctions don't impede growth; they just make sure that the public gets paid appropriately for what is theirs. Modern auction theory has shown how changing the design of the auction can generate much more revenue for the government. These theories were tested out in the auction of the spectrum used for telecommunications beginning in the 1990s, and they worked remarkably well, generating billions for the government.

Sometimes government munificence, instead of handing over resources for pennies on the dollar, takes the form of rewriting the rules to boost profits. An easy way to do this is to protect firms from foreign competition. Tariffs, taxes paid by companies abroad but not by domestic firms, are in effect a gift to domestic producers. The firms demanding protection from foreign competition always provide a rationale, suggesting that society as a whole is the beneficiary and that any benefits that accrue to the companies themselves are incidental. This is self-serving, of course, and while there are instances in which such pleas contain some truth, the widespread abuse of the argument makes it hard to take seriously. Because tariffs put foreign producers at a disadvantage, they enable domestic firms to raise their prices and increase their profits. In some cases, there may be some incidental benefits such as higher domestic employment and the opportunity for companies to invest in R&D that will increase productivity and competiveness. But just as often, tariffs protect old and tired industries that have lost their competitiveness and are not likely to regain it, or occasionally those that have made bad bets on new technologies and would like to postpone facing competition.

The ethanol subsidy offers an example of this phenomenon. A plan to reduce our dependence on oil by replacing it with the energy of the sun embedded in one of America's great products, its corn, seemed irresistible. But converting plant energy into a form that can provide energy for cars instead of people is hugely expensive. It is also easier to do with some plants than others. So successful has Brazil's research on sugar-based ethanol been that in order for America to compete, for years it had to tax Brazilian sugar-based ethanol 54 cents a gallon.[50] Forty years after the introduction of the subsidy, it was still in place to support an infant technology that seemingly would not grow up. When oil prices fell after the 2008 recession, many ethanol plants went bankrupt, even with massive subsidies.[51] It wasn't until the end of 2011 that the subsidy and tariff were allowed to expire.

The persistence of such distortionary subsidies stems from

a single source: politics. The main—and for a long while, effectively the only—*direct* beneficiary of these subsidies were the corn-ethanol producers, dominated by the megafirm Archer Daniels Midland (ADM). Like so many other executives, those at ADM seemed to be better at managing politics than at innovation. They contributed generously to both parties, so that as much as those in Congress might rail against such corporate largesse, lawmakers were slow to touch the ethanol subsidies.[52] As we've noted, firms almost always argue that the true beneficiaries of any largesse they receive lie elsewhere. In this case, ethanol advocates argued that the real beneficiaries were America's corn farmers. But that was, for the most part, not the case, especially in the early days of the subsidy.[53]

Of course, why American corn farmers, who were already the recipients of massive government handouts, receiving almost half of their income from Washington rather than from the "soil," should receive still further assistance is hard to understand, and hard to reconcile with principles of a free-market economy. (In fact, the vast preponderance of government money subsidizing agriculture does not go, as many believe, to poor farmers or even family farms. The design of the program reveals its true objective: to redistribute money from the rest of us to the rich and corporate farms.)[54]

Sadly, government munificence toward corporations does not end with the few examples we have given, but to describe each and every instance of government approved rent seeking would require another book.[55]

CHAPTER THREE

MARKETS AND INEQUALITY

THE PRECEDING CHAPTER EMPHASIZED THE ROLE of rent seeking in creating America's high level of inequality. Another approach to explaining inequality emphasizes abstract market forces. In this view, it's just the bad luck of those in the middle and at the bottom that market forces have played out the way they have—with ordinary workers seeing their wages decline, and skilled bankers seeing their incomes soar. Implicit in this perspective is the notion that one interferes with the wonders of the market at one's peril: be cautious in any attempt to "correct" the market.

The view I take is somewhat different. I begin with the observation made in chapters 1 and 2: other advanced industrial countries with similar technology and per capita income differ greatly from the United States in inequality of pretax income (before transfers), in inequality of after tax and transfer income, in inequality of wealth, and in economic mobility. These countries also differ greatly from the United States in the *trends* in these four variables over time. If markets were the principal driving force, why do seemingly similar advanced industrial countries differ so much? Our hypothesis is that market forces are real, but that they are shaped by political processes. Markets are shaped by laws, regulations, and institutions. Every law, every regulation, every institutional arrangement has distributive consequences—and the way we have been shaping America's market economy works to the advantage of those at the top and to the disadvantage of the rest.

There is another factor determining societal inequality, one that we discuss in this chapter. Government, as we have seen, shapes market forces. But so do societal norms and social institutions. Indeed, politics, to a large extent, reflects and amplifies societal norms. In many societies, those at the bottom consist disproportionately of groups that suffer, in one way or another, from discrimination. The extent of such discrimination is a matter of societal norms. We'll see how changes in social norms—concerning, for instance, what is fair compensation—and in institutions, like unions, have helped shape America's distribution of income and wealth. But these social norms and institutions, like markets, don't exist in a vacuum: they too are shaped, in part, by the 1 percent.

THE LAWS OF SUPPLY AND DEMAND

Standard economic analysis looks to demand and supply to explain wages and wage differences and to shifts in demand and supply curves to explain changing patterns of wages and income inequality. In standard economic theory, wages of unskilled workers, for example, are determined so as to equate demand and supply. If demand increases more slowly than supply,[1] then wages fall. The analysis of changes in inequality then focuses on two questions: (a) What determines shifts in demand and supply curves? and (b) What determines individuals' endowments, that is, the fraction of the population with high skills or large amounts of wealth?

Immigration, legal and illegal alike, can increase the supply of labor. Increasing the availability of education may reduce the supply of unskilled labor and increase the supply of skilled labor. Changes in technology can lead to reduced demands for labor in some sectors, or reduced demands for some types of labor, and increases in the demand for labor of other types.

In the background of the global financial crisis were major structural changes in the economy. One was a shift in the U.S. job market structures over some twenty years, especially the destruction of millions of jobs in manufacturing,[2] the very sector that had helped create a broad middle class in the years after World War II. This was partly a result of technological change, advances in productivity that outpaced increases in demand. Shifting comparative advantages compounded the problem, as the emerging markets, especially China, gained competencies and invested heavily in education, technology, and infrastructure. The U.S. share of global manufacturing shrank in response. Of course, in a dynamic economy jobs are always being destroyed and created. But this time it was different: the new jobs typically were often not as well-paying or as long-lasting as the old. Skills that made workers valuable—and highly paid—in manufacturing were of little value in their new jobs (if they could get new jobs), and, not surprisingly, their wages reflected the changed status, as they went from being a skilled manufacturing worker to being an unskilled worker in some other sector of the economy. American workers were, in a sense, victims of their own success:

their increased productivity did them in. As the displaced manufacturing workers fought for jobs elsewhere, wages in other sectors suffered.

The stock market boom and the housing bubble of the early twenty-first century helped to hide the structural dislocation that America was going through. The real estate bubble offered work for some of those who lost their jobs, but it was a temporary palliative. The bubble fueled a consumption boom that allowed Americans to live beyond their means: without this bubble, the weakening of incomes of so many in the middle class would have been readily apparent.

This sectoral shift was one of the key factors in the increase in inequality in the United States. It helps explain why ordinary workers are doing so badly. With their wages so low, it's not a surprise that those at the top, who get the lion's share of the profits, are doing so well.

A second structural shift stemmed from changes in technology that increased the demand for skilled workers, and replaced many unskilled workers with machines. This was called skill-biased technological change. It should be obvious that innovations or investments that reduce the need for unskilled labor (for example, investments in robots) weaken the demand for unskilled labor and lead to lower unskilled wages.

Those who attribute the decline of wages at the bottom and in the middle to market forces then see it as the normal working of the balance of these forces. And, unfortunately, if technological change continues as it has, these trends may persist.

Market forces haven't always played out this way, and there is no theory that says that they necessarily should. Over the past sixty years, supply and demand for skilled and unskilled labor have shifted in ways that at first decreased, and then increased, wage disparities.[3] In the aftermath of World War

II, large numbers of Americans received a higher education thanks to the GI Bill. (College graduates formed only 6.4 percent of the labor force in 1940, but the percentage had doubled, to 13.8 percent, by 1970.)[4] But the growth of the economy and the demand for high-skill jobs kept pace with the increase in supply, so the return to education remained strong. Workers with a college education still received 1.59 times what a high school graduate received, almost unchanged from the ratio in 1940 (1.65). The diminished *relative* supply of unskilled workers meant that even these workers benefited, so wages across the board increased. America enjoyed broadly shared prosperity, and in fact at times incomes at the bottom increased faster than those at the top.

But then U.S. educational attainment stopped improving, especially relative to the rest of the world. The fraction of the U.S. population graduating from college increased much more slowly, which meant the relative supply of skilled workers, which had increased at an average annual rate of almost 4 percent from 1960 to 1980, instead increased at the much smaller rate of 2.25 percent over the next quarter century.[5] By 2008 the U.S. high school graduation rate was 76 percent, compared with 85 percent for the EU.[6] Among the advanced industrial countries, the United States is only average in college completion; thirteen other countries surpass it.[7] And average scores of American high school students, especially in science and mathematics, were at best mediocre.[8]

In the past quarter century, technological advances, particularly in computerization, enabled machines to replace jobs that could be routinized. This increased the demand for those who mastered the technology and reduced the demand for those who did not, leading to higher relative wages for those who had the skills required by the new technologies.[9] Globalization compounded the effects of technology's advances: jobs that could be routinized were sent abroad, where labor that could handle the work cost a fraction of what it cost in the United States.[10]

At first, the balance of supply and demand kept wages in the middle rising, but those at the bottom stagnated or even fell. Eventually, the deskilling and outsourcing effects dominated. Over the past fifteen years, wages in the middle have not fared well.[11]

The result has been what we described in chapter 1 as the "polarization" of America's labor force. Low-paying jobs that cannot be easily computerized have continued to grow—including "care" and other service sectors jobs—and so have high-skilled jobs at the top.

This skill-biased technological change has obviously played a role in shaping the labor market—increasing the premium on workers with skills, deskilling other jobs, eliminating still others. However, skill-biased technological change has little to do with the enormous increase in wealth at the very top. Its *relative* importance remains a subject of debate, upon which we will comment later in this chapter.

There is one more important market force at play. Earlier in the chapter, we described how increases in productivity in manufacturing—outpacing the increase in demand for manufactured goods—led to higher unemployment in that sector. Normally, when markets work well, the workers displaced easily move to another sector. The economy as a whole benefits from the productivity increase, even if the displaced worker doesn't. But moving to other sectors may not be so easy. The new jobs may be in another location or require different skills. At the bottom, some workers may be "trapped" in sectors with declining employment, unable to find alternative employment.

A phenomenon akin to what happened in agriculture in the Great Depression may be happening in large swaths of today's job market. Then increases in agricultural productivity raised the supply of agricultural products, driving down prices and farm incomes relentlessly, year after year, with an occasional exception from a bad harvest. At points, and especially at the beginning of the Depression, the fall was precipitous—a decline of half or more in farmers' income in three years. When incomes were declining more gradually, workers migrated to new jobs in the cities, and the economy went through an orderly, if difficult, transition. But when prices fell precipitously—and the value of housing and other assets that the farmers owned fell concomitantly—people were suddenly trapped on their farms. They couldn't afford to move, and their decreased demand for goods made in urban factories caused unemployment in the cities as well.

Today America's manufacturing workers have been experiencing something similar.[12] I recently visited a steel mill near where I was born, in Gary, Indiana, and although it produces the same amount of steel that it did several decades ago, it does so with one-sixth the labor. And once again there is neither the push nor the pull to move people to new sectors: higher costs of education make it difficult for people to obtain the skills they need for jobs that would pay a wage comparable to their old wage; and among the sectors where there might have been growth, low demand from the recession creates few vacancies. The result is stagnant, or even declining, real wages. As recently as 2007, the base wage of an autoworker was around $28 an hour. Now, under a two-tier wage system agreed upon with the United Automobile Workers union, new hires can expect to earn only about $15 an hour.[13]

Back to the role of government

This broad narrative of what has happened to the market and the contribution of market forces to increasing inequality ignores the role that government plays in shaping the market. Many of the jobs that have not been mechanized, and are not likely to be soon, are public-sector jobs in teaching, public hospitals, and so on. If we had decided to pay our teachers more, we might have attracted and retained better teachers, and that might have improved overall long-term economic performance. It was a public decision to allow public-sector wages to sink below those of comparable private-sector workers.[14]

The most important role of government, however, is setting the basic rules of the game, through laws such as those that encourage or discourage unionization, corporate governance laws that determine the discretion of management, and competition laws that *should* limit the extent of monopoly rents. As we have already noted, almost every law has *distributive* consequences, with some groups benefiting, typically at the expense of others.[15] And these distributive consequences are often the most important effects of the policy or program.[16]

Bankruptcy laws provide an example. Later, in chapter 7, I describe how "reforms" in our bankruptcy laws are creating partially indentured servants. That reform, together with the law prohibiting the discharge of student debt in bankruptcy,[17] is causing immiseration for large parts of America. Like the effects on distribution, the effects on efficiency have been adverse. The bankruptcy "reform" reduced the incentives of creditors to assess creditworthiness, or to ascertain whether the individual is likely to get a return from the education commensurate with its costs. It increased the incentives for predatory lending, since lenders could be more certain of recovering the loans, no matter how onerous the terms and how unproductive the uses to which the money was put.[18]

In later chapters, we'll also see other examples of how government helps shape market forces—in ways that help some, at the expense of others. And too often, the ones who are helped are those at the top.

It is, of course, not just laws that have large distributive effects, but also policies. We've considered several policies in the previous chapter—for example, on the enforcement of laws against anticompetitive practices. In chapter 9 we'll look at monetary policies, which affect the level of employment and the stability of the economy. We'll see how they have been set in ways that weakened the income of workers and enhanced that of capital.

Finally, public policy affects the direction of innovation. It is not inevitable that innovation be skill biased. Innovation could, for instance, be biased toward the saving of natural resources. Later in this book, we'll describe alternative policies that might succeed in redirecting innovation.

GLOBALIZATION

One aspect of the "market forces" theory has been the center of attention now for more than a decade: globalization, or the closer integration of the economies of the world. Nowhere do politics shape market forces more than in the globalization arena. While the lowering of transportation and communication costs has promoted globalization, changes in the rules of the game have been equally important: these include reducing impediments to the flow of capital across borders and trade barriers (for instance, reducing tariffs on imported Chinese goods that allow them to compete with American ones on an almost even playing field).

Both trade globalization (the movement of goods and services) and capital markets globalization (international financial market integration) have contributed to growing inequality, but in different ways.

Financial liberalization

Over the past three decades, U.S. financial institutions have argued strongly for the free mobility of capital. Indeed, they have become the champions of the rights of capital—over the rights of workers or even political rights.[19] Rights simply specify what various economic players are entitled to: the rights workers have sought include, for instance, the right to band together, to unionize, to engage in collective bargaining, and to strike. Many nondemocratic governments severely restrict these rights, but even democratic governments circumscribe them. So too, the owners of capital may have rights. The most fundamental right of the owners of capital is that they not be deprived of their property. But again, even in a democratic society, these rights are restricted; under the right of eminent domain, the state can take away somebody's property for public purpose, but there must be "due process" and appropriate compensation. In recent years, the owners of capital have demanded more rights, like the right to move freely into or out of countries. Simultaneously, they've argued *against* laws that might make them more accountable for human rights abuses in other countries, such as the Alien Torts Statute, which enables victims of those abuses to bring suit in the United States.

As a matter of simple economics, the efficiency gains for world output from the free mobility of labor are much, much larger than the efficiency gains from the free mobility of capital. The differences in the return to capital are minuscule compared with those on the return to labor.[20] But the financial markets have been driving globalization, and while those who work in financial markets constantly talk about efficiency gains, what they really have in mind is something else—a set of rules that benefits them and increases their advantage over workers. The threat of capital outflow, should workers get too demanding about rights and wages, keeps workers' wages low.[21] Competition across countries for investment takes on many forms—not just lowering wages and weakening worker protections. There is a broader "race to the bottom," trying to ensure that business regulations are weak and taxes are low. In one arena, finance, this has proven especially costly and especially critical to the growth in inequality. Countries raced to have the least-regulated financial system for fear that financial firms might decamp for other markets. Some in the U.S. Congress worried about the consequences of this deregulation, but they felt helpless: America would lose jobs and a major industry if it didn't comply. In retrospect, however, this was a mistake. The loss to the country from the crisis that resulted from inadequate regulation was orders of magnitude larger than the number of jobs in finance that were saved.

Not surprisingly, whereas a decade ago it was part of conventional wisdom that everyone would benefit from free capital movements, in the aftermath of the Great Recession many observers have their doubts. These concerns are coming not just from those in developing countries but also from some of globalization's strongest advocates. Indeed, even the IMF (the International Monetary Fund, the international agency responsible for ensuring global financial stability) has now recognized the dangers of unencumbered and excessive financial integration:[22] a problem in one country can rapidly spread to another. In fact, fears of contagion have motivated bailouts of banks in the magnitude of tens and hundreds of billions of dollars. The response to contagious diseases is "quarantine," and finally, in the spring of 2011, the IMF recognized the desirability of the analogous response in the financial markets. This takes the form of capital controls, or limiting the volatile movement of capital across borders, especially during a crisis.[23]

The irony is that in the crises that finance brings about, workers and small businesses bear the brunt of the costs. Crises are accompanied by high unemployment that drives down wages, so workers are hurt doubly. In earlier crises, not only did the IMF (typically with the support of the U.S. Treasury) insist on huge budget cuts from troubled nations, converting downturns into recessions and depressions, but it also demanded the fire sales of assets, and the financiers then swooped in to make a killing. In my earlier book *Globalization and Its Discontents,* I described how Goldman Sachs was one of the winners in the 1997 East Asia crisis, as it was in the 2008 crisis. When we wonder how it is that the financiers get so much wealth, part of the answer is simple: they've helped write a set of rules that allows them to do well, even in the crises that they help create.[24]

Trade globalization

The effects of trade globalization have not been as dramatic as those of the crises associated with capital and financial market liberalization, but they have nonetheless been operating slowly and steadily. The basic idea is simple: the movement of goods is a substitute for the movement of people. If the United States imports goods that require unskilled workers, it reduces the demand for unskilled workers to make those goods in the United States, and that drives down unskilled workers' wages. American workers can compete by accepting lower and lower wages—or by getting more and more skilled.[25] This effect would arise no matter how we managed globalization, so long as it led to more trade.

The way globalization has been managed, however, has itself led to still lower wages because workers' bargaining power has been eviscerated. With capital highly mobile—and with tariffs low—firms can simply tell workers that if they don't accept lower wages and worse working conditions, the company will move elsewhere. To see how asymmetric globalization can affect bargaining power, imagine, for a moment, what the world would be like if there was free mobility of labor, but no mobility of capital.[26] Countries would compete to attract workers. They would promise good schools and a good environment, as well as low taxes on workers. This could be financed by high taxes on capital. But that's not the world we live in, and that's partly because the 1 percent doesn't want it to be that way.

Having succeeded in getting governments to set the rules of globalization in ways that enhance their bargaining power vis-à-vis labor, corporations can then work the political levers and demand lower taxation. They threaten the country: unless you lower our taxes, we will go elsewhere, where we are taxed at lower rates. As corporations have pushed a political agenda that shapes market forces to work for them, they have not, of course, revealed their hand. They don't argue for globalization—for free capital mobility and investment protections—saying that doing so will enrich them at the expense of the rest of society. Rather, they make specious arguments about how *all* will benefit.

There are two critical aspects to this contention. The first is that globalization will increase the country's overall output as measured, for instance, by GDP. The second is that if GDP is increased, trickle-down economics will ensure that all will benefit. Neither argument is correct. It is true that when markets work perfectly, free trade allows people to move from protected sectors to more efficient unprotected export sectors. There *can* be, as a result, an increase in GDP. But markets often don't work so nicely. For example, workers displaced by imports often can't find another job. They become unemployed. Moving from a low-productivity job in a protected sector to unemployment lowers national output. This is what has been happening in the United States. It happens when there is bad macroeconomic management, so the economy faces a high unemployment rate, and it happens when financial sectors don't do their jobs, so new businesses aren't created to replace the old businesses that are destroyed.

There is another reason why globalization may lower overall output; it typically increases the risks that countries face.[27] Opening up a country can expose it to all kinds of risks, from the volatility of capital markets to that of commodity markets. Greater volatility will induce firms to move to less risky activities, and these safer activities often have a lower return. In some cases, the risk-avoidance effect can be so large that everyone is made worse-off.[28]

But even if trade liberalization leads to a higher overall output for a given economy, large groups in the population can still be worse off. Consider for a moment what a fully integrated global economy (with both knowledge and capital moving freely around the world) would entail: all workers (of a given skill) would get the same wage everywhere in the world. America's unskilled workers would get the same wage that an unskilled worker gets in China. And that would mean, in turn, that America's workers' wages would fall precipitously. The prevailing wage would be the average of that of America and the rest of the world and, unfortunately, much closer to the lower wage prevailing elsewhere. Not surprisingly, advocates of full liberalization, who typically believe that markets function well, don't advertise this outcome. In fact, unskilled workers in the United States have already taken a beating. As globalization proceeds, there will be further downward pressures on their wages. I don't think markets work so well that wages will be fully equalized, but they will move in that direction, and far enough to be of serious concern.[29] The problem is particularly severe today in the United States and Europe: at the same time that labor-saving technological change has reduced the demand for many of the "good" middle-class blue-collar jobs, globalization has created a global marketplace, putting the same workers in direct competition with comparable workers abroad. Both factors depress wages.

How, then, can globalization's advocates claim that everybody will be better off? What the theory says is that everybody *could* be better off. That is, the winners could compensate the losers. But it doesn't say that they will—and they usually don't. In fact, globalization's advocates often claim that globalization means that they can't and shouldn't do this. The taxes that would have to be levied to help the losers would, they claim, make the country less competitive, and in our highly competitive globalized world countries simply can't afford that. In effect, globalization hurts those at the bottom not only directly but also indirectly, because of the induced cutbacks in social expenditures and progressive taxation.

The result is that in many countries, including the United States, globalization is almost surely contributing significantly to our growing inequality. I have emphasized that the problems concern *globalization as it has been managed*. Countries in Asia benefited enormously through export-led growth, and some (such as China) took measures to ensure that significant portions of that increased output went to the poor, some went to provide for public education, and much was reinvested in the economy, to provide more jobs. In other countries, there have been big losers as well as winners—poor corn farmers in Mexico have seen their incomes decline as subsidized American corn drives down prices on world markets.

In many countries, poorly functioning macroeconomies have meant that the pace of job destruction has exceeded that of job creation. And that's been the case in the United States and Europe since the financial crisis.

Among the winners from globalization in the United States and some European countries, as it's been managed, are the people at the top. Among the losers are those at the bottom, and increasingly even those in the middle.

BEYOND MARKET FORCES: CHANGES IN OUR SOCIETY

So far, we have discussed the role that market forces, politics, and rent seeking play in creating the high level of inequality in our society. Broader societal changes are also important, changes both in norms and in institutions.[30] These too are shaped by, and help shape, politics.

The most obvious societal change is the decline of unions, from 20.1 percent of wage- and salary-earning U.S. workers in 1980 to 11.9 percent in 2010.[31] This has created an imbalance of economic power and a political vacuum. Without the protection afforded by a union, workers have fared even more poorly than they would have otherwise. Market forces have also limited the effectiveness of the unions that remain. The threat of job loss by the moving of jobs abroad has weakened their power. A bad job without decent pay is better than no job. But just as the passage of the Wagner Act during Franklin Delano Roosevelt's presidency encouraged unionization, Republicans at both the state and the federal levels, in the name of labor flexibility, have worked to weaken them. President Reagan's breaking of the air traffic controllers strike in 1981 represented a critical juncture in the breaking of the strength of unions.[32]

Part of the conventional wisdom in economics of the past three decades is that flexible labor markets contribute to economic strength. I would argue, in contrast, that strong worker protections correct what would otherwise be an imbalance of economic power. Such protection leads to a higher-quality labor force with workers who are more loyal to their firms and more willing to invest in themselves and in their jobs. It also makes for a more cohesive society and better workplaces.[33]

That the American labor market performed so poorly in the Great Recession and that American workers have done so badly for three decades should cast doubt on the mythical virtues of a flexible labor market. But in the United States unions have been seen as a source of rigidity and thus of labor market inefficiency. This has undermined support for unions both inside and outside of politics.[34]

Inequality may be at once cause and consequence of a

breakdown in social cohesion over the past four decades. The pattern and magnitude of changes in labor compensation as a share of national income are hard to reconcile with any theory that relies *solely* on conventional economic factors. For instance, in manufacturing, for more than three decades, from 1949 to 1980, productivity and real hourly compensation moved together. Suddenly, in 1980, they began to drift apart, with real hourly compensation stagnating for almost fifteen years, before starting to rise, again almost at the pace of productivity, until the early 2000s, when compensation again began essentially stagnating. One of the interpretations of these data is that in effect, during the periods when wages grew so much slower than productivity, corporate managers seized a larger share of the "rents" associated with corporations.[35]

The extent to which this occurs is affected not just by economics and societal forces (the ability and willingness of CEOs to garner for themselves a larger fraction of the corporate revenues), but also by politics and how they shape the legal framework.

Corporate governance

Politics—and in particular how politics shapes the laws governing corporations—is a major determinant of the fraction of a corporation's revenues that its top executives take for themselves. U.S. laws provide them considerable discretion. This meant that when social mores changed in ways that made large disparities in compensation more acceptable, executives in the United States could enrich themselves at the expense of workers or shareholders more easily than could executives in other countries.

A significant fraction of U.S. output occurs in corporations whose shares are publicly traded. Corporations have numerous advantages—legal protection afforded by limited liability,[36] advantages of scale, often long-established reputations—that allow them to earn excess returns over what they have to pay to raise capital. We call these excess returns "corporate rents," and the question is how these rents are divided among the various "stakeholders" in the corporation (in particular, between workers, shareholders, and management). Before the mid-1970s there was a broad social consensus: executives were well paid, but not fabulously so; the rents got divided largely between loyal workers and management. Shareholders never had much say. America's corporate law gives wide deference to management. It's hard for shareholders to challenge what the management does, hard to wage a takeover battle,[37] hard even to wage a proxy battle for control. Over the years, managers learned how to entrench and protect their interests. There were numerous ways for them to do this, including investments shrouded in uncertainty that made the value of the firm less certain and a takeover battle that much riskier; poison pills that decreased the value of the firm in the event of a takeover; and golden parachutes that guaranteed managers a lifetime of comfort should the firm be taken over.[38]

Gradually, beginning in the 1980s and 1990s, management realized that the measures taken to fend off outside attacks, combined with weaker unions, also meant that they could take a larger share of the corporate rents for themselves with impunity. Even some financial leaders recognized that "executive compensation in our deeply flawed system of corporate governance has led to grossly excessive executive compensation."[39]

Norms of what was "fair" changed too: the executives thought little of taking a bigger slice of the corporate pie, awarding themselves large amounts *even as they claimed they had to fire workers and reduce wages to keep the firm alive*. In some circles, so engrained did these schizophrenic attitudes to "fairness" become that early in the Great Recession an Obama administration official could say, with a straight face, that it was necessary to honor AIG bonuses, even for the officials who had led the company to need a $182 billion bailout, because of the sanctity of contracts; minutes later he could admonish autoworkers to accept a revision of their contract that would have lowered their compensation enormously.

Different corporate governance laws (even modest ones, like giving shareholders some say in the pay of their CEO)[40] might have tamed the unbridled zeal of executives, but the 1 percent didn't—and still don't—want such reforms in corporate governance, even if they would make the economy more efficient. And they have used their political muscle to make sure that such reforms don't occur.

The forces we have just described, including weaker unions and weaker social cohesion working with corporate governance laws that give management enormous discretion to run corporations for their own benefit, have led not only to a declining wage share in national income but also to a change in the way our economy responds to an economic downturn. It used to be that when the economy went into recession, employers, wanting to maintain the loyalty of their workers and concerned about their well-being, would keep as many as they could on their payroll. The result was that labor productivity went down, and the share of wages went up. Profits bore the brunt of the downturn. Wage shares would then fall after the end of a recession. But in this and the previous (2001) recession, the pattern changed; the wage share declined in the recession. Firms prided themselves on their ruthlessness—cutting out so many workers that productivity actually increased.[41]

Discrimination

One other major societal force affects inequality. There is economic discrimination against major groups in American society—against women, against African Americans, against Hispanics. The existence of large differences in income and wealth across these groups is clear. Wages of women, African Americans, and Hispanics are all markedly lower than those of white males.[42] Differences in education (or other characteristics) account for a portion of the disparity, but only a portion.[43]

Some economists have argued that discrimination was impossible in a market economy.[44] In a competitive economy, so the theory went, as long as there are some individuals who do not have racial (or gender or ethnic) prejudices, they will hire members of the discriminated-against group because their wages will be lower than those of similarly qualified members of the not discriminated-against group. This process will continue until the wage/income discrimination is eliminated. Prejudice might lead to segregated workplaces, but not to income differentials. That such arguments gained currency in the economics profession says a lot about the state of the discipline. To an economist like me who grew up in the midst of a city and country where discrimination was *obvious*, such arguments provided a challenge: something was wrong with a theory that said discrimination couldn't exist. Over the past forty years, a number of theories have been developed to help explain the persistence of discrimination.[45]

Game-theoretic models, for instance, have shown how tacit collusive behavior of a dominant group (whites, men) can be used to suppress the economic interests of another group. Individuals who break with the discriminatory behavior are punished: others will refuse to buy from their store, work for them, supply them inputs; social sanctions, like ostracism, can also be effective. Those who don't punish transgressors are subjected to the same punishment.[46]

Related research has shown how other mechanisms (associated with imperfect information) can lead to discriminatory equilibria even in a competitive economy. If it is difficult to assess the true ability of an individual and the quality of his education, then employers may turn to race, ethnicity, or gender—whether justified or not. If employers believe that those who belong to a particular group (women, Hispanics, African Americans) are less productive, then they will pay them lower wages. The result of discrimination is to reduce incentives for members of the group to make the investments that would lead to higher productivity. The beliefs are self-reinforcing. This is sometimes called statistical discrimination—but of a particular form, where the discrimination actually leads to the differences that are believed to exist between groups.[47]

In the theories of discrimination just described, individuals *consciously* discriminate. Recently, economists have suggested an additional driver of discriminatory behavior: "implicit discrimination," which is unintentional and outside the awareness of those engaging in discrimation and at variance with what they (explicitly) think or favor for their organization.[48] Psychologists have learned to measure implicit attitudes (that is, attitudes of which individuals are not consciously aware). There is preliminary evidence that these attitudes predict discriminatory behavior better than explicit attitudes, especially in the presence of time pressure. That finding sheds new light on studies that have shown systematic racial discrimination.[49] This is because many real-world decisions, such as job offers, are often made under time pressure, with ambiguous information—conditions that give greater scope for implicit discrimination.

A striking example, from a study by the sociologist Devah Pager, is of the stigmatizing effect of a criminal record.[50] In her field study, matched pairs of twenty-three-year-olds applied for real entry-level jobs in order to test the degree to which a criminal record (a nonviolent drug offense) affects subsequent employment opportunities. All the individuals presented roughly identical credentials, including a high school diploma, so that differences experienced among groups can be attributed to the effects of race or criminal status. After an invited interview, the ratio of callbacks for white nonoffenders to white ex-offenders is 2:1, this same ratio for blacks is nearly 3:1. And a white man *with* a criminal record is slightly more likely to be considered for a job than a black man with no criminal past. Thus, on average, being black reduces employment opportunities substantially, and more so for ex-offenders. These effects can represent important barriers to black men trying to become economically self-sufficient, since roughly one in three black men will spend time in prison in his lifetime.

There are strong interactions between poverty, race, and government policies. If certain minorities are disproportionately poor, and if the government provides poor education and health care to the poor, then members of the minority will suffer disproportionately from poor education and health. Health statistics, for instance, are telling: life expectancy at birth for blacks in 2009 was 74.3 compared with 78.6 for whites.[51]

The Great Recession has not been good for members of the groups that have been traditionally discriminated against, as we saw in chapter 1. The banks saw them as easy targets, because they had aspirations of upward mobility; owning a home was a sign that they were making it into America's middle class. Unscrupulous vendors pushed mortgages on households that were beyond their ability to pay, ill-suited for their needs, and carrying high transactions costs. Today large fractions of these populations have lost not only their homes but also their life savings. The data on what has happened to their wealth are truly disturbing: in the aftermath of the crisis, the typical black household had a net worth of only $5,677, a twentieth of that of a typical white household.[52]

Our economic system rewards profits, no matter how they're made, and in a money-centric economy it's not surprising to see moral scruples put to the side. Occasionally, our system holds those who have behaved wrongly accountable, though only after a long and expensive legal battle. Even then, it's not always clear whether the penalties do more than take back a part of the profits that the banks have made by their unscrupulous behavior. In that case, even among those who are punished, crime pays.[53] In December 2011, four to seven years after the subprime lending occurred, Bank of America agreed to a $335 million settlement for its discriminatory practices against African Americans and Hispanics, the largest settlement ever over residential fair lending practices. Wells Fargo and other lenders have been similarly accused of discriminatory practices; Wells, the country's largest home mortgage lender, paid the Fed $85 million to settle charges that it had brought. In short, discrimination in lending was not limited to isolated instances, but was a pervasive practice.

Lending and housing discrimination has thus contributed

to lowering standards of living of African Americans and their wealth, compounding the effects of the labor market discrimination discussed earlier.

ROLE OF GOVERNMENT
IN REDISTRIBUTION

We have examined how market forces, shaped by politics and societal changes, have played a role in bringing about the level of inequality in *before-tax incomes and transfers*.

The irony is that just as markets started delivering more unequal outcomes, tax policy asked less of the top. The top marginal tax rate was lowered from 70 percent under Carter to 28 percent under Reagan; it went up to 39.6 percent under Clinton and down finally to 35 percent under George W. Bush.[54]

This reduction was supposed to lead to more work and savings, but it didn't.[55] In fact, Reagan had promised that the incentive effects of his tax cuts would be so powerful that tax revenues would *increase*. And yet, the only thing that increased was the deficit. George W. Bush's tax cuts weren't any more successful: savings did not increase; instead the household savings rate fell to a record low (essentially zero).

The most egregious aspect of recent tax policy was the lowering of tax rates on capital gains. This happened first under Clinton and again under Bush, making the long-term capital gains tax rate only 15 percent. In this way we have given the very rich, who receive a large fraction of their income in capital gains, close to a free ride. It doesn't make sense that investors, let alone speculators, should be taxed at a lower rate than someone who works hard for his living, yet that's what our tax system does. And capital gains are not taxed until they are realized (that is, until the asset is sold), so there is an enormous benefit from this deferral of taxes, especially when interest rates are high.[56] Furthermore, if the assets are passed on at death, the capital gains made during the individual's lifetime escape taxation. Indeed, the tax lawyers for rich people like Ronald Lauder, who inherited his fortune from his mother, Estée Lauder, even figured out how to "have your cake and eat it too," that is, in effect, sell your stock and not pay the tax.[57] Their plan, and other similar tax-avoidance schemes, involves complicated transactions including short selling (selling borrowed stock) and derivatives. Though this particular loophole was eventually closed, tax lawyers for the rich are always seeking to outsmart the IRS.

The inequality in dividends is greater than that in wages and salaries, and the inequality in capital gains is greater than that in any other form of income, so giving a tax break to capital gains is, in effect, giving a tax break to the very rich. The bottom 90 percent of the population gets less than 10 percent of all capital gains.[58] Under 7 percent of households earning less than $100,000 receive any capital gains income, and for these households capital gains and dividend income combined make up an average of 1.4 percent of their total income.[59] Salaries and wages accounted for only 8.8 percent of the income of the top 400, capital gains for 57 percent, and interest and dividends for 16 percent—so 73 percent of their income was subject to low rates. Indeed, the top 400 taxpayers garner close to 5 percent of the country's entire dividends.[60] They posted an average of $153.7 million in gains each (a total of $61.5 billion in gains) in 2008, $228.6 million each (for a total of $91.4 billion) in 2007. Lowering the tax on capital gains from the ordinary rate of 35 percent to 15 percent thus gave each of these

400, on average, a gift of $30 million in 2008 and $45 million in 2007, and it lowered overall tax revenues by $12 billion in 2008 and $18 billion in 2007.[61]

The net effect is that the superrich actually pay on average a lower tax rate than those less well-off; and the lower tax rate means that their riches increase faster. The average tax rate in 2007 on the top 400 households was only 16.6 percent, considerably lower than the 20.4 percent for taxpayers in general. (It increased slightly in 2008, the last year for which data are available, to 18.1 percent.) While the average tax rate has decreased little since 1979—going from 22.2 percent to 20.4 percent, that of the top 1 percent has fallen by almost a quarter, from 37 percent to 29.5 percent.[62]

Most countries have adopted estate taxes, not just to raise revenue from those who are more able to afford it but also to prevent the creation of inherited dynasties. The ability of one generation to pass on its wealth to another more easily tilts the playing field of life chances. If the wealthy escape taxation (as they increasingly do) and if estate taxes are lowered (as they were under President Bush—actually abolished in 2010, though only for one year), then the role of inherited wealth will become more important.[63] Under these circumstances, and with more and more of the wealth concentrated in the upper 1 percent (or the upper 0.1 percent), America has the potential of becoming increasingly a land of an inherited oligarchy.

The rich and superrich often use corporations to protect themselves and shelter their income, and they have worked hard to ensure that the corporate income tax rate is low and the tax code is riddled with loopholes. Some corporations make such extensive use of these provisions that they don't pay any taxes.[64] Even though the United States supposedly has a higher corporate tax rate than much of the world, reaching 35 percent according to statute, the real average tax that firms pay is on par with that of many other countries, and corporate tax revenues as a share of GDP are smaller than they are, on average, in other advanced industrial countries. Loopholes and special provisions have eviscerated the tax to such a degree that it has gone from providing 30 percent of federal revenues in the mid-1950s to less than 9 percent today.[65] If an American firm invests abroad through a foreign subsidiary, its profits are not taxed by the United States until the money is brought home. While a great deal for the firm (if it invests in a low-tax jurisdiction like Ireland), it has the perverse effect of encouraging reinvestment abroad—creating jobs outside the United States but not in it. But then the corporations duped President Bush into giving them a tax holiday—money they brought back during the holiday, supposedly for investment, would be taxed at only 5.25 percent; they would bring the money back and reinvest it in America. When Bush put in place a one-year holiday at that rate, they did bring their money back; Microsoft alone brought back more than $32 billion.[66] But the evidence shows that little additional investment was generated. All that happened is that they managed to avoid paying most of the taxes that they should have paid.[67]

At the state level, things are even worse. Many states don't even make a pretense at progressivity, that is, having a tax system that makes the 1 percent, who can afford it, pay a larger fraction of their income than the poor have to pay. Instead, the sales tax offers a major source of revenue, and because the poor spend a larger fraction of their income, such taxes are often regressive.[68]

While tax policies can either let the rich get richer or restrain the growth of inequality, expenditure programs can play an especially important role in preventing the poor from becoming poorer. Social Security has almost eliminated poverty among the elderly. Recent research has shown how large these effects can be: the earned-income tax credit, which supplements the income of poor working families, by itself lowers the poverty rate by 2 percentage points. Housing subsidies, food stamps, and school lunch programs all have big effects in lowering poverty.[69] A program like the provision of health insurance for poor kids can bring benefits to millions and help ensure that these children have a lower risk of being handicapped for life by an illness or other health problem; this stands in marked contrast to some of the corporate subsidies or tax loopholes that cost much more and the benefits of which go to far fewer people. The United States spent far more on its big bank bailout, which helped the banks to maintain their generous bonuses, than it spent to help those who were unemployed as a result of the recession that the big banks brought about. We created for the banks (and other corporations, like AIG) a much stronger safety net than we created for poor Americans.

What is striking about the United States is that while the level of inequality generated by the market—a market shaped and distorted by politics and rent seeking—is higher than in other advanced industrial countries, it does less to temper this inequality through tax and expenditure programs. And as the market-generated inequality has increased, our government has done less and less.[70]

Government and opportunity

Among the more disturbing findings recited in chapter 1 is that the United States has become a society in which there is less equality of opportunity, less than it was in the past, and less than in other countries, including those of old Europe. Market forces described earlier in this chapter play a role: as the returns to education have increased, those with a good education have fared well, those (and especially men) with a high school education or less have done miserably. This is even more true today, in our deep economic downturn. While the unemployment rate among those with a college degree or higher was only 4.2 percent, those with less than a high school diploma faced an unemployment rate three times higher, at 12.9 per cent. The picture for recent high school dropouts and even graduates not enrolled in college is far more dismal: jobless rates of 42.7 percent and 33.4 percent, respectively.[71]

But access to good education depends increasingly on the income, wealth, and education of one's parents, as we saw in chapter 1, and for good reason: a college education is becoming more and more expensive, especially as states cut back on support, and access to the best colleges depends on going to the best high schools, grade schools, and kindergartens. The poor can't afford high-quality private primary and secondary schools, and they can't afford to live in the rich suburbs that provide high-quality public education. Many of the poor have traditionally lived in close proximity to the rich—partly because they provided services to them. This phenomenon in turn led to public schools with students from diverse social and economic backgrounds. As a recent study by Kendra Bischoff and Sean Reardon of Stanford University shows, that is changing: fewer poor are living in proximity to the rich, and fewer rich are living in proximity to the poor.[72]

U.S. neighborhoods are even segregated between homeowners and renters. This pattern cannot be explained by race or the presence of children in the household, because it occurs within racial groups and among households with children. The segregation in American metropolitan areas into homeowner communities and renter communities can produce communities with starkly different civic environments. Community quality depends on residents' efforts to prevent crime and improve local governance, and the payoff to an individual making that effort is greater for homeowners than for renters, and generally greater for those who live in communities where many other residents make similar efforts to render local government more responsive to community members. Thus there are economic forces that lead from differences in household wealth (and homeownership) to differences in the civic quality of the community in which a household lives.[73] U.S. policy to increase low-income ownership rates reflects the understanding that homeownership rates affect neighborhood quality and that growing up in a violent, crime-ridden neighborhood impairs health, personal development, and school outcomes. But homeownership—a major way in the United States that households access better neighborhoods and also accumulate wealth—is not sustainable for households with no wealth to start with and little income.

We also noted in chapter 1 that even among college graduates, those who are fortunate enough to have wealthier and better-educated parents have better prospects. This may be partly because of networking—making connections—which may become especially important when jobs are scarce, as now. But it is also partly because of the increasing role of internships. In a labor market such as the one we have had since 2008, there are many job seekers for every job, and having experience counts. Firms are exploiting this imbalance by providing unpaid or low paid internships, which adds an important element to a resume. But not only are the rich in a better position to get the internship; they are in a better position to *afford* unpaid work for a year or two.[74]

While government has been doing less to countervail these market forces that lead to greater inequality of opportunity, on the basis of differential access to "human capital" and jobs, it has also, as we have noted, been doing less to level the playing field in financial capital, as a result of less progressive taxation and especially lower inheritance taxes. In short, we have created an economic and social system, and a politics, in which, going forward, current inequalities are not only likely to be perpetuated but to be exacerbated: we can anticipate in the future more inequality both in human capital and in financial capital.

THE BIG PICTURE

Earlier in this chapter and in chapter 2 we saw how the rules of the game have helped create the riches of those at the top and have contributed to the miseries of those at the bottom. Government today plays a double role in our current inequality: it is partly responsible for the inequality in *before-tax distribution of income*, and it has taken a diminished role in "correcting" this inequality through progressive tax and expenditure policies.

As the wealthy get wealthier, they have more to lose from attempts to restrict rent seeking and redistribute income in order to create a fairer economy, and they have more resources with which to resist such attempts. It might seem strange that as inequality has increased we have been doing less to diminish its impact, but it's what one might have expected. It's certainly what one sees around the world: the more egalitarian societies work harder to preserve their social cohesion; in the more unequal societies, government policies and other institutions tend to foster the persistence of inequality. This pattern has been well documented.[75]

Justifying inequality

We began the last chapter by explaining how those at the top have often sought to justify their income and wealth, and how "marginal productivity theory," the notion that those who got more did so because they had made a greater contribution to society, had become the prevailing doctrine, at least in economics. But we noted, too, that the crisis had cast doubt on this theory.[76] Those who perfected the new skills of predatory lending, who helped create derivatives, described by the billionaire Warren Buffett as "financial weapons of mass destruction," or who devised the reckless new mortgages that brought about the subprime mortgage crisis walked away with millions, sometimes hundreds of millions, of dollars.[77]

But even before that, it was clear that the link between pay and societal contribution was, at best, weak. As we noted earlier, the great scientists who have made discoveries that provided the basis of our modern society have typically reaped for themselves no more than a small fraction of what they have contributed, and received a mere pittance compared with the rewards reaped by the financial wizards who brought the world to the brink of ruin.

But there is a deeper philosophical point: one can't really separate out any individual's contributions from those of others. Even in the context of technological change, most inventions entail the synthesis of preexisting elements rather than invention de novo. Today, at least in many critical sectors, a large fraction of all advances depend on basic research funded by the government.

Gar Alperovitz and Lew Daly concluded in 2009 that "if much of what we have comes to us as the free gift of many generations of historical contribution, there is a profound question as to how much can reasonably be said to be 'earned' by any one person, now or in the future."[78] So too, the success of any businessperson depends not just on this "inherited" technology but on the institutional setting (the rule of law), the existence of a well-educated workforce, and the availability of good infrastructure (transportation and communications).

Is inequality necessary to give people incentives?

Another argument is often proffered by those who defend the status quo: that we need the current high level of inequality to give people incentives to work, save, and invest. This confuses two positions. One is that we should have no inequality. The other is that we would be better-off if we had less inequality than we have today. I and, as far as I know, most progressives—do not argue for full equality. We realize that that would weaken incentives. The question is, How seriously would incentives be weakened if we had a little bit less inequality? In the next chapter, I will explain why, to the contrary, less inequality would actually enhance productivity.

Of course, much of what is called incentive pay isn't really that. It's just a name given it to justify the huge inequality, and to delude the innocent to think that without such inequality our economic system wouldn't work. That was made evident when, in the aftermath of the financial debacle of 2008, the banks were so embarrassed about calling what they paid their executives "performance bonuses" that they felt compelled to change the name to "retention bonus" (even if the only thing being retained was bad performance).

Under incentive compensation schemes, pay is supposed to increase with performance. What the bankers did was common practice: when there was a decline in *measured* performance according to the yardsticks that were supposed to be used to determine compensation, the compensation system changed. The effect was that, in practice, pay was high when performance was good, and pay was high when performance was bad.[79]

Parsing out the sources of inequality

Economists are prone to quibble about the relative importance of various factors leading to America's growing inequality. Increasing inequality in wages and capital income and an increasing share of income going to those forms of income that are more unequally distributed contributed to greater inequality in market income, and, as we saw earlier in the chapter, less progressive tax and expenditure policies contributed to an even larger increase in after-tax and transfer income.

The explanation for the increase in dispersion of wages and salaries has been particularly contentious. Some focus on changes in technology—skill-biased technological change. Others on social factors—the weakening of unions, the breakdown of social norms restraining executive pay. Still others focus on globalization. Some focus on the increasing role of finance. Strong vested interests inform each of these explanations: those fighting to open up markets see globalization as playing a minor role; those arguing for stronger unions see the weakening of unions as central. Some of the debates have to do with the different aspects of inequality that are being focused upon: the increasing role of finance may have little to do with the polarization of wages in the middle, but a great deal to do with the increases of income and wealth at the top. At different times, different forces have played different roles: globalization has probably played a more important role since, say, 2000 than it did in the preceding decade. Still, there is a growing consensus among economists that it is hard to parse out cleanly and precisely the roles of different forces. We can't conduct controlled experiments, to see what inequality would have been if, keeping everything else the same, we had had stronger unions. Moreover, the forces interact: the competitive forces of globalization—the threat of jobs moving elsewhere—has been important in weakening unions.[80]

To me, much of this debate is beside the point. The point is that inequality in America (and some other countries around the world) has grown to where it can no longer be ignored. Technology (skill-biased technological change) may be central to certain aspects of our current inequality problem, especially to the polarization of the labor market. But even if that is the case, we don't have to sit idly by and accept the consequences. Greed may be an inherent part of human nature, but that doesn't mean there is nothing we can do to temper the consequences of unscrupulous bankers who would exploit the poor and engage in anticompetitive practices. We can and should regulate banks, forbid predatory lending, make them accountable for their fraudulent practices, and punish them for abuses of monopoly power. So too, stronger unions and better education might mitigate the consequences of skill-biased technological change. And it's not even inevitable that technological change continues in this direction: making firms pay for the environmental consequences of their production might encourage firms to shift away from skill-biased technological change to resource-saving technological change. Low interest rates may encourage firms to robotize, replacing unskilled jobs that can easily be routinized; so alternative macroeconomic and investment policies could slow the pace of the deskilling of our economy. So too, while economists may disagree about the precise role that globalization has played in the increase in inequality, the *asymmetries* in globalization to which we call attention put workers at a particular disadvantage; and we can manage globalization better, in ways that might lead to less inequality.

We have also noted how the growth in the financial sector as a share of total U.S. income (sometimes referred to as the increased financialization of the economy) has contributed to increased inequality—to both the wealth created at the top and the poverty at the bottom. Jamie Galbraith has shown that countries with larger financial sectors have more inequality, and the link is not an accident.[81] We have seen how deregulation and hidden and open government subsidies distorted the economy, not only leading to a larger financial sector but also enhancing its ability to move money from the bottom to the top. We don't have to know precisely the fraction of inequality that should be attributed to the increased financialization of the economy to understand that a change in policies is needed.

Each of the factors that have contributed to inequality has to be addressed, with especial emphasis on those that simultaneously contribute *directly* to the weakening of our economy, such as the persistence of monopoly power and of distortionary economic policies. Inequality has become ingrained in our economic system, and it will take a comprehensive agenda—described more fully in chapter 10—to uproot it.

Alternative models of inequality

In this chapter, we have explained that there are alternative theories of inequality, in some of which inequality seems more "justified," the income of those at the top more deserved, and the costs of checking the inequality and redistribution greater than others. The "achievement" model of income determination focuses on the efforts of each individual; and if inequality were largely the result of differences in effort, it would be hard to fault it, and it would seem unjust, and inefficient, not to reward it. The Horatio Alger stories that we described in the preface belong to this tradition: in the more than a hundred tales of rags to riches, it was by dint of the individual's own efforts that the hero of each tale pulled himself out of poverty. They may contain a grain of truth, but it is only a grain. We saw in chapter 1 that the major determinant of an individual's success was his initial conditions—the income and education of his parents. Luck also plays an important role.

The central thesis of this chapter and the preceding one is also that inequality is not just the result of the forces of nature, of abstract market forces. We might like the speed of light to be faster, but there is nothing we can do about it. But inequality is, to a very large extent, the result of government policies that shape and direct the forces of technology and markets and broader societal forces. There is in this a note of both hope and despair: hope because it means that this inequality is not inevitable, and that by changing policies we can achieve a more efficient and a more egalitarian society; despair because the political processes that shape these policies are so hard to change.

There is one source of inequality, especially at the bottom, about which this chapter has had little to say: as this book goes to press, we are still in the worst economic downturn since the Great Depression. Macro-mismanagement, in all of its guises, is a major source of inequality. The unemployed are more likely to join those in poverty, the more so, the longer the economic downturn. The bubble gave a few of the poor an illusion of wealth, but only for a moment; as we have seen, when the bubble burst, it wiped out the wealth of those at the bottom, creating new levels of wealth inequality and heightening the fragility of those at the bottom. Chapter 9 will lay out how the macroeconomic (and especially monetary) policies that the United States and many other countries pursued reflected the interests and ideologies of the top.

Another theme of this book is that of "adverse dynamics," "vicious circles." We saw in the last chapter how greater inequality led to less equality of opportunity, leading in turn to more inequality. In the next chapter, we'll see some further examples of downward spirals—how more inequality undermines support for collective action, the kinds of actions that ensure that everyone lives up to his or her potential, as a result, for instance, of good public schools. We'll explain how inequality fosters instability, which itself gives rise to more inequality.

CHAPTER FOUR

WHY IT MATTERS

WE SAW IN CHAPTER 1 THAT THE AMERICAN economy has not been delivering for most citizens for years, even though, with the exception of 2009, GDP per capita has been increasing. The reason is simple: growing inequality, an increasing gap between the top and the rest. We saw in chapter 2 that one of the reasons that the top has done so well is *rent seeking*—which entails seizing a larger share of the pie and, in doing so, making the size of the pie smaller than it otherwise would be.

We are paying a high price for our large and growing inequality, and because our inequality is likely to continue to grow—unless we do something—the price we pay is likely to grow too. Those in the middle, and especially those at the bottom, will pay the highest price, but our country as a whole—our society, our democracy—also will pay a very high price.

Widely unequal societies do not function efficiently, and their economies are neither stable nor sustainable in the long term. When one interest group holds too much power, it succeeds in getting policies that benefit itself, rather than policies that would benefit society as a whole. When the wealthiest

use their political power to benefit excessively the corporations they control, much-needed revenues are diverted into
the pockets of a few instead of benefiting society at large.

But the rich do not exist in a vacuum. They need a functioning society around them to sustain their position and to
produce income from their assets. The rich resist taxes, but
taxes allow society to make investments that sustain the country's growth. When little money is invested in education, for
lack of tax revenues, schools do not produce the bright graduates that companies need to prosper. Taken to its extreme—
and this is where we are now—this trend distorts a country
and its economy as much as the quick and easy revenues of
the extractive industry distort oil- or mineral-rich countries.

We know how these extremes of inequality play out
because too many countries have gone down this path before.
The experience of Latin America, the region of the world with
the highest level of inequality,[1] foreshadows what lies ahead.
Many of the countries were mired in civil conflict for decades,
suffered high levels of criminality and social instability. Social
cohesion simply did not exist.

This chapter explains the reasons why an economy like
America's, in which most citizens' wealth has fallen, median
incomes have stagnated, and many of the poorest citizens have
been doing worse year after year, is not likely to do well over
the long haul. We will look first at the effects of inequality on
national output and economic stability, then at its impact on
economic efficiency and on growth. The effects are multiple
and occur through a number of channels. Some are caused by
the increase in poverty; others can be attributed to the evisceration of the middle class, still more to the growing disparity between the 1 percent and the rest of us. Some of these
effects arise through traditional economic mechanisms, while

others are the consequence of inequality's broader impact on our political system and society.

We'll also examine the fallacious ideas that inequality is good for growth, or that doing anything about inequality—like raising taxes on the rich—would harm the economy.

INSTABILITY AND OUTPUT

It is perhaps no accident that this crisis, like the Great Depression, was preceded by large increases in inequality:[2] when money is concentrated at the top of society, the average American's spending is limited, or at least that would be the case in the absence of some artificial prop, which, in the years before the crisis, came in the form of a housing bubble fueled by Fed policies. The housing bubble created a consumption boom that gave the appearance that everything was fine. But as we soon learned, it was only a temporary palliative.

Moving money from the bottom to the top lowers consumption because higher-income individuals consume a smaller proportion of their income than do lower-income individuals (those at the top save 15 to 25 percent of their income, those at the bottom spend all of their income).[3] The result: until and unless something else happens, such as an increase in investment or exports, total demand in the economy will be less than what the economy is capable of supplying—and that means that there will be unemployment. In the 1990s that "something else" was the tech bubble; in the first decade of the twentieth-first century, it was the housing bubble. Now the only recourse is government spending.

Unemployment can be blamed on a deficiency in aggregate demand (the total demand for goods and services in the economy, from consumers, from firms, by government, and by exporters); in some sense, the entire shortfall in aggregate demand—and hence in the U.S. economy—today can be blamed on the extremes of inequality. As we've seen, the top 1 percent of the population earns some 20 percent of U.S. national income. If that top 1 percent saves some 20 percent of its income, a shift of just 5 percentage points to the poor or middle who do not save—so the top 1 percent would still get 15 percent of the nation's income—would increase aggregate demand *directly* by 1 percentage point. But as that money recirculates, output would actually increase by some 1½ to 2 percentage points.[4] In an economic downturn such as the current one, that would imply a decrease in the unemployment rate of a comparable amount. With unemployment in early 2012 standing at 8.3 percent, this kind of a shift in income could have brought the unemployment rate down close to 6.3 percent. A broader redistribution, say, from the top 20 percent to the rest, would have brought down the unemployment further, to a more normal 5 to 6 percent.

There's another way of seeing the role of growing inequality in weakening macroeconomic performance. In the last chapter, we observed the enormous decline in the wage share in this recession; the decline amounted to more than a half trillion dollars a year.[5] That's an amount much greater than the value of the stimulus package passed by Congress. That stimulus package was estimated to reduce unemployment by 2 to 2½ percentage points. Taking money away from workers has, of course, just the opposite effect.

Since the time of the great British economist John Maynard Keynes, governments have understood that when there is a shortfall of demand—when unemployment is high—they need to take action to increase either public or private spending. The 1 percent has worked hard to restrain government spending. Private consumption is encouraged through tax cuts, and that was the strategy undertaken by President Bush, with three large tax cuts in eight years. It didn't work. The burden of countering weak demand has thus been placed on the U.S. Federal Reserve, whose mandate is to maintain low inflation, high growth, and full employment. The Fed does this by lowering interest rates and providing money to banks, which, in normal times, lend it to households and firms. The greater availability of credit at lower interest rates often spurs investment. But things can go wrong. Rather than spurring *real* investments that lead to higher long-term growth, the greater availability of credit can lead to bubbles. A bubble can lead households to consume in an unsustainable way, on the basis of debt. And when a bubble breaks, it can bring on a recession. While it is not inevitable that policy makers will respond to the deficiency in demand brought about by the growth in inequality in ways that lead to instability and a waste of resources, it happens often.

How the government's response to weak demand from inequality led to a bubble and even more inequality

For instance, the Federal Reserve responded to the 1991 recession with low interest rates and the ready availability of credit, helping to create the tech bubble, a phenomenal increase in the price of technology stocks accompanied by heavy investment in the sector. There was, of course, something *real* underlying that bubble—technological change, brought about by the communications and computer revolution. The Internet was rightly judged to be a transformative innovation. But the irrational exuberance on the part of investors went well beyond anything that could be justified.

Inadequate regulation, bad accounting, and dishonest and incompetent banking also contributed to the tech bubble. Banks famously had touted stocks that they knew were "dogs." "Incentive" pay provided CEOs with incentives to distort their accounting, to show profits that were far larger than they actually were. The government could have reined this in by regulating the banks, by restricting incentive pay, by enforcing better accounting standards, and by requiring higher margins (the amount of cash that investors have to put down when they buy stock). But the beneficiaries of the tech bubble—and especially the corporate CEOs and the banks— didn't want the government to intervene: there was a party going on, and it was a party that lasted for several years. They also believed (correctly, as it turned out) that somebody else would clean up the mess.

But the politicians of the era were also beneficiaries of the bubble. This irrational investment demand during the tech boom helped to offset the otherwise weak demand created by the high inequality, making the Bill Clinton era one of *seeming* prosperity. Tax revenues from capital gains and other income generated by the bubble even gave the appearance of fiscal soundness. And, to some extent, the administration could claim "credit" for what was going on: Clinton's policies of financial market deregulation and cuts to capital gains tax rates (increasing the returns to speculating on the tech stocks) added fuel to the fire.[6]

When the tech bubble finally burst, the demand by firms (especially technology firms) for more capital diminished markedly. The economy went into recession. Something else would have to rekindle the economy. George W. Bush succeeded in getting a tax cut targeted at the rich through Congress. Much of the tax cut benefited the very rich: a cut in the rate on dividends, which was reduced from 35 percent to 15 percent, a further cut in capital gains tax rates, from 20 percent to 15 percent, and a gradual elimination of the estate tax.[7] But because, as we have noted, the rich save so much of their income, such a tax cut provided only a limited stimulus to the economy. Indeed, as we discuss next, the tax cuts had even some perverse effects.

Corporations, realizing that the dividend tax rate was unlikely to remain so low, had every incentive to pay out as much as they felt that they could do safely—without jeopardizing too much the future viability of the firm. But that meant smaller cash reserves left on hand for any investment opportunities that came along. Investment, outside of real estate, actually fell,[8] contrary to what some on the right had predicted.[9] (Part of the reason for the weak investment, of course, was that during the tech bubble many firms had *overinvested*.) By the same token, the cut in the estate tax may have discouraged spending; the rich could now safely stow away more money for their children and grandchildren, and they had less incentive to give away money to charities that would have spent the money on good causes.[10]

Strikingly, the Fed and its chairman at the time, Alan Greenspan, didn't learn the lessons of the tech bubble. But this was in part because of the politics of "inequality," which didn't allow alternative strategies that could have resuscitated the economy without creating another bubble, such as a tax cut to the poor or increased spending on badly needed infrastructure. This alternative to the reckless path the country took was anathema to those who wanted to see a smaller government—one too weak to engage in progressive taxation or redistributive policies. Franklin Delano Roosevelt had tried these policies in his New Deal, and the establishment pilloried him for it. Instead, low interest rates, lax regulations, and a distorted and dysfunctional financial sector came to the rescue of the economy—for a moment.

The Fed engineered, unintentionally, another bubble, this one temporarily more effective than the last but in the long run more destructive. The Fed's leaders didn't see it as a bubble, because their ideology, their belief that markets were always efficient, meant that there *couldn't* be a bubble. The housing bubble was more effective because it induced spending not just by a few technology companies but by tens of millions of households that thought that they were richer than they were. In one year alone, close to a trillion dollars were taken out in home equity loans and mortgages, much of it spent on consumption.[11] But the bubble was more destructive partly for the same reasons: it left in its wake tens of millions of families on the brink of financial ruin. Before the debacle is over, millions of Americans will lose their homes, and millions more will face a lifetime of financial struggle.

Overleveraged households and excess real estate have already weighed down the economy for years and are likely to do so for more years, contributing to unemployment and a massive waste of resources. At least the tech bubble left something useful in its wake—fiber optics networks and new technology that would provide sources of strength for the economy. The housing bubble left shoddily built houses, located in the wrong places and inappropriate to the needs of a country where most people's economic position was in decline. It's the culmination of a three-decade stretch spent careening from one crisis to another without learning some very obvious lessons along the way.

In a democracy where there are high levels of inequality, politics can be unbalanced, too, and the combination of an unbalanced politics managing an unbalanced economy can be lethal.

Deregulation

There is a second way that unbalanced politics driven by extremes of inequality leads to instability: deregulation. Deregulation has played a central part in the instability that we, and many other countries, have experienced. Giving corporations, and especially the financial sector, free rein was in the *shortsighted* interest of the wealthy; they used their political weight, and their power to shape ideas, to push deregulation, first in airlines and other areas of transportation, then in telecom, and finally, and most dangerously, in finance.[12]

Regulations are the rules of the game that are designed to make our system work better—to ensure competition, to prevent abuses, to protect those who cannot protect themselves. Without restraints, the kinds of market failures described in the last two chapters—where markets fail to produce efficient outcomes—are rampant. In the financial sector, for instance, there will be conflicts of interest and excesses, excess credit, excess leverage, excess risk taking, and bubbles. But those in the business sector see things differently: without the restraints, they see increases in profits. They think not of the broad, and often long-term, social and economic consequences, but of their narrower, short-term self-interest, the profits that they might garner now.[13]

In the aftermath of the Great Depression, an event preceded by similar excesses, the country enacted strong financial regulations, including the Glass-Steagall Act in 1933 (the law separated investment banks, which managed rich people's money and issued bonds and stocks, from commercial banks, which are concerned with ordinary people's money and make loans). These laws, effectively enforced, served the country well: in the decades following passage, the economy was spared the kind of financial crisis that had repeatedly plagued this country (and others). With the dismantling of these regulations in 1999, the excesses returned with even greater force: bankers quickly put to use advances in technology, finance, and economics. The innovations offered ways to increase leverage that circumvented the regulations that remained and that the regulators didn't fully understand, new ways of engaging in predatory lending, and new ways to deceive unwary credit card users.

The losses from the underutilization of resources associated with the Great Recession and other economic downturns are enormous. Indeed, the sheer waste of resources brought on by this crisis caused by the private sector—a shortfall of trillions of dollars between what the economy could have produced and what it has produced—is greater than the waste of any democratic government, ever. The financial sector claimed that its innovations had led to a more productive economy—a claim for which there is no evidence—but there is no doubting the instability and inequality for which it is responsible. Even if the financial sector had led to a quarter percent higher growth for three decades—a claim that is beyond that of even the most exaggerated supporters of the sector—it would barely have made up for the losses that its misbehavior precipitated.

We have seen how inequality gives rise to instability, as a result of both the deregulatory policies that are enacted and the policies that are typically adopted in response to the deficiencies in aggregate demand. Neither is a *necessary* consequence of inequality: if our democracy worked better, it might have resisted the political demand for deregulation and might have responded to the weaknesses in aggregate demand in ways that enhanced sustainable growth rather than creating a bubble.[14]

There are further adverse effects of this instability: it increases risk. Firms are risk averse, which means that they demand compensation for bearing the risk. Without compensation, firms will invest less, and so there will be less growth.[15]

The irony is that while inequality gives rise to instability, the instability itself gives rise to more inequality, one of the vicious cycles that we identify in this chapter. In chapter 1, we saw how the Great Recession has been particularly hard on those at the bottom, and even those in the middle, and this is typical: ordinary workers face higher unemployment, lower wages, declining house prices, a loss of much of their wealth. Since the rich are better able to bear risk, they reap the reward that society provides for compensating for the greater risk.[16] As always, they seem to be the winners from the policies that they advocated and that imposed such high costs on others.

In the wake of the 2008 global financial crisis, there is now an increasing global consensus that inequality leads to instability, and that instability contributes to inequality.[17] The International Monetary Fund (IMF), the international agency charged with maintaining global economic stability, which I have strongly criticized for paying insufficient attention to the consequences of its policies for the poor, belatedly acknowledged that it cannot ignore inequality if it is to fulfill its mandate. In a 2011 study, the IMF concluded, "We find that longer growth spells are robustly associated with more equality in the income distribution. . . . Over longer horizons, reduced inequality and sustained growth may thus be two sides of the same coin."[18] In April of that year its then–managing director, Dominique Strauss-Kahn, emphasized, "Ultimately, employment and equity are building blocks of economic stability and prosperity, of political stability and peace. This goes to the heart of the IMF's mandate. It must be placed at the heart of the policy agenda."[19]

HIGH INEQUALITY MAKES FOR A LESS EFFICIENT AND PRODUCTIVE ECONOMY

Beyond the costs of the instability to which it gives rise, there are several other reasons why high inequality—the kind that now characterizes the United States—makes for a less efficient and productive economy. We discuss in turn (a) the reduction in broadly beneficial public investment and support for public education, (b) massive distortions in the economy (especially associated with rent seeking), in law, and in regulations, and (c) effects on workers' morale and on the problem of "keeping up with the Joneses."

Lowering public investment

The current economic mantra stresses the role of the private sector as the engine of economic growth. It's easy to see why: when we think of innovation we think of Apple, Facebook, Google, and a host of other companies that have changed our lives. But behind the scenes lies the public sector: the success of these firms, and indeed the viability of our entire economy, depends heavily on a well-performing public sector. There are creative entrepreneurs all over the world. What makes a difference—whether they are able to bring their ideas to fruition and products to market—is the government.

For one thing, the government sets the basic rules of the game. It enforces the laws. More generally, it provides the soft and hard infrastructure that enables a society, and an economy, to function. If the government doesn't provide roads, ports, education, or basic research—or see to it that someone else does, or at least provides the conditions under which someone else could—then ordinary business cannot flourish. Economists call such investments "public goods," a technical term referring to the fact that everyone can enjoy the benefits of, say, basic knowledge.

A modern society requires collective action, the country acting together to make these investments. The broad societal benefits that flow from them cannot be captured by any private investor, which is why leaving it to the market will result in underinvestment.

The United States and the world have benefited greatly from government-sponsored research. In earlier decades research conducted through our state universities and agricultural extension services contributed to enormous increases in agricultural productivity.[20] Today, government-sponsored research has promoted the information technology revolution and advances in biotechnology.

For several decades America has suffered from underinvestment in infrastructure, basic research, and education at all levels. Further cutbacks in these areas lie ahead, given the commitment by both parties to bringing down the deficit and the refusal of the House of Representatives to raise taxes. The cuts come despite evidence that the boost these investments give to the economy far exceeds the average return in the private sector, and is certainly higher than the cost of funds to the government.[21] Indeed, the boom years of the 1990s were buoyed by innovations made in previous decades that finally took their place in our economy. But the well from which the private sector can draw—for the next generation of transformational investments—is drying up. Applied innovations depend on basic research, and we simply haven't been doing enough of it.[22]

Our failure to make these critical public investments should not come as a surprise. It is the end result of a lopsided wealth distribution in society. The more divided a society becomes in terms of wealth, the more reluctant the wealthy are to spend money on common needs. The rich don't need to rely on government for parks or education or medical care or personal security. They can buy all these things for themselves. In the process, they become more distant from ordinary people.

The wealthy also worry about a strong government—one that could use its power to adjust the imbalances in our society by taking some of their wealth and devoting it to public investments that would contribute to the common good or that would help those at the bottom. While the wealthiest Americans may complain about the kind of government we have in America, in truth many like it just fine: too gridlocked to redistribute, too divided to do anything but lower taxes.

Living up to potential: the end of opportunity

Our underinvestment in the common good, including public education, has contributed to the decline in economic mobility that we noted in chapter 1. This in turn has important consequences for the country's growth and efficiency. Whenever we diminish equality of opportunity, we are not using one of our most valuable assets—our people—in the most productive way possible.

In earlier chapters we saw how the prospects of a good education for the children of poor and middle-income families were far bleaker than those of the children of the rich. Parental income is becoming increasingly important, as college tuition increases far faster than incomes, especially at public colleges, which educate 70 percent of Americans. But, one might ask, don't expanded student loan programs fill the gap? The answer, unfortunately, is no; and again, the financial sector is more than a little at fault. Today, the market is characterized by a set of perverse incentives, which, together with the absence of regulations that prevent abuse, mean that the student loan programs, rather than uplifting the poor, can (and too often do) lead to their further immiseration. The financial sector succeeded in making student loans non-dischargeable in bankruptcy, which meant that the lenders had little incentive to see to it that the schools for which the students were borrowing money were actually providing them with an education that would enhance their income. Meanwhile, private for-profit schools with richly compensated executives have defeated attempts to impose high standards that would make schools that exploit the poor and ill informed—by taking their money and not providing them with an education that enables them to get jobs to repay the loans—ineligible for loans.[23] It is totally understandable that a young person, seeing how the burden of debt is crushing his parents' lives, would be reluctant to take on student loans. It is, in fact, remarkable that so many are willing to do so, to the point that the average college graduate now has a debt of over $26,000.[24]

There may be another factor at play that is decreasing mobility and that, over the long run, will decrease the nation's productivity. Studies of educational attainment stress the importance of what happens in the home. As those in the middle and at the bottom struggle to make a living—as they have to work more to get by—families have less time to spend together. Parents are less able to supervise their children's homework. Families have to make compromises, and among them is less investment in their children (though they wouldn't use those words).

A distorted economy—rent seeking and financialization—and a less well-regulated economy

A central theme of the preceding chapters was that much of the inequality in our economy was the result of rent seeking. In their simplest form, rents are just redistributions from the rest of us to the rent seekers. That's the case when oil and mining companies succeed in getting rights to oil and minerals at prices well below what they should be. The main waste of resources is only on lobbying: there are more than 3,100 lobbyists working for the health industry (nearly 6 for every congressperson), and 2,100 lobbyists working for the energy and natural resources industries. All told, more than $3.2 billion was spent on lobbying in 2011 alone.[25] The main distortion is to our political system; the main loser, our democracy.

But often rent seeking involves a real waste of resources that lowers the country's productivity and well-being. It distorts resource allocations and makes the economy weaker. A byproduct of efforts directed toward getting a larger share of the pie is shrinkage of the pie. Monopoly power and preferential tax treatment for special interests have exactly this effect.[26]

The magnitude of "rent seeking" and the associated distortions in our economy, while hard to quantify precisely, are clearly enormous. Individuals and corporations that excel at rent seeking are amply rewarded. They may garner immense profits for their firms. But this does not mean that their *social* contribution is even positive. In a rent-seeking economy such as ours is becoming, private and social returns are badly misaligned. The bankers who gained large profits for their companies were amply rewarded, but, as I have repeatedly said, those profits were ephemeral and unconnected to sustainable improvements in the *real* economy. That something was wrong should have been evident: the financial sector is supposed to *serve* the rest of the economy, not the other way around. Yet before the crisis, 40 percent of all corporate profits went to the financial sector.[27] Credit card companies would extract more money from transaction fees than the grocery store would profit from the sale of its goods. For the movement of a few electrons upon the swipe of a card, something that costs at most a few pennies, the finance company received as much money as the store did for managing a complex operation that made a wide variety of food available at a low price.[28]

Rent seeking distorts our economy in many ways—not the least of which is the misallocation of the country's precious talent. It used to be that bright young people were attracted to a variety of professions—some to serving others, as in medicine or teaching or public service; some to expanding the frontiers of knowledge. Some always went into business, but in the years before the crisis an increasingly large fraction of the country's best minds chose finance. And with so many talented young people in finance, it's not surprising that there would be innovation in that sector. But many of these "financial innovations" were designed to circumvent regulations, and actually lowered long-run economic performance. These financial innovations do not compare with real innovations like the transistor or the laser that increase our standard of living.

The financial sector is not the only source of rent seeking in our economy. What is striking is the prevalence of limited competition and rent seeking in so many key sectors of the economy. Earlier chapters referred to the hi-tech sector (Microsoft). Two others that have drawn attention are the health care sector and telecommunications. Drug prices are so much higher than the costs of production that it pays drug companies to spend enormous amounts of money to persuade doctors and patients to use them, so much so that they now spend more on marketing than on research.[29] And much of the so-called research itself is rent seeking—producing a me-too drug that will divide the high profits of a rival firm's blockbuster drug. Imagine how competitive our economy might be—and how many jobs might be created—if all that money was invested in *real* research and *real* investments to increase the nation's productivity.

Whenever rents are generated by monopoly power, a large distortion in the economy occurs. Prices are too high. Restrictions in production induce a shift from the monopolized product to others. It is remarkable that even though the United States is allegedly a highly competitive economy, certain sectors seem to continue to reap excess profits.

Economists marvel at our health care sector and its ability to deliver less for more: health outcomes are worse in the United States than in almost all other advanced industrial countries, and yet the United States spends absolutely more per capita, and more as a percentage of GDP, by a considerable amount. We've been spending more than one-sixth of GDP on health care, while France has been spending less than an eighth. Per capita spending in the United States has been two and a half times higher than the average of the

advanced industrial countries.[30] This inefficiency is so large
that after it is taken into account, the gap between income
per capita in the United States and in France shrinks by about
a third.[31] While there are many reasons for this disparity in
the efficiency of the health care system, rent seeking, in particular on the part of health insurance companies and drug
companies, plays a significant role.

Earlier, we cited the most notorious example: a provision in
the 2003 Bush Medicare expansion that led to much higher
drug prices in the United States and to a windfall gain (a rent)
for the drug companies estimated at $50 billion or more a
year. Well, one might say, what is $50 billion among friends?
In a $15 trillion economy,[32] it amounts to less than a third
of 1 percent. But as Everett Dirksen, the senator from Illinois, is reputed to have said: a billion here, a billion there,
and pretty soon you're talking real money.[33] In the case of our
rent-seeking corporations, it's more like $50 billion here, $50
billion there, and pretty soon you're talking very big money.

When competition is very restricted, the real effect of competition is often waste, as the competitors fight over who gets
to exploit the consumer. Accordingly, high profits are not the
only sign of rent seeking. Indeed, distorted, oligopolistic competition among firms can even lead to dissipation of rents, but
not economic efficiency; when profits (above a normal return)
are driven to or near zero (or to where the return on capital
is normal), it is not necessarily evidence of an efficient economy. We see evidence of rent seeking in the high expenditures
to recruit credit card or cell phone customers. Here the object
becomes to exploit customers as much and as fast as possible,
with fees and charges that are neither understandable nor
predictable. Companies work hard to make it difficult to compare the costs of using, say, one credit card versus another

because to do so would enhance competition, and competition would erode profits.

American businesses, too, have to pay much more to the credit card companies than do businesses in other countries that have managed to curb some of the anticompetitive practices—and the higher costs faced by businesses get passed on to American consumers, lowering standards of living.

The same holds for cell phones: Americans pay higher cell phone rates, and get poorer service, than people in countries that have succeeded in creating a more truly competitive marketplace.

Sometimes the distortions of the rent seekers are subtle, not well captured in the diminution of GDP. This is because GDP doesn't adequately capture costs to the environment. It doesn't assess the sustainability of the growth that is occurring. When GDP arises from taking resources out of the ground, we should make note that the country's wealth is diminished, unless that wealth is reinvested above ground in human or physical capital. But our metrics don't do that. Growth that arises from depleting fish stocks or groundwater is ephemeral, but our metrics don't tell us that. Our price system is flawed, because it doesn't reflect accurately the scarcity of many of these environmental resources. And since GDP is based on market prices, our GDP metrics are also flawed.

Industries like coal and oil want to keep it that way. They don't want the scarcity of natural resources or the damage to our environment to be priced, and they don't want our GDP metrics to be adjusted to reflect sustainability. Not charging them for the costs they impose on the environment is, in effect, a hidden subsidy, little different from the other gifts the industry receives in favorable tax treatment and acquiring resources at below fair market prices.

When I was chair of the Council of Economic Advisers under President Clinton, I tried to have the United States issue a "Green GDP account," which would reflect the depletion of our resources and the degradation of our environment. But the coal industry knew what it would mean—and it used its enormous influence in Congress to threaten to cut off funding for those engaged in this attempt to define Green GDP, and not just for this project.

When the oil industry pushes for more offshore drilling and simultaneously pushes for laws that free companies from the full consequences of an oil spill, it is, in effect, asking for a public subsidy. And such subsidies do more than provide rents; they also distort resource allocations. GDP, and more broadly, societal welfare, is diminished—as was made so evident by the 2010 BP oil spill in the Gulf of Mexico. Because of the oil and coal companies that use their money to influence environmental regulation, we live in a world with more air and water pollution, in an environment that is less attractive and less healthy, than would otherwise be the case. The costs show up as lower standards of living for ordinary Americans, the benefits as higher profits for the oil and coal companies. Again, there is a misalignment between social returns (which may in fact be negative, as a result of the lowering of our standard of living in the wake of environmental deterioration) and private rewards (which are often huge).[34]

As we explained in the last two chapters, one objective of rent seekers is to shape laws and regulations to their benefit. To do that, you need lawyers. If it can be said that America has a government of the 1 percent, by the 1 percent, and for the 1 percent, it can be said with even more conviction that America has a government of the lawyers, by the lawyers, and for the lawyers. Twenty-six of America's forty-four presidents have been lawyers, and 36 percent of the legislators in the House have a background in law. Even if they are not narrowly pursuing what is in the financial interests of lawyers, they may be "cognitively captured."

The legal framework is *supposed* to make our economy more efficient by providing incentives for individuals and firms not to behave badly. But we have designed a legal system that is an arms race: the two protagonists work hard to out-lawyer each other, which is to say outspend each other, since good and clever lawyers are expensive. The outcome is often determined less by the merits of the case or issue than by the depth of the pockets. In the process, there is massive distortion of resources, not just in the litigation but in actions taken to affect the outcome of litigation and to prevent litigation in the first place.

The macroeconomic effect of America's litigious society was suggested by some studies that showed that countries with fewer lawyers (relative to their population) grew faster.[35] Other research suggests that the main channel through which a high proportion of lawyers in a society hurts the economy is the diversion of talent away from more innovative activities (like engineering and science), a finding consistent with our earlier discussion of finance. [36]

But I should be clear: given the success of the financial sector and corporations more generally in stripping away the regulations that protect ordinary citizens, the legal system is often the only source of protection that poor and middle-class Americans have. But instead of a system with high social cohesion, high levels of social responsibility, and good regulations protecting our environment, workers, and consumers, we maintain a very expensive system of *ex post accountability*, which to too large an extent relies on penalties for those that do injury (say, to the environment) *after the fact* rather than restricting action *before the damage is done.*[37]

Corporations successfully beat back regulations in their battle with the rest of society, but have met their match with the lawyers. Both groups spend heavily on lobbying to ensure that they can continue their rent-extracting activities. In the course of this arms race, a balance appears to have been struck—there are at least some countervailing powers checking the behavior of corporations. While the balance is better than what would emerge if, say, the corporations wrote their own rules—where the victims of their actions would have no recourse—the current system is still enormously costly to our society.

The 1 percent that shapes our politics not only distorts our economy by not doing what it should, in aligning private and social incentives, but also by encouraging it to do what it shouldn't. The recurrent bank bailouts, which encourage banks to engage in excessive risk taking,[38] offer the most obvious example. But many argue that even more costly are the distortions in foreign policy. More persuasive as an explanation of the Iraq War than Bush's avowed determination to eliminate one dictator was the attraction of Iraqi oil (and perhaps the huge profits that would accrue to Bush devotees, including Vice President Richard Cheney's Halliburton Corporation).[39]

While those at the top may disproportionately be among the beneficiaries of war, they bear disproportionately less of the cost. Members of the top 1 percent rarely serve in the military—the reality is that the all-volunteer army does not pay enough to attract their sons and daughters. The wealthiest class feels no pinch from higher taxes when the nation goes to war: borrowed money pays for it,[40] and if budgets get tight, middle-class tax benefits and social programs are given the ax, not the preferential tax treatment and manifold loop-holes for the rich.

Foreign policy is, by definition, about the balancing of national interests and national resources. With the top 1 per-cent in charge and paying no price for wars, the notion of bal-ance and restraint goes out the window. There is no limit to the adventures we can undertake; corporations and contrac-tors stand only to gain. At the local level around the world, contractors love roads and buildings, from which they can benefit enormously, especially if they make the right political contributions. For U.S. contractors, the military has provided a bonanza beyond imagination.

Efficiency wage theory and alienation

A central theme of this chapter is that much of the inequality in our society arises because private rewards differ from social returns, and that the high level of inequality that now char-acterizes the United States, and the *widespread acceptance* of that level of inequality (despite the encouraging signs from the Occupy Wall Street movement), makes it difficult in the United States to adopt good policies. Policy failures include those in macroeconomic stabilization, industry deregulation, and underinvestment in infrastructure, public education, social protection, and research.

We now consider an altogether different reason why the high inequality makes for a less efficient and productive economy than we could otherwise achieve. People are not like machines. They have to be motivated to work hard. If they feel that they are being treated unfairly, it can be hard to moti-vate them. This is one of the central tenets of modern labor economics, encapsulated in the efficiency wage theory, which argues that how firms treat their workers—including how much they pay them—affects productivity. It was, in fact, a theory elaborated nearly a century ago by Alfred Marshall, the great economist who wrote in 1895 that "highly paid labour is generally efficient and therefore not dear labour," though he admitted that this was "a fact which, though it is more full of hope for the future of the human race than any other that is known to us, will be found to exercise a very complicating influence on the theory of distribution."[41]

The revival of this theory began in development economics, where theorists recognized that malnourished workers are less productive.[42] But the insight applies as well to more advanced industrial countries, as America discovered in World War II when it found that many recruits were sufficiently malnourished that it might impair their effectiveness in the military. Education scholars have shown that hunger and inadequate nutrition impede learning.[43] That's why school lunch programs are so important. With one of seven Americans facing food insecurity, many poor American children also face impaired learning.

In a modern economy, efficiency is affected not so much by malnutrition as by a host of other factors. The immiseration of the bottom and the middle of the population has forced upon them a host of anxieties: Will they lose their home? Will they be able to give their children an education that will allow them to succeed in life? How will their parents survive in retirement? The more energy that is focused on these anxieties, the less energy there is for productivity at the workplace.

The economist Sendhil Mullainathan and psychologist Eldar Shafir have found evidence from experiments that living under scarcity often leads to choices that exacerbate the conditions of scarcity: "The poor borrow at great cost and stay poor. The busy [the time-poor] postpone when they have little time only to become busier."[44] Results of a very simple survey illustrate the cognitive resources that the poor expend for day-to-day survival and that the better-off do not. In the survey, individuals who have just exited a grocery store are asked what they had spent in total at the store and what the price of a few of the items in their shopping bags were. The poor typically could answer these questions precisely, whereas the non-poor often did not know. An individual's cognitive resources are limited. The stress of not having enough money to meet urgent needs may actually impair the ability to take decisions that would help alleviate the situation. The limited stock of cognitive resources is depleted and this can lead people to make irrational decisions.

Stress and anxiety can also impair the acquisition of new skills and knowledge. If that learning is impaired, productivity increases will be slower, and this bodes ill for the long-run performance of the economy.

Equally important in motivating workers is their sense that they are being fairly treated. While it is not always clear what is fair, and people's judgments of fairness can be biased by their self-interest, there is a growing sense that the present disparity in wages is unfair. When executives argue that wages have to be reduced or that there have to be layoffs in order for corporations to compete, but simultaneously increase their own pay, workers rightly consider that what is going on is unfair. That will affect their effort today, their loyalty to the firm, their willingness to cooperate with others, and their willingness to invest in its future. As any firm knows, a happier worker is a more productive worker; and a worker who believes that a firm is paying senior employees too much relative to what everyone else receives is not likely to be a happy worker.[45]

A detailed case study by Krueger and Mas of the plants that manufactured Bridgestone/Firestone tires provides a particularly chilling illustration. After a profitable year management demanded moving from an eight-hour to a twelve-hour shift, which would rotate between days and nights, and cutting pay for new hires by 30 percent. The demand created the conditions that led to the production of many defective tires. Defective tires were related to over one thousand fatalities and injuries until the recall of Firestone tires in 2000.[46]

In Russia under communism, the widespread sense by workers that they were not being adequately paid played a major role in the collapse of their economy. As the old Russian adage had it, "They pretended to pay us, and we pretended to work."

Recent experiments in economics have confirmed the importance of fairness. One experiment showed that raising wages of workers who felt that they were being treated unfairly had a substantial effect on productivity—and no effect on those who felt they were being treated fairly. Or take another situation, involving a group of workers performing a similar job. One might have expected that increasing the wages of some and lowering that of others would increase productivity of the higher-wage worker, and lower that of the lower-wage workers in offsetting ways. But economic theory—confirmed by the experiments—holds that the decrease in productivity of the low-wage worker is greater than the increase in productivity of the high-wage worker, so total productivity diminishes.[47]

Consumerism

We have described how inequality adversely affects the economy's growth and efficiency—and societal well-being, in both the short and the long run—through a variety of what might be viewed as *economic* mechanisms, reinforced and shaped by politics and public policy. But there are deeper, distorting effects of inequality on our society. Trickle-down economics may be a chimera, but trickle-down behaviorism is very real. People below the top 1 percent increasingly aspire to imitate those above them. Of course, for those at the very bottom, living like the wealthiest 1 percent is unimaginable. But for those in the second percentile, the 1 percent provides an aspiration, for those in the third percentile, the second percentile provides an aspiration, and so on down the line.

Economists talk about the importance of "relative income" and relative deprivation. What matters (for an individual's sense of well-being, for instance) is not just an individual's absolute income, but his income relative to that of others.[48] The importance of relative income in developed countries is so great that it is a completely unsettled question among economists whether there is *any* long-run relationship between GDP growth and subjective well-being in those countries.[49] Individuals' concerns with their consumption relative to that of others—the problem of "keeping up with the Joneses"— helps explain why so many Americans live beyond their means—and why so many work so hard and so long.

Many years ago Keynes posed a question. For thousands of years, most people had to spend most of their time working just to survive—for food, clothing, and shelter. Then, beginning with the Industrial Revolution, unprecedented increases in productivity meant that more and more individuals could be freed from the chains of subsistence living. For increasingly large portions of the population, only a small fraction of their time was required to provide for the necessities of life. The question was, How would people spend the productivity dividend?[50]

The answer was not obvious. They could decide to enjoy

more and more leisure, or they could decide to enjoy more and more goods. Economic theory provides no clear prediction, though one might have assumed that reasonable people would have decided to enjoy both more goods and more leisure. That is what happened in Europe. But America took a different turn—less leisure (per household, as women joined the labor force) and more and more goods.

America's high inequality—and individuals' sensitivity to others' consumption—may provide an explanation. It may be that we are working more to maintain our consumption relative to others, and that this is a rat race, which is individually rational but futile in terms of the goal that it sets for itself. Adam Smith pointed out that possibility 250 years ago: in "this general scramble for preeminence, when some get up, others must necessarily fall undermost."[51] While there is no "right" answer to Keynes's question according to standard economic theory, there is something disturbing about America's answer.[52] Individuals say they are working so hard *for the family*, but as they work so hard there is less and less time for the family, and family life deteriorates. Somehow, the means prove inconsistent with the stated end.

THE ALLEGED INEQUALITY EFFICIENCY TRADE-OFF

In the previous pages, I explained how inequality—in all of its dimensions—has been bad for our economy. As we saw in earlier chapters, there is also a counternarrative, advanced primarily by those on the political right, which focuses on incentives. In this view incentives are essential for making an economy work, and inequality is the inevitable consequence of any incentive system, since some will produce more than others. Any program of redistribution will accordingly necessarily attenuate incentives. Proponents of this view argue, too, that it is wrong to fixate on the inequality of outcomes, particularly in any single year. What matters is lifetime inequality, and what matters even more is opportunity. They then maintain that there is a trade-off between efficiency and equality. While different people may differ in how much efficiency one would be willing to give up to get more equality, in the view of the Right the price we have to pay for any more equality in America is just too great. Indeed, it's so high that even the middle and the bottom, especially those who depend on government programs, would likely suffer; with a weaker economy, incomes for all would be down, tax revenues would be lower, and government programs would have to be cut.

We have argued in this chapter, to the contrary, that we could have a more efficient and productive economy with more equality. In this section, I recap the essential points of divergence: The Right has in mind a perfectly competitive economy with private rewards equal to social returns; we see an economy marked by rent seeking and other distortions. The Right underestimates the need for public (collective) action, to correct pervasive market failures. It overestimates the importance of financial incentives. And, as a result of all of these mistakes, the Right overestimates the costs and underestimates the benefits of progressive taxation.

Rent seeking and the inequality/efficiency trade-off

A central thesis of this book is that rent seeking is pervasive in the American economy, and that it actually impairs overall economic efficiency. The large gaps between private rewards and social returns that characterize a rent-seeking economy mean that incentives that individuals face often misdirect their actions, and that those who receive high rewards are not necessarily those who have made the largest contributions. In those instances where private rewards of those at the top exceed by a considerable amount their marginal social contribution, redistribution could both reduce inequality and increase efficiency.[53]

Making markets work better, by aligning the two and reducing the scope for rent seeking, and by correcting other market failures, whose effects are especially hard felt at the bottom and in the middle, would also simultaneously reduce inequality and increase efficiency—just the opposite of what the Right contends.

Market failures and the inequality/efficiency trade-off

The Right has underestimated the importance of other imperfections in our economy: if capital markets were perfect, then each individual would be able to invest in himself up to the point where additional returns equal the cost of capital. But capital markets are far from perfect. Individuals do not have easy access to capital and cannot divest themselves of risk.

A lack of wealth restricts families' opportunities to be productive in a variety of ways. It reduces their ability to invest in their children, to become homeowners and thereby participate in the financial rewards of improving their neighborhoods, and to offer collateral that can credibly show lenders that the uses to which they will put borrowed funds are sound—which is useful for obtaining bank credit on affordable terms.

Wealth in the form of collateral plays a kind of catalytic role rather than a role of input that gets used up in the process of producing output.[54] The most important consequence of these imperfections is that in a world in which many families have little or no wealth, and in which only limited educational opportunity is provided by the government, there is underinvestment in human capital.

The result is that, especially without a good public education system, parental wealth (education, income) will be a primary determinant of that of their children. It is not a surprise, then, that America, with its high level of wealth and income inequality, is also a society with a lack of equality of opportunity, as we saw in chapter 1. Increasing equality and equality of opportunity, by the same token, would enhance the nation's productivity.

There is still another reason why the alleged inequality/ inefficiency trade-off may not exist. Risk markets—giving individuals the ability to buy insurance in the private market against the important risks that individuals face, like unemployment—are imperfect and absent; that imposes a huge burden on those with limited resources. Because risk markets are imperfect, in the absence of social protection, individual welfare is lower—and the willingness to undertake high-return and high-risk ventures is lower. Providing better social protection can help create a more dynamic economy.

The adverse effects of so-called incentive pay

The Right, like many economists, tends to overestimate the benefits and underestimate the costs of incentive pay. There are certainly contexts in which monetary prizes have the potential to focus minds on a thorny problem and deliver a solution. A famous example is detailed in Dava Sobel's *Longitude: The True Story of a Lone Genius Who Solved the Greatest Scientific Problem of His Time.* As she reports, in the Longitude Act of 1714, the British Parliament set "a prize equal to a king's ransom (several million dollars in today's currency) for a 'Practicable and Useful' means of determining longitude." This was critical to the success of transoceanic navigation. John Harrison, a watchmaker with no formal education but a mechanical genius, devoted his life to this quest and ultimately claimed the prize in 1773.[55] However, it is a great leap from the power of monetary incentives to focus minds on a great quest to the idea that monetary incentives are the key to high performance in general.

The absurdity of incentive pay in some contexts is made clear by thinking of how it might apply to medical doctors. Is it conceivable that a doctor performing heart surgery would exert more care or effort if his pay depended on whether the patient survived the surgery or if the heart valve surgery lasts for more than five years? Doctors work to make sure each surgery is their absolute best, for reasons that have little to do with money. Interestingly, in some areas we recognize the dangers of incentive pay: expert witnesses in litigation are not allowed to be paid contingent on the outcome of the case.

Because financial incentive systems can never be perfectly designed, they often lead to distorted behavior, an overemphasis on quantity and an underemphasis on quality.[56] As a result, in most sectors of the economy simplistic (and distorting) incentive schemes like those used in finance and those provided to CEOs are not used. Instead, assessments take into account performance relative to others in a similar position; there is an evaluation of long-term performance and potential. Rewards often take the form of promotions. But it is assumed, especially for higher-level jobs, that employees will do their best and not hold back, even in the absence of "incentive pay."[57]

Incentive pay, especially as it was implemented in the financial sector, illustrates how distorting such compensation can be: the bankers had an incentive to engage in excessive risk taking, shortsighted behavior, and deceptive and non-transparent accounting.[58] In good years the bankers could walk off with a large fraction of the profits; in bad years the shareholders were left with the losses; and in really bad years so were the bondholders and taxpayers. It was a one-sided pay system: heads the bankers won, tails everyone else lost.

Even if the bankers' pay system had made sense before the Great Recession, it didn't afterward, when the banks were put on life-support systems provided by the public. I described earlier how the government essentially gave them blank checks—lending them money at near-zero interest rates that they could "invest" in bonds paying much higher returns. As one banker friend put it to me, anyone, even his twelve-year-old son, could have made a fortune if the government had been willing to lend money to him at those terms. But the bankers treated the resulting profits as if they were a result of their genius, fully deserving of the same compensation to which they had become accustomed.

But while the bankers' compensation schemes demonstrated some of what was wrong with the so-called incentive pay systems, the problems were more pervasive. Stock options were as one-sided as bankers' compensation—executives did well when things went well, but didn't suffer commensurately when stocks went down. But stock options also encouraged dishonest accounting that made it seem that the company was doing well, so the stock price would go up.

Part of the creatively dishonest accounting involved accounting for the stock options themselves, so shareholders wouldn't know how much the value of their shares was being diluted by newly issued options. When the Financial Accounting Standards Board (the nominally independent board that sets accounting standards), supported by the Securities and Exchange Commission and the Council of Economic Advisers, tried to force companies to provide honest accounting of what they were giving their executives, the CEOs replied with a vehemence that demonstrated their commitment to deception. The proposed reforms didn't require firms to do away with stock options, but only to reveal what was being given to their executives in a way that their shareholders could easily grasp. We wanted to make markets work better, by having better information.

It is because accounting standards affect how markets perceive firms' future prospects, and because firms want standards that make them look good—leading to a higher stock price, at least in the short run—that we created an independent board to set these standards. But then corporations used their trump card—their political influence—as senior government officials weighed in, in a process that is *supposed to be independent and nonpolitical*, to maintain the deception.[59] The pressure worked.

Indeed, if one were really interested in incentives—and not in deception—one would have designed a quite different compensation system. Stock option incentive pay rewarded executives when there was a stock market boom for which they could fairly claim no credit. It also gave CEOs a big bonus whenever the price of what they sold soared or the price of a critical input fell—regardless of whether there was anything they had done to bring these price changes about.

Fuel costs are critical for airlines, meaning that airline CEOs got a bonus anytime the price of oil fell. A good incentive system might base pay on how the company performs relative to others in the industry, but few firms do this. That's testimony either to their lack of understanding of incentives or to their lack of interest in having a reward structure that is related to performance, or to both.[60]

The lack of well-designed compensation schemes, such as one based on relative performance, compared to a group of comparable peers, reflects *another* market failure, to which we called attention in the last chapter: deficiencies in corporate governance that provide scope for executives to do what is in their interests—including adopting compensation systems that enrich themselves—rather than in the interests of society, or even of shareholders.

The criticisms of incentive pay that I have discussed so far are well within the confines of traditional economic analysis. But incentives are about *motivating* people, for instance, to work hard. Psychologists, labor economists, and other social scientists have studied closely what motivates people, and it appears that, at least in many circumstances, economists have gotten it all wrong.

Individuals can often be better motivated by intrinsic rewards—by the satisfaction of doing a job well—than by extrinsic rewards (money). To take one example, the scientists whose research and ideas have transformed our lives in the past two hundred years have, for the most part, not been motivated by the pursuit of wealth. This is fortunate, for if they had, they would have become bankers and not scientists. It is the pursuit of truth, the pleasure of using their minds, the sense of achievement from discovery—and the recognition of their peers—that matters most.[61] Of course, that doesn't mean that they will turn down money if it's given to them. And, as we noted earlier, an individual preoccupied with where his and his family's next meal will come from will be too distracted to do good research.

In some circumstances, a focus on extrinsic rewards (money) can actually diminish effort. Most (or at least many) teachers enter their profession not because of the money but because of their love for children and their dedication to teaching. The best teachers could have earned far higher incomes if they had gone into banking. It is almost insulting to assume that they are not doing what they can to help their students learn, and that by paying them an extra $500 or $1,500, they would exert greater effort. Indeed, incentive pay can be corrosive: it reminds teachers of how bad their pay is, and those who are led thereby to focus on money may be induced to find a better-paying job, leaving behind only those for whom teaching is the only alternative. (Of course, if teachers perceive themselves to be badly paid, that will undermine morale, and that will have adverse incentive effects.)

An often told story provides another example: a cooperative day center had a problem with certain parents' picking up their children in a timely way. It decided to impose a charge, to provide an incentive for them to do so. But many parents, including those who had occasionally been late, had struggled to pick up their children on time; they did as well as they did because of social pressure, the desire to do the "right thing," even if they were less than fully successful. But charging a fee converted a social obligation into a monetary transaction. Parents no longer felt a social responsibility, but assessed whether the benefits of being late were greater or less than the fine. Lateness increased.[62]

There is another defect of standard incentive pay compen-

sation schemes. In business school we emphasize the importance of teamwork. Most employers recognize that teamwork
is absolutely essential for the success of the company. The
problem is that *individual* incentives can undermine this kind
of teamwork. There can be destructive as well as construc-
tive competition.[63] By contrast, cooperation can be facilitated
by pay that depends on "team performance."[64] Ironically, standard economic theory always disparaged such reward systems,
arguing that individuals would have no incentives, because
typically the impact of each individual's efforts on team performance (if the team is of even moderate size) is negligible.

The reason that economic theory failed to gauge accurately
the effectiveness of team incentives is that it underestimated
the importance of personal connectiveness.[65] Individuals work
hard to please others in their team—and because they believe
it is the right thing to do. Economists overestimate, too, the
selfishness of individuals (though there is considerable evidence that economists are more selfish than others, and that
economics training does make individuals more selfish over
time).[66] It is thus perhaps not surprising that firms owned by
their workers—and who therefore share in the profits—have
performed better in the crisis and laid off fewer employees.[67]

The blinders in economic theories in this arena are related
to a broader deficiency in the field. The prevailing approach to
behavior in standard economic theory focuses on rational *indi-
vidualism*. Each individual assesses everything from a perspective that pays no attention to what others do, how much they
get paid, or how they are treated. Human emotions such as
envy, jealousy, or a sense of fair play do not exist or, if they do,
have no role in *economic* behavior; and if they do appear, they
shouldn't. Economic analysis should proceed as if they did not
exist. To noneconomists, this approach seems nonsensical—

and to me, it does too. I have explained, for instance, how individuals may decrease effort if they feel they are being unfairly treated, and how team spirit can spur them on. But this individual-centered, bottom-line economics, tailor-made for America's short-term financial markets, is undermining trust and loyalty in our economy.

In short, contrary to the assertion of the Right that incentive pay is *necessary* to the country's maintaining its high level of productivity, the kinds of incentive pay schemes employed by many corporations, while they create more inequality, are actually counterproductive.

Overestimating the costs, and underestimating the benefits, of more-progressive taxation

The Right has not only underestimated the costs of inequality and ignored the benefits that we have described in eliminating the market distortions that give rise to it. It has also overestimated the costs of correcting inequality through progressive taxation, and underestimated the benefits of public spending.

We observed in the last chapter that President Reagan, for instance, claimed that by making the tax system less progressive—lowering taxes at the top—one would actually raise more money, because savings and work would increase. He was wrong: tax revenues fell significantly. President Bush's tax cuts fared no better; they, like those of Reagan, simply increased the deficit. President Clinton raised taxes at the top, and America experienced a period of rapid growth and a slight diminution in inequality. Of course, the Right is right in noting that if marginal tax rates were near 100 percent tax rates, incentives would be significantly weakened, but these examples show that we're nowhere near the point where this should be of concern. Indeed, University of California professor Emmanuel Saez, Thomas Piketty of the Paris School of Economics, and Stefanie Stantcheva of the MIT Department of Economics, carefully taking into account the incentive effects of higher taxation and the societal benefits of reducing inequality, have estimated that the tax rate at the top should be around 70 percent—what it was before President Reagan started his campaign for the rich.[68]

But even these calculations do not fully reflect, I believe, the benefit from more-progressive taxation, for three reasons. First, we noted earlier that increasing fairness (and the perception of fairness) increases productivity, and in keeping with most economic analyses, those calculations ignored this.

Second, the sense that our economic and political system is unfair undermines trust, which is essential for the functioning of our society. In the next chapter, we'll explain in greater detail how inequality and the way in which it has arisen in the United States has undermined trust, and how the weakening of trust weakens our economy and our democracy. A more-progressive tax system might contribute a little to a restoration in confidence that our system is, after all, fair. That could have enormous societal benefits, including to our economy.

Third, as we noted in the last chapter, much of the lack of progressivity—the low rates faced by those at the top, including the presidential candidate Mitt Romney—comes from special provisions of the tax code, like the low rates on capital gains taxation, the broad definition of capital gains,[69] and loopholes in both corporate and individual income taxes. These distort the economy, lowering productivity. As we commented, one of the reasons that so many of our corporations pay so little is that they are not taxed on income of foreign subsidiaries until they bring it home, a provision of the tax code that encourages these firms to invest abroad rather than in the United States. Eliminating these provisions would both increase progressivity and strengthen the U.S. economy.

Moreover, to the extent that incomes at the top arise from rents and to the extent that it is possible to target these rents, again one can have a more-progressive tax system without any adverse effects on incentives.

The fact that tax cuts for the rich have increased the deficit and the national debt substantially has another effect: it has created pressure to reduce government support for investments in education, technology, and infrastructure. The Right has underestimated the importance of these public investments, which not only can yield high returns directly but provide the basis of high-return private-sector investment. Earlier I mentioned the contribution that government investments in research and technology had made (including the first telegraph line that spanned North America in the nineteenth century, and the creation of the Internet and the foundations of the first browser in the twentieth). Recent research has shown that the years before World War II were years of high productivity increase, which set the stage for even more productivity increases in subsequent years. Among the reasons for this is government investment in roads (which interestingly played an important role in increasing productivity in railroads).[70] Such public investments can be financed sustainably only through taxation, and given the level of inequality, what is required is well-designed progressive taxation that can be less distortionary than regressive taxation. A corporate CEO will not exert less effort to make the company work well simply because his take-home pay is $10 million a year rather than $12 million. In any case, the possible loss of effort in socially productive activities from taxing the few in the top 1 percent—which, because of the huge inequality in our society, raises large amounts of money—pales in comparison with the effects on the many more numerous who would have to face higher tax rates to raise the same amount of money.[71]

CONCLUDING COMMENTS

Some of the adverse effects of inequality might be smaller if those who are poor today were rich tomorrow, or if there were true equality of opportunity. As the Occupy Wall Street movement drew attention to the growing inequality, the response of the Right was to say, almost proudly, that unlike the Democrats, who believe in equality of outcomes, they were committed to equality of opportunity. According to Paul Ryan, the Wisconsin Republican who heads the House Budget Committee, responsible for making the critical budgetary decisions affecting the country's future, a central difference between the parties is "[w]hether we are a nation that still believes in equality of opportunity, or whether we are moving away from that, and towards an insistence on equality of outcome."[72] He went on to say, "Let's not focus on redistribution; let's focus on upward mobility."

There are two factual problems with this perspective. First, it suggests that while we are failing in equality of outcomes, we are succeeding in equality of opportunity. Chapter 1 showed that that was not true. The quip of Jonathan Chait seems to fit here: "The facts shouldn't get in the way of a pleasant fantasy."[73]

The second factual problem is the claim that the progressive perspective argues for equality of outcome. As Chait expressed it, the reality is that the Democrats are not arguing for equality of outcome, only for policies "that leave in place skyrocketing inequality of income, just ever so slightly amelio- rated by government."[74]

Perhaps the most essential point is this: no one succeeds on his own. There are plenty of bright, hardworking, ener- getic people in developing countries who remain poor—not because they lack abilities or are not making sufficient effort, but because they work in economies that don't function well. Americans all benefit from the physical and institutional infrastructure that has developed from the country's collec- tive efforts over generations. What's worrying is that those in the 1 percent, in attempting to claim for themselves an unjust proportion of the benefits of this system, may be willing to destroy the system itself to hold on to what they have.

This chapter has explained that we are paying a high price for the inequality that is increasingly scarring our economy— lower productivity, lower efficiency, lower growth, more insta- bility—and that the benefits of reducing this inequality, at least from the current high levels, far outweigh any costs that might be imposed. We have identified numerous channels through which the adverse effects of inequality operate. The bottom line, though, that higher inequality is associated with lower growth—controlling for all other relevant factors—has been verified by looking at a range of countries and looking over longer periods of time.[75]

Of all the costs imposed on our society by the top 1 per- cent, perhaps the greatest is this: the erosion of our sense of identity in which fair play, equality of opportunity, and a sense of community are so important. America has long prided itself on being a fair society, where everyone has an equal chance of getting ahead, but the statistics today, as we've seen, suggest otherwise: the chances that a poor or even a middle-class American will make it to the top in America are smaller than in many countries of Europe. And as inequality itself creates a weaker economy, the chance can only grow slimmer.

There is another cost of America's inequality, beyond this loss of a sense of identity and beyond the way it is weakening our economy: our democracy is being put at peril, a subject to which we turn in the next two chapters.

CHAPTER FIVE

A DEMOCRACY
IN PERIL

WE HAVE SEEN HOW AMERICA'S CURRENT inequality, and that of many other countries, did not arise spontaneously from abstract market forces but was shaped and enhanced by politics. Politics is the battleground for fights over how to divide nation's economic pie. It is a battle that the 1 percent have been winning. That isn't how it's supposed to be in a democracy. In a system of one person one vote, 100 percent of the people are supposed to count. Modern political and economic theory predicted that the outcomes of electoral processes with one person having one vote would reflect the views of the average citizen—not that of the elites. More precisely, standard theory, based on individuals with well-defined preferences who are voting in their self-interest, predicts that the outcome of democratic elections would reflect the views of the "median" voter—the person in the middle. In the case of public expenditures, for instance, it says that half would want more spending and half less.[1] But polls consistently show that there are large discrepancies between what most voters want and what the political system delivers.

In the aftermath of the Great Recession there is disillusionment not only with the global economic system but also with how the political systems in many Western democracies have been working. This disillusionment found expression in the Occupy Wall Street and *indignado* movements around the world. That there are major failures in our economic system is obvious; but it is equally evident that the American political system has not even begun to fix them. Most Americans don't think the new financial regulations (Dodd-Frank) went far enough, and they're right. Even before the crisis, there was an awareness of widespread predatory lending practices. It was in the interests of most Americans to curb those as well as the abusive credit card practices. But that didn't happen. The federal government has done little to prosecute banks that violated the law—as we will see in chapter 7, much less than it did in the much less serious Savings and Loan crisis two decades ago. The *New York Times* has described how the Securities and Exchange Commission, which is supposed to protect investors from fraud, "has repeatedly allowed the biggest firms to avoid punishments specifically meant to apply to fraud cases."[2]

Why hasn't the middle had the political influence that standard theory predicts it should have, and why does our current system seem to operate on "one dollar" one vote instead of one person one vote? In earlier chapters, we saw how markets are shaped by politics: politics determines the rules of the economic game, and the playing field is slanted in favor of the 1 percent. At least part of the reason is that the rules of the political game, too, are shaped by the 1 percent.

This story has two critical elements. One, shaping individuals' perceptions—so that the 99 percent adopt the interests of the 1 percent as their own—is the focus of the next chapter. The current chapter focuses on the economics and politics of voting itself.

Undermining Democratic Political Processes

The voting paradox and voter disillusionment

One of the puzzles in modern political economy is why anyone votes at all. Very few elections actually turn on the vote of a single individual. There is a cost to voting—although no American state has an explicit charge for voting today, it takes time and effort to get to the voting booth. Registration can also be a burden, requiring planning well in advance of elections. People who live in sprawling Western cities with poor public transportation may be at a disadvantage for reaching their polling stations. People with limited mobility may find it difficult to get to the polling station even when it is nearby. For voters' troubles, there is little personal benefit. Indeed, it almost never happens that the individual's vote is pivotal, that is, makes any difference to the final outcome. Modern political and economic theories assume rational self-interested actors. On that basis, why anyone votes is a mystery.

The answer, of course, is that we've been indoctrinated with notions of "civic virtue." It is our responsibility to vote. Each individual contemplating not voting worries about what would happen if everyone acted like him: "If I and other like-minded people didn't vote, that would leave the outcome to be determined by others with whom I disagree."

Such civic virtue should not be taken for granted. If the belief takes hold that the political system is stacked, that it's unfair, individuals will feel released from the obligations of civic virtue. When the social contract is abrogated, when trust between a government and its citizens fails, disillusionment, disengagement, or worse follows.³ In the United States today, and in many other democracies around the world, mistrust is ascendant.⁴

The irony is that the wealthy who seek to manipulate the political system for their own ends welcome such an outcome. Those who turn out to vote are those who see the political system working, or at least working for them. So if the political system works systematically in favor of those at the top, it is they who (disproportionately) are induced to engage in politics, and inevitably the system serves best those whose voices are heard.

Moreover, if voters have to be *induced* to vote because they are disillusioned, it becomes expensive to turn out the vote; the more disillusioned they are, the more it costs. But the more money that is required, the more power that the moneyed interests wield. For those with money, spending it to shape the political process is not a matter of civic virtue; it is an investment, from which they demand (and get) a return. It is only natural that they end up shaping the political process *in their interests*. That, in turn, increases the sense of disillusionment that pervades the rest of the electorate and boosts the power of money further.

Lowering trust

I have emphasized how the country has to act together, cooperatively, if the country's problems are to be solved. Government is the formal institution through which we act together, collectively, to solve the nation's problems. Inevitably, individuals will differ in their views of what should be done. That's one of the reasons that collective action is so difficult. There needs to be compromise, and compromise has to be based on trust: one group gives in today, in the understanding that another does in another year. There must be trust that all will be treated fairly, and if matters turn out differently from how the proponents of a measure claim it will, there will be change to accommodate the unexpected circumstances.

But it's easier to act together if the interests and perspectives of the members of a group are at least loosely aligned; if everyone is, as it were, in the same boat. But it is evident that the 1 percent and the rest are not in the same boat.

Cooperation and trust are important in every sphere of society. We often underestimate the role of trust in making our economy work or the importance of the social contract that binds us together. If every business contract had to be enforced by one party's taking the other to court, our economy, and not just our politics, would be in gridlock. The legal system enforces certain aspects of "good behavior," but most good behavior is voluntary. Our system couldn't function otherwise. If we littered every time we could get away with it, our streets would be filthy, or we would have to spend an inordinate amount on policing to keep them clean. If individuals cheated on every contract—so long as they could get away with it—life would be unpleasant and economic dealings would be fractious.

Throughout history the economies that have flourished are those where a man's word is his honor, where a handshake is a deal.[5] Without trust, business deals based on an understanding that the complex details will be worked out later are no longer feasible. Without trust, each participant in a deal looks around to see how and when those with whom he is dealing will betray him. To protect against these outcomes, individuals spend energy and resources obtaining insurance, making contingency plans, and taking actions to ensure that, should they be "betrayed," the consequences are limited.

Some social scientists try to account for the effect of "trust" on the overall economy by referring to social capital. An economy with more "social capital" is more productive, just like an economy with more human or physical capital. Social capital is a broad concept that includes those factors that contribute to good governance in both the public and the private sectors. But the idea of trust underlies all notions of social capital; people can feel confident that they will be treated well, with dignity, fairly. And they reciprocate.

Social capital is the glue that holds societies together. If individuals believe the economic and political system is unfair, the glue doesn't work and societies don't function well. As I've traveled around the world, partly in my job as chief economist of the World Bank, I've seen instances where social capital has been strong and societies have worked together. I've also seen instances where social cohesion has been destroyed and societies have become dysfunctional.

Bhutan, the remote Himalayan state to the northeast of India, for instance, is protecting its forests as part of a broader commitment to the environment. Each family is allowed to cut down a fixed number of trees for its own use. In this sparsely populated country, I asked, how could one enforce such an edict? The answer was simple and straightforward: in our jargon, social capital. The Bhutanese have internalized what is "right" when it comes to the environment. It would be wrong to cheat, and so they don't.

Communities that rely on irrigation—whether it's in the

hills and mountains of Bali or in the Atacama Desert of northern Chile—have to work together to manage their water and to maintain the irrigation canals. These communities, too, seem to develop strong bonds, a strong sense of social capital, with little or no cheating on the "social contract."

At the other extreme, when I visited Uzbekistan after the fall of the Soviet empire, I saw the consequences of the erosion of social capital. Most greenhouses had no glass, making them totally ineffective. I was told that as Uzbek society and economy decayed, each family looked out for itself. The glass was stolen from the greenhouses. Nobody was sure what they would do with the stolen glass, but it provided some limited security, and they were sure that if they didn't steal it, somebody else would.

More generally, in the aftermath of the breakdown of the Soviet Union, Russia experienced a marked decline in output. This puzzled most economists. After all, there was the same physical, human, and natural capital after the breakdown that there had been before the crisis. Eliminating the old distortionary centralized planning system and replacing it with a market economy should have meant that those resources would, at last, be more efficiently used. But what the analysis failed to incorporate was how seventy-four years of Communist Party rule, along with the suppression of civil society institutions, had eroded social capital. The only thing that had held the country together was a central planning system and an oppressive dictatorship. When these institutions crumbled, the social capital required to hold the country and the economy together just wasn't there. Russia became the "Wild East," more lawless than America's Wild West before it was tamed. Russia was "caught up in a systemic vacuum with neither the plan nor the market."[6]

Recent advances in the study of social norms show that

many or even a majority of people will abstain from an individually beneficial but socially harmful action if they perceive that most people do too. But the converse is also true. This has an important consequence: desirable behavior can quickly degrade when people are exposed to a sufficient number of "transgressions."[7]

In America there has been an enormous erosion of trust in recent years.[8] Within the economy the banking sector has been at the forefront of the trend. An entire industry that was once based on trust has lost it. Pick up the newspaper on a random day, and there will almost surely be more than one article describing some bank or someone from another part of the financial sector being accused or convicted of engaging in some fraud, aiding and abetting some tax evasion scheme, or participating in some credit card abuse, some insider trading, some mortgage scandal.

The head of Goldman Sachs, Lloyd Blankfein, made it perfectly clear: sophisticated investors don't, or at least shouldn't, rely on trust. Those who bought the products the banks sold were consenting adults who should have known better. They should have known that Goldman Sachs had the means, and the incentives, to design products that would fail, that they had the means and the incentives to create asymmetries of information—where they knew more about the products than the buyers did—and that they had the means and the incentives to take advantage of these asymmetries. Those who fell victim to the investment banks were, for the most part, well-off investors (though they included pension funds managing the money of ordinary citizens). But deceptive credit card practices and predatory lending have made every American understand that the banks are not to be trusted. One has to read the fine print—and even that won't be enough.

Shortsighted financial markets, focusing on quarterly returns, have also been central in undermining trust within the workplace. In *old* economics, most firms held on to their good workers through the ups and downs of the business cycle, and those workers returned the favor with loyalty and investment of human capital in the firm, to increase the firm's productivity. This was called "labor hoarding," and it made good economic sense.[9] But as markets became more short-sighted, such humane polices no longer seemed profitable. The extra profitability—from investments in human capital, from lower turnover costs, and from greater loyalty among workers—wouldn't be felt for years to come, especially if the downturn went on for some time. Sloughing off workers was relatively easy in America's flexible labor market, and that rendered them another disposable input. That helps explain one of the unusual aspects of the 2008 recession (and other recent downturns) that I discussed in the beginning of chapter 2. Under the old model, in an economic downturn, productivity would go down because so many workers were retained. Instead of going down at the bottom of the cycle, productivity now went up: all those good workers about whom the firm worried, wondering whether they should or should not be terminated, were given the ax. The task of restoring team spirit, loyalty, and human capital would be left to a future manager.[10]

More broadly, not only are workers happier in workplaces that treat them well—including during downturns—but productivity is enhanced.[11] The importance of a sense of well-being in the workplace should not be underestimated: most people spend a substantial fraction of their lifetime at the workplace, and what happens there spills over strongly into the rest of their lives.[12]

The breaking of the social bonds and trust—seen in our

politics, in our financial sector, and in the workplace—will, inevitably, have broader societal consequences. Trust and reciprocal goodwill are necessary not only for the functioning of markets but also for every other aspect of societal cooperation. We have explained how the long-term success of any country requires social cohesion—a kind of social contract that binds members of society together. Experiences elsewhere have shown, however, the fragility of social cohesion. When the social contract gets broken, social cohesion quickly erodes.

Governments and societies make decisions—expressed through policies, laws, and budgetary choices—that either strengthen that contract or weaken it. By allowing inequality to metastasize unchecked, America is choosing a path of the destruction of social capital, if not social conflict.

As we have emphasized, the arena in which social cooperation is absolutely essential is politics, for it is here that collective decisions affecting all are taken. Of course, there are other ways of organizing life: police states provide rules and punishments for disobeying. It is a system of compliance based on "incentives"—the incentives of threats. But such societies typically do not function well. The enforcers cannot be everywhere to make good on the threats, and if there is a sense that the rules and regulations are unfair, there will be attempts at circumvention. It will be expensive to achieve compliance, and even then it will be only partial. Productivity will be low, and life will be unpleasant.

The democratic alternative entails trust and a social compact, an understanding of the responsibilities and rights of different individuals. We tell the truth because it is the *right* or *moral* thing to do—knowing the costs imposed on others of the breakdown of the system of trust. We've seen how the erosion of trust hurts the economy. But what is happening in the sphere of politics may be even worse: the breaking of the social contract may have even more invidious effects on the functioning of our democracy.

Fairness and disillusionment

To most Americans it is *obvious* that fairness is important. Indeed, one of the aspects of our society that Americans were most proud of was that our economic system was fair—it gave opportunity to everybody.

Recent research has illuminated just how important fairness is to most individuals (though economists continue to focus almost exclusively on efficiency). In a series of experiments initially conducted by three German economists, Werner Güth, Rolf Schmittberger, and Bernd Schwarze, a subject was given a certain amount of money, say $100, and was told to divide it between himself and the other player in the game.[13] In the first version, called the dictator game, the second player has to accept what he is given. Standard economic theory provides a clear prediction: the first player keeps all of the $100 for himself. Yet in practice, the first player gives the second *something*, though usually less than half.[14]

A related experiment gives even stronger evidence of the importance that individuals attach to fairness: most individuals would rather accept an inefficient outcome—even hurting themselves—than an unfair one. In what is known as the ultimatum game, the second player has the right to veto the division proposed by the first player. If the second player exercises his veto, neither party gets anything. Standard economic theory suggests a clear strategy: the first player keeps

99 dollars for himself, giving 1 dollar to the other player, who accepts it, because 1 dollar is better than zero. In fact, offers typically average about 30 to 40 dollars (or 30–40 percent of the total sum in a game with different quantities), and the second player tends to veto the allocation if he is offered less than 20 dollars.[15] He is willing to accept some inequity—he realizes he is in the less powerful position—but there is a limit to how much inequity he will stand for. He would rather have zero than, say, $20—a 4-to-1 split is too unfair.[16]

Perceptions of unfairness affect behavior. If individuals believe that their employer is treating them unfairly, they are more likely to shirk on the job.[17] In the last chapter, we described experimental results confirming the importance of perceptions of fairness to productivity.

But, as chapter 1 pointed out, America's economic system is, in a fundamental sense, no longer fair. Equality of opportunity is just a myth; and Americans are gradually realizing this. One poll showed that 61 percent of Americans now believe that our economic system favors the wealthy; only 36 percent—a little over one out of three Americans—think our system is generally fair.[18] (And, perhaps not surprisingly, by similar numbers, they think unfairness in the economic system that favors the wealthy is a more serious problem than overregulation.)[19]

Other research, comparing individuals' views about what a good distribution of income might look like with their *perceptions* of inequality in the United States confirms that most think there is too much inequality. And these views were held broadly across very different demographic groups, men and women, Democrats and Republicans, and those at the top and those with lower incomes. Indeed, in most people's ideal distribution, the top 40 percent had less wealth than the top

20 percent currently holds. Equally striking, when asked to choose between two distributions (shown on a pie chart), participants overwhelmingly chose one that reflected the distribution in Sweden over that in the United States (92 percent to 8 percent).[20]

Views that our political system is rigged are even stronger than those that our economic system is unfair. The poor, especially, believe that their voice is not being heard. The widespread support expressed for the Occupy Wall Street movement (discussed in the preface) bears testimony to these concerns. The belief (and the reality) that our political and economic system is unfair weakens both.

While the most immediate symptom is disillusionment leading to a lack of participation in the political process, there is always a worry that voters will be attracted to populists and extremists who attack the establishment that has created this unfair system[21] and who make unrealistic promises of change.

Distrust, the media, and disillusionment

Among economists, no one doubts the importance of a competitive marketplace for goods and services. Even more important for our society and our politics is a competitive marketplace of ideas. And unfortunately, that marketplace is—and is perceived to be—distorted.[22] Citizens can't make informed decisions as voters if they don't have access to the requisite information. But if the media are biased, they won't get information that is balanced. And even if the media were balanced, citizens know that the information that the government discloses to the media may not be.

John Kenneth Galbraith some sixty years ago, recognizing that few markets were anywhere close to the economists' idea of "perfect competition," wrote about the importance of "countervailing powers."[23] We'll never have truly competitive media in the United States, with a plethora of newspapers and TV stations representing a diversity of views, but we could do better. We could have more forceful policing of antitrust laws, recognizing that what is at stake is more than just control over, say, the market for advertising, but also control over the market for ideas. We could be especially vigilant about attempts by media firms to control newspapers, TV, and radio. And we could provide public support for the media that would help diversify it. After all, the public good is a public good—that is, all benefit from ensuring that our government performs well. A basic insight of economics is that private markets, on their own, spend too little on public goods, since the societywide benefits are far greater than the benefits the individual himself enjoys. Ensuring that we have a well-informed public citizenry is important for a well-functioning democracy, and that in turn requires an active *and diverse* media. Other countries have attempted to ensure this diversity—with some success—by providing broad public support for media, ranging from national public broadcasting stations to community radio stations to support for second newspapers, even in smaller communities.[24]

We could also have more balanced media. As it is, the media are a realm where those in the 1 percent have the upper hand. They have the resources to buy and control critical media outlets, and some of them are willing to do so at a loss: it's an investment in maintaining their economic position.[25] Like the political investments of the banks, these investments may yield far higher *private* returns than ordinary investments—if one includes impacts on the political process.[26]

This is another element in the creation of distrust and disillusionment: not only isn't there trust in the fairness of our political and economic system; there isn't even trust in the information that is provided about our political and economic system.[27]

Disenfranchisement

The political battle is not just fought over getting supporters and getting them to vote. It's also fought over *not allowing those who disagree with you to vote*—a return to the mindset of two centuries ago, when the voting franchise was severely restricted.

The reluctance of the elites to extend the voting franchise, however objectionable from current perspectives, is understandable. In the UK, until the Reform Act of 1832, only large property owners or people of considerable wealth could vote. The elites didn't trust what might happen if voting rights were extended. In the Jim Crow South at the end of the nineteenth century, white politicians devised poll taxes that were designed to disenfranchise the former slaves and their descendants, who wouldn't have the wherewithal to pay.[28] Those taxes, combined with literacy tests and sometimes violence and terror, succeeded both in substantially lowering electoral turnouts and in increasing the Democratic vote share.[29]

In Ecuador, before 1979, only the literate could vote, and the ruling elite made sure that the indigenous people didn't have sufficient education to qualify. In each case elites feared they would lose their position of power and privilege, and even their wealth, if they extended the voting franchise.

Many of the efforts at disenfranchisement, now and in the past, have been directed at disenfranchising the poor; in the 1930s, pauper exclusion laws disenfranchised jobless men and women who were receiving relief.[30] The political science scholar Walter Dean Burnham has detailed the long history of what he calls efforts at voter "demobilization" targeted at various groups: against urban workers, by upstate agrarians and small towners; against leftist parties, by the major parties; against populists, by the urban corporate elites; against the poor, by the middle- and upper-income groups.[31] Many of these measures may be thought of as *disenfranchisement by stealth*.

Of course, those trying to disenfranchise the poor don't describe it that way. Economists and statisticians distinguish two kinds of errors: someone who is qualified to vote not being allowed to vote, and someone who is not qualified to vote being allowed to vote. Republicans tend to claim that the latter is the more important problem, Democrats that it's the former. But the Republican claim is disingenuous: the barriers that they seek to create to catch the latter mistake are really *economic* barriers, not barriers based on the likelihood of being qualified to vote. Requiring a government-issued photo ID—typically a driver's license or an identification card issued by the Department of Motor Vehicles—discriminates between those who have sufficient means, time, and access to information to get to the DMV, and those who do not.[32] Obtaining voter identification may also necessitate having a birth certificate or other documentation, which requires even more time, money, and knowledge of bureaucracy.

While the days of outright exclusion from the voting process are mostly behind us in the United States, there remains a steady stream of initiatives to limit participation, invariably targeting the poor and less well connected. Authorities can use even more subtle methods to discourage certain groups' political participation, whether it is conducting inadequate voter outreach to poor or immigrant neighborhoods, poorly staffing polling places, or preventing some felons from voting. In some cases, it is difficult to distinguish neglect from willful disenfranchisement, but the effects are the same: depressing voter turnout, often of a targeted group. These measures will chip away at voter participation, even when they do not present absolute barriers to registering or voting—especially among the least privileged parts of the population, where enthusiasm for voting is already low and mistrust of the official system runs high. The result is that one in four of those eligible to vote—51 million Americans or more—are not registered.[33]

On the other hand, certain measures can make it easier to register and will make it more likely that those who are qualified to vote do so. Allowing individuals to register to vote at the same time that they apply for a driver's license lowers transactions cost, and thus facilitates voter registration. More flexible schedules at polling centers and more voting booths facilitate the act of voting itself.

These attempts at disenfranchisement have a double effect. To the extent that they succeed, they ensure that the voices of some citizens are not heard; and the perception that there is such a struggle to reverse a long-accepted principle that all citizens have effective access to the vote reinforces disillusionment in the political system and increases political alienation.

Disempowerment

We saw earlier how the rules of the economic game, set by the political process, stack the cards in favor of the 1 percent. So too for the rules of the political game. The perception that they are set in ways that are unfair—that they give disproportionate power to economic elites, in a way that further strengthens the economic power of those at the top—reinforces political alienation and a sense of disempowerment and disillusionment. The sense of disempowerment occurs at myriad levels of engagement with government.

The 2010 decision in the case of *Citizens United v. Federal Election Commission*, in which the Supreme Court essentially approved unbridled corporate campaign spending, represented a milestone in the disempowerment of ordinary Americans.[34] The decision allows corporations and unions to exercise "free speech" in supporting candidates and causes in elections to the same degree as individual human beings. Since corporations have many millions of times the resources of the vast majority of individual Americans, the decision has the potential to create a class of super-wealthy political campaigners with a one-dimensional political interest: enhancing their profits.

It was hard to justify the Court's decision on philosophical terms. Corporations are legal entities, created for a specific purpose and endowed by man-made laws with specific rights and obligations. They have the advantage, for instance, of limited liability, but in certain instances the corporate veil can be pierced. There can still be individual culpability for criminal acts. But corporations aren't people, and they don't have any *inalienable* rights. The Supreme Court, in giving them carte blanche to shape power and our political system, seemed to think otherwise.

The Court's decision in balancing the interests of free speech with the interests of a balanced democracy, gave short shrift to the latter. It is generally recognized that providing money (support) conditional on a candidate's providing a favor (supporting a bill) is corruption. Corruption undermines faith in our democracy. But there is little difference between that and what actually occurs—candidates who, say, support a bill that an oil company wants to have immunity from liability from an oil spill are given money, and the candidate, and everyone else, knows that that money will be withdrawn if he votes differently. There is no *formal* quid pro quo; but the effect is the same. And most importantly, the perception by ordinary citizens is the same, so it weakens faith in our democracy little less than blatant corruption does.[35]

The Court's action was, in a sense, just another reflection of the success of the moneyed interests in creating a system of "one dollar one vote": they had succeeded in electing politicians who in turn appointed judges who would enshrine a corporation's right to unbridled spending in the political arena.[36]

The rules of the political game can also make individuals feel, rightly, that they are disenfranchised. Gerrymandering can make it more likely that an individual's vote *doesn't* count: the outlines of voting districts are drawn so that the outcome of the election is almost preordained. The filibuster gives inordinate power to a minority of senators. In the past, it was used with discretion. There was an understanding that it would be used only on issues that were of intense concern: ironically, it was used most frequently to stop the passage of civil rights laws that would ensure everyone the right to vote. But those days are gone. Now the filibuster is used as a matter of course to obstruct legislation.[37]

Later we'll discuss one more example of disempowerment, the role of the Federal Reserve Bank in setting macroeconomic policy. Government has entrusted the responsibility for a matter of vital concern to ordinary citizens—monetary policy, which affects the level of unemployment and economic activity—to a group that consists in significant measure of those elected by banks and the business community themselves, with insufficient democratic accountability.

The pattern of growing inequality in the United States may be particularly bad for our democracy. There is a widespread understanding that the middle class is the backbone of our democracy. The poor are often so alienated that getting them to vote proves especially hard. The rich don't need a rule of law; they can and do shape the economic and political processes to work for themselves. The middle class is most likely to understand why voting is so important in a democracy and why a *fair* rule of law is necessary for our economy and society. In the middle of the last century, its members believed that the economic and political system was basically fair, and their belief in "civic engagement" was seemingly rewarded by a burst of growth that benefited them—and everyone else. But now all that is changing. As we saw in chapter 3, the polarization of our labor market has been hollowing out the middle class, and the dwindling middle class is itself becoming disillusioned with a political process that is obviously not serving its members well.

Why we should care

In this chapter we have described the construction of a political system that, though nominally based on the principle of one person one vote, has turned out to serve the interests of those at the top. Another vicious circle has been set in play: political rules of the game have not only *directly* benefited those at the top, ensuring that they have a disproportionate voice, but have also created a political process that *indirectly* gives them even more power. We have identified a whole series of forces contributing to the disillusionment with politics and distrust of the political system. The yawning divide in our society has made it difficult to reach compromise, contributing to our political gridlock.

This, in turn, has contributed to undermining trust in our institutions, both their effectiveness and their fairness. Attempts at disenfranchisement, a recognition that our political and economic systems are unfair, the knowledge that the flow of information is controlled by a media that itself is controlled by those at the top, and the apparent role of money in politics, reflected in unbridled campaign contributions, have only enhanced disillusionment with our political system. Disillusionment has decreased political participation, especially at the bottom, every bit as effectively as the outright attempts at disenfranchisement in tilting the electorate toward the top. This has provided more scope for influence of those in the 1 percent and their money—reinforcing the lack of trust, and the disillusionment. With such disillusionment, it costs money to get out the vote—and efforts to get out the vote can be targeted at those whose interests coincide with the top.

The effect can be seen in the United States, where voter turnout looks dismal in comparison with that of other advanced societies. Average voter turnout for the presidential elections has been 57 percent in recent years,[38] but voting for the House of Representatives in nonpresidential years has averaged only 37.5 percent.[39] Given the extent of youth disillusionment—especially after the 2008 elections, when expectations were so high—it is no wonder that in the 2010 election youth turnout was even more dismal, at around 20 percent.[40]

Turnouts in primary elections are even poorer—and biased[41]—with the result that the electoral choices voters face in the general elections seem disappointing, contributing in turn to low voter turnout in those elections.

Disillusionment with our political system—and the belief that it is unfair—can give rise to agitation outside the political system, evidenced in the Occupy Wall Street movement. When this then leads to a reform of the political system, the effects can be positive. When the political system rebuffs these reforms, it reinforces alienation.

Earlier in the chapter, I discussed the importance of trust, cooperation, social capital, and a sense of fairness to the functioning of the economy and society more generally. These failures in our political system have important spillovers. It is another channel through which our society and our economy will pay a great price for the high and growing inequality.

Reforming our political process

Most Americans now realize how essential it is that our political process be reformed in ways that make it more responsive to the wishes of the majority and that diminish the power of money. We have described how the political rules of the game give those at the top outsize influence. Changing the rules of the game can create a more democratic democracy.

We can, and should, for instance, change the rules to make sure the electorate reflects our citizenry—stopping the efforts at disenfranchisement, making it easier, even for the poor, to vote. Practices like gerrymandering, designed to reduce the responsiveness of the political system, need to be circumscribed. So must practices like revolving doors (which allow someone from the banking sector to move smoothly between Wall Street and Washington and back to Wall Street). Rules like mandatory voting (as in Australia) lead, not surprisingly, to higher voter participation, and a greater likelihood that the out-comes of elections reflect the views of society more generally.[42] Most importantly, there is a need for campaign finance reform. Even if *Citizens United* is not reversed, corporations should be allowed to make campaign contributions only if their owners—the shareholders—vote to do so. It shouldn't be just left to the top managers, who have used their power not merely to pay themselves outsize rewards but then also to use their power to maintain a system that allows them to do so. And the govern-ment should use its financial resources to make sure that there is a level playing field in the "marketplace of ideas," or at least a more level playing field than exists today.[43]

We know what to do—and even if the reforms would not fully create the one-person-one-vote democracy that we would like, they could move us in that direction. But efforts to do so have been stymied, for the obvious reason: moneyed interests have the incentives and resources to ensure that the system continues to serve those interests. When I was chair of the Council of Economic Advisers, the Clinton adminis-tration made a valiant effort to curb the need for campaign finance. The public owns the airwaves that the TV stations use. Rather than giving these away to the TV stations without restriction—a blatant form of corporate welfare—we should sell access to them; and we could sell it with the condition that a certain amount of airtime be made available for cam-paign advertising. With free advertising politicians would need less money, and we could constrain those accepting the free advertising in the amount and nature of campaign con-tributions that they accepted. But the TV stations that make such money from campaign advertising—and from their free gifts of spectrum—vehemently and successfully opposed the reform.

The evisceration of our democracy

Democracy—at least as most of us conceive of it—is based on the principle of one person one vote. Much of the political rhetoric focuses on the "middle" "independent" voter, as standard political theory suggests should be the case. But no one would suggest that the outcome of America's politics really reflects the median voter's interests. The median voter has no interest in corporate welfare. The median voter didn't prevail in the battle over financial regulatory reform, where the vast majority (some two-thirds according to some opinion polls)[44] wanted tighter regulation, but the big banks didn't. In the end, we got regulatory reform that was like Swiss cheese—full of holes, exceptions, and exemptions that couldn't be justified by any set of principles. There was no good reason for tighter consumer protection on all loans *except* auto loans; it was just that those lenders succeeded in making the necessary political investments.

It was no wonder that the House Financial Services Committee, charged with writing the new regulations, had sixty-one members, almost 15 percent of all the representatives. The Dodd-Frank bill passed in 2010 represented a carefully balanced compromise between the ten biggest banks and the 200 million Americans who wanted tighter regulation. (History, I am afraid, will prove that the vast majority of Americans were right.)

Paul Krugman put it forcefully when he wrote, "[E]xtreme concentration of income is incompatible with real democracy. Can anyone seriously deny that our political system is being warped by the influence of big money, and that the warping is getting worse as the wealth of a few grows ever larger?"[45]

In the Gettysburg Address, President Abraham Lincoln said that America was fighting a Great Civil War so that "Government of the people, by the people, and for the people shall not perish from this earth." But if what has been happening continues, that dream is in peril.[46]

We began this chapter with a discussion of the puzzle of the median voter—why our democracy seems not to reflect the views of those in the middle as much as the views of those at the top. This chapter has provided a partial explanation: the median voter (the voter such that half the voters have an income higher than his, half lower) is richer than the median American. We have a *biased* electorate, tilted toward the top.

But this doesn't fully explain what's been going on in American politics. The bias in the outcomes—the extent to which the political system favors those at the top—is greater than can be explained by the bias in the electorate. Another part of this puzzle is explained by the bias in perceptions and beliefs—that the top has persuaded those in the middle to see the world in a distorted way, leading them to perceive policies that advance the interests of those at the top as consonant with their own interests. How the top does this is the subject of the next chapter.[47] But first I want to discuss globalization, how it has been mismanaged by our elites in ways that have benefited them at the expense of most Americans, but, even more importantly, how the way it has been managed in the United States, and even more so elsewhere, has undermined democracy. Moreover, the weakening and distortion of our democracy that I've just described is undermining our role in global leadership, and thus our ability to create a world that is more in accord with our values and our interests, more broadly understood.

GLOBALIZATION, INEQUALITY, AND DEMOCRACY

These outcomes should not be surprising: globalization, if managed for the 1 percent, provides a mechanism that simultaneously facilitates tax avoidance and imposes pressures that give the 1 percent the upper hand not just in bargaining within a firm (as we saw in chapter 3) but also in politics. Increasingly, not only have jobs been offshored but so, in a sense, has politics. This trend is not limited to the United States; it is a global phenomenon, and in some countries matters are far worse than in the United States.

The most vivid examples have arisen in countries that have become overindebted.[48] The loss of "control" by debtor countries of their own destiny—turning over power to creditors—dates back to the earlier days of globalization. In the nineteenth century, poor countries that owed money to banks in the rich nations were confronted with a military takeover, or bombardment: Mexico, Egypt, and Venezuela were all victims. This continued through the twentieth century: in the 1930s Newfoundland gave up its democracy as it went into receivership and became administered by its creditors.[49] In the post–World War II era, the IMF was the instrument of choice: countries turned over, in effect, their economic sovereignty to an agency that represented the international creditors.

It was one thing for these events to occur in poor developing countries; it's another for them to occur in advanced industrial economies. That's what has been happening lately in Europe, as first Greece and then Italy allowed the IMF, together with the European Central Bank and the European Commission (all unelected), to dictate parameters of policy and then appoint technocratic governments to oversee the implementation of the program.[50] When Greece proposed to submit the tough austerity program that had been prepared to a popular referendum, there arose a shout of horror from European officials and the bankers:[51] Greek citizens might reject the proposal, and that might mean that the creditors would not be repaid.

The surrender to the dictates of financial markets is broader and more subtle. It applies not only to those countries on the brink of disaster but also to any country that has to raise money from capital markets. If the country doesn't do what the financial markets like, they threaten to downgrade the ratings, to pull out their money, to raise interest rates; the threats are usually effective. The financial markets get what they want. There may be free elections, but, as presented to the voters, there are no real choices in the matters that they care most about—the issues of economics.

Twice in the 1990s Luiz Inácio Lula da Silva was on the verge of being elected president of Brazil, and twice Wall Street objected, exercising what amounted to a veto. It signaled that if he were elected, it would pull money out of the country, the interest rates that the country would have to pay would soar, the country would be shunned by investors, and its growth would collapse. The third time, in 2002, the Brazilians said, in effect, that they would not be dictated to by international financiers.[52] And President Lula made an excellent president, maintaining economic stability, promoting growth, and attacking his country's extreme inequality. He was one of the few presidents around the world who, after eight years, still enjoyed the popular support that he had in the beginning.

This is just one of many instances in which the judgments of the financial markets were badly flawed. Proponents of financial markets like to claim that one of the virtues of open capital markets is that they provide "discipline." But the markets are a fickle disciplinarian, giving an A rating one moment and turning around with an F rating the next. Even worse, the financial markets' interests frequently do not coincide with those of the country. The markets are shortsighted and have a political and economic agenda that seeks the advancement of the well-being of financiers rather than that of the country as a whole.

It doesn't have to be this way. Financial markets can threaten to pull money out of a country overnight largely because of their total openness, especially to short-term capital flows. But in spite of the financial market's ideological commitment to what is called capital market liberalization (allowing capital to move freely in and out of a country)— an ideology consistent with the markets' self-interest—in fact such liberalization doesn't promote economic growth; it does, however, lead to increased instability and inequality.[53]

The problems that I've outlined run deeper and are in fact more widespread. As one of the world's experts on globalization, the Harvard University professor Dani Rodrik has pointed out, one cannot simultaneously have democracy, national self-determination, and full and unfettered globalization.[54]

Often, international companies have attempted to obtain in the international arena what they cannot get at home. The Financial Services Agreement of the World Trade Organization (WTO) has tried to force financial market liberalization, requiring governments to allow foreign banks into their countries and restraining the ability to impose regulations that would ensure that the financial system is stable and actually serves the economy and society in the way it should. The Uruguay Round Trade Agreement has successfully forced upon countries around the world a version of intellectual property rights that is bad for American science, bad for global science, bad for developing countries, and bad for access to health. Designed by corporate interests to prevent the free flow of knowledge, the agreement strengthens monopoly power— helping create rents, and, as we saw in chapter 2, rents are the source of so much of today's inequality.[55] Whether one agrees or not with this assessment of this particular international agreement, it is clear that it has imposed severe— unnecessarily severe—strictures on the design of each country's intellectual property regime. It has undermined the countries' self-determination and the power of their democracies. They cannot choose an intellectual property regime that reflects their view of what will best promote the advance of knowledge in their country, balancing concerns about access to knowledge and to life-saving medicines with the necessity of providing incentives for research and innovation; they have to choose a regime that conforms with the dictates of the WTO.[56]

Other examples abound. The United States, in its bilateral trade agreement with Singapore, attempted to restrict that country's regulations concerning chewing gum: it was worried that they might discourage U.S. exports of one of our "major" export commodities, chewing gum. In its bilateral agreement with Chile, the United States attempted to prevent the imposition of capital controls, rules that the country had used successfully to stabilize its economy. Other agreements have tried to prevent countries from discouraging the purchase of gasoline-guzzling vehicles, because those are the kinds of cars in which America specializes. Chapter 11 of the North

American Free Trade Agreement and other bilateral investment agreements (and other economic agreements that the
United States and Europe have signed with developing countries) arguably provides compensation to firms for loss of profits incurred as a result of a regulatory change, something that
both Congress and the U.S. courts have refused to do. It is a
provision designed to discourage environmental regulations by
making the imposition of such regulations costly to the government's budget.[57]

For many developing countries—and, more recently, even
for European countries—that are indebted and have to turn
to the IMF, the consequences of their loss of economic sovereignty have been serious. At least within the United States
and most European countries, the 1 percent normally doesn't
get its way without a fight. But finance ministries often use
the IMF to enforce their perspectives, to adopt the institutional arrangements and the regulatory and macroeconomic
frameworks that are in the interests of the 1 percent. Even
Greece, to secure its 2011 bailout by the European Union,
was forced to pass laws affecting not only the budget but also
the health sector, the rights of unions in collective bargaining,
and the minimum wage.

Even when globalization doesn't circumscribe democracy through global agreements or as part of an international
"rescue," it circumscribes democracy through competition.
One of the reasons, we were told, that we *had* to have weak
financial regulations was that if we didn't, financial firms would
move overseas. In response to a proposal to tax bank bonuses,
London firms threatened to leave the country. In these cases,
one might argue: good riddance. The cost to society—the bailouts, the economic disruption, the inequality—of the financial
sector's excesses far outweighs the few jobs that companies

in the sector create. The speculators will leave; but those engaged in the kind of finance that really matters—lending to local firms—will stay. These *have* to be here.

The arena in which democracy is most circumscribed is in taxation, especially in the design of tax systems that reduce inequality. What is called tax competition—the race between different polities to have the lowest taxes around—limits the scope for progressive taxation. Firms threaten to leave if taxes are too high. So do wealthy individuals. Here the United States has at least one advantage over other countries: we are taxed on our worldwide income. A Greek citizen, having benefited from that country's public schools and universities, and having enjoyed the benefit of its hospitals and health care system, can take up residence in Luxembourg, do business in all of Europe freely, and avoid any responsibility of paying taxes to Greece—even to repay the costs of her education.

We are often told that this is the way it has to be, that globalization gives us no choice. This fatalism, which serves those benefiting from the current system, obscures reality: the predicament is a choice. The governments of our democracies have chosen an economic framework for globalization that has actually tied the hands of those democracies. The 1 percent was always worried that democracies would be tempted to enact "excessively" progressive taxation under the influence, say, of a populist leader. Now citizens are told they can't do so, not if they want to partake of globalization.

In short, globalization, as it's been managed, is narrowing the choices facing our democracies, making it more difficult for them to undertake the tax and expenditure policies that are necessary if we are to create societies with more equality and more opportunity. But tying the hands of our democracies is exactly what those at the top wanted: we can have a democracy with one person one vote, and still get outcomes that are more in accord with what we might expect in a system with one dollar one vote.[58]

Diminishing America's influence

America's global strength is its soft power, the power of its ideas, an educational system that educates leaders from all over the world, the model that it provides for others to follow. Iraq and Afghanistan have shown the limits of military power; not even a large country spending as much on the military as all of the rest of the world combined can truly pacify or conquer a country with one-tenth its population and 0.1 percent of its GDP. The country has long exerted its influence by the strength of its economy and the attractiveness of its democracy.

But the American model is losing some of its luster. It's not just that the American model of capitalism didn't provide sustained growth. It's more that others are beginning to realize that most citizens have not benefited from that growth, and such a model is not very politically attractive. And they are sensing, too, the corruption (American style) of our political system, rife with the influence of special interests.

Of course, there's more than a little schadenfreude here. We lectured countries all around the world about how to run their economy, about good institutions, about democracy, about fiscal rectitude and balanced budgets. We even lectured them about their excessive inequality and rent seeking. Now our creditability is gone: we are seen to have a political system in which one party tries to disenfranchise the poor, in which money buys politicians and policies that reinforce the inequalities.

We should be concerned about the risk of this diminished influence. Even if things had been going better in the United States, the growth of the emerging markets would necessitate a new global order. There was just a short period, between the fall of the Berlin Wall and the collapse of Lehman Brothers, when the United States dominated in virtually every realm. Now the emerging markets are demanding a larger voice in international forums. We moved from the G-8, where the richest industrial countries tried to determine global economic policy, to the G-20, because we had to: the global recession provided the impetus, but one could not deal with global issues, like global warming or global trade, without bringing others in. China is already the second-largest global economy, the second-largest trading economy, the largest manufacturing economy, the largest saver, and the largest contributor to greenhouse gas emissions.

America has been extraordinarily influential in spreading ideas—of equality, of human rights, of democracy, of the market. Having a world that shares these values has been part of the country's mission. But it is also in our self-interest. I observed earlier that our real source of power is our soft power; but that power arises only because others see things through lenses that are not too dissimilar from ours. We may try to enforce a pax Americana, but we have seen how difficult and costly that is. Far better for others to see their interests as coincident with ours, in creating democratic and prosperous societies. The management of globalization requires global agreements, in trade, finance, investment, the environment, health, and the management of knowledge. In the past the United States had enormous influence in shaping these agreements. We have not always used that influence well; we have often used it to advance some of our special interests, aiding and abetting the rent-seeking activities that play such a large role in the creation of inequalities. Although in the early days of modern globalization, that was not fully grasped, today it is. There is a demand for a change in the governance of the global economic institutions and arrangements, and, combined with the new balance of global economic power, changes are inevitable. Even then, our influence is likely to remain large, almost surely disproportionate to our population or our economy. But the extent to which the global economy and polity can be shaped in accord with our values and interests will depend, to a large extent, on how well our economic and political system is performing *for most citizens*. As democracies grow in many other parts of the world, an economic and political system that leaves most citizens behind—as ours has been doing—will not be seen as a system to be emulated, and the rules of the game that such a country advocates will be approached with jaundiced eyes.

CONCLUDING COMMENTS

The United States played a central role in creating the current rules of the game and the United States, still the world's largest economy, can use its economic power and influence to shape new rules that create a fairer global economy. It may or may not be in the interests of the 1 percent to do so,[59] but it is in our broader national interests. As we saw earlier, current rules of globalization are contributing to our growing inequality. Someday, perhaps soon, we too will see how globalization *as currently managed* promotes neither global efficiency nor equity; even more importantly, it puts our democracy in peril. *Another world is possible*: there are alternative ways of managing globalization that are better for both our economy and our democracy; but they do not entail *unfettered* globalization. We have learned the risks of unfettered markets for our economy and how to temper capitalism so that it serves *the majority* of citizens, not a tiny, powerful fraction. So too, we can temper globalization; indeed, we must if we want to preserve our democracy, prevent our rampant inequality from growing worse, and maintain our influence around the world.

CHAPTER SIX

1984 IS UPON US

THE BIG PUZZLE WE PRESENTED IN THE LAST chapter was how, in a democracy supposedly based on one person one vote, the 1 percent could have been so victorious in shaping policies in its interests. We described a process of disempowerment, disillusionment, and disenfranchisement that produces low voter turnout, a system in which electoral success requires heavy investments, and in which those with money have made political investments that have reaped large rewards—often greater than the returns they have reaped on their other investments.

There is another way for moneyed interests to get what they want out of government: convince the 99 percent that they have shared interests. This strategy requires an impressive sleight of hand; in many respects the interests of the 1 percent and the 99 percent differ markedly.

The fact that the 1 percent has so successfully shaped public perception testifies to the malleability of beliefs. When others engage in it, we call it "brainwashing" and "propaganda."[1] We look askance at these attempts to shape public views, because they are often seen as unbalanced and manipulative, without realizing that there is something akin going on in democracies, too. What is different today is that we have far greater understanding of how to shape perceptions and beliefs—thanks to the advances in research in the social sciences.

In contradistinction to the reality that perceptions and preferences can be shaped, mainstream economics assumes that individuals have well-defined preferences and fully rational expectations and perceptions. Individuals know what they want. But in this respect, traditional economics is wrong. If it were true, there would be little scope for advertising.[2] Corporations use recent advances in psychology and economics that extend our understanding of how preferences and beliefs can be shaped to induce people to buy their products. In this chapter we'll see how those in the 1 percent have shaped beliefs about what is fair and efficient, about the strengths and weaknesses of government and the market, and even about the extent of inequality in America today.

It is clear that many, if not most, Americans possess a limited understanding of the nature of the inequality in our society: They believe that there is less inequality than there is, they underestimate its adverse economic effects,[3] they underestimate the ability of government to do anything about it, and they overestimate the costs of taking action. They even fail to understand what the government is doing—many who value highly government programs like Medicare don't realize that they are in the public sector.[4]

In a recent study respondents on average thought that the top fifth of the population had just short of 60 percent of the wealth, when in truth that group holds approximately 85 percent of the wealth. (Interestingly, respondents described an ideal wealth distribution as one in which the top 20 percent hold just over 30 percent of the wealth. Americans recognize that some inequality is inevitable, and perhaps even desirable if one is to provide incentives; but the level of inequality in American society is well beyond that level.)[5]

Not only do Americans misperceive the level of inequality; they underestimate the changes that have been going on. Only 42 percent of Americans believe that inequality has increased in the past ten years, when in fact the increase has been tectonic.[6] Misperceptions are evident, too, in views about social mobility. Several studies have confirmed that perceptions of social mobility are overly optimistic.[7]

Americans are not alone in their misperceptions of the degree of inequality. Looking across countries, it appears that there is an inverse correlation between trends in inequality and perceptions of inequality and fairness. One suggested explanation is that when inequality is as large as it is in the United States, it becomes less noticeable—perhaps because people with different incomes and wealth don't even mix.[8]

These mistaken beliefs, whatever their origins, are having an important effect on politics and economic policy.

Perceptions have always shaped reality, and understanding how beliefs evolve has been a central focus of intellectual history. Much as those in power might like to shape beliefs, and much as they do shape beliefs, they do not have full control: ideas have a life of their own, and changes in the world—in our economy and technology—impact ideas (just as ideas have an enormous effect in shaping our economy). What is different today is that the 1 percent now has *more* knowledge about how to shape preferences and beliefs in ways that enable the wealthy to better advance their cause, and more tools and more resources to do so.

In this chapter, I describe some of the research in economics and psychology that extends our understanding of the links between perceptions and reality. I show how the 1 percent has used these advances to alter perceptions and achieve its aims—to make our inequality seem less than it is and more acceptable than it should be.

SOME BASICS OF MODERN PSYCHOLOGY AND ECONOMICS

Understanding how people actually behave—rather than how they would behave if, for instance, they had access to perfect information and made efficient use of it in their attempts to reach their goals, which they themselves understood well— is the subject of an important branch of modern economics called behavioral economics. This school holds that even if behavior is not consistent with the standard tenets of *rationality*, it still may be predictable. And if we can understand what determines behavior, we can shape it.[9]

Work in modern psychology and behavioral economics has observed that, in certain arenas, there are systematic misperceptions. There are consistent biases in judgments. And the work has set out to explain what determines those biases and misperceptions.

Framing and misperceptions

This research has emphasized how much our perceptions are affected by "framing," for instance, the context in which the analysis is posed. Police lineups are notorious: even if none of the accused could have been at the scene of the crime, eyewitnesses will identify one of them as the culprit, with conviction. Much of the battle in politics today is over framing. The frames that different parts of our society bring to bear affect their judgments.

One can manipulate frames and thus perceptions and behavior. These frames and perceptions can be self-reinforcing.[10]

One set of experiments shows how "fragile" and easily affected our beliefs can be. Individuals are asked to draw a number out of a hat. They are then asked a question about which they have relatively little information, such as the number of ships that passed through the Panama Canal last year. The answer, it turns out, is systematically related to the random number they previously pulled out of the hat—those who pulled out a larger number *systematically* respond with a higher number.[11]

Standard economic theory begins, as we have noted, with the presumption that individuals have well-defined preferences and beliefs. They make decisions about how much to save on the basis of a careful evaluation of the benefits of consuming today versus consuming in the future. The reality is otherwise. When employers ask individuals how much of their income they would like to put into their retirement accounts, the answer depends heavily on how the employer "frames" the question. If she says, for instance, that 10 percent will be deducted from income and put into a retirement account unless the employee elects to save more (15 percent) or less (5 percent), overwhelmingly the worker chooses 10 percent. But if the employer says that 15 percent will be deducted unless the employee chooses a smaller number (5 percent or 10 percent), the number 15 percent is chosen much more frequently. If she poses the question still differently, giving additional options of 20 percent or 25 percent, these options—irrelevant for most individuals, because they wouldn't, in any case, be chosen—still affect the employee's choice.[12]

Such behavior should not come as a surprise (at least not to someone who is not an economist). Individuals don't really know what life will be like forty years from now and therefore have little basis for making a judgment about how much to save now. The standard model in economics has individuals making choices repeatedly—say, between red lettuce and green lettuce, experimenting and discovering what they truly like. But unless there is reincarnation, there is no way that an individual can repeatedly go through the savings experiment over time: if he saves too little, he may live to regret it, but he won't be able to live his life over again; the same applies if he saves too much. And today's world is so different from yesterday's that there is little that he can learn from his parents about life cycle savings and little that his children can learn from him.

Equilibrium fictions

There is a second important proposition from psychological research: individuals process information that is consistent with their prior beliefs differently from how they process information that is inconsistent.[13] Information that is consistent is remembered, seen as relevant, and reinforces beliefs. Information that is inconsistent is more likely to be ignored, discounted, or forgotten. This distortion is called "confirmatory bias."[14]

The "equilibrium fictions" that can result from this process are beliefs that are maintained strongly because the evidence that people see—as they perceive and process it—is fully consistent with those beliefs.[15]

Behavioral economics and modern marketing

Shaping behavior is a central goal of marketing. Over the years, firms have worked hard to understand what determines consumers' buying decisions; for if they understand that, they can induce people to buy more of their products. Thus, the major objective of advertising is not to convey information, but to shape perceptions. The best-known examples conjure a lifestyle—which may even be at odds with that of the real users of the product—that consumers aspire to. The Marlboro Man offers an egregious example of this strategy.[16]

Perceptions affect behavior and market equilibrium

Beliefs and *perceptions*, whether they are grounded in reality or not, affect behavior. If people see the "Marlboro man" as the type of person they aspire to be, they may choose that cigarette over others. If individuals overestimate some risk, they may take excessive precautions.

But important as perceptions and beliefs are in shaping individual behavior, they are even more important in shaping *collective* behavior, including political decisions affecting economics. Economists have long recognized the influence of ideas in shaping policies. As Keynes famously put it,

The ideas of economists and political philosophers, both when they are right and when they are wrong, are more powerful than is commonly understood. Indeed the world is ruled by little else. Practical men, who believe themselves to

be quite exempt from any intellectual influence, are usually
the slaves of some defunct economist.[17]

Social sciences like economics differ from the hard sciences in that beliefs affect reality: beliefs about how atoms
behave don't affect how atoms actually behave, but beliefs
about how the economic system functions affect how it actually functions. George Soros, the great financier, has referred
to this phenomenon as reflexivity,[18] and his understanding
of it may have contributed to his success. Keynes, who was
famous not just as a great economist but also as a great investor, described markets as a beauty contest where the winner
is the one who assessed correctly what the other judges would
judge to be the most beautiful.

Markets can sometimes create their own reality. If there is
widespread belief that markets are efficient and that government regulations only interfere with efficiency, then it is more
likely that government will strip away regulations, and this
will affect how markets actually behave. In the most recent
crisis what followed from deregulation was far from efficient,
but even here a battle of interpretation rages. Members of
the Right tried to blame the seeming market failures on government; in their mind the government effort to push people
with low incomes into homeownership was the source of the
problem. Widespread as this belief has become in conservative circles, virtually all serious attempts to evaluate the evidence have concluded that there is little merit in this view.
But the little merit that it had was enough to convince those
who believed that markets could do no evil and governments
could do no good that their views were valid, another example
of "confirmatory bias."[19]

Perceptions of inequality and individual behavior

As we discussed in chapter 4, if individuals believe that they are being treated unfairly by their employer, they are more likely to shirk on the job. If individuals from some minority are paid lower wages than other equally qualified individuals, they will and should feel that they are being treated unfairly—but the lower productivity that results can, and likely will, lead employers to pay lower wages. There can be a "discriminatory equilibrium."[20]

Even perceptions of race, caste, and gender identities can have significant effects on productivity. In a brilliant set of experiments in India, low- and high-caste children were asked to solve puzzles, with monetary rewards for success. When they were asked to do so anonymously, there was no caste difference in performance. But when the low caste and high caste were in a mixed group *where the low-caste individuals were known to be low caste* (they knew it, and they knew that others knew it), low-caste performance was much lower than that of the high caste.[21] The experiment highlighted the importance of social perceptions: low-caste individuals somehow absorbed into their own reality the belief that lower-caste individuals were inferior—but only so in the presence of those who held that belief.

Perceptions of fairness and the politics of inequality

I explained earlier how our perceptions are affected by "framing," and thus it's not surprising that much of the battle today is over the framing of inequality. Fairness, like beauty, is at least partly in the eyes of the beholder, and those at the top want to be sure that the inequality in the United States today is framed in ways that make it seem fair, or at least acceptable. If it is perceived to be unfair, not only may that hurt productivity in the workplace but it might lead to legislation that would attempt to temper it.

In the battle over public policy, whatever the realpolitik of special interests, public discourse focuses on efficiency and fairness. In my years in government, I never heard an industry supplicant looking for a subsidy ask for it simply because it would enrich his coffers. Instead, the supplicants expressed their requests in the language of fairness—and the benefits that would be conferred on others (more jobs, high tax payments).

The same goes for the policies that have shaped the growing inequality in the United States—both those that have contributed to the inequality in market incomes and those that have weakened the role of government in bringing down the level of inequality. The battle about "framing" first centers on how we *see* the level of inequality—how large is it, what are its causes, how can it be justified?

Corporate CEOs, especially those in the financial sector, have thus tried to persuade others (and themselves) that high pay can be justified as a result of an individual's larger contribution to society, and that it is necessary to motivate him to continue making those contributions. That is why it is called *incentive pay*. But the crisis showed to everyone what economic research had long revealed—the argument was a sham. As we noted in chapter 4, what was called incentive pay was anything but that: pay was high when performance was high, but pay was still high when performance was low.

Only the name changed. When performance was low, the name changed to "retention pay."

If the problems of those at the bottom are mainly of their own making and if those collecting welfare checks were really living high on the rest of society (as the "welfare deadbeats" and "welfare queen" campaign in the 1980s and 1990s suggested), then there is little compunction in not providing assistance to them. If those at the top receive high incomes because they have contributed so much to our society—in fact, their pay is but a fraction of their social contribution—then their pay seems justified, especially if their contributions were the result of hard work rather than just luck. Other ideas (the importance of incentives and incentive pay) suggest that there would be a high price to reducing inequality. Still others (trickle-down economics) suggest that high inequality is not really that bad, since all are better off than they would be in a world without such a high level of inequality.

On the other side of this battle are countering beliefs: fundamental beliefs in the value of equality, and analyses such as those presented in earlier chapters that find that the high level of inequality in the United States today increases instability, reduces productivity, and undermines democracy, and that much of it arises in ways that are unrelated to social contributions, that it comes, rather, from the ability to exercise market power—the ability to exploit consumers through monopoly power or to exploit poor and uneducated borrowers through practices that, if not illegal, ought to be.

The intellectual battle is often fought over particular policies, such as whether taxes should be raised on capital gains. But behind these disputes lies this bigger battle over perceptions and over big ideas—like the role of the market, the state, and civil society. This is not just a philosophical debate but a battle over shaping perceptions about the competencies of these different institutions. Those who don't want the state to stop the rent seeking from which they benefit so much, and don't want it to engage in redistribution or to increase economic opportunity and mobility, emphasize the state's failings. (Remarkably, this is true even when they are in office and could and should do something to correct any problem of which they are aware.) They emphasize that the state interferes with the workings of the markets. At the same time that they exaggerate the failures of government, they exaggerate the strengths of markets. Most importantly for our purposes, they strive to make sure that these perceptions become part of the common perspective, that money spent by private individuals (presumably, even on gambling) is better spent than money entrusted to the government, and that any government attempts to correct market failures—such as the proclivity of firms to pollute excessively—cause more harm than good.[22]

This big battle is crucial for understanding the evolution of inequality in America. The success of the Right in this battle during the past thirty years has shaped our government. We haven't achieved the minimalist state that libertarians advocate. What we've achieved is a state too constrained to provide the public goods—investments in infrastructure, technology, and education—that would make for a vibrant economy and too weak to engage in the redistribution that is needed to create a fair society. But we have a state that is still large enough and distorted enough that it can provide a bounty of gifts to the wealthy. The advocates of a small state in the financial sector were happy that the government had the money to rescue them in 2008—and bailouts have in fact been part of capitalism for centuries.[23]

These political battles, in turn, rest on broader ideas about

human rights, human nature, and the meaning of democracy and equality. Debates and perspectives on these issues
have taken a different course in the United States in recent
years than in much of the rest of the world, especially in other
advanced industrial countries. Two controversies—the death
penalty (which is anathema in Europe) and the right to access
to medicine (which in most countries is taken as a basic
human right)—are emblematic of these differences. It may be
difficult to ascertain the role the greater economic and social
divides in our society has played in creating these differences
in beliefs; but what is clear is that if American values and perceptions are seen to be out of line with those in the rest of
the world, our global influence will be diminished, as we suggested in the last chapter.

How ideas evolve

Changing ideas about these fundamentals are both cause and
consequence of a changing society and economy—including
changes in societal inequality.

The history of ideas describes how ideas evolve. No one
controls the evolution.[24] Change is more organic. Ideas
emerge from a variety of sources—often in response to the
events of the moment, sometimes as part of a natural evolutionary process.[25] Ideas get thrown out (one can think of them
as intellectual mutations), and some find fertile ground: they
help people understand the world, especially *as it is in their
self-interest to understand it.*

In the past, beliefs sometimes changed in ways that
enhanced the well-being of the elites, as when ideas that justified slavery or inequality became prevalent. Sometimes beliefs
changed in ways that worked against their interests. Surely

elites in the UK would have preferred that Enlightenment ideas had not crossed the Atlantic. Slave owners in the South would have liked to keep the expression "all men are created equal" more narrowly defined. That there were at least some instances in which beliefs evolved in ways that were counter to the interests of the elites suggests that, at least in the past, the elites didn't in fact dictate how they evolved.

Globalization has, for instance, brought new ideas to many countries, including ideas about democracy, human rights, and equality. A change in technology or market structure—the move from agriculture to manufacturing, or from manufacturing to a service sector economy—inevitably is accompanied by societal changes of enormous magnitude, including ideas about how society and the economy should be organized. The development of manufacturing required a more educated labor force, and it was difficult to make an argument *not* to extend voting rights to the well educated, even if they were not members of earlier elites.

Successes and failures of governments and markets have played an important role in the evolution of ideas about the role of each in the past century. With the Great Depression, when one out of four workers was out of a job, it was hard for anyone but a devoted ideologue to see markets as always efficient. It was not surprising that under those circumstances, the idea that government should play a more important role in macromanagement gained strength. Before 1960, in most developing countries around the world, markets (at least as shaped by colonial powers) by themselves were not delivering growth. It was natural that many in these societies came to the conclusion that government should play a more important role in development. With the failures of communism, though, it was similarly hard for any but a devoted ideologue to believe that government should take a *dominant* role in the economy. Out of these experiences, out of observations that markets often fail, but so do governments, the idea advocated here—that there needs to be a balanced role between markets, the state, and civil society—naturally evolved. What that balance would be could differ across countries and over time. In East Asia there arose the idea of the *developmental state,* one that orchestrated development, but used market mechanisms. There were some enormous successes, the fastest sustained growth ever, with huge reductions in poverty, and large gains for the vast majority of citizens.

But ideas and interpretations of historical events are always contested. Some look at these experiences and, somehow, come up with alternative interpretations. Some (like the Nobel laureate and University of Chicago economist Milton Friedman) constructed an interpretation of the Great Depression that focused on government failure, just as the Right looks at the Great Recession and seeks to put blame on government efforts to promote housing for the poor. Some looked at the enormous successes of the United States in the years after World War II—its relative stability, its rapid growth, a growth from which all shared—and said that growth could be even faster, if only we deregulated and lowered taxes. (Of course, as earlier chapters pointed out, that didn't happen: growth in the era of deregulation and lower taxes was slower, and the country grew apart.)

As our discussion of equilibrium fictions emphasized, evidence doesn't always resolve these disputes: the advocates of different perspectives see evidence in different ways. Even if growth in the era of deregulation and low taxes was slower and most Americans didn't do well, something else can be blamed—there were still too many regulations and too much uncertainty caused by those advocating more regulations. Analyses showing that Fannie Mae and Freddie Mac were not at the center of the Great Recession are simply dismissed.[26]

Some ideas are transformative, but for the most part societal change and change in beliefs occurs slowly. Sometimes, there is a disparity between the pace of change of ideas and of society; sometimes the disparity between beliefs and reality is so startling it forces a rethinking of ideas—or a change in society.

Change often occurs less rapidly than it seems that it should, and the slow evolution of ideas is one of the reasons that societies sometimes change slowly. The Declaration of Independence may have enunciated clearly in 1776 the principle that all men were created equal, but it would be almost two centuries before the United States adopted civil rights legislation that would embrace this principle, and full equality has yet to be achieved.

One of the reasons that ideas change slowly is that ideas and perceptions are *social constructs*. My willingness to hold a belief is related to others' holding similar beliefs. As I travel around the country and the world, I am often struck how in some places one set of ideas is part of conventional wisdom—such as that government is necessarily inefficient or that government caused the recession or that global warming is a fiction—and in others just the opposite is taken to be the "truth." Most individuals don't themselves examine the evidence. Few have the capabilities of assessing the evidence on global warming even if they had the time. But the fact that others that they talk to and trust hold certain beliefs reinforces their conviction in their correctness.

Some of these socially constructed ideas and perceptions provide the lens through which we see the world. Categories, like race and caste, are relevant in some societies, but not in others. But as we have noted, these "ideas" have real consequences, which can persist.

Societies can get "stuck" in a particular set of beliefs, with each individual's beliefs changing only if enough others' change; but *those* beliefs won't change, if those of the rest don't.

The notion that ideas and perceptions are social constructs also helps explain how societal beliefs sometimes can change rather rapidly. If, somehow, enough people find the idea attractive, there may be a tipping point: it becomes part of a new "social construction of reality," the new conventional wisdom. The notion of racial differences moves then from a concept to be proven to a concept to be disproved. Or there is a switch in beliefs from the notion that inequality is necessary for the functioning of a market economy to the belief that the level of inequality in America today impairs the functioning of our economy and our society. The new ideas become part of the conventional wisdom—until some other intellectual or real current arrives to disturb the intellectual equilibrium.

The social context of beliefs is critical. If different groups interact little, they can develop differing perceptions of reality. So it is with the debate about the legitimacy and even the magnitude of inequality. In some groups (including both rich and poor), the rich are believed to have obtained their wealth largely through their own hard work, with contributions from others and luck playing merely a minor role; among others, the belief is just the opposite.[27] Not surprisingly, these groups have different views about tax policy. If an individual believes what he has is a result just of his own efforts, he is less willing to share that wealth with others who he thinks *chose* to exert less effort. If an individual sees his success as a result largely of good luck, he is more willing to share that good fortune.

Shaping perceptions about policies

Today those who wish to preserve societies' inequalities actively seek to shape perceptions and beliefs to make such inequalities more acceptable. They have the knowledge, the tools, the resources, and the incentives to do so. Even if, in the past, there were many attempts to shape societal perceptions, today there is increased sophistication in doing so. Those who seek to do so know, for instance, more about how to manipulate ideas and preferences. They don't have to just hope and pray that the evolution of ideas works out in their favor.[28]

The fact that those at the top can shape perceptions represents an important caveat to the idea that no one controls the evolution of ideas. Control can happen in several ways, which we will explore in greater depth in this section. One is through access to education and the media. If one group is greatly disadvantaged in opportunities for education or access to public office and to the media, then it will not participate on equal terms in the deliberative space in which the "conventional wisdom" emerges. Some ideas will therefore not emerge; other ideas can be effectively suppressed.

A second way is through the creation of social distance. If one group's economic opportunities leave it much poorer than other groups, then the interactions of the first group with people from other groups will be limited, and it is likely to develop a different culture. Then ideas about intrinsic differences of the poor group are more likely to take root and to persist. As I noted in earlier work on cognitive frames,[29] part of the power of socially constructed categories depends upon their not seeming to be socially constructed. People put in different categories come to act differently and thus to appear intrinsically different.

Most importantly, if goods can be marketed, so can ideas and especially the ideas that underpin policies. Modern marketing has taught the art and science of shaping perceptions—and for those with enough resources (disproportionately the wealthy) there are tools to do so.

In promoting products, many firms have felt few qualms about providing distorted information—or even lying. Thus the cigarette companies succeeded in casting doubt on the scientific evidence of the health hazards of smoking, even though they had in their own possession evidence to the contrary. Similarly, Exxon exhibited no compunction in supporting so-called think tanks casting doubt on the scientific evidence on the risks of global warming—even though there was overwhelming evidence to the contrary. Truth-in-advertising laws try to circumscribe firm behavior, but in promoting ideas and policies, there is no such thing.[30] We've already seen several examples—such as the claim that while America may not be as equal as others, it offers more equality of opportunity, or that it was government efforts to promote housing for the poor that were at the root of the Great Recession—and we'll take a closer look at others.

Education, of course, also shapes beliefs and perceptions, and perhaps with no group is that more the case than with economists. There is now considerable evidence that economists' perceptions, say, about fairness, are markedly different from those of the rest of society. The Chicago economist Richard Thaler reports that while 82 percent of respondents in the general population believed it was unfair to increase the price of snow shovels after a storm, among his MBA students, only 24 percent held that view.[31] It could be partly because economics attracts those who, among the population, put less weight on notions of fairness. But there is evidence as well that training in economics shapes perceptions—and given the role that economists have increasingly had in public policy, their perceptions of what is fair and their views of trade-offs between equity and efficiency may have had disproportionate consequences.

The Right has recognized the importance of education in shaping perceptions, which is why it has been active in trying to influence the design of curricula in schools and embarked on an "education" program to make judges more "economic literate," that is, to see the world through the narrow lens of conservative economics.[32]

One of the most effective ways of influencing public opinion is to capture politicians. After all, politicians are merchants of ideas. (Persuading politicians to adopt one's perspectives and perceptions has a double advantage: not only do they sell the ideas to the public; they translate the ideas into legislation and regulation.) For the most part, politicians don't originate ideas; rather, they take those emanating from academia and from public intellectuals, and from within governments and from nongovernmental organizations (NGOs). They put together a pastiche of these ideas that accord with their worldview, or at least that they think their constituents will favor. In America's moneyed politics, not all constituents are created equal. Politicians have an incentive to espouse ideas that serve the moneyed interests.

In some other countries, politicians can be directly bought. But American politicians are, for the most part, not so crass. They don't accept stuffed brown envelopes. Money goes to their election campaigns and into the coffers of their party. This has come to be called "corruption American style." Some will reap monetary rewards after they leave office, part of the process of revolving doors that is endemic in the United States; for others, the pleasures of power today suffice.

Backing up these ideas are armies of "experts" willing to provide testimony, arguments, and stories to show the right-ness of these views. This battle of ideas occurs, of course, in many playing fields. The politicians have their surrogates, their minions who are not running for office but who advance variants of these ideas, and challenge those of rivals. Evidence and argumentation on both sides are assembled.

This "battle of ideas" has two objectives (like advertis-ing more generally)—to mobilize those who are already true believers and to persuade those who have not yet made up their minds. The former entails rallying the troops and rein-vigorating commitment. In an expensive electoral democ-racy like the United States, arousing the "base" is important because the outcome of elections often hinges on raising campaign funds and getting out the vote. Labeling a rival as a "liberal" or a "neoconservative" can help motivate voting, even when one's own candidate is lackluster.

Much of the battle of persuasion is for "independent voters." To win them over simple, distorted stories, often repeated, can be more effective than longer and more subtle ones. Messaging that appeals to feelings is often more effective than appeals to reason. Advertisers are good at distilling a message down to a sixty-second ad that strikes just the right notes—an emotional response seemingly reinforced by "reason."[33]

THE WEAPONS OF WAR

There is a real battlefield of ideas. But it does not, for the most part, involve a battle of ideas as academics would understand it, where evidence and theory on both sides are carefully weighed. It is a battlefield of "persuasions," of "framing," of attempts not necessarily to get to the truth of the matter but to understand better how ordinary citizens' perceptions are formed and to influence those perceptions.

In this battle of ideas, certain weapons play a central role. In the last chapter, we discussed one of these weapons—the media. It should be obvious that imbalances in the media can lead to a battlefield in the war of ideas that is far from level.

However ideas get disseminated, much of the battle is, as I have suggested, over framing; and in that battle, words are pivotal. The words we use can convey notions of fairness, legitimacy, *positive* feelings; or they can convey notions of *divisiveness* and *selfishness* and *illegitimacy*. Words also frame issues in other ways. In American parlance, "socialism" is akin to communism, and communism is the ideology we battled for sixty years, triumphing only in 1989 with the fall of the Berlin Wall. Hence, labeling anything as "socialism" is the kiss of death. America's health care system for the aged, Medicare, is a single-payer system—the government pays the bill, but the individual gets to choose the provider. Most of the elderly love Medicare. But many are also so convinced that government *can't* provide services efficiently that they believe that Medicare must be private. In the tumultuous discussion of health care reform during President Obama's first year in office, one man was heard to say, "Keep your government hands off my Medicare."[34] The Right attacks extending the Medicare program to the rest of the population as "socialism." That ends the debate. One doesn't have to discuss whether it's efficient or inefficient, whether the quality of care is good or bad, or whether there is choice or not.

Americans have come to believe in markets, and incentives make markets work. Hence labeling pay as "incentive pay" puts a halo over it; it provides justification regardless of the amount. The issue of outsize pay has come up episodically. In 1993, at the beginning of the Clinton administration, the intensity of criticism was so high that the administration decided to impose a surtax on salaries in excess of a million dollars. But then an exception was made for pay related to performance.[35] That, of course, provided an incentive to label all high payments incentive pay. But as we saw earlier, it also provided a whole set of distorted incentives that had impacts beyond mere compensation.

To take another example, credit card companies impose rules on merchants that accept their cards. One such rule is known as the "no surcharge rule." It forbids merchants from passing on the cost of credit card transaction fees to their customers. But the price system works only if individuals see the costs associated with the choices they make. When individuals make a purchase, they make a choice of a payment mechanism. No one would say it is a "surcharge" to charge more for an expensive product than a cheap one. But by labeling *any* charge as a surcharge, credit card companies are attempting to "frame" the charge, to make it seem unreasonable. They want customers to believe that such a charge is so unreasonable as to warrant switching away from merchants who do impose such charges, and thus to induce merchants not to "charge." The absence of an explicit (sur)charge means that the credit card companies can raise the fees they charge merchants to high levels—near to the "breaking point," where the merchant would rather lose the customer than pay the fee.

A final example concerns the price discovery function of markets. In well-functioning markets, demand is equated to supply, and the resulting equilibrium price "reveals" the marginal value of the good to the buyer and the marginal cost to the seller. This information is of value in making decisions. Many economists argued, by analogy, that in a stock market, the prices that emerge reflect the true value of the asset. This is called the "price discovery" role of markets. The words are emotive: discovering the true value of an asset is presumably valuable, and markets are to be commended for performing this important social function. Indeed, market advocates claimed that markets were fully efficient—prices revealed *all* the information available to market participants. This was a matter of religious belief, an article of faith. The use of language was important: because "efficiency" was good, it was obvious that fully efficient markets were good. But this notion was based on deeply flawed logic. Indeed, if markets fully revealed all the information to all market participants, no one would have any incentive to gather information about publicly traded assets, since those who did not spend the money would have equal access to the information. If the efficient-markets hypothesis were true, it would ironically mean that stock markets would necessarily be very inefficient, since no one would gather any information.[36]

In the aftermath of the Great Recession, the efficient-markets model has taken a beating.[37] In the meanwhile, though, some market advocates continue to use the "price discovery" argument for defending changes in markets that were actually making it more volatile and less efficient.

A major change occurred in markets around the turn of this century: most trading (some 61 percent in 2009, 53 percent in 2010) on the stock exchange was done by computers trading with other computers, using certain algorithms. Offers to buy and sell were based not on market research, on informed views about the prospects of, say, steel or the efficiency of a particular steel company, but rather on extracting information from the pattern of prices and trades, and on whatever other information a computer could absorb and process on the fly. Offers to buy and sell were held open for a nanosecond. The response to the suggestion that any firm making an offer to, say, buy a stock at a particular price hold open that offer for one second was: "Do you want to go back to the Middle Ages." Of course, the prices that were determined in those nanoseconds were of no relevance to any *real* decision making. No steel firm would base its decision on whether to expand or contract on these microadjustments of stock prices. The algorithmic traders claimed that they were making markets more liquid ("deeper"), but it was a liquidity that disappeared when it was needed, when a *real* disturbance occurred to which the market needed to adjust. The result was that the market began to exhibit unprecedented volatility. On one day alone, May 6, 2010, stock market prices plummeted so much that the Dow Jones temporarily lost about 10 percent of its value, including a nearly 600-point drop in a five-minute period.[38] Before the end of the day, the market regained much of its value nearly as fast as it had been lost. No one could claim that the real value of the country's assets had diminished in that short period of time. Yet, constant reference to "price discovery" and "efficient markets" provided the halo that made this kind of flash trading seem not only acceptable but even desirable.

In fact, there are reasons to believe that flash trading actually makes markets not just more volatile but also less "informative." Computers attempt to use complex mathematical algorithms to extract whatever information is in the market, in a modern and more sophisticated version of front running, the old-style illegal activities by which brokers try to use information they glean from those placing orders to enhance their own profits. Of course, market participants know this. If some market researcher discovered that some company was going to do well (had just made a valuable discovery), he might rush, placing a large order. But the computer traders would immediately sense this and try to use *his* information for their own purpose. Today, of course, the first trader knows the game he's playing, so he would never place a large order, but would place a myriad of small orders. There's been an arms race, where those doing the hard work of research try to keep their information away from the algorithmic traders, and the algorithmic traders try to break their code. One might say it's just a waste of resources—a fight over the rents associated with early information. But it's worse than that. To the extent that the algorithmic traders succeed in outwitting those who do the real research, the returns to research fall; there will be less investment in information, and markets actually will convey less of the information that we care about.

The Battle over Policies as a Battle over Perceptions

The extent to which the battle over policies is a battle over *perceptions* is particularly striking. The following paragraphs consider three big battles that occurred in recent years— over the repeal of the estate tax, the bank bailout, and mortgage restructuring. The latter two were, of course, front and center in discussions over the response to the 2007–08 financial crisis. All are critical to our understanding of how America has come to be so unequal. Without an estate tax, we create a new plutocracy, marked by dynasties that are self-perpetuating. The bailout provided money to the financial sector—one of the important sources of money at the top. And the failure to do enough about mortgage restructuring has contributed to economic stress at the bottom and in the middle.

Estate taxes[39]

As we've seen, the Right has been able to persuade many Americans to support policies that are *not* in their self-interest. The estate tax, which is imposed on those who have large estates passed on to heirs, provides the quintessential example. Critics of the estate tax call it a death duty and suggest that it is unfair to tax death. Under current law, the tax is levied only on the amount passed on that is *in excess of $5 million* (usually $10 million for a married couple),[40] so that it is unlikely that most Americans would ever be touched by the tax, even with their overoptimistic view of mobility in American society.[41] Yet, because of the concentration of wealth in our society, the tax can raise large amounts of money. Moreover, in theory a "fair" society would put everyone on a level playing field at the start. We know that that's impossible; but the tax is designed to limit the extent of "inherited" inequality—to create a slightly more level playing field. It should be obvious that the tax is in the interests of most Americans, and yet the Right has persuaded large numbers to oppose it[42]—against their own interests. For a brief moment, in 2010, it was totally repealed as a result of tax cuts passed in 2001 under the George W. Bush administration. The Right talks about how much the tax affects small businesses, yet the vast majority of small businesses are too small to be touched; and provisions within the estate tax allow for spreading the payment over fourteen years, precisely so that it will not be disruptive.[43]

Bank recapitalization

As the financial crisis unfolded, we saw how the banks managed perceptions. We were told that we had to save the banks to save the economy—to protect *our* jobs no matter how unsavory the bailouts felt at the time; that if we put conditions on the banks it would roil the markets, and we would all be the worse for it; and that we needed to save not only the banks but also the bankers, the bank's shareholders, and the banks' bondholders. There were, of course, countries like Sweden that had done otherwise, that had played by the rules of "capitalism" and put banks whose capital was inadequate into conservatorship, a process akin (for banks) to bankruptcy, focused on protecting depositors and "conserving" the banks assets; but those were "socialist" countries. To follow Sweden was not the "American way." Obama not only bought into this line; by repeating it, he lent it an aura of authenticity.[44] But this line had no factual basis and was designed to make the world's most massive transfer of wealth acceptable: never in the history of the planet had so many given so much to so few who were so rich without asking anything in return.

The question could have been framed very differently. It could have been argued that the real American way is the rule of law. The law was clear: if a bank can't pay what it owes and what depositors demand back, then it is restructured; shareholders lose everything. Bondholders are made the new shareholders. If there is still not enough money, the govern-

211 IS UPON US   *211*

ment steps in. Bondholders and unsecured creditors then lose everything, but insured depositors get back what they have been promised. The bank is saved, but the government, as the new owner of the bank, will eventually decide to wind it down, reprivatize it, or merge it with a healthier bank. Its objective in part is to recover as much for the taxpayer as possible. We don't wait, of course, until the bank has no money to take these drastic actions. When you go to the bank and put in your ATM card, if the light flashes, "insufficient funds," we want it to be because your account, rather than the bank itself, had insufficient funds. This is the way banking is supposed to work; but it wasn't the way things worked in the United States during the Bush and Obama administrations. They saved not only the banks—there was a rationale for doing that—but also the shareholders, bondholders, and other unsecured creditors. This was a victory in the battle of perceptions.

There was an alternative way to frame the policy question. This narrative would have begun not with the suggestion that what Sweden did was not in our "tradition" but with an analysis of what economic theory and history had shown. That analysis would have demonstrated that we could have saved the banking sector, protected depositors, and maintained a flow of credit, all at less cost to the government, by following the ordinary rules of capitalism. This was, in fact, what Sweden and the United States had done in other situations when banks got into trouble.

Put simply, the economy's interest could have been better protected and a sense of fairness in our system better preserved, if Obama and Bush had played by the rules of ordinary capitalism, rather than making up the rules as they went along—if they had, in a sense, abided by the rule of law.

Instead, the bankers got their money without conditions. The money was *supposed to recapitalize the banks*, and *recapitalizing the banks was supposed to lead to more lending*. But money given to the banks that went to pay bonuses couldn't simultaneously be used to recapitalize the banks. The bankers and their backers won the momentary battle—they got the money into the coffers of the banks and the bankers. But they lost the long-run battle of perceptions: virtually everyone sees what was done as *unfair*—and unjustified even by the unusual economic circumstances. It is this, as much as anything else, that has provided the impetus to the current backlash.[45]

Restructuring mortgages

When the housing bubble burst, many homeowners found themselves "underwater": they owed more on their home than the home was worth. The bank bailout and the case for mortgage restructuring provide a clear contrast in the battle of perceptions: in one case, the perception that shaped government action was that a large bailout is *desirable*, while in the other, the perception that shaped government action was that a large restructuring is *undesirable*. Today the bailouts of the banks are widely seen as far from desirable. And ironically, there is increasing recognition that without doing more for the housing/mortgage market, our economy won't recover.

What has happened in the mortgage market has been far from efficient. When foreclosure forces families out of their homes, everyone loses. The cost to the family—the disruption to their lives, the loss of their life savings—is obvious. Worse still, an empty home, uncared for, decreases the value of neighboring homes. More of them will go underwater.

Communities with large numbers of foreclosures inevitably suffer. The bank loses too: the most important determinant of foreclosures is the extent to which the home is underwater. Foreclosures beget foreclosures: by making more houses go underwater, the banks increase foreclosures and their resulting losses; they lose still more from the substantial legal fees that accompany each foreclosure.

There are better ways of dealing with this unfortunate spiral: a write-down of the principal (what the homeowner owes), perhaps with a debt-to-equity conversion that gives the lender a share in the capital gain when the house is sold. Homeowners still have an incentive to maintain their homes; houses aren't thrown onto the market, depressing housing prices; the costly foreclosure process is averted. Communities are protected. It's to everyone's advantage to give homeowners a fresh start. The lender gets as much or more than she would have otherwise. Executing this strategy would have required modifications to existing law, but the bankers—and the Obama administration—rejected this approach out of hand, at least until the 2012 election approached.[46]

The banks saw that restructuring mortgages would make them *recognize* their losses, an outcome they had successfully kept at bay with deceptive but legal accounting maneuvers that treated impaired mortgages—those in which the borrower was not keeping up with his payments—as if they eventually would be repaid. The true market value of these nonperforming mortgages was often a fraction of the face value. But recognizing the losses would have required the banks to come up with more capital, and they were struggling to get enough capital under the current regulations, let alone the new regulations (called Basel III) adopted in fall 2010.

Of course, the Obama administration and the bankers didn't present their case this way.[47] Two main arguments were advanced for not doing much for homeowners. It would be "unfair" to help those who were struggling with their mortgages when there were so many good and responsible citizens who had worked hard and paid off their mortgage, or were able to make their current payments. Furthermore, offering relief to homeowners would exacerbate the problem of moral hazard: if individuals were left off the hook, it would undermine incentives to repay.[48]

What was curious about these arguments was that they could have applied just as easily, and with greater force, to the banks. The banks had repeatedly been bailed out. The Mexican bailout of 1995, the Indonesian, Thai, and Korean bailouts of 1997–98, the Russian bailout of 1998, the Argentinean bailout of 2000, these and others were all really bank bailouts, though they carried the name of the country where banks had lent excessively. Then, in 2008–09, the U.S. government was engaged in yet another bailout, this one the most massive ever. The banks had proven the relevance of moral hazard—bank bailouts had repeatedly and predictably led to excessive risk taking by banks—and yet both the Bush and the Obama administrations ignored it and refused to discourage future bad behavior by, for instance, firing executives (as the UK did)[49] or making shareholders and bondholders take a hit.[50] Unlike the banks, most of the people losing their homes were not repeat offenders. Yet they were asked to lose all of the equity that they had put into their home, while bank shareholders and bondholders were given a massive gift.[51] Moreover, few homeowners would have been willing to put themselves through the anguish that they have experienced—worries about losing their life savings as well as their home—had they known what was in store for them; their mistake was to trust the bankers, who seemed to understand markets and risk, and who had assured them that the risks they were undertaking were easily manageable.

The bankers and their allies unleashed tirades against the homeowners who were losing their homes. They were labeled as having been reckless. A small percentage had bought multiple houses, and, in an attempt to tarnish all of those losing their homes, they were labeled "speculators." Of course, what else might one call the gambling of so many of the banks? Their reckless speculation lay at the heart of the crisis.

But the greatest irony was the claim that helping some poor homeowners and not helping others would be "unfair." Yet these inequities pale in comparison with those that arose from the hundreds of billions of dollars thrown at the financial sector. Inequities related to the bank bailouts were never mentioned, and if a critic raised them, they were dismissed as the unfortunate but necessary price to resuscitate the economy. There was no mention of the idea that stopping the flood of foreclosures might be a good thing for resuscitating the economy—and helping ordinary citizens.

There were ways of helping homeowners that would not have cost taxpayers a dime and that would have left homeowners who had managed their debts prudently far better-off than those who hadn't; but the bankers resisted any and all such proposals.[52]

We saw in chapter 1 part of the consequence of the combination of the bank bailout without constraints and the absence of help for homeowners: the increase in the inequality of wealth, including the dramatic reduction in the wealth of those in the bottom half of the population.[53]

THE BATTLE OVER THE BIG IDEAS: GOVERNMENT VERSUS MARKET FAILURE

I have illustrated the fight over perceptions in the context of quite specific battles, but the battles rage most intensely in the field of big ideas. One such battle involves on one side those who believe that markets *mostly* work well on their own and that most market failures are in fact government failures. On the other side are those who are less sanguine about markets and who argue for an important role for government. These two camps define the major ideological battle of our time. It is an *ideological* battle, because economic science—both theory and history—provides a quite nuanced set of answers.

This battle plays out in every realm of public policy. It affects the role that government takes in ensuing macrostability, in regulating markets, in investing in public goods, in protecting consumers, investors, and the environment, and in providing social protection. Our focus here, though, is more narrow: this is the big battle the outcome of which will have much to say about the evolution of inequality in the United States, whether it continues to increase, as it has been, or starts to diminish.

A central thesis of chapters 2 and 3 is that market failures—and the failure of government to circumscribe them—play a key role in explaining inequality in America. At the top there are rents (such as monopoly rents); at the bottom there is underinvestment in human capital. Hidden subsidies that distort the market and rules of the game that give an upper hand to those at the top have compounded the problems.

As we noted in chapter 3, economic theory has shown that

markets don't exist in the abstract. At the very least, there is a need for government to enforce contracts and to provide the basic legal structure. But how governments do this makes a difference, both for efficiency and for distribution. The Right wants the "right" rules of the game—those that advantage the wealthy at the expense of the rest. They've tried to shape the debate, to suggest that there is a *single* set of rules that would be best for all. But, throughout the book, we've seen how that's just not true.

Economic theory has shown that markets work well when private and social returns are well aligned, and don't when they are not. Market failures are pervasive. Externalities, for instance, are not limited to the environment. Our banks polluted the global economy with toxic mortgages, and their failures brought the global economy to the brink of ruin, imposing huge costs on workers and citizens throughout the world. Some of these market failures are easy, in principle, to correct: a firm that is polluting can be charged for the pollution it creates. But the distortions caused by imperfect and asymmetric information are present everywhere, and are not so easily corrected. Managers do not always act in the interests of "stakeholders" (including shareholders), and there's little that they can do about it. As we saw in chapter 4, incentive pay that was supposed to align their interests didn't do so; the managers benefited, at the expense of everyone else.[54]

But if you listened only to arguments from the Right, you would have thought that markets *always* worked and government always failed. They worked hard to create this perception within the public, most simply by ignoring private market failures and government successes. And they've tried to ignore—and to get others to ignore—the distributive consequences of these market failures, who gains and who loses when private rewards and social returns are not well aligned. The crisis provided an instance where it was easy to see the winners and losers; but in almost every case, whether it's environmental pollution or predatory lending or abuses of corporate governance, it is those at the top who are the winners, and the rest who are the losers.

Of course, not every government effort is successful, or as successful as its advocates would have liked. Indeed, when the government undertakes research (or supports new private-sector ventures), there *should* be some failures. A lack of failures means you are not taking enough risks. Success occurs when the returns from those projects that succeed are more than enough to offset the losses on those that fail. And the evidence in the case of government research ventures is unambiguously and overwhelmingly that the returns from government investments in technology *on average* have been very, very high—just think about the Internet, the Human Genome Project, jet airplanes, the browser, the telegraph, the increases in productivity in agriculture in the nineteenth century, that provided the basis for the United States' moving from farming to manufacturing. When I was chairman of the Council of Economic Advisers, we assessed the average social returns on government R&D, and it turned out to be well in excess of 50 percent, far higher in other areas of investment (including private sector R&D).[55]

Governments are human institutions, and all people, and the institutions they create, are fallible. There are government failures just as there are market failures. Recent economic theory has explained when each of these is more likely to fail, and how governments and markets (and other civil institutions, including those that serve as watchdogs on both corporations and government) can complement each other and provide a system of checks and balances. We have seen myriad instances of this kind of complementarity: a government initiative created the Internet, but private-sector firms like Google built many of products and applications that have placed it at the center of people's lives and our economy. Government may have created the first web browser, but the private sector and open-source movement have refined it.

That there are successes and failures in both the public and the private sector is clear. And yet many on the right seem to think only the government can fail. Part of the reason for these disparate perceptions about markets and governments has to do with the theory of equilibrium fictions described earlier. Those who believe in markets discount information about market failure while assigning high saliency to examples of government failure. They can easily recall examples of failed government programs, but the massive failures of our financial system in the run-up to the Great Recession are quickly forgotten, described as an anomaly, or blamed on the government.

The fact of the matter is that there has been no successful large economy in which the government has not played an important role, and in the countries with the most rapid growth (such as China) and in those with the highest standards of living (such as those in Scandinavia),[56] the government plays a very important role. Yet the prevailing ideology on the right is so strong that there continues to be a push for a small government, for contracting out government services and privatization and even a resistance to regulation.

This Right fails to note not only the successes of government but the failures of markets. In the aftermath of the crisis of 2008, however, it is hard to ignore the *repeated* financial crises that have marked capitalism since its origins.[57]

Repeated bank bailouts have imposed high costs on taxpayers. If we add up the losses from the financial sector's misalloca- tion of capital before the crisis and the shortfall between the economy's potential output and actual output after the bubble burst, we get a number in the trillions of dollars.

After the Great Depression, government succeeded in reg- ulating the financial sector, producing almost four decades of financial stability and rapid growth, with banks focusing on lending, providing the money needed for the rapid expansion of our enterprises. Government helped make markets act the way markets are *supposed* to function, by reducing the scope for fraud and consumer deception and enhancing competi- tion. But beginning with President Reagan and continuing through President Clinton, government stepped back. The deregulation led to instability; with less oversight, there was more fraud and less competition.

Nor is this the only example. Private health insurance com- panies are much less efficient than the government-run Medi- care program.[58] Private life insurance companies are much less efficient than the government's Social Security program.[59]

To take another example: a recent study showed that, on average, contractors "charged the federal government more than twice the amount it pays federal workers" for perform- ing comparable services.[60] As much as one out of four dol- lars spent on contracting in Iraq and Afghanistan was wasted or misspent, according to the Commission on Wartime Con- tracting in Iraq and Afghanistan.[61] In an earlier study, Linda Bilmes and I showed how the government could have saved billions by having the armed forces provide these services.[62] But this—and other experiences—suggests that it was not just ideology that drove the contracting/privatization agenda: it was rent seeking.

Liberalization and privatization

The irony is that advocates of privatization (turning over previously publicly run enterprises to the private sector) and liberalization (stripping away regulations) have long claimed that these policies are necessary to restrain rent seeking. They note corruption in the public sector but seldom acknowledge that on the other side of every public-sector employee who takes a bribe is a briber, and that briber is typically a private party. The private sector is fully involved in the corruption. Worse still, in a fundamental sense, the agenda of privatization and liberalization has itself been corrupt: it has garnered high rents for those who used their political influence to push it.[63]

Around the world, the examples of failed privatizations are legion—from roads in Mexico to railroads in the UK.

The major privatization in the United States of recent years—of the company that makes enriched uranium, used for nuclear power plants and making atomic bombs (USEC, the U.S. Enrichment Corporation)—has been plagued with criticisms of dishonest dealing. While the former government officials who engineered the privatization and the investment bank that facilitated it made millions, the company was never able to turn a profit. For more than a decade and a half after privatization, government subsidies were at the center of their business model. The results have been so troubling that there have been proposals to renationalize USEC.[64]

But had President George W. Bush had his way, there would have been a much, much bigger privatization—the (partial) privatization of Social Security, at the center of his State of the Union address of 2005. Americans are, of course, now thankful that his efforts failed. For if they had succeeded, America's elderly would have been in an even worse position than they are today: those who had put their money in the stock market would have seen much of their retirement wealth gone; those who put their money in safe T-bills would be struggling to survive, as the Fed pushes interest rates down to near-zero levels. But even before the crisis, it should have been obvious that privatization was a bad deal for most Americans. We noted before that Social Security is more efficient than private providers of annuities. Private insurance companies have much higher transactions costs. In fact, that was the whole point of privatization: for the elderly, transactions costs are a bad thing; but for the financial sector, they are a good thing. That's their income. That's what they live off of. Their hope was to get a slice of the hundreds of billions of dollars[65] that people put every year into their Social Security accounts.[66]

Liberalization/deregulation initiatives have had as mixed a record as those of privatization—with the most notorious being financial sector deregulation and capital market liberalization. For those devoted to the ideology of the Right, these failures are a mystery. To those more apprised of the limitations of the market, they are predictable—and often predicted. This also applies to other liberalization initiatives, including the disastrous liberalization of electric power in California. Enron, one of the big advocates of the liberalization and an outspoken advocate of the wonders of the market (before it went down in 2001, the largest corporate bankruptcy ever recorded up to that point), manipulated the California electricity market to make millions and millions for itself, a transfer of money from ordinary citizens of that state to Ken Lay, its CEO, and the others who ran the company. Bush officials blamed the shortages that Enron had managed to create on excessive environmental regulation that discouraged new construction. The reality was otherwise: as soon as

Enron's market manipulations to inflate prices were exposed and regulations were restored, the shortages disappeared.

Innovation and the resistance to regulation

Opponents of regulation always complain that it's bad for business. Regulations that prevent pollution, of course, are bad for businesses that would have otherwise polluted. Regulations that prevent child labor are bad for businesses that would have exploited children. Regulations that prevent American companies from engaging in bribery or abuses of human rights may be bad for businesses that engage in bribery or human rights abuses. As we've seen, private rewards and social returns often differ; and when they do, markets don't work well. The task of government is to align the two.

If it were true, as some have claimed, that new banking regulations will stifle innovation, we still would have to weigh the benefits of the regulation against the costs. If regulations can prevent another near-collapse of the banking system, the benefits would be enormous, possibly in the trillions of dollars. And well-designed regulations did succeed in ensuring the stability of our financial system for decades, *so regulations can work.* Moreover, this period of tight financial regulation was also one of rapid economic growth, a period in which the fruits of that growth were more widely shared than they are today. By contrast, in the period of "liberalization" the growth of a typical citizen's income was far lower than in the period of regulation.

There is a simple reason for the failure of liberalization: when social returns and private rewards are misaligned, all economic activity gets distorted, including innovation. The innovation of the financial sector was directed not to improving the well-being of Americans but to improving the well-being of bankers. At least for a time, it succeeded in doing that; but it failed miserably in improving the plight of the ordinary American or even spurring growth in the American economy as a whole.

SUCCESSES IN THE BATTLE OF IDEAS

I have described the war of ideas—including those ideas that are central to the policies that determine societal inequality—and while the wealthy (and corporations) have been enormously successful in shaping perceptions in ways that benefit them, they have lost, or are losing, at least some of the battles. The marketplace of ideas, while far from perfect, is still competitive. This is a reason for hope.

In the following paragraphs I describe three such battles in which the tide has been turning: that over corporate welfare; that over the IMF, its governance, and some of the policies that it used to pursue; and that over the ultimate objectives of public policy.

Class warfare and corporate welfare

When President Clinton entered office, there was both high unemployment and a large deficit, though the unemployment and debt levels pale in comparison with those of today. It was natural for us to look for budget cuts that would increase efficiency without endangering the core agenda of "putting people first" and perhaps, by redirecting spending, even stimulate the economy. Obvious candidates for cutting were large expenditures on what Robert Reich (then secretary of labor) and I called *corporate welfare,* subsidies to American corporations. The Council of Economic Advisers was tasked with drawing up a list of cuts—not as easy as it might seem, because much of the corporate welfare is hidden within the tax code. Even then, toward the top of the list were subsidies to the banks (for instance, via IMF bailouts), to agriculture, and to the coal and other natural resource companies.

I thought that there would be broad consensus within the administration on the principle, but considerable reservation on the politics. I expected the departments that doled out the subsidies to try to defend their turf. What surprised me was the strong reaction from the head of the National Economic Council (later, secretary of Treasury) Bob Rubin: he suggested that we were trying to wage class warfare. It was, of course, nothing of the kind. For a Democratic administration trying to focus its attention on economic recovery and helping people, expensive subsidies that distorted the economy and increased inequality made no sense. Besides, to pretend that there were not large inequalities, large divisions, in our society was putting one's head in the sand. Warren Buffett put it correctly when he said, "There's been class warfare going on for the last 20 years and my class has won."[67] But the accusation of class warfare suggested that those who were trying to reduce corporate welfare were being *divisive.*

In the Clinton administration, we made only a little progress in cutting out corporate welfare. The big subsidies for agriculture and energy remained. So did the smaller, but highly symbolic, subsidies for corporate jets.

But during the 2008 crisis, corporate welfare reached new heights. In the great bailout of the Great Recession, one corporation alone, AIG, got more than $180 billion—more than was spent on welfare to the poor from 1990 to 2006.[68]

As deficits have become larger, there has been increasing scrutiny of the budget, and cutbacks of corporate welfare—whether by that name or not—have been on the table. Some cutbacks have already occurred—as we noted earlier, at the end of 2011 the $6 billion ethanol subsidy, in place for three decades, ended. But I suspect that the more powerful industries and firms will be able to retain much of what they receive.

There is a role for government in providing a safety net, in "social protection," but it should be protecting *individuals and families* against the risks that they face, especially those against which they cannot insure; it should not be protecting corporations from facing the consequences of bad business judgments or providing subsidies to enrich their coffers. Markets can't work if there isn't some discipline—if companies get only the upside of the risks, with taxpayers bearing the losses.

The IMF: the emperor has no clothes

In *Globalization and Its Discontents*, I described the intense battles between the IMF and some of those in developing countries and emerging markets in a variety of arenas—in developmental policy, in the policies of transition from communism to a market economy, and in the management of the East Asia crisis. I explained how the IMF had imposed contractionary policies on countries facing economic downturns, and I explained how its "structural adjustment" policies—forcing privatization and liberalization—had often led not to growth but instead to hardship, especially among the poor.

At the time I wrote the book, the IMF was viewed as *the* authority on these matters, especially in the West. Many in the developing world were skeptical: they saw that the policies pushed by the IMF often failed. They perceived the IMF as advancing the interests of the global financial sector and corporate interests in the advanced industrial countries. But they typically felt they had no choice except to follow the IMF's strictures. They needed its money. I set out to show that *the emperor had no clothes*: that the favored IMF policies were not based on the best economic science; to the contrary, many of the doctrines that they had pushed had been thoroughly discredited by research in economics over the preceding quarter century.

I also sought to expose both some of the intellectual inconsistencies and the failures in governance. Over this period, the IMF increasingly had focused on "governance," yet its own governance left much to be desired. The financial sector had too much influence, the developing countries had too little. The excessive influence of the financial sector helped explain the IMF's devotion to contractionary policies—its first priority was to get Western creditors repaid, and that meant countries had to cut back their spending, so that more money would be left to repay debts. It also helped explain its advocacy of capital market liberalization, the stripping away of regulations that affected the flows of money (especially short-term hot money) into and out of a country. While there was little evidence that capital market liberalization led to faster growth, there was ample evidence that it led to more instability. But from the perspective of the advanced industrial countries, it was still desirable, because it gave more scope for Western financial firms to come into developing countries—and make more profits there. Evidently, the IMF had been captured by a self-reinforcing combination of ideology and interests.

Not surprisingly, the IMF did not take kindly to these perspectives—and the response was personal and vituperative.

The suggestion that under certain circumstances capital controls might be desirable was greeted with suggestions that I was trying to sell snake oil.

Ten years later, the battlefield looks different. There has been a major change in perceptions, to which my book may have contributed, and there is a broad consensus on the need for governance reform—with some already under way, and more scheduled for the future.

The IMF has admitted that capital controls may be desirable under certain circumstances.[69] In some of its programs, such as that for Iceland, it has accepted capital controls and has pushed for much less austerity than was its wont. Behind the scenes, in some of the European countries in crisis, it pushed for debt restructurings—making creditors bear more of the costs, taxpayers less. But there have been powerful forces on the other side, including the European Central Bank. While in Greece the notion that a deep debt restructuring was finally accepted, in Ireland even unsecured bondholders were protected—they got the high return, supposedly for bearing risk, but in the end, they were protected, at great expense to Irish taxpayers.

In pursuit of the wrong goals

America has been hot in pursuit of the wrong goals. We've lost our way. We thought that simply by increasing GDP all would benefit, but that has not been the case. Even if the American economy produces more goods and services, if, year after year, most Americans have lower and lower incomes, our economy is *not* performing well.

It is obvious now that the standard way of measuring economic performance, the level of real per capita GDP (the sum of all of the goods and services produced inside the country, divided by the number of people in the country, adjusted for inflation) and the rate at which it is growing, is not a good measure of success. America has been doing fairly well in terms of real per capita GDP, and those numbers lulled it into thinking that all was going well. (Even then, the United States was not the top performer—Luxembourg Norway, Switzerland, Denmark, and "socialist" Sweden[70] had a higher GDP per capita in 2010.)[71]

To take one example of how GDP can give a false impression of a country's success, GDP per capita mismeasures the value of goods and services produced in several sectors, including health and the public sector—two sectors whose importance today is much greater than when GDP first started to be measured a half century ago. America, for instance, gets worse health outcomes, in terms of longevity or virtually any other measure of health performance, but spends more money. If we were measuring *performance*, the lower efficiency of America's sector would count against the United States, and France's health care sector output would be higher. As it is, it's just the reverse: the inefficiency helps inflate America's GDP number.

Our standard measure of performance, GDP, doesn't take into account sustainability—both individuals and countries can live beyond their means, but only for a time. That, of course, was the case for the United States. Not only were most individuals borrowing to sustain their living standards; so was the country as a whole. A housing bubble kept the economy going for much of the first decade of this century—a kind of artificial life-support system that gave rise to unsustainable consumption.

Most importantly for the purposes of this book, our con-

ventional measures of income don't adequately reflect a
broader sense of what's happening to most citizens. As we saw
in chapter 1, GDP per capita could be going up, and yet most
citizens in the country could be stagnating or even becoming
worse-off, year after year: precisely what has been happening
in the United States.

And just as there are large inequalities in income, there are
large disparities in almost all of the other dimensions that contribute to our general welfare, and none of these are reflected
in GDP as a measure of economic performance. Take, for
instance, health, education, or the environment. The environmental justice movement has called attention to the adverse
environmental conditions under which many of the poor live—
the only housing they can afford is near polluting factories or
noisy airports and trains.[72]

How we measure performance is an aspect of the battle
over perceptions and makes a difference, especially in our
performance-oriented society. Our systems of measurement
affect our perception of how well we are doing—and of the
relative performance of different economic systems. If we
measure the wrong thing, we will be tempted to do the wrong
thing, and to make the wrong inferences about what is a good
economic system.

If we measure our success by GDP, that's what we'll push
for, and we'll pay insufficient attention to what's happening
to *most* Americans. To take another example: critics of, say,
environmental regulations suggest that they are costly, that
they reduce growth. But how we see that trade-off depends
on how we measure output. If in our measurements of GDP,
we take into account the cost of environmental degradation,
then better environmental regulation may actually improve
GDP *correctly measured.*

For years the standard measure of economic performance was GNP, gross national product, roughly equal to the gross income of the citizens of a country. But then, around 1990, there was a switch to GDP, gross domestic product, the value of the goods and services produced within a country. For a country in isolation, not trading with other countries or receiving inward investments, the two numbers are equivalent. But the switch occurred just as the pace of globalization was increasing. This had some profound effects: if the income associated with goods produced in the country went elsewhere, GDP could go up while GNP decreased. And this was not just a theoretical nicety. Papua New Guinea's (PNG) gold mines were developed by foreign companies, from Australia, Canada, and elsewhere. Most of the value of what was produced accrued to the foreign companies. PNG got a pittance—not enough even to compensate it for the destruction of its environment, or other adverse effects on its economy or the health of its people.[73] A focus on GDP encouraged countries to undertake such projects—the measure of their success was improved. But had the old measure, GNP, been the focus, such projects might have been rejected.

When I was chairman of the Council of Economic Advisers, I tried to encourage the United States to address some of these problems, for instance, by constructing "Green GDP" accounts, which would take into consideration the depletion of natural resources and the degradation of the environment. I knew that I had hit on something important when the coal industry responded with vehemence, and when congressional representatives of the coal states even threatened to cut off funding for work on this area. The coal industry realized that perceptions mattered: if it became widely recognized that, correctly measured, the coal industry might have been making a negative contribution to the nation's output, that would have had significant policy implications.

Today there is almost universal recognition that we have to change our metrics. President Sarkozy of France set up the International Commission on the Measurement of Economic Performance and Social Progress, which I chaired.[74] Experts were drawn from statistics, economics, political science, and psychology, and the group included three Nobel Prize winners. We unanimously agreed not only that GDP was a bad, and potentially badly misleading, measure but that it could be improved upon.[75] I cannot say, at this point, that we have fully won this battle, but the tide has turned. Even the United States has begun work in broadening its measures. The G-20 endorsed work to find better metrics. The OECD, the organization of the advanced industrial countries, has undertaken a large project following up on our work. And countries around the world—Australia, New Zealand, Scotland, the UK, Germany, France, Korea, Italy, and many others—have begun initiatives along these lines.

In democratic societies, even given the power of the wealthy to control the media and shape perceptions, it is impossible to completely suppress ideas. And when these ideas resonate with so many citizens, they can take on a life of their own.

CONCLUDING COMMENTS

In politics, perceptions are crucial. Devoted ideologues on each side will cherry-pick examples and draw from them broad generalizations. As we've tried to argue, many individuals will perceive or remember only the evidence that is consistent with their initial beliefs. This is so perhaps especially in ideologically charged issues, such as the role of government, particularly in dealing with inequality. That itself may be a reflection of the high inequality in the United States. A great deal of money is at stake for the 1 percent in winning this debate. Given that, it becomes harder, not easier, to weigh all considerations in a balanced way.

In this chapter, I've tried to present a case for a nuanced and balanced approach to the proper role of the market and the government. We don't decide whether a given medical intervention is good or bad by considering only the successes or only the horror stories. Instead, we try to understand the conditions under which a medical intervention is likely to work or not. What are the risks of doing nothing? What are the limitations of intervening? The same care should be taken with both the "big" ideas we have been discussing and the more specific policy interventions.

The powerful try to frame the discussion in a way that benefits their interests, realizing that, in a democracy, they cannot simply impose their rule on others. In one way or another, they have to "co-opt" the rest of society to advance their agenda.

Here again the wealthy have an advantage. Perceptions and beliefs are malleable. This chapter has shown that the wealthy have the instruments, resources, and incentives to shape beliefs in ways that serve their interests. They don't always win—but it's far from an even battle.

We've seen how the powerful manipulate public perception by appeals to fairness and efficiency, while the real outcomes benefit only them. In the next chapter, we'll see how they achieve this not only in the court of public opinion but also in America's courts.

CHAPTER SEVEN

JUSTICE FOR ALL? HOW INEQUALITY IS ERODING THE RULE OF LAW

E VERY MORNING, STUDENTS THROUGHOUT AMER-
ica pledge their allegiance to the flag of the United
States and "to the Republic for which it stands, one nation,
under God, with liberty and justice for all." That implicit
promise, liberty and justice for all, captures one of the essential values that help define America's sense of identity. At our
best, we are a country where the rule of law prevails, where
an individual is innocent until proven guilty, and where all
people stand equal before the law. These values also are central to our understanding of America's place in the world.
We have championed them to other countries. Yet what the
pledge really means is seldom taken up. Nor is a still larger
question broached: whether America has really delivered on
its promises.

This chapter explores one of three crucial battlefields upon which the fight to create a more equal, or more unequal, society is fought—the battle over the laws and regulations that govern our economy and how they are enforced. The next chapter considers the battle of the budget, and chapter 9 examines the conduct of monetary policy and macroeconomics.

The chapter begins by asking a rather abstract, but key, set of questions: What is the purpose of the laws and regulations that are central to the functioning of our economy? Why do we need a rule of law? Is there more than one possible "rule of law," and, if so, what differences do the choices make? The central message echoes that of earlier chapters: There are alternative legal frameworks. Each has consequences for efficiency and distribution. The *wrong* kind of rule of law can help preserve and extend inequities.

While a good "rule of law" is supposed to protect the weak against the powerful, we'll see how these legal frameworks have sometimes done just the opposite, and the effect has been a large transfer of wealth from the bottom and middle to the top.[1] Ironically, while the advocates of these legal frameworks argued for them as promoting an efficient economy, they have actually led to a distorted economy.

WHY WE NEED A RULE OF LAW

As the old poem goes, "No man is an island." In any society what one person does may hurt, or benefit, others. Economists refer to these effects as externalities. When those who injure others don't have to bear the full consequences of their actions, they will have inadequate incentives not to injure them, and to take precautions to avoid risks of injury. We have laws to provide incentives for each of us to avoid injuries to others—to their property, their heath, and the public goods (such as nature) that they enjoy.

Economists have focused on how best to provide incentives so that individuals and firms take into account their externalities: steel producers should be forced to pay for their pollution, and those who cause accidents should pay for the consequences. We embody these ideas, for instance, in the "polluter pays principle," which says that polluters should pay for the full consequences of their actions. Not paying the full consequences of one's action—for instance, for the pollution caused by production—is a subsidy. It is equivalent to not paying the full cost of labor or capital. Some corporations that resist paying for the pollution that they create talk about the possible loss of jobs. No economist would suggest that distortionary subsidies to labor or capital should be preserved to save jobs. Not paying the costs imposed on the environment is a form of subsidy that should be no more acceptable. The responsibility for maintaining the economy at full employment lies elsewhere—with monetary and fiscal policy.

The success corporations often have had in avoiding the full consequences of their actions is an example of how they shape the rules of the economic game in their favor. As a result of laws that limit the extent of their liabilities, nuclear power plants and offshore oil rigs are shielded from bearing the full costs should they explode.[2] The consequence is that we have more nuclear power plants and offshore rigs than we would otherwise—in fact, it's questionable whether, without a whole set of government subsidies, there would be any nuclear power plants at all.[3]

Sometimes, the costs that firms impose on others aren't apparent right away. Corporations often take big risks, and nothing may go wrong for years and years. But when something does go wrong (as with the TEPCO nuclear power plant in Japan or with the Union Carbide plant in Bhopal, India), thousands can suffer. Forcing corporations to compensate those injured doesn't really undo the harm. Even if the family of someone who dies because of unsafe work conditions is compensated, the person isn't brought back to life. That's why we can't rely just on incentives. Some people are risk takers—especially when others bear most of the risk. The explosion aboard the Deepwater Horizon in April 2010 began a spill that spewed millions of barrels of British Petroleum oil into the Gulf of Mexico. BP executives had gambled: skimping on safety increased immediate profits. In this case, they gambled and lost—but the environment and residents of Louisiana and the other Gulf states lost even more.

In the resulting litigation, corporations that do cause damage may have a stronger hand than the people who are hurt. They may be in a position to nickel-and-dime those who suffer damage, since many people cannot hold out for adequate compensation, nor can they afford lawyers to match those of the company. One role of government is to rebalance the scales of justice—and in the case of the BP disaster, it did, but very gently, and in the end, it became clear that many of the victims were likely to receive compensation that was but a fraction of what they suffered.[4]

Ronald Coase, a Chicago Nobel Prize–winning economist, explained how different ways of assigning property rights were equally efficient for addressing externalities, or at least would be in a hypothetical world with no transactions costs.[5] In a room with smokers and nonsmokers, one could assign the "air rights" to the smokers, and if the nonsmokers valued clean air more than the smokers valued smoking, they could bribe the smokers not to smoke. But one could alternatively assign the air rights to the nonsmokers. In that case, smokers could bribe the nonsmokers to allow them to smoke so long as they valued the right to smoke more than the nonsmokers valued clean air. In a world of transactions costs—the real world, where, for instance, it costs money to collect money from one group to pay another—one assignment can be much more efficient than the other.[6] But more to the point, there can be large distributive consequences of alternative assignments. Giving nonsmokers the air rights benefits them at the expense of the smokers.

Try as one might, one cannot escape issues of distribution, even when it comes to the simplest problems in organizing an economy.[7] The flip side of the intertwining of these "property rights"/externalities issues and distribution is that notions of "liberty" and "justice" cannot be separated. Each individual's liberties have to be curtailed when they impose harms on others. One person's liberty to pollute deprives another of her health. One person's liberty to drive fast deprives another of his right not to be injured.[8] But whose liberties are paramount? To answer this fundamental question, societies develop rules and regulations. These rules and regulations both affect the efficiency of the system and distribution: some gain at the expense of others.

That's why "power"—political power—matters so much. If economic power in a country becomes too unevenly distributed, political consequences will follow. While we typically think of the rule of law as being designed to protect the weak against the strong, and ordinary citizens against the privileged, those with wealth will use their political power to shape the rule of law to provide a framework within which they can exploit others.[9] They will use their political power, too, to ensure the preservation of inequalities rather than the attainment of a more egalitarian and more just economy and society. If certain groups control the political process, they will use it to design an economic system that favors them: through laws and regulations that apply specifically to an industry, through those that govern bankruptcy, competition, intellectual property or taxation, or, indirectly, through costs of accessing the court system. Corporations will argue, in effect, that they have the right to pollute—and they will ask for subsidies not to pollute; or that they have the right to impose the risk of nuclear contamination on others—and they will ask for, in effect, hidden subsidies, limitations in liability to protect themselves against being sued if their plant explodes.

My experience in government suggests that those who hold positions of power want to believe that they are doing the right thing—that they are pursuing the public interest. But their beliefs are at least malleable enough for them to be convinced by "special interests" that what they want is in the public interest, when it is in fact in *their own* interests to so believe. In the rest of this chapter, we examine this theme in three contexts where rules and regulations play a central role in determining how America's market economy has been working in recent years: predatory lending, bankruptcy law, and the foreclosure process.

PREDATORY LENDING

Early on in the housing bubble, it became clear that the banks were engaged not only in reckless lending—so reckless that it would endanger the entire economic system—but also in predatory lending, taking advantage of the least educated and financially unsophisticated in our society by selling them costly mortgages and hiding details of the fees in fine print incomprehensible to most people. Some states tried to do something about it. For instance, in October 2002 the Georgia legislature, after observing that mortgage lending in the state was riddled with fraud and predation, tried to call a halt to it with a consumer protection law. The response from the financial markets was quick and furious.

The ratings agencies, today best known for their role in calling pools of F-rated mortgages A-rated securities, also had a hand in sustaining fraudulent lending practices. They should have welcomed the actions of states like Georgia: the law meant that the agencies would not need to assess whether mortgages in a given pool were fraudulent or inappropriate. Instead, Standard & Poor's, one of the leading rating agencies, threatened not to rate any of Georgia's mortgages. Without these ratings, the mortgages would have been hard to securitize and without securitization (in the business model of the day) mortgage lending in the state might dry up. Evidently, the rating agencies were worried that if the practice spread to other states, the flow of bad mortgages from which they made so much money "rating" would be greatly diminished. S&P's threat was effective: the state quickly reversed the law.[10]

In some other states, too, there were attempts to stop predatory lending, and in each of these instances banks used all their political muscle to stop states from enacting laws aimed at curtailing predatory lending.[11] The result, as we know now, was not only massive fraud but also bad lending: too much indebtedness, with financial products that could explode with a change in interest rates or in the broader economic conditions, and indeed many did explode.[12]

In a simpler world, the adage caveat emptor ("let the buyer beware") might have been appropriate; but not in today's complex world. A regulatory agency for financial products is needed to prevent not just fraud but also abusive, deceptive, and inappropriate products.[13]

Even many financial institutions recognized that *some* regulation was needed: without bank and insurance regulations ensuring the soundness of these institutions, individuals would be reluctant to turn over their money to banks and insurance companies, lest they never get it back. Individuals on their own would never be able to assess the financial conditions of these large and complex institutions; it has proven hard enough for experienced government regulators to do so.[14]

But the U.S. banking sector resisted the suggestion that regulation be extended to protect consumers, in spite of its terrible record of bad lending and poor credit practices before the crisis, which had led to widespread public support for an agency to do so. And when a provision creating such an agency was included in the Dodd-Frank bill, financial institutions campaigned to make sure that Elizabeth Warren, a Harvard law professor with all the credentials necessary to run such an agency, including the expertise and commitment to protect consumers, was not chosen to head it. The banks won. (She was in, in fact, widely cited as the originator of the idea of such an agency, and a tireless campaigner for it, a sin for which the financial community could not forgive her. Even worse, she served as chair of the Congressional Oversight Panel, overseeing the government's bailout program. The panel revealed that the administration was giving the banks a great deal—getting back from the banks preferred shares worth about half of what the government was giving them.)[15]

BANKRUPTCY LAW

A host of other laws and regulations shape the market and thereby affect the distribution of income and well-being. Bankruptcy law (which specifies what happens when an individual or a corporation can't pay back what is owed) has particular relevance to two parts of our society—those at the top (the bankers) and those at the bottom, who struggle to make ends meet.

Bankruptcy law is designed to give individuals a fresh start. The notion that under certain conditions debts should be forgiven has a long tradition that goes back at least as far as the Book of Leviticus, where debts were forgiven in the Jubilee year. Virtually every modern economy has a bankruptcy law. These laws can be either more debtor or more creditor friendly, making it easier or more difficult to discharge debts. How they are shaped obviously has strong distributional consequences, but the incentive effects can be equally powerful. If debts can't be discharged, or can't be discharged easily, lenders have less of an incentive to be careful in lending—and more of an incentive to engage in predatory lending.

In 2005, just as subprime mortgages were starting to boom, Congress passed a new creditor-friendly bankruptcy law that gave the banks even more of an upper hand, making it more difficult for distressed borrowers to discharge their debts. The change in the law introduced a system of "partial indentured servitude." An individual with, say, debts equal to 100 percent of his income could be forced to hand over to the bank 25 percent of his gross, pretax income for the rest of his life. This is because the bank could add on, say, 30 percent interest each year to what a person owed. In the end, a mortgage holder would owe far more than the bank ever lent. The debtor would end up working, in effect, one-quarter time for the bank.[16]

Every loan has a willing lender and a willing borrower; the banks are supposed to be financially sophisticated, to know how much debt individuals can manage. But a distorted financial system put more emphasis on the up-front fees that showed up quickly in the banks' bottom line than on the losses that might be incurred further down the line. Emboldened by the new bankruptcy law, they felt they could somehow squeeze money out of their hapless borrowers, whatever happened to the housing market and unemployment. This reckless lending, combined with deceptive practices and sometimes usurious interest rates, has put many households on the brink of financial ruin. In spite of so-called reforms, banks still sometimes charge rates nearing 30 percent a year (which means that a $100 debt can grow to $1,000 in a short span of nine years). On top of this, they can impose crippling fees. While some of the worst abuses have been curbed, such as those associated with overdrafts (which generated literally billions of dollars a year in profits[17]—money taken out of the pockets of ordinary citizens), many continue.

When the new bankruptcy law was passed, property rights were changed, but in a way that favored the banks. At the time the borrowers had incurred their debt, a more humane bankruptcy law gave them a chance for a fresh start if the burden of debt repayment became too onerous. The banks didn't complain about this change in property rights; after all, they had pushed for it vociferously. When things go the other way, of course, the owners of property complain that the rules of the game are being changed midcourse and demand compensation.[18]

Student loan programs

We saw earlier that inequality in the United States has been rising steeply and is likely to continue to increase. One of the reasons is the growing inequality of opportunity, related in part to educational opportunity. Young people and their parents know the importance of education, but we have created a system where the striving for education may actually be leading to more inequality. One reason for this is that over the past twenty-five years, the states have been withdrawing support from higher education.[19] This problem grew in the recession.

Another reason is that aspiring students are becoming increasingly indebted.[20] The 2005 bankruptcy law made it impossible for students to discharge their student debts even in bankruptcy.[21] This eviscerates any incentives for banks, and the for-profit schools that they work with, to provide an education that will yield a return.[22] Even if the education is worthless, the borrower is still on the hook. And for many students, the education is frequently almost worthless. Some 80 percent of the students do not graduate,[23] and the real financial rewards of education come only upon completion of the programs—and even then they may not materialize. But in this conspiracy between the for-profit schools (many owned partly or largely by Wall Street firms) and the for-profit banks, the students are never warned. Rather than "Satisfaction guaranteed or your money back," the reality is "Dissatisfaction is almost guaranteed, but you will be saddled with these debts for the rest of your life." Neither the schools nor the lenders say, "You are almost certain *not* to get a good job, of the kind you dream of. We exploit your dreams; we don't deliver on our promise." When the government proposed standards—schools would qualify for government backed loans only if there was an adequate completion rate and enough student satisfaction, with at least a minimal number of students getting the jobs that were promised—the schools and the banks fought back, largely successfully.

It wasn't as if the government was trying to regulate a private industry that was seemingly doing well on its own (though partly by exploiting the poor and less informed). The for-profit schools existed largely because of the federal government. Schools in the $30 billion a year for-profit education industry receive as much as 90 percent of their revenue from federal student loan programs and federal aid. They were enjoying the more than $26 billion they were getting from the federal government; it was enough money to make it worthwhile to invest heavily in lobbying and campaign contributions, to make sure that they were not held accountable.[24]

In the case of student loans, the banks managed for years to get rewards with almost no risk: in many instances, the government guaranteed the loans; in others, the fact that the loans can never be discharged—they are bankruptcy proof—makes them safer than other loans to similar individuals. And yet the interest rate charged to students was incommensurate with these risks: the banks have used the student loan programs (especially those with government guarantees) as an easy source of money—so much so that when the government finally scaled down the program in 2010, the government and the students could, between them, pocket tens of billions of dollars that previously had gone to the banks.[25]

America sets the pattern

Usury (charging exorbitant interest rates),[26] of course, is not limited to the United States. In fact, around the world the poor are sinking in debt as a result of the spread of the same rogue capitalism. India had its own version of a subprime mortgage crisis: the hugely successful microcredit schemes that have provided credit to poor farmers and transformed their lives turned ugly once the profit motive was introduced. Initially developed by Muhammad Yunus of the Grameen Bank and Sir Fazle Hasan Abed of BRAC in Bangladesh, microcredit schemes transformed millions of lives by giving the poorest, who had never banked, access to small loans. Women were the main beneficiaries. Allowed to raise chickens and engage in other productive activities, they were able to improve living standards in their families and their communities. But then for-profit banks discovered that there "was money at the bottom of the pyramid."[27] Those on the bottom rung had little, but they were so numerous that taking a small amount from each of them was worth it. Banks all over the world enthusiastically embraced microfinance for the poor. In India the banks seized upon the new opportunities, realizing that poor Indian families would pay high interest rates for loans not just to improve livelihoods but to pay for medicines for sick parents or to finance a wedding for a daughter.[28] They could cloak these loans in a mantle of civic virtue, describing them as "microcredit," as if they were the same thing that Grameen and BRAC were doing in neighboring Bangladesh—until a wave of suicides from farmers overburdened with debt called attention to the fact that they were *not* the same.

THE MORTGAGE CRISIS AND THE ADMINISTRATION OF THE RULE OF LAW

When the subprime mortgage crisis finally broke wide open, precipitating the Great Recession of 2008, the country's response to the ensuing flood of foreclosures provided a test of America"s "rule of law." At the core of property rights and consumer protection are strong procedural safeguards (such as record keeping) to protect those who enter into contracts. Such safeguards were in place to protect homeowners as well as lenders. If the bank claimed that a person owed it money, then by law it had to provide proof before it could just throw someone out into the streets. When a mortgage (an IOU from a homeowner to a lender) is transferred from one lender to another, then by law a clear record of what the borrower has repaid, and what he owes, must accompany the mortgage.

The banks had issued so many mortgages, so rapidly, that they had given short shrift to basic procedural safeguards. And as the banks and other lenders rushed to lend more and more money, not surprisingly fraudulent practices became endemic. FBI investigations spiked.[29] The combination of frequent fraudulent practices and a disregard of procedural safeguards was lethal.

The banks wanted a speedier and less costly way of transferring claims, so they created their own system, called MERS (Mortgage Electronic Registry System), but, like so much of what the banks had done in the gold rush days, it proved to be a deficient system, without safeguards, and amounted to an end run around a legal system intended to protect debtors. As one legal expert put it, "MERS and its members believed that they could rewrite property law without a democratic mandate."[30]

When the housing bubble finally burst, the dangers of banks' recklessness in lending and record keeping became apparent. By law, banks were supposed to be able to prove the amounts owed. It turned out that in many cases, they simply could not.

All of this has complicated the process of cleaning up the ensuing mess. The sheer numbers of mortgages in default, running in the millions, made the task even worse. The immensity of the task led the banks to invent "robo-signing." Instead of hiring people to examine records, to verify that the individual did owe the amount claimed, signing an affidavit at the end that they had done so, many banks arranged for a single person to sign hundreds of these affidavits without even looking at the records. Checking records to comply with legal procedure would hurt the bank's bottom line. The banks adopted a policy of *lying to the court*. Bank officers knew this—the system was set up in a way that made it impossible for them to examine the records, as they claimed to have done.

This brought a new twist to the old doctrine of too-big-to-fail. The big banks knew that they were so big that if they lost on their gambles of risky lending they would have to be bailed out. They also knew that they were so big that if they got caught lying, they were too big and powerful to be held accountable. What was the government to do? Reverse the millions of foreclosures that had already occurred? Fine the banks billions of dollars—as the authorities should have done? But this would have put the banks again in a precarious position, requiring another government bailout, for which it had neither the money nor the political will. Lying to a court is normally a very serious matter. Lying to the court routinely, hundreds of times, should have been an even greater offense. There was a true pattern of crime. If corporations had been people[31] in a state that enforced a "three strikes" rule (three instances of shoplifting, and one faces a mandatory life sentence), these repeat offenders would have been sentenced to multiple life sentences, without parole. In fact, no bank officer has gone to jail for these offenses. Indeed, as this book goes to press, neither Attorney General Eric Holder nor any of the other U.S. district attorneys have brought suits for foreclosure fraud. By contrast, following the savings and loan crisis, by 1990, the Department of Justice had been sent 7,000 criminal referrals, resulting in 1,100 charges by 1992, and 839 convictions (of which around 650 led to a prison sentence).[32] Today, while the banks have made a partial settlement of some $26 billion over foreclosure fraud, the cost will be borne by the banks' shareholders, not by the bank officers whose bonuses were inflated by their fraudulent behavior.[33]

What the banks did was not just a matter of failing to comply with a few technicalities. This was not a victimless crime. To many bankers, the perjury committed as they signed affidavits to rush the foreclosures was just a detail that could be overlooked. But a basic principle of the rule of law and property rights is that you shouldn't throw someone out of his home when you can't prove he owes you money. But so assiduously did the banks pursue their foreclosures that some people were thrown out of their homes who did not owe any money. To some lenders this is just collateral damage as the banks tell millions of Americans they must give up their homes—some eight million since the crisis began, and an

estimated three to four million still to go.[34] The pace of foreclosures would have been even higher had it not been for government intervention to stop the robo-signing.

The banks' defense—that most of the people thrown out
of their homes did owe money—was evidence that America
had strayed from the rule of law and from a basic understanding of it. One is supposed to be innocent until proven guilty.
But in the banks' logic, the homeowner had to prove that he
was not guilty, that he didn't owe money. In our system of justice it is unconscionable to convict an innocent person, and it
should be equally unconscionable to evict anyone who doesn't
owe money on her home. We are supposed to have a system
that protects the innocent. The U.S. justice system requires a
burden of proof and establishes procedural safeguards to help
meet that requirement. But the banks short-circuited these
safeguards.

In fact, the system we had in place made it easy for them
to get away with these shortcuts—at least until there was a
popular uproar. In most states, homeowners could be thrown
out of their homes without a court hearing. Without a hearing, an individual cannot easily (or at all) forestall an unjust
foreclosure. To some observers, this situation resembles what
happened in Russia in the days of the "Wild East" after the
collapse of communism, where the rule of law—bankruptcy
legislation in particular—was used as a legal mechanism
to replace one group of owners with another. Courts were
bought, documents forged, and the process went smoothly. In
America, the venality operates at a higher level. It is not particular judges who are bought but the laws themselves, through
campaign contributions and lobbying, in what has come to
be called "corruption, American-style." In some states judges
are elected, and in those states there's an even closer con-

nection between money and "justice." Monied interests use campaign contributions to get judges who are sympathetic to their causes.[35]

The administration's response to the massive violations of the rule of law by the banks reflects our new style of corruption: the Obama administration actually fought *against* attempts by states to hold the banks accountable. Indeed, one of the federal-government controlled banks[36] threatened to cease doing business in Massachusetts when that state's attorney general brought suit against the banks.

Massachusetts attorney general Martha Coakley had tried to reach a settlement with the banks for over a year, but they had proved intransigent and uncooperative. To them the crimes they had committed were just a matter for negotiation. The banks (she charged) had acted both deceptively and fraudulently; they had not only improperly foreclosed on troubled borrowers (citing fourteen instances), relying to do so on fraudulent legal documentation, but they had also, in many cases, promised to modify loans for homeowners and then reneged on the promise. The problems were not accidental but systematic, with the MERS recording system "corrupting" the framework put into place by the state for recording ownership. The Massachusetts attorney general was explicit in rejecting the "too big to be accountable" argument: "The banks may think that they are too big to fail or too big to care about the impact of their actions, but we believe they are not too big to have to obey the law."[37]

In late February 2012, the *Wall Street Journal* uncovered another unsavory aspect of America's foreclosure crisis. Just as we noted in chapter 3 that there had been discrimination in the issuance of mortgages, so too in the foreclosure process—this time not on the basis of race but on the basis of income. On average, it took banks two years and two months to foreclose on mortgages over $1 million, six months longer than on those under $100,000. There were many reasons for this, including banks' exerting greater efforts to accommodate these big debtors and borrowers' being better armed with lawyers to defend themselves.[38]

The discussion of this chapter, along with that of chapter 6, has shown how the financial sector made sure that the "rule of law" works in its favor *almost always*, and against ordinary Americans. It has the resources, the organization, and the incentives to do so; and it accomplished what it set out to do, through a multifaceted attack that included reforming bankruptcy laws to increase their power over borrowers, ensuring that private, for-profit schools could get access to student loans, almost regardless of standards, abolishing usury laws, preventing legislation to curtail predatory lending, and circumventing the procedural safeguards, weak as they were, to make sure that only individuals who really owed money would lose their homes. But in lending and in foreclosures they targeted the weak, the poorly educated, the poor. Moral scruples were set aside in the grand quest to move money from the bottom to the top.

In chapter 6 we explained how the foreclosure crisis could itself have been largely avoided, if we had only not let the banks have so much influence, by allowing an orderly restructuring of debt, just as we do for large corporations. At each step of the way, from the initial making of loans to the final foreclosure, there were alternatives and regulations that would have curtailed the reckless and predatory lending and enhanced economic stability—perhaps even avoiding the Great Recession itself—but with a political system where money matters, these alternatives had no chance.

The mortgage debacle and the persistence of predatory lending and bankruptcy "reform" have raised deep questions about "the rule of law," which is the universally accepted hallmark of an advanced, civilized society. The rule of law is supposed to protect the weak against the strong and ensure fair treatment for all. In the wake of the subprime mortgage crisis, it has done neither. Instead of a rule of law that protected the weak, we had laws and regulations and a system of enforcement that further empowered the already powerful banks. In moving money from the bottom to the top, they worsened the problems of inequality in both tails of the income and wealth distribution.

DE FACTO VS. DE JURE

Running a judicial system is costly, and the rules of the game determine how large those costs are and who bears them. If one designs a costly system in which the parties themselves bear the cost, then one is designing an unfair system, even if in principle it seems otherwise. If one designs a slow judicial system, that too can be unfair. It's not just that "justice delayed is justice denied," but that the poor can't bear the costs of delay as well as the rich. Corporations know this. In their negotiations with less wealthy opponents a standard tactic is to make a small up-front offer and threaten to impose a long and costly process with an uncertain outcome if the offer is not accepted.[39]

Even access to the legal system is expensive, and that gives an advantage to large corporations and the wealthy. We talk about the importance of intellectual property, but we have designed an expensive and unfair intellectual property regime that works more to the advantage of patent lawyers and large corporations than to the advancement of science and small innovators.[40] Large firms can trespass on the intellectual property rights of smaller ones almost with impunity, knowing that in the ensuing legal fight they can outgun them. Rogue patent trolls (law firms) can buy sleeping patents (patents that have not yet been used to bring products to the market) at a low price, and then when a firm is successful in the same field, claim trespass, and threaten to shut it down as a form of extortion.

That's what happened to Research in Motion, the producer of the popular BlackBerry, which became the target of a patent suit from "patent-holding company" NTP, Inc. That company is currently also in litigation involving Apple, Google, Microsoft, Verizon Wireless, AT&T, Yahoo! and T-Mobile USA.[41] It wasn't even clear whether the patents that were supposedly infringed were valid. But until their claims are reviewed and declared invalid—which may take years and years—the "owners" of the patent can shut down any firm that might trespass, unless it pays *whatever* fee and accepts *whatever* conditions are imposed upon it, including the condition that the patent not be challenged. In this case, BlackBerry gave in to the demands and paid more than $600 million to NTP.[42]

More recently, the cell phone industry has been engaged in a tangle of patent disputes (involving Apple, Samsung, Ericsson, Google, Microsoft, Motorola, Nokia, RIM, LG, HP, and a patent holder, Acacia Research Corporation), in a variety of legal forums in different countries. While the outcome is uncertain—if certain parties win, the range of choices consumers face may be dramatically reduced and prices increased—what is certain is that the big winners in these battles will be the lawyers.

The legal system itself extracts large rents, as we noted in chapter 2. The big legal battles to enforce the laws that exist—say, over whether Microsoft violated the laws designed to maintain a competitive marketplace or whether the banks committed fraud—entail battalions of lawyers. There has been an arms race; and it's an arms race in which the banks that engage in fraud or the firms that engage in anticompetitive practices have the big advantage, especially since private firms do what they can to circumscribe government's ability to spend. The consequence is illustrated by how the Securities and Exchange Commission has pursued repeated occurrences of fraud by America's banks.

The SEC and securities fraud

I have described how the banks tried to take advantage of ordinary homeowners in the mortgage market. The banks tried to take advantage of the more financially sophisticated as well. The SEC (the U.S. Securities and Exchange Commission, which is in charge of enforcing the federal securities laws) has repeatedly brought civil enforcement actions against Citibank and other major banks for violations of the fraud laws.

What happens after that has generally followed this path: The banks threaten a never-ending legal battle. Compromise follows: the banks pay a large fine, neither admitting nor denying guilt. They also promise never to do such a thing again. But soon after their promise, they engage in similar behavior again. Then they incur another scolding and a fine they can afford.

It's a convenient solution: the government has limited resources to prosecute legal cases, and there are many instances of fraud. Having reached a settlement on one, the government can then go on to attack another. The system also suits the banks: the cost is low relative to the profits they reap from their fraudulent behavior, and, had they admitted guilt, the evidence could have been used against them in private litigation brought by those the fraud injured in their attempt to recover their losses. The banks know that most of their victims don't have the legal resources to challenge them without the government's help. No one can claim that justice is really being done in this system. An economic system in which there is a pattern of such abuses can't work well: fraud distorts the economy and undermines trust.

A court has to approve the SEC settlements, and the courts typically approve them pro forma. But for one judge the level of fraud finally proved too much. In late November 2011, Judge Rakoff of the U.S. District Court in Manhattan rejected a proposed $285 million settlement from Citigoup on a fraud charge. He noted that the bank had been a repeated offender, a "recidivist." It was clear that the SEC enforcement actions were having little effect on its behavior, partly because the SEC didn't bring contempt charges against repeated offenders like Citibank for violating their promises.

In this case, Citibank (like many of the other banks, including Goldman Sachs) had constructed securities consisting of mortgages that it believed would fail, partly so that it (or, in the case of some other banks, favored customers) could bet against the securities. When the values declined, the bank (or its favored customers) made huge profits at the expense of the bank's clients who purchased the securities. Many of the banks didn't disclose what they were doing. One variant of their defense was caveat emptor: "No one *should* trust us, and anyone who does is a fool." But in the case whose settlement Judge Rakoff rejected, Citibank and some of the other banks had gone beyond keeping silent on the risks: they had falsely told investors that an independent party was choosing the portfolio's investments. While investors lost $700 million in the deal, Citibank made $160 million.

If this were an isolated instance, it could be blamed on a few individuals. But the *New York Times*, in an analysis of SEC fraud settlements, "found 51 instances, involving 19 companies, in which the agency claimed that a company had broken fraud laws that they previously had agreed never to breach."[43]

It would seem we have an economic and legal system that provides incentives for bad behavior: the executives' pay goes up when profits go up, even if the profits are based on fraud; but the company's shareholders pay the fines. In many cases the executives who were responsible for the fraudulent behavior have been long gone. There is something to be said here for criminal prosecutions against executives. If the shareholders pay the fines, and management pays itself compensation based on short-term performance and hiding risks in the tails of the return distribution (the events that occur with small likelihood, like getting caught, prosecuted, *and* fined), we shouldn't be surprised at these persistent patterns of fraud. In such circumstances, we have to go beyond fining the company: it is people who make decisions and take actions, and they should bear responsibility for their actions. Those who commit these crimes can't just shift their accountability to an abstract entity called the "corporation."

CONCLUDING COMMENTS

The need for a strong rule of law is widely accepted, but it also matters what kind of rules there are and how they are administered. In designing the system of laws and regulations that govern an economy and a society, there are trade-offs: some laws and regulations favor one group, others another.

We have examined several examples where what has happened was perhaps predictable: the laws and regulations, and how they are implemented and enforced, reflect the interests of the top layer of society more than those of the people in the middle and at the bottom.

Growing inequality, combined with a flawed system of campaign finance, risks turning America's legal system into a travesty of justice. Some may still call it the "rule of law," but in today's America the proud claim of "justice for all" is being replaced by the more modest claim of "justice for those who can afford it." And the number of people who can afford it is rapidly diminishing.

CHAPTER EIGHT

THE BATTLE OF
THE BUDGET

WITH THE ONSET OF THE GREAT RECESSION, government revenues plummeted, and the nation's deficit and debt soared. A cry soon went out in the United States and Europe that deficits had to be brought under control as soon as possible, typically by drastic cuts in expenditures—in programs referred to as *austerity*.

President Obama set up a bipartisan deficit reduction commission, headed by the former Wyoming senator Alan K. Simpson and President Bill Clinton's former chief of staff Erskine Bowles.[1] A Washington think tank, the Bipartisan Policy Center, came out with its own proposal.[2] The head of the Budget Committee in the House of Representatives, Paul Ryan of Wisconsin, offered another.[3] By the summer of 2011 debate over the budget had turned rancorous, and House Republicans effectively held the country for ransom, refusing to allow an increase in the debt ceiling, unless it was accompanied by a commitment to substantial deficit reduction—either cutting expenditures or raising taxes.[4]

This budget brinkmanship obscured the real economic challenges facing the country: the immediate problem posed by the high level of unemployment and the gap between the economy's potential output and its actual output, and the long-term problem of growing inequality. The brinkmanship shifted attention away from these problems to the issues of deficit and debt reduction.

As the recommendations of the various commissions came in, some actually proposed lowering taxes at the top and increasing taxes in the middle. They ignored how the deficit—the gap between the governments expenditures and revenues—had come about in the first place. If they had focused on the true origins of the deficit, they would have realized that there were more straightforward ways of getting it under control. In this chapter, I seek to recast the debate. I will show how budget, tax, and expenditure policies can actually be used to reduce our country's inequality at the same time that they promote economic growth and bring the deficit under control.

The History of the Deficits

It may be hard to remember now, but just a decade before seemingly out-of-control deficits rose to the top of the nation's policy agenda, the country had large surpluses, some 2 percent of GDP. So large were the surpluses that Fed chairman Alan Greenspan fretted that the entire national debt would soon be repaid, and that would make the conduct of monetary policy difficult. (The way the Federal Reserve increases or decreases interest rates is to sell or buy government Treasury bills, but if there was no government debt, there would be no Treasury bills to buy and sell.) There was (according to him) an answer to this potential crisis: Bush's proposed tax cut, most of the benefits of which went to the rich. Greenspan's support for the 2001 tax cut was pivotal.[5]

The argument should have been viewed with skepticism: had the forecasts been accurate, with the national debt at some future date in danger of being paid off, he and the president could have appealed to Congress to increase spending or cut taxes. It is inconceivable that they would not have complied quickly enough to avoid the alleged looming disaster of the elimination of the national debt. For the critics of these tax cuts, it seemed that Greenspan's agenda had less to do with monetary policy and more to do with downsizing government. And for those concerned about the country's increasing inequality, the combination of tax cuts targeted at the top and weakened social protection programs for lower- and middle-income Americans that would inevitably follow as fiscal constraints tightened was particularly troubling.

It wasn't long before the surpluses turned to deficits under the influence of four major forces. The first was the tax cuts themselves. The intervening years have shown the magnitude by which they exceeded what the country could afford: by 2010 the Congressional Budget Office (CBO) was predicting that if the tax cuts were extended for the next decade, the budgetary costs for 2011–20 would be $3.3 trillion.[6] Of the 2012 budget deficit, around a fifth is attributed to the Bush tax cuts.[7]

The second contributor to the dramatic change in the country's fiscal position was the expenses incurred in the wars in Iraq and Afghanistan, with budgetary costs (over the long run) estimated to exceed $2 to $3 trillion. The budgetary costs will, in fact, go on for decades: almost 50 percent of returning troops are eligible to receive some level of disability payment, and such payments and health care costs for these veterans are likely to approach or exceed a trillion dollars.[8] Even as the Iraq war was being brought to an end in 2011, war spending still accounted for at least 15 percent of the 2012 budget deficit.[9] Instead of raising taxes to pay for these ventures, we put them on the credit card, with compounding consequences for the debt, especially in the years before the Great Recession. At a 5 percent interest rate, a $2 trillion national debt requires $100 billion to service it (even if no attempt were made to repay), year after year. Right now, that interest bill is low, because interest rates are so low; but it is a bill that will grow much larger when the economy recovers and interest rates return to normal.

While the United States was fighting those wars, it increased its other military spending by hundreds of billions of dollars[10]—including spending for what critics said were weapons that didn't work, against enemies that didn't exist. You might not have suspected that the Cold War was over by looking at the Defense Department and CIA spending. America was spending as if it was still ongoing: its military expenditures totaled that of the entire rest of the world put together.[11]

While the tens of thousands of Iraqis and Afghanis, and the thousands of young Americans who became disabled or died fighting in these wars have paid a high price, every public expenditure, every venture, has winners as well as losers, and this is the case here too: defense contractors walked away with excess profits, some of which got "recycled" in the form of campaign contributions. Some of this spending took the form of "rents" (as we called them in chapter 2), with government paying prices greater than competitive market rates. The $7 billion Halliburton no-bid contract at the start of the Iraq war was a classic example. We described in chapter 6 the high costs associated with contracting, in which the government pays more than it would if government employees provided the services. The cost of weapons systems has soared even as the government has tried to rein it in: the $382 billion Lockheed Martin F-35 Joint Striker Fighter by itself costs half of the entire Obama stimulus program.[12] (One can understand why so many people are upset with current budget priorities: there is money for a fighter jet that critics say doesn't help in the types of conflicts the United States finds itself in, and likely will in the future, but there's no more money to help homeowners stay in their homes.)

The third large source of the increase in the deficit was the new Medicare drug benefit, and while the benefit itself made sense, part of the cost was another huge "rent"—this time not to the military contractors but to the pharmaceutical industry. We noted earlier that a small detail—a provision in the bill providing the drug benefit to Medicare recipients which said that the government, the largest buyer of drugs in the world, couldn't negotiate prices with the drug companies—was a gift worth, by some estimates, a half trillion dollars over ten years.[13]

The biggest difference between the world of 2001, when we expected a large federal budget surplus, and the world of 2011, when we faced yawning deficits as far as the eye could see, though, was the Great Recession. Any recession causes a decrease in revenues and an increase in expenditures (for unemployment insurance and social programs), and a recession of the magnitude of the Great Recession of 2008 causes a major reversal in the fiscal position of a country. Spain and Ireland also had budget surpluses before the crisis and now are on the verge of fiscal collapse. Even as the American economy was supposedly entering into recovery, in 2012 the downturn accounted for almost two-thirds of the deficit—16 percent of the deficit was for measures to stimulate the economy (the stimulus package that included tax cuts, aid to states, and public investment); but almost half (48 percent) of the entire deficit was a result of the underperformance of the economy, which led to lower tax revenues and higher expenditures on unemployment insurance, food stamps, and other social protection programs. These shortfalls reflect the fact that the U.S. GDP in 2012 is predicted to be nearly $900 billion short of its potential.[14]

The critical point to bear in mind in thinking about deficit reduction is that the recession caused the deficits, not the other way around. More austerity will only worsen the downturn, and the hoped-for improvement in the fiscal position will not emerge.

KILLING THREE BIRDS WITH ONE STONE

The *causes* of the reversal in the U.S. fiscal position provide a clear prescription for how to put it on a firm foundation: reverse the Bush era tax cuts for millionaires, end the wars and scale back defense spending, allow the government to negotiate drug prices, and, most importantly, put the country back to work. Restoring the country to full employment would do more than anything else to improve the country's fiscal position. While all of these actions would help to address current budget woes, improve the distribution of income, and make money available for investments that could improve future growth, there are a few other reforms that would go still further.[15]

Making the tax system *fair* is one such reform. Right now, as we noted in chapter 3, speculators are taxed at a fraction of the rate of those who work for their living. It's a prime example of how those in the 1 percent have convinced the rest of society that what is in their interests is in the interests of all. The lower tax rates on capital gains didn't lead to higher sustainable growth, but rather fed two speculative booms: it's not an accident that, in quick succession, after the capital gains tax cuts of 1997 and the early 2000s, America experienced both a tech bubble and a housing bubble.[16]

So too, Bush argued successfully in 2003 for a (temporary) cut on the tax on dividends, to a maximum of 15 percent, less than half the rate paid by someone who receives a comparable income in the form of wages and salaries. The claim was that it would lead to more investment by firms in plant and equipment, but it didn't. Arguably, it may have had the opposite effect. As we observed in chapter 4, firms were, in effect, encouraged to pay out dividends while the tax rates were low, leaving fewer funds inside the corporation for a good investment project, should one have turned up.[17]

Beyond this, making the tax system not only more fair but more progressive would involve closing loopholes and enacting increases in the tax rates at the top and reductions in tax rates at the bottom. The exemption of interest on municipal bonds is an example of an inefficient "loophole" of far more benefit to the rich than to the municipalities, the *alleged* beneficiaries. The tax deductibility allows cities to borrow at a lower rate—but only slightly lower. If, for simplicity of arithmetic, the interest rate had been 10 percent, the tax exemption might lower the rate that a city could borrow to 9 percent. On a $100 million bond, the city then saves $1 million a year. The bondholders, many of them in the top tax bracket, get $9 million in interest payments and owe no taxes on their interest income. But suppose they had faced a combined federal and state tax of 40 percent. They would have had to pay $4 million in taxes and reaped after-tax returns of $6 million. In our current system they take home $9 million. While it's true the city saves $1 million, to deliver that $1 million of assistance, the state and federal government have to give up $4 million in tax revenues. Wealthy bondholders get three times the benefit that is received by cities. It would have been far more efficient to give the cities a direct subsidy from the federal government.[18]

A basic principle of economics holds that it is highly efficient to tax rents because such taxes don't cause any distortion. A tax on land rents doesn't make the land go away. Indeed, the great nineteenth-century progressive Henry George argued that government should rely solely on such a tax.[19] Today, of course, we realize that rents can take many forms—they can be collected not just on land, but on the value of natural resources like oil, gas, minerals, and coal.[20] There are other sources of rents, such as those derived from the exercise of monopoly power. A stiff tax on all such rents would not only reduce inequality but also reduce incentives to engage in the kind of rent-seeking activities that distort our economy and our democracy.

The Right suggests that all taxes are distortionary, but that's simply not true: the rent taxes would actually improve economic efficiency. But there are some new taxes that might do so even more.

A basic principle in economics is that it is better to tax bad things than good things. Compared with taxing work (a productive thing), it is better to tax pollution (a bad thing, whether it's oil that pollutes our oceans from spills of oil companies, toxic wastes produced by chemical firms, or toxic assets created by financial firms). Those who pollute do not bear the costs they impose on the rest of society. The fact that those who generate water or air pollution (including greenhouse gas emissions) do not pay the social costs of their actions is a major distortion in the economy; a tax would help correct this distortion, discouraging activities that create negative externalities, shifting resources into areas where social contributions are higher. Firms that are not paying the full costs they impose on others are, in effect, being subsidized. At the same time, such a tax could raise literally trillions of dollars over a ten-year period.

Oil, gas, coal, chemical, paper, and many other companies have polluted our environment. But the financial companies polluted the global economy with toxic mortgages. The financial sector has imposed enormous externalities on the rest of society—as we noted, the total costs of the financial crisis for which they bear significant responsibility is in the trillions of dollars. In earlier chapters we saw how flash trading and other speculation may create volatility, but not really create value: the overall efficiency of the market economy may even be reduced.

The polluter pay principle says that polluters should pay the costs that they impose on others. Through our bailouts and a myriad of hidden subsidies, we have in fact been effectively subsidizing the financial sector. There is a growing demand for the imposition of a variety of taxes on the financial sector, including a financial transactions tax, a tax on all financial transactions at a very low rate, or at least on a selected set of such transactions, like foreign exchange transactions. France is already in the process of adopting one. The UK has a more limited variant. The heads of Spain and Germany and the

European Commission have advocated such a tax. Even at very low rates, it would raise substantial revenues.

There are other ways of raising revenues—simply stop giving away resources at below-market prices to oil, gas, and mining companies. The giveaways can be thought of as a subsidy to these companies. The government needs to make sure that it's not giving away willy-nilly billions of dollars, as it does when it allows TV stations to use spectrum without charge, when it allows mining companies to pay a minimal royalty, rather than auctioning off the rights to exploit these natural resources, when it conducts a fire sale on oil and gas leases, rather than a well-designed auction to maximize the revenue to the public.[21]

There are still other ways of raising more revenue: closing the hidden subsidies to corporations buried in our tax code (what we referred to in chapter 6 as corporate welfare), or eliminating the loopholes and other special provisions that have enabled so many American corporations to escape so much of the taxes that they should be paying.

In chapter 6 we presented evidence on the importance that most Americans give to fairness. Earlier chapters showed that, with many of those at the very top paying a smaller percentage of their income in taxes than those who are not so well-off, our tax system is not fair—and is widely perceived not to be fair. Our tax system relies, to some extent at least, on voluntary compliance; but if the tax system is viewed not to be fair, such compliance will not be forthcoming. We will become like so many other countries where compliance is either weak or attained only through intrusive and forceful measures. But creating a fairer tax system can also raise substantial additional revenues.

Levying additional taxes involves a simple principle: go where the money is. Since money has been increasingly going to the top, that's where additional tax revenues have to come from. It's really that simple. It used to be said that the top didn't have enough money to fill the hole in the deficit; but that's becoming less and less true. With those in the top 1 percent getting more than 20 percent of the nation's income, an incremental 10 percent tax on their income (without loopholes) would generate revenues equal to some 2 percent of the nation's GDP.

In short, *if* we were serious about deficit reduction, we could easily raise trillions of dollars over the next ten years simply by (a) raising taxes on people in the top—because they get so much of the nation's economic pie, even small increases in tax rates raises substantial revenues; (b) eliminating loopholes and special treatment of the kind of income earned disproportionately by the top—from lower tax rates for speculators and dividends to exemption of municipal interest; (c) eliminating the loopholes and special provisions of the individual and corporate tax system that subsidize corporations; (d) taxing rents at higher rates; (e) taxing pollution; (f) taxing the financial sector, at least to reflect in part the costs it has repeatedly imposed on the rest of the economy; and (g) making those who get to use or exploit our nation's resources—resources that rightfully belong to *all* Americans—pay full value. These revenue raisers would not only make for a more efficient economy and substantially reduce the deficit but also reduce inequality. That's precisely why these simple ideas have not been front and center in the budget debate. Because so many in the 1 percent derive too much of their income from the sectors that get these gifts—

from oil, gas, and other forms of environmentally polluting activities, from the subsidies hidden in the tax code, from the ability to obtain our nation's resources on the cheap, from myriad special benefits given to the financial sector—these proposals have not been focal points of the standard deficit reduction agenda.

Just as we can design a tax system that raises more money and enhances efficiency and equality, so too for expenditures. In chapter 2 we saw the role of rents in enhancing incomes at the top and noted that some rents are just gifts from the government. In earlier chapters I described the important functions the government needs to perform. One of these is social protection—helping the poor and providing insurance to all Americans when the private sector fails to do so adequately or on reasonable terms. But while some welfare programs for the poor have been curtailed in recent years, what we described in chapter 6 as corporate welfare, subsidies to corporations, have increased.

Of course, whenever proposals to reduce or eliminate subsidies (hidden or open) are broached, the recipients of those subsidies try to defend them as being *in the public interest.* There is here a certain irony, in that many of these corporations and recipients of government largesse simultaneously argue against government spending—for a small government. It is human nature that self-interest shapes judgments of fairness. The influence can, in fact, be subconscious. But as we have repeatedly observed, these subsidies and the efforts to get them distort our economy and our political system.

In the next section, we'll explain how, by cutting these subsidies, and spending the money elsewhere, we can actually increase employment.[22]

SQUARING THE CIRCLE: STIMULATING THE ECONOMY IN AN ERA OF BUDGET DEFICITS AND INADEQUATE DEMAND

If the economy were at full employment, we would focus on the "supply side" effects of reforms to the tax code and expenditure programs, reforms like the elimination of corporate welfare that reduce distortions, thereby increasing productivity and GDP, *even as they raise more revenue.*

Today, however, the Right advocates a curious combination of supply- and demand-side measures: deficit reduction, it is somehow argued, will restore confidence in the country and its economy, and thus be positive; and tax reductions will improve the efficiency of the economy and put money in the hands of those who can spend it well. Of course, if deficits are to be reduced at the same time that taxes are being reduced, it means expenditures have to be reduced by a lot. And that's the true agenda—downsizing government. Indeed, since most on the Right want to protect military expenditures, the necessary reductions in education, research, infrastructure—all the nondefense expenditures—would eviscerate these programs.

But this agenda would not only jeopardize the country's future growth; it would deepen the current economic downturn. In this section I explain how the government can stimulate the economy even while it keeps its focus on debt, and how the agenda of the Right almost surely will be disastrous.

The government could borrow today to invest in its future—for example, ensuring quality education for poor and middle-class Americans and developing technologies that increase the demand for America's skilled labor force, and simultaneously protect the environment. These high-return investments would improve the country's balance sheet (which looks simultaneously at assets *and* liabilities) and yield a return more than adequate to repay the very low interest at which the country can borrow. All good businesses borrow to finance expansion. And if they have high-return investments, and face low costs of capital—as the United States does today—they borrow liberally.

The United States is in an especially good position to pursue this strategy, both because returns to public investments are so high, as a result of underinvestment for a quarter century, and because it can borrow so cheaply *long term.* Unfortunately, especially among the Right (but even, alas, among many in the center) *deficit fetishism* has gained ground. The rating agencies—still trusted in spite of their incredibly bad performance in recent decades—have joined the fray, downgrading U.S. debt. But the test of the quality of debt is the risk premium that investors demand. As this book goes to press, there is a demand for U.S. T-bills at interest rates near zero (and in real terms, negative).

Although deficit fetishism can't be justified on the basis of economic principles, it may be becoming part of the reality. The strategy of investing in the country's future would in the medium to long run reduce the national debt; but in the short run, the government would have to borrow, and those under the influence of deficit fetishism argue that doing so is reckless.

There is another strategy that can stimulate the economy, even if there is an insistence that the deficit *now* not increase; it is based on a long-standing principle called the *balanced-budget multiplier.* If the government simultaneously increases taxes and increases expenditure—so that the *current* deficit remains unchanged—the economy is stimulated. Of course, the taxes by themselves dampen the economy, but the expenditures stimulate it. The analysis shows *unambiguously* that the stimulative effect is considerably greater than the contractionary effect. If the tax and expenditure increases are chosen carefully, the increase in GDP can be two to three times the increase in spending.[23] And while the deficit is neither increased nor decreased immediately—by assumption— the national debt is decreased over the intermediate term, because of the increased tax revenues from the increased growth that is brought about.

There is a final way of squaring the circle—stimulating the economy within the confines of the debt and deficit—that works even if government can't increase its overall size. And that's where the reforms we discussed in the preceding section become particularly relevant.

We can take advantage of the extent to which different taxes and expenditures stimulate the economy, spending more on programs that have large multipliers (where each dollar of spending generates more overall GDP) and less on programs that have small multipliers; raising taxes from sources with low multipliers while cutting taxes on those with high multipliers. Money spent paying for foreign contractors in Afghanistan doesn't stimulate the American economy; money spent paying unemployment benefits to the long-term unemployed does, simply because these individuals are so strapped that they tend to spend every dollar given to them. Raising taxes on the very rich reduces spending by at most around 80 cents on the dollar; lowering taxes at the bottom increases spending at almost 100 cents on the dollar. Hence making the tax system more progressive not only reduces inequality but stimulates the economy as well. *Trickle-up economics can work, even when trickle-down economics doesn't.*

Even the rich can benefit from the increased GDP, in some cases even enough to offset the increased taxes they would have to pay. Because government programs that increase rents (whether paying too much in government procurement, subsidies for rich farmers, or corporate welfare) go dispro-portionately to those at the top, cutbacks in these—with the money going for increased investments and improved social protection—increase equity, efficiency, and growth; and in the current situation the overall economy is also stimulated.

The Greek factor

The unfolding debt crisis in Greece and other problems elsewhere in Europe have instilled a fear of debt in many quarters. Many people who look at Europe's crisis see it con-firming their prejudices: it's what happens when one has high taxes and debt and an excessively generous welfare system. But this interpretation of what has been happening in Europe is simply wrong, and there are marked differences between Greece's situation (and the situation of other European coun-tries) and that of the United States—differences arising from the monetary system.

Greece can be convicted of overspending—though, again, there is some culpability of the financial sector; one of Amer-ica's banks helped an earlier government hide its fiscal posi-tions both from its citizens and the EU by using derivatives. But other crisis countries cannot be accused of fiscal profli-gacy: Ireland and Spain had fiscal surpluses before the crisis.

One of the big differences between the United States and Greece (and those other countries) is that while those other countries owe money in euros, over which they have no direct control, U.S. debt is denominated in dollars—and the United

States controls the printing presses. That's why the notion that the United States would default (suggested by one of the rating agencies) borders on the absurd. Of course, there is some chance that, to pay off what's owed, so many dollars would have to be printed that they wouldn't be worth much. But then the issue is *inflation*, and at present the markets just don't think that inflation is a significant risk. One can infer that both from the very low interest rate that the government has to pay on its long-term debt and even more from what it has to pay for inflation-protected bonds (or more accurately, the difference between the returns on ordinary bonds and inflation-protected bonds). Now, the market could be wrong, but then the rating agencies giving a downgrade to the United States should have explained why the market was wrong, and why they believed that there is a much higher risk of inflation than the market believed. The answers have not been forthcoming.

Before the euro, Greece owed money in drachmas. Now it owes money in euros. Not only does Greece owe money in euros, but control of the central bank is vested in Europe. The United States knows that the Fed will buy U.S. government bonds. Greece can't even be sure that the European Central Bank (ECB) will buy Greek bonds owned by its own banks. In fact, the ECB continually threatens not to buy the sovereign bonds of the countries of the eurozone, unless they do as it says.

The Right's alternative

Europe's crisis is not an accident, but it's not caused by excessive long-term debts and deficits or by the "welfare" state. It's caused by excessive austerity—cutbacks in government expenditures that predictably led to the recession of 2012—and a flawed monetary arrangement, the euro. When the euro was introduced, most disinterested economists were skeptical. Changes in exchange rates and interest rates are critical for helping economies adjust. If all of the European countries were buffeted by the same shocks, then a single adjustment of the exchange rate and interest rate would do for all. But different European economies are buffeted by markedly different shocks. The euro had taken away two adjustment mechanisms, and put nothing in its place. It was a political project; politicians thought that sharing a currency would move the countries closer together, but there wasn't enough cohesion within Europe to do what needed to be done to make the euro work. All they agreed upon was not to have too large deficits and debts. But as Spain and Ireland so aptly showed, that wasn't enough. There was hope that over the years, the political project would be finished. But when things were going well, there was no momentum to do anything further; and after the crisis, which affected different countries so differently, there was no will. The countries could agree only on further belt tightening, which forced Europe into a double-dip recession.

Looking across Europe, among the countries that are doing best are Sweden and Norway, with their strong welfare states and large governments, but they chose not to join the euro. Britain is not in crisis, though its economy is in a slump: it too chose not to join the euro, but it too decided to follow the austerity program.

Unfortunately, many members of Congress want the United States to join that same "austerity and small government" bandwagon—to cut back taxes and expenditures. We saw that balanced increases in taxes and expenditures stimulate the economy. By the same token, balanced cutbacks in expenditures and taxes will lead to a contraction in the economy. And if we go one step farther, as the Right wants to do, to cut back expenditures even more, in a valiant if possibly fruitless attempt to reduce the deficit, the contraction will be even greater.

UNMASKING THE DEFICIT AGENDA: PRESERVING AND EXTENDING INEQUALITIES

It might seem strange, in a country where tax rates at the top are already lower than they are in most of the other advanced industrial countries, to have a *deficit reduction program* emphasize the reduction of top tax rates and tax rates on corporations, but that's exactly what the Bowles-Simpson Deficit Reduction Commission did.[24] It proposed limiting the top marginal tax rate to between 23 percent and 29 percent, part of its broader agenda of limiting the size of government, capping overall tax revenues at 21 percent of GDP. Indeed, about three-fourths of the deficit reduction is achieved by cutbacks in government spending.

Reagan supply-side economics, which held that lowering tax rates would increase economic activity, so much so that tax revenues would actually increase, has (as we noted in chapter 3) been disproved by what happened after both the Bush and the Reagan tax cuts. Today individual tax rates are much lower than they were in 1980, suggesting that further reductions in tax rates would lower tax revenues even more.

The argument that the corporate tax rate should be lowered (to between 23 percent and 29 percent, from the current 35 percent)[25] was even less convincing, though the

Bowles-Simpson commission's proposals to close the myriad loopholes, if actually implemented, would mean that many corporations would pay more taxes even though the official rate was lowered. We noted in chapter 3 that the effective tax rate—the fraction of their income that corporations actually pay in taxes—is much less than 35 percent, with some of the country's premier corporations, like GE, paying no taxes. But while there is a compelling case for closing the loopholes, even focusing simply on investment and job creation, there was little case for an across-the-board lowering of the corporate tax rate. After all, with the tax deductibility of interest, the tax lowers the cost of borrowing and the return proportionately. There is no adverse effect on investment for any investment financed through borrowing, and once one takes into account the favorable rates at which capital could be depreciated (businesses are allowed to deduct from their income an amount to reflect the fact that their machines are wearing out), the tax code actually encourages investment.[26] If the commission was concerned about the tax's effect on investment, there were more precise ways to tweak the tax code than an across-the-board cut: it could have suggested lowering the tax on firms that created jobs and invested in America and raising taxes on those that didn't. Such a policy would raise revenues and provide incentives for more investment and job creation in the United States.

Each of the deficit reduction groups sought to address distortionary aspects of the tax code—provisions, many of them deliberately placed by special interests, that encourage specific sectors in the economy. No group, however, suggested a frontal attack on corporate welfare and the hidden subsidies (including to the financial sector) that we've stressed in this book, partly because, as we saw in chapter 6, the Right has succeeded in convincing many Americans that an attack on corporate welfare is "class warfare."

Deductions

Many of the advocates of deficit reduction have given particular attention to a set of deductions that have been of special benefit to the middle class—the interest deduction for mortgages and the deduction for health care benefits.[27] But eliminating these deductions would be an effective increase in taxation on the middle class, whose income has been stagnating or declining for years. Anyone concerned with the plight of the middle class should have seen that if deductions were eliminated, they—not those at the top—should have been compensated with lower tax rates.

Most economists would have supported the elimination of the home mortgage deduction, which leads to too much spending on housing. Additionally, the mortgage deduction can be faulted for encouraging excessive indebtedness. The government was, in effect, subsidizing debt—another hidden subsidy to the bankers who were among the true beneficiaries. And because richer individuals face higher tax rates, they benefit more from the mortgage deduction than do lower-income individuals. The tax deduction, as currently designed, is both distortionary and inequitable. And it may not even be effective in increasing homeownership in urban areas, where so many lower-income individuals live. In those localities, where the supply of housing is limited, the mortgage subsidies may raise prices, making homeownership less affordable.[28]

But the timing of the elimination is a concern: eliminating the deduction would have made housing more expensive, depressing housing prices. Because a quarter of all Americans with mortgages owe more on their mortgages than the value of their houses—some eleven million families—the crisis in the housing sector would have become only worse. There would have been more foreclosures, more depressed communities, and this key sector of the economy would have remained in the doldrums for years to come. The longer the housing market stays depressed, the longer the economy remains in its current state of near-recession.

There is a way around the quandary. In 2009 a first-time home buyer tax credit of $10,000 helped to prop up the housing market by providing first-time buyers with *equity*. Renewing and extending this program to all low-income families would simultaneously help stimulate the housing market, help restore the economy to health, and make it possible for lower-income families to afford homes.

More generally, a variety of tax provisions (like special treatment of retirement accounts) are designed to encourage individuals to save more; whether they actually lead to more savings is questionable, but because they are of much greater benefit to upper-income individuals, they do help enrich the rich who do save. But there is nothing comparable for low-income individuals. If the government provided a cashable tax credit for investments by low-income households (that is, supplemented their savings, even if they didn't pay any taxes), it would provide them with increased incentives to save and might even reduce some of the disparity between the bottom and the top.

An equitable approach to deficit reduction

In short, while deficit reduction is not the major immediate problem facing the economy today, the task of reducing the deficit is not that difficult. Simply reverse the measures that led to the reversal of the government's fiscal position from 2000 to today; raise taxes at the top; cut out corporate welfare and the hidden subsidies; increase taxes on corporations that don't invest and create jobs in the United States relative to those that do; impose taxes and charges on polluters; stop the giveaways of our country's resources; cut back on military waste; and don't overpay for procurement, whether from the drug companies or defense contractors. There's more than enough money in this agenda to meet the most ambitious deficit reduction target set by any of the deficit reduction commissions.

Contrasting this agenda with the reforms proposed by the various commissions, one comes to one of two conclusions: either some of them were deliberately seeking to continue the path of restructuring our economy in ways that benefit the top at the expense of the rest; or they were taken in by some of the myths that have distorted rational economic policy making.

MYTHS

The debate over the budget has been clouded by a set of myths, some of which we have already discussed. The supply-side myth argues that taxing the rich will reduce work and savings and that everyone—not just the rich—will be hurt. Every industry has its own version of the myth that helping them helps everyone: cutting back on military expenditures will cost jobs. Cutting back on tax benefits to the coal or oil industry will cost jobs. Industries that contribute to air or water pollution or that create toxic wastes claim that forcing polluters to pay for the costs they impose on others will cost jobs.

As we've explained, history and theory argue strongly against supply-side economics, but today that's almost beside the point. Today our problem is not supply but demand: large firms at least have the cash on hand to make any investment that they want; but without demand for their products, such investments won't be forthcoming. To stimulate investment, we must focus on how best to stimulate demand. Getting more money into the pockets of those in the middle and at the bottom would do that. That's why deficit reduction proposals that would, in effect, impose much of the burden of tax increases on the middle would simply make things worse.[29]

It is the responsibility of macropolicy—monetary and fiscal policy—to maintain the economy at full employment. When things are going well, and the economy is operating near full employment, excessive military spending and lavish corporate welfare don't create jobs. They just distort the economy by moving labor from more-productive uses to less-productive uses. It is true that if we correct these distortions, some workers with sector-specific skills will suffer, as their skills will no longer be in demand. But that is not an argument for keeping them in place. It is an argument for robust adjustment assistance for the affected workers—assistance that the Right has typically resisted.

Perhaps the myth that's been most effective is the claim that raising taxes on millionaires or corporations will hurt small businesses and therefore cost jobs. In reality very few small businesses would even be affected by such taxes— under 1 percent. But it's only their *profits* that would be slightly reduced. If it were profitable to hire a worker or buy a new machine before the tax, it would still be profitable to do so after the tax. Say hiring a worker yielded the firm a return of $100,000, and the firm had to pay (inclusive of all taxes) $50,000, the firm (small or large) makes a neat profit of $50,000. If the owner now had to pay an extra tax on that profit of 5 percent, it would lower what he netted by $2,500, but it would still be very profitable for him to hire the worker. What is so striking about claims to the contrary is that they fly in the face of elementary economics: no investment, no job that was profitable before the tax increase, will be unprofitable afterward.

There may be a slight concern that in this era of limited credit availability for small firms, a higher tax on millionaires might reduce their *ability* to make desirable investments (simply because they would have less money *after tax* to spend). Ironically, the banks that were so amply supported in the Great Recession claim that it is not the case—good small businesses with good projects can, they say, get the money they need. According to the bankers, the lack of lending to small businesses is not due to the banks' failure to fulfill their side of the bargain (when money was given so freely to the banks, the understanding was that it was so that they could and would continue to lend); it is due to the recession's elimination of good lending opportunities. But even if there is a problem with the ability to invest, there are better ways of handling it than giving a blank check to the corporations and hoping that somehow some of that money will trickle down and eventually create jobs.[30]

Cutbacks to social insurance

When the Right is not viciously defending against even modest increases in taxes for the wealthy, those in the 1 percent and their allies advocate cuts to social insurance—both health care and Social Security (pensions) for the aged, often

disparagingly called *middle-class entitlements*. The Right
fought against the adoption of both of these programs. Now
it's blaming these programs for the country's fiscal difficulties.

In its most hopeful scenarios, the Right would privatize
both services. Privatization, of course, is based on yet another
myth: that government-run programs *must* be inefficient, and
privatization accordingly *must* be better. In fact, as we noted
in chapter 6, the transaction costs of Social Security and
Medicare are much, much lower than those of private-sector
firms providing comparable services. This should not come
as a surprise. The objective of the private sector is to make
profits—for private companies, transactions costs are a good
thing; the difference between what they take in and what they
pay out is what they want to maximize.[31]

The gap between revenues and expenditures for public programs does create problems over the long run. In the case of
Social Security, the gap is probably relatively small, with a high
degree of uncertainty. Social Security's fiscal position depends
heavily on forecasts of wages, population, and longevity. Economic forecasters didn't do a very good job of predicting the
Great Recession even a year before it occurred, so no one
should put much credence in economic forecasts forty years
out. It is even possible that the program will be in surplus,
especially if the level of immigration continues at its prerecession pace, relative to the size of the population. Of course, we
have to be attuned to the possibility that there will be a large
long-term deficit in the Social Security program and that there
will have to be changes to either contributions or benefits.

A few adjustments now do make sense: increasing the maximum income for which contributions are made (in 2011 contributions were only made up to $106,800 of income, with the
result that less than 86 percent of wages were subject to the

payroll tax); continuing the adjustment of the age of retirement as longevity increases (but this must be accompanied by
increased support for those who have to retire early as a result
of partial disability); and increasing the progressivity of the
system to better reflect the increasing inequality in our society. Those at the top currently get slightly less than they contribute; those at the bottom slightly more. Tilting the balance
a little more would, with the extension of the contributions to
upper-income individuals, both help those at the bottom and
put Social Security on firmer financial footing. In the longer
run, there may have to be some additional adjustments, say, a
slight increase in taxes, a slight decrease in benefits; but even
in the standard scenarios the gap is moderate.[32]

Social Security has been an impressively successful program, which has not only almost eliminated poverty among
the elderly[33] but also provided a kind of security that no private insurance program can match, protecting against volatility in the stock market as well as against inflation. Many
Americans who have relied on private pensions know what
I'm talking about: even as government programs attempt to
make sure that private pensions are adequately capitalized,
firms have gamed their employees. Before the companies go
bankrupt, their CEOs walk off with large pay; but the pension
funds are put at risk.

President Bush's agenda for privatization of Social Security
was not about providing more money to America's retirees or
more security or about increasing efficiency. It was about
one thing only: providing more money to the 1 percent at
the expense of the 99 percent—more money to Wall Street.
The magnitudes involved are potentially enormous. Think of
the $2.6 trillion in the Social Security fund. If Wall Street
could get just 1 percent per year for managing that money,

that would be an extra bonanza for the managers of $26 billion *a year*.

Medicare

The issues involved with the Medicare program are more complicated, but only slightly so. America has an inefficient health care system that delivers first-rate health care to those who are lucky enough to have good health insurance or wealthy enough to afford it without insurance. A system riddled with distortions and rents, health care's high transactions costs feed the profits of the insurance companies, and its high drug prices feed the profits of the pharmaceutical industry. There is one way to solve the long-term deficit associated with Medicare and Medicaid: make the health care sector more efficient. If the cost of delivering health care in the United States were comparable to that of other advanced industrial countries *that achieve better outcomes*, as evidenced, for instance, by longevity or infant or maternal mortality, America's budgetary problems would be solved.[34]

Instead, the deficit reduction commissions and proposals on offer in 2011 either waved their hands—saying that the growth in Medicare spending would have to be capped, without saying how that would be achieved—or, as in the Ryan plan, suggested converting Medicare to a voucher program, in which individuals would be given a chit that they could use to pay for health insurance *in the private market*.[35] Those who couldn't supplement the voucher with their own money would have to make do with the best policy that they could get with the voucher. The implication was clear: if costs of medical care in general increased but spending on the aged was capped, those who could afford to pay more out of their own pocket would have to; and those that could not would have do without—for them, there would be, in effect, rationing.

Most of the reforms in Social Security and Medicare have to be phased in gradually over time, which is why these cutbacks will not have an immediate big effect on current deficit. On the one hand, that's the big advantage: one can talk about fiscal responsibility but not crimp the economy *now*.[36] On the other hand, for the true deficit hawks, that's the big disadvantage. Talk is cheap. The Right wants real cuts in spending now, *and* a promise of future cuts in social programs. But enacting real cuts now will exacerbate the economic downturn and worsen the plight of those in the middle and at the bottom.

Blame the victim

Still another myth is that the poor have only themselves to blame. The unemployed are jobless because they are lazy. They haven't searched hard enough.[37] When faced with a proposal to extend unemployment benefits, advocates of these ideas worry about moral hazard. Providing insurance to the unemployed, they think, reduces their incentive to look for a job, which in turn leads to higher unemployment. Whether such claims are valid when the economy is operating near full employment is not my concern here. With four applicants for every job, however, it should be obvious that the problem today is not the lack of applicants for jobs, but the lack of jobs.[38] If more people searched, there would just be that many more people applying for the few jobs that were available. There would essentially be no change in the level of employment.[39]

Standard fare among central bankers (and others on the

right) maintains that it is not that *they* have failed to manage total demand to keep the economy fully functioning. Instead, they shift blame elsewhere, particularly to workers, for demanding excessive job security and too high wages, undermining the functioning of the labor market. The crisis demonstrated how wrong their views about the labor market were: the United States, with allegedly the most flexible labor market, performed far worse than countries with stronger labor protections (like Sweden and Germany).[40] And the reason is obvious: cuts in wages reduce total demand and deepen the downturn.

AUSTERITY

The worst myths are that austerity will bring recovery and that more government spending will not. The argument is that businessmen, seeing that the government's books are in better shape, will be more confident; more confidence will lead to more investment. Interestingly, on the basis of this argument, the advocates should support our first strategy for economic recovery: higher public investment. Since there are public investment opportunities that are widely believed to have very high expected returns—much higher than the interest rate government has to pay to borrow—more public investment would lead to a lower long-run national debt; and the belief that that was so should instill confidence, bringing on an even stronger burst of economic activity. But the advocates of austerity do not support higher public investment.[41]

Another way to consider the merits of austerity is to look at history. History shows that austerity has almost never worked, and theory explains why we shouldn't be surprised by this. Recessions are caused by *lack of demand*—total demand is less than what the economy is capable of producing. When the government cuts back on spending, demand is lowered even more, and unemployment increases.

Underlying the myth that austerity will bring confidence is often another myth—the myth that the national government's budget is like a household's budget. Every household, sooner or later, has to live within its means. When an economy has high unemployment, the simple rule does not apply to the national budget. This is because an expansion of spending can actually expand production by creating jobs that will be filled by people who would otherwise be unemployed. A single household, by spending more than its revenues, cannot change the macro-economy. A national government can. And the increase in GDP can be a multiple of the amount spent by the government.

Those in finance stress the importance of confidence, but confidence can't be restored by policies that lead to more unemployment and lower output. Confidence can be restored only through policies that lead to growth—and austerity does just the opposite.

Austerity's advocates present evidence of countries in a downturn that have imposed austerity and recovered. But a careful look shows that those countries were all small and had trading partners that were experiencing a boom.[42] Thus, increased exports could easily replace reduced government expenditures. That is not the case today for the United States and Europe, many of whose trading partners are themselves in a slump.[43]

One might have thought that those who advocate austerity would have learned from the plethora of earlier experiences where austerity had disastrous consequences: Herbert Hoover's austerity converted the 1929 stock market crash into the Great Depression, IMF austerity converted the downturns in East Asia and Latin America into recessions and depressions; the self-imposed and forced austerity in several European countries (the UK, Latvia, Greece, Portugal) is now having exactly the same effect. But austerity's advocates haven't seemed to come to terms with this overwhelming evidence. Like the doctors of the Middle Ages who believed in bloodletting, but when the patient didn't get better argued that what they really needed was another round, the blood letters of twenty-first-century economics will not waver. They will demand ever more austerity, and they will find myriad excuses for why the first dosage didn't work as predicted. Meanwhile, unemployment will increase, wages will decrease, and government programs upon which those in the middle and at the bottom rely will wither away.

By contrast, government spending has succeeded. It was ultimately government spending in anticipation of World War II that pulled the country out of the Great Depression. Although the New Deal provided some stimulus, and helped the economy recover between 1933 and 1936, the stimulus was not large enough to overcome the combined effect of the contraction of spending at the state and local levels and the weaknesses in agriculture (incomes of those in that sector, constituting a quarter of the population, fell dramatically in this period—by 50 percent between 1929 and 1932 alone).[44] Then, at the end of Roosevelt's first term, in 1936, worries about the deficit and pressures from fiscal conservatives induced him to cut back federal spending. The economy's recovery was halted, and growth turned negative.[45]

The myth of the failed stimulus

The advocates of austerity counter those who argue for more government spending by saying that such spending will not stimulate the economy. They begin their critique by observing that the almost $800 billion stimulus package enacted in February 2009 didn't save the economy from a deep recession—and neither would more government spending. But the stimulus *did* work: if it hadn't been for the stimulus, the unemployment rate would have peaked in excess of 12 percent, more than 2 percentage points higher than the levels eventually reached.

The administration did make several mistakes. First, it underestimated the depth and duration of the downturn. It thought that without the stimulus unemployment would peak at around 10 percent. Administration economists, some of whom had been connected with the creation of the bubble, underestimated its size. They simply couldn't believe that real estate prices were *that* overinflated; so they believed that the fall in prices would be only temporary, and with the recovery of housing prices consumption would be restored. As businesses saw a quick recovery, they would be reluctant to let their good employees go. The reality was otherwise: there had been an enormous bubble, and with prices still 30 percent below precrisis levels going on five years after the bubble broke—in some places more than 50 percent below precrisis levels—it has become increasingly clear that the real estate sector could be depressed for some time to come, even if the financial sector were perfectly back to health.[46] That's a problem, because before the crisis some 40 percent of all investment was in real estate.

A second mistake was that the administration believed that the primary problem was the financial crisis—not recognizing the underlying need for structural transformation. The enormous increases in productivity in manufacturing, outpacing the increase in demand, inevitably meant that labor

would have to move out of that sector—just as the enormous
increases in agricultural productivity in the years before the
Great Depression meant that labor had to move out of agriculture into manufacturing. Moreover, with globalization an
increasingly large fraction of the jobs in manufacturing would
reside in developing countries and emerging markets, compounding the need for structural transformation.

The administration failed, too, to grasp another fundamental problem, the growing inequality and its impact on what
had happened before the crisis, and what was likely to happen
subsequently. Before the crisis, the average household savings rate was near zero, and that meant that many Americans
were dissaving—had negative savings. With the upper 20 percent of the population holding approximately 40 percent of
the national income and saving approximately 15 percent of
that income (for a total of approximately 6 percent of national
income being saved), it meant that the bottom 80 percent,
with the remaining 60 percent of the national income, had
to be *dissaving* at a rate of 10 percent of their income. Again,
even if the banks were perfectly restored to health and even if
the deleveraging of the household sector (that is, paying down
their excessive indebtedness) was complete, these households shouldn't return to their wayward ways of consuming
persistently beyond their income, and banks shouldn't lend
to them. That's why it's unrealistic to think that the consumption excesses of the precrisis level will resume.

And, of course, the declining share of wages—the increasing inequality—will make the recovery all the more difficult,
without government assistance.

These mistakes in economic analysis had consequences.
The belief that the economy would recover quickly on its
own—once the banks had been brought back to health with

government assistance—led to a stimulus package that was too small and too short-lived. Because the administration thought the downturn would be short, it thought firms would hold on to their workers; but businesses knew otherwise, and hence the layoff of workers was greater than the administration anticipated. Moreover, the stimulus was not as well designed as it could have been; there could have been more stimulus per dollar of spending. But the belief that only a short-term palliative was needed, while the financial sector recovered, may have made the administration more relaxed about these weaknesses.[47]

The administration's misjudgments in this area were compounded by one more: the thought that if its spokesmen could talk up the economy and "restore confidence," the almighty American consumer would somehow return. In March of 2009 they started talking about green shoots; but by summer these shoots had turned brown. In the years that followed, glimmers of hope would occasionally appear, but these attempts to repeatedly exude confidence may actually have undermined confidence (and especially in both the administration and the Fed): clearly, the country's leaders hadn't grasped what was going on.[48]

Why government spending can be very effective

The logic of why government spending can be—and has been—effective in stimulating the economy is compelling. If government, say, increases spending, GDP increases by a multiple of that amount. The relationship between the increase in GDP and the increase in government spending is called the multiplier. Not surprisingly, those on the right say that the multiplier is small—and maybe even near zero. Of course, when the economy is at full employment, more government spending won't increase GDP. It *has* to crowd out other spending. If the Fed increases interest rates or reduces credit availability, as it works to ensure that the increased government spending is not inflationary, investment will be crowded out. But these experiences are irrelevant for the question of assessing the impact of government spending when unemployment is high (and it's likely to be high for years to come) and when the Fed has committed itself to not increasing interest rates in response. In these circumstances—the conditions of the Great Recession—multipliers are likely to be large, far in excess of one.[49]

The government spending can, of course, be even more effective if it goes to high productivity investments, including those that facilitate the restructuring of the economy. Beyond the high direct returns to such investments, there are other benefits—returns to private investments are increased, so that private investments are "crowded in"; the deficit is reduced in the medium term, and not only should that instill confidence but consumers, realizing that their future tax burdens will be lower than they might otherwise be, may consume more today.[50] Even private consumption is "crowded in."

Government money spent on structural reform—helping move resources from old, less competitive sectors to new sectors—stimulates the economy, and the higher incomes give individuals and firms the resources to adapt to the changed economy.

In many of the European countries facing austerity, there is simultaneously a demand for faster structural reforms. The structural reforms that they often focus upon do not entail government assistance in moving the economy into new sectors. Rather, what is referred to is a mixture of counterproductive measures (lowering minimum wages) and rent-reducing measures (like more effective enforcement of competition laws and reducing licensing restrictions), with measures of ambiguous effect—rushed privatizations that have, in many countries, actually increased rents and impaired efficiency. These reforms are topped off with aspirational messages—to be more competitive. Even were these reforms to occur at historically unprecedented paces, it would be years before the full benefits were realized. But these reforms at best (when they are well designed, and many are not) improve the supply side of the economy; as we have repeatedly noted, however, the weaknesses in the economy today stem from the demand side, and a cutback in workers' income, either as a result of firing workers or lower wages, simply lowers total demand, lowering GDP and weakening the capacities of those who have to make the structural transformations to do so. Adjustment is likely to be impaired. In fact, unless something is done about demand and growth *now* (and most of the European programs seem to be doing little or nothing), structural reforms that increase efficiency imply that fewer workers will be required to produce whatever output the economy generates. Desirable as the structural reforms are for the long run, they run the risk of increasing unemployment and lowering output in the short run.

CONCLUDING COMMENTS

The views of the bankers and others of the 1 percent on how to respond to the crisis—cut wages and cut budgets—won't restore our economies to prosperity. It's not even clear that the policies they advocate will be very successful in reducing the deficit in the current conditions of economic weakness: lower GDP and higher unemployment will mean lower tax revenues and higher expenditures. Nor is it even clear that they're in the interests of the 1 percent, though it's easy to see why they might think that. Lowering wages ("more labor market flexibility") would increase profits, if only sales held up. The bankers, moreover, are always focused on getting paid back. They think of a household that owes them money. If the household cuts back on spending on itself, it has more money to give the bank. But as I've explained, the analogy between the household and the economy is false: cutting back on government spending destroys demand and destroys jobs. The household won't have the money to repay the banker if its income falls concomitantly with cutbacks in expenditure. And repayment will be even more difficult if income falls by a multiple of the cutback in expenditures—which is precisely what economics has shown to be the case.

What's striking is how many people—pundits and ordinary citizens alike, those in government and those outside—have been seduced by the myth of austerity and the myth that the government budget is like a household's budget. Many people have been captured by a subtle, parallel argument that the Right makes about macroeconomics: There was a stimulus. The economy didn't get better. It even got worse. Ergo, the stimulus didn't work. But the stimulus did work; it prevented the unemployment rate from being even higher.

The 1 percent has captured and distorted the budget debate—using an understandable concern about overspending to provide cover for a program aimed at downsizing the government, an action that would weaken the economy today, lower growth in the future, and, most importantly for the focus of this book, increase inequality. It has even used the occasion of the budget battle to argue for reduced progressivity in our tax system and a cutback in the country's already limited programs of social protection.

Given the weaknesses in the economy (both the lack of demand today and the lack of investment in our future), deficit fetishism focuses on the wrong problem, at least for now. But even if one gave in to deficit fetishism, we've shown that there are alternative tax and expenditure policies that can simultaneously increase economic efficiency, increase the nation's output and lower its unemployment rate, and address one of the country's most troublesome problems, its growing inequality.

A major source of inequality, at the bottom, is unemployment. Those without jobs suffer, and so do those with jobs, as high unemployment puts strong downward pressure on wages. Since America's political gridlock is constraining the use of fiscal policy (taxes and expenditures) to restore the economy to full employment, hope has shifted to monetary policy. As this chapter has pointed out, matters may get even worse: deficit fetishism could lead to austerity, which will weaken the economy further and put an even greater burden on monetary policy. But is monetary policy up to the task? The next chapter explains why monetary policy hasn't really served our nation as well as it should: to too large an extent, it's been designed to serve the financial sector and other interests of those at the top.

CHAPTER NINE

A MACROECONOMIC POLICY AND A CENTRAL BANK BY AND FOR THE 1 PERCENT

SOME READERS MIGHT BE SURPRISED TO SEE A chapter on macroeconomics—the branch of economics that deals with the overall level of economic activity, with output (GDP) and employment, with interest rates and inflation—in a book on inequality. Nothing affects the well-being of most citizens more than the state of the macroeconomy—whether there is full employment and growth. And when macroeconomic policies fail, and unemployment soars, those at the bottom are among those that suffer the most. More broadly, macroeconomic policy greatly affects the distribution of income. Policymakers should be aware of this, but they often act as if they aren't. Indeed, the distribution of income is seldom mentioned in macroeconomics, and that's exactly the point.

The most important responsibility of policy makers is to maintain the overall stability of the economy. The Great Recession offers evidence of a colossal failure. And this failure has imposed an enormous burden on ordinary Americans— as workers, as homeowners, as taxpayers, as we described in Chapter 1. We explained how the failure of macroeconomics finally brought to the fore the problems with our economic system. When things were going well, most people were prospering and could persuade themselves that those who weren't had only themselves to blame. But with the recession of 2008, the story stopped making sense. Too many people who "played by the rules, studied hard, worked hard" were just getting by, or not even getting by. *The system wasn't working.*

This book has argued that, in many ways, our economic system has benefited those at the top, at the expense of the rest, and that this system is far removed from what has been called "the achievement model of income determination," in which incomes reflect contributions to society. In this chapter we focus on the contribution of our macroeconomic policy to this outcome—before, during, and after the crisis.

Policy entails choices. There are distributive consequences of all policies. A central theme of this book is that some of the policy choices have simultaneously increased inequality— benefiting those at the top—and hurt the economy.

But many choices are more complicated and involve trade-offs. If there is a trade-off between inflation and unemployment, pursuing lower inflation means higher unemployment and workers suffer; lower unemployment means higher inflation, and bondholders see the value of their assets erode. A focus on inflation puts the bondholders' interests at center stage. Imagine how different monetary policy might have been if the focus had been on keeping unemployment below 5 percent, rather than on keeping the inflation rate below 2 percent.

Different policies also impose different risks on different segments of society. If things go wrong, who will bear the consequences? If things go right, who reaps the benefits? The Fed gambled, in trusting that banks on their own could manage risk—a gamble that paid off handsomely for the banks, and especially for the bankers, but in which the rest paid the price. The Fed could have curbed the reckless and predatory lending, the abusive credit card practices, but chose not to do so. Again, the banks were the winners; the rest the losers.

Monetary and macroeconomic policy and Fed action thus contributed to the country's growing problem of inequality in several ways. At the bottom and in the middle, higher unemployment than was necessary at times (implying lower wages) meant lower incomes for workers. Less protection from the abusive practices of the banks hurt their standards of living. We'll even see how current macroeconomic policies may even be contributing to creating a jobless recovery—when the recovery actually gets really under way. Hidden subsidies to banks and support for deregulation that contributed so much to the financialization of the economy contributed to the increasing inequality at the top, and aggressive policies fighting inflation meant that rich bondholders didn't have to worry that inflation would erode their value.

These failures are not an accident. The institutional arrangements by which monetary policy is set are designed to give disproportionate voice to the bankers and their allies. This was even reflected in the models that became part of the standard tool kit of central banks. While they focused on inflation (something bondholders cared a great deal about), they ignored distribution (something bankers wouldn't want central bankers to think too much about)—even though, as we have argued, growing inequality was critical in creating the economy's instability.

Just as the Great Recession drew attention to America's growing inequality—destroying the myth that all were benefiting from the growth that had occurred in the preceding quarter century—it destroyed two other myths: that a focus on inflation was the cornerstone to economic prosperity, and that the best way of ensuring economic stability was to have an independent central bank. This chapter will explain how the monetary policies that were pursued simultaneously weakened overall economic performance and increased inequality.

There is an alternative set of policies and institutional arrangements that holds out the promise of not only better and more stable growth but also of a more equitable sharing of the benefits of that growth.

How Modern Macroeconomics and Monetary Policies Have Hurt the 99 Percent

The central focus of much of modern macroeconomics and monetary policy is on inflation—keeping inflation low and stable allegedly provides the macroeconomic conditions under which a market economy can flourish. Inflation—especially very high and erratic levels of inflation—can be a problem, but the United States and Western Europe have not faced a serious problem of inflation in more than a third of a century.[1] Focusing on yesterday's problems can distract one from the more pressing issues of today. In the years before the Great Recession, of far more concern than a possible slight loss of efficiency from a slight increase in inflation should have been the very big loss from the collapse of the financial system.[2] In the years after the onset of the Great Recession, of far more concern than a possible slight loss of efficiency from a slight increase in inflation should have been the very big losses from the waste of resources as a result of the economy's not living up to its potential.

As we noted in chapter 4, those who suffer the most in crises are workers and small businesses, and that's been especially true in this crisis, where corporate profits remain high in many sectors[3] and banks and bankers are doing well. High unemployment hurts those who depend on working for their living; most of those with jobs face shorter hours and lower incomes. But it particularly hurts those at the bottom. The more skilled workers displace the less skilled, and the less skilled displace the unskilled. While each of these groups suffers with lower incomes, those that are displaced from their jobs are hurt the most.[4]

A high level of joblessness doesn't just affect those who lose their jobs or have their working hours cut: it hurts the bottom 99 percent by forcing down wages as workers compete for jobs. And the way most central banks conduct monetary policy creates a ratchet effect that has been working ruthlessly for the past several decades. As soon as wages start to recover, the central bankers, with their single-minded focus on inflation, raise the specter of price increases. They raise interest rates and tighten credit, *to maintain unemployment at an unnecessarily high level.* Too often they succeed in choking off wage increases—with the result that productivity has been growing *six times* faster than wages.[5] (At the time of the 2008 crisis, workers had not yet recovered what they had lost in the last recession.)[6]

Central bankers have a hard time limiting their opinions to monetary and bank regulatory policy. (If they had stuck to their knitting, and gotten monetary and regulatory policy right, the economy would be in far better shape.) A central theme of these bankers is that there should be more "labor market flexibility," which typically means lowering wages, and especially minimum wages and job protections. But the weakening of systems of social protection has amplified the adverse effects on the 99 percent of mistaken macropolicies. Minimum wages have not kept up with inflation (so that the *real* federal minimum wage in the United States in 2011 is 15 percent *lower* than it was almost a third of a century ago, in 1980); and this has obviously made lowering wages easier, especially at the bottom.[7] Unemployment insurance also has not kept up with the times, so those who lose their jobs and are lucky enough to have unemployment insurance receive a fraction of their previous pay.[8] And, as we saw in chapter 1, the number of unemployed who are not receiving benefits has risen to staggering levels.

But the weakening of the system of social protection and the push for more flexible labor markets may itself have amplified the macroeconomic consequences of flawed monetary policies. The central economic problem in the Great Recession, as we have noted, is lack of total (or aggregate) demand. With good systems of social protection, workers' income and consumption are sustained, even in the face of a downward "shock" to the economy. Economists refer to these shock absorbers as automatic stabilizers. On the other hand, wage declines in response to an adverse shock to the economy amplify its effects. The central bankers who were simultaneously calling for more "wage flexibility," focusing on inflation, and ignoring the risks of financial fragility were simultaneously pursuing a policy that exposed the economy to a risk of a major shock and advocating policies that would ensure that the shock, when it occurred, would have deep and serious consequences.

Oblivious to the distributional consequences of monetary policy

As I noted, the standard macroeconomic models don't even recognize that the distribution of income matters, and so it's not surprising that the Fed in its policies has often seemed oblivious to the distributional implications of its decisions. Even when it does focus on employment, its failure to take into account the distributional consequences of its actions lead it to adopt policies that may be counterproductive.

For instance, the Fed focuses on interest rates in the mistaken belief that changes in the interest rates are a simple "lever" by which it can control the economy—lower the interest rate and the economy expands; raise the interest rate and it slows down. And though there are times and circumstances in which the interest rate may have those effects, at other times the links are at best weak and other instruments might have been more effective. For instance, in response to the real estate bubble, it would have made more sense to raise the down payment requirements for mortgages than to raise interest rates; one didn't want to slow down productive investments, just to dampen the bubble. Such regulations were anathema to the Fed, with its religious devotion to the price system and the wonders of the market.

When the economy went into a tailspin, the lowering of

interest rates may have saved the banks, but it clearly didn't reignite the economy. Even if the lower rates that banks paid for funds had been passed on to borrowers, in most sectors there wouldn't have been much increased investment, given the low level of capacity utilization—the economy already had more than enough capacity to produce whatever was demanded. So, besides cheap money for the banks—a hidden subsidy—there really wasn't much benefit to lowering the interest rate. When the Fed lowered interest rates in response to the collapse of the tech bubble, it didn't lead to much business investment, but it did lead to the real estate bubble. But in 2008–2009, with real estate prices down as much as they were, it was almost inconceivable that lower interest rates would have much effect there.

There was a cost, however: all those retired individuals who had invested prudently in government bonds suddenly saw their incomes disappear. In this way, there was a large transfer of wealth from the elderly to the government, and from the government to the bankers. But little mention of the harm to the elderly was made, and little was done to offset it.[9]

The lower interest rates might have dampened spending in other ways. Persons nearing retirement, seeing that they would have to put away that much more in safe government bonds to get the retirement income they desired, would have to save more. As would parents saving to put their kids through school. Even cursory attention to the distributional consequences of such policies would have raised doubt about the effectiveness of the low interest rate policy.[10]

The Fed, with its focus ever on the 1 percent, did however suggest that lower interest rates would increase stock market prices—helping those at the top, who, as we have seen, own a disproportionate share of the stock market—and

higher stock market prices would lead to more consumption, because people would feel wealthier. But interest rates
would not remain at such a low level forever, which meant
the gain in stock prices was not likely to be permanent. It was
unlikely that any temporary increases in stock prices caused
by a temporary lowering of interest rates, of benefit particularly to the rich, would translate into substantial increases in
consumption.[11]

Although the Fed's low interest rate policy hadn't led to
the resurgence of investment as it had hoped, it did encourage those who were planning investments to substitute cheap
capital for labor. Capital was, in effect, at a temporary arti-
ficially low price, and one might as well take advantage of
this unusual situation. This reinforced distorted patterns of
innovation that focused on saving labor at a time when it was
increasingly in abundance. It is curious that at a time when
unemployment among the unskilled is so high, grocery and
drug stores are replacing checkout clerks with automatic
machines. The Fed was making it more and more likely that,
when a recovery set in, it would be a jobless one. Indeed, this
turned out to be the hallmark of the recovery from the 2001
recession, during which the Fed had again put interest rates
at low levels.[12]

Helping the top

We've already noted a number of ways that the Fed helped the
banks and the bankers, especially in the crisis. The Federal
Reserve lends to the banks *at very low interest rates*, rates that,
especially in times of crisis, are far below the market rate. If a
bank can borrow at close to zero, and buy a long-term government bond yielding, say, 3 percent, it makes a nifty 3 percent

profit *for doing nothing*.[13] Lend the banking system a trillion dollars a year, and that's a $30 billion gift. But banks can often do better—they can lend to triple A–rated firms, prime customers, at much higher interest rates. If they can lend at just 10 percent, then the government's willingness to lend them a trillion dollars at close to zero interest rate is a $100 billion a year gift.[14]

Banks can also deposit money into the Federal Reserve, and they now, for the first time, receive interest on those deposits—another hidden transfer from taxpayers to the banks.[15] Curiously, this latest gift may have discouraged lending. Paying banks *not to lend* meant that the incremental returns banks got from lending were lowered.[16]

More broadly, the bailout strategy put the interests of the banks (and especially the large banks) and bankers ahead of the rest of our economy.[17] Money was given to the banks *allegedly* so that the flow of credit would not be interrupted, but no conditions were imposed on the financial institutions receiving funds. No conditions to maintain the flow of lending, no conditions not to use the money to pay bonuses. Much of the money given to the banks went to bonuses, not to bank recapitalization. Money went disproportionately to the large banks, which were more interested in speculation and trading than in lending. To the extent that they lent money at all, it was disproportionately to large international firms. The government's money, for the most part, didn't go to the smaller regional and community banks that focus on lending to small and medium-size enterprises.[18] Not surprisingly, hundreds of these smaller banks went bankrupt,[19] and hundreds more were in such a precarious position that they had to curtail lending.[20] For a strategy aimed at maintaining the flow of credit, the Fed's decisions (together with Treasury) were deeply flawed.

Deregulation: key to the increasing financialization of the economy

This deference to the banks lies at the center of the Fed's, and other central banks', greatest contribution to inequality: their failure to impose adequate regulation and to adequately enforce regulations that existed—the culmination of two decades of financial deregulation that had begun under President Reagan. The Fed and its chairman Alan Greenspan were instrumental in stripping away the regulations that had been so important in ensuring that the financial system served the country well in the decades after the Great Depression. They were also instrumental in preventing new regulations to reflect changes in the financial sector, such as the development of derivatives, that posed threats to the stability of the financial and economic system.[21]

This deregulation had two related consequences, both of which we noted earlier. First, it led to the increasing financialization of the economy—with all the associated distortions and inequities. Second, it allowed the banks to exploit the rest of society—through predatory lending, abusive credit card fees, and other practices. The banks shifted risk toward the poor and toward the taxpayer: when things didn't go as the lenders had predicted, others had to bear the consequences. The Fed not only didn't discourage this; it encouraged it.[22] It is clear that, *from a societal perspective*, the banks did not help people manage risk; they created it. But when it came to managing their own risk, the bankers were more successful. They didn't bear the downside of their actions.

In the aftermath of the crisis, the Fed's position in the regulatory debate showed where their allegiance was. Regulations should have been designed to encourage banks to go back to the boring business of lending. Recognizing that the too-big-to-fail banks had perverse incentives, they should have focused on how to limit the size and interconnectedness of the banks. Moreover, too-big-to-fail banks have a competitive advantage over other banks—those who provide them finance know that they can count, in effect, on a government guarantee, and thus they are willing to provide them funds at lower interest rates. The big banks can thus prosper not because they are more efficient or provide better service but because they are in effect subsidized by taxpayers. Our failure to impose a tax to offset this advantage is just giving the too-big-to-fail banks *another* large gift.[23] The recognition that outsize bonuses gave financial professionals incentives to engage in excess risk taking and shortsighted behavior should also have led to tight regulations on the design of bonuses. And in acknowledgment of the risk of undercapitalized banks—where small changes in the value of assets can be enough to cause bankruptcy—there should have been tight regulation on the size of bonuses and dividends until the banking system was fully recovered. Recognizing the role that lack of transparency and derivatives had played in the banking crisis, the Fed should have insisted that something be done about both.

Little of the above was done, and what was done was often achieved over the opposition of the Federal Reserve. The new regulatory bill (Dodd-Frank) signed into law in July 2010 gave much of the responsibility for implementing regulations to the Fed, and at least in some areas it again showed where its loyalties were. To cite but a few examples: in the discussion preceding the passage of the Dodd-Frank bill, the Senate committee with responsibility for oversight of derivatives had recommended that government-insured banks not be allowed to write derivatives. While it wasn't clear whether derivatives were insurance products or gambling instruments, it was clear that they weren't loans. If they were insurance products, they should be regulated by state insurance authorities; if they were gambling products, they should be regulated by state gambling authorities; but in no circumstances should they be underwritten by the U.S. government, through the Federal Deposit Insurance Corporation, the government agency that insures *bank depositors.* But Ben Bernanke, the Fed chief, argued otherwise (over the opposition of two regional Fed presidents, who seemed to harbor the quaint notion that banks should focus on banking). Bernanke and the big banks that made billions a year from the credit default swaps, or CDSes, won.

Meanwhile, there emerged a broad consensus among economists and policy makers (including at least one Federal Reserve regional governor and the governor of the Bank of England, Mervyn King) that something ought to be done about the too-big-to-fail banks. King pointed out that if they were too big to fail, they were too big to exist. Even earlier, Paul Volcker, former chairman of the Federal Reserve, had observed that these banks were also too big to be managed. But the Federal Reserve Board's current and past chairmen (Greenspan and Bernanke, responsible for bringing on the crisis) have never seemed even to recognize the problem, at least not enough to suggest that something be done. And there was much that could be done: from regulatory solutions limiting bank size and what they could do, to taxes to offset the advantages described earlier.

The Fed, of course, never set out to increase inequality—either by the benefits it proffered to those at the top or by what it did and what it countenanced the banks to do to those in the middle and at the bottom. Indeed, as we shall explain later, most of its board members probably truly believed that its policies—lax regulation, fighting inflation, helping banks that are so essential to the functioning of our economy—would promote growth from which *all* would benefit. But that's just testimony to the extent to which the Fed was "captured" by the perspectives and worldview of the bankers.

TOWARD A MORE DEMOCRATIC CENTRAL BANK[24]

A central thesis of current conventional wisdom is that central banks should be independent. If they are subject to political forces, so the thinking goes, politicians will manipulate monetary policy for their short-run advantage at a long-run cost; they will stimulate the economy excessively before an election, with the price—higher inflation—to be paid after the election. Moreover, with an independent central bank committed to low inflation, markets will not build inflationary expectations into their behavior, so inflation will be contained, and there will be better overall economic performance.

The failure of independent central banks

The independent central banks of the United States and Europe didn't perform particularly well in the last crisis. They certainly performed far more poorly than less independent central banks like those of India, China, and Brazil. The reason was obvious: America's and Europe's central banks had, in effect, been captured by the financial sector. They might not have been democratically accountable, but they did respond to the interests and perspectives of the bankers. The bankers wanted low inflation, a deregulated financial sector, with lax supervision, and that's what they got—even though the economic losses from inflation were minuscule compared with the losses that arose from the excessively deregulated financial market. The losses to ordinary consumers from predatory lending were given short shrift—indeed, the additional profits increased the financial strength of the banks. The soundness of the banking system was, after all, the central banks' first charge.

Capture

We saw in chapter 2 that a regulatory agency is captured by those that it is supposed to regulate when the policies it pursues and regulations that it adopts reflect more the interests and perspectives of those that it is supposed to regulate rather than the public interest. Capture occurs partially as a result of revolving doors, where the regulators come from regulated sector and, after their brief stint in government, return to it. "Capture" is partly what is called cognitive capture—in which the regulator comes to adopt the mindset of the regulated. In the United States capture also occurred more directly, as when Wall Street weighed in strongly on potential appointees to the central bank. I saw that during the Clinton administration, where two excellent appointments were in effect vetoed by the financial markets, one because she had demonstrated a concern about discrimination in lending, the other because he seemed too concerned about encouraging economic growth and full employment. The most curious case was the one that occurred during the Obama administration, which nominated a brilliant Nobel Prize winner who had done pathbreaking work extending our understanding of unemployment and its determinants—something that should have been of central concern to the Fed. Perhaps some in the financial markets realized that having a critical thinker, who might cast doubt on certain conventional central bank doctrines that were not grounded in economic theory or evidence, would be *inconvenient*. His nomination never even got through the Senate Banking Committee.[25]

In spite of such pressures, there has been considerable diversity of perspectives among the Fed governors. There was even one Fed governor[26] who warned about the bad lending to the housing sector, but he was effectively ignored by the others. In this recession, several of the Fed governors have been adamant that unemployment is the *key* issue, and there is a recognition that the underlying problem is a lack of demand. Some have even made the heretical (for central bankers) suggestion that until the economy's unemployment rate is substantially lower, unemployment, not inflation, ought to be the "target" of monetary policy.

A lack of faith in democracy

The lack of faith in democratic accountability on the part of those who argue for independent central banks should be deeply troubling. Where does one draw the line in turning over the central responsibilities of government to independent authorities? The same arguments about politicization could be applied to tax and budgetary policies. I suspect some in the financial market would be content to turn those responsibilities over to "technical experts." But here's the hidden agenda: the financial markets would not be content with just any set of technical experts. They prefer, as we have seen, "experts" who shared their views—views that support their interests and ideology. The Federal Reserve and its chairmen like to pretend that they are above politics. It is convenient not to be accountable, to be independent. They see themselves as simply wise men and women, public servants, helping to steer the complex ship of the economy.

But if there was any doubt of the political nature of the Fed and its chairmen, it should have been resolved by observing the seemingly shifting positions of the central bank over the past twenty years. In 1993, when the United States had a large fiscal deficit and high unemployment, the chairman of the Fed, Alan Greenspan, urged the government to take strong actions to reduce the deficit, with the understanding that interest rates would then be reduced to restore the economy to full employment. But the economy was facing unemployment; it was not overheated. There was no reason to make the lowering of interest rates conditional on a reduction of the deficit; indeed, lowering interest rates and increasing the availability of credit could have worked hand in hand to help get the economy growing, and that would have done wonders for the deficit. But interest rates were lowered only to a little below 3 percent—presumably if they had been lowered further, the economy would have had a more robust recovery. Then, in 2001, Greenspan urged Congress to cut taxes, *creating a massive deficit*, and responded to the recession by lowering interest rates to a much lower level—eventually to under 1 percent. One interpretation of these seemingly inconsistent positions was that the real objective was to downsize government and reduce tax progressivity.[27]

In any democracy a public institution—and pretend as it might, a central bank is a public institution—must have some degree of accountability. There must be oversight to make sure that there is no malfeasance, and that the central bank functions in accordance with its mandate, and that the mandate in question is in accord with the public interest. In a modern democratic society, governance is a central concern. How are those responsible for making critical decisions chosen? How are the decisions made? Is there sufficient transparency that there can be meaningful public scrutiny?

Few matters are of greater concern to citizens than the performance of the economy, and monetary policy is a central determinant of that performance. Indeed, standard models in political science show that especially the level of unemployment and its rate of change is the most important determinant of presidential and congressional electoral outcomes. And yet, it seems that under current arrangements public officials are being held accountable for something over which they do not control one of the main levers.

In the United States our system of governance and accountability for our central bank should in fact be an embarrassment. Monetary policy is set by a committee (called the Open Market Committee) of the seven members of the Federal Reserve Board, plus the twelve regional Federal Reserve Bank presidents, of whom only the head of the New York Fed and four others have the right to vote. But the regional Federal Reserve Bank presidents are chosen in a nontransparent process that gives the public little say, and in which the banks (which they are supposed to be regulating) have too much influence.[28]

While the current Fed chairman, Ben Bernanke, has written forcefully about the virtue of transparency,[29] he seems to have changed his mind once the task of providing hidden assistance to the banks moved more to the center of the Fed's agenda. When the media requested information, of the kind that other government agencies are required to disclose under the Freedom of Information Act, the Fed claimed that the Fed was not subject to the act. The Federal District Court disagreed, but the Fed was unrepentant—it refused to disclose what the press wanted to know. The Fed appealed the decision, and the appellate court reaffirmed that the Fed was accountable. Reportedly, the Fed would have appealed to the Supreme Court, had the White House not told the Fed that it was in fact part of the government and had to obey the laws that applied to other government agencies. Congress, independently, demanded an audit of what the Fed was doing—including who was getting its money.

Eventually, the Fed succumbed to the pressure from courts and Congress, and when the information was disclosed, the American people understood better why the Federal Reserve had not wanted to disclose the information. The real reason for secrecy, it turned out, was to hide policies that would not meet with popular support—and to conceal inconsistencies between what the Fed was saying and what was going on.[30]

In the great bailout that marked the beginning of the Great Recession, the head of the New York Fed was one of the triumvirate (along with the head of the Federal Reserve and the secretary of Treasury) that shaped the bailout, determined who got saved and who got executed, and who got how much and on what terms. And he, in turn, had been nominated by a committee that consisted of bankers and CEOs from some of the same firms that were bailed out *on most favorable terms*.[31] There is the appearance, if not the reality, of a conflict of interest. Americans never fully understood why AIG got a bailout of the magnitude that it did or why, when its derivatives were bought back, they were paid off at 100 cents on the dollar—far higher than was necessary. But when the ultimate beneficiaries of the AIG bailout were revealed, all became clearer: the biggest beneficiary was Goldman Sachs, and other recipients were large foreign banks, some of which were suspected of having complex financial dealings with Goldman Sachs. It seemed especially strange that the United States was bailing out foreign banks. If foreign banks were in trouble, it should have been the responsibility of the foreign governments to bail out their own banks.

As more information was given out, it became clear that the Fed had been lending massively to foreign banks long before the September 2008 crisis.[32] Evidently, the U.S. Fed was the lender of last resort not only for U.S. banks but for foreign banks as well.[33] Had American banks undertaken such complex and large-risk exposures with these other banks that if they sank, American banks would be at risk? If so, it was evident that the Fed had failed in its supervisory job as well as in its regulatory responsibilities. It also grew clear that in spite of statements from the Fed claiming that the problems of the subprime mortgage and the breaking of the bubble were well contained,[34] global financial markets had been going through trauma for months.

The data that the Fed was forced to reveal also showed that in the months after Lehman Brothers collapsed, large banks, like Goldman Sachs, were borrowing large amounts from the Fed, while simultaneously claiming publicly that they were in excellent health.

None of this should be surprising: an independent central bank, captured by the financial sector, is going to make decisions that represent the beliefs and interests of the financial sector.

Even if it were desirable to have a central bank that was independent from the democratic political process, the board should at least be representative and not dominated by members of the financial sector. Several countries do not allow those from the financial sector to serve on their central bank board—they see it as an obvious conflict of interest. There exists a wealth of expertise outside the financial sector. Indeed, those in the financial sector are attuned to making deals and are not experts in the complexities of macroeconomic interdependencies. Today, fortunately, there are real experts in a variety of institutions other than the financial sector—including academia, NGOs, and unions.

Those who favor an independent central bank often assume that no trade-offs are involved in the decisions the bank takes. Technical experts can figure out the best way of managing the economy just as they can decide on the best design of a bridge. But trade-offs are the essence of economic policy making. There are, as we have argued, choices to be made; some will benefit from these choices while others lose. It is evident now that the Fed failed to maintain economic stability—and after the crisis, it failed to restore the economy to health; it is evident, too, that the economic doctrines on which its policies were based were badly flawed. No policy is without risk. But the policies chosen by the Fed forced the brunt of the risk to be borne by homeowners, workers, and taxpayers, while the upside was captured by the banks. There were other policies, with other risks, in which the rest of our society would have fared far better, and the banks worse. We need to recognize that a central bank's decisions are essentially political; they should not be delegated to technocrats, and they certainly can't be left to those who disproportionately represent one of the vested interests.[35]

The euro crisis—an example

The institutional flaws in the design of the central banking system for regulating banks and determining interest rates in the United States also arise in countries around the world. Before the crisis America was held up as a model of good institutional design, and countries elsewhere imitated it. In the aftermath of the crisis, the flaws in the system have become apparent, and the United States, and others that have adopted similar institutional arrangements, should be thinking of a redesign.

Critical as I am of the Fed, I find matters even worse in Europe. America's central bank *officially* is supposed to look at inflation, growth, and employment. The European Central Bank (ECB), Europe's equivalent of the Federal Reserve that rules over the seventeen-country eurozone, is supposed to focus only on inflation. It also reflects the mindset of the banks and financial community even more than the Fed does. The ECB response to the great debt crisis that began with Greece in January 2010 offers an example. First Greece, then Ireland and Portugal, later followed by Spain and Italy, faced interest rates on their debt that were unsustainable. The specter of a Greek default shifted from a remote possibility in January 2010 to an inevitability by July 2011, though somewhat gentler words like "a debt restructuring" were used. Greece owed more than it could possibly pay without inflicting politically unacceptable pain on the citizens of the country. When the only problem seemed to be that of Greece, a simple patch on the European system could have done the trick. But when large countries like Spain and Italy faced difficulties financing their debt at reasonable interest rates, it was clear that the problem would require more resolute action.

The ECB played, at best, an ambiguous role.[36] For instance, in the case of Greece, it insisted that any restructuring of the debt (asking creditors to take a debt write-down and postpone repayment) be voluntary. They said whatever agreement was reached couldn't be allowed to set off a "credit event," meaning an event that would trigger a payment on credit default swaps, the risky securities that would pay off if Greece defaulted. In saying that, the ECB seemed to be placing the interests of the banks well above that of the Greek people. Greece needed a deep restructuring (another way of saying a large reduction in its debt burden), well beyond that which might emerge from a voluntary restructuring, but only a voluntary write-down would not be considered a credit event.

There was something even more curious about the ECB position. Credit default swaps are supposed to provide insurance. If you have an insurance policy, you want the insurance company to be generous and declare that an "insurable event" has occurred: it is the only way that you can collect on your policy. In fact, sometimes people do something to create such an event (that's how the term "moral hazard" arose). In the Greek case the ECB said that it didn't want these insurance policies to be triggered. If the derivatives had been purchased as insurance products, then the banks would have wanted to collect on the insurance, and the ECB, as protector of the banks, would have wanted that as well. One explanation was that the ECB had failed in its regulatory role, and some banks, rather than buying insurance, were engaged in gambling and stood to lose if the CDSes had to pay off. The ECB seemed to be putting the interests of these banks ahead not only of the citizens of Greece but also of those banks that had been more prudent and purchased insurance.[37]

Of course, the responsibility of the ECB and the European financial authorities was to make sure that the banks were adequately capitalized and were not excessively exposed to risk. That they had failed miserably was evident: weeks after European financial institutions were given a clean bill of health (from the passage of a stress test, supposedly designed to ensure that the banks could survive a major economic stress), the Irish banks collapsed. A few weeks after they were given a second seal of approval, having supposedly tightened their standards, another major European bank (Dexia) failed.[38]

MONETARY POLICY AND THE
BATTLE OF IDEAS

A central theme of this book is that there has been a battle of ideas—over what kinds of society, what kinds of policies, are best for *most citizens*—and that this battle has seen an attempt to persuade everyone that what's good for the 1 percent, what the top cares about and wants, is good for everyone: lower tax rates at the top, reduce the deficit, downsize the government.

It is not a coincidence that currently fashionable monetary/ macroeconomics finds its origins in the work of the influential Chicago school economist Milton Friedman, the strong advocate of so-called free-market economics, which downplayed the importance of externalities and ignored information imperfections and other "agency" issues.[39] While his pioneering work on the determinants of consumption rightly earned him a Nobel Prize, his free-market beliefs were based more on ideological conviction than on economic analysis. I remember long discussions with him on the consequences of imperfect information or incomplete risk markets; my own work and that of numerous colleagues had shown that in these conditions, markets typically didn't work well. Friedman simply couldn't or wouldn't grasp these results. He couldn't refute them. He simply *knew* that they had to be wrong. He, and other free-market economists, had two other replies: even if the theoretical results were true, they were "curiosities," exceptions that proved the rule; and even if the problems were pervasive, one couldn't rely on government to fix them.

Friedman's monetary theory and policy reflected his commitment to making sure that government was small and its discretion limited. The doctrine that he pushed, called monetarism, held that government should simply increase the money supply at a fixed rate (the rate of growth of output, equal to the rate of growth of the labor force plus the rate of growth of productivity). That monetary policy could not be used to stabilize the *real* economy—that is, to ensure full employment—was not of much concern. Friedman believed that on its own the economy would remain at or near full employment. Any deviation would be quickly corrected as long as the government didn't muck things up.

In Friedman's eyes, the Great Depression was not a market failure, but a government failure: the Fed had failed to do what it should have done. It let the monetary supply decrease. In economics we don't have the opportunity to do experiments. We can't relive the Great Depression again, changing monetary policy to see the consequences. But in some ways, the Great Recession has provided a wonderful, if costly, opportunity to test some of the ideas. Ben Bernanke, a student of the Great Depression, knew the criticisms of the Federal Reserve, and he didn't want to be accused of ignoring lessons learned. He flooded the economy with liquidity. A standard measure of monetary policy action is the size of the Fed's balance sheet— how much it has lent out to the banking system and bought in government and other bonds. The balance sheet nearly tripled, from $870 billion (June 28, 2007) before the crisis to $2.93 trillion as this book goes to press (February 29, 2012).[40] This liquidity increase—together with the massive Treasury bailout—may have saved the banks, but it failed to prevent the recession. The Fed may have caused the crisis through its loose monetary policy and lax regulations, but there was little it could do to prevent or reverse the downturn. Finally, its chairman admitted as much.[41]

Friedman also had views about banking regulations—like most other regulations, he thought, they interfered with economic efficiency. He advocated "free banking," the idea that banks should be effectively unrestrained, an idea that had been tried, and failed, in the nineteenth century. He found a willing student in the Chilean dictator Augusto Pinochet. Free banking did lead to a burst of economic activity as new banks were opened and credit flowed freely. But just as it didn't take long for America's deregulated banking industry to bring the American economy to its knees, Chile, too, experienced its deepest downturn in 1982. It would take Chile more than a quarter century to pay back the debts that the government incurred in fixing the problem.

In spite of these experiences, the view that financial markets work well on their own—that government should not interfere—became a dominant theme during the past quarter century, pushed, as we have seen by Fed chairman Alan Greenspan and a succession of Treasury secretaries. And, again as we have noted, it served the interests of the financial sector and others at the top well, even as it distorted the economy. Moreover, even though the collapse of the financial system seemed to hit the Fed by surprise, it shouldn't have. Bubbles have been part of Western capitalism since the beginning—from the tulip bulb mania of 1637 in the Netherlands to the housing bubble of 2003–07.[42] And one of the responsibilities of monetary authorities, in ensuring economic stability, is to discourage the formation of such bubbles.[43]

Monetarism was based on the assumption that the velocity of circulation—the number of times a dollar bill turns over in a year—was constant. And while in some countries and in some places that had been true, in the rapidly changing global economy of the end of the twentieth century, it was not. The theory became deeply discredited just years after it was the rage among all the central bankers. As they quickly abandoned monetarism, they looked for a new religion consistent with their faith in minimal intervention in the markets. They found it in inflation targeting. Under this scheme central banks should pick an inflation rate (2 percent was a fashionable number), and whenever inflation exceeded that rate, they should raise interest rates. The higher interest rates would dampen growth, and thereby dampen inflation.[44]

The obsession with inflation

Inflation targeting was based on three questionable hypotheses. The first is that inflation is the supreme evil; the second is that maintaining low and stable inflation was necessary and almost sufficient for maintaining a high and stable *real* growth rate; the third is that all would benefit from low inflation.[45]

High inflation—such as the hyperinflation that plagued Germany's Weimar Republic in the early 1920s—is a real problem; but it is not the *only* economic problem, and it is often not the most important one.[46] Inflation, as we have noted, has not been a major problem in the United States and Europe for a third of a century. At least in the United States, the Fed had a balanced mandate—*inflation, employment, and growth*—but in practice the focus was on inflation, and until recently any central banker who suggested otherwise risked becoming a pariah. Even as the United States faced unemployment of 9 percent—and hidden unemployment that meant that the true unemployment was much higher—three "inflation hawks" on the Fed board voted to raise interest rates because of their single-minded concern with inflation.

In 2008, shortly before the global economy collapsed, inflation targeting was put to the test. Most developing countries faced higher rates of inflation not because of poor macromanagement but because oil and food prices were soaring, and these items represent a much larger share of the average household budget in developing countries than in rich ones. In China, for example, inflation approached 8 percent or more. In Vietnam it reached 23 percent.[47] Inflation targeting meant that these developing countries should have raised their interest rates, but inflation in these countries was, for the most part, *imported*. Raising interest rates wouldn't have much impact on the international price of grains or fuel.[48]

As long as countries remain integrated into the global economy—and do not take measures to restrain the impact of international prices on domestic prices—domestic prices of food and energy are bound to rise markedly when international prices do.[49] Raising interest rates can reduce aggregate demand, which can slow the economy and tame increases in prices of some goods and services, especially nontraded goods and services. But unless they are taken to an intolerable level, these measures by themselves cannot bring inflation down to the targeted levels. If global food and energy prices are going up at 20 percent a year, for the *overall* inflation rate to be 2 percent would require wages and prices elsewhere to be falling. That would almost surely entail a marked economic slow-down and high unemployment. The cure would be worse than the disease.[50]

For inflation hawks the economy is always at the edge of a precipice: once inflation starts, it will be difficult to control. And since the cost of reversing inflation—disinflation, as it's called—is so large, it is best to address it immediately. But these views are not based on a careful assessment of the evidence. There is no precipice, and mild upticks in inflation, if they look as if they might become persistent, can easily be reversed by tightening credit availability.[51] In short, it was simply wrong that the best way to maintain high employment and strong growth was to focus on inflation. The focus on inflation distracted attention from things that were far more important: the losses from even moderate inflation were negligible in comparison to the losses from the financial collapse.

Doing someone else a favor

As we've seen, there is a rationale in standard economic models for keeping inflation low, but those models are misleading. On the basis of those models, advocates for keeping inflation low argue for low inflation because it would be good for the economy as a whole. They don't single out the bond-holders as the big recipients of the benefits of low inflation. Inflation, as it is put, is the cruelest tax. It affects everybody indiscriminately and especially the poor, who are least able to bear it. But ask someone who has been out of a job for four years what he would prefer—another year of unemployment or a slight increase in inflation from, say, 1 percent to 2 percent. The answer is unambiguous. The toll unemployment takes on workers is high and hard to manage. Better some job whose pay has declined in real terms by a few percent than no job.

Wall Street pundits used to argue that inflation hurt poor retirees, but that argument was also incorrect, since Social Security goes up with inflation[52] and recipients are therefore protected. In periods in which markets work well, workers are also protected. Higher prices increase the (marginal) return to workers, and so should increase their pay commensurately.[53] It is mainly because in periods in which inflation has historically been high, there were also large shocks to the real economy, that inflationary episodes were often accompanied by decreases in real income for workers.

Bondholders aren't doing anyone else a favor when they maintain vigilance over inflation, and especially not when they persuade the monetary authorities to increase interest rates. They are merely helping themselves. And it's a one-sided bet: if the central bankers are overly vigilant, and inflation is lower than they expected, or prices are actually induced to decline, bondholders win both because of the higher interest payments they receive and because of the higher value of the money that they get back when the bond comes to maturity.

No trade-offs

Precrisis economic analysis argued not only that government intervention was not needed—because markets by and large were efficient and stable—but also that it was ineffective. Bubbles, so the logic went, didn't exist. But even if there were a bubble, government couldn't be sure whether there was one until after it broke; and even if it could tell, the only instrument at its disposal was the blunt instrument of interest rates. It was better just to let the bubble run its course, since cleaning up the mess afterward would be cheaper than distorting the economy to prevent a bubble from surfacing.

If the leaders of the Fed hadn't been so wedded to the notion that there were no bubbles, it would have been obvious to them (as it was to economists like Robert Shiller, of Yale, one of the country's leading experts on housing),[54] that the unprecedented rise in housing prices relative to incomes *almost surely represented a bubble.* In addition, the Fed didn't have to rely on interest rate changes to dampen the bubble—it could have increased down payment requirements or tightened lending standards. Congress had given the Fed authority to do so in 1994. The Fed in its allegiance to market fundamentalism had tied its own hands.

Economists have, similarly, provided the Fed with reasons not to attempt to address unemployment. People in a dynamic economy have to move from job to job, and that takes time, which creates a *natural* rate of unemployment. To push the economy beyond that natural rate pushes the economy to ever-accelerating inflation (in this view). As the unemployment rate falls even briefly below the natural rate, inflation increases; but then market participants come to expect that rate of inflation, and so they build that into their wage and price increases. Eventually—and, in the eyes of these economists, soon—the central bank will have to give in, allowing unemployment to return to the natural rate. But then, according to this view, a further price will have to be paid to bring down the inflation rate. To do that, unemployment will have to be higher than the natural rate. Otherwise inflation will simply persist. Their contention is that the benefits of the temporary low unemployment are far smaller than the costs—in higher inflation and subsequent high unemployment.

These ideas provided intellectual comfort to central bankers who didn't want to do anything about unemployment. But there were strong grounds for skepticism about these ideas: some countries, like Ghana and Israel, have managed to bring down their inflation rates very quickly at little cost. The underlying hypothesis that there is a stable relationship between the unemployment level and the rate of *acceleration* of inflation has not withstood the test of time, and the even stronger hypothesis underlying the claim that the costs of disinflation are greater than the benefits of allowing slightly higher inflation has really never been well established.[55]

The use of the term "natural" unemployment rate suggests that it is "natural" and natural things are good, or at least unavoidable. Yet there is nothing natural about the high level of unemployment we see today. And these ideas are being used by those that don't want government to take steps to do anything about it. There is, I believe, considerable scope for lowering the unemployment rate. There are millions of Americans who have jobs but are working part-time or short hours *simply because there is not enough total demand in the economy.* Whatever one's guess about the level of the "natural" unemployment rate today—and whether one believes that the concept of natural unemployment is at all relevant—it is clear that increases in aggregate demand would be beneficial.[56]

Of course, government needs to do more than just increase total demand; it has to help individuals change sectors, from where they were needed yesterday to where they will be needed tomorrow. These "active labor market policies" have proven effective in several countries, especially in Scandinavia. Cutbacks in government spending for such programs will not only lower total income by lowering demand but also lead to a higher level of natural unemployment, if such a thing exists. State funding cuts in higher education—which have been especially large in science, engineering, and health care fields because these fields are especially expensive to teach— mean that some jobs in these fields are going unfilled, and the cuts disproportionately reduce the ability for the poor to receive more training and get good jobs.[57]

CONCLUDING COMMENTS

For most people, wages are the most important source of income. Macroeconomic and monetary policies that result in higher unemployment—and lower wages for ordinary citizens— are a major source of inequality in our society today. Over the past quarter century macroeconomic and monetary policies and institutions have failed to produce stability; they failed to produce sustainable growth; and, most importantly, they failed to produce growth that benefited most citizens in our society.

In light of these dramatic failures, one might have antici- pated a quest for an alternative macroeconomic and mone- tary framework. But just as the banks—which argue that no system is accident proof, that they have been the victims of a once-in-a-century flood, and that our current recession is no reason to change a system that works—have been remarkably successful in resisting reregulation, many of those who held the erroneous beliefs about macroeconomics that led to the flawed monetary policies have been unrepentant. They have been reluctant to change those beliefs. The theory was correct, they claim; there were only a few flaws in implementation.[58]

In truth the macroeconomic models placed too little atten- tion on inequality and the consequences of policies for dis- tribution. Policies based on these flawed models both helped create the crisis and have proven ineffective in dealing with it. They may even be contributing to ensuring that when the recovery occurs, it will be jobless. Most importantly, for the purposes of this book, macroeconomic policies have contributed to the high level of inequality in America and elsewhere.

While the advocates of these policies may claim that they are the *best* policies for all, this is not the case. There is no single, best policy. As I have stressed in this book, policies have distributive effects, so there are trade-offs between the interests of bondholders and debtors, young and old, financial sectors and other sectors, and so on. I have also stressed, however, that there are alternative policies that would have led to better overall economic performance—especially so if we judge economic performance by what is happening to the well-being of most citizens. But if these alternatives are to be implemented, the institutional arrangements through which the decisions are made will have to change. We cannot have a monetary system that is run by people whose thinking is captured by the bankers and that is effectively run for the benefit of the those at the top.

CHAPTER TEN

THE WAY FORWARD: ANOTHER WORLD IS POSSIBLE

THERE'S NO USE IN PRETENDING. IN SPITE OF THE enduring belief that Americans enjoy greater social mobility that their European counterparts, America is no longer the land of opportunity.

Nothing illustrates what has happened more vividly than the plight of today's twenty-year-olds. Instead of starting a new life, fresh with enthusiasm and hope, many of them confront a world of anxiety and fear. Burdened with student loans that they know they will struggle to repay and that would not be reduced even if they were bankrupt, they search for good jobs in a dismal market. If they are lucky enough to get a job, the wages will be a disappointment, often so low that they will have to keep living with their parents.[1]

While fifty-something parents worry about their children, they also worry about their own future. Will they lose their home? Will they be forced to retire early? Will their savings, greatly diminished by the Great Recession, carry them through? They know that if they face hardship, they may not be able to turn to their children for help. From Washington comes even worse news: cutbacks in Medicare that will make access by some groups to health care unaffordable are widely discussed. Social Security, too, seems to be on the cutting table. As older Americans face their sunset years, the dreams of a comfortable retirement seem a mirage. The dreams of a prosperous, better life for their children may be as antiquated as something out of a 1950s movie.

What's been happening in America has also been happening in many countries around the world. But it is not inevitable. It is not the inexorable workings of the market economy. There are societies that have managed things far better, even in a world where market forces and the dominant policy paradigm lead to substantial inequality because of differences in ability, effort, and luck. Those societies produce a standard of living higher than that of the United States for most of their citizens, measured not just in terms of income but in terms of health, education, security, and many other aspects that are key to determining the quality of life. And some societies where inequality was far worse than in the United States have looked over the precipice, seen what might lie ahead, and retreated: they have managed to reduce the degree of inequality, to help the poor and to extend education.

Another world is possible. We can achieve a society more in accord with our fundamental values, with more opportunity, a higher total national income, a stronger democracy, and higher living standards for most individuals. It won't be easy. There are some market forces pulling us the other way. Those market forces are shaped by politics, by the rules and regulations that we as a society adopt, by the way our institutions (like the Federal Reserve, our central bank, and other regulatory agencies) behave. We have created an economy and a society in which great wealth is amassed through rent seeking, sometimes through direct transfers from the public to the wealthy, more often through rules that allow the wealthy to collect "rents" from the rest of society through monopoly power and other forms of exploitation.

This book is not about the politics of envy: the bottom 99 percent by and large are not jealous of the social contributions that some of those among the 1 percent have made, of their well-deserved incomes. This book is instead about the politics of efficiency and fairness. The central argument is that the model that best describes income determination at the top is not one based on individuals' contributions to society (the "marginal productivity theory" introduced earlier), even though, of course, some at the top have made enormous contributions. Much of the income at the top is instead what we have called rents. These rents have moved dollars from the bottom and middle to the top, and distorted the market to the advantage of some and to the disadvantage of others.

A more efficient economy and fairer society will also come from making markets work like markets—more competitive, less exploitive—and tempering their excesses. The rules of the game matter not just for the efficiency of the economic system but also for distribution. The wrong rules lead to a less efficient economy and a more divided society.

Investing more in our society—in education, technology, and infrastructure—and providing more security to ordinary citizens will lead to a more efficient and dynamic economy, one more consistent with what we claim to be and offering more opportunity to a wider segment of the society. Even the 1 percent (those who are there now) may benefit when the capabilities of so many at the bottom are not squandered. And many more people will have a shot at one day being in the 1 percent.

Finally, making the society more equal is likely to affect the prevailing ideology that influences our microeconomic and macroeconomic policies. We have identified several myths on which this ideology depends. We can break out of the vicious cycle where the political domination of the top leads to beliefs and policies that enhance economic inequality and reinforce their political domination.

For a third of a century American workers have seen their standard of living first stagnate and then erode. To those who, in the depths of the Great Depression, said that market forces would eventually prevail and restore the economy to full employment, Keynes retorted to the effect that, yes, in the long run markets may work, but in the long run we're all dead. But I'm not sure that even he had in mind a long run as long as the period that American workers have seen their standard of living being ground down.

In this chapter, I will review what has to be done to create this *other world*—the reforms we need in our economics and our politics. Unfortunately, we are headed in the *wrong* way; there is a risk that political and economic changes will make things worse. I end on a note outlining what has to happen if we are to change course—a cautious note of optimism.

As we think about how to strengthen our economy, it is imperative that we not succumb to GDP fetishism. We've seen (in chapters 1 and 4) that GDP is not a good measure of economic performance; it doesn't reflect accurately changes in the standard of living, broadly defined, of most citizens, and it doesn't tell us whether the growth we experience is sustainable.

THE ECONOMIC REFORM AGENDA

A real economic reform agenda would simultaneously increase economic efficiency, fairness, and opportunity. Most Americans would gain; the only losers might be some of the 1 percent—those whose income, for instance, depends on rent seeking and those who are excessively linked to them. The reforms follow closely from our diagnosis: we have a problem at the top, the middle, and the bottom. Simple solutions won't suffice. We identified multiple factors contributing to the country's current high level of inequality and low level of opportunity. While economists often argue about the relative importance of each of the factors, we explained why resolving the question is an almost impossible task. Besides, inequality of opportunity in America has grown to the point where we have to do everything we can. Some of the causes of inequality may be largely beyond our control, others we can affect only gradually, in the long run, but there are still others that we can address immediately. We need a comprehensive attack, some of the key elements of which I lay out below.

Curbing the excesses at the top

Chapter 2 showed how so much of the wealth at the top is derived, in one way or another, from rent seeking and rules of the game that are tilted to advantage those at the top. The distortions and perversions of our economic system are pervasive, but the following seven reforms would make a big difference.

Curbing the financial sector. Since so much of the increase in inequality is associated with the excesses of the financial sector, it is a natural place to begin a reform program. Dodd-Frank is a start, but only a start. Here are six further reforms that are urgent:

(a) Curb excessive risk taking and the too-big-to-fail and too-interconnected-to-fail financial institutions; they're a lethal combination that has led to the repeated bailouts that have marked the last thirty years. Restrictions on leverage and liquidity are key, for the banks somehow believe that they can create resources out of thin air by the magic of leverage. It can't be done. What they create is risk and volatility.[2]

(b) Make banks more transparent, especially in their treatment of over-the-counter derivatives, which should be much more tightly restricted and should not be underwritten by government-insured financial institutions. Taxpayers should not be backing up these risky products, no matter whether we think of them as insurance, gambling instruments, or, as Warren Buffett put it, financial weapons of mass destruction.[3]

(c) Make the banks and credit card companies more competitive and ensure that they *act* competitively. We have the technology to create an efficient electronics payment mechanism for the twenty-first century, but we have a banking system that is determined to maintain a credit and debit card system that not only exploits consumers but imposes large fees on merchants for every transaction.

(d) Make it more difficult for banks to engage in predatory lending and abusive credit card practices, including by putting stricter limits on usury (excessively high interest rates).

(e) Curb the bonuses that encourage excessive risk taking and shortsighted behavior.

(f) Close down the offshore banking centers (and their onshore counterparts) that have been so successful both at circumventing regulations and at promoting tax evasion and avoidance. There is no good reason that so much finance goes on in the Cayman Islands; there is nothing about it or its climate that makes it so conducive to banking. It exists for one reason only: circumvention.

Many of these reforms are interrelated: a more competitive banking system is less likely to engage in abusive practices, less likely to be successful in rent seeking. Curbing the financial sector will be hard, because the banks are so clever at circumvention. Even if banks are limited in size—a hard enough task—they will make contracts with each other (such as derivatives) that will ensure that they are too intertwined to fail.

Stronger and more effectively enforced competition laws. While every aspect of our legal and regulatory code is important for both efficiency and equity, the laws governing competition, corporate governance, and bankruptcy are especially relevant.

Monopolies and imperfectly competitive markets are a major source of rents. Banking is not the only sector in which competition is weaker than it should be. As we look across the sectors of the economy, it is striking how many are dominated by at most two, three, or four firms. At one time, it was thought that that was OK—that in the dynamic competition associated with technological change, one dominant firm would replace another. There was competition for the market rather than competition in the market. But we now know that this won't suffice. Dominant firms have tools with which to suppress competition, and often they can even suppress innovation. The higher prices that they charge not only distort the economy but also act like a tax, the revenue from which doesn't, however, go to public purposes, but rather enriches the coffers of the monopolists.

Improving corporate governance—especially to limit the power of the CEOs to divert so much of corporate resources for their own benefit. Too much power, too much deference to their supposed wisdom, is given to corporate executives. We have seen how they use that power for their own benefit. Laws that give shareholders a say on pay would make a difference. So would accounting rules that let shareholders know clearly how much they're giving away to their executives.

Comprehensive reform of bankruptcy laws—from the treatment of derivatives to underwater homes and to student loans. Bankruptcy law offers another example of how the basic rules of the game that determine how markets work have strong distributional consequences, as well as effects on efficiency. As in many other areas, the rules have increasingly favored those at the top.

Every loan is a contract between a willing borrower and a willing lender, but one side is supposed to understand the market far better than the other; there is a massive asymmetry in information and bargaining power. Accordingly, the lender should bear the brunt of the consequences of a mistake, not the borrower.

Making bankruptcy law more debtor-friendly would give banks an incentive to be more careful in lending. We would have fewer credit bubbles and fewer Americans deeply in debt. One of the most egregious examples of bad lending, as we've noted, is the student loan programs; and bad lending there has been encouraged by the nondischargeability of the debt.

In short, an unbalanced bankruptcy law has contributed to a bloated financial sector, to economic instability, to exploitation of the poor and less financially sophisticated, and to economic inequality.

End government giveaways—whether in the disposition of public assets or in procurement. The preceding four reforms focus on restricting the ability of those at the top, including those in the financial sector, from exploiting consumers, borrowers, shareholders, and others in *private* transactions. But much of the rent seeking takes the form of exploiting taxpayers. This exploitation assumes many different guises, some that are best described simply as giveaways and others that fall under the rubric of corporate welfare.

As we saw in chapter 2, the amounts of government giveaways to corporations are huge, ranging from the no-bargaining provision in drugs, to the cost-plus Halliburton contracts in defense, to the poorly designed auctions for oil, to the giving away of spectrum to TV and radio, to the below-market royalty rates for minerals. These giveaways are a pure transfer, from the rest of the population to corporations and the wealthy; but in a world of budget constraints, they are more than that, for they result in less spending on high-return public investments.

End corporate welfare—including hidden subsidies. We explained in earlier chapters how the government too often, rather than helping people who need assistance, spends its valuable money helping corporations, through corporate welfare. Many of the subsidies are buried in the tax code. While all the loopholes, exceptions, exemptions, and preferences reduce the progressivity of the tax system and distort incentives, this is especially true of corporate welfare. Corporations that can't make it on their own should come to an end. Their workers may need assistance moving to another occupation, but that's a matter far different from corporate welfare.

Much of corporate welfare is far from transparent—perhaps because if citizens really knew how much they were giving away, they would not allow it. Beyond the corporate welfare embedded in the tax code is that embedded in cheap credit and government loan guarantees. Among the most dangerous forms of corporate welfare are ones that limit liability for the damage the industries can cause—whether it's limited liability for nuclear power plants or for the environmental damage of the oil industry.

Not bearing the full cost of one's action is an implicit subsidy, so all those industries that impose, for instance, environmental costs on others are, in effect, being subsidized. Like so many of the other reforms discussed in this section, these would have a triple benefit: a more efficient economy, fewer of the excesses at the top, improved well-being for the rest of the economy.

Legal reform—democratizing access to justice, and diminishing the arms race. The legal system generates enormous rents at the expense of the rest of society. We don't have a system in which there is justice for all. We have a system in which there's an arms race, and those with the deepest pockets are in the best position to fight and to win. The details of the reform of our legal system would take me beyond the confines of this book—or even a much longer tome. Suffice it to say that the required reform is far more extensive than, and very different from, the litigation reform advocated by the Right. Embracing the conservative reform agenda, as trial lawyers correctly point out, would leave ordinary Americans unprotected. But other countries[4] have, for instance, developed systems of accountability and protection—where doctors that engage in malpractice are held accountable, and where those who suffer injury, whether as a result of malpractice or simply bad luck, are compensated appropriately.

Tax reform

Each of the seven reforms that we have described yields a double dividend: enhanced economic efficiency and increased equality. But even after we do that, large inequalities will remain, and to provide revenues for public investment and other public needs, to help the poor and the middle class, to ensure the existence of opportunity for all segments of the population, we'll have to impose progressive taxes and, most importantly, do a better job in closing loopholes.

In recent decades, we've been creating a less progressive tax system.

Create a more progressive income and corporate tax system—with fewer loopholes. Our tax system, while nominally progressive, is much less progressive than it seems. It is riddled with loopholes, exemptions, exceptions, and preferences. A fair tax system would tax speculators at at least the same rate as those who work for their income. It would ensure that those at the top pay at least as large a percentage of their income in taxes as those with lower incomes.[5] The corporate tax system should be reformed, both to eliminate loopholes and to encourage more job creation and investment.

In chapter 4, I explained that, contrary to the assertion of the Right, we could have a more efficient tax system that is, in fact, more progressive. Earlier I cited studies that showed, on the basis of the response of savings and labor supply, that the top tax rate should be well in excess of 50 percent, and plausibly in excess of 70 percent.[6] And these studies have not fully taken into account the extent to which very high incomes arise from rents.[7]

Create a more effective and effectively enforced estate tax system, to prevent the creation of a new oligarchy. The restoration of a meaningful estate tax would help in the prevention of a new American oligarchy or plutocracy, and so would the elimination of the preferential treatment of capital gains. The adverse effects are likely to be minimal: most of those who accumulate these large estates do so as a result of luck or the exercise of monopoly power, or are motivated by nonpecuniary incentives.[8]

HELPING THE REST

We can judge our system by its results, and if we do so, we have to give it a failing grade: a little while ago those at the bottom and in the middle got a glimpse of the American dream, but today's reality is that for a large segment of the population that dream has now vanished.

Some of the reforms described earlier would not only curb the top but help the rest. For instance, ending some of the abusive and monopolistic practices will, by itself, increase the *real* well-being of most Americans. Ordinary people will pay less for credit cards, telephones, computers, health insurance, and a host of other products.

Several additional actions would, I think, make a big difference in the plight of the 99 percent. Some of them require resources, and the reforms described above, and amplified in chapter 8, would generate the required revenue.

Improving access to education. Opportunity is shaped, more than anything else, by access to education, and the direction we have been going (income-segregated residential communities, sharply decreased public support for higher education—and the resulting sharp increases in tuition in public colleges and restrictions on places available in engineering and other high-demand but high-cost fields) can be reversed as well, but it will take a concerted *national* effort. What can be done to improve access to education, and, in particular, to improve the quality of public education, would require a much longer discussion.[9]

But there is one thing that can be done quickly: the for-profit schools, whether financed by government loans, government-guaranteed loans, or private loans, with the noose of nondischargeability, have failed to increase opportunity, and have in fact been a major force dragging down poor aspiring Americans. A few may emerge with better jobs, but the vast majority simply emerge encumbered with greater debt. It is unconscionable that we allow this predatory activity to continue, and even more unconscionable that it is, in effect, supported by public money. Public money should be used to expand support for state and nonprofit higher educational systems and to provide scholarships to ensure that the poor have access.

Helping ordinary Americans save. Wealth dynamics are affected, both at the top and the bottom, by government policies. We described how the tax system helps the rich accumulate and bequeath money to their heirs though a variety of incentives. The poor get no such assistance from the tax system. Government incentives for the poor to save (say, a matching grant or expansion of first-time homeowner programs)[10] would, over time, help create a fairer society, with more security and opportunity, with a larger fraction of the nation's wealth at the bottom and in the middle.

Health care for all. The two most important sources of economic trauma for an American family are the loss of a job and an illness. Together they are a lethal combination, one often associated with bankruptcy. Health care in America has traditionally been provided by employers. This inefficient and antiquated system has contributed greatly to the reality that the United States has the most inefficient and poorest-performing, overall, health care system among the advanced industrial countries. The problem with our health care system is not that we spend too much; it's that we don't get value for our money and that too many people don't have access to health care. Obama's health care reform partially addressed the latter problem, though court challenges[11] combined with cutbacks in public support may undermine the effectiveness of the reforms. But it did little (at least in the short run) to improve efficiency.[12] Our high costs are due in part to rent seeking by insurance companies and the pharmaceutical industry. Other countries have curbed these rents. We have not. Other countries not as well-off as the United States have managed to provide universal access to health care. Most countries treat access to medicine as a basic human right. But even if one doesn't approach the issue from this principled perspective, our failure to provide access to health care increases the inefficiency of our health care system. In the end, with much delay, we do provide some health care to those who are in desperate need. But it happens in emergency rooms, and costs are often much increased as a result of the delay in treatment.

Lack of access to health care contributes significantly to inequality, and this aspect of inequality in turn is especially important in undermining the performance of our economy.

Strengthening other social protection programs. The crisis has shown how woefully inadequate our unemployment insurance system is. We shouldn't have to have a major political battle, in which the unemployed are held hostage, every few months as financial support for extended unemployment insurance comes to an end.[13] The new reality is that, given the magnitude of the recession of 2008 and given the magnitude of the structural transformation our economy is going through, there will be large numbers of long-term unemployed for the foreseeable future.

Government programs (like the earned-income tax credit, Medicaid, food stamps, and Social Security) have proven very effective in reducing poverty. More spending on these programs could reduce poverty even more.

Tempering globalization: creating a more level playing field and ending the race to the bottom

Globalization and technology both contribute to the polarization of our labor market, but they are not abstract market forces that just arrive from on high; rather, they are shaped by our policies. We have explained how globalization—especially our *asymmetric globalization*—is tilted toward putting labor in a disadvantageous bargaining position vis-à-vis capital. While globalization may benefit society as a whole, it has left many behind—not a surprise given that, to a large extent, globalization has been managed by corporate and other special interests for their benefit. Too often, the response to the threat of globalization is to make workers even worse off, not just by cutting their wages but also by lowering social protections. The growth of the antiglobalization movement is, under these circumstances, totally understandable.

There are myriad ways in which globalization could be brought back into a better balance.[14]

In many countries the onslaught of hot money moving in and out of the country has been devastating; it has caused havoc in the form of economic and financial crises. There is a need for regulations on cross-border capital flows, especially of the short-term, speculative kind. For most countries some restrictions in the unbridled flow of capital would create not only a more stable economy but also one in which capital markets would exert a less heavy hand over the rest of our society. This may not be a policy that is easily available to the United States. But because of the dominant role we play in the global economy, we do have opportunities to help shape globalization—opportunities not available to others.

In reshaping globalization, we have to realize that there has occurred a race to the bottom from which we have all suffered. The United States is in the best position to stop this (if its politics would allow it); it can fight for better worker rights and conditions, better financial regulations, better environmental conditions. But other countries, working together, can also fight against the race to the bottom.

Even the advocates of globalization should understand that tempering globalization is in their interests. For if globalization is not managed better than it has been, there is a real risk of a retreat, into protectionism or forms of beggar-thy-neighbor policies.

There are specific policies that the United States can undertake to rebalance globalization in ways that are consistent with increasing global equity and efficiency. For instance, current U.S. tax law, where U.S. corporations are taxed only on profits that they bring back home, encourages outsourcing of jobs. Our system of global competition encourages firms to locate on the basis not of global efficiency but of tax competition; while it's understandable why corporations like this, since tax competition increases their after-tax profits, it distorts the global economy and undermines the ability to impose fair taxation on capital. The United States is in a position, for instance, to tax corporations that operate in the United States on the full basis of the profits they derive from their sales in the United States, regardless of where their production occurs.[15]

Restoring and maintaining full employment

A fiscal policy to maintain full employment—with equality. The most important government policy influencing well-being, with the most important consequences for distribution, is maintaining full employment. Unless the United States is careful, it could move into a situation similar to that of some European countries, with permanently higher unemployment—a vast waste of resources, which would simultaneously lead to more inequality and weaken both our economic and our fiscal situation. For seventy-five years we've known the basic principles of how to maintain the economy at or near full employment. Chapter 8 explained how well-designed macropolicies can actually achieve all three objectives simultaneously—lower debts and deficits, faster growth and employment, and an improved distribution of income.

A monetary policy—and monetary institutions—to maintain full employment. Historically there has been greater reliance on monetary policy than on fiscal policy for short-term stabilization, simply because it can adjust to changing circumstances more rapidly. But deficiencies in governance, and in the prevailing economic models, have led to a massive failure of monetary policy. Chapter 9 explained the reforms in theory, in governance, and in policy that are needed: a more accountable and a more representative central bank, and a shift away from the excessive focus on inflation to a more balanced focus on employment, growth, and financial stability.

Correcting trade imbalances. One of the reasons that total demand is so weak is that the United States imports so much—more than half a trillion dollars more than we export.[16] If exports create jobs, then imports destroy jobs; and we've been destroying more jobs than we've been creating. For a while, a long while, government spending (deficits) made up the difference, allowing the United States to maintain full employment in spite of the gap. But how long can we continue to borrow at such a clip? As I argued in chapter 8, the benefits of borrowing, especially for high-return investment, still well exceed the costs; but sometime in the future, perhaps the not-too-distant future, this may not be true. In any case, politics in the United States is making sustaining deficits, even for financing investment, difficult. If that continues, and our trade deficit continues, maintaining full employment will prove virtually impossible.[17] Moreover, and perhaps more importantly, with an aging population, America should be saving for the future, not living beyond its means.

From a global perspective, there is another reason to try to correct trade imbalances: global imbalances—the large discrepancies between imports and exports (deficits in the case of the United States, surpluses in the case of China, Germany, and Saudi Arabia) have long been a worry. They (or more accurately, a "disorderly unwinding" of these unbalances, as markets come to believe that they are unsustainable and exchange rates adjust abruptly) may not have been the cause of the last Great Recession, but they could be of the next.

Restoring trade balance has proven extraordinarily difficult. The United States has tried competitive devaluation—lowering interest rates below that of its competitors, which normally lowers exchange rates. But I've likened exchange rates to negative beauty contests: bad as American politics and economic management are, Europe seems to have surpassed us; and the trade imbalances have persisted.[18]

Exchange rates are determined largely by capital flows, and finance pays little attention to its consequences: as capital seeks a safe harbor in the United States, the exchange rate is driven up, exports are hurt, imports encouraged, the trade imbalance increases, and jobs are destroyed. But even if workers' livelihoods are put at risk, the financier's money feels safer. This is, of course, just the consequence of market forces working themselves out—but market forces shaped by rules and regulations that allow the free flow of money without restraint. This is just another example of how the well-being of finance is put over the interests of ordinary working people.

There are some interesting proposals that would restore trade balance and help restore the economy to full employment. One of the problems, though, is that the rules of globalization—designed largely by trade lawyers focusing on impediments facing particular industries rather than on big-picture issues associated with systemic performance—are such that some of the reforms *may* contravene existing rules.[19]

Active labor market policies and improved social protection. Our economy is going through a large structural transformation.[20] The changes brought about by globalization and technology require large movements across sectors and jobs by workers, and markets by themselves don't handle these changes well. To make sure that there are more winners from this process and fewer losers, government will have to play an active role. Workers will require active assistance to help them move from jobs that are being lost to new jobs that are being created, with heavy investments in education and technology to ensure that the new jobs are at least as good as the lost ones. Active labor market policies can work, but only, of course, if there are jobs for people to move into. If we can't succeed in reforming our financial system to make it return to its core function of providing finance for the new businesses of the future, then the government may even need to take a more active role in financing the new enterprises.

A *new social compact*

Supporting workers' and citizens' collective action. The rules of the game affect the bargaining strength of different participants. We have created rules of the game that weaken the bargaining strength of workers vis-à-vis capital, and workers have suffered as a result. The dearth of jobs and the asymmetries in globalization have created competition for jobs in which workers have lost and the owners of capital have won. Whether that is the result of an accidental evolution or of a deliberate strategy, it is now time to recognize what has happened and to reverse course.

Maintaining the kind of society and the kind of government that serve all the people—consistent with principles of justice, fair play, and opportunity—doesn't happen by itself. Somebody has to look after it. Otherwise our government and our institutions get captured by special interests. At the very least, we need countervailing powers. But our society and our polity have grown off kilter. All human institutions are fallible; all have their weaknesses. No one proposes abolishing large corporations because so many exploit their workers or damage the environment or engage in anticompetitive practices. Rather, we recognize the dangers, we impose regulations, we attempt to alter behavior, knowing that we will never fully succeed, but that these reforms can *improve* behavior.

And yet, our attitude toward unions has been the opposite. They are vilified, and in many states there are explicit attempts to undermine them, but there is no recognition of the important role that they can play in countervailing other special interests and in defending the basic social protections that are necessary if workers are to accept change and to adjust to the changing economic environment.[21]

Affirmative action, to eliminate the legacy of discrimination. One of the most invidious—and hardest to eradicate—sources of inequality is discrimination, both ongoing discrimination today and the legacy of past discrimination. In different countries it takes on different forms, but almost everywhere there is racial and gender discrimination. Market forces on their own won't eradicate it. We've described how, together with social forces, they can enable it to persist. But such discrimination corrodes our basic values, our basic sense of identity, the notion of nationhood. Strong laws prohibiting discrimination are essential; but the effects of past discrimination continue, and so even if we were successful in eliminating discrimination today, its consequences would still be with us. Fortunately, we've learned how to improve matters through affirmative action programs—softer than hard quotas, but when implemented with good intentions, they can help our society evolve in ways that are consistent with our basic principles. Because education is the key to opportunity, such programs are perhaps even more important there than elsewhere.

Restoring sustainable and equitable growth

A growth agenda, based on public investment. We explained why trickle-down economics doesn't work: growth doesn't automatically benefit all. But growth does provide the resources with which to tackle some of society's most intractable problems, including those posed by poverty. Right now the main problem confronting the U.S. and European economies is lack of demand. But eventually, when total demand is enough to fully use our resources—putting America back to work—the supply side will matter. Supply, not demand, will then be the constraint. But it's not the supply-side economics emphasized by the Right. One can raise taxes on corporations that don't invest and lower taxes on those that do, and on those that create jobs. Doing that is more likely to lead to growth than the kinds of across-the-board tax reductions that some businesses demand. While the supply-side economics of the Right has exaggerated the importance of tax incentives, especially when it comes to the corporate income tax, it has underestimated the importance of other policies. Government investments—in infrastructure, education, and technology—underpinned growth in the last century, and they can form the basis of growth in this century. These investments will expand the economy and make private investment even more attractive. As the economic historian Alex Fields has pointed out,[22] the decades of 1930s, '40s, '50s, and '60s were periods of high productivity increases—higher than the decades before and after—and much of this success had to do with *public* investments.

Redirecting investment and innovation—to preserve jobs and the environment. We need to redirect investment and innovation from saving labor (a euphemism under current circumstances for creating unemployment) to saving resources. This won't be easy; there will have to be both a push and a pull. For instance, in innovation, we can do this both by the kind of basic and applied research that the government funds and by forcing firms to pay for their full environmental damage. That will provide them with incentives to save on resources, diverting their attention away from replacing workers. Rather than across-the-board low interest rates (as now), which encourage the replacement even of low-skilled workers by machines, we could use investment tax credits to encourage investment; but the credits would be given only for investments that save resources and preserve jobs, not for investments that destroy resources and jobs.

Throughout this book, I've emphasized that what matters is not just growth, but *what kind of growth* (or, as it's sometimes put, the quality of growth). Growth in which most individuals are worse-off, where the quality of our environment suffers, where people endure anxiety and alienation, is *not* the kind of growth that we should be seeking. The good news is that sometimes we can both shape market forces for the better *and* derive revenues that can be used to promote growth and enhance societal well-being.

THE IMMEDIATE ISSUES

I have laid out a long-term economic reform agenda, but right now the largest causes of suffering among the 99 percent are in the labor market and housing.

In housing, we saw how accounting standards were a major impediment to restructuring, and that government programs for restructuring were designed not to force, or not even to encourage, principal write-downs. The rules of the game favored the banks over the homeowners, and those rules must be changed. We saw that in our discussion of foreclosures in chapter 7.

The banks need to be given incentives, and perhaps be required, to restructure mortgages. Requiring them to recognize the losses of their mortgages—which is called "marking to market"—would eliminate a major obstacle to restructuring. Tax incentives—allowing favorable treatment of losses if incurred as part of a restructuring now, and less favorable treatment of losses that result from foreclosure—might provide a carrot. And if that doesn't work, forcing a restructuring may be necessary.

We have a provision in our bankruptcy code, Chapter 11, that gives corporations that have become overindebted (even as a result of foolishness on their part) a fresh start; we recognize the value of keeping enterprises going, the value of the jobs that are retained. But, as we argued in chapter 6, if it's desirable to give corporations a fresh start, it's equally valuable to give families a fresh start. Current policy is devastating families and communities. We need a homeowners' Chapter 11 that would write down what the family owes, in return for a share of the capital gain when the house is sold.

The Obama administration, through Fannie Mae and Freddie Mac, the two private mortgage companies[23] that the government took over as they collapsed at the beginning of the crisis, now owns a substantial fraction of all mortgages. It is unconscionable that they have not restructured the mortgages that they hold.[24] Taxpayers, homeowners, and our economy would all be better-off.

Fixing the mortgage problem is necessary to get our economy going, but it's not sufficient. The labor market, too, is in shambles, with close to one in six workers who would like a full-time job unable to get one. More aggressive stimulation of the economy, through fiscal policy, as described in chapter 8, could substantially lower the unemployment rate, and more active labor market policies could train workers for the new jobs that the economy will create as it recovers—which may be different from the old jobs in manufacturing and real estate that have been destroyed.

THE POLITICAL REFORM AGENDA

The economics is clear: the question is, What about the politics? Will our political processes allow the adoption of even the barest elements of this agenda? If that is to occur, major political reforms must precede it.

We all benefit from having a well-functioning democracy and society. But because we all benefit, anyone can be a free rider.[25] As a result, there will be underinvestment in the smooth functioning of our democracy, perhaps the most important public good of all. In effect, we've privatized to a large extent the support and maintenance of the public good, with disastrous consequences. We've let private corporations and rich individuals spend money to "inform" us of the merits of alternative policies and candidates. And they have every incentive to distort the information they provide.

Alternative institutional arrangements are possible, but, again, we may be moving in the wrong direction. Campaign finance reform would limit the scope for corporate funding of campaigns, but the Supreme Court in its *Citizens United* case removed strictures on big firms' contributions.[26] We could make corporations more accountable to their shareholders, forcing them to go to their shareholders for a vote on campaign contributions, but with corporations controlling Congress, it's been impossible to get this and similar legislation curbing the political power of corporations adopted, or even seriously discussed. We could diminish the need for campaign contributions, by having more public funding or by requiring broadcasters to provide free airtime. But neither the broadcasters (who make large amounts of money from campaign advertising) nor the corporations (who like things the way they are, for obvious reasons) support such reforms, and their opposition makes congressional passage of such reforms all but impossible.

We could try to ensure greater access to less biased information, as several of the Scandinavian countries do. Rather than just having media controlled by moguls—drawn disproportionately from the 1 percent, and mostly reflecting their views—they've tried, with some success, to create a more democratic media. We could, as many of the European countries do, provide public support for a variety of independent think tanks, to ensure a more balanced debate about the wisdom of alternative policies.

We could make money less important in the political process by requiring voting (with financial penalties for not complying), as Australia, Belgium, and Luxembourg do. This also shifts the focus of the political parties from turning out voters to informing voters. Not surprisingly, voter participation (surpassing 90 percent in Australia) far exceeds that in the United States.[27] And there are political reforms that would make voter registration and voting easier, and make voting more meaningful—and thus increase voter turnout, by ensuring that the political process is more responsive to the concerns of the 99 percent. Some reforms would represent fundamental changes in our political system,[28] but others, such as reducing the scope for gerrymandering or the scope for filibuster, could be accomplished within our current political structure.

None of these are foolproof recipes; all of them are likely to diminish only slightly the political power of the 1 percent. And yet, taken together with the economic reform agenda of the previous section, they offer the prospect of a new era—for our economy, our politics, and our society.

And that leads us to a final question.

IS THERE HOPE?

The political and economic reform agenda in this chapter assumes that while market forces play some role in the creation of our current level of inequality, market forces are ultimately shaped by politics. We can reshape these market forces in ways that promote *more* equality. We can make markets work, or at least work better. The Great Recession did not create the country's inequality, but it made it much worse, so much so that it made it hard to ignore, and it further limited a large segment of the population's access to opportunity. With the right policies, along the lines of the agenda laid out earlier in this chapter, we can make things better. It's not a matter of eliminating inequality or creating full equality of opportunity. It's just a matter of reducing the level of inequality and increasing the extent of equality of opportunity. The question is, can we get there?

Our democracy, tilted as it may be, provides two routes by which reform might happen. Those in the 99 percent could come to realize that they have been duped by the 1 percent: that what is in the interest of the 1 percent is *not* in their interests. The 1 percent has worked hard to convince the rest that an alternative world is not possible; that doing anything that the 1 percent doesn't want will inevitably harm the 99 percent. Much of this book has been devoted to destroying this myth and to arguing that we could actually have a more dynamic and more efficient economy *and* a fairer society.

In 2011 we watched people take to the streets by the millions to protest political, economic, and social conditions in the oppressive societies they inhabit. Governments toppled in Egypt, Tunisia, and Libya. Protests erupted in Yemen, Bahrain, and Syria. The ruling families elsewhere in the region looked on nervously from their air-conditioned penthouses. Will they be next? They are right to worry. These are societies where a minuscule fraction of the population—less than 1 percent—controls the lion's share of the wealth; where wealth is a main determinant of power, both political and economic; where entrenched corruption of one sort or another is a way of life; and where the wealthiest often stand actively in the way of policies that would improve the lives of people in general. As we gaze out at the popular fervor in the streets, we might ask ourselves some questions. When will it come to America? When will it come to other countries of the West? In important ways, our own country has become like one of these disturbed places, serving the interests of a tiny elite. We have a big advantage—we live in a democracy—but it's a democracy that has increasingly not reflected the interests of large fractions of the population. The people sense this—it's reflected in the low support they express for Congress and in the abysmally low voter turnout.

And that's the second way that reform could happen: the 1 percent could realize that what's been happening in the United States is not only inconsistent with our values but not even in the 1 percent's own interest. Alexis de Tocqueville once described what he saw as a chief element of the peculiar genius of American society, something he called "self-interest properly understood." The last two words were key. Everyone possesses self-interest in a narrow sense: I want what's good for me right now! Self-interest "properly understood" is different. It means appreciating that paying attention to everyone else's self-interest—in other words, to the common welfare—is in fact a precondition for one's own ultimate well-being.[29] Tocqueville was not suggesting that there was anything noble or idealistic about this outlook. Rather, he was suggesting the opposite: it was a mark of American pragmatism. Those canny Americans understood a basic fact: looking out for the other guy isn't just good for the soul; it's good for business.

The top 1 percent have the best houses, the best educations, the best doctors, and the best lifestyles, but there is one thing that money doesn't seem to have bought: an understanding that their fate is bound up with how the other 99 percent live. Throughout history, this has been something that the top 1 percent eventually do learn. Often, however, they learn it too late.

We have seen that politics and economics are inseparable, and that if we are to preserve a system of one person one vote—rather than one dollar one vote—reforms in our political system will be required; but we are unlikely to achieve a fair and responsive political system within an economic system that is characterized by the degree of inequality that marks ours. We have seen most recently that our political system can't work if there isn't a deeper sense of community; but how can we have such a sense of community if our country is so divided? And seeing the increasing divide in our economy, we can only ask, What will it portend for the future of our politics?

There are two visions for America a half century from now.

One is of a society more divided between the haves and the have-nots, a country in which the rich live in gated communities, send their children to expensive schools, and have access to first-rate medical care. Meanwhile, the rest live in a world marked by insecurity, at best mediocre education, and in effect rationed health care—they hope and pray they don't get seriously sick. At the bottom are millions of young people alienated and without hope. I have seen that picture in many developing countries; economists have even given it a name, a dual economy, two societies living side by side, but hardly knowing each other, hardly imagining what life is like for the other. Whether we will fall to the depths of some countries, where the gates grow higher and the societies split farther and farther apart, I do not know. It is, however, the nightmare toward which we are slowly marching.

The other vision is of a society where the gap between the haves and the have-nots has been narrowed, where there is a sense of shared destiny, a common commitment to opportunity and fairness, where the words "liberty and justice for *all*" actually mean what they seem to mean, where we take seriously the Universal Declaration of Human Rights, which emphasizes the importance not just of civil rights but of economic rights, and not just the rights of property but the economic rights of ordinary citizens. In this vision, we have an increasingly vibrant political system far different from the one in which 80 percent of the young are so alienated that they don't even bother to vote.

I believe that this second vision is the only one that is consistent with our heritage and our values. In it the well-being of our citizens—and even our economic growth, especially if properly measured—will be much higher than what we can achieve if our society remains deeply divided. I believe it is still not too late for this country to change course, and to recover the fundamental principles of fairness and opportunity on which it was founded. Time, however, may be running out. Four years ago there was a moment where most Americans had the audacity to hope. Trends more than a quarter of the century in the making might have been reversed. Instead, they have worsened. Today that hope is flickering.

NOTES

Preface to the Paperback Edition

1. Parts of this paperback preface are taken from op-eds that I have written in the last few months in *USA Today* ("Fallacies of Romney's Logic," September 19, 2012), the *New York Times* ("Political Causes, Political Solutions for Inequality," October 18, 2012), the *Los Angeles Times* ("America's Prosperity Requires a Level Playing Field," July 22, 2012), the *Financial Times* ("America Is No Longer a Land of Opportunity," June 26, 2012), and the *Washington Post* ("How Policy Has Contributed to the Great Economic Divide," June 22, 2012) and from the prefaces to the Spanish and Japanese translations of my book.

2. As the *New York Times* has reported, federal bankruptcy law does provide for the discharging of student debt when a debtor can show that "undue hardship" because of repayment. That threshold is often absurdly high: in August 2012, the *Times* reported the heart-wrenching story of an unemployed blind man stuck with $89,000 in student loans because he had been unable to prove to the bankruptcy court that there was "a certainty of hopelessness." In practice, the discharging of student loans is rare. The same report noted that it is hard to come by thorough data

on the number of debtors who successfully discharge student loans by claiming undue hardship, but claims alone seem to number fewer than 1,000 a year throughout the United States. See Ron Lieber, "Last Plea on School Loans: Proving a Hopeless Future," *New York Times*, August 31, 2012.

3. National Center for Education Statistics data, available at http://nces .ed.gov/fastfacts/display.asp?id=76. The figure is adjusted for inflation. Between 1981 and 2011, tuition and fees at public four-year universities increased by some 368 percent, adjusted for inflation. See College Board, "Trends in College Pricing 2011," available at http://trends.collegeboard .org/downloads/College_Pricing_2011.pdf (accessed October 10, 2012).

4. Rajashri Chakrabarti, Maricar Mabutas, and Basit Zafar of the Federal Reserve Bank of New York report that "from 2000 to 2010, real net average tuition at public universities and colleges rose by 33.1 percent, from $3,415 to $4,546." They note that, in the same period, "data from the State Higher Education Executive Officers (SHEEO) show that, from 2000 to 2010, public funding per pupil, defined as state and local support for public higher education per pupil (excluding loans), fell by 21 percent, from $8,257 to $6,532 (all numbers presented in this post have been adjusted for inflation and reported in 2011 dollars . . .)." See Rajashri Chakrabarti, Maricar Mabutas, and Basit Zafar, "Soaring Tuitions: Are Public Funding Cuts to Blame?," 2012 blog post on the website of the New York Fed, available at http://libertystreeteconomics. newyorkfed.org/2012/09/soaring-tuitions-are-public-funding-cuts-to-blame.html (accessed December 3, 2012). The College Board, "Trends in College Pricing 2011," reports that state support fell (in inflation-adjusted dollars) by a quarter between 2006–07 and 2011–12.

5. College fees are five and a half times what they were in 1985. See Catherine Rampell, "Why Tuition Has Skyrocketed at State Schools," *New York Times*, March 2, 2012, available at http://economix.blogs .nytimes.com/2012/03/02/why-tuition-has-skyrocketed-at-state-schools/ (accessed November 29, 2012), citing Bureau of Labor Statistics. The College Board, "Trends in College Pricing 2011," reports, "Over the decade from 2001–02 to 2011–12, published tuition and fees for in-state students at public four-year colleges and universities increased at an average rate of 5.6% per year beyond the rate of general inflation. This rate of increase compares to 4.5% per year in the 1980s and 3.2% per year in the 1990s." The increasing inequality, decline in median income,

and increasing tuition meant that by 2011 (the last year for which data
are available) the average annual cost at a four-year public university was
50 percent *greater* than the average income of the bottom 20 percent of
families. There was no way that families, on their own, could send their
children to college.

6. "Trends in College Pricing," p. 17.

7. Pew Research Center, *Trends in Political Values and Core Attitudes:
1987–2009* (May 21, 2009), p. 56, available at http://www.people-press
.org/files/legacy-pdf/517.pdf.

8. See data from the Economic Policy Institute's *The State of Working America*, available at http://stateofworkingamerica.org/chart/swa-
wealth-table-6-6-wealth-groups-shares/. The EPI reports, "In 2010, less
than half (46.9 percent) of all households had stock holdings, and less
than a third (31.1 percent) had stock holdings of $10,000 or more."
See H. Shierholz, "The 'Democratization of the Stock Market' That
Never Happened" (2012), available at http://www.epi.org/publication/
wealth-stock-market-holdings/.

9. See "True Progressivism," *Economist*, October 13, 2012, p. 13.
Thomas Piketty and Emmanuel Saez, whose work I frequently cite in
this book, show that save for a brief couple of years immediately preceding the crash of 1929, the concentration of income in America's top .01
percent is unprecedented in the twentieth century. See Thomas Piketty
and Emmanuel Saez, "Income Inequality in the United States, 1913–
1998," *Quarterly Journal of Economics* 118, no. 1 (2003): 1–39, and
the paper's updated tables, available at http://elsa.berkeley.edu/~saez/
(accessed November 27, 2012).

10. See Warren Buffett, "A Minimum Tax for the Wealthy," *New York
Times*, November 25, 2012. Buffett apparently made an approximation
based on Internal Revenue Service data and a 40-hour workweek. In
the same op-ed, he provides a useful chronicle of the declining tax rates
on the wealthy—and a persuasive argument that raising those rates is a
fiscal and economic imperative.

11. See "The 400 Individual Income Tax Returns Reporting the Largest Adjusted Gross Incomes Each Year, 1992–2009," a publication of
the Internal Revenue Service, available at http://www.irs.gov/pub/irs-
soi/09intop400.pdf (accessed November 29, 2012).

12. The data on wealth here and in the following paragraphs come from
the Federal Reserve Board's Survey of Consumer Finances for 2010,

"Changes in U.S. Family Finances from 2007 to 2010: Evidence from the Survey of Consumer Finances," *Federal Reserve Bulletin* 98, no. 2 (2012): 1–80.

13. The median for the bottom fourth of net worth fell from $1,300 to zero. See ibid., p. 20.

14. Census table P-53, available at http://www.census.gov/hhes/www/income/data/historical/people/.

15. Census table H-6, available at http://www.census.gov/hhes/www/income/data/historical/household/.

16. Census Table H-13, available at http://www.census.gov/hhes/www/income/data/historical/household/.

17. Julian P. Cristia, "Rising Mortality and Life Expectancy Differentials by Lifetime Earnings in the United States," Inter-American Development Bank Working Paper no. 665, January 2009, available at http://www.iadb.org/res/publications/pubfiles/pubWP-665.pdf.

18. Human Mortality Database, available at http://www.ceda.berkeley.edu/News/NAS_WilmothBB_GeogDiff_e50.html#NASe0f.

19. See S. Jay Olshansky et al., "Differences in Life Expectancy Due to Race and Educational Differences Are Widening, and Many May Not Catch Up," *Health Affairs* 31, no. 8 (2012): 1803–13. Life expectancy numbers for those with only a high school education need to be interpreted with caution, since the fraction of the population with only a high school education has been changing.

20. These differences are approximate, and relate to the younger cohorts that Olshansky et al. examined (differences in life expectancy according to education attainment have been less marked for sixty-year-olds than for forty-year-olds and twenty-year-olds). The data can be viewed in the appendix to the Olshansky study, available at http://content.health affairs.org/content/suppl/2012/07/31/31.8.1803.DC1/2011-0746_Olshansky_Appendix.pdf (accessed November 28, 2012). The Schwarz Center for Economic Policy Analysis at the New School has collected additional studies that essentially corroborate the story told by the data presented in Olshansky et al. See, e.g., "Differences in Life Expectancy: Is Working Longer a Solution for Everyone," available at http://www.economicpolicyresearch.org/guaranteeing-retirement-income/560-differences-in-life-expectancy-is-working-longer-a-solution-for-everyone.html (accessed November 28, 2012), and the references cited there.

21. Sabrina Tavernise, "Life Spans Shrink for Least-Educated Whites in

the U.S.," *New York Times*, 20 September 2012, available at http://www
.nytimes.com/2012/09/21/us/life-expectancy-for-less-educated-whites-
in-us-is-shrinking.html?pagewanted=all.

22. According to Tavernise, "Life Spans Shrink," among working-age
adults with less than a high school diploma, 43 percent did not have
health insurance in 2006, up 8 percentage points from just thirteen years
earlier.

23. *National Federation of Independent Business v. Sebelius.*

24. Indeed, several publications in the last year have supported, strength-
ened, or expanded on these theses. They include Timothy Noah's *The
Great Divergence: America's Growing Inequality Crisis and What We Can
Do about It* (New York: Bloomsbury Press, 2012); *Inequality in Amer-
ica: Facts, Trends, and International Perspectives*, by Uri Dadush, Kemal
Dervis, Sarah Puritz Milsom, and Bennett Stancil (Washington, DC:
Brookings Institution Press, 2012); and *Inequality and Instability: A Study
of the World Economy Just before the Great Crisis*, by James K. Galbraith
(New York: Oxford University Press, 2012).

25. For instance, this is one of the arguments of the right-wing Heritage
Foundation, which tried to claim that inequality is good for us, in a report
by David Azerrad and Rea S. Hederman Jr. that it released in September
2012, "Defending the Dream: Why Income Inequality Doesn't Threaten
Opportunity," available at http://thf_media.s3.amazonaws.com/2012/pdf/
SR119.pdf (accessed November 28, 2012).

26. There are complicated issues in assessing the accuracy of medical
care inflation numbers, because in some areas (like heart surgery) there
have been marked improvements in outcomes. This is just one of a large
number of measurement problems that bedevil assessments of what is
happening to standards of living, and in comparing standards of living
across countries. Our metrics don't account, for instance, for increases
in insecurity (the greater risk of unemployment, or of losing one's home).
If household income increases mainly because people work longer hours,
then improvements in household income overstate the improvement in
living standards. For a more extensive discussion of these issues, see
J. E. Stiglitz, J. Fitoussi, and A. Sen, *Mismeasuring Our Lives: Why GDP
Doesn't Add Up* (New York: New Press, 2010).

27. Richard Lambert, "Paying for Inequality," *Prospect*, July 19, 2012.

28. "True Progressivism."

29. The report observes, e.g., "America's top 25 hedge-fund managers

make more than all the CEOs of the S&P 500 combined." See "The Rich and the Rest," *Economist*, October 13, 2012, pp. 12–15, citing research by Steven N. Kaplan and Joshua Rauh, in "Wall Street and Main Street: What Contributes to the Rise in the Highest Incomes?," *Review of Financial Studies* 23, no. 3 (2010): 1004–50. The same *Economist* article cites the work of Thomas Philippon and Ariell Reshef, who found in their "Wages and Human Capital in the U.S. Financial Industry: 1909–2006" (working paper forthcoming in the *Quarterly Journal of Economics*) that wages in finance were "excessively high" from the mid-1990s until 2006, and that "rents accounted for 30% to 50% of the wage differential between the financial sector and the rest of the private sector" (p. 1).

30. "True Progressivism," p. 13.

31. See Sean F. Reardon "The Widening Academic Achievement Gap between the Rich and the Poor: New Evidence and Possible Explanations," in R. Murnane and G. Duncan, eds., *Whither Opportunity? Rising Inequality and the Uncertain Life Chances of Low-Income Children* (New York: Russell Sage Foundation, 2011), pp. 91–116.

32. "True Progressivism," p. 13.

33. Ibid.

34. E. Conard, *Unintended Consequences: Why Everything You've Been Told about the Economy Is Wrong* (New York: Penguin, 2012).

35. Apple has 47,000 current U.S.-based employees (a large proportion of whom were in sales), but it has identified a further "257,000 jobs at 'other companies' that touch and support its products." See C. Guglielmo, "Apple Touts Itself as Big Job Creator in the U.S.," *Forbes*, March 2, 2012, available at http://www.forbes.com/sites/connieguglielmo/2012/03/02/apple-touts-itself-as-big-job-creator-in-the-u-s/.

36. Mitt Romney said, "There are 47 percent of the people who will vote for the president no matter what. All right, there are 47 percent who are with him, who are dependent upon government, who believe that they are victims, who believe the government has a responsibility to care for them, who believe that they are entitled to health care, to food, to housing, to you-name-it—that that's an entitlement. And the government should give it to them. And they will vote for this president no matter what. . . . These are people who pay no income tax. . . . [M]y job is not to worry about those people. I'll never convince them they should take personal responsibility and care for their lives." See L. Madison, "Fact-checking Romney's '47 percent' comment," CBS News, September 18, 2012, avail-

able at http://www.cbsnews.com/8301-503544_162-57515033-503544/
fact-checking-romneys-47-percent-comment/.

37. The Congressional Budget Office, estimates that individual income
taxes accounted for about 46 percent of federal tax revenues in fiscal
year 2012, while social insurance receipts (including a category that
includes Social Security and payroll taxes, Medicare payroll taxes, and
unemployment insurance) accounted for about 35 percent. Corporation
income taxes made up around 10 percent of receipts. See Congressional Budget Office, "Monthly Budget Review: Fiscal Year 2012: A Congressional Budget Office Analysis," October 5, 2012, available at http://
www.cbo.gov/sites/default/files/cbofiles/attachments/2012_09_MBR.pdf
(accessed December 3, 2012).

38. The *Economist* has highlighted another inequity in our system: the
government spends four times as much on subsidizing housing for the
richest through the tax system as it does on public housing for the poor.
See "True Progressivism," p. 13.

39. In the book, I borrow a phrase from Alexis de Tocqueville, "self-
interest properly understood."

40. This is the term used by the International Labor Organization to
describe the work that society should be aspiring toward. See the description at ILO, "Decent Work Agenda," http://www.ilo.org/global/about-the-
ilo/decent-work-agenda/lang--en/index.htm.

41. "The Rich and the Rest," *Economist*, p. 15.

42. Not all were successful. In Pennsylvania, for example, a judge struck
down—at least temporarily—parts of a draconian law requiring state-
approved photo identification to vote. Many social scientists and civil
rights activists consider voter identification laws—billed as a way to stop
the nearly nonexistent threat of voter fraud at polling places—an insidi-
ous tool for suppressing the vote of the poor and disadvantaged, another
episode in the continuing saga of disenfranchisement that I describe in
chapter 5.

43. For example, average annual Greek wages declined nearly 13.7 percent from 2009 to 2011; for Portugal the decline in the same period was
6.8 percent, according to the "Average annual wages, 2011 constant
prices and NCU" data series published by the Organization for Economic Co-operation and Development, available at http://stats.oecd.org/
(accessed December 3, 2012).

44. This pattern is referred to as the Kuznets curve, after Simon Kuznets's

1955 paper "Economic Growth and Income Inequality," *American Economic Review* 45, no. 1 (1955): 1–28. The idea has since been elaborated and refined; see, e.g., Susmita Dasgupta, Benoit Laplante, Hua Wang, and David Wheeler, "Confronting the Environmental Kuznets Curve," *Journal of Economic Perspectives* 16, no. 1 (2002): 147–68.

45. "The top 0.1%—about 315,000 individuals out of 315 million—are making about half of all capital gains on the sale of shares or property after 1 year; and these capital gains make up 60% of the income made by the Forbes 400," according to R. Lenzner, "The Top 0.1% of the Nation Earn Half of All Capital Gains," *Forbes*, November 20, 2011, available at http://www.forbes.com/sites/robertlenzner/2011/11/20/the-top-0-1-of-the-nation-earn-half-of-all-capital-gains/.

46. J. Stewart, "In Superrich, Clues to What Might Be in Romney's Returns," *New York Times*, August 10, 2012, available at http://www.nytimes.com/2012/08/11/business/in-the-superrich-clues-to-romneys-tax-returns-common-sense.html?pagewanted=all.

Preface

1. May 2011, available at http://www.vanityfair.com/society/features/2011/05/top-one-percent-201105 (accessed February 28, 2012).

2. See chapter 1 for a description of how unequal the United States has become, and for citations.

3. The nature of the market failures differed, of course, across countries. In Egypt, for instance, neoliberal market reforms had brought some growth, but the benefits of that growth had not trickled down to most individuals.

4. Not all of them show up in the "official" unemployment statistic, which stood at 8.3 percent. Some were actively looking for a full-time job and couldn't get any job, some had accepted a part-time job because a full-time job was not available, some were so discouraged by the lack of jobs that they had dropped out of the labor force. The numbers in Europe are similar.

5. Widely reported in the media; see, e.g., http://www.dailymail.co.uk/news/article-2048754/Occupy-Wall-Street-Bloomberg-backs-dawn-eviction.html (accessed December 3, 2011).

6. *USA Today*, available at http://www.usatoday.com/news/nation/story/2011-10-17/poll-wall-street-protests/50804978/1.

7. Non-Americans may be surprised to find out that the U.S. unemployment insurance normally extends for only six months. Chapter 1 describes both the battles to get it extended during the recession and the large numbers of people not covered.

8. Such divisions smacked of Marxian analysis, which was anathema during the Cold War, and in some places even after it.

9. As we show in chapter 1. Sociologists emphasize that there is more to class than just income.

10. We'll provide evidence on this in later chapters.

11. One response would be to stop talking about values. Rhetoric about equality, fairness, due process, and the like don't have anything to do with how the world works. In politics we would call this emphasis on reality realpolitik. Advocates of "realism" in economics often support a kind of economic Darwinism; let the system evolve and let the fittest survive. Systems that are flawed, like communism, won't survive. For now, American-style capitalism is the best system. In the nineteenth century these ideas were referred to as "social Darwinism." A variant of this concept was popularized among the Right. Such an argument (often unexpressed) sometimes seems to have influenced advocates of American-style capitalism. There are, however, a number of problems with this perspective. At a theoretical level, this teleological take on evolution—that it leads to the best-possible system—has no justification. Nor is it certain that a system that works now will have the resilience to meet future challenges. It is precisely this inability to assess resilience that is one of the flaws of the modern market economy. See also J. E. Stiglitz, *Whither Socialism?* (Cambridge: MIT Press, 1994).

12. As of July 2012, for 16- to 24-year-olds. See Bureau of Labor Statistics website, http://www.bls.gov/news.release/youth.nr0.htm (accessed November 14, 2012).

13. That our judicial system has been undermined by the growing inequality has been the subject of recent discussions. See, e.g., Glenn Greenwald, *With Liberty and Justice for Some: How the Law Is Used to Destroy Equality and Protect the Powerful* (New York: Metropolitan Books/Henry Holt, 2011). Others have also called attention to how the failure of our politics—the undue influence of special interests—is

undermining our economy, and did so even before the financial crisis made it self-evident. See Robert Kuttner, *The Squandering of America: How the Failure of Our Politics Undermines Our Prosperity* (New York: Knopf, 2007).

14. This is the perspective that I argued for in my earlier books *Globalization and Its Discontents* (New York: W. W. Norton, 2002), *Making Globalization Work* (New York: W. W. Norton, 2006), *The Roaring Nineties* (New York: W. W. Norton, 2003), and *Freefall* (New York: W. W. Norton, 2010). Others who have sounded similar themes include the excellent books by Robert Kuttner, *Everything for Sale: The Virtues and Limits of Markets* (New York: Knopf, 1997); John Cassidy, *How Markets Fail: The Logic of Economic Calamities* (New York: Farrar, Straus and Giroux, 2009); Michael Hirsh, *Capital Offense: How Washington's Wise Men Turned America's Future Over to Wall Street* (New York: Wiley, 2010); and Jeff Madrick, *The Age of Greed: The Triumph of Finance and the Decline of America, 1970 to the Present* (New York: Knopf, 2011).

15. New York: Simon and Schuster, 2010.

16. New York: Twelve, 2011.

17. New York: Russell Sage, 2008.

18. New York: MIT Press, 2008. These books follow in a long tradition, including Greg Palast, *The Best Democracy Money Can Buy*, rev. ed. (New York: Plume, 2004).

19. An alternative interpretation, which I discuss briefly in chapter 5, is that of Thomas Frank, in his *What's the Matter with Kansas? How Conservatives Won the Heart of America* (New York: Metropolitan Books, 2004).

20. This chapter of my thesis was published as "The Distribution of Income and Wealth Among Individuals," *Econometrica* 37, no. 3 (July 1969): 382–97. Other papers growing out of this early work include two with George Akerlof, with whom I shared the 2001 Nobel Prize, "Investment, Income, and Wages" (abstract), *Econometrica* 34, no. 5, suppl. issue (1966):118, and "Capital, Wages and Structural Unemployment," *Economic Journal* 79, no. 314 (June 1969): 269–81; one with my thesis supervisor, Robert Solow, "Output, Employment and Wages in the Short Run," *Quarterly Journal of Economics* 82 (November 1968): 537–60; and another chapter from my thesis, "A Two-Sector, Two Class Model of Economic Growth," *Review of Economic Studies* 34 (April 1967): 227–38.

21. I describe some of the influences contributing to the evolution of my thinking, especially about the role of information imperfections, in my

Nobel lecture, "Information and the Change in the Paradigm in Economics," in *Les Prix Nobel; The Nobel Prizes 2001*, ed. Tore Frängsmyr (Stockholm: Nobel Foundation, 2002), pp. 472–540. Also available at http://www.nobelprize.org/nobel_prizes/economics/laureates/2001/stiglitz-lecture.pdf (accessed February 28, 2012) and in abbreviated form as "Information and the Change in the Paradigm in Economics," *American Economic Review* 92, no. 3 (June 2002): 460–501. See also the brief autobiography written for the Nobel Foundation, "Nobel Memoirs," in *Les Prix Nobel; The Nobel Prizes 2001*, pp. 447–71, and "Reflections on Economics and on Being and Becoming an Economist," in *The Makers of Modern Economics*, vol. 2, ed. Arnold Heertje (New York: Harvester Wheatsheaf, 1994), pp. 140–83.

Chapter One AMERICA'S 1 PERCENT PROBLEM

1. From January 2007 to December 2011 there were more than 8.2 million foreclosure starts and 4 million completed foreclosures. See Realtytrac, 2012, "2012 Foreclosure Market Outlook," February 13, available at http://www.realtytrac.com/content/news-and-opinion/slideshow-2012-foreclosure-market-outlook-7021 (accessed March 28, 2012). There are still many foreclosures in the pipeline—some 5.9 million properties are 30 or more days delinquent or in foreclosure; see Mortgage Monitor Report, Lender Processing Services (March 2012), available at http://www.lpsvcs.com/LPSCorporateInformation/NewsRoom/Pages/20120321.aspx (accessed March 28, 2012). Additionally, 11.1 million, or 22.8 percent, of all residential properties with a mortgage in the United States were underwater (had negative equity at the end of the fourth quarter of 2011); see "Negative Equity Report," Corelogic (Q4, 2011), available at http://www.corelogic.com/about-us/researchtrends/asset_upload_file360_14435.pdf (accessed March 28, 2012).

2. The exact amount varies from year to year. For data on income inequality, I rely heavily on the work of Emmanuel Saez and Thomas Piketty. The important initial work is T. Piketty and E. Saez, "Income Inequality in the United States, 1913–1998," *Quarterly Journal of Economics* 118, no. 1 (2003): 1–39. A longer and updated version is published in A. B. Atkinson and T. Piketty, eds., *Top Incomes over the Twentieth Century: A Contrast between Continental European and English-Speaking Countries* (New

York: Oxford University Press, 2007). Tables and figures updated to 2010
in Excel format are available at Saez's website, http://www.econ.berkeley
.edu/~saez/. Saez has an accessible summary of this work on his website,
"Striking It Richer: The Evolution of Top Incomes in the United States."
Note that the Saez data are based on income tax returns, and thus are
high quality, but also therefore cover only reported income. To the extent
that upper-income taxpayers are better able to avoid reporting income,
e.g., through keeping income abroad in corporations they control, the data
may underestimate the extent of inequality. I also draw on a recent CBO
report, "Trends in the Distribution of Household Income between 1979
and 2007," October 2011, available at http://www.cbo.gov/sites/default/
files/cbofiles/attachments/10-25-HouseholdIncome.pdf; and on recent
work by J. Bakija, A. Cole, and B. T. Hein in "Jobs and Income Growth
of Top Earners and the Causes of Changing Income Inequality: Evidence
from U.S. Tax Return Data," working paper, January 2012, available at
http://web.williams.edu/Economics/wp/BakijaColeHeimJobsIncome
GrowthTopEarners.pdf. The Census Historical Tables provide data on
median household incomes over time, available at http://www.census.gov/
hhes/www/income/data/historical/household/index.html. Basic sources of
data for across-country comparisons are OECD, "Divided We Stand: Why
Inequality Keeps Rising," December 5, 2011; World Bank, World Bank
Development Indicators, available at http://data.worldbank.org/indica
tor; and the Luxembourg Income Study. The Economic Policy Institute
provides excellent interpretations and updates of the data at its website,
http://www.epi.org/.
3. Laurence Mishel and Josh Bivens, "Occupy Wall Streeters Are Right
about Skewed Economic Rewards in the United States," EPI Briefing Paper 331, October 26, 2011, available at https://docs.google.com/
viewer?url=http://www.epi.org/files/2011/BriefingPaper331.pdf&hl=en_
US&chrome=true (accessed February 28, 2012). Another manifestation of
the growing inequality that in 1979 the ratio of the average income in the
top 0.1 percent, including capital gains, was "only" around 50 times greater
than that of the average in the bottom 90 percent. By 2010 the ratio was
164 times that of the average bottom 90 percent of income earners. Meanwhile, the ratio of the average household income of the top 1 percent to
that of the bottom 90 percent has tripled, from 14:1 to 42:1. Based on data
from Piketty and Saez, "Income Inequality in the United States, 1913–
1998," and the updates on Saez's website, cited in n. 2, above.

4. More precisely, the top 1 percent control about 35 percent of the wealth. If the value of the home is excluded, i.e., "nonhome wealth," the number is considerably larger: the top 1 percent owns two-fifths of the nation's wealth. Edward N. Wolff compares both figures in "Recent Trends in Household Wealth in the United States: Rising Debt and the Middle-Class Squeeze—an Update to 2007," Levy Institute Working Paper no. 589, March 2010, available at http://www.levyinstitute.org/pubs/wp_589.pdf (accessed February 28, 2012). The Federal Reserve is the original source for the net-worth figures, including home wealth; see Arthur B. Kennickell, "What's the Difference? Evidence on the Distribution of Wealth, Health, Life Expectancy and Health Insurance Coverage," paper prepared for the 11th Biennial CDC/ATSDR Symposium, September 23, 2007, available at http://www.federalreserve.gov/pubs/oss/oss2/papers/CDC.final.pdf (accessed February 28, 2012). Note that the top 1 percent income may not perfectly overlap the top 1 percent wealth holders—these are two different categories. The top 1 percent of income earners own "only" about 25 percent of the nation's wealth. See Arthur B. Kennickell, "Ponds and Streams: Wealth and Income in the U.S., 1989 to 2007," staff working paper in the Finance and Economics Discussion Series, Federal Reserve Board, Washington, DC, January 7, 2009, p. 36, available at http://www.federalreserve.gov/pubs/feds/2009/200913/200913pap.pdf (accessed February 29, 2012).

5. Based on data from Piketty and Saez's, "Income Inequality in the United States, 1913–1998," and the updates on Saez's website, cited in n. 2, above.

6. The top 1 percent of income earners received some 60 percent of the gains during the country's economic expansion between 1979 and 2007. While the real after-tax household income of the 1 percent grew by 275 percent in that period, the bottom fifth's average real after-tax household income rose only 18 percent. *Indeed, the bottom 90 percent of earners got just a fourth of what the top 0.1 percent gained.* Based on data from, Piketty and Saez, "Income Inequality in the United States, 1913–1998," and the updates on Saez's website, cited in n. 2, above. See EPI Briefing Paper, October 26, 2011, cited in n. 3, above; and Josh Biven, "Three-Fifths of All Income Growth from 1979–2007 Went to the Top 1%," Economic Policy Institue, October 27, 2011, available at http://www.epi.org/publication/fifths-income-growth-1979-2007-top-1/ (accessed February 28, 2012). The CBO 2011 study, cited in n. 1, above, presents a similar picture.

378 NOTES TO PAGES 3-4

7. We use the term "typical" to refer to the median income, i.e., the income such that half of all workers have an income higher than that number, half below. Median household income was actually lower in 2011 ($50,054) than it was in 1996, adjusted for inflation ($50,661 in 2011 dollars). Over the longer period, 1980–2010, median family income essentially stagnated, growing at an annual rate of only 0.36 percent. Based on table H-9 of Census historical tables, available at http://www.census.gov/hhes/www/income/data/historical/household/index.html.

8. Adjusted for inflation, male median income in 2011 was $32,986; in 1968 it was $33,880. See table P-5 of the U.S. Census Bureau's income report, available at http://www.census.gov/hhes/www/income/data/historical/people/index.html (accessed November 27, 2012). (Of course, the median worker today is a different person from the median person in 1968, and these numbers can be affected by immigration of unskilled workers.)

9. By April 2010, stock market prices (S&P 500), which had fallen 56 percent between the peak, in October 2007, and the trough, in March 2009, were up 78 percent from the trough (though at the time of writing, they are still 13 percent below the peak).

10. See the 2012 update to the data for Piketty and Saez, "Income Inequality in the United States, 1913–1998."

11. House prices are, at the time of writing (February 2012), still down 33 percent, and for those living in some parts of the country (e.g., Miami, Florida), the decline is still more than 50 percent (using S&P/Case-Shiller Home Price Indices). See "All Three Home Price Composites End 2011 at New Lows According to the S&P/Case-Shiller Home Price Indices," press release of S&P/Case-Shiller Home Price Indices, February 28, 2012, available at http://www.standardand poors.com/servlet/BlobServer?blobheadername3=MDT-Type&blobcol=urldocumentfile&blobtable=SPComSecureDocument&blobheadervalue2=inline%3B+file name%3Ddownload.pdf&blobheadername2=Content-Disposition&blob headervalue1=application%2Fpdf&blobkey=id&blobheadername1=con tent-type&blobwhere=1245329497678&blobheadervalue3=abinary%3B +charset%3DUTF-8&blobnocache=true (accessed March 2, 2012).

12. According to Lawrence Mishel and Josh Bivens, "Occupy Wall Streeters Are Right about Skewed Economic Rewards in the United States," Economic Policy Institute Briefing Paper no. 331, available at http://www.epi.org/files/2011/BriefingPaper331.pdf (accessed Febru-

ary 10, 2012). Some other studies give slightly different numbers—all, though, show correspondingly high ratios of CEO pay to that of the median worker.

13. Figures are from 1983. See Piketty and Saez, cited in n. 2, above. There are some problems in estimating changes in income share over long periods of time. Prior to 1986, thanks to the relatively low corporate income tax rate, it paid some high-income individuals to shelter their income inside a corporation, because it allowed the deferral of paying the high individual income tax rates so long as money remained within the corporation. This changed in 1986, leading to higher incomes reported on individuals' own tax returns. While this explains a substantial portion of the increase in reported incomes around 1986, looking beyond this period—1988 onward—it is clear that there have been huge increases in the share of income going to the top. See Jon Bakija et al., "Jobs and Income Growth of Top Earners and the Causes of Changing Income Inequality: Evidence from U.S. Tax Return Data;" Roger Gordon and Joel Slemrod, "Are 'Real' Responses to Taxes Simply Income Shifting between Corporate and Personal Tax Bases?," in *Does Atlas Shrug? The Economic Consequences of Taxing the Rich*, ed. Joel Slemrod (Cambridge: Harvard University Press, 2000); and Joel Slemrod, "High Income Families and the Tax Changes of the 1980s: The Anatomy of Behavioral Response," in *Empirical Foundations of Household Taxation*, ed. Martin Feldstein and James Poterba (Chicago: University of Chicago Press, 1996). It is important to note that the composition of the 1 percent (or the 0.1 percent) is changing over the years. It's not that the income of those who were in the 1 percent in 2002 were 65 percent richer on average in 2007. There is some mobility—but, as we discuss later in this chapter, much less than is widely assumed. The statistic says only that those who were in the top in more recent years seized a much larger fraction of the nation's economic pie than those who were in the top positions ten years ago, or twenty-five years ago.

14. While those at the bottom and middle have seen their income fall in this century, the divide between the rich and the poor has been growing for a third of a century. Between 1979 and 2007, the after-tax income for the top 1 percent income earners increased 275 percent. For the 21st through 80th percentiles, the increase was just below 40 percent. For the bottom 20 percent, the increase was only 18 percent. The net result of this is that "the share of household income after transfers and federal

taxes going to the highest income quintile grew from 43 percent in 1979 to 53 percent in 2007" (for the 1 percent the increase was from 8 percent to 17 percent), whereas the share of after-tax and transfer income for all other quintiles fell (all by between 2 and 3 percentage points). See CBO, "Trends in the Distribution of Household Income." The *threshold* for belonging to the top 1 percent of income earners in 2010 when capital gains are included, according to Piketty and Saez, "Income Inequality in the United States, 1913–1998," and the related data updated on Saez's website, is $352,055. For the top 0.1 percent, the threshold was $1,492,175. (The data have not been updated past 2010.) In contrast, the median *household* income in 2010 was $49,455 (in 2010 dollars), according to census data, table H-9, cited in n. 7, above. Different studies have used slightly different calculations to assess the cutoff point for the top 1 percent, but the picture is essentially the same.

15. Assuming a 2,000-hour work year, the $1.3 million per year converts into approximately $650 per hour, or some 80 times greater than the minimum wage. The figures come from CBO, *Average Federal Tax Rates in 2007*, June, available at http://www.cbo.gov/sites/default/files/cbofiles/ftpdocs/115xx/doc11554/average federaltaxrates2007.pdf (accessed February 29, 2012). See table 1. Again, different data sources provide slightly different numbers—but the picture is essentially the same. According to Piketty and Saez, "Income Inequality in the United States, 1913–1998," the "top 1 percent" (those with incomes above $352,055 in 2010) had an average income, including *realized* capital gains, of $1.4 million in 2007 (dropping to $1.0 million in 2010).

16. See CBO, *Average Federal Tax Rates in 2007*. Table 1 reports the average after-tax income of the highest quintile as $198,300, whereas the sum of the after-tax income averages of the other quintiles is $77,700 + $55,300 + $38,000 + $17,700 = $188,700.

17. Poverty was reduced by 40 percent. Using the national poverty standard, the percentage in poverty fell from almost 36 percent in 2003 to 21 percent in 2009. Also reduced was the income share of the top 10 percent, from 46.7 percent to 42.5 percent between 2001 and 2009. See http://www.unicef.org/infobycountry/brazil_statistics.html#0; http://web.worldbank.org/wbsite/external/countries/lacext/brazilextn/0,menuPK:322367~pagePK:141132~piPK:141109~theSitePK:322341,00.html; World Bank Development Indicators: http://data.worldbank.org/indicator.

18. From 2004 to 2010, the Brazilian economy expanded at an average rate of 4.4 percent per year; if the global recession year of 2009 is excluded, the average is nearly 5.3 percent, much higher than it was, say, from 1985 to 1994. See World Bank Indicators, available at http://data .worldbank.org/indicator/ny.gdp.mktp.kd.zg?page=2 (accessed March 5, 2012).

19. Growth in the past thirty years (1981–2011) was not as strong as in the preceding thirty years (an average annual growth of 2.8 percent versus 3.6 percent). Federal Reserve Bank of St Louis, Real Gross Domestic Product growth rate, available at http://research.stlouisfed.org/fred2/series/ GDPC1/downloaddata?cid=106.

20. From 1992 to 2000, the lowest quintile grew at 2.6 percent, faster than any of the other quintiles except the top fifth, which grew at 3.5 percent. U.S. Census Bureau, cited by Alan B. Krueger, "The Rise and Consequences of Inequality in the United States," address delivered at the Center for American Progress, January 12, 2012.

21. There's been redistribution *away* from the bottom and middle, and almost all of what's been redistributed has gone to the *very* top, the top 1 percent. This is a direct corollary of the fact that incomes at the bottom and in the middle have been falling, while those at the very top have been rising. CBO, "Trends in the Distribution of Household Income."

22. See also Krueger, "The Rise and Consequences of Inequality."

23. See National Center for Education Statistics, "Fast Facts," on the question "What is the average income for young adults?," available at http://nces.ed.gov/fastfacts/display.asp?id=77.

24. Based on median income for households with a householder who is at least 25 and has a bachelor's degree or more. See Census Household Income Historical Table H-13, "Table H-13. Educational Attainment of Householder—Households with Householder 25 Years Old and Over by Median and Mean Income: 1991 to 2011," available at http:// www.census.gov/hhes/www/income/data/historical/household/ (accessed November 28, 2012). Median incomes for college-educated women over the same time period have been flat and are today at two-thirds the level of male earnings. See U.S. Census Bureau, Historical Income Table P-16, available at http://www.census.gov/hhes/www/income/data/ historical/people/.

25. As Paul Krugman has pointed out, "almost two-thirds of the rising share of the top percentile in income actually went to the top 0.1 per-

cent . . . who saw their real incomes rise more than 400 percent" from 1979 to 2005. "Oligarchy, American Style," *New York Times*, November 4, 2011, available at http://www.nytimes.com/2011/11/04/opinion/oligarchy-american-style.html (accessed March 1, 2012). According to data from Piketty and Saez, "Income Inequality in the United States, 1913–1998," and Saez's website, cited in n. 2, above, the income of the top 0.1 percent in 1979 accounted for just 3.44 percent of the total income, but by 2005 its share had more than tripled, to 10.98 percent. Bakija et al., "Jobs and Income Growth of Top Earners," report that the increase of the top 0.1 percent in pretax income share was from 2.2 percent to 8 percent from 1981 to 2006. Other data series give slightly different numbers, but corroborate the enormous increase in the share of the top 0.1 percent.

26. That is, household income consists of wages and salaries and returns on capital. There is a third determinant, which we will discuss later in the chapter—government can augment incomes (through transfer programs) or diminish them (through taxes). As we note below, government programs have become less progressive, that is, taken less from the top and given less to the bottom.

27. More precisely, over the period 1979–2006, the top 1 percent saw wages grow by 144 percent; the top 0.1 percent, by 324 percent. Even the top 1 percent gets more than 20 times that of the bottom 90 percent. Lawrence Mishel, Jared Bernstein, and Heidi Shierholz, *The State of Working America 2008/2009* (Ithaca, NY: ILR Press, an imprint of Cornell University Press, 2009), table 3.10, cited in Mishel and Biven, "Occupy Wall Streeters Are Right."

28. When the numbers were already large—125 to 1 and 131 to 1, respectively. From Mishel and Bivens, "Occupy Wall Streeters Are Right," based on analysis of Edward Wolff, unpublished analysis of the U.S. Federal Reserve Board, Survey of Consumer Finances and Federal Reserve Flow of Funds, prepared for the Economic Policy Institute, in Sylvia Allegretto, *The State of Working America's Wealth, 2011: Through Volatility and Turmoil the Gap Widens*, Economic Policy Institute Brief Paper 292 (Washington, D.C.: EPI, 2010).

29. Mishel and Biven, "Occupy Wall Streeters Are Right," based on data from CBO, p. 8. This is why the data on *income* inequality show so much more inequality than the data focusing just on wage and earnings inequality.

30. From 1979 to 2007. Mishel and Biven, "Occupy Wall Streeters Are Right," p. 9, EPI analysis of data from the CBO collection of data on effective federal taxes.

31. The Economic Policy Institute has found that the Walton wealth was larger than the wealth of the bottom 40 percent of all American families combined in 2010. See www.epi.org/blog/inequality-exhibit-walmart-wealth-american/ (accessed November 14, 2012).

32. Larry Katz of Harvard has popularized the term in a number of papers written with coauthors (and cited in the next chapter). See David H. Autor, Lawrence F. Katz, and Melissa S. Kearney, "The Polarization of the Labor Market," *American Economic Review* 96, no. 2 (May 2006): 189–94; and Claudia Goldin and Lawrence F. Katz, "Long-Run Changes in the Wage Structure: Narrowing, Widening, Polarizing," *Brookings Papers on Economic Activity* 2 (2007): 135–64, and the references cited there. Autor, Katz, and Kearney cite Maarten Goos and Alan Manning, "Lousy and Lovely Jobs: The Rising Polarization of Work in Britain," London School of Economics, Center for Economic Performance Discussion Papers: No. DP0604, 2003, as the first source of the term "polarization."

33. One way of saying this numerically is the following: the ratio of the income of those at the top (say, at the 95th percentile, i.e., only 5 percent of the population has a higher income) to those in the middle has increased, while the ratio of the income of those in the middle to those at the bottom (say, at the 20th percentile) has not changed. Data from Piketty and Saez, "Income Inequality in the United States, 1913–1998," compared to U.S. Census Historical Tables (H-9 and H-1), shows that the ratio of the 95th percentile households to the median in 1980 was 2.6; the ratio of the median income households to the 20th percentile was 2.4. In 2010, the ratio of the 95th percentile income to the median income was 3.0; the ratio of the median income to the 20th percentile income was still 2.4.

34. Another way of seeing the evisceration of the middle class is that the fraction of those with incomes that are close to the middle—within a range that goes from 50 percent greater than the median to 50 percent less than the median—has fallen since 1970 from just over 50 percent to just over 42 percent. Krueger, "The Rise and Consequences of Inequality," citing Council of Economic Adviser calculations based on the Current Population Survey.

35. Bureau of Labor Statistics, Employment Situation Summary, November 2011, available at http://www.bls.gov/news.release/empsit .nr0.htm.

36. For an excellent telling of some of these stories, see Peter Goodman, *Past Due: The End of Easy Money and the Renewal of the American Economy* (New York: Times Books, 2009). See also Lisa A. Goodman, Leonard Saxe, and Mary Harvey, "Homelessness as Psychological Trauma: Broadening Perspectives," *American Psychologist* 46, no. 11 (November 1991): 1219–25.

37. See U.S. Census Bureau, "Income, Poverty, and Health Insurance Coverage in the United States: 2010," issued September 2011, P60-239.

38. Himmelstein et al. "conservatively" estimate that "62.1% of all bankruptcies in 2007 were medical," that is, had important medical factors as a contributor. Furthermore, "most medical debtors were well educated, owned homes, and had middle-class occupations. Three quarters had health insurance. Using identical definitions, between 2001 and 2007, the share of bankruptcies attributable to medical problems rose by 49.6%." D. Himmelstein, D. Thorne, E. Warren, and S. Woolhandler, "Medical Bankruptcy in the United States, 2007: Results of a National Study," *American Journal of Medicine* 122, no. 8 (2009): 741–46. In terms of getting at a more causal measure, i.e., estimating the direct effect of a health shock on the decision of whether or not to declare bankruptcy, Gross and Notowidigdo find "that out-of-pocket medical costs are pivotal in roughly 26 percent of personal bankruptcies among low-income households." Tal Gross and Matthew J. Notowidigdo, "Health Insurance and the Consumer Bankruptcy Decision: Evidence from Expansions of Medicaid," *Journal of Public Economics* 95, nos. 7–8 (2011): 767–78.

39. Washington State Child Care Resource and Referral Network, 2010 data reports. Average statewide cost for one preschooler and one toddler. Assumes children are in full-time, full-year center care. Available at http://www.child carenet.org/partners/data (accessed February 2, 2012).

40. Bureau of Labor Statistics, Employment Situation, available at http://www.bls.gov/news.release/empsit_nr.htm (accessed November 15, 2012). By October 2012, an additional 3.3 million Americans had full-time jobs.

41. See, e.g., Stephane Pallage, Lyle Scruggs, and Christian Zimmermann, "Unemployment Insurance Generosity: A Trans-Atlantic Comparison," IZA Discussion Papers 3869, Institute for the Study of Labor (IZA), 2008.

42. Most recently, before this book went to press, in February 2012.

43. A Congressional Research Service report notes that 2 million of the 14.4 million unemployed in June 2011 were unemployed for more than 99 weeks. G. Mayer, "The Trend in Long-Term Unemployment and Characteristics of Workers Unemployed for More Than 99 Weeks," September 12, 2011, available at http://big.assets.huffingtonpost.com/crsreport.pdf. The BLS reports that 9 percent of the 2010 unemployed had reached a duration of 99 weeks of unemployment. See R. Ilg, "How Long before the Unemployed Find Jobs or Quit Looking?," Bureau of Labor Statistics, May 2011, available at http://www.bls.gov/opub/ils/summary_11_01/unemployed_jobs_quit.htm.

44. As of October 2011. In December 2007, that ratio was 1.8; at the peak of the Great Recession, it reached 6.1. Bureau of Labor Statistics, "Job Openings and Labor Turnover Survey—October 2011," December 13, 2011, available at http://www.bls.gov/web/jolts/jlt_labstatgraphs.pdf.

45. Some politicians, and a few economists, worried that unemployment insurance would discourage search. But more search would have just meant longer lines, not more employment.

46. Michael Cooper and Allison Kopicki, "Jobless Go Without, But Stay Hopeful, Poll Finds," New York Times, October 27, 2011, pp. A1, A16.

47. For those 45 to 54, the average duration of unemployment in January 2012 was 43 weeks, for those 55 to 64, the average already exceeds a year, at almost 57 weeks. See Household Data Table A-6 from the Bureau of Labor Statistics, "Unemployed Persons by Age, Sex, Race, Hispanic or Latino Ethnicity, Marital Status, and Duration of Unemployment," January 2012, available at http://www.bls.gov/web/empsit/cpseea36.pdf (accessed March 6, 2012).

48. See, e.g., Steven J. Davis and Till von Wachter, "Recessions and the Costs of Job Loss," November 2011, prepared for the Brookings Papers on Economic Activity, available at http://www.columbia.edu/~vw2112/papers//Recessions_and_the_Costs_of_Job_Loss_23_November_2011.pdf (accessed March 5, 2012). See also P. Oreopoulos, T. von Wachter, and A. Heisz, "The Short- and Long-Term Career Effects of Graduating in a Recession: Hysteresis and Heterogeneity in the Market for College Graduates," NBER Working Paper, no. 12159 (2006); or L. Kahn, "The Long-Term Labor Market Consequences of Graduating from College in a Bad Economy," Labour Economics 12, no. 2 (April 2010): 303–16.

49. A point explained in Domenico Delli Gatti, Mauro Gallegati, Bruce

C. Green-wald, Alberto Russo, and Joseph E. Stiglitz, "Sectoral Imbalances and Long Run Crises," proceedings of the Beijing 2012 World Congress of the International Economic Association.

50. One in four mortgage owners, some 14 million Americans, are underwater, for a net negative equity total of $700 billion. M. Zandi, "To Shore Up the Recovery, Help Housing," Special Report, Moody's Analytics, May 25, 2011.

51. Those receiving mortgages between 2004 and 2008 were particularly hard hit; of those receiving loans in this period, 2.7 million households have already been foreclosed upon, and another 3.6 million are at serious risk. D. Gruenstein Bocian, W. Li, and C. Reid, "Lost Ground, 2011: Disparities in Mortgage Lending and Foreclosures," Center for Responsible Lending, November 2011, available at http://www.responsiblelending .org/mortgage-lending/research-analysis/Lost-Ground-2011.pdf.

52. Zandi, "To Shore Up the Recovery."

53. Pew Research Center, "Wealth Gaps Rise to Record Highs between Whites, Blacks, Hispanics Twenty-to-One" (2011), available at http:// www.pewsocialtrends.org/2011/07/26/wealth-gaps-rise-to-record-highs-between-whites-blacks-hispanics/. The 2010 Fed Survey of Consumer Finances, released after publication of the hardcover version of this book, shows that median white American wealth has rebounded somewhat but is still below 2005 levels. The overall picture remains bleak.

54. World Bank, Life Expectancy at Birth (years), available at http://data .worldbank.org/indicator/SP.DYN.LE00.IN?order=wbapi_data_value_ 2009+wbapi_data_value+wbapi_data_value-last&sort=desc.

55. According to the World Bank, the United States' mortality rate for under-5's in 2010 was 8 per 1000. This places it 45th in the world on this metric, worse, e.g., than Cuba (6), Belarus (6), Lithuania (7), and the United Arab Emirates (7). In Iceland the rate is four times better (at 2). Data available at http://data.worldbank.org/indicator/SH.DYN .MORT?order=wbapi_data_value_2010+wbapi_data_value+wbapi_ data_value-last&sort=asc. The pictures for maternal mortality ratio data from the World Bank are similar, where, e.g., the performance of Germany is three times better than that of the United States.

56. In 2002 the bottom decile's life expectancy was 73.2, as opposed to 79.8 for the top. The gap between the top and the bottom has actually been growing. In 1982 the highest decile had an expected life of 76.3 compared with 71.0 for the lowest decile. (Some measures of

inequality in health, however, such as the Gini coefficient, do show an improvement.) S. Peltzman, "Mortality Inequality," *Journal of Economic Perspectives* 23, no. 4 (Fall 2009): 175–90. Inequalities in health are long-standing and widespread. As reported in David Cutler, Angus Deaton, and Adriana Lleras-Muney, "The Determinants of Mortality," *Journal of Economic Perspectives* 20, no. 3 (Summer 2006): 97–20, "Americans in the bottom 5 percent of the income distribution in 1980 had a life-expectancy at all ages that was about 25 percent lower than the corresponding life-expectancies of those in the top 5 percent of the income distribution (Rogot, Sorlie, Johnson and Schmitt, 1992)" (p. 98). They continue (p. 99), "American blacks had a life expectancy in 2002 that was 5.4 years less than that of American whites. In England and Wales in 1997–2001, male manual workers could expect to live 8.4 years less than professionals, a gap that has increased since the early 1970s."

57. Some 5.9 million aged 25 to 34 were living at home, up 14 percent from a prerecession figure of 4.7million. See "America's Families and Living Arrangements: 2011," a series of tables from the 2011 Current Population Survey. K. Newman, *The Accordion Family* (Boston: Beacon Press, 2012), reports that there is a higher proportion of U.S. parents living with children than at any other time since the 1950s.

58. Carol Morello, "Married Couples at a Record Low," *Washington Post*, December 14, 2011, citing data provided by Rose Kreider, a Census Bureau demographer. The trend, of course, was present before the recession, but the magnitude of the change was dramatic, and had much to do with the recession. The total number of couples living together without being married was 7.5 million in 2010. In many poorer countries, lack of economic resources is a barrier to marriage or leads to marriage later in life; in some ways, American mores are following the same pattern.

59. Part of the problem is that individuals without a history of violent crime can be given long prison terms for possession of drugs. But part of the problem reflects high levels of violence. But the pattern of incarceration suggests that other social forces (including discrimination) are at play. See Robert Perkinson, *Texas Tough* (New York: Metropolitan Books, 2010) and Michelle Alexander, *The New Jim Crow* (New York: New Press, 2010).

60. FBI, "Crime in the US, 1991–2010," Uniform Crime Reports, available at http://www.fbi.gov/about-us/cjis/ucr/crime-in-the-u.s/2010/crime-in-the-u.s.-2010/tables/10tbl01.xls. Homicides rose sharply in the 1970s,

to peak at 10.2 per 100,000 in 1980, falling slightly in the mid-1980s before rising again to 9.8 per 100,000 in 1991 and falling off since. In 2010 the rate was 4.8 per 100,000. U.S. Department of Justice, *Homicide Trends in the United States, 1980–2008*, November 2011. The violent-crime rate reached its highest level of 758 per 100,000 people in 1991 (the data cover 1960–2010). By 2009 that rate was down to 429. FBI, Uniform Crime Reports as prepared by the National Archive of Criminal Justice Data, available at UCR data tool, http://www.ucrdatatool.gov/index.cfm (accessed January 1, 2012).

61. The rates of incarceration and supervision are from L. Glaze, *Correctional Populations in the United States, 2010*, United States Bureau of Justice Statistics, NCJ 231681, 2011. According to the same report, the total number under correctional supervision as of 2010 is even larger— more than seven million. International comparisons are from the International Centre for Prison Studies, available at http://www.prisonstudies .org/info/worldbrief/wpb_stats.php?area=all&category=wb_poprate, according to which the United States incarcerates 730 per 100,000 people; the world's next highest incarceration rates are Rwanda, at about 595, and Russia, with a rate of 542. For more within-U.S. cross-state comparisons, see also Pew Center on the States, 2008, *One in 100: Behind Bars in America 2008*, available at http://www.pewcenteronthe states.org/uploadedFiles/One%20in%20100.pdf.

62. Between 1987 and 2007 the ratio of (general fund) spending on corrections to that on higher education increased across all states except two. In New York that ratio increased by 0.61. Oregon spends a $1.06 on corrections for every dollar of spending on higher education; Michigan, $1.19. Pew Center on the States, *One in 100: Behind Bars in America 2008*, available at http://www.pewcenteronthestates.org/uploadedFiles/8015PCTS_ Prison08_FINAL_2-1-1_FORWEB.pdf.

63. That GDP gives a misleading impression of the economy's health is the main message of the Commission on the Measurement of Economic Performance and Social Progress. Jean-Paul Fitoussi, Amartya Sen, and Joseph E. Stiglitz, with J. Fitoussi and A. Sen, *Mismeasuring Our Lives: Why GDP Doesn't Add Up* (New York: New Press, 2010), also available at http://www.stiglitz-sen-fitoussi.fr/en/index.htm (accessed March 1, 2012).

64. America's prison population is about 2.27 million, according to the Department of Justice. See "Correctional Population in the United

NOTES TO PAGE 20   389

States, 2010," U.S. Department of Justice, Bureau of Justice Statistics, December 2011, NCJ 236319, available at http://bjs.ojp.usdoj.gov/con tent/pub/pdf/cpus10.pdf (accessed March 1, 2012). If that population, which is not employed, was added to the January 2012 civilian labor force of 154.40 million and to those 12.76 million currently counted as unemployed, it would increase the unemployment rate from 8.3 percent to 9.5 percent. Unemployment figures are from the Bureau of Labor Statistics' "Unemployment Situation Report—January 2012, available at http://www.bls.gov/news.release/pdf/empsit.pdf (accessed March 1, 2012). One study, written in 1999, when the prison population was somewhat lower, showed that the unemployment rate might be as much as 2 percent higher if prison populations were included in the count. See, e.g., Bruce Western and Katherine Beckett, "How Unregulated Is the U.S. Labor Market? The Penal System as a Labor Market Institution," *American Journal of Sociology* 104, no. 4 (January 1999): 1030–60. Incarceration itself, however, may contribute to higher unemployment rates among the nonimprisoned population, because, as we note in chapter 3, those who have been incarcerated have much poorer job prospects, and this is especially true for African Americans.

65. Federal poverty *thresholds* were developed in the mid-1960s by Mollie Orshansky at the Social Security Administration. On the basis of survey work that indicated that households at the time spent roughly a third of their income on food, the poverty line was calculated as three times the cost of the USDA's economy food plan. The thresholds are used by the Census Bureau and are annually updated for inflation. The federal poverty *guidelines* are an administrative tool (issued by the Department of Health and Human Services) and have been institutionalized in a variety of important welfare programs. The measures obviously have problems (as Orshansky herself has noted), notably that the cost of food relative to, e.g., housing and health care has changed dramatically. In 2011 the poverty level for a family of four was $22,350. The U.S. Department of Health and Human Services Poverty Guidelines, available at http://aspe.hhs.gov/poverty/11poverty.shtml.

66. H. Luke Shaefer and Kathryn Edin, "Extreme Poverty in the United States, 1996 to 2011," National Poverty Center Policy Brief no. 28, February 2012, available at http://npc.umich.edu/publications/policy_ briefs/brief28/policybrief28.pdf (accessed March 1, 2012). The numbers increased from 636,000 to 1.46 million. Families spent at least

390 NOTES TO PAGES 20-21

one month in the year in extreme poverty. The study includes only cash income, and thus does not include in-kind benefits. Still, only one in five received rent vouchers or lived in public housing. Even if the household spent nothing on food or medical care, just obtaining housing for a family of three at $180 a month—and having nothing left over for anything else—is a near-impossibility. Poverty rate figures are from the U.S. census.

67. See OECD Factbook 2011–2012: Economic, Environmental and Social Statistics, available online at http://www.oecd-ilibrary.org/ (accessed March 5, 2012).

68. Some 46.3 million are on food stamps as of fall 2011, yet 14.5 percent of Americans still face food insecurity. See "Supplemental Nutrition Assistance Program: Number of Persons Participating," data provided by the U.S. Department of Agriculture, available at http://www.fns.usda .gov/pd/29snapcurrpp.htm (accessed March 1, 2012), and "Food Security in the United States: Key Statistics and Graphics," U.S. Department of Agriculture, available at http://www.ers.usda.gov/briefing/foodsecurity/ stats_graphs.htm (accessed March 1, 2012). Food insecurity is measured as follows: "At times during the year, these households were uncertain of having, or unable to acquire, enough food to meet the needs of all their members because they had insufficient money or other resources for food."

69. Under the new measure, the numbers in poverty increased from 43.6 million in 2009 to 46.2 million in 2010, and the numbers in poverty under the new measure were actually higher than under the old. The poverty threshold level in 2010 was $17,568 for a single mother with two children. As the discussion earlier in the chapter should have made clear, living in most of our cities, providing child care, food, shelter, and clothing for that amount—leaving a little for the amenities of a modern life—is hard to imagine. Food stamps ease the burden, giving the family a maximum of $526 a month, or $6 per day per person. See U.S. Census, "The Research Supplemental Poverty Measure: 2010," November 2011. This discussion has not emphasized enough the many dimensions of poverty. When I was chief economist of the World Bank, we conducted a survey of 10,000 people, to assess what aspects of their life most weighed them down. The lack of income was obvious. But repeatedly, they emphasized insecurity and the lack of voice, their inability to shape the decisions that affected their lives. Deepa Narayan et al., *Can Anyone Hear Us? Voices of the Poor* (New York: Published by Oxford University Press for the World Bank,

2000); and World Bank, *World Development Report 2000–2001: Attacking Poverty* (New York: Oxford University Press, 2000–01).

70. Of the 46.2 million people living below the poverty line, only 3.5 million are aged 65 and over, some 7.6 percent of those in poverty. In the general population, people aged 65 and over compose some 13 percent. The reduction in old-age poverty is due mainly to Social Security. According to the Census Bureau, "In 2010, the number of people aged 65 and older in poverty would be higher by almost 14 million if social security payments were excluded from money income, quintupling the number of elderly people in poverty" (p. 22). U.S. Census Bureau, "Income, Poverty, and Health Insurance Coverage in the United States: 2010," issued in September, and U.S. Census, "The Research Supplemental Poverty Measure: 2010," November 2011.

71. See U.S. Census 2011, "Child Poverty in the United States 2009 and 2010: Selected Race Groups and Hispanic Origin," available at http://www.census.gov/prod/2011pubs/acsbr10-05.pdf (accessed March 6, 2012). For some groups the rate is much higher: nearly 40 percent of African American children lived in poverty in 2010.

72. Katharine Bradbury (p. 26) concludes, on the basis of the data from the Panel Study of Income Dynamics, that a "variety of measures indicate that U.S. family income mobility has decreased over the 1969–2006 time span, and especially since the 1980s." K. Bradbury, "Trends in U.S. Family Income Mobility, 1969–2006," Federal Reserve Bank of Boston, Working Papers, no. 11-10, 2011, available at http://www.bos.frb.org/economic/wp/wp2011/wp1110.pdf.

73. "Does America Promote Mobility As Well As Other Nations?," Economic Mobility Project of the Pew Charitable Trusts (November 2011), p.2, available at http://www.economicmobility.org/assets/pdfs/CRITA_FINAL.pdf (accessed March 26, 2012).

74. E.g., Mark Huggett, Gustavo Ventura, and Amir Yaron, "Sources of Lifetime Inequality," *American Economic Review* 101, no. 7 (December 2011): 2923–54, show that "differences in initial conditions account for more of the variation in lifetime earnings, lifetime wealth, and lifetime utility than do differences in shocks received over the working lifetime." The relationship between parents' income and that of their children is, in fact, very similar to that between parents' height and that of their children. Alan Krueger, chairman of President Obama's Council of Economic Advisers and a distinguished Princeton Univer-

sity professor, has pointed out, "The chance of a person who was born to a family in the bottom 10 percent of the income distribution rising to the top 10 percent as an adult is about the same as the chance that a dad who is 5' 6" tall having a son who grows up to be over 6' 1" tall. It happens, but not often." Krueger, "The Rise and Consequences of Inequality." The correlation between a child's height or income and that of his parents is around .5.

75. Krueger, "The Rise and Consequences of Inequality," refers to this systematic relationship between inequality and a standard measure of mobility (the intergenerational income elasticity) as the *Great Gatsby Curve.*

76. Jason DeParle, "Harder for Americans to Rise from Lower Rungs," *New York Times,* January 4, 2012, citing work by Markus Jäntti. In particular, see M. Jäntti, B. Bratsberg, K. Røed, O. Raaum, R. Naylor, E. Österbacka, A. Björklund, and Tor Eriksson, "American Exceptionalism in a New Light: A Comparison of Intergenerational Earnings Mobility in the Nordic Countries, the United Kingdom and the United States," IZA Discussion Paper no. 1938, 2006, available at http://users.abo.fi/mjantti/dp1938.pdf.

77. With full equality of opportunity, only 40 percent of those in the bottom rung would remain in the bottom 40 percent. Numbers from DeParle, "Harder for Americans to Rise from Lower Rungs," citing work by Markus Jäntti et al., "American Exceptionalism in a New Light."

78. Some 62 percent of the children of those in the top quintile wind up in the top 40 percent. DeParle, "Harder for Americans to Rise from Lower Rungs," citing J. B. Isaacs, I. V. Sawhill, and R. Haskins, "Getting Ahead or Losing Ground: Economic Mobility in America," *Brookings/Pew Economic Mobility Project,* February 2008, available at http://www.economicmobility.org/assets/pdfs/PEW_EMP_GETTING_AHEAD_FULL.pdf.

79. Jonathan Chait, "No Such Thing as Equal Opportunity," *New York,* November 7, 2011, pp. 14–16.

80. Some 29 percent of low-income students with high eighth-grade test scores complete college, compared with 30 percent of high-income students with low eighth-grade test scores who earn a degree.

81. Some 19 percent of children born in the lowest income fifth who earn a college degree make it into the highest fifth, whereas 23 percent of children born in highest group who don't graduate remain in highest bracket.

82. Based on standardized tests. *OECD Programme for International Student Assessment (PISA)* 2009 results, especially the rankings available at http://www.pisa.oecd.org/dataoecd/54/12/46643496.pdf (accessed March 2, 2012).

83. Using different definitions of what makes a "top school," various studies have provided telling numbers about the lack of economic diversity in elite universities. Research by Anthony P. Carnevale and Stephen J. Rose, cited by Lawrence Mishel, Jared Bernstein, and Heidi Shierholz in *The State of Working America 2008/2009* (Ithaca, NY: ILR Press), showed earlier in the last decade that some 74 percent of top-school freshmen hailed from first-quartile families, while only 6 percent and 3 percent were from the bottom third and fourth quartiles, respectively. (It is also striking that there is so little difference between the bottom quarter and the next. This is partly because the colleges have focused their efforts at recruiting the very poor and minorities.) Other studies support this trend; see for instance Alexander Astin and Leticia Osequera, "The Declining 'Equity' of Higher Education," *Review of Higher Education* 27, no. 3 (2004): 321–41.

84. Janet Currie provides compelling evidence that "children born to less educated and minority mothers are more likely to be exposed to pollution in utero." She studied a dataset containing 11 million births across five states between 1989 and 2003, combined with information about the location of Superfund sites and information from EPA Toxic Release Inventory (TRI) facilities. Whereas 61 percent of black mothers live within 2,000 meters of such a site, only 41 percent of white mothers do. Her analysis leads her to conclude (p. 12), "These estimates strongly support the claims of the environmental justice literature that minorities and people of lower socioeconomic status are more likely to be exposed to potentially harmful pollutants for reasons that cannot be explained by their broad geographical distribution, education, or other observable characteristics." See Currie, "Inequality at Birth: Some Causes and Consequences," *American Economic Review: Papers and Proceedings* 101, no. 3 (2011): 1–22. Earlier, we provided data showing the large fraction of Americans that face insecurity and the large fraction of children in poverty. It is well established that hunger and lack of adequate nutrition impede learning.

85. See, e.g., Samuel Bowles, Steven N. Durlauf, and Karla Hoff, eds., *Poverty Traps* (New York: Russell Sage Foundation; Princeton: Princeton University Press, 2006).

86. Pew Economic Mobility Project, "Economic Mobility and the American Dream: Where Do We Stand in the Wake of the Great Recession?" Washington, DC: Pew Charitable Trusts, 2011, available at http://www .economicmobility.org/poll2011.

87. "Companies listed on Japan's stock exchanges paid their chief executives an average of $580,000 in salary and other compensation last fiscal year, PWC estimates, about 16 times more than the typical Japanese worker. Average CEO pay at the 3,000 largest U.S. companies is $3.5 million, including stock options and bonuses, according to the Corporate Library, a research group." J. Clenfield, "In Japan, Underpaid—and Loving It," *Bloomberg Businessweek*, 2010, available at http://www.business week.com/magazine/content/10_28/b4186014341924.htm.

88. As we noted, different sources give slightly different numbers, but all present the same picture. One (at http://www.ips-dc.org/reports/exec utive_excess_2010) reports CEO pay of major U.S. corporations as some 263 times that of the income of the average worker. They report that, in inflation-adjusted terms, CEO pay in 2009 was nearly 8 times higher than in the 1970s. Earlier, we presented data from Mishel, Bernstein, and Shierholz, *The State of Working America*. This showed CEO compensation to that of the typical worker for large firms, up tenfold from 24 to 1 in 1965 to 243 to one in 2010. Whereas CEO compensation grew by only 0.8 precent a year from 1950 to 1975, since then it has grown more than 10 percent per year. See C. Frydman and D. Jenter, "CEO Compensation," *Annual Review of Financial Economics* 2, no. 1 (December 2010): 75–102. Frydman and Saks report "Ratio of Average Top 3 Compensation to Average Workers" between 1970 and 1979 as 33. That ratio (which should be slightly lower than that of the CEO compensation to that of the average workers) grew at a rate of 4.7 percent in the 1980s, 8.9 percent in the 1990s, and 6 percent between 2000 and 2003, rising to a level of 219 (see table 6, p. 45). C. Frydman and R. Saks, "Historical Trends in Executive Compensation 1936–2003," working paper, November 2005, available at http://faculty.chicagobooth.edu/workshops/ AppliedEcon/archive/pdf/FrydmanSecondPaper.pdf (accessed January 27, 2012).

89. See Joseph E. Stiglitz, *The Roaring Nineties* (New York: Norton, 2003).

90. See "Cheques with Balances: Why Tackling High Pay Is in the National Interest," final report of the UK High Pay Commission, p. 24,

available at http://highpaycommission.co.uk/wp-content/uploads/2011/11/
HPC_final_report_WEB.pdf (accessed March 1, 2012).

91. Ibid., p. 21. Even the Institute of Directors (the U.K. organization
of Corporate Directors) suggests that something is out of line. See Institute of Directors press release, "The Answer to High Executive Pay Lies
with Shareholders and Boards, Says IoD," October 28, 2011, available at
http://press.iod.com/2011/10/28/the-answer-to-high-executive-pay-lies-
with-shareholders-says-iod/ (accessed March 6, 2012).

92. OECD, "Divided We Stand." Among OECD countries, Turkey and
Mexico both have substantially greater inequality as measured by the
Gini coefficient. See the discussion of this measure below.

93. These comparisons are based on Gini coefficient data provided by
the United Nations International Human Development Indicators, but
are also supported by other databases. The Gini coefficient is an imperfect measure of inequality, but is useful for general international comparisons such as this one. I discuss some of the difficulties of comparing
Gini data in subsequent footnotes in this chapter.

94. See United Nations Human Development Report statistics, available online at http://hdr.undp.org/en/statistics/ (accessed March 6,
2012). The only country where inequality had a larger negative effect on
ranking was Colombia.

95. See World Bank Indicators, available at http://data.worldbank.org/
indicator.

96. United Nations Human Development Indicators database, available
at http://hdrstats.undp.org/en/tables/ (accessed March 6, 2012).

97. Some caution must be used in making comparisons across countries. Data necessary for calculating the Gini coefficient are difficult
to collect, especially in poor countries. Moreover, inequality in income
may not adequately capture inequality in "well-being," especially
in comparing governments that provide strong safety nets and systems of social protection. Moreover, some of the inequality in larger
countries (like China) may be related to geography. There are various
sources for data comparing Gini coefficients across countries, including the World Bank, the United Nations, the CIA, and the Global
Peace Index. See respectively http://data.worldbank.org/indicator/
SI.POV.GINI?page=2&order=wbapi_data_value_2009%20wbapi_
data_value%20wbapi_data_value-last&sort=asc, http://hdrstats.undp
.org/en/indicators/67106.html, https://www.cia.gov/library/publications/

the-world-factbook/rankorder/2172rank.html, and http://www.visionof
humanity.org/.

98. Calculated between 1999 and 2011 on the basis of data from the
U.S. Census Bureau. See Historical Table H-4, Gini Ratios for Households, by Race and Hispanic Origin of Householder, available at http://
www.census.gov/hhes/www/income/data/historical/household/index
.html.

99. See UN Human Development Indicators database. It should be
noted that data are quite incomplete for recent years, and that the UN's
calculation of the Gini coefficient in the United States in 2000 (40.8) is
different from the U.S. census calculation for that year (46.2). I attempt
to make comparisons only within one dataset at a time.

100. See Eurostat data on European Gini coefficients, available at http://
appsso.eurostat.ec.europa.eu/nui/show.do?dataset=ilc_di12&lang=en
(accessed March 5, 2012).

101. Based on comparison of World Bank data, available at http://data.
worldbank.org/indicator/NY.GDP.PCAP.KD?page=6 (accessed February
14, 2012). The U.S. GDP per capita in 2010 in constant 2000 dollars
was $35,527, and in 1980 it was $20,004.

102. There is a standard theory in economics that consumption should
reflect differences in lifetime (or permanent) income. See Milton Friedman, *A Theory of the Consumption Function* (Princeton: Princeton University Press, 1957). The large inequalities in consumption thus suggest
large inequalities in lifetime incomes. Note that year-to-year variations in
income can still have welfare consequences, if capital markets are imperfect (as they are) so that individuals can't smooth consumption. Using
annual earnings data from the Social Security Administration, Wojciech
Kopczuk, Emmanuel Saez, and Jae Song find that "most of the increase
in the variance of (log) annual earnings is due to increases in the variance
of (log) permanent earnings with modest increases in the variance of
transitory (log) earnings." Thus, in fact, the increase in earnings inequality is in permanent income. Furthermore, they find that it remains difficult for someone to move up the earnings distribution (though they do
find upward mobility for women in their lifetime). See their "Earnings
Inequality and Mobility in the United States: Evidence from Social Security Data since 1937," *Quarterly Journal of Economics* 125, no. 1 (2010):
91–128. To the extent that consumption inequality may have been less
than income inequality before the crisis, and that it grew more slowly

than did income inequality, it was partly because of unbridled borrowing. With the collapse of the housing market, the ability to consume beyond one's income has been reduced. This provides an important critique of earlier analyses of consumption inequality, e.g., Dirk Krueger and Fabrizio Perri, "Does Income Inequality Lead to Consumption Inequality? Evidence and Theory," *Review of Economic Studies* 73 (January 2006): 163–92.

103. In 1995, Congress requested that a panel of experts from the National Academy of Sciences issue a report investigating revisions to the poverty threshold. National Research Council. *Measuring Poverty: A New Approach* (Washington, DC: The National Academies Press, 1995).

104. The Heritage Foundation has recently complained, "In 2005, the typical household defined as poor by the government had a car and air conditioning. For entertainment, the household had two color televisions, cable or satellite TV, a DVD player, and a VCR. If there were children, especially boys, in the home, the family had a game system, such as an Xbox or PlayStation. In the kitchen, the household had a refrigerator, an oven and stove, and a microwave. Other household conveniences included a clothes washer, a clothes dryer, ceiling fans, a cordless phone, and a coffee maker." R. Rector and R. Sheffield, 2011, "Air Conditioning, Cable TV, and an Xbox: What Is Poverty in the United States Today?," July 19, 2011, available at http://www.heritage.org/research/reports/2011/07/what-is-poverty. Of course, selling the TV (or one of these other appliances) would not go far to provide food, medical care, housing, or access to good schools. There is another important area, exploring the relationship between consumption and happiness, going back at least to Veblen's (1899) *Theory of the Leisure Class*, which introduced the concept of "conspicuous consumption." More recently, Richard Wilkinson and Kate Pickett, in *The Spirit Level: Why Greater Equality Makes Societies Stronger* (New York: Bloomsbury Press, 2009), argue that more equality can improve happiness through reducing "social evaluation anxieties" and associated stresses.

105. See U.S. Census, "The Research Supplemental Poverty Measure: 2010," November 2011.

106. As we'll explain in chapter 3, there are two sides of this argument (both wrong). The first is that taxing the top at higher rates will reduce their incentives to work and save, so much that tax revenues may even fall; the second is that helping the poor will just breed more poverty—inducing those at the bottom not to work.

107. Mitt Romney on the *Today Show*, January 11, 2012, "I think it's fine to talk about those things in quiet rooms . . . . It's a very envy-oriented . . . approach and I think it'll fail." Available at http://blogs.chicagotribune .com/news_columnists_ezorn/2012/01/shhhhh.html (accessed January 25, 2012).

Chapter Two RENT SEEKING AND THE MAKING OF AN UNEQUAL SOCIETY

1. That's one of the reasons that good stock market performance is no longer a good indicator of a healthy economy. Stocks can do well because wages are low and the Fed, worried about the economy, keeps interest rates at near zero.

2. Thucydides, *The Peloponnesian War*, trans. Richard Crawley (New York: Modern Library, 1951), p. 331 (book 5.89).

3. That's why the cases where those in power voluntarily give some of it up are so interesting. In some of them, it's because those in power have an understanding of their own long-term interests—and the long-term interests of those they are supposed to serve. That was the case, e.g., when the king of Bhutan, in 2007, insisted on converting his country into a constitutional monarchy. He had to persuade his citizens that that was the right course for them. The elites of nineteenth-century countries that extended education must have known that there was a risk that this would over the long run weaken their dominance of the political franchise; yet the short-term economic advantages of having a more educated workplace seem to have dominated the long-term political consequences. See François Bourguignon and Sébastien Dessus, "Equity and Development: Political Economy Considerations," pt. 1 of *No Growth without Equity?*," ed. Santiago Levy and Michael Walton (New York: Palgrave Macmillan, 2009). Daron Acemoglu and James Robinson theorize that democratization is a way for ruling elites to commit to future redistribution, and thus avoid the extreme of revolution when faced with social unrest. If there is not sufficient strength in the rebellion, repression or temporary reform (or transfers) might suffice. Acemoglu and Robinson, *Economic Origins of Dictatorship and Democracy* (Cambridge: Cambridge University Press, 2006).

4. See Karl Polyani, *The Great Transformation* (New York: Rinehart,

1944). Even before Marx, scholars had attempted to explain and justify inequality and the seeming high returns to capital. Nassau Senior, the first holder of the Drummond Chair at Oxford University, who argued that the return capitalists earned was compensation for their "abstinence" (i.e., saving, or *not consuming*).

5. The formalization of this idea is called the "first welfare theorem of economics." It asserts that under certain conditions—when markets work well—no one can be made better-off without making someone else worse-off. But, as we shall explain shortly, there are many instances in which markets do not work well. A recent popular analysis is Kaushik Basu, *Beyond the Invisible Hand: Groundwork for a New Economics* (Princeton: Princeton University Press, 2011). Basu uses the metaphor of a magic show to describe the way the discussion of economics on the political right draws attention to the conclusion of this theorem—that markets are efficient—and away from the very special and unrealistic conditions under which the conclusion holds—perfect markets. Like a good magician, a free-market economist succeeds by drawing spectators' attention to what he wants them to see—the rabbit jumping out of the hat—while distracting their attention from other things—how the rabbit got into the hat in the first place.

6. Adam Smith, *The Wealth of Nations* (1776; New York: P. F. Collier, 1902), p. 207.

7. See Carmen Reinhart and Kenneth Rogoff, *This Time Is Different: Eight Centuries of Financial Folly* (Princeton: Princeton University Press, 2009).

8. A derivative is just a financial instrument the return to which is *derived* on the basis of something else, e.g., the performance of a stock or the price of oil or the value of a bond. A few banks have profited enormously by keeping this market nontransparent, garnering for themselves an amount widely estimated at more than $20 billion a year.

9. On October 31, 2011, MF Global Holdings, a brokerage firm run by Jon Corzine, filed for bankruptcy protection in New York. It was the eighth-largest corporate bankruptcy in U.S. history and the biggest failure by a securities firm since Lehman Brothers Holdings Inc. filed for Chapter 11 in September 2008.

10. While there may be some debate about when taking advantage of information asymmetries is unethical (reflected in the maxim "caveat emptor," putting the obligation on the buyer to beware of the possibility

of information asymmetries), there is no doubt that the banks stepped over the line. See the discussion in later chapters over the large fines paid by the banks for practices that were fraudulent and deceptive.

11. This predatory behavior took a number of forms. One way was to charge *very* high interest rates, sometimes obfuscated by fees. The abolition of usury laws (which limit the interest rates lenders can charge) provided lenders greater scope for charging exorbitant interest rates; and lenders found ways of circumventing whatever regulations there were. Rent-a-Center claimed to be renting furniture; it was really selling furniture and simultaneously lending money—at extraordinarily high interest rates. Many states tried to circumscribe its activities, but it used its political influence (it had senior ex-politicians, including a former leader of the Republicans in the House of Representatives, on its board) to try to get federal preemption (whereby weaker federal rules preempt the rights of states to regulate). In 2006 Rent-a-Center (with nationwide revenues in excess of $2 billion) was successfully sued by the state of California for deceptive business practices. See http://oag.ca.gov/news/press_release?id=1391. Credit cards and payday loans provided other venues for predatory practices. Among many discussions, see, e.g., Robert Faris, "Payday Lending: A Business Model That Encourages Chronic Borrowing," *Economic Development Quarterly* 17, no. 1 (February 2003): 8–32; James H. Carr and Lopa Kolluri, *Predatory Lending: An Overview* (Washington, DC: Fannie Mae Foundation, 2001).

12. A well-performing financial sector is absolutely essential for a well-performing economy. It allocates capital, manages risk, and runs the payments mechanism. As I explain in *Freefall* (New York: Norton, 2010), in the run-up to the 2008–09 crisis, it did not perform these functions well. Part of the reason is that it was focused more on circumventing regulations and exploitive activities, like predatory lending. The negative-sum nature is reflected in the immense losses in the real estate sector. The financial sector likes to claim that it has been highly innovative, and that these innovations are at the root of the economy's overall success. But as Paul Volcker, former chairman of the Federal Reserve, pointed out, there is little evidence of any significant effect of these innovations on economic growth or societal well-being (with the exception of the ATM machine). But even if the financial sector had contributed slightly to the country's growth in the years before the crisis, the losses associated with the crisis more than offset any of these gains.

13. A recent study has shown that people of higher status/income have fewer qualms about breaking the rules, are more likely to be driven by self-interest, more likely to cheat, and more likely to behave in other ways that would generally be viewed as unethical. Paul K. Piff, Daniel M. Stancato, Stephane Cote, Rodolfo Menoza-Denton, and Dacher Keltner, "Higher Social Class Predicts Increased Unethical Behavior," *Proceedings of the National Academy of Sciences*, February 27, 2012. While what is "unfair" or "unethical" depends on "norms," and there may be disagreements about what is or is not fair, the experiment focused on situations where there would be broad consensus on what was fair or ethical. Similarly, much of the financial sector behavior that I criticize below violates virtually any sense of "fairness" or "ethics."

14. This problem has come to be called the "natural resource curse." There are other reasons that such countries have not done well: managing natural resources can be difficult (prices fluctuate and exchange rates can become overvalued). For a recent review of some of the problems and how they can be addressed see *Escaping the Resource Curse*, ed. M. Humphreys, J. Sachs, and J. E. Stiglitz (New York: Columbia University Press, 2007). See also, e.g., Michael Ross, *The Oil Curse: How Petroleum Wealth Shapes the Development of Nations* (Princeton: Princeton University Press, 2012); and idem, *Timber Booms and Institutional Breakdown in Southeast Asia* (New York: Cambridge University Press, 2001).

15. According to World Bank Indicators, available at http://data.worldbank.org/indicator, 50 percent of the population was living under the national poverty line in 1998 before Chavez took office in 1999.

16. He shared the 1964 Nobel Prize in Physics with the Soviet scientists Nikolay Basov and Aleksandr Prokhorov for "fundamental work in the field of quantum electronics, which has led to the construction of oscilators and amplifiers based on the maser-laser principle."

17. They received the 1956 Nobel Prize in Physics "for their researches on semiconductors and their discovery of the transistor effect."

18. The World Wide Web Consortium he founded decided that its standards should be based on royalty-free technology, so that they could easily be adopted by anyone. Like Jobs, Bill Gates is often heralded as an innovator, but even though the adoption of his products is nearly universal now, that is due more to his business acumen—and near-monopoly of the market—than to the uniqueness of the technology he sells.

19. Bakija et al. found (p. 3) that "executives, managers, supervisors, and financial professionals account for about 60 percent of the top 0.1 percent of income earners in recent years, and can account for 70 percent of the increase in the share of national income going to the top 0.1 percent of the income distribution between 1979 and 2005." The composition of the top 1 percent in 2005 was 31 percent "Executives, managers, supervisors (non-finance)"; 15.7 percent "Medical," 13.9 percent "Financial professionals, including management," and 8.4 percent "Lawyers." The share of finance almost doubled over the period, rising from 7.7 percent in 1979 to 13.9 percent in 2005. (Nonfinance executives and medical fell slightly; lawyers increased marginally.) These statistics are based on an income measure that *excludes* capital gains. This is very important because about half of all capital gains accrue to the top 0.1 percent. For the top 400 income earners, 60 percent of their income is in the form of capital gains. J. Bakija, A. Cole, and B. T. Hein, "Jobs and Income Growth of Top Earners and the Causes of Changing Income Inequality: Evidence from U.S. Tax Return Data." See also comments by C. Rampell, "The Top 1%: Executives, Doctors and Bankers" *New York Times*, October 17, 2011, available at http://economix .blogs.nytimes.com/2011/10/17/the-top-1-executives-doctors-and-bank ers/; and Laura D'Andrea Tyson, "Tackling Income Inequality," *New York Times*, November 18, 2011, available at http://economix.blogs.nytimes .com/2011/11/18/tackling-income-inequality/.
20. See Forbes World's Billionaires list at http://www.forbes.com/wealth/ billionaires /; ranking is from 2011.
21. Slim's Grupo Carso, France Telecom, and Southwestern Bell paid $1.7 billion in December 1990 to acquire "a controlling 20.4 percent stake in Telmex, which includes 51 percent of the votes in the company." See Keith Bradsher, "Regulatory Pitfall in Telmex Sale," *New York Times*, December 7, 1990, available at http://www.nytimes.com/1990/12/27/business/ talking-deals-regulatory-pitfall-in-telmex-sale.html?scp=1&sq=telmex%20 southwestern%20bell%201990&st=cse (accessed March 3, 2012).
22. In the midnineties, Russia borrowed large amounts of money from the private sector, putting up shares in its oil and natural resource companies as collateral. But it was all a ruse to turn over state assets to the oligarchs. This was called "loans for shares." See Chrystia Freeland, *Sale of the Century: Russia's Wild Ride from Communism to Capitalism* (New York: Crown Business, 2000). A variety of specious arguments are often

put forward for these privatizations. Most recently, Greece has been pushed to privatize, as a condition for getting assistance from Europe and the IMF. For a discussion of privatization and the arguments used for it, see chapters 6 and 8, below, and J. E. Stiglitz, *Globalization and Its Discontents* (New York: Norton, 2002). Not every country and not every privatization has suffered from transferring state assets to private parties at below fair market prices. Many believe that the privatizations in the UK under Margaret Thatcher, with shares publicly floated and with the number of shares any one person or company could buy strictly limited, were conducted deliberately in a manner to avoid such outcomes.

23. See Forbes America's Highest Paid Chief Executives 2011, available at http://www.forbes.com/lists/2011/12/ceo-compensation-11_rank.html.

24. This is obviously a controversial claim: the CEOs might argue that in fact they receive but a small fraction of what they contribute to shareholder value. But, as we argue below, the so-called incentive structures are poorly designed, providing little link between that part of the increase in market value that is attributable to the efforts of the CEO and that which is the result of broader market forces—lower costs of inputs or higher stock market prices in general. Some studies have suggested, moreover, that once total compensation is taken into account (including adjustments of bonuses when the stock market doesn't do well), there is little relationship between firm performance and compensation. For a broader discussion of this issue, see J. E. Stiglitz, *Roaring Nineties* (New York: W. W. Norton, 2003); and especially Lucian Bebchuk and Jesse Fried, *Pay without Performance: The Unfulfilled Promise of Executive Compensation* (Cambridge: Harvard University Press, 2004).

25. Still one more group is real estate moguls, who benefit from special provisions of the tax code and often get rents as a result of local government variances in zoning laws.

26. These are sometimes called natural monopolies. They include the examples given earlier where network externalities are very large.

27. The advocates of stronger intellectual property rights, of course, claim otherwise. Interestingly, in the United States many of the most innovative firms, those in Silicon Valley, have been among those opposing certain proposals by those in the drug and entertainment industries to strengthen intellectual property rights. Recent revisions of patent law arguably gave large corporations an advantage over new firms, illustrating the fact, repeated in the next chapter, that there are strong distributive

consequences of any legal framework. For a discussion of how our current intellectual property framework may actually inhibit innovation, see J. E. Stiglitz, *Making Globalization Work* (New York: Norton, 2006), and Claude Henry and J. E. Stiglitz, "Intellectual Property, Dissemination of Innovation, and Sustainable Development," *Global Policy* 1, no. 1 (October 2010): 237-51.

28. See, e.g., A. Dixit, "The Role of Investment in Entry-Deterrence," *Economic Journal* 90, no. 357 (March 1980): 95-106; and J. Tirole and D. Fudenberg, "The Fat Cat Effect, the Puppy Dog Ploy and the Lean and Hungry Look," *American Economic Review* 74 (1984): 361-68. The practices Microsoft used to rid itself of its rivals (described below) also helped prevent entry of new competitors.

29. It's clear that one wants standards; one doesn't want to be operated on by an unqualified doctor. But, for instance, the supply of qualified doctors could have been increased simply by increasing the number of places in medical school.

30. In 1890 Congress passed the Sherman Anti-Trust Act, and its enforcement speeded up in the twentieth century. In 1911 the Supreme Court ordered the dissolution of the Standard Oil Company and the American Tobacco Company, which brought down the two powerful industrial trusts. In 1984 the Court broke up AT&T's monopoly following *United States v. AT&T.* See Charles R. Geisst, *Monopolies in America: Empire Builders and Their Enemies from Jay Gould to Bill Gates* (New York: Oxford University Press, 2000).

31. The term "Chicago school" is often applied to this group of economists, partially because the high priest of this religion, Milton Friedman (and many of his acolytes), taught at the University of Chicago. But it should be understood that many at that great university are not devotees of this school of thought, and that there are many devotees in other universities around the world. The term has, however, become a commonly used shorthand.

32. One group even went so far as to argue that markets will behave competitively even if there is only one firm, so long as there is potential competition. This argument played an important role in airline deregulation, where it was contended that even if there was only one airline on a given route, it would be disciplined from charging monopoly prices by the threat of entry. Both theory and experience have shown that this argument is wrong, so long as there are sunk costs (costs that

NOTES TO PAGES 55-58   405

won't be recovered if a firm enters and subsequently leaves), no matter how small those costs. See Joseph Farrell, "How Effective Is Potential Competition?," *Economics Letters* 20, no. 1 (1986): 67–70; J. E. Stiglitz, "Technological Change, Sunk Costs, and Competition," *Brookings Papers on Economic Activity* 3 (1987), pp. 883–947; and P. Dasgupta and J. E. Stiglitz, "Potential Competition, Actual Competition, and Economic Welfare," *European Economic Review* 32, nos. 2–3 (March 1988): 569–77.

33. For discussion and examples of conservative foundations' contribution to the Chicago school law and economics programs, see Alliance for Justice, *Justice for Sale: Shortchanging the Public Interest for Private Gain* (Washington, DC: Alliance for Justice, 1993).

34. The Department of Justice brought a case against American Airlines in the early years of this century. I thought the evidence that American Airlines had engaged in predatory behavior was especially compelling, but the judge didn't need to look at the evidence: the Supreme Court had ruled that there was just too strong a presumption *against* the existence of predatory pricing to make prosecution possible.

35. One of Netscape's founders, Marc Andreessen, was part of the team at the University of Illinois at Urbana-Champaign that developed Mosaic, the first widely used web browser, which was a project of the university's National Center for Supercomputing Applications (one of the original sites of the National Science Foundation's Supercomputer Centers Program). See the website of the NCSA, http://www.ncsa.illinois.edu/Projects/mosaic.html (accessed March 3, 2012); and John Markoff, "New Venture in Cyberspace by Silicon Graphics Founder," *New York Times,* May 7, 1994, available at http://www.nytimes.com/1994/05/07/business/new-venture-in-cyberspace-by-silicon-graphics-founder.html?ref=marcandreessen (accessed March 3, 2012).

36. For an overview of the Microsoft case, see Geisst, *Monopolies in America.*

37. See Steven C. Salop and R. Craig Romaine, "Preserving Monopoly: Economic Analysis, Legal Standards, and Microsoft," *George Mason Law Review* 4, no. 7 (1999): 617–1055.

38. See Microsoft's annual report.

39. As the late Oxford professor and Nobel Prize winner John Hicks said, "The best of all monopoly profits is a quiet life." J. R. Hicks, "Annual Survey of Economic Theory: The Theory of Monopoly," *Econometrica* 1,

no. 8 (1935). Kenneth Arrow pointed out that because monopolists restrict production, the saving they get from reducing costs is diminished. See Arrow, "Economic Welfare and the Allocation of Resources for Invention," in *The Rate and Direction of Inventive Activity: Economic and Social Factors* (Princeton: Princeton University Press, 1962), pp. 609–26. Monopolies, of course, don't last forever: new technologies and the open-source movement are already beginning to challenge Microsoft's dominance.

40. Calculated by total assets of commercial banks, as of September 3, 2011. See FDIC Statistics on Banking, available at http://www2.fdic.gov/ SDI/SOB/index.asp; and Federal Reserve Statistical Release Large Commercial Banks, available at http://www.federalreserve.gov/releases/lbr/ current/default.htm.

41. Moreover, banks don't compete on price for the services they offer. If you want to do a merger or acquisition, every major bank charges the same percentage fee. When takeovers were hundreds of millions of dollars, the resulting charges were large; when they became billions, charges became astronomical, for essentially the same amount of work by the same number of people.

42. From 2010 Q4 to 2011 Q3 (the most recently available year), FDIC-insured institutions made an aggregate profit of $115 billion. See *FDIC Quarterly*, available at http://www.fdic.gov/bank/analytical/quarterly/index .html. But these numbers don't really capture the magnitude of bank profits, since they are the profits after paying out the mega-bonuses to the executives, which can push compensation at some firms above 50 percent of revenues after other costs have been taken out, i.e., the "true" profits may be as much as double the above number. The *profits and bonuses* of the banking sector exceed 1 percent of the country's entire national output. Such numbers lead many to conclude that the financial sector, which is supposed to be the servant of the rest of the economy, has become its master.

43. Microsoft tried to exert political influence through a variety of channels. It has made campaign contributions of $13,516,304 from 1999 to present. See campaignmoney.com, compiled from campaign finance reports and data disclosed by Federal Election Commission, lists of contributions available at http://www.campaignmoney.com/Microsoft .asp?pg=88 (accessed March 6, 2012). The remedies put forward by President Bush's Justice Department in response to Microsoft's conviction on anticompetitive behavior were mild and did not effectively cur-

tail its market power. See, e.g., Andrew Chin's account of the outcome of *United States v. Microsoft Corp.*: "Decoding Microsoft: A First Principles Approach," *Wake Forest Law Review* 40, no. 1 (2005):1–157. In the case of antitrust laws, there's a partial remedy for the absence of effective public enforcement: private antitrust action (which was introduced because of worries about the willingness of public authorities to take enforcement action).

44. The late Nobel Prize–winning economist George Stigler wrote extensively about this. See, e.g., Stigler, "The Economic Theory of Regulation," *Bell Journal of Economics* 11 (1971): 3–21.

45. Data from the OpenSectrets.org, a website of the Center for Responsive Politics, counting lobbyists for commercial banks, finance, and credit companies. When all lobbyists are counted in the finance, insurance, and real estate industries, the number balloons to nearly five per congressman. See http://www.opensecrets.org/lobby/indus.php?id=F&year=a (accessed March 24, 2012).

46. The latest instance was the veto by the Senate Banking Committee chairman of the nomination of Nobel Prize–winning economist Peter Diamond. Diamond would have provided a critical voice on some of the doctrines that prevail among some of the governors. (Diamond was first nominated to the Fed by President Obama in April 2010; he was renominated in September and again in January 2011, after Senate Republicans blocked a floor vote on his confirmation. On June 5, 2011, Diamond withdrew his nomination, ending a fourteen-month nomination effort resisted by Senator Richard Shelby of Alabama, who, with party colleagues repeatedly criticized Diamond for supporting the central bank's monetary stimulus. Diamond responded that his opponents failed to appreciate that understanding the determinants of unemployment is essential to effective monetary policy.)

47. The Medicare Prescription Drug, Improvement, and Modernization Act of 2003.

48. The economist Dean Baker's research shows that $332 billion could be saved between 2006 and 2013 (around $50 billion a year) in the most conservative high-cost scenario, if Medicare were allowed to negotiate prices; in the middle-cost scenario, $563 billion could be saved for the same budget window. See Baker, *The Savings from an Efficient Medicare Prescription Drug Plan* (Washington, DC: Center for Economic and Policy Research, January 2006).

49. It is estimated that four banks in the United States take home a windfall of some $20 billion a year in derivatives.

50. The market for ethanol was distorted in other ways—such as ethanol requirements and subsidies for gasoline refiners who blended gasoline with ethanol—most of which came from America's corn producers. See the 2010 CBO study "Using Biofuel Tax Credits to Achieve Energy and Environmental Policy Goals," available at http://www.cbo.gov/sites /default/files/cbofiles/ftpdocs/114xx/doc11477/07-14-biofuels.pdf (accessed March 2, 2012); and "The Global Dynamics of Biofuel," Brazil Institute Special Report, April 2007, issue no. 3, available at http://www .wilsoncenter.org/sites/default/files/Brazil_SR_e3.pdf (accessed March 2, 2012).

51. Congress finally allowed the subsidy to expire at the end of 2011.

52. Famously, ADM was fined a then record $100 million for lysine price fixing in 1997, a result of a lengthy federal investigation that also led to convictions and prison time for three executives. (This became a book by Kurt Eichenwald and then a 2009 movie starring Matt Damon, *The Informant.*)

53. In the early days of corn-based ethanol, this was flatly wrong: the demand for corn by ethanol producers was so low that the corn farmers received almost no benefit from the subsidy. Because usage of corn for ethanol production was such a small fraction of global supply, it had a neglible effect on corn prices. ADM and other ethanol producers were the true beneficiaries.

54. The U.S. government paid a total of $261.9 billion for agriculture subsidies from 1995 to 2010. According to USDA, 63 percent of farms do not receive any payments. Among those payments, a large chunk (62 percent in 2009) goes to large-scale commercial farms (with gross annual sales of $250,000 or more). Between 1995 and 2010, the top 10 percent of farms received $30,751 average per year, while the bottom 80 percent of farms received $587 average per year. See USDA Economic Research Service, "Farm Income and Cost: Farms Receiving Government Payments," available at http://www.ers.usda.gov/Brief ing/FarmIncome/govtpaybyfarmtype .htm; Environmental Working Group, Farm Subsidy Database, available at http://farm=.ewg.org/region.php?fips=00000&regname=UnitedStatesFarm SubsidySummary.

55. And indeed, many books have been written on the subject. See, e.g.,

Glenn Parker, *Congress and the Rent-Seeking Society* (Ann Arbor: University of Michigan Press, 1996).

Chapter Three MARKETS AND INEQUALITY

1. More precisely, if the demand curve shifts more than the supply curve.
2. Employment in manufacturing dropped from 18 million in 1988 to less than 12 million now. See Department of Labor, Bureau of Labor Statistics.
3. For an excellent discussion of these issues, see David H. Autor, Lawrence F. Katz, and Melissa S. Kearney, "Measuring and Interpreting Trends in Inequality," *American Economic Review* 96 (May 2006): 189–94; and Claudia Goldin and Lawrence F. Katz, "Long-Run Changes in the Wage Structure: Narrowing, Widening, Polarizing," *Brookings Papers on Economic Activity* 2 (2007): 135–64, and the references cited there.
4. David H. Autor, Lawrence F. Katz, and Alan B. Krueger, "Computing Inequality: Have Computers Changed the Labor Market?," *Quarterly Journal of Economics* 113 (November 1998): 1169–213; and L. F. Katz, "Technological Change, Computerization, and the Wage Structure," in *Understanding the Digital Economy*, ed. E. Brynjolfsson and B. Kahin (Cambridge: MIT Press, 2000), 217–44.
5. Goldin and Katz, "Long-Run Changes in the Wage Structure," 153. They attribute most of the difference to the decline in educational attainment of native-born Americans.
6. See OECD, Education at a Glance: OECD Indicators, 2011, p. 54, available at http://www.oecd.org/dataoecd/61/2/48631582.pdf (accessed March 2, 2012).
7. Ibid., p. 68.
8. For data, see the *OECD Programme for International Student Assessment (PISA)* 2009 results.
9. Even by 1998, college graduate wages had risen to 1.75 times that of high school graduate wages (up from 1.59 in 1970).
10. See, e.g., David H. Autor, Frank Levy, and Richard J. Murnane, "The Skill Content of Recent Technological Change: An Empirical Exploration," *Quarterly Journal of Economics* 118 (2003): 1279–333.
11. According to Autor et al., "Measuring and Interpreting Trends in

Inequality," since 1988 the most rapid rise in wages has occurred at the top, and the slowest growth in the middle two quartiles.

12. See Domenico Delli Gatti, Mauro Gallegati, Bruce C. Greenwald, Alberto Russo, and Joseph E. Stiglitz, "Sectoral Imbalances and Long Run Crises" (forthcoming 2012); and J. E. Stigltiz, "The Book of Jobs," *Vanity Fair*, January 2012, available at http://www.vanityfair.com/politics/2012/01/stiglitz-depression-201201 (accessed February 15, 2012).

13. See Bill Vlasic, "Detroit Sets Its Future on a Foundation of Two-Tier Wages," *New York Times*, September 12, 2011, available at http://www.nytimes.com/2011/09/13/business/in-detroit-two-wage-levels-are-the-new-way-of-work.html?pagewanted=all (accessed March 6, 2012). The 2007 GM annual report confirms some of the details on wages, available at http://bigthreeauto.procon.org/sourcefiles/GM_AR_2007.pdf (accessed March 6, 2012), see pp. 62–63. For a longer discussion of wages, see Bruce C. Greenwald and Judd Kahn, *Globalization: The Irrational Fear That Someone in China Will Take Your Job* (Hoboken, NJ: John Wiley, 2009).

14. Some on the right compare wages in public-sector jobs to those in private-sector jobs *unadjusted for education*—that is, not taking account of differences in the level of education between the public and private sectors—and complain that public-sector wages are too high. But education-adjusted public sector pay (that is, taking into account differences in education between the two sectors) is lower than private. Some contend that more generous (and less risky) pensions and other benefits in the public sector compensate for this differential. Munnell et al. find instead that private sector workers enjoy a "modest" 4 percent premium even net of benefits. A. Munnell, J.-P. Aubry, J. Hurwitz, and L. Quimby, "Comparing Compensation: State-Local versus Private Sector Workers," Center for Retirement Research at Boston College, no. 20, September 2011.

15. Traditionally many economists have been uncomfortable in dealing with these distributive changes, because of the difficulties of making interpersonal comparisons. Economists often focus on "Pareto efficient" equilibria—where no one can be made better-off without making someone else worse-off; or on "Pareto improvements," where someone is made better-off, but no one is harmed. But few policy changes are of that sort. Generally, some gain and some lose. A Pareto efficient equilibrium, as is learned in elementary economics courses (and then perhaps

forgotten), might be very undesirable because it left many people at bare subsistence.

16. Several hundred years ago, in England and Scotland, the large landowners enclosed the common land. Some economists have argued that this was desirable, because it avoided the problem of overgrazing, a problem that was called the "tragedy of the commons." But far larger than the efficiency effect were the distributive effects: large numbers lost their livelihood and became impoverished. As the Nobel Prize–winning economist/political scientist Elinor Ostrom has pointed out, there are other ways to avoid the tragedy of the commons and to ensure that the resources are well managed—such as simply regulating the number of sheep that can graze. These can do just as well in attaining efficiency, but with far better social consequences. The true tragedy of the commons was that with the privatization of the commons by the lords, thousands became destitute and had to migrate either to the cities of Britain or abroad. A system of use rights—allowing each family to graze, say, ten sheep—would have prevented the problem of overgrazing as well as the further immiseration of the peasants. Virtually every society in which water is very scarce (such as the indigenous people of the Atacama Desert) or which relies on irrigation has developed complex regulatory schemes for allocating water, balancing out equity and efficiency—and with only limited use of prices. For a more extensive discussion of some of these issues, see Stigltiz, *Making Globalization Work*, chap. 4.

17. That was another iniquitous aspect of the 2005 bankruptcy act: it made even loans from for-profit banks for for-profit schools nondischargeable.

18. We'll discuss predatory education loans in a later chapter. Another bankruptcy "reform" (discussed in chapter 2), giving derivatives seniority in bankruptcy, not only distorted the economy by encouraging these gambling instruments but did so at the expense of others—including workers and pensioners, whose claims against the bankrupt firm were correspondingly weakened.

19. The Universal Declaration of Human Rights, adopted by the United Nations on December 10, 1948, recognized both economic rights and political rights; but the economic rights that were identified pertained to the ordinary citizen. "(1) Everyone has the right to a standard of living adequate for the health and well-being of himself

and of his family, including food, clothing, housing and medical care and necessary social services, and the right to security in the event of unemployment, sickness, disability, widowhood, old age or other lack of livelihood in circumstances beyond his control." The Universal Declaration of Human Rights, available at http://www.un.org/en/documents/udhr/index.shtml#a25. Implicitly, it was realized that individuals whose survival was at risk could and would not effectively exercise their political rights. In the years of the Cold War, those on the left emphasized the importance of these economic rights, while the U.S. government centered its attention on political rights. Ironically, when economic rights were finally discussed, it was the rights not of workers and citizens but of capital; it was property rights, intellectual property rights, the rights of capital to move freely across borders. In other countries, however, there has been increasing recognition of the economic rights of ordinary citizens, e.g., in the constitution of South Africa, where even the right to housing is accepted. See Chapter 2, Bill of Rights, Section 26: "26 (1) Everyone has the right to have access to adequate housing. (2) The state must take reasonable legislative and other measures, within available resources to achieve the progressive realisation of this right. (3) No-one may be evicted from their home, or have their home demolished, without an order of the court made after considering all the relevant circumstances," available at http://www.info.gov.za/documents/constitution/1996/96cons2.htm#26. The Indian supreme court has recognized rights to education; in 2002, through the 86th Amendment Act, Article 21(A) was incorporated in the constitution to make education a fundamental right for children, and rights to pollution-free-air (under Article 21). It also recognizes fundamental rights, particularly the Right to Life guaranteed in Article 21. Around the world, the rights-based approach has received increasing attention. See, e.g., the work done by the former head of the UN Human Rights Commission (and former president of Ireland) Mary Robinson's organization, Realizing Rights, available at http://www.realizingrights.org/.

20. This ignores, however, the many social and other consequences of labor migration, both to the country that the migrant leaves and the country to which he comes.

21. Of course, some, perhaps many, of those advocating the liberalization of financial markets look only at the *direct* increase in their profitability from their ability to invest in places where returns are higher.

They don't think about the systemic effects of asymmetric liberalization on wages.

22. Financial market integration entails not just the free movement of capital across borders but also the free movement of financial institutions across borders. See chapter 6 for a fuller discussion of these issues.

23. A similar problem arises in the design of electric networks. More integrated networks are subject to systemic breakdowns—a problem in one little place, like a substation in Ohio, can bring down the whole East Coast. The response is the design of effective circuit breakers, to isolate—or quarantine—the problem.

24. Banks spend a lot of money lobbying both against regulations and for bailouts that serve their interests. Lobbying expenditures in 2009 jumped 12 percent from 2008, to $29.8 million, among the eight banks and private equity firms that spent the most to influence legislation, and much of the increase happened in the last three months when Congress voted on finance reform bills. See "Banks Step Up Spending on Lobbying to Fight Proposed Stiffer Regulations," Los Angeles Times, February 16, 2010. As an example of the impact of bank lobbyists, the Federal Reserve set a 24-cent maximum on the fee banks can charge retail merchants for debit card transactions in June 2011, an amount that was a multiple of reasonable estimates of the cost of the transaction, and roughly double the 12 cents tentatively proposed by the Fed in December 2010. See "Fed Halves Debit Card Bank Fee," New York Times, June 29, 2011, available at http://www.nytimes.com/2011/06/30/business/30debit.html.

25. Developing countries also have many complaints against globalization, which I've discussed elsewhere. For instance, they rightly complain that the trade agreements are not fair: the bargaining power is all on the side of the developed countries. Consider the so-called Free Trade Agreements, which the United States has with many other countries around the world. These agreements are not really free-trade agreements. If they were, they would be a few pages long, with each side agreeing to eliminate its tariffs, its nontariff barriers, and its subsidies. But the agreements go to hundreds of pages, because they are in fact managed-trade agreements, and managed for the benefit of special interests. They are agreements in which hosts of industries insist on one form of favorable treatment or another. Companies' focus is naturally on rules that increase their profits. When trade liberalization helps their profits, then they're in favor of it; but when it works the other way, they oppose it. And for the

414   NOTE TO PAGE 77

most part, the U.S. trade representative and trade ministers from other advanced industrial countries represent the interests of the country's companies. Opening up trade is, however, only one part of the focus of trade negotiations. Today much attention is centered on inducing other countries to open up their markets to foreign investment and protecting the investments that are made there—that is, providing conditions that enhance the movement of jobs overseas. In short, much of the focus is on enhancing corporate profits, rather than on increasing jobs at home. And this is not surprising, given where the campaign contributions and lobbying is coming from. (It's not an accident that sometimes, the U.S. trade representative has been a presidential campaign manager.) Everybody believes that exports are good—but that imports are bad. (Such a position, of course, is intellectually incoherent.) Our firms claim that if some other firm undercuts them, it must be playing unfair. It must be selling goods below cost, or be subsidized by its government. U.S. firms use these arguments to advocate for the imposition of duties to "level the playing field." When international trade agreements prevent the imposition of tariffs, the United States (and other countries) turn aggressively to using what are called nontariff barriers, and especially dumping duties. But the fact of the matter is that many American industries are not the most efficient in the world. Many have not invested what they should either in people or in machines, and that's why their costs are higher. For a discussion of the importance of innovation in the American automobile manufacturing, and how U.S. firms have stacked up against foreign competitors, see McKinsey & Company, "Increasing Global Competition and Labor Productivity: Lessons from the US Automotive Industry," a report of the McKinsey Global Institute, 2005, available at http://www.mckinsey.com/Insights/MGI/Research/Productivity_Competitiveness_and_Growth/Increasing_global_competition_and_labor_productivity (accessed March 6, 2012).
26. In its early history, the United States had such conditions, and indeed a very different process played out. Territories and the new western states of the Union competed for settlers with the older states on the Eastern Seaboard. This led across the nation to the expansion of voting rights, in the right to run for political office, and in public education, which in turn contributed to the vast expansion of literacy in the United States (relative to what it had been before, and what it was in Europe). See S. Engerman and K. Sokoloff, "Factor Endowments, Inequality, and

Paths of Development among New World Economies," *Economia* 3, no. 1 (2002): 41–109; and S. Engerman and K. Sokoloff, "The Evolution of Suffrage Institutions in the New World," *Journal of Economic History* 65, no. 4 (December 2005): 891–921.

27. This is especially true for smaller countries. Most of the adverse shocks they face come from abroad.

28. See D. Newbery and J. E. Stiglitz, "Pareto Inferior Trade," *Review of Economic Studies* 51 (1984): 1–12.

29. These ideas have been at the center of trade theory for more than sixty years. See P. A. Samuelson, "International Trade and the Equalisation of Factor Prices," *Economic Journal* 58 (June 1948): 163–84; and W. F. Stolper, W. F. and P. A. Samuelson, "Protection and Real Wages," *Review of Economic Studies* 9, no. 1 (1941): 58–73. For a more extensive discussion of these issues, see Stiglitz, *Making Globalization Work*, chap. 3. A standard implication of these theories is that the differential between unskilled and skilled workers' wages should narrow in developing countries, reducing inequality. This has not happened. One of the reasons is that the most unskilled workers in developing countries—those who are, e.g., subsistence farmers—may be made even worse-off as a result of trade agreements that open up their markets to highly subsidized agricultural goods. There is no agreement among economists who have attempted to quantify the relative importance of trade globalization on inequality. It used to be part of the conventional wisdom that a small part (at most a fifth) of the increase in inequality was due to globalization. (For instance, Florence Jaumotte and Irina Tytell, "How Has the Globalization of Labor Affected the Labor Share in Advanced Countries?," *IMF Working Paper*, 2007, argues that technological change was more important than globalization, especially on the wages of low skilled workers.) But more recently, Paul Krugman has argued that the impact of globalization may be larger than was previously thought. "Trade and Inequality, Revisited," *Vox*, June 15, 2007; see also his paper "Trade and Wages, Reconsidered," Brookings Panel on Economic Activity, Spring 2008. Part of the difficulty is that globalization is intertwined with the changing productivity within the United States, the weakening of unions, and a host of other economic and societal changes. There is no obvious way to specify the counterfactual: what would the degree of inequality have been, if we had not had globalization, but everything else had been the same?

30. The relative importance of these societal changes and the market forces described earlier (especially the role of skill-biased technical change) has been a subject of some contention in labor economics. David Card and John DiNardo, "Skill-Biased Technological Change and Rising Wage Inequality: Some Problems and Puzzles," *Journal of Labor Economics* 20 (2002): 733–83, and Thomas Lemieux, "Increased Residual Wage Inequality: Composition Effects, Noisy Data, or Rising Demand for Skill?," *American Economic Review* 96, no. 3 (2006): 461–98, focus on the timing of the increase in inequality—in the 1980s—suggesting it is caused by the institutional/societal changes, including those we focus on here. Piketty and Saez, "Income Inequality in the United States, 1913–1998," *Quarterly Journal of Economics* 118, no. 1 (2003): 1–39, "The Evolution of Top Incomes: A Historical and International Perspective," *American Economic Review* 96 (2006): 200–206, and Frank Levy and Peter Temin, "Inequality and Institutions in 20th Century America," working paper, MIT 2007, focusing on the rise of inequality at the very top, advance an explanation based on social norms and regulatory and institutional changes, along the lines presented in this section. Other societal changes have contributed to inequality *among households,* e.g., increases in the number of female-headed households, and an increase in associative mating (where higher-income males are more likely to marry higher-income females). See R. Fernandez and R. Rogerson, "Sorting and Long-Run Inequality," *Quarterly Journal of Economics* 116 (2001): 1305–41. Differences among households in hours worked (partly related to differences in gender participations and changes in patterns of gender discrimination) also played a role. These changes, while important, are less significant than the other changes on which we have focused. See OECD, "Divided We Stand: Why Inequality Keeps Rising," December 5, 2011.

31. See http://www.bls.gov/news.release/union2.nr0.htm.

32. See details in Joseph A. McCartin, *Collision Course: Ronald Reagan, the Air Traffic Controllers, and the Strike That Changed America* (New York: Oxford University Press, 2011).

33. See chapter 4 for a more extensive discussion. Critics ask, If it's so profitable to pay workers high wages, why don't firms do it on their own? A central thesis of this book is that managerial incentives are not well aligned either with real economic returns or even with the interests of shareholders.

34. Part of the reason for the differing interpretations is that there are

instances where inefficient work rules do interfere unnecessarily with efficiency. All human institutions are fallible; it makes no more sense to condemn all unions for the failings of some than to condemn all corporations for the failings of some. For a discussion of circumstances under which unionization increases productivity, see Richard B. Freeman and James L. Medoff, "Trade Unions and Productivity: Some New Evidence on an Old Issue," *Annals of the American Academy of Political and Social Science* 473 (1984): 149–64.

35. See Susan Fleck, John Glaser, and Shawn Sprague, "The Compensation-Productivity Gap: A Visual Essay," *Monthly Labor Review*, January 2011, pp. 57–69. Movements in the share of labor (or labor compensation) in national income are also affected by changes in sector composition and government wage policies.

36. Which means that if the firm makes losses, the most that a shareholder can lose is the amount he has spent on his shares. By contrast, with unlimited liability partnerships, a partner can lose not only his original investment, but much more.

37. A takeover battle occurs when some outside firm tries to buy enough shares to get control of the firm and displace existing management.

38. The notion that management may not pursue the interests of shareholders—that there is, in modern America, a separation of ownership and control—was advanced by A. A. Berle and G. C. Means, *The Modern Corporation and Private Property* (New York: Macmillan, 1932). An explanation for this separation, in terms of costly and imperfect information, was provided by J. E. Stiglitz, "Credit Markets and the Control of Capital," *Journal of Money, Banking, and Credit* 17, no. 2 (1985): 133–52. There is a large subsequent literature on these topics. See, e.g., Aaron S. Edlin and Joseph E. Stiglitz, "Discouraging Rivals: Managerial Rent-Seeking and Economic Inefficiencies," *American Economic Review* 85, no. 5 (December 1995): 1301–12; and Andrei Shleifer and Robert W. Vishny, "A Survey of Corporate Governance," *Journal of Finance* 52, no. 2 (June 1997): 737–83.

39. John Bogle, the founder of Vanguard Group, an investment management company that manages approximately $1.6 trillion in funds, in his comments on Bebchuk and Fried, *Pay without Performance*. The Bogle quotation is from p. 483 of a review and summary of Bebchuk and Fried by Henry Tosi in *Administrative Science Quarterly* 50, no. 3 (September 2005): 483–87.

40. Australia has such legislation. Our corporate executives fought even a "say in pay" provision that would have not been binding on corporations. Shareholders are supposed to "own" the company, but our corporate officers somehow think it's right that the owners have absolutely no say in the pay of those who are supposedly working for them.

41. In manufacturing the decline in the share of wages was from a peak in excess of 65 percent at the beginning of the century to 58 percent in 2010; for business income as a whole, from 63 percent in 1990 to 61 percent in 2005; but it then fell further, to 58 percent by mid-2011. One has to treat the data with some caution. The data at the top are distorted by the fact that bankers' (and other CEOs') compensation is treated like any other wage, when in fact it's part of the rents they garner from their positions. To the extent that pay at the top is so distorted, what is going on is in fact not well described by a conventional demand and supply model.

42. In 2010 a woman's median wage was 80 percent of a man's, up from 62 percent in 1979; the median wage among African Americans and Hispanics is 80 percent and 70 percent, respectively, of that among white people.

43. There is a huge literature on labor market discrimination; see, e.g., Joseph G. Altonji and Rebecca M. Blank, "Race and Gender in the Labor Market," in *Handbook of Labor Economics*, ed. Orley C. Ashenfelter and David Card, vol. 3, pt. C (New York: Elsevier, 1999), pp. 3143–259. (Of course, there is also a feedback loop in "statistical" discrimination—differences in education, too, are a result of discrimination.) See note 47 in this chapter for further discussion of statistical discrimination.

44. See, in particular, the Nobel Prize–winning economist Gary Becker's *The Economics of Discrimination* (Chicago: University of Chicago Press, 1957).

45. Of course, for a long time, Jim Crow laws reinforced market processes of discrimination. Inadequate public education ensured that those from certain groups began life with a handicap—and that problem continues today.

46. See, e.g., Dilip Abreu, "On the Theory of Infinitely Repeated Games with Discounting," *Econometrica* 56, no. 2 (March 1988): 383–96. See also George A. Akerlof, "Discriminatory, Status-Based Wages among Tradition-Oriented, Stochastically Trading Coconut Producers," *Journal of Political Economy* 93, no. 2 (April 1985): 265–76.

47. This is another example of the notion of reflexivity discussed in chapter 5. Psychological phenomena, where individuals' perceptions are affected by their beliefs, reinforce the result—a phenomenon also discussed further in chapter 5. For a discussion of statistical discrimination, see Edmund S. Phelps, "The Statistical Theory of Racism and Sexism," *American Economic Review* 62 (1972): 659–61. For a discussion of the kinds of discriminatory equilibrium just described, see Joseph Stiglitz, "Approaches to the Economics of Discrimination," *American Economic Review* 6, no. 2 (1973): 287–95; Stiglitz, "Theories of Discrimination and Economic Policy," in *Patterns of Racial Discrimination*, ed. G. von Furstenberg et al. (Lexington, MA: Lexington Books, 1974), pp. 5–26; and K. J. Arrow, "The Theory of Discrimination," in *Discrimination in Labor Markets*, ed. O. Ashenfelter and A. Rees (Princeton: Princeton University Press, 1973).

48. See M. Bertrand, D. Chugh, and S. Mullainathan, "Implicit Discrimination," *American Economic Review* 95, no. 2 (2005): 94–98.

49. These studies are often called "audit" studies. See M. Bertrand and S. Mullainathan, "Are Emily and Greg More Employable Than Lakisha and Jamal? A Field Experiment on Labor Market Discrimination," *American Economic Review* 94, no. 4 (September 2004): 991–1013; and J. Braucher, D. Cohen, and R. M. Lawless, "Race, Attorney Influence, and Bankruptcy Chapter Choice," *Journal of Empirical Legal Studies* (forthcoming).

50. See D. Pager, "The Mark of a Criminal Record," *American Journal of Sociology* 108, no. 5 (2003): 937–75; and Devah Pager, *Marked: Race, Crime, and Finding Work in an Era of Mass Incarceration* (Chicago: University of Chicago Press, 20007).

51. Centers for Disease Control and Prevention, "Deaths: Preliminary Data for 2009," *National Vital Statistics Reports* 59, no. 4 (March 2011): 16.

52. In 2009 a typical Hispanic had wealth of only $6,325, while, as we noted in chapter 1, a typical white had $113,149. Four years earlier a typical white household had "only" ten times that of blacks. About a third of Hispanics (31 percent) and blacks (35 percent) had zero or negative net worth in 2009, compared with half that number (15 percent) for whites. (In 2005 the numbers were 29 percent for blacks, 23 percent for Hispanics, and 11 percent for whites.) Pew Research Center, "Wealth Gaps Rise to Record Highs between Whites, Blacks, and Hispanics," July 26, 2011.

420   NOTES TO PAGES 88-90

53. For more discussion of discrimination see chapter 4.

54. See Tax Policy Center: Urban Institute and Brookings Institution, table available at http://www.taxpolicycenter.org/taxfacts/displayafact .cfm?Docid=213. Most of the benefits of the Bush tax cuts went to those at the very top—two-thirds to the top quintile, one-third to the top 1 percent.

55. Theoretically, the effect of lower taxes on savings is ambiguous because while higher tax rates reduce the return to savings, they force those who are attempting to save for a particular target—like retirement or financing the college education of their children—to save more. (More formally, economists say that there are income and substitution effects that pull in different directions, with ambiguous net effects.) From the perspective of national savings, even if the tax cut in capital gains induced more private savings (which is dubious), it increases the federal deficit. It is particularly unlikely that the gain in private savings is so great as to offset the latter effect.

56. As chairman of Clinton's Council of Economic Advisers, I was actively involved in the debate over lowering capital gains, actively opposing it: it was inequitable, the gap between how capital gains and other returns to capital were taxed was distortionary, and the alleged benefits were illusionary. Particularly objectionable was extending the preferential treatment (under both Bush and Clinton) to investments that had already been made. In these cases it was hard to argue that there was any "incentive" benefit to offset the adverse distributional consequences.

57. D. Kocieniewski, "A Family's Billions, Artfully Sheltered," *New York Times*, November 26, 2011, available at http://www.nytimes.com /2011/11/27/business/estee-lauder-heirs-tax-strategies-typify-advantages-for-wealthy.html?pagewanted=all.

58. CBO, "Trends in the Distribution of Household Income between 1979 and 2007," October 2011. Data is for 2007. Numbers vary from year to year.

59. These numbers refer to capital gains and dividends subject to tax. From Joel Friedman and Katherine Richards, "Capital Gains and Dividend Tax Cuts: Data Make Clear That High-Income Households Benefit the Most," Center on Budget and Policy Priorities, January 30, 2006.

60. See James B. Steward, "Working All Day for the IRS," *New York Times*, February 17, 2012, available at http://www.nytimes.com/2012/02/

18/business/working-all-day-for-the-irs-common-sense.html?pagewanted= 1&ref=jamesbstewart (accessed March 3, 2012).

61. See "Richest 400 Took Record Share of Capital Gains during Market Meltdown Year," *Forbes*, May 11, 2011.

62. Ethan Pollack and Rebecca Thiess (based on data from CBO and IRS): Economic Policy Institute, "Taxes on the Wealthy Have Gone Down Dramatically," April 14, 2011. The famous investor Warren Buffett even called for higher tax payment in his op-ed in the *New York Times*, saying that the very wealthy people like himself pay lower tax rates than the middle class, thanks to special tax categories for investment income. "Stop Coddling the Super-Rich," *New York Times*, August 14, 2011, available at http://www.nytimes.com/2011/08/15/opinion/stop-coddling-the-super-rich.html (accessed March 2012).

63. Conservatives, with their obsession with incentives, should have worried about the peculiar incentives to which having a zero tax rate on inheritances for one year might give rise.

64. And some, like GE, actually get money back from the government. See David Kocieniewski, "G.E.'s Strategies Let It Avoid Taxes Altogether," *New York Times*, March 24, 2011. Its success is based both on effective lobbying for tax provisions that benefit it and on effective exploitation of tax provisions (which it can do, with a tax department of almost one thousand). Multinationals like GE often shift income around, so that it appears that more of their profits originate in low taxed countries. (In the case of GE, e.g., in recent years 46 percent of its revenues originate in the United States, but it claims that only 18 percent of its profits do.) A U.S. Government Accountability Office (GAO) study found that 55 percent of U.S. companies paid no federal income taxes during at least one year in a seven-year period it studied. See GAO, "Comparison of the Reported Tax Liabilities of Foreign- and U.S.-Controlled Corporations, 1998–2005," June 2008, available at http://www.gao.gov/new.items/d08957.pdf.

65. Corporate income tax revenue accounted for 30 percent of total government receipts in 1954 and had declined to 9 percent by 2010. See Tax Policy Center: Urban Institute and Brookings Institution, table available at http://www.taxpolicycenter.org/taxfacts/displayafact.cfm?Docid=203. At $191 billion in 2010, corporation tax was equal to 1.3 percent of the nation's GDP; internationally corporate income tax revenues in OECD countries averaged 2.8 percent of GDP in 2009, the latest year for which statistics were published. See *OECD (2011), Revenue Statistics 2011*,

OECD Publishing, available at http://dx.doi.org/10.1787/rev_stats-2011-en-fr (accessed March 2, 2012).

66. See "Microsoft Outlines Quarterly Dividend, Four-Year Stock Buy-back Plan, and Special Dividend to Shareholders," Microsoft press release, July 20, 2004, available at http://www.microsoft.com/presspass/press/2004/jul04/07-20boardpr.mspx (accessed March 2, 2012).

67. According to an IRS study in 2008, during 2004–05, 843 corporations brought into the United States almost $362 billion of their overseas profits, at the special 5.25 percent tax rate, a savings (over the normal tax they would have had to pay) of more than $100 billion. See Melissa Redmiles, "The One-time Received Dividend Deduction," 2008 IRS, available at http://www.irs.gov/pub/irs-soi/08codivdeductbul.pdf. The Levin report released on October 2011 studied the top 15 corporations claiming the largest qualifying overseas dividends under the 2004 American Jobs Creation Act; it found that after repatriating $155 billion, these firms firms reduced their overall U.S. workforce by nearly 21,000 jobs, and their R&D spending slightly decreased after the tax break. See Permanent Subcommittee on Investigations, Senator Carl Levin, "Repatriating Offshore Funds: 2004 Tax Windfall For Select Multinationals," available at http://levin.senate.gov/download/repatriating-offshore-funds.

68. It is understandable why there is less redistribution at the state level. States have to compete for people and firms.

69. Housing subsidies lower it by .9 percentage points, the Supplemental Nutrition Assistance Program lowers it by 1.7 percentage points, and the school lunch program by .4 percentage points. See U.S. Census Bureau, "The Research Supplemental Poverty Measure, 2010," issued November 2011.

70. The CBO, "Trends in the Distribution of Household Income," concluded, "The equalizing effect of transfers and taxes on household income was smaller in 2007 than it had been in 1979." For instance, while the share of the market (before taxes and transfers) income of the top 1 percent doubled between 1979 and 2007, the after-tax and transfer share *more* than doubled, from 8 percent to 17 percent. At the other end of the spectrum, the bottom 20 percent of the population's share of after-tax and transfer income fell from 7 percent to 5 percent.

71. Bureau of Labor statistics, Table A-4, Employment status of the civilian population 25 years and over by educational attainment, seasonally adjusted, February 2012, http://www.bls.gov/news.release/empsit.t04

.htm (accessed March 25, 2012) and Bureau of Labor Statistics, "College Enrollment and Work Activity of 2010 High School Graduates," http://www.bls.gov/news.release/hsgec.nr0.htm (accessed March 25, 2012).

72. K. Bischoff and S. F. Reardon, "Growth in the Residential Segregation of Families by Income, 1970–2009," November 2011, available at http://cepa.stanford.edu/sites/default/files/RussellSageIncomeSegregation report.pdf; and Sean F. Reardon and Kendra Bischoff, "Income Inequality and Income Segregation," *American Journal of Sociology* 116, no. 4 (January 2011): 1092–53.

73. K. Hoff and A. Sen, "Homeownership, Community Interactions, and Segregation," *American Economic Review* 95, no. 4 (2005): 1167–89.

74. As Ross Perlin has described in *Intern Nation* (London: Verso, 2011).

75. In the New World colonies with higher inequality at the outset of colonization, institutions tended to evolve in ways that restricted to a narrow elite access to political power and opportunities for economic advancement. New World colonies with lower initial inequality followed a very different path of institutional development. Engerman and Sokoloff have discerned this pattern in a wide range of public policies over many centuries: in the right to vote, public schooling, the distribution of land and other public natural resources, banking laws, taxation, and patent institutions. See Kenneth L. Sokoloff and Stanley L. Engerman, "History Lessons: Institutions, Factor Endowments, and Paths of Development in the New World," *Journal of Economic Perspectives* 14, no. 3 (2000): 217–32; and Sokoloff and Engerman, "Factor Endowments, Inequality, and Paths of Development among New World Economies," *Economia* 3, no. 1 (2002): 41–109. An overview of the effects of initial inequality on institutional development is K. Hoff, "Paths of Institutional Development: A View from Economic History," *World Bank Research Observer* 18, no. 22 (2003): 2205–26.

76. Kenneth R. Feinberg, whom President Obama appointed to oversee bank executive compensation, has argued that nearly 80 percent of the $2 billion in 2008 bonus pay doled out by troubled banks was unmerited. By 2010 bonus pay had fully recovered—at just the twenty-five top public traded banks and security firms, it had hit $135.5 billion, or almost 1 percent of GDP. Louise Story, "Executive Pay," *New York Times*, December 5, 2011, available at http://topics.nytimes.com/top/reference/timestopics/subjects/e/executive_pay/index.html. See press release of the report at U.S. Treasury's website, "The Special Master for Tarp Executive

Compensation Concludes the Review of Prior Payments," July 23, 2010, available at http://www.treasury.gov/press-center/press-releases/Pages/tg786.aspx (accessed February 15, 2012).

77. Warren Buffett, Chairman and CEO of Berkshire Hathaway, in a 2002 letter to his shareholders wrote that "derivatives are financial weapons of destruction, carrying dangers that, while now latent, are potentially lethal" on page 15 of the report. That report can be accessed here: http://www.berkshirehathaway.com/letters/2002pdf.pdf (accessed on March 21, 2012).

Angelo Mozilo, former Countrywide CEO, one of the worst purveyors of the kinds of mortgages that brought on the crisis, earned around $470 million between 2001 and 2006. *Wall Street Journal*, November 20, 2008, available at http://online.wsj.com/public/resources/documents/st_ceos_20081111.html. Now deceased, Roland Arnall, former Ameriquest founder (and ambassador to the Netherlands under President George W. Bush), had an estimated wealth of $1.5 billion. The parent of that company paid a settlement in 2006 of $325 million in relation to deceptive loan practices—for which it admitted no wrongdoing. When that company failed, the divisions of the parent were folded into Citigroup. See http://www.nytimes.com/2008/03/19/business/19arnall.html.

78. *Unjust Deserts: How the Rich Are Taking Our Common Inheritance and Why We Should Take It Back* (New York: New Press, 2009), p. 97.

79. The problems with executive compensation have been highlighted—and explained—by Bebchuk and Fried, *Pay without Performance*. They point out that managerial discretion—the ability of executives to set their own compensation schedules—has resulted in pay structures that effectively decouple pay from performance and misalign incentives. Michael Jensen and Kevin Murphy, "Performance Pay and Top-Management Incentives," *Journal of Political Economy* 98, no. 2, (1990): 225–64, provide empirical evidence of the very loose link between pay (including options, stockholdings, and dismissal) and performance. Henry Tosi Jr. and Luis Gomez-Mejia provide an explanation, related to the separation of ownership and control (agency theory) discussed above. I also discuss these issues in greater detail in *The Roaring Nineties*.

80. So too, the banks have connived with the CEOs, to help them "extract" more money out of their firms, in return ensuring that the banks make excessive profits. The bank-CEO collusion was exposed by the scandals that marked the beginning of the century (involving bank

analysts, Woldçom, Enron, accounting firms, etc.) and is described more fully in Stiglitz, *The Roaring Nineties*.

81. James K. Galbraith, *Inequality and Instability: A Study of the World Economy Just before the Great Crisis* (New York: Oxford University Press, 2012).

Chapter Four WHY IT MATTERS

1. A few countries in transition from communism to a market economy, as well as some resource-rich countries, are making strides to usurp its unfortunate position.

2. Arjun Jayadev, "Distribution and Crisis: Reviewing Some of the Linkages," *Handbook on the Political Economy of Crisis*, ed. G. Epstein and M. Wolfson (forthcoming), based on T. Piketty and E. Saez, "Income Inequality in the United States, 1913–1998," *Quarterly Journal of Economics* 118, no. 1 (2003): 1–39.

3. Karen E. Dynan, Jonathan Skinner, and Stephen P. Zeldes, "Do the Rich Save More?," *Journal of Political Economy* 112, no. 2 (2004): 397–444.

4. For the United States the short-run multiplier is normally estimated to be around 1.5; but what is relevant in a long-term downturn is the multiperiod, long-term multiplier, which is larger, more like 2. (Note that many conservative economists argue that the multiplier is smaller, but this is because much of the data upon which they draw entails periods in which the economy is at or near full employment, so that as the government spends more, monetary authorities engage in offsetting contractionary actions. In the current context, the Fed has committed itself not to increase interest rates.) There are a number of other technical reasons to expect the multiplier in the current context to be large: (a) much of the money that is not spent in the United States ("recycled" here) goes to buy imports, and with so much of the world's economy weak, this spending increases incomes abroad, leading in turn to more purchases from the United States; (b) individuals and firms, seeing incomes rise, may become more confident in the economy, leading to more investment and consumption (this is sometimes referred to as the "confidence multiplier"); and (c) in particular, households, anticipating high incomes in the future, are more willing to spend today.

5. Peter Orzsag, "As Kaldor's Facts Fall, Occupy Wall Street Rises,"

Bloomberg, October 18, 2011. The wage share declined by 5 percentage points from 1990 to 2011, but 3 percentage points from 2005 to 2011 alone. Nicholas Kaldor, a noted Cambridge University economist of the midtwentieth century, had claimed that, by and large, the share of labor was constant. While technological change may increase the demand for some types of labor and decrease it for others, there is no general theory about what should happen to the share of labor. If technological change increases the "effective" supply of labor, and labor and capital are not very substitutable, then technological change drives down the share of labor. But the pattern of increase of wages—with wages at the very top (e.g., of bankers) increasing so much relative to that of others—is consistent with the view that something else besides technological change is causing the decline in the wage share.

6. For a more complete telling of this story, see J. E. Stiglitz, *The Roaring Nineties* (New York: Norton, 2003).

7. For a closer look at how these tax cuts benefited the rich, see Joel Friedman and Isaac Shapiro, "Tax Returns: A Comprehensive Assessment of the Bush Administration's Record on Cutting Taxes," Center on Budget and Policy Priorities, April 23, 2004. Friedman and Shapiro estimate that in 2004 the middle 20 percent income earners reaped about 8.9 percent of the tax cut windfall, while the top 1 percent got 24.2 percent. Those earning over a million dollars alone gained 15.3 percent of the benefit. See also "Extending the Bush Tax Cuts Is the Wrong Way to Stimulate the Economy," report by the Joint Economic Committee Majority Staff, Chairman Charles E. Schumer; Vice Chair Rep. Carolyn B. Maloney, April 2008.

8. In 2004 private non–real estate investment was 11.59 percent of GDP, as compared with 13.97 percent in 2000. See "Flow of Funds Accounts of the United States, 1995–2004," Board of Governors of the Federal Reserve, table F.6, p. 4, available at http://www.federalreserve .gov/releases/z1/Current/annuals/a1995-2004.pdf (accessed March 3, 2012).

9. The theory (and some of the evidence) explaining why the dividend tax cut may have been bad for investment is set out in Anton Korinek and Joseph E. Stiglitz, "Dividend Taxation and Intertemporal Tax Arbitrage," *Journal of Public Economics* 93, nos. 1–2 (February 2009): 142–59. See also the references cited there.

10. See, e.g., "The Estate Tax and Charitable Giving," Congressional Budget

Office, July 2004, available at http://www.cbo.gov/doc.cfm?index=5650 (accessed February 15, 2012).

11. See J. E. Stiglitz, *Freefall* (New York: Norton, 2010), for a more complete telling of the housing bubble and its immediate aftermath.

12. While many of the big instances of deregulation are well known, deregulation has had pervasive effects. Even though the government had, in effect, given a gift worth billions of dollars to the TV companies, it became reluctant to impose restrictions. In 1985, guidelines for minimal amounts of nonentertainment programming on TV were abolished. FCC guidelines on how much advertising can be carried per hour were eliminated. See http://www.pbs.org/now/politics/mediatimeline.html.

13. The distinction between the short term and the long term is important, for two reasons. When restraints are removed, others too engage in similar practices, and *if* markets are competitive, the seeming profits quickly disappear. In the long run, at least in the financial sector, the banks may actually have lost substantial amounts (or would have, had the government not given them so much money), because of the instability to which their excesses gave rise.

14. The link between inequality, the credit bubble, and the economic crisis was laid out in Stiglitz, *Freefall*, and "Report of the Commission of Experts of the President of the United Nations General Assembly on Reforms of the International Monetary and Financial System," September 21, 2009, available as *The Stiglitz Report* (New York: New Press, 2010). Since then, a large literature on the subject has developed. See, e.g., M. Kumhof and R. Ranciere, "Inequality, Leverage and Crises," IMF working paper, 2010; and Raghuram G. Rajan, *Fault Lines: How Hidden Fractures Still Threaten the World Economy* (Princeton: Princeton University Press, 2010). For a survey and references, see J. E. Stiglitz, "Macroeconomic Fluctuations, Inequality, and Human Development," *Journal of Human Development and Capabilities* (2012).

I've argued that inequality, even high inequality, may not necessarily lead to crises; there are other ways of responding to the deficiency in aggregate demand that may result, and other fortuitous circumstances that can fill the gap. That is not inconsistent with the empirical findings in Michael D. Bordo and Christopher M. Meissner, "Does Inequality Lead to a Financial Crisis?," NBER Working Paper No. 17896, March 2012.

15. At least in the short to medium term. Modern growth theory—see

Robert M. Solow, "A Contribution to the Theory of Economic Growth," *Quarterly Journal of Economics* 70, no. 1 (February 1956): 65–94—has emphasized that in the long run the growth rate is determined by the pace of innovation (productivity increase) and population growth. Higher instability may lead to less investment in research and development, and thus a slower pace of increase in productivity.

16. Some parts of the market, in particular the large banks, act in a risk-loving way and have been a major source of the volatility in the economy. There are four possible explanations for this behavior: (a) Organizational incentives: the large banks actually push off much of the risk to government, because they are too big to fail. (b) Individual incentives (agency problems): those inside the bank have incentives that encourage risk taking. (c) Self-selection: in any society there are those who are risk loving, and they are especially attracted to the financial sector. (d) Pervasive irrationality: those in the financial sector systematically underestimate risk; and their investors do not understand the risks of leverage and underestimate its consequences.

17. See, e.g., the findings the report of the UN commission charged with analyzing the causes of the crisis and coming up with remedies. Report of the Commission of Experts of the President of the United Nations General Assembly on Reforms of the International Monetary and Financial System, September 21, 2009, available as *The Stiglitz Report* (New York: New Press, 2010).

18. Andrew G. Berg and Jonathan D. Ostry, "Inequality and Unsustainable Growth: Two Sides of the Same Coin?," IMF Staff Discussion Note, April 8, 2011, p. 3, available at http://www.imf.org/external/pubs/ft/sdn/2011/sdn1108.pdf (accessed March 25, 2012).

19. Dominique Strauss-Kahn, "The Global Jobs Crisis—Sustaining the Recovery through Employment and Equitable Growth," April 13, 2011, available at http://www.imf.org/external/np/speeches/2011/041311.htm.

20. There are, of course, many ways of *producing* these goods. Basic research could, for instance, be financed by the government and produced either in private laboratories, universities, or government-run laboratories. The United States has traditionally employed all of these.

21. A report of the Council of Economic Advisers documented the high returns to government support for research and development. Council of Economic Advisers, "Supporting Research and Development to Promote Economic Growth: The Federal Government's Role," October 1995. A

large body of literature documents the value of government investments. See, e.g., David Alan Aschauer, "Is Government Spending Stimulative?" *Contemporary Economic Policy* 8, no. 4 (1990): 30–46. Aschauer has also shown that public capital investment can improve returns to private capital, along with the direct benefits it provides. See Aschauer, "Does Public Capital Crowd Out Private Capital," *Journal of Monetary Economics* 24, no. 2 (1989): 121–88.

22. This is something that Ben Bernanke highlighted in a May 16, 2011, speech, "Promoting Research and Development: The Government's Role," available at http://www.federalreserve.gov/newsevents/speech/bernanke20110516a.htm (accessed March 3, 2012). "First, since the 1970s, R&D spending by the federal government has trended down as a share of GDP, while the share of R&D done by the private sector has correspondingly increased. Second, the share of R&D spending targeted to basic research, as opposed to more applied R&D activities, has also been declining. These two trends—the declines in the share of basic research and in the federal share of R&D spending—are related, as government R&D spending tends to be more heavily weighted toward basic research and science. The declining emphasis on basic research is somewhat concerning because fundamental research is ultimately the source of most innovation, albeit often with long lags. Indeed, some economists have argued that, because of the potentially high social return to basic research, expanded government support for R&D could, over time, significantly boost economic growth." Indeed, real federal investment in basic research decreased from $4.3 billion in 2003 to $3.9 in 2008, adjusted for inflation. See table 6 of National Science Board, "Science and Engineering Indicators: 2010," National Science Foundation, 2010, available at http://www.nsf.gov/statistics/nsf10314/content.cfm?pub_id=4000&id=2 (accessed March 3, 2012). Albert M. Link and others have shown that there is a direct link between basic research and productivity growth. See Link, "Basic Research and Productivity Increase in Manufacturing: Additional Evidence," *American Economic Review* 71, no. 5 (1981): 1111–12.

23. Studies by the Health, Education, Labor and Pensions (HELP) Committee have shown that for-profit colleges are drastically more expensive, spend less per student than nonprofit and public institutions, lead the nation in withdrawal rates—up to 84 percent for some associate's degree programs—and account for 50 percent of all student loan

defaults, even though they enroll only about 13 percent of American higher education students. These findings and others can be viewed at http://harkin.senate.gov/help/forprofitcolleges.cfm (accessed February 15,.2012).

24. According to FinAid.org, "Some 66 percent of four-year undergraduate students graduated with some debt in 2007–08, and the average cumulative debt incurred was $27,803." Average cumulative debt has been increasing at a rate in excess of 5 percent per year. See www .finaid.org/loans (accessed November 15, 2012). These figures were calculated by FinAid.org using the data analysis system for the 2007–08 National Postsecondary Student Aid Study (NPSAS), conducted by the National Center for Education Statistics at the U.S. Department of Education.

25. This included 784 lobbyists (nearly 2 per U.S. representative) from the oil industry and 262 from the mining industry; total spending for the energy and natural resources industry's lobbying was $387.8 million in 2011. Financial-sector spending on lobbying is even greater. Data is from OpenSectrets.org, the website of the Center for Responsive Politics; see in particular http://www.opensecrets.org/lobby/top.php?indexType=c (accessed March 5, 2012).

26. Classic references on rent seeking, demonstrating their dissipative effects and estimating their costs, are Gordon Tullock, "The Welfare Costs of Tariffs, Monopolies, and Theft," *Economic Inquiry* 5, no. 3, (1967): 224–32; and Ann Krueger, "The Political Economy of the Rent-Seeking Society," *American Economic Review* 64, no. 3 (1974): 291–303. Interestingly, even the efforts of those with greater ability to appropriate for themselves returns commensurate with their abilities can lead to an equilibrium in which not only others are less well-off but even they are too, as they spend money (stay in school longer) and take other actions to differentiate themselves. See J. E. Stiglitz, "The Theory of Screening, Education and the Distribution of Income," *American Economic Review* 65, no. 3 (June 1975): 283–300.

27. See Bureau of Economic Analysis, National Income and Product Accounts Table, "Table 6.16D. Corporate Profits by Industry," available at http://www.bea .gov/National/nipaweb/SelectTable.asp.

28. This is based on plausible industry assertions about the fees. Tim Hammonds, president and CEO of Food Marketing Institute, has said, "How big is the problem? The interchange fee a supermarket pays when

a customer pays with plastic is more than the money that flows to the retailer's bottom line; it's often double. Does that seem right to you? The service provider using a computerized payment network is getting more dollars from the transaction than the net profit for the merchant who provides the labor, the land, the fixtures, the light and the heat, and the store that stocks the products." Hammonds, speech to the FMI Midwinter Executive Conference (January 24, 2006), available at http://c0462491.cdn.cloudfiles.rackspacecloud.com/Hammonds_Interchange_Speech.pdf (accessed March 6, 2012).

29. See Marc-André Gagnon and Joel Lexchin, "The Cost of Pushing Pills: A New Estimate of Pharmaceutical Promotion Expenditures in the United States," *PLoS Medicine* 5, no. 1 (January 2008): 1–6.

30. In 2009 the United States spent about 17.4 percent of GDP, amounting to almost $8,000 per capita. The Netherlands and France were the next two highest countries, spending 12.0 percent and 11.8 percent of GDP, respectively. The average OECD spending was $3,223. OECD Health Data 2011, database available at http://www.oecd.org/document/30/0,3746,en_2649_37407_12968734_1_1_1_37407,00.html (accessed March 3, 2012).

31. "The Measurement of Economic Performance and Social Progress Revisited—Reflections and Overview," September, 16, 2009, CMEPSP, available at http://www.stiglitz-sen-fitoussi.fr/documents/overview-eng.pdf (accessed February 15, 2012), a follow-up to the report of the Commission on the Measurement of Economic Performance and Social Progress. Also available as Joseph Stiglitz, Amartya Sen, and Jean-Paul Fitoussi, *Mismeasuring Our Lives* (New York: New Press, 2010).

32. Figures are available from the IMF World Economic Outlook Database, available at http://www.imf.org/external/pubs/ft/weo/2011/02/weodata/index.aspx (accessed February 12, 2012).

33. Some claim, however, that the quotation is only apocryphal. See http://www.dirksencenter.org/print_emd_billionhere.htm.

34. See the Commission on the Measurement of Economic Performance and Social Progress.

35. Stephen P. Magee, William A. Brock, and Leslie Young, *Black Hole Tariffs and Endogenous Policy Theory: Political Economy in General Equilibrium* (New York: Cambridge University Press, 1989). Not surprisingly an army of lawyers is ready to come to the defense of the legal profession and to challenge these findings. See George L. Priest, "Lawyers, Liabil-

ity, and Law Reform: Effects on American Economic Growth and Trade Competitiveness" (1993), Faculty Scholarship Series, available at 624. http://digitalcommons.law.yale.edu/fss_papers/624.

36. See Andrei Shleifer and Robert W. Vishny, *The Grabbing Hand: Government Pathologies and Their Cures* (Cambridge: Harvard University Press, 1998).

37. The theory is that fear of punishment after the fact will provide incentives for firms to behave well. But firms well armed with lawyers know that they often will escape punishment. And besides, taking risks with the environment increases profits today, and shortsighted managers are more concerned with the reality of today's profits than what might happen to profits sometime in the future. The interests of the managers may not be well aligned with the interests of the firm, and the interests of the firm are not well aligned with those of society more broadly.

38. Known as the problem of moral hazard.

39. For a fuller discussion of these issues, see L. Bilmes and J. E. Stiglitz, *The Three Trillion Dollar War* (New York: Norton, 2008).

40. The Iraq war was put entirely on the credit card: when the war started, the United States already had a deficit. But instead of raising taxes to pay for it, the government lowered taxes in 2003.

41. Quotation is from Marshall's 1895 *Principles of Economics*. It appears on p. 555 of the 8th ed. (London: Macmillan, 1920).

42. H. Leibenstein, *Economic Backwardness and Economic Growth* (New York: Wiley, 1957).

43. See Paul Glewwe, Hanan G. Jacoby, and Elizabeth M. King; "Early Childhood Nutrition and Academic Achievement: A Longitudinal Analysis," *Journal of Public Economics* 81, no. 3 (September 2001): 345–68. For a recent review of literature, see Douglas Almond and Janet Currie, "Human Capital Development before Age Five," in *Handbook of Labor Economics*, vol. 4b, ed. Orley Ashenfelter and David Card (New York: Elsevier, 2011), 1315–486.

44. Mullainathan and Shafir are writing a book, *The Packing Problem: Time, Money, and the Science of Scarcity.* The quotation in the text is from their manuscript as reported on http://westallen.typepad.com/idealawg/2011/07/are-you-money-poor.html. Their argument is vividly explained in http://www.youtube.com/watch?v=5Aw_czU1bm0.

45. My own work has focused on a broad analysis of how higher wages can increase productivity, through lowering labor turnover, improv-

ing incentives, improving the quality of the labor force, and improving morale. The theories are known collectively as "efficiency wage theories" and were discussed in my review paper "The Causes and Consequences of the Dependence of Quality on Prices," *Journal of Economic Literature* 25 (1987): 1–48, as well as in my Nobel Prize lecture, published as "Information and the Change in the Paradigm in Economics," *American Economic Review* 92, no. 3 (June 2002): 460–501. George Akerlof (who shared with me the 2001 Nobel Prize in Economics) and Janet Yellen (currently vice chair of the Federal Reserve) have further articulated how the perception of unfairness can undermine effort. See Akerlof and Yellen, "The Fair-Wage Effort Hypothesis and Unemployment," *Quarterly Journal of Economics* 105 (1990): 255–83. Joseph W. Harder looked at a context in which there were objective measures of performance— baseball and basketball—and showed that "underrewarded individuals behaved less cooperatively and more selfishly." "Play for Pay: Effects of Inequity in a Pay-for-Performance Context," *Administrative Science Quarterly* 37 (1992): 321–35.

46. Alan B. Krueger and Alexandre Mas, "Strikes, Scabs, and Tread Separations: Labor Strife and the Production of Defective Bridgestone/ Firestone Tires," *Journal of Political Economy* 112, no. 2 (2004): 253–89.

47. Alain Cohn, Ernst Fehr, and Lorenz Goette, "Fairness and Effort— Evidence from a Field Experiment," Working Paper, October 2008; and Alain Cohn, Ernst Fehr, Benedikt Herrmann, and Frederic Schneider, "Social Comparison in the Workplace: Evidence from a Field Experiment," IZA Working Paper 5550, March 2011.

48. Marianne Bertrand and Adair Morse have used an expression similar to our "trickle-down behaviorism." They've documented the importance of trickle-down consumerism, showing that not only does spending increase if one lives in a community with higher income inequality, but so do bankruptcy and self-reported financial distress. Interestingly, they also show that politicians in such communities support measures to make credit more available—perhaps in a short-sighted attempt to make poorer individuals feel better by being able to (temporarily) consume more. See "Trickle-down consumption," working paper, February 2012, available at ⟨http://isites.harvard.edu/fs/docs/ icb.topic964076.files/BertrandMorseTrickleDown_textandtables.pdf⟩. Robert Frank of Cornell University, Adam Seth Levine of the University of Michigan, and Oege Dijk of the European University Institute

have put forward a similar hypothesis, called "expenditure cascades." They provide empirical evidence that increased income inequality is associated with "overspending," reflected in, for instance, higher bankruptcy rates. See "Expenditure Cascades," available at http://ssrn.com/abstract=1690612, Oct 12, 2010.

49. A survey of the evidence for both developed and developing countries is in Andrew E. Clark and Claudia Senik, "Will GDP Growth Increase Happinenss in Developing Countries?," Paris School of Economics, Working Paper no. 2010-43, March 2011.

50. John Maynard Keynes, *Economic Possibilities for Our Grandchildren: Essays in Persuasion* (originally published 1930) (New York: Norton, 1963), pp. 358–73. The discussion here draws upon my reflections on that essay: "Toward a General Theory of Consumerism: Reflections on Keynes' *Economic Possibilities for Our Grandchildren*," in *Revisiting Keynes: Economic Possibilities for Our Grandchildren*, ed. G. Piga and L. Pecchi (Cambridge: MIT Press, 2008), pp. 41–87. See also the other essays in that volume.

51. Adam Smith, *Lectures on Jurisprudence*, ed. Ronald L. Meek, D. D. Raphael, and Peter Stein (New York: Clarendon Press, 1978), (A) vi.54. The citation and analysis are in Daniel Luban, "Adam Smith on Vanity, Domination, and History," *Modern Intellectual History*, forthcoming.

52. For the long-run survival of the planet, there's something else wrong with America's answer: excessive consumption of material goods leads to global warming and puts the earth in peril.

53. Though incentives are at the core of the conservative justification for inequality, they also appeal to "fairness." See chapter 2 for a critique.

54. Wealth in the form of collateral plays a kind of catalytic role rather than a role of input that gets used up in the process of producing output. See K. Hoff, "Market Failures and the Distribution of Wealth: A Perspective from the Economics of Information," *Politics and Society* 24, no. 4 (1996): 411–32; and Hoff, "The Second Theorem of the Second Best," *Journal of Public Economics* 25 (1994): 223–42.

55. The exciting story is told in the bestseller by Dava Sobel, *Longitude: The True Story of a Lone Genius Who Solved the Greatest Scientific Problem of His Time* (New York: Walker, 1995).

56. Technically, the problems with incentive pay arise when there are information asymmetries. The employer doesn't fully know the quality of the products produced by the worker (otherwise, he would specify that). In a

trial, the judge and jury worry that the strength of an expert's opinion might be affected if his compensation depended on the outcome of the trial.

57. Given this, one might ask, why are those in finance, supposedly experts in economics, so wedded to these distortionary incentive schemes. The answer, as we explained earlier, relates to failures in corporate governance: these schemes allow them to more easily divert more of the corporate revenue to themselves.

58. See Patrick Bolton, Jose Scheinkman, and Wei Xiong, "Executive Compensation and Short-Termist Behaviour in Speculative Markets," *Review of Economic Studies* 73, no. 3 (2006): 577–610.

59. Opponents claimed that there was no way that one could accurately value the options, but at the Council of Economic Advisers we devised a way of providing at least a lower bound on the estimate—a far better estimate than the zero value associated with current accounting practices.

60. See B. Nalebuff and J. E. Stiglitz, "Information, Competition and Markets," *American Economic Review* 73, no. 2 (May 1983): 278–84; B. Nalebuff and J. E. Stiglitz, "Prizes and Incentives: Toward a General Theory of Compensation and Competition," *Bell Journal* 14, no. 1 (Spring 1983): 21–43; and J. E. Stiglitz, "Design of Labor Contracts: Economics of Incentives and Risk-Sharing," in *Incentives, Cooperation and Risk Sharing*, ed. H. Nalbantian (Totowa, NJ: Rowman & Allanheld, 1987), pp. 47–68.

61. Dasgupta Partha and Paul A. David, "Toward a New Economics of Science," *Research Policy* 2, no. 5 (September 1994): 487–521.

62. The study was conducted in Haifa, Israel, by two economists, Uri Gneezy and Aldo Rustichini, and published as "A Fine Is a Price," *Journal of Legal Studies* 29, no. 1 (January 2000): 1–17. A variety of experiments confirm the power of intrinsic rewards, in comparison with extrinsic rewards. See, e.g., Gneezy and Rustichini, "Pay Enough or Don't Pay At All," *Quarterly Journal of Economics* 115, no. 3 (2000): 791–810. One explanation for why "high-performance work systems" (in which workers are given more responsibility) perform better is that they enhance trust and a perception of intrinsic reward. See Eileen Appelbaum, Thomas Bailey, Peter Berg, and Arne Kalleberg, *Manufacturing Advantage: Why High-Performance Work Systems Pay Off* (Ithaca: Cornell University Press, 2000). See also J. E. Stiglitz, "Democratic Development as the Fruits of Labor," in *The Rebel Within*, ed. Ha-Joon Chang (London: Wimbledon Publishing, 2001), pp. 279–315. (Originally key-

note address at the Industrial Relations Research Association, Boston, January 2000.)

63. A key insight of modern industrial organization is that in imperfectly competitive markets—and most markets are imperfectly competitive—one can get ahead and increase profits not just by performing better but also by ensuring that one's rival performs more poorly. Profits—and bonuses—can increase, but societal welfare can be decreased. This theory is called "raising rivals costs." See Steven C. Salop and David T. Scheffman "Raising Rivals' Costs," *American Economic Review* 73, no. 2 (May 1983): 267–71.

64. A good empirical review is "Team-Based Rewards: Current Empirical Evidence and Directions for Future Research," *Research in Organizational Behavior* 20 (1998): 141–83. A more recent study has shown how competition among workers undermines workplace productivity. See Jeffrey Carpenter, Peter Hans Matthews, and John Schirm, "Tournaments and Office Politics: Evidence from a Real Effort Experiment," *American Economic Review* 100, no. 1 (2010): 504–17.

65. Again, well-being at the workplace was something that the Committee for the Measurement of Economic Social Progress emphasized.

66. See Gerald Marwell and Ruth E. Ames, "Economists Free Ride, Does Anyone Else?," *Journal of Public Economics* 15 (June 1981): 295–310; John R. Carter and Michael D. Irons, "Are Economists Different, and If So, Why?," *Journal of Economic Perspectives* 5, no. 2 (Spring 1991): 171–77; Günther Schulze and Bjorn Frank, "Does Economics Make Citizens Corrupt?," *Journal of Economic Behavior and Organization* 43, no. 1 (2000): 101–13; Robert H. Frank, Thomas Gilovich, and Dennis T. Regan, "Does Studying Economics Inhibit Cooperation?," *Journal of Economic Perspectives* 7, no. 2 (Spring 1993): 159–71; Reinhard Selten and Axel Ockenfels, "An Experimental Solidarity Game," *Journal of Economic Behavior and Organization* 34, no. 4 (March 1998): 517–39.

67. Fidan Ana Kurtulus and Doug Kruse show that in this recession, and in past ones, employee-owned firms did better, maintaining higher levels of employment, than did others. See "How Did Employee Ownership Firms Weather the Last Two Recessions? Employee Ownership and Employment Stability in the US: 1999–2008," PowerPoint presentation given at Mid-Year Fellows Workshop in Honor of Louis O. Kelso, February 24–25, 2011, at Rutgers School of Management and Labor Relations.

68. See Peter Diamond and Emmanuel Saez, "The Case for a Progressive Tax: From Basic Research to Policy Recommendations," *Journal of Economic Perspectives* 25, no. 4 (2011): 165–90; and Thomas Piketty, Emmanuel Saez, and Stefanie Stantcheva, "Optimal Taxation of Top Labor Incomes: A Tale of Three Elasticities," NBER Working Paper 17616, 2011, available at http://www.nber.org/papers/w17616 (accessed March 1, 2012). For an accessible discussion of the second paper's findings, see the same authors' article "Taxing the 1%: Why the Top Tax Rate Could Be over 80%," *Vox*, December 8, 2011, available at http://www.voxeu.org/index.php?q=node/7402 (accessed March 6, 2012). Some earlier, idealized economic models suggested that it was optimal not to tax interest income (income from capital), but subsequent research showed that this result was not robust: capital taxation is desirable. See, e.g., Thomas Piketty and Emmanuel Saez, "A Theory of Optimal Capital Taxation," working paper, 2011, Paris School of Economics and University of California at Berkeley, available at http://elsa.berkeley.edu/~saez/piketty-saez1_1_11optKtax.pdf (accessed February 27, 2012); and J. E. Stiglitz, "Pareto Efficient Taxation and Expenditure Policies, with Applications to the Taxation of Capital, Public Investment, and Externalities," presented at conference in honor of Agnar Sandmo, Bergen, Norway, January 1998.

69. Which allowed those in private equity firms and hedge funds to be taxed on their returns—including what they received from managing other people's money—at the favorable capital gains tax rate.

70. Alexander J. Field, *A Great Leap Forward: 1930s Depression and U.S. Economic Growth* (New Haven: Yale University Press, 2011).

71. This is the thrust of the analysis of "optimal redistributive taxation," discussed in an earlier footnote.

72. In a speech (October 26, 2011) entitled "Saving the American Idea: Rejecting Fear, Envy, and the Philosophy of Division" delivered in response to the CBO report detailing America's growing inequality, as cited in Jonathan Chait, "No Such Thing as Equal Opportunity," *New York*, November 7, 2011, pp. 14–16.

73. Ibid.

74. Ibid.

75. See Torsten Persson and Guido Tabellini, "Is Inequality Harmful for Growth?," *American Economic Review* 84, no. 3 (June 1994): 600–21.

Chapter Five A DEMOCRACY IN PERIL

1. For a textbook exposition, and a discussion of the implications, for instance, for education expenditures or the progressivity of the tax system, see J. E. Stiglitz, *The Economics of the Public Sector*, 3rd ed. (New York: W. W. Norton, 2000). For earlier theoretical discussions, see Anthony Downs, "An Economic Theory of Political Action in a Democracy," *Journal of Political Economy* 65, no. 2 (1957): 135–50; Harold Hotelling, "Stability in Competition," *Economic Journal* 39, no. 153 (1929): 41–57; and Kenneth J. Arrow, *Social Choice and Individual Values*, 2nd ed. (New York: Wiley, 1963).

2. Edward Wyatt, "S.E.C. Is Avoiding Tough Sanctions for Large Banks," *New York Times*, February 3, 2012, p. A1. The article provides a detailed analysis, citing as an example JPMorganChase, which "has settled six fraud cases in the last 13 years, including one with a $228 million settlement last summer, but it has obtained at least 22 waivers, in part by arguing that it has 'a strong record of compliance with securities laws.'"

3. This is undoubtedly one of the reasons why, in the United States, voter turnout among African Americans has so frequently lagged behind that of whites, and turnout among the poor has lagged behind that of better-off other groups. America had so long excluded African Americans from enjoying full rights that even when voting restrictions were lifted,the community's faith in the electoral process remained seriously harmed. See, e.g., Mark Lopez and Paul Taylor, "Dissecting the 2008 Electorate: Most Diverse in U.S. History," Pew Research Center, April 30, 2009, available at http://pewresearch.org/assets/pdf/dissecting-2008-electorate.pdf.

4. The strength of faith in democratic processes is, however, remarkable. One interpretation for why it took so long for the Occupy Wall Street protests to emerge was that many hoped that the political process would "work" to rein in the financial sector and redress the country's economic problems. It was only when it was evident that they did not that protests became widespread. The strong voter turnout in 2008 (the highest since 1968) reflects the power of hope. War, too, elicits a strong sense of civic identity, perhaps accounting for the relatively high voter turnout in 2004.

5. Economic historians have emphasized the role of trust in the development of modern capitalism. See, e.g., D. McCloskey *The Bourgeois Virtues: Ethics for an Age of Commerce* (Chicago: University of Chicago

Press, 2006); and J. Mokyr, *The Enlightened Economy* (New Haven: Yale University Press, 2011). They have argued that Britain's success in the Industrial Revolution depended on its norms against opportunism. As Mokyr puts it, "opportunistic behavior was made so taboo that in only a few cases was it necessary to use the formal institutions to punish deviants. . . . Entrepreneurial success was based less on multi-talented geniuses than on successful cooperation between individuals who had good reason to think they could trust one another" (pp. 384–86). Trust was also one of the reasons that certain close-knit ethnic communities and certain other communities took on a pivotal role in the early development of capitalism. See, e.g., Avner Greif, "Reputation and Coalitions in Medieval Trade: Evidence on the Maghribi Traders," *Journal of Economic History* 49, no. 4 (1989): 857–82; and Greif, "Contract Enforceability and Economic Institutions in Early Trade: The Maghribi Traders' Coalition," *American Economic Review* 83, no. 3 (1993): 525–48. Albert Hirschman, a great economist whose insights reached beyond economics, has made similar observations. See, e.g., his *The Passions and the Interests* (Princeton: Princeton University Press, 1977).

6. The quotation is from G. W. Kolodko, *From Shock to Therapy: The Political Economy of Postsocialist Transformation* (New York: Oxford University Press, 2000). The absence of trust made it difficult not only to be productive, particularly when chains of production linked many specialized producers, but also to build the kind of rule-of-law institutions that would make the economy productive under a free market. That is, building institutions itself requires trust. See O. Blanchard and M .Kremer, "Disorganization," *Quarterly Journal of Economics* 112, no. 4 (November 1997): 1091–126; K. Hoff and J. E. Stiglitz, "After the Big Bang? Obstacles to the Emergence of the Rule of Law in Post-Communist Societies," *American Economic Review* 94, no. 3 (June 2004): 753–63; and K. Hoff and J. E. Stiglitz, "Exiting a Lawless State," *Economic Journal* 118, no. 531 (August 2008): 1474–97.

7. Thus, to put it in somewhat more technical terms, people's preferences are *conditional*; what they want to do depends on what they believe other people do. What matters is often not the legal norm (what you are supposed to do) but the descriptive norm (what you believe most other people do). For this reason, as the philosopher Cristina Bicchieri points out, "beneficial descriptive norms are fragile." Bicchieri, *The Grammar of Society* (New York: Cambridge University Press, 2006), p. 68.

8. A poll conducted by Gallup and the Better Business Bureau found that the trust Americans have in the businesses they deal with every day declined 14 percent between September 2007 and April 2008 alone. See "BBB/Gallup Trust in Business Index: Executive Summary—Survey Results Consumers' Rating of Companies They Regularly Deal With, April 2008," available at http://www.bbb.org/us/storage/0/Shared%20 Documents/Survey%20II%20-%20BBB%20Gallup%20-%20Execu tive%20Summary%20-%2025%20Aug%2008.pdf (accessed March 4, 2012). A *New York Times*/CBS News poll in October 2011 similarly found that Americans' trust in Congress and in Washington more generally had dipped to all-time lows. Just 9 percent of Americans approved of Congress, and just 10 percent thought they could "trust the government in Washington to do what is right" all or most of the time. See "Americans' Approval of Congress Dips to Single Digits," *New York Times*, October 25, 2011, available at http://www.nytimes.com/interac tive/2011/10/25/us/politics/approval-of-congress-drops-to-single-digits .html (accessed March 4, 2012).

9. See Walter Y. Oi, "Labor as a Quasi-fixed Factor," *Journal of Political Economy* 70 (1962): 538–55; and Robert M. Solow, "Distribution in the Long and Short Run," in *The Distribution of National Income: Proceedings of a Conference Held by the International Economics Association at Palermo*, ed. Jean Marchal and Bernard Ducrois (New York: St. Martin's Press, 1968), pp. 449–66. See also Truman Bewley, *Why Wages Don't Fall during Recessions* (Cambridge: Harvard University Press, 1999); and Craig Burnside, Martin Eichenbaum, and Sergio Rebelo, "Labor Hoarding and the Business Cycle," *Journal of Political Economy* 101, no. 2 (April 1993): 245–73.

10. See the discussion in chapter 4 and the references cited there.

11. This, as we noted in chapter 4, is one of the central tenets of efficiency wage theory. For broader discussions of what is sometimes called the "high quality workplace," see chapter 4. Other references can be found in my paper "Democratic Development as the Fruits of Labor," in *The Rebel Within*, ed. Ha-Joon Chang (London: Wimbledon Publishing, 2001), pp. 279–315. Ernst Fehr and Klaus M. Schmidt show that workplaces that uses bonuses to promote effort—a system that relies on trust for compensation (workers trust that they will receive the bonus)—perform better than those that rely on standard performance-based piece rate incentive schemes. Ernst Fehr and Schmidt, "Fairness

and Incentives in a Multi-task Principal-Agent Model," *Scandinavian Journal of Economics* 106, no. 3 (2004): 453–74. See chapter 4 for more discussion of how workplaces that treat workers better also do well in downturns.

12. Again, a point emphasized by the Commission on the Measurement of Economic Performance and Social Progress.

13. See Werner Güth, Rolf Schmittberger, and Bernd Schwarze, "An Experimental Analysis of Ultimatum Bargaining," *Journal of Economic Behavior and Organization* 3 (December 1982): 367–88.

14. The experiment also shows that an individual's construct of fairness is shaped by the circumstances. Even if he knows he was randomly chosen to be the "dictator," he acts as if he believes it is appropriate to keep more than half for himself. Interestingly, if the second player begins the game with some money, and the first has the right to take away something from the second, then the first player is much less likely to give the second player anything. In an experiment by John List, the fraction of positive offers from the first player fell from 71 percent to 10 percent. This reflects the motivation to avoid the most selfish feasible action with the other player. It shows that fairness is construed not, or not only, in terms of what the other player gets, but also in terms of what the other player gets relative to his worst possible outcome. The realization that he could abuse the second player even more, by taking something from him, makes the first player feel better about a more unfair division. See List, "On the Interpretation of Giving in Dictator Games," *Journal of Political Economy* 115, no. 3 (2007): 482–93.

15. For a discussion of these outcomes (and the sums people will accept or veto in ultimatum games), see Colin Camerer and Richard Thaler, "Anomalies: Ultimatums, Dictators and Manners," *Journal of Economic Perspectives* 9, no. 2 (1995): 209–19.

16. For a sample of the large literature, see, e.g., Daniel Kahneman, Jack L. Knetsch, and Richard H. Thaler, "Fairness and the Assumptions of Economics," *Journal of Business* 59, no. 4 (1986): S285–S300; Gary E. Bolton and Axel Ockenfels, "ERC: A Theory of Equity, Reciprocity, and Competition," *American Economic Review* 90, no. 1 (March 2000): 166–93; Armin Falk, Ernst Fehr, and Urs Fischbacher, "On the Nature of Fair Behavior," *Economic Inquiry* 41, no. 1 (January 2003): 20–26; Daniel Kahneman, Jack L. Knetsch, and Richard H. Thaler, "Fairness as a Constraint on Profit Seeking: Entitlements in the Market," *American*

Economic Review 76, no. 4 (1986): 728–41; Amartya Sen, "Moral Codes and Economic Success," in *Market Capitalism and Moral Values*, ed. C. S. Brittan and A. Hamlin (Brookfield, VT: Aldershot, 1995).

17. Morale is destroyed. The implications have been explored in the branch of the literature in economics noted earlier, called the efficiency wage theory, describing how wages affect productivity. See, in particular, George A. Akerlof and Janet L. Yellen, "The Fair Wage-Effort Hypothesis and Unemployment," *Quarterly Journal of Economics* 105, no. 2 (1990): 255–83.

18. See "Frustration with Congress Could Hurt Republican Incumbents," Pew Research Center for the People and the Press, p. 13, based on poll conducted December 7–11, 2011, available at http://www.people-press .org/files/legacy-pdf/12-15-11%20Congress%20and%20Economy%20 release.pdf (accessed March 4, 2012).

19. *Washington Post*/ABC poll, January 12–15, 2012, available at http:// www.washingtonpost.com/wp-srv/politics/polls/postabcpoll_011512.html (accessed March 4, 2012).

20. Michael I. Norton and Dan Ariely, "Building a Better America–One Wealth Quintile at a Time," *Perspectives on Psychological Science* 6, no. 1 (2011): 9–12.

21. As we explain at greater length below, it is not that there is an "establishment," which has gotten together to create the current system as it exists today. Rather, our economic and political system evolves, but moneyed interests use their wealth and influence as they can to shape it. And the shape that has emerged is much like that which might have emerged had they gotten together to shape it in their own interests.

22. See, e.g., Ben H. Bagdikian, *The New Media Monopoly* (Boston: Beacon Press, 2004); Robert W. McChesney, *The Political Economy of Media: Enduring Issues, Emerging Dilemmas* (New York: Monthly Review Press, 2008).

23. See John Kenneth Galbraith, *American Capitalism: The Concept of Countervailing Power* (New York: New American Library, 1952).

24. For an excellent discussion of these issues, see André Schiffrin, *Words and Money* (New York: Verso, 2010).

25. In a sense, the problem is worse: the media depend heavily on advertising, and the threat of withdrawal of advertising (or the worry over a loss of advertising revenues) can inhibit full coverage of corporate misdeeds.

26. See Stefano DellaVigna and Ethan Kaplan, "The Fox News Effect:

Media Bias and Voting," *Quarterly Journal of Economics* 122, no. 3 (2007): 1187–234. The case of the former Italian prime minister Silvio Berlusconi, who used his television empire to solidify his hold on power for seventeen years, provides an excellent illustration of how control of the media can affect political outcomes.

27. The Internet has exposed the biases and distortions in mainstream media, but also provided more extensive access to a diversity of viewpoints. At the same time, the "business model" of the Internet doesn't provide the resources for the kind of in-depth investigative reporting that has enabled the press to serve as an effective check on abuses in both the public and the private sectors. Finally, as we note in chapter 6, the Internet can lead to the polarization of perspectives that inhibits democratic compromise.

28. Indeed, Democratic primaries were restricted to whites, and since the Democratic Party dominated the electoral process, African Americans were effectively disenfranchised.

29. Suresh Naidu of Columbia University shows that "poll taxes and literacy tests each lowered overall electoral turnout by 10–23% and increased the Democratic vote share in national elections by 5%–10%." His clever and careful research methodology entails comparing adjacent county-pairs that straddle state boundaries. See his "Suffrage, Schooling, and Sorting in the Post-Bellum U.S. South," working paper, Columbia University, 2010, available at http://iserp.columbia.edu/sites/default/files/suresh_naidu_working_paper.pdf.

30. Other targeted groups (with similar political objectives) include immigrants and blue-collar workers. See Alexander Keyssar, "The Squeeze on Voting," *International Herald Tribune*, February 15, 2012, p. 9; and Keyssar, *The Right to Vote: The Contested History of Democracy in the United States* (New York: Basic Books, 2000). He cites instances of voters' being required to "bring their sealed naturalization papers to the polls or to present written evidence that they had canceled their registration at any previous address or to register annually, in person, on one of only two Tuesdays." More recently, attempts to effectively disenfranchise Hispanic voters center on bilingual ballots. See, e.g., Adam Serwer, "Gingrich and Romney Want to Say Adios to Bilingual Ballots," *Mother Jones*, January 30, 2012, available at http://motherjones.com/politics/2012/01/gingrich-and-romney-want-say-adios-bilingual-ballots. Of course, the most significant disenfranchisement was that of women,

whose attitudes, e.g., to war and to social issues are often markedly different from those of men. Clearly, the disenfranchisement affected the outcome of political processes.

31. See Walter Dean Burnham, "Democracy in Peril: The American Turnout Problem and the Path to Plutocracy," Roosevelt Institute Working Paper no. 5, December 1, 2010; Frances Fox Piven and Richard A. Cloward, "Government Statistics and Conflicting Explanations of Non-voting," PS: Political Science and Politics 22, no. 3 (September 1989): 580–88; and Piven and Cloward, "National Voter Registration Reform: How It Might Be Won," ibid. 21, no. 4 (Autumn 1988): 868–75.

32. Even someone with the means to vote but without a car will have less of an incentive to get the driver's ID to vote, since the marginal cost of voting is higher. More than a dozen states have passed ID laws since 2005. See Keyssar, "The Squeeze on Voting."

33. See "Inaccurate, Costly, and Inefficient: Evidence That America's Voter Registration System Needs an Upgrade," Pew Center on the States, report released February 14, 2012, available at http://www.pewcenteron thestates.org/uploadedFiles/Pew_Upgrading_Voter_Registration.pdf (accessed March 4, 2012). The report also identifies large numbers of inaccuracies or invalid registrations, some one in eight.

34. It was one of many 5-to-4 decisions under Chief Justice Roberts. Another, equally important decision was the Court's 2011 striking down (in Arizona Free Enterprise Club v. Bennett) the state of Arizona's attempt to redress the imbalance of political power created by an imbalance of economic power by providing additional funds to the candidates who were less successful in raising private campaign money. Trust in the Court is important, because in any society there will be disputes, and it is vital that the courts be viewed as fair arbiters of such disputes. But if the Court is viewed as not fair—as taking sides, even before the arguments have been presented—then the Court's main source of strength, its credibility and the influence it has in the court of public opinion, will quickly disappear. In other countries marked by high levels of divisiveness, the notion of an independent judiciary is looked upon with skepticism, and the court's pronouncements are seen as essentially political as that of any other branch of government.

35. In fact, economists refer to such arrangements as "implicit" contracts, enforced sometimes even more effectively than explicit contracts,

through the design of repeated games, where participants know of the severe consequences of failure to live up to the tacit understandings.

36. Congress could have required that, before any such contributions were made, shareholders had to vote. But Senator Schumer and others trying to limit the impact of *Citizens United* were unable to pass this or other legislation circumscribing the political power of corporations. The increased power of monied interests is already being felt in the election of 2012, where noncandidate political action committees (working on behalf of particular candidates) were spending more money than the candidates themselves, and often engaged in very negative advertising.

37. In effect, with the filibuster, the "decisive" voter (in the Senate) is not the median but the voter at the 40th percentile. Since the filibuster rules are not a matter of the Constitution, but decided by each Congress, there is an interesting question: Why does the "median" voter cede control to the 40th percentile voter? The filibuster was created to protect minority rights on issues that the minority believed were of critical importance but not protected by the Bill of Rights. The irony is that it was used mostly in issues of civil rights, to abrogate the rights of African Americans. Ezra Klein, "Breaking the Filibuster in One Graph," *Washington Post*, December 23, 2010, available at http://voices.washingtonpost .com/ezra-klein/2010/12/breaking_the_filibuster_in_one.html, provides data showing the "shocking" rise in the number of filibusters—a negligible number a quarter century ago, but around 140 filings to end a filibuster in the last Congress. Today the filibuster is used as a matter of routine and, together with campaign contributions, enhances the ability of moneyed interests to exercise their political influence even when what they want is counter to the interests of the majority.

38. Many factors contribute to voter participation. Disillusionment and disenfranchisement, upon which this chapter focuses, are important. Personalities matter. So too does war (note, e.g., the relatively high turnout in 2004).

39. Burnham, "Democracy in Peril," cites data showing that those states where disenfranchasement and disempowerment have been the strongest (the South) have also had the worst voter turnout. The rate has been as low as 1.8 percent in South Carolina (in the house election of 1926) and fallen below 30 percent—usually well below that number—in many of the southern states in elections held over the past 110 years.

Although there was a slight increase in voter turnout in the 2008 presidential election, the last time voter turnout in a presidential election exceeded 60 percent was 1968, and the last time it exceeded 70 percent was 1900. See http://www.presidency.ucsb.edu/data/turnout.php. Compare this to countries such as Germany, where turnout for parliamentary elections has never dipped below 70 percent in the last 60 years, or France, where parliamentary election turnout has only dipped below 60 percent once in the last 60 years, and where turnout for presidential elections has always been at least 77 percent and often much more since 1965. See Voter Turnout database of the International Institute of Democracy and Electoral Assistance, available at http://www .idea.int/vt/.

40. Such a low turnout is especially striking given that young people have so much more at stake—a lifetime of consequences as a result of government policies that might be enacted now.

41. This was evident, e.g., in the turnout in early Republican primaries and caucuses in 2012: 1 percent of Maine's registered voters turned out for its caucuses, 16 percent in Florida, 3 percent in Nevada. The nature of the bias is illustrated by South Carolina's primary: 98 percent of voters were white (66 percent of the population is white), 72 percent were 45 or older (median age is 36), two-thirds were evangelical Christians (exit polls in the 2008 general election had 40 percent evangelicals). Similar biases are reflected in stances on particular issues. While evidently among Republican primary voters there is strong opposition to mandated health insurance coverage of contraception, a *New York Times* poll in February 2012 suggests that such provisions have a two-to-one popular support. See Erik Eckholm, "Poll Finds Wide Support for Birth Control Coverage," *New York Times*, March 1, 2012, available at http://www.nytimes.com/2012/03/02/us/politics/americans-divided-on-birth-control-coverage-poll-finds.html (accessed March 4, 2012).

42. Citizens are not required to vote, only to come to the polling station. The mandate largely resolves the "voting paradox" we discussed earlier in the chapter.

43. This means a reversal of the Court decision in *Arizona Free Enterprise Club v. Bennett* and in *Citizens United v. Federal Election Commission*.

44. See *Washington Post*/ABC News poll from April 26, 2010, which showed two-thirds of Americans favored stricter financial regulation.

Available at http://abcnews.go.com/images/PollingUnit/1109a1Financial Regulation.pdf (accessed March 4, 2012).

45. Paul Krugman, "Oligarchy, American Style," *New York Times*, November 4, 2011, available at http://www.nytimes.com/2011/11/04/ opinion/oligarchy-american-style.html (accessed March 1, 2012).

46. President Obama put it equally forcefully in his Osawatomie, Kansas, address on December 6, 2011: "[I]n 1910, Teddy Roosevelt came here to Osawatomie. . . . Our country," he said, ". . . means nothing unless it means the triumph of a real democracy. . . of an economic system under which each man shall be guaranteed the opportunity to show the best that there is him." The president went on to say, "Inequality also distorts our democracy. It gives an outsized voice to the few who can afford high-priced lobbyists and unlimited campaign contributions, and it runs the risk of selling out our democracy to the highest bidder. It leaves everyone else rightly suspicious that the system in Washington is rigged against them, that our elected representatives aren't looking out for the interests of most Americans."

47. There is a third explanation that may play some role. Politics in a democracy requires the formation of coalitions. Our analysis has proceeded as if the only issues that individuals cared about were economic issues. But voters also care about social issues, and they choose candidates that reflect their perspectives, weighting in different ways social and economic issues. At least for a while, Republicans formed a coalition of social and economic conservatives, which though it advanced an agenda that was consistent with the desires of the social conservatives, was often against their economic interests. See Thomas Frank, *What's the Matter with Kansas? How Conservatives Won the Heart of America* (New York: Metropolitan Books, 2004).

48. There are many parallels between global financial problems and those in the United States: in many cases, it is the banks that actively encouraged the excess indebtedness, that persuaded individuals and countries to take on more debt than they should have. In some cases, matters are even worse: East Asia, with its high savings rate, had no need to borrow from abroad. But the United States and other advanced industrial countries (both directly, and indirectly, through the IMF) put pressure on these countries to allow their firms to borrow freely from Western banks. Money flowed in. But when attitudes changed about the

prospects of the region, money rushed out the door, and thus the region faced the 1997 East Asia crisis. The banks made large profits as money flowed in, but, through the good offices of the IMF and the U.S. Treasury, they also made money *after* the crisis, by forcing the countries to have fire sales of their assets. See J. E. Stiglitz, *Globalization and Its Discontents* (New York: Norton, 2002).

49. For a more extensive discussion, see J. E. Stiglitz, 2006, *Making Globalization Work* (New York: Norton, 2003), chap. 8; and David Hale, "Newfoundland and the Global Debt Crisis," *Globalist*, April 28, 2003, available at http://www.theglobalist.com/StoryId.aspx?StoryId=3088 (accessed March 7, 2012).

50. Technically, the governments were voted in by their parliament; but many, if not most, of the parliamentarians felt they had little choice.

51. For an account of officials and banks' reactions—and the impact on banks and the stock market—see Quentin Peel, Richard Milne, and Karen Hope, "EU Leaders Battle to Save Greek Deal," *Financial Times*, November 1, 2011, available at http://www.ft.com/intl/cms/s/0/cc377942-0472-11e1-ac2a-00144feabdc0.html#axzz1oBCs0Dlj (accessed March 4, 2012).

52. In that election, Goldman Sachs went so far as to create the Goldman Sachs "Lulameter" to measure risks associated with Mr. da Silva's chances of becoming president, with the implicit notion that his election put at risk investments in that country. See http://moya.bus.miami.edu/~sandrade/Lulameter_GS.pdf. Apparently that report (link above) got them into a bit of trouble as they subsequently backed off. The *New York Times* reported, "Goldman, Sachs seems to have distanced itself from a report its strategists released earlier this year using a 'Lulameter.' Since then, Paulo Leme, its managing director for emerging markets research, has presented a relatively balanced view of Brazil's prospects." Available at http://www.nytimes.com/2002/10/12/business/worldbusiness/12BRAZ.html?pagewanted=all.

53. As we noted in chapter 3, even the IMF has now conceded that at times capital controls may be desirable. There is a large literature on the subject. See, e.g., Jonathan D. Ostry et al., "Capital Inflows: The Role of Controls," IMF Staff Position note 10/04, February 19, 2010, available at http://www.imf.org/external/pubs/ft/spn/2010/spn1004.pdf (accessed December 28, 2011), and the more extensive discussion of the issue in the next chapter.

54. *The Globalization Paradox: Democracy and the Future of the World Economy* (New York: W. W. Norton, 2011).

55. The high costs of medicine that result also play an important role in the immiseration of those at the bottom. See Stiglitz, *Making Globalization Work*, chap. 4, for a fuller discussion of the issues surrounding intellectual property rights.

56. As an example, no one believes that any incentive was provided by the extension of copyright to seventy years after the author's death *for works already created under the older, more restrictive regime*. It was simply a provision that enhanced rents for Disney and other owners of copyrighted material. Developing countries have worried, in particular, about how intellectual property regimes imposed on them have restricted access to generic drugs, forcing them to pay prices beyond those they can afford, leading to untold numbers of unnecessary deaths.

57. These provisions are called "regulatory takings." For a discussion of this controversy, see, e.g., Stiglitz, *Making Globalization Work*, chap. 7, and J. E. Stiglitz, "Regulating Multinational Corporations: Towards Principles of Cross-border Legal Frameworks in a Globalized World Balancing Rights and Responsibilities," *American University International Law Review* 23, no. 3 (2007): 451–58, Grotius Lecture presented at the 101st Annual Meeting of the American Society for International Law, Washington, DC, March 28, 2007, and the references cited there.

58. I should emphasize that it is not that the 1 percent has "conspired" to ensure that this would happen; rather, it pushed for rules of games that have had that effect—and that have served its interests well. See the discussion of chapter 6.

59. Later we argue that to a large extent the 1 percent (like the bankers) have been shortsighted—they have pushed for policies that may be in their short-run interests, but not in their long-run interests.

Chapter Six 1984 Is upon Us

1. Lenin saw the shaping of public opinion as essential in bringing on the revolution, but to some extent all countries and all leaders develop narratives that shape how people perceive their government and country. Anticolonial leaders had an easier time persuading the citizens of their country of the illegitimacy of colonial rule.

2. Ads could provide information, e.g., about what goods are available at what prices. But statements about the attributes of a product by the seller (unless accompanied by a money-back guarantee) would be taken as just self-serving. There are Ptolemaic attempts to describe ads, like that of the old Marlboro cowboy (retired in the United States around the turn of the century after a forty-five-year stint), as providing consumers information: most individuals who buy the cigarettes are not cowboys, but may identify themselves as hardy, like a cowboy. The ad conveyed information about what kind of person enjoys this brand of cigarette, and the ad would have been successful, and persisted, only if those who self-identify themselves in this way do in fact enjoy the product.

3. In chapter 4 we argued for the importance of publicly provided goods and a sense of social cohesion and economic fairness and justice. A major divide in voting patterns across states is among the affluent, with more of the more affluent in "liberal" states seemingly recognizing this (and treating social justice as a basic value in its own right) than in the conservative states. Paul Krugman, "Moochers against Welfare," *New York Times*, February 16, 2012 , available at http://www.nytimes .com/2012/02/17/opinion/krugman-moochers-against-welfare.html?_ r=1&scp=1&sq=krugman%20moochers&st=cse (accessed February 20, 2012). Krugman cites the work of Andrew Gelman of Columbia University, who has shown that the rich everywhere vote more conservatively, but it is the rich in poor states who vote much more conservatively— leading to the phenomenon of Republicans' often representing poorer states. See Gelman, *Red State, Blue State, Rich State, Poor State: Why Americans Vote the Way They Do* (Princeton: Princeton University Press, 2010).

4. Suzanne Mettler of Cornell University cites statistics showing that 44 percent of Social Security recipients, 43 percent of recipients of unemployment benefits, and 40 percent of those on Medicare say that they "have not used a government program." Cited in Krugman, "Moochers against Welfare." See Suzanne Mettler, "Reconstituting the Submerged State: The Challenges of Social Policy Reform in the Obama Era," *Perspectives on Politics* 8, no. 3 (2010): 803–24. This partially accounts for the quandary that states that are the largest recipients of federal assistance tend to be most against government programs. See also the anecdote described below, in the next section, involving the elderly objecting to Obama-care because it threatened to socialize Medicare.

5. See Michael I. Norton and Dan Ariely, "Building a Better America—One Wealth Quintile at a Time," *Perspectives on Psychological Science* 6, no. 1 (2011): 9–12.

6. See the survey on the perception of inequality in the world, conducted by the Fondation Jean-Jaurès, available at (in French) http://www.jean-jaures.org/Publications/Dossiers-d-actualite/Enquete-sur-la-perception-des-inegalites-dans-le-monde (accessed March 4, 2012).

7. See R. Benabou and E. A. Ok, "Social Mobility and the Demand for Redistribution: The POUM Hypothesis," *Quarterly Journal of Economics* 116 (2001): 447–87; K. K. Charles and E. Hurst, "The Correlation of Wealth across Generations," *Journal of Political Economy* 111, no. 6 (2003): 1155–82; and L. A. Keister, *Getting Rich: America's New Rich and How They Got That Way* (Cambridge: Cambridge University Press, 2005).

8. From Charlotte Cavaille, "Perceptions of Inequalities in the World: Food for Thought," available at inequalitiesblog.wordpress.com/2011/09/27/perceptions-of-inequality-in-the-world-food-for-thought (accessed December 19, 2011). She provides an interesting interpretation, quoting Alexis de Tocqueville's classic work: "When inequality of conditions is the common law of society, the most marked inequalities do not strike the eye; when everything is nearly on the same level, the slightest are marked enough to hurt it. Hence the desire for equality always becomes more insatiable in proportion as equality is more complete." *Democracy in America* (Middlesex, UK: Echo Library, 2007), p. 428.

9. The tenets of rationality, in the jargon of economics, are that individuals maximize a well-defined utility function (or have a well-defined set of preferences) and maximize that with rational expectations. The alternative perspective of behavioral economics is expressed in the title of the popular book by Dan Ariely, *Predictably Irrational: The Hidden Forces That Shape Our Decisions* (New York: HarperCollins, 2008).

10. These ideas have begun to be used in the context of politics. See George Lakoff, *Don't Think of an Elephant! Know Your Values and Frame the Debate* (White River Junction, VT: Chelsea Green, 2004).

11. This is called the anchoring effect. See discussions of anchoring and framing effects on judgments and preferences in Daniel Kahneman, Paul Slovic, and Amos Tversky, eds., *Judgment under Uncertainty: Heuristics and Biases* (Cambridge: Cambridge University Press, 1982); and

Daniel Kahneman and Amos Tversky, eds., *Choices, Values and Frames* (New York: Cambridge University Press, 2000). For a popular and recent discussion, see Daniel Kahneman, *Thinking, Fast and Slow* (New York: Farrar, Straus and Giroux, 2011); and Richard Thaler and Cass Sunstein, *Nudge: Improving Decisions about Health, Wealth, and Happiness* (New Haven and London: Yale University Press, 2008).

12. See the discussion of framing effects in the case of the introduction of lifecycle funds in U.S. 401(k) plans in Ning Tang, Olivia S. Mitchell, Gary R. Mottola, and Stephen P. Utkus, "The Efficiency of Sponsor and Participant Portfolio Choices in 401(k) Plans," *Journal of Public Economics* 84, nos. 11–12 (2010): 1073–85; and Olivia S. Mitchell, Gary R. Mottola, Stephen P. Utkus, and Takeshi Yamaguchi, "Default, Framing and Spillover Effects: The Case of Lifecycle Funds in 401(k) Plans," NBER Working Papers 15108, 2009.

13. Thus, the Right wanted to believe that it was the government that caused the problem, and not the market; so it discounted evidence that it was the markets that had failed—that, for instance, the subprime mortgage debacle *began* in the private sector, and that even at the peak, the performance of Fannie Mae mortgages was better than that of the private sector.

14. There is by now a large literature on confirmatory bias. See, e.g., Matthew Rabin and Joel Schrag, "First Impressions Matter: A Model of Confirmatory Bias," *Quarterly Journal of Economics* 114, no. 1 (1999): 37–82.

15. See, in particular, Karla Hoff and Joseph E. Stiglitz, "Equilibrium Fictions: A Cognitive Approach to Societal Rigidity," *American Economic Review* 100, no. 2 (May 2010): 141–46; Hoff and Stiglitz, "The Role of Cognitive Frames in Societal Rigidity and Change," World Bank, 2011, available at http://www.ewi-ssl.pitt.edu/econ/files/seminars/110405_sem 814_Karla%20Hoff.pdf (accessed March 4, 2012), and the references cited there. The authors explain how equilibrium fictions may play a role in sustaining discrimination. Those who believe in caste differences are cognitively more sensitive to failures of the purported inferior caste and ignore their successes. Even worse, individuals who believe that they are inferior will behave that way.

16. Persuasive marketing is the gentlest and most honest way that corporations try to manipulate behavior. The cigarette companies secretly made their products more addictive, rendering it more likely that smok-

ers would continue to smoke. David Kessler, the former head of the Food and Drug Administration who led the U.S. government charge against the cigarette companies, points out that producers of fast foods, snacks, and other products do quite similar things (even if it isn't precisely addiction), through their fine understanding of how smells and tastes stimulate the brain and create cravings. See Kessler, *The End of Overeating: Taking Control of the Insatiable American Appetite* (New York: Rodale Books, 2009).

17. John Maynard Keynes, *The General Theory of Employment, Interest, and Money* (New York: Harcourt, Brace & World, 1936), p. 383.

18. See George Soros, *The Soros Lectures: At the Central European University* (New York: Public Affairs, 2010).

19. See in particular the report *The Financial Crisis Inquiry Report* of the bipartisan National Commission on the Causes of the Financial and Economic Crisis in the United States, which concluded that Fannie Mae and Freddie Mac "contributed to the crisis, but were not a primary cause" (p. xxvi). The report is available at http://www.gpo.gov/fdsys/pkg/GPO-FCIC/pdf/GPO-FCIC.pdf (accessed February 20, 2012). Only one member, Peter J. Wallison of the American Enterprise Institute, dissented. Other, more academic studies have confirmed and supported their findings.

20. See the discussion of statistical discrimination in chapter 5.

21. See Karla Hoff and Priyanka Pandey, "Discrimination, Social Identity, and Durable Inequalities," *American Economic Review* 96, no. 2 (May 2006): 206–11; and Hoff and Pandey, "Making Up People: The Behavioral Effects of Caste," Working Paper, World Bank. A large literature in social psychology shows that "priming" a stereotyped identity (that is, making it salient) shifts performance in the direction of the stereotype. See C. M. Steele, *Whistling Vivaldi and Other Clues to How Stereotypes Affect Us* (New York: W. W. Norton, 2010); and Michael Inzlicht and Toni Schmader, eds., *Stereotype Threat: Theory, Process, and Application* (New York: Oxford University Press, 2012).

22. Of course, neither government nor markets are perfect. As I'll explain later in the chapter, while there are many instances of government failures, they pale in comparison with the losses from private sector failures—in particular, those surrounding the Great Recession.

23. In 1772 the East India Company was lent hundreds of thousands of pounds by the Bank of England after a combination of factors, including

a famine in Bengal and a stock market crash in London, threatened the company's survival. From Nick Robins, *The Corporation That Changed the World* (London: Pluto Press, 2006), p. 97.

24. While it might be in the interests of an individual or group to work to alter perceptions in ways that advance particular interests, typically change doesn't happen in such a concerted way. There is no general forum in which plots are hatched, no opportunity for a conspiracy.

25. See Richard Dawkins, *The Selfish Gene*, 30th anniversary ed. (Oxford: Oxford University Press, 2006).

26. See *The Financial Crisis Inquiry Report*.

27. In January 2012, the Pew Research Center released a poll that found an even divide in perceptions: about 46 percent of the respondents (Americans) believed that rich people obtained their wealth because they were "fortunate enough to be from wealthy families or have the right connections," while 43 percent thought they were wealthy because of "their own hard work, ambition, or education." The same poll found that 58 percent of Democrats "say wealth is mainly due to family money or knowing the right people. An identical proportion of Republicans say wealth is mainly a consequence of hard work, ambition or having the necessary education to get ahead." See "Rising Share of Americans See Conflict between Rich and Poor," report of the Pew Research Center, January 11, 2012, available at http://www.pew socialtrends.org/2012/01/11/rising-share-of-americans-see-conflict-between-rich-and-poor/?src=prc-headline (accessed March 4, 2012).

28. One other change has occurred recently that may affect the future evolution of ideas and beliefs and reinforces the problems posed by confirmatory bias noted earlier: the rise and proliferation of the Internet has made it easier for individuals to create their own "communities"—groups that share the same information. In the past, most Americans would have had a shared experience of watching the national TV news on CBS, ABC, or NBC. But now there exists a plethora of cable channels, some appealing to the left, some to the right. An individual who wants to be reinforced in his conservative views can turn to Fox News. The views to which he is exposed have been preselected to conform to his beliefs. The consequence is the risk of further polarization of beliefs. The fact that beliefs about inequality are thus so polarized has obvious implications for the ability of our society to deal with the problem on the basis of a national consensus. For a discussion of these issues, see, e.g., Cass Sun-

stein, *Infotopia: How Many Minds Produce Knowledge* (New York: Oxford University Press, 2006), where he suggests that people are trapped in "information cocoons," shielded from information at odds with their preconceptions. Charles Lord and coauthors carried out important research on belief polarization: they showed research results on the death penalty to two groups of people, pro– and anti–capital punishment. They found that people tended to hold that research that agreed with their original views had been better conducted and was more convincing than research that conflicted with their original views, and they tended to have a stronger position after reading about research that supported their position. Charles Lord, Lee Ross, and Mark Lepper, "Biased Assimilation and Attitude Polarization: The Effects of Prior Theories on Subsequently Considered Evidence," *Journal of Personality and Social Psychology* 37, no. 11 (1979): 2098–109.

29. Hoff and Stiglitz, "Equilibrium Fictions" and "The Role of Cognitive Frames." See also Glenn C. Loury, *Anatomy of Racial Inequality* (Cambridge: Harvard University Press, 2002).

30. The "Swift boat" attack on Senator Kerry is a legendary example of "marketing" with no basis in fact, which nonetheless was extraordinarily effective. For a discussion of this case and a list of resources from the *New York Times*, see the *New York Times* "Times Topic" on "Swift Boat Veterans for Truth," available at http://topics.nytimes.com/topics/reference/timestopics/organizations/s/swift_boat_veterans_for_truth/index.html (accessed March 4, 2012).

31. See Richard H. Thaler, "When Business Can't Foresee Outrage," *New York Times*, November 19, 2011, p. BU4. See Daniel Kahneman, Jack Knetsch, and Richard H. Thaler, "Fairness and the Assumptions of Economics," *Journal of Business* 59, no 4 (1986): S285–300. Amelie Goosens and Pierre-Guillaume Meon, "The Impact of Studying Economics, and Other Disciplines, on the Belief That Voluntary Exchange Makes Everyone Better Off," University of Brussels working paper, 2010, show that there are both selection and learning effects. For an overview, see John R. Carter and Michael D. Irons, "Are Economists Different, and If So, Why?" *Journal of Economic Perspectives* 5, no. 2 (Spring 1991): 171–77; and Alexandra Haferkamp, Detlef Fetchenhauer, Frank Belschak, and Dominik Enste, "Efficiency versus Fairness: The Evaluation of Labor Market Policies by Economists and Laypeople," *Journal of Economic Psychology* 30, no. 4 (August 2009): 527–39. See also Robert

Kuttner, *Everything for Sale: The Virtues and Limits of Markets* (New York: Knopf, 1997); and William Lazonick, *Business Organizations and the Myth of the Market Economy* (New York: Cambridge University Press, 1991). For a somewhat different perspective, see Bryan Caplan, "Systematically Biased Beliefs about Economics: Robust Evidence of Judgemental Anomalies from the Survey of Americans and Economists on the Economy," *Economic Journal*, April 2002, pp. 433–58.

32. The John M. Olin Foundation, named after the industrialist who endowed it, funded a huge array of research that injected law schools and other academic dialogue with conservative economic ideas until its closing in 2003. The *National Review* writer John J. Miller, who has written a book celebrating the foundation titled *A Gift of Freedom: How the John M. Olin Foundation Changed America* (San Francisco: Encounter Books, 2006), described the foundation's influence this way: "If conservative intellectuals and organizations were NASCAR vehicles, then just about every one of them would sport at least an Olin bumper sticker—and a good number would have O-L-I-N splashed across their hoods." See Miller, "Foundation's End," *National Review*, April 6, 2005, available at http://www.nationalreview.com/articles/214092/foundations-end/john-j-miller (accessed March 4, 2012).

33. It is interesting how little effort is made to persuade those of the other side. The reason is that the person on the other side has already such a strong frame, a perspective, through which he sees the world, that the contrary evidence is highly discounted and the confirming evidence given undue weight.

34. According to the *Washington Post*, this incident occurred at a town hall meeting interaction in Simpsonville, North Carolina, in 2009, where a man stood up and made this complaint to the then Representative Robert Inglis. See Philip Rucker, "Sen. DeMint of S.C. Is Voice of Opposition to Health-Care Reform," *Washington Post,* July 28, 2009, available at http://www.washingtonpost.com/wp-dyn/content/article/2009/07/27/AR2009072703066.html?hpid=topnews&sid=ST2009072703107 (accessed February 20, 2012).

35. It was perhaps not coincidental that a key member of the Clinton economics team had received a substantial bonus well above the $1 million threshold prior to joining the administration.

36. See Sanford Grossman and J. E. Stiglitz, "Information and Competitive Price Systems," *American Economic Review* 66, no. 2 (May 1976):

246–53; and Sanford Grossman and J. E. Stiglitz, "On the Impossibility of Informationally Efficient Markets," *American Economic Review* 70, no. 3 (June 1980): 393–408.

37. See Justin Fox, *The Myth of the Rational Market* (New York: Harper Business, 2009).

38. This was equivalent to a loss of more than a trillion dollars. The stocks of eight major companies in the S&P 500 (including Accenture) fell to one cent per share; the prices of other stocks (including Sotheby's, Apple, and Hewlett-Packard) increased to over $100,000. Obviously, nothing *real* could account for such changes. Markets were clearly not being efficient. A report of the U.S. Securities and Exchange Commission and the Commodity Futures Trading Commission "portrayed a market so fragmented and fragile that a single large trade could send stocks into a sudden spiral." "Findings Regarding the Market Events of May 6, 2010," report dated September 30, 2010. I served on an advisory panel to the SEC/CFTC on market reforms motivated by the flash crash. Its report is available at http://www.sec.gov/news/stud ies/2010/marketeventsreport.pdf.

39. Tax changes are an arena where framing is particularly contentious: does one express, say, a tax cut in terms of the percent reduction in their tax rate, in the absolute reduction in their tax rate, or in terms of the absolute dollar value that goes to each group. In one way of presenting the Bush tax cuts, the top 1 percent were the big beneficiaries, with one-third of the benefits going to the top 1 percent (two-thirds of the benefits went to the top 20 percent) and 1 percent of the benefits going to the bottom 20 percent. Andrew Fieldhouse, "The Bush Tax Cuts Disproportionately Benefitted the Wealthy," Economic Policy Institute, June 4, 2011. But defenders of the tax cut point out that the top pays a large fraction of overall taxes.

40. Under the law that was passed on December 17, 2010, this is the tax-exempt amount for 2012 (adjusted upward for inflation). See the website of the IRS, http://www.irs.gov/businesses/small/article/0,,id=164871,00 .html (accessed March 26, 2012). At the time of this writing, unless Congress passes new legislation (which is likely) the exemption will revert to $1 million in 2013.

41. Larry Bartels, "Homer Gets a Tax Cut: Inequality and Public Policy in the American Mind," *Perspectives on Politics* 3, no. 1 (2005): 15–31, argues that "most ordinary citizens are remarkably ignorant and uncertain

about the workings of the tax system and the policy options under consideration, or actually adopted." In the case of the estate tax, Joel Slemrod, "The Role of Misconceptions in Support for Regressive Tax Reform," *National Tax Journal* 59, no. 1 (2006): 57–75, finds that a majority of people either believe that the estate tax affects "most" families (49 percent) or do not know how many families it affects (20 percent). In fact, it affects only 2 percent of families. John Sides, "Stories, Science, and Public Opinion about the Estate Tax," George Washington University, 2011, shows that correct information about who actually pays the estate tax does increase support for the estate tax.

42. In an ABC News and the *Washington Post* poll in December 2010, 52 percent of the participants favored increasing the exemption on inheritance taxes. See http://abcnews.go.com/Politics/obama-gop-tax-deal-abc-news-washington-post-poll-support/story?id=12382152#.TvzvAjXWark.

43. A little-known provision of current law allows capital gains to totally escape taxation upon death. The provision is called "step up of basis," i.e., those inheriting the asset are taxed only on the capital gain from the time they inherit it. There is no economic justification for this; in fact, it leads to large distortions in behavior. Legislation in 2010 provided some limitations to the step up of basis.

44. Obama defended the bank bailouts by arguing that nationalization of banks (which might better have been described as "playing by the rules of capitalism," since it would put banks with insufficient capital into conservatorship) might have worked well for Sweden, but was not a good option in the United States, because of the smaller numbers of banks in Sweden and because we "have different traditions in this country." Terry Moran interview with President Obama, *Nightline*, ABC News, transcript, February 10, 2009, available at http://abcnews.go.com/Politics/Business/story?id=6844330&page=1#.T3CknDEgcs1 (accessed March 26, 2012).

45. The administration and the banks have tried to shape perceptions about the bailout, by arguing that in fact the money was fully repaid. We explain in chapter 9 what's wrong with their contention. Most Americans have remained outraged at the bailout.

46. In February 2012 the administration, recognizing that its housing programs had so far failed to do much to stem the flood of foreclosures, let alone to resuscitate the housing market, proposed a multibillion-dollar program for homeowner refinancing. See "Fact Sheet: President

Obama's Plan to Help Responsible Homeowners and Heal the Housing Market," White House release, available at http://www.whitehouse.gov/the-press-office/2012/02/01/fact-sheet-president-obama-s-plan-help-responsible-homeowners-and-heal-h (accessed March 26, 2012).

47. There was another possible reason for the reluctance to help homeowners. They understood that there was a limit to the government's largesse, to how much it would spend to support the banks and to help homeowners with their mortgages. The more money to homeowners, the less there would be for the banks. Given the precarious financial position of the banks—at the time, it was uncertain just how much they would need to stay afloat—their first imperative was securing as much money as possible for the banks. They did set aside about $50 billion from the Toxic Asset Relief Program for mortgage restructuring, but interestingly, the Obama administration has spent only about $3.4 billion of this amount—suggesting that it was the resistance of the banks, more than the money itself, that has been the real impediment to restructuring.

48. Even the use of the term "moral hazard" (as opposed the more neutral term "incentive effects") has emotive overtones, suggesting that there is something *immoral* about these particular incentive responses. As the University of Pennsylvania law professor Tom Baker put it, the term "helps deny that refusing to share [the burdens of life] is mean-spirited or self-interested." (Quoted in Shaila Dewan, "Moral Hazard: A Tempest-tossed Idea," *New York Times,* February 26, 2012, p. BU1.) In fact, there is little evidence that there would be serious "moral hazard consequences" even of a generous program to help homeowners. Shaun Donovan, secretary of the Department of Housing and Urban Development, argues that "only about 10 or 15 percent of Americans who can still pay their mortgages try to walk away from their debt." Ibid. The general theory of moral hazard was developed in the midsixties and seventies by Arrow, Mirrlees, Ross, and Stiglitz. See, e.g., Kenneth Arrow, *Aspects of the Theory of Risk Bearing* (Helsinki, Finland: Yrjö Jahnssonin Säätiö, 1965); James Mirrlees, "The Theory of Moral Hazard and Unobservable Behaviour I," *Review of Economic Studies* 66, no. 1 (1999): 3–21; S. Ross, "The Economic Theory of Agency: The Principal's Problem," *American Economic Review* 63, no. 2 (1973): 134–39; and J. E. Stiglitz, "Incentives and Risk Sharing in Sharecropping," *Review of Economic Studies* 41, no. 2 (1974): 219–55. For a broader discussion of the term, see Tom Baker, "On the Genealogy of Moral Hazard," *Texas Law Review* 75 (1996): 237.

49. Also UK regulators are pushing for new power of automatic sanctions of senior bank executives for poor decisions they make that lead to bank failures. See "The Failure of the Royal Bank of Scotland: Financial Services Authority Board Report," Financial Services Authority (December 2011), available at http://www.fsa.gov.uk/static/pubs/other/rbs.pdf (accessed March 26, 2012).

50. Initially, there was even a reluctance to limit bonuses or compensation more generally, although, after the uproar over bank bonuses, some constraints were imposed.

51. The fervor with which the banks discussed homeowners' moral hazard is reminiscent of Andrew Mellon's advice to Herbert Hoover, "liquidate labor, liquidate stocks, liquidate farmers, liquidate real estate . . . it will purge the rottenness out of the system. High costs of living and high living will come down. People will work harder, live a more moral life. Values will be adjusted, and enterprising people will pick up from less competent people." Herbert Hoover, *Memoirs*, vol. 3 (New York: Macmillan, 1952), p. 30. The bankers did not perceive the same moral force for themselves when it was time for them to be bailed out.

52. For instance, a debt-to-equity conversion that gives the lender a share in the capital gain when the house is sold in return for a write-down of the principal. Homeowners still have an incentive to maintain their homes, houses aren't thrown onto the market, depressing housing prices; families are given a "fresh start" (a basic principle in all bankruptcy law); the costly foreclosure process is avoided. The homeowner pays a price—the loss of (a substantial fraction) of his capital gain, so "moral hazard" is averted. In *Freefall* (New York: Norton, 2010), I refer to this as a homeowners' Chapter 11, by way of analogy to laws governing corporations, that give corporations a fresh start by allowing a similar conversion of debt to equity.

53. There is one more consequence of the failure to address the mortgage crisis. Not only didn't we give a fresh start to America's families, we didn't give a fresh start to the mortgage industry itself, which remains on government life support. While the Right talks about the virtues of the private sector, this vital sector of the economy remains dominated by government as no other sector of the economy. Today, nearly 90 percent of new mortgages are being backed by the U.S. government, mostly through Fannie Mae and Freddie Mac, which are now government owned.

54. As we noted earlier, Adam Smith, the founder of modern economics, was far more skeptical about the ability of markets to lead to efficient

outcomes than his latter-day followers; he was, for instance, concerned about monopolies and was aware of many of the other market imperfections to which modern economics has called attention.

55. In a study with Scott Wallsten prepared while I was chairman of President Clinton's Council of Economic Advisers: "Supporting Research and Development to Promote Economic Growth: The Federal Government's Role," Council of Economic Advisers, October 1995.

56. As measured, e.g., by the UNDP Human Development Indicators. See the discussion in the final section of this chapter.

57. Kenneth Rogoff and Carmen M. Reinhardt, *This Time Is Different: Eight Centuries of Financial Folly* (Princeton: Princeton University Press, 2009), describe hundreds of financial crises in the last eight hundred years, eighteen banking crises in the developed world since World War II alone. Earlier, the late Charles Kindleberger of MIT described repeated crises in his classic *Manias, Panics, and Crashes: A History of Financial Crises* (New York: Basic Books, 1978).

58. The Congressional Budget Office (CBO) has found that administrative costs under the public Medicare plan are less than 2 percent of expenditures, compared with approximately 11 percent for private plans under Medicare Advantage. (CBO, "Designing a Premium Support System for Medicare," November 2006, 12.) According to Centers for Medicare and Medicaid Services, Medicare's inflation-adjusted cost per beneficiary increased 500 percent from 1969 to 2009, while the private insurance companies' real-cost increased 800 percent for the same period. See https://www.cms.gov/nationalhealthexpenddata/02_national healthaccountshistorical.asp. Similarly, several studies suggest that the cost of Medicaid, the health program for the poor, is lower than if the services were provided privately. See Jack Hadley and John Holahan, "Is Health Care Spending Higher under Medicaid or Private Insurance?" *Inquiry* 40, no. 4 (Winter 2003–04): 323–42; and "Medicaid: A Lower-Cost Approach to Serving a High-Cost Population," policy brief by the Kaiser Commission on Medicaid and the Uninsured, March 2004. See also Paul Krugman, "Medicare Saves Money," June 12, 2011, available at http://www.nytimes .com/2011/06/13/opinion/13krugman.html.

59. A study of partial privatization of social security (pensions) in the UK showed that these transactions' costs in effect lowered pensions by 40 percent; taking an extra 1 percent out in one year might not seem like a lot, but when taken year after year, the amounts cumulate. See

Mamta Murthi, Michael Orszag, and Peter Orszag "Administrative Costs under a Decentralized Approach to Individual Accounts: Lessons from the United Kingdom," in *New Ideas about Old Age Security*, ed. R. Holzmann and J. Stiglitz (Washington, DC: World Bank: 2001).

60. See Project on Government Oversight's report, "Bad Business: Billions of Taxpayer Dollars Wasted on Hiring Contractors," September 13, 2011, available at http://www.pogo.org/pogo-files/reports/contract-oversight/bad-business/co-gp-20110913.html (accessed February 22, 2012). Reported in Ron Nixon, "Government Pays More in Contracts, Study Finds," *New York Times*, September 12, 2011.

61. See the commission's final report, "Transforming Wartime Contracting: Controlling Costs, Reducing Risks," issued August 31, 2011, available at http://www.wartimecontracting.gov/docs/CWC_FinalReport-lowres.pdf. Reported by Nathan Hodge, "Study Finds Extensive Waste in War Contracting," *Wall Street Journal*, September 1, 2011, available at http://online.wsj.com/article/SB10001424053111904716604576542703010051380.html (accessed March 26, 2012).

62. Stiglitz and Bilmes, *The Three Trillion Dollar War: The True Cost of the Iraq Conflict* (New York: Norton, 2008).

63. We noted in chapter 2 that the world's richest person, Carlos Slim, had his fortune built in the privatization of Mexico's telephone monopoly. So pervasive is corruption in the privatization process that in my book *Globalization and Its Discontents* I referred to it as "briberization."

64. I describe the earlier episodes of this unfortunate drama in *Globalization and Its Discontents*. The saga of what happened since—repeated attempts to get government subsidies—with the company on the verge of bankruptcy today, confirms the criticisms leveled at the time. For other discussions, see Peter R. Orszag, "Privatization of the U.S. Enrichment Corporation: An Economic Analysis," presented at the Brookings Institution, February 2000. See also Daniel Guttman, "The United States Enrichment Corporation: A Failing Privatization," *Asian Journal of Public Administration* 23, no. 2 (2001): 247–72. The most recent episodes are described in Geoffrey Sea, "USEC Pushback on Coffin Lid of Uranium Project," available at http://ecowatch.org/2011/usec-pushback-on-coffin-lid-of-uranium-project/.

65. In 2010 total contributions were $639 billion. See http://www.ssa.gov/policy/docs/statcomps/supplement/2011/oasdi.html.

66. Moreover, no private insurance company provides insurance against

the risk of inflation, which, though low now, could become once again high, as it was in the 1970s.

67. See http://www.nytimes.com/2006/11/26/business/yourmoney/26every .html. Chris Leonard, who describes more fully how those at the top try to affect perceptions of the rest, devotes a chapter to class warfare. He notes that, in the usual characterization, it "is always waged upward, never downward," an all-purpose weapon to be brought out whenever redistributive policies or taxes on the top are put on the table. He observes that it "references a conflict without any conceivable mobilized army." *Rich People Things: Real Life Secrets of the Predator Class* (New York: Haymarket Books, 2010), pp. 53–55.

68. The U.S. federal government spent about $140 billion on its Temporary Assistance to Needy Families and Assistance and Aid to Families with Dependent Children programs in the form of "Expenditures on Cash Benefits and Administration" between 1990 and 2006. See "2008 Indicators of Welfare Dependence, Appendix A, Program Data," provided by the U.S. Department of Health and Human Services, available at http://aspe.hhs .gov/hsp/indicators08/apa.shtml#ftanf2 (accessed March 4, 2012).

69. See, e.g., the keynote address by Dominique Strauss-Kahn, managing director, International Monetary Fund, Nanjing, March 31, 2011 "In the IMF, in particular, while the tradition had long been that capital controls should not be part of the toolbox, we are now more open to their use in appropriate circumstances, although of course countries should be careful not to use them as substitutes for good macroeconomic policies." Available at http://www.imf.org/external/np/speeches/2011/033111.htm (accessed February 22, 2011).

70. Dwight Eisenhower remarked about Sweden at a Republican National Committee breakfast in 1960, "I have been reading quite an article on the experiment of almost complete paternalism in a friendly European country. This country has a tremendous record for socialistic operation, following a socialistic philosophy, and the record shows that their rate of suicide has gone up almost unbelievably and I think they were almost the lowest nation in the world for that. Now, they have more than twice our rate. Drunkenness has gone up. Lack of ambition is discernible on all sides." Dwight D. Eisenhower: Remarks at the Republican National Committee Breakfast, Chicago, Illinois, July 27, 1960. *Public Papers of the Presidents of the United States, Dwight D. Eisenhower* (Washington, DC: Government Printing Office, 1999), p. 605.

71. In making comparisons across countries, one has to adjust for differences in cost of living. At current exchange rates (e.g., how many euros trade for a dollar), living may be cheaper in one country than in another. (The difference can depend, of course, on what one spends one's money on. Someone having to buy health care in the United States has a much lower standard of living that a comparably sick person in France.) Economists refer to the comparisons attempting to make (albeit imperfect) adjustments for cost of living as PPP (purchasing power parity) comparisons. For instance, in terms of official exchange rates, per capita GDP in 2010 in the United States was more than 10 times that in China; adjusting for PPP, it is 6 times that in China. See World Bank Indicators database, available at http://databank.worldbank.org/ddp/home .do?Step=12&id=4&CNO=2 (accessed March 26, 2012).

72. See Janet Currie of Princeton University, "Inequality at Birth: Some Causes and Consequences," and the discussion of her work in chapter 1.

73. For a discussion of some of these costs (not all easy to quantify) to the people of Papua New Guinea, see the 2011 Human Rights Watch report "Gold's Costly Dividend: Human Rights Impacts of Papua New Guinea's Porgera Gold Mine," available at http://www.hrw.org/sites/ default/files/reports/png0211webwcover.pdf (accessed March 7, 2012).

74. Convened by President Sarkozy of France. Its report is available as Jean-Paul Fitoussi, Amartya Sen, and Joseph E. Stiglitz, *Mismeasuring Our Lives: Why GDP Doesn't Add Up* (New York: New Press, 2010), and available at http://www.stiglitz-sen-fitoussi.fr/en/index.htm. (Translations are available in Chinese, Korean, Italian, and other languages.)

75. This point was made right at the start, by the early developer of the national income accounts, Simon Kuznets, who noted that "the welfare of a nation can scarcely be inferred from a measure of national income." Kuznets, "National Income, 1929–1932," 73rd U.S. Cong., 2d sess., 1934, Senate doc. no. 124, p. 7.

Chapter Seven JUSTICE FOR ALL? HOW INEQUALITY IS ERODING THE RULE OF LAW

1. There are many instances where laws can be seen as preserving inequities. The laws that protected and preserved slavery offer the most profound example. Although slaves couldn't vote, the Constitution treated

each slave as three-fifths of a person for purposes of congressional representation, thus guaranteeing disproportionate representation in government for the white slave owners of the South. In the aftermath of the Civil War, Jim Crow laws ensured segregation and the economic disempowerment of African Americans. Like feudalism in Europe centuries earlier, landowners were able to hire labor at more favorable terms: in this case, the rule of law was used to enhance the wealth and income of white landowners. There is a large literature describing labor coercion and legal frameworks that helped enforce it. See, e.g., S. Naidu, "Recruitment Restrictions and Labor Markets: Evidence from the Postbellum U.S. South," *Journal of Labor Economics* 28, no. 2 (2010): 413–45; Stanley Engerman, "Economic Adjustments to Emancipation in the United States and British West Indies," *Journal of Interdisciplinary History* 13 (1982): 191–220; S. Naidu and N. Yuchtman, "How Green Was My Valley? Coercive Contract Enforcement in 19th Century Industrial Britain," NBER Working Paper no. 17051, 2011, available at http://www.nber.org/papers/w17051 (accessed March 4, 2012).

2. The as yet totally unsolved problem of nuclear waste disposal is another example of nuclear power plants' not having to fully internalize the costs of their operations. With material that remains dangerous for tens of thousands of years, the cost of dealing with the waste is bequeathed to future generations, whether or not the company that runs the plant is around by that time.

3. The question is made more complex because of the hidden and open subsidies to other forms of energy production, such as coal. The market is so distorted that it's hard to judge what might emerge in an efficient market place.

4. The settlement process is still under way. BP spent $20 billion to establish the Gulf Coast Claims Facility. The fund, which is administered by Kenneth Feinberg, has paid or approved for payment a total of $7.96 billion as of February 2012, according to the BP website, available at http://www.bp.com/sectiongenericarticle.do?categoryId=9036580&contentId=7067577 (accessed March 4, 2012). The structure of the fund has not been without criticism. One legal scholar characterized it thus: "The Gulf Coast Claims Facility represents an unnoticed incremental trend toward the lawless, private resolution of mass claims. This resolution (in the case of the GCCF) was created by a culpable defendant, unbounded by legal norms, and administered by a heroic special master with limit-

less unreviewable discretion, who also is in the employ of the malefactor. Whatever else may be argued on behalf of the GCCF, this cannot be a good development." L. Mullenix, "Prometheus Unbound: The Gulf Coast Claims Facility as a Means for Resolving Mass Tort Claims—A Fund Too Far," *Louisiana Law Review* 71 (2011): 823. As this book goes to press, an out-of-court settlement between BP and the lawyers for the plaintiffs is being considered. "Accord Reached Settling Lawsuit over BP Oil Spill," *New York Times*, March 3, 2012, p. A1. *Propublica* maintained an active media oversight of the aftermath of the BP spill, including corruption in the clean-up process. See http://www.propublica.org/topic/gulf-oil-spill/.

5. R. H. Coase, "The Problem of Social Cost," *Journal of Law and Economics* 3 (1960): 1–44.

6. This is especially the case when there are information asymmetries—where one party has easier access to information. If one group has less information about the harm than another (a common situation), then the more informed is in a better position to avoid the harm. Other market imperfections can also affect the efficiency of alternative assignments of property rights. For example, if one group is credit constrained, it may not be able to pay.

7. In many cases, it is not always clear who is exerting an externality on whom. The driver who collides with another vehicle would not have got into an accident if the other driver had not been on the road. Other people's smoking could not lead to cancer in a nonsmoker if the nonsmoker had not exposed himself to the "secondary" effects of smokers by being in the vicinity of the smoker. In these and most other cases, there is a broad consensus: those who drive safely should have the right to drive without worrying about the risk of an accident from a reckless driver; ordinary citizens should have the right to breathe clean air.

8. John Stuart Mill in *On Liberty* (1869) distinguishes between other-regarding and self-regarding spheres of action. In his theory, individuals have the right to perform an action insofar as they do not harm others.

9. And to shape beliefs and perceptions that shape the presumptions that are so critical as judges and juries make judgments about the merits of either side in a court case.

10. For a discussion, see G. Morgenson and Joshua Rosner, *Reckless Endangerment: How Outsized Ambition, Greed, and Corruption Led to Economic Armageddon* (New York: Times Books, 2011). More specifically, the ratings agencies claimed that they could not rate RMBS based

on mortgages originated in New Jersey and Georgia, on the grounds that the RMBS holder would be liable under state Consumer Protection or Predatory Lending Law. Under the Georgia law, unlimited punitive damages for predatory lending under the Georgia Fair Lending Act would extend to RMBS holders in due course. This led to the amendment of the Georgia predatory lending statute in 2003. A similar chain of events happened in New Jersey, leading to the amendment of the New Jersey Homeownership Security Act of 2002 to appease lenders in June 2004. See also the discussion in B. Keys, T. Mukherjee, A. Seru, and V. Vig, "Did Securitization Lead to Lax Screening? Evidence from Subprime Loans," *Quarterly Journal of Economics* 125, no. 1 (2010): 307–62.

11. One of the most important additional aspects was the preemption by federal bank regulators, notably the Office of the Controller of the Currency (OCC), which is the agency in the Treasury charged with overseeing banks, and OTS (the Office of Thrift Supervision, originally set up to oversee the savings and loans institutions), of stricter state regulation by claiming jurisdiction over national banks. This meant that if a state tried to regulate banks in its state more strictly, the tighter standards would extend only to state-chartered banks, which would then be less competitive than the nationally chartered institutions. Making matters worse, "some states, such as Georgia, have parity or wild card laws that exempt state-chartered banks and thrifts and their subsidiaries from state anti-predatory lending laws to the same extent as national banks and federal thrifts. . . ." P. McCoy and E. Reunart, "The Legal Infrastructure of Subprime and Nontraditional Home Mortgages," Joint Center for Housing Studies Harvard University, UCC08-05. The head of the OCC tried to allay worries about this preemption: "Our approach . . . protects consumers where abusive practices are found." Speech available at http://www.occ.gov/static/news-issuances/news-releases/2003/nr-occ-2003-57.pdf. See the broader discussion of the role of preemption in Mike Konczal at http://rortybomb.wordpress.com/2010/03/01/cfpa-i-preemption-or-what-a-bad-cfpa-would-look-like/.

12. See my *Freefall* (New York: Norton, 2010) for a fuller discussion of the whole variety of bad financial products and the consequences.

13. Just as the Food and Drug Administration protects consumers against deceptive, dangerous, and ineffective drugs.

14. Evidenced by the fact that just shortly after European regulators subjected one of Europe's larger banks to a stress test—to see how well

it would do in adverse conditions—and it passed brilliantly, the bank collapsed. Private rating agencies, too, have demonstrated that they are not up to the task.

15. In the first set of deals, taxpayers got back about 65 cents on the dollar, but in later deals, especially with AIG and Citbank, they got back about 41 cents on the dollar. See Congressional Oversight Panel, "Valuing Treasury's Acquisitions," February Oversight Report, February 6, 2009, available at http://cop.senate.gov/reports/library/report-020609-cop.cfm. While the legal system is stacked against ordinary citizens, the magnitude of the banks' bad behavior was so large that there was *some* accountability—though not enough to offset the huge profits they had made in their predatory lending, which was often targeted at poor African Americans and Hispanics. See chapter 3 for a more extensive discussion.

16. While many mortgages were nonrecourse (that is, creditors could claim only the house—they couldn't go after the borrower's other assets), and thus might not be affected by this provision, most of the subprime lending involved second mortgages, which were recourse. The change in the bankruptcy law applied to such loans.

17. Overdraft fees average between $30 and $35 a transaction and have risen by almost a fifth over the past five years. In 2011 they were estimated to increase bank earnings by $30 billion. Ninety percent of the fees are paid by 10 percent of the customers, mostly low income. The attempt to curb the fees in 2010 failed, partly because customers were misled by the banks. The director of the new consumer agency, Richard Cordray, criticized bank practices designed to ensure that customers did not understand the fees they faced. A *New York Times* editorial described bank practices that "deliberately buried information, requiring consumers to visit three Web pages and scroll through 50 pages of text to find fee information." "A Further Look at Overdraft Fees," *New York Times,* February 27, 2012, p. A16 (available at http://www.nytimes.com/2012/02/27/opinion/a-further-look-at-overdraft-fees.html, accessed March 4, 2012), citing in part data from Moebs Services, a research company that has conducted studies for both government and some banks. See also FDIC Study of Bank Overdraft Programs, November 2008. Executive Summary available at http://www.fdic.gov/bank/analytical/overdraft/FDIC138_ExecutiveSummary_v508.pdf (accessed February 22, 2012).

18. They call it a regulatory taking. But any change in law that affects contracts or property has redistributive consequences.

19. See, e.g., "Where the Jobs Are, the Training May Not Be," *New York Times*, March 2 2012, p. A1. The article reports, "Technical, engineering, and health care expertise are among the few skills in huge demand even in today's lackluster job market. They are also, unfortunately, some of the most expensive subjects to teach." As a result, the article, notes seven states have eliminated engineering and computer science departments. It describes a community college in North Carolina—a state with a severe nursing shortage—where "nursing program applicants so outnumber available slots that there is a waiting list just to get on the waiting list."

20. In chapter 4 we presented data showing the high level of indebtedness of the two-thirds of students graduating with debts—in excess of $25,000. If parental loans were included, the numbers were more than a third higher. On average, students at these for-profit schools have 45 percent more debt than students at other schools. These average numbers mask the fact that large numbers have extraordinarily high student debts, especially at the for-profit schools. Almost one-quarter of those who received bachelor's degrees at for-profit schools in 2008 borrowed more than $40,000, compared with 5 percent at public institutions and 14 percent at not-for-profit colleges. Indebtedness has increased markedly over the past decade. Students who earned a bachelor's degree in 2008 borrowed 50 percent more, in inflation-adjusted dollars, than those who graduated in 1996; for those earning an associate's degree, indebtedness had doubled. See "Subprime Opportunity: The Unfulfilled Promise of For-Profit Colleges and Universities," Education Trust, November 2010, available at http://www.edtrust.org/sites/edtrust.org/files/publications/files/Subprime_report.pdf; "The Rise of College Student Borrowing," study of the Pew Research Center, released November 23, 2010, available at http://www.pewsocialtrends.org/files/2010/11/social-trends-2010-student-borrowing.pdf (accessed March 4, 2012); and the Project on Student Debt, "Student Debt and the Class of 2010," November 2011, available at http://projectonstudentdebt.org/pub_view.php?idx=791 (accessed March 4, 2012). For excellent reporting on these issues, see Tamar Lewin, "Report Finds Low Graduation Rates at For-Profit Colleges," *New York Times*, November 23, 2010, accessible at http://www.nytimes.com/2010/11/24/education/24colleges.html (accessed January 29, 2012); and Tamar Lewin, "College Graduates' Debt Burden Grew, Yet Again, in 2010," *New York Times*, November 2, 2011.

21. More accurately, it extended nondischargeability to private sector lenders, and that's where the perverse incentives set in with particular force.

22. If this part of the education market worked better, reputation effects would exert discipline and provide incentives. *U.S. News* even reports loan default rates for large online-oriented for-profit schools, with Kaplan University scoring a remarkable 17.2 percent (in contrast to the private not-for-profit school average of 4 percent). The University of Phoenix has a 12.9 percent default rate. Yet these numbers don't seem to deter enrollment, or not enough. See http://www.usnews.com/education/online-education/articles/2010/09/15/loan-default-rates-at-prominent-online-universities (accessed March 5, 2012).

23. Only 22 percent of the first-time, full-time bachelor's degree students at for-profit colleges graduate within six years, 55 percent at public institutions, and 65 percent at private nonprofit colleges. See "Subprime Opportunity," Education Trust, 2010.

24. The schools have not only large drop out rates but, given that, also large default rates. Some 8.8 percent of student loan borrowers who entered repayment in 2009 had defaulted by the end of 2010, up from 7 percent for the previous cohort, with more than half of the increase coming from for-profit schools. See Eric Lichtblau, "With Lobbying Blitz, For-Profit Colleges Diluted New Rules," *New York Times*, December 9, 2011, and Project on Student Debt, "Sharp Uptick in Federal Student Loan Default Rates," September 12, 2011. A *New York Times* editorial ("Fraud and Online Learning," October 5, 2011) points out the rampant fraud in the for-profit education sector: "The Department of Education's Office of the Inspector General claims it has opened 100 investigations since 2005 and is reviewing 49 complaints."

25. As a result of legislation signed by President Obama in March 2010, private banks no longer handled federally backed student loans. The CBO (Congressional Budget Office) estimated that the net savings was in excess of $60 billion over a decade—in effect, the amount that taxpayers had handed the banks as a gift. CBO, "Costs and Policy Options for Federal Student Loan Programs," March 2010, available at http://www.cbo.gov/sites/default/files/cbofiles/ftpdocs/110xx/doc11043/03-25-student loans.pdf (accessed February 22, 2012).

26. High interest rates predictably lead to more risk for several reasons. Only those engaged in high-risk activities are willing to pay the high

interest rates (the "selection" effect); to get returns to pay back the loan with interest requires the borrower to undertake highly risky activities (the incentive effect); and lenders, comforted by the high returns they get from those loans that are paid back, may put less effort into screening. See J. E. Stiglitz and A. Weiss, "Credit Rationing in Markets with Imperfect Information," *American Economic Review* 71, no. 3 (June 1981): 393–410. In the United States beginning in 1980, federal laws increasingly preempted state laws that attempted to restrict usury.

27. See C. K. Prahalad, *The Fortune at the Bottom of the Pyramid: Eradicating Poverty through Profits* (Upper Saddle River, NJ: Prentice Hall, 2005).

28. The former governor of the Reserve Bank of India explicitly made the link between microcredit in India and America's subprime lending: Y. V. Reddy "Microfinance in India Is like Subprime Lending," *Economic Times*, November 23, 2010, available at http://articles.economictimes.indiatimes .com/2010-11-23/news/27602978_1_priority-sector-lending-sks-micro finance-microfinance-industry.

29. The FBI's mortgage fraud unit reports that fraud continued to be elevated into 2010. Mortgage fraud–related suspicious activity reports (SARs) rose sixfold from 2003 to 2007. (Of course, with the popping of the housing bubble, buyers were more sensitive to having been deceived.) See FBI Mortgage Fraud Reports, data from 2007 and 2010 reports, available at http://www.fbi.gov/stats-services/publi cations/mortgage-fraud-2010 and http://www.fbi.gov/stats-services/publi cations/mortgage-fraud-2007/mortgage-fraud-2007.

30. The legal issues this gave rise to are surveyed in Christopher L. Peterson, "Two Faces: Demystifying the Mortgage Electronic Registration System's Land Title Theory," *William and Mary Law Review* 53, no. 1 (2011): 111–61 (quoted material is from p. 138), available at http:// scholarship.law.wm.edu/wmlr/vol53/iss1/4 (accessed March 4, 2012).

31. As the Supreme Court seems to have claimed in the *Citizens United* case.

32. Phil Angelides, who headed the Financial Crisis Inquiry Commission into the causes of the crisis, noted that "today the rate of federal prosecutions for financial fraud is less than half of what it was" during the savings and loan crisis. He also noted that his budget for investigating the crisis, including the misdeeds of the banks, was $9.8 million—roughly one-seventh of the budget of Oliver Stone's *Wall Street: Money Never*

Sleeps. See "Will Wall Street Ever Face Justice?," *New York Times*, March 2, 2012, available at http://www.nytimes.com/2012/03/02/opinion/will-wall-street-ever-face-justice.html (accessed March 6, 2012). See W. K. Black, K. Calavita, and H. N. Pontell, "The Savings and Loan Debacle of the 1980s: White-Collar Crime or Risky Business?," *Law and Policy* 17, no. 1 (1995): 23–55. On our current crisis, see Matt Stoller, "Treat Foreclosure as a Crime Scene," *Politico*, December 15, 2011. Jamie Galbraith of the University of Texas has been forcefully making the same case. The banks violated other laws as well—with limited prosecution. The Office of the Comptroller of the Currency, the federal national bank regulator, reported in November 2011 that 5,000 active-duty members of the U.S. military may have been unlawfully foreclosed upon (this was in a study of just ten national banks). S. Nasiripour, "US Lenders Review Military Foreclosures," *Financial Times*, November 28, 2011.

33. The failure to prosecute the banks is only one aspect of the failure to hold the financial sector accountable. The Financial Inquiry Commission described how Clayton Holdings, hired by more than twenty major financial institutions to do "due diligence" on the mortgages that the banks were handling (ensuring, e.g., that they were not fraudulent and there had been compliance with legal procedures) sampled 2 to 3 percent, and even in this small sample, detected significant numbers of defective loans. But the banks didn't insist that the other 97 percent be investigated, and didn't disclose information about defective loans to investors, as required by securities law. Evidently, there is still no prosecution for this aspect of the violation of the law. See Phil Angelides, "Will Wall Street Ever Face Justice?," *New York Times*, March 1, 2012.

34. It is hard to get precise numbers. At the time of the foreclosure agreement in January 2012, reports put the numbers in foreclosure since the bursting of the housing bubble at nearly 8 million. See D. Kravitz, "Banks' Agreement to Overhaul Mortgage Industry Sent to States," *Associated Press*, January 24, 2012. The New York Fed governor William Dudley suggested that the pace of foreclosures in 2012 and 2013 could increase (technically, real estate transferred into the hands of the banks)—to as high as 1.8 million per year, up from around 1.1 million in 2011 and around 600,000 in 2010. Dudley, "Housing and the Economic Recovery," Remarks at the New Jersey Bankers Association Economic Forum, Iselin, NJ, available at http://www.newyorkfed.org/newsevents/speeches/2012/dud120106.html (accessed January 29, 2012).

35. Campaign fundraising on judicial elections more than doubled in the last decade—it rose to $206.9 million in 2000–09 from $83.3 million in 1990–99. Chief justices have been defeated by well-monied challengers; "attack ads" have increasingly found their way onto television. See J. Sample, A. Skaggs, J. Blitzer, and L. Casey, "The New Politics of Judicial Elections, 2000–2009: Decade of Change," Brennan Center for Justice, New York University School of Law. There is also an increasing perception that justice is being bought: while as, expected, citizens fear that "campaign contributions affect the outcome of courtroom decisions," what is even more striking is that "nearly half of state judges agree." See the website http://www.brennancenter.org/content/resource/the_new_politics_of_judicial_elections/(accessed March 7, 2012).

36. Ally, formerly GMAC, in which the government has 74 percent ownership.

37. Quoted in Gretchen Morgenson, "Massachusetts Sues 5 Major Banks over Foreclosure Practices," *New York Times*, December 2, 2011, pp. B1, B9. New York State's attorney general Eric Schneiderman also sued Bank of America, Wells Fargo, and JPMorgan Chase, describing what they did as "bizarre and complex," an end run around the traditional public recording system. The motive was clear: saving $2 billion in recording fees. MERS, of course, denied the charges. "New York Sues 3 Big Banks Over Mortgage Database," *New York Times*, February 4, 2012, p. B6.

38. Based on an analysis of data from Lender Processing Services. On average, it took 792 days for large loans, 611 for small loans. The differences were especially large in states that required court proceedings. Still, in California, a state that doesn't, foreclosures on large mortgages took 50 percent longer than on small ones, 671 days vs. 445. Interestingly, before the mortgage crisis, when the "ordinary" rule of law was working, there was essentially no difference, 251 days for large mortgages, 260 for small ones. See Shelly Banjo and Nick Timiraos, "For the Costliest Homes, Foreclosure Comes Slowly," *Wall Street Journal*, February 28, 2012, available at http://online.wsj.com/article/SB100014240529 70204369404577209181305152266.html.

39. Our complex legal system contributes to the costs and uncertainty. The oil companies have tried (in part successfully) to limit their liability for, e.g., offshore oil disasters. Courts have limited liability for economic damages resulting from, say, an oil spill to those most directly affected. In

474 NOTES TO PAGE 254

the case of the *Exxon Valdez* oil spill, this meant that many of those who were injured by the destruction of the fishing industry couldn't recover their lost profits. The Oil Pollution Act of 1990 tried to correct some of these limitations. But the full testing of the legal framework—with the legions of lawyers that likely will be mounted by BP, attempting to limit what it has to pay out—will take years. For a discussion exemplifying the complexity of the legal framework, see Ronen Perry, "The Deepwater Horizon Oil Spill and the Limits of Civil Liability,"*Washington Law Review* 86, no. 1 (2011): 1–68.

40. The patent system has long been used in such an unfair and discriminatory way. Patent fees in the UK from the start made access to the patent system available only to the wealthy. See Z. Kahn and K. Sokoloff, "Patent Institutions, Industrial Organization and Early Technological Change: Britain and the United States, 1790–1850," in *Technological Revolutions in Europe*, ed. M. Berg and K. Bruland (Cheltenham, UK: Elgar, 1998). B. Zorina Kahn has noted, "Prohibitively high costs . . . limited access to property rights in invention. These constraints favoured the elite classes of those with wealth or exceptional technical qualifications. Inventors who wished to obtain protection throughout the realm had to contend with the bureaucracy of three patent systems, and to pay fees that ranged from £100 for an English patent to £300 for property rights that extended to Ireland and Scotland." Khan, "Intellectual Property and Economic Development: Lessons from American and European History," mimeo, 2003. See also B. Zorina Khan, *The Democratization of Invention: Patents and Copyrights in American Development, 1790–1920* (New York: Cambridge University Press, 2005).

41. Lower courts sometimes rule one way, higher courts the other, with the entire legal process stretching out for a very long time. Moreover, some jurisdictions may recognize the patent, others reject it. See S. Decker, "NTP Wins Court Ruling on 7 Patents from Apple, AT&T Cases," *Bloomberg*, August 1, 2011. For an earlier and broader discussion of these issues, see J. E. Stiglitz, *Making Globalization Work* (New York: W. W. Norton, 2006).

42. There are alternative ways of organizing the patent system that can avoid the scope for extortion, such as the liability system, where individuals have the right to use any patent, upon payment of a "reasonable" fee. (The Supreme Court decision in *eBay Inc. v. MercExchange L.L.C.* limited the extent of extortion.) Alternative ways of organizing the intellec-

tual property regime can create a more level playing field. Small changes in the rules can have large distributive consequences. There was a heated debate in the United States concerning the move from a system where the patent was given to the "first to file" rather than "first to invent." The first to file gives a big advantage to big corporations that have on their staffs large numbers of patent lawyers, ready to file a patent application the second a patentable innovation occurs. See the work of Jerome H. Reichman, including his "Saving the Patent Law from Itself: Informal Remarks concerning the Systemic Problems Afflicting Developed Intellectual Property Regimes," *Advances in Genetics* 50 (2003): 289–303, and the references cited there.

43. Edward Wyatt, "Judge Blocks Citigroup Settlement with S.E.C.," *New York Times,* November 28, 2011.

Chapter Eight THE BATTLE OF THE BUDGET

1. The report of the commission is available at http://www.fiscalcom mission.gov/sites/fiscalcommission.gov/files/documents/TheMoment ofTruth12_1_2010.pdf.

2. Bipartisan Policy Center Debt Reduction Task Force (chaired by former Senate Budget Committee chairman Pete Domenici and former White House budget director and Federal Reserve vice chair Alice Rivlin, and included nineteen former White House and Cabinet officials, former Senate and House members, former governors and mayors, and business, labor, and other leaders). Their report, "Restoring America's Future," is available at http://www.bipartisanpolicy.org/sites/default/files/BPC%20 FINAL%20REPORT%20FOR%20PRINTER%2002%2028%2011.pdf (accessed March 5, 2012).

3. Titled "Roadmap for America's Future," the proposals are available at http://www.roadmap.republicans.budget.house.gov/ (accessed March 5, 2012). The House of Representatives passed a variant of his budget on April 15, 2011, available at http://budget.house.gov/UploadedFiles/PathTo ProsperityFY2012.pdf (accessed March 5, 2012).

4. The ceiling limits how much the government can borrow. But Congress had also passed laws mandating expenditures and assessing certain taxes. Although Congress legislates tax rates, the tax revenues depend on how well the economy is doing. If the economy is doing well, revenues

are high; in recessions, revenues are low. As the government borrows more year after year, the total amount of *debt* increases. Congress, somewhat inconsistently, also sets a limit on the amount that the government can borrow. Without an agreement to increase the ceiling, some thought, the government would be forced to shut down. In any case, it would face an impossible situation: either the law specifying what was to be spent had to be broken, or the law specifying how much could be borrowed had to be violated.

5. During testimony in Congress on January 25, 2001, Greenspan gave support for near-term tax cuts and expressed worries about the government's paying off its debt too quickly. "But continuing to run surpluses beyond the point at which we reach zero or near-zero federal debt brings to center stage the critical longer-term fiscal policy issue of whether the federal government should accumulate large quantities of private (more technically nonfederal) assets. At zero debt, the continuing unified budget surpluses currently projected imply a major accumulation of private assets by the federal government. This development should factor materially into the policies you and the Administration choose to pursue. . . . In today's context, where tax reduction appears required in any event over the next several years to assist in forestalling the accumulation of private assets, starting that process sooner rather than later likely would help smooth the transition to longer-term fiscal balance," he said. "And should current economic weakness spread beyond what now appears likely, having a tax cut in place may, in fact, do noticeable good." See "Testimony of Chairman Alan Greenspan: Outlook for the Federal Budget and Implications for Fiscal Policy," before the Committee on the Budget, U.S. Senate, January 25, 2001, available at http://www.federalreserve.gov/boarddocs/testimony/2001/20010125/default.htm (accessed March 5, 2011).

6. See the CBO's "Current Budget Projections: Selected Tables from CBO's Budget and Economic Outlook: An Update," August 2010, pp. 9–10, available at http://www.cbo.gov/sites/default/files/cbofiles/ftpdocs/117xx/doc11705/budgetprojections.pdf (accessed February 22, 2012). This estimate includes an adjustment for the magnified effect of both the Economic Growth and Tax Relief Reconciliation Act of 2001 and the Jobs and Growth Tax Relief Reconciliation Act of 2003.

7. Economic Policy Institute, "Economic Snapshot," May 18, 2011, available at http://www.epi.org/publication/what_goes_into_a_budget_deficit/ (accessed March 5, 2012), based on CBO data. The Tax Relief, Unem-

ployment Insurance Reauthorization, and Job Creation Act of 2010, not only extended the Bush tax cuts by two years; it introduced other tax expenditures. The CBO estimated that the act would expand the deficit by $390 billion in 2011, and by $407 billion in 2012. See "The Budget and Economic Outlook: Fiscal Years 2011 to 2021," CBO 2011, available at http://budget.senate.gov/democratic/index.cfm/files/serve?File_id=94312aeb-8a73-41cd-b774-8533403f83a6 (accessed March 5, 2012). In January 2012 the CBO projected a deficit for the year of about $1.1 trillion. See "The Budget and Economic Outlook: Fiscal Years 2012 to 2022," CBO 2012, available at http://cbo.gov/sites/default/files/cbofiles/attachments/01-31-2012_Outlook.pdf (accessed March 5, 2012).

8. In present discounted terms, expressed in today's dollars. See J. E. Stiglitz and Linda Bilmes, Testimony before the U.S. Congress Hearing on the Economic Costs of the Iraq War, October 24, 2007, http://www.hks.harvard.edu/news-events/news/testimonies/linda-bilmes-testifies-before-us-house-of-representatives-commitee-on-the-budget-on-the-economic-costs-of-the-iraq-war); and Linda J. Bilmes and J. E. Stiglitz, *The Three Trillion Dollar War: The True Cost of the Iraq Conflict* (New York: Norton, 2008). Others have provided even higher numbers. The Eisenhower Study Group Research Project estimates that as of June 2011, $3.2–$4 trillion had been spent or obligated in the wars in Iraq, Afghanistan, and Pakistan since 2001. See "The Costs of War since 2001: Iraq, Afghanistan, and Pakistan," available at http://costsofwar.org/sites/default/files/Costs%20of%20War%20Executive%20Summary.pdf (accessed March 5, 2012).

9. "Funding for Operations in Afghanistan and Iraq and for Related Activities" was projected to cost $145 billion for 2012. See "The Budget and Economic Outlook: Fiscal Years 2012 to 2022," CBO 2012, available at http://cbo.gov/sites/default/files/cbofiles/attachments/01-31-2012_Outlook.pdf (accessed March 5, 2012). See the next footnote for why this almost surely represented an under-estimate of war spending.

10. Bilmes and Stiglitz, in *The Three Trillion Dollar War*, estimate that the cumulative increase in defense spending between 2003 and 2008 *beyond* costs attributed to the war at $600 billion. A substantial fraction of this was, in fact, hidden war spending.

11. See "Defence Costs," *Economist*, June 8, 2011, available at http://www.economist.com/blogs/dailychart/2011/06/military-spending (accessed March 7, 2012). For an additional discussion see Bilmes and Stiglitz, *The Three Trillion Dollar War*.

12. See "Lockheed F-35 Cost Controls in $662 Billion Defense Bill," *Businessweek*, December 15, 2011, available at http://www.business week.com/news/2011-12-15/lockheed-f-35-cost-controls-in-662-billion-defense-bill.html.

13. See the discussion in chapter 3 for cost estimates of this provision.

14. CBO estimate, see p. 117 of "The Budget and Economic Outlook: Fiscal Years 2012 to 2022," CBO 2012, available at http://cbo .gov/sites/default/files/cbofiles/attachments/01-31-2012_Outlook.pdf (accessed March 5, 2012).

15. The U.S. government benefited from the bubble, for a while, which masked its true financial position, as it did that of ordinary Americans: some of the revenues were from artificial capital gains and profits from bubble prices, so that even after reversing the four actions described above, there might still be a deficit. Besides, health care inflation has exceeded overall inflation, necessitating further expenditures for Medicare and Medicaid.

16. Of course, the capital gains tax cut was only part of the story of the creation of the bubble. Lax regulations and low interest rates also played a role.

17. See Anton Korinek and J. E. Stiglitz, "Dividend Taxation and Intertemporal Tax Arbitrage," *Journal of Public Economics* 93 (2009): 142–59. The advocates of the preferential tax treatment for dividends made one other argument: it was *unfair* to tax both corporate profits and dividends. Originally, the preferential treatment was supposed to extend only to firms that actually paid taxes; but then in one of those frequent last-minute switches, that restriction was dropped. The result is an even greater inequity—income that escapes corporate profits taxes and, then, when it's paid out, is taxed at a lower rate than comparable income of wage earners.

18. The actual inefficiency of the municipal tax provision is less than this hypothetical example suggests. One study suggested that some "20 percent of the benefit from the municipal-bond exemption unintentionally leaks to bond buyers from higher-income tax brackets." See Jordan Eizenga and Seth Hanlon, "Tax Expenditure of the Week: Tax-Exempt Bonds," March 2, 2011, website of the Center for American Progress, http://www .americanprogress.org/issues/2011/03/te030211.html (accessed March 5, 2012), citing T. J. Atwood, "Implicit Taxes: Evidence from Taxable, AMT, and Tax-Exempt State and Local Government Bond Yields," *Journal of the American Taxation Association* 25, no. 1 (2003): 1–20.

19. See Henry George, *Progress and Poverty: An Inquiry into the Cause of Industrial Depressions and of Increase of Want with Increase of Wealth: The Remedy* (1879). With Richard Arnott, I showed that there were conditions in which a 100 percent tax on such rents was, in fact, the optimal tax. See our "Aggregate Land Rents, Expenditure on Public Goods and Optimal City Size," *Quarterly Journal of Economics* 93, no. 4 (November 1979): 471–500. There is one qualification that is important when producers can't adequately insure themselves against the risks they bear. Then government should not rely heavily on a land tax or any other tax based on fixed quantities, because it will impose a high burden relative to income in bad years, and a low burden in good years. See K. Hoff, "Land Taxes, Output Taxes, and Sharecropping: Was Henry George Right?" *World Bank Economic Review* 5 (1991): 93–112; and X. Meng, N. Qian, and P. Yared, "The Institutional Causes of China's Great Famine," Yale University manuscript, 2010, available at http://papers.ssrn.com/sol3/papers.cfm?abstract_id=1671744 (accessed March 5, 2012).

20. The price of such resources can be decomposed into two parts—a rent, plus the cost of extraction.

21. It is even possible to auction off subsidies, to make sure that they go to where they are valued the most. A provision giving the Department of Agriculture discretion to do so was included in the 1995 farm bill, but never implemented.

22. As we noted in earlier chapters, a defense of these subsidies is that they increase employment. But as we noted there, too, the responsibility for maintaining the economy at full employment lies with macroeconomic policy (monetary policy and fiscal policy). If macroeconomic policy is managed well, we can have an economy at full employment, without these subsidies. If macroeconomic policy is not managed well, we won't have full employment, even with the subsidies.

23. The balanced-budget multiplier is normally assumed to be around unity. But if taxes are increased on the rich, who otherwise would have saved a lot, and expenditure increases are focused on "high multiplier" activities, like investments in education, then the balanced-budget multiplier can be much larger.

24. Members of the commission do pay homage to the need for a more progressive tax system, but what they recommended was almost surely a less progressive one. They provide an illustrative distributional analysis (which focuses only on the individual income tax changes, not on the

impact of the corporate income tax changes or on cutbacks in expenditures). Even in their analysis, the largest percentage increase in average federal taxes is imposed on the second quintile—13.5 percent, compared with 10.4 percent for the top quintile. At the same time, some of their loophole-closing reforms do make an important contribution to increasing progressivity. Almost half of their increased tax revenues come from the top 1 percent—consistent with the recommendations made earlier in this chapter.

25. For small corporations, there would be a tax increase under their proposal.

26. For a standard textbook treatment of this issue, see J. E. Stiglitz, *The Economics of the Public Sector*, 3rd ed. (New York: Norton, 2000). For the original theoretical analysis, see Joseph E. Stiglitz, "Taxation, Corporate Financial Policy, and the Cost of Capital," *Journal of Public Economics* 2 (February 1973): 1–34.

27. The Bowles-Simpson Commission, in its final report, was more careful. It argued that the new tax code "must include provisions (in some cases permanent, in others temporary) for . . . mortgage interest only for principal residences; employer-provided health insurance; charitable giving; [and] retirement savings and pensions."

28. There is evidence that in densely populated areas—which are precisely the areas in which homeownership is likely to improve communities through higher voting rates and more participation in collective action—the mortgage interest deduction does not increase homeownerhip rates and may actually lower them. Because the supply of housing in such areas is inelastic, much of the mortgage interest deduction is capitalized into housing prices in those areas. At the higher housing price, fewer low- to moderate-income households gain from homeowning rather than renting. See C. A. Hilber and T. M. Turner, "The Mortgage Interest Deduction and Its Impact on Homeownership Decisions," SERC Discussion Papers, 55, London School of Economics, 2010, available at http://personal.lse.ac.uk/hilber/hilber_wp/Hilber_Turner_2010_08.pdf (accessed March 5, 2012).

29. Most of the proposals did take some account of this, by postponing the implementation of their cuts, but only briefly, perhaps because they had an excessively optimistic view of recovery. Under Bowles-Simpson, cuts (relative to what public spending otherwise would have been) begin in 2012. Yet, as this book goes to press, the Congressional Budget Office

projects that the economy will not be back to full employment before 2018, and the Fed is so pessimistic that it has said that interest rates will remain near zero through the end of 2014.

30. As an obvious example, a tax credit to corporations that do invest provides incentives for firms to invest and provides them the cash to do so.

31. In a world of perfect competition, prices are driven down ruthlessly to marginal costs, and marginal costs are driven down ruthlessly to the lowest level consistent with current technology. But for a variety of reasons, competition in the health care sector, and especially in health insurance, is far from perfect. One of the reasons that the private sector has such high transactions costs is that companies devote considerable efforts to "cream skimming," to ensuring that those whom they insure are healthy, or at least healthier than average. Another reason is that, in the presence of excess profits, they spend considerable resources recruiting good customers, e.g., through advertising.

32. Many of these recommendations are consistent with those of Bowles-Simpson.

33. Gary Engelhardt and Jonathan Gruber show that increases in Social Security benefits can explain all of the 17 percentage point decline in poverty that occurred between 1960 and 2000. "Social Security and the Evolution of Elderly Poverty," NBER Working Paper 10466 (2004).

34. Thomas Ferguson and Robert Johnson, "A World Upside Down? Deficit Fantasies in the Great Recession," Roosevelt Institute Working Paper no. 7, 2010.

35. The Obama health care program contains a number of provisions that are designed to bring down the costs of health care. It is too soon to tell for sure how effective these will be.

36. That's not quite true: even promised future cuts, if they are credible, may be a damper on the economy now, as households, knowing that Social Security and Medicare are being cut, will have to save more now, to protect themselves; and even though higher saving in the long run is good, the short-run impact—less consumption—will not be good for recovery.

37. A variant of this, remarkably held by some serious economists, is that they aren't really unemployed; they're just "enjoying" leisure. Of course, normally, someone enjoying leisure should be happy, which is not the case for most of those out of a job. But, in this view, that's a problem for psychology, not for economics.

38. This is, of course, better than at the worst of the recession, when there were seven applicants for every job. (Bureau of Labor Statistics http://www.bls.gov/news.release/jolts.htm). Reportedly, when McDonald's advertised that it was going to hire 50,000 workers, 1 million applicants showed up! See Leslie Patton, "McDonald's Hires 62,000 in U.S. Event, 24% More Than Planned," *Bloomberg*, April 28, 2011, available at http://www.bloomberg.com/news/2011-04-28/mcdonald-s-hires-62-000-during-national-event-24-more-than-planned.html (accessed March 5, 2012).

39. Indeed, there is an argument that unemployment insurance might actually enhance the efficiency of the labor search market, since those who were least desirous of a job and least likely to get a job would be the first to drop out. In doing so, search costs were lowered for others, and those who did get a job were more likely to be better matched. I am indebted to George Akerlof for discussions on this point.

40. Growth of real GDP (percent change from preceding year) for 2010: United States (2.9), Sweden (5.3), Germany (3.5). Employment growth (percent change from preceding year) for 2010: United States (–0.6), Sweden (1.0), Germany (0.5).

See OECD at http://www.oecd.org/document/22/0,3746,en_2649_39023495_43221014_1_1_1_1,00.html#taxes. Chapter 4 explained a variety of short- and longer-term benefits of greater social protection—greater risk taking, greater stability, and more political support for measures, like trade opening, that, if well managed, can help improve economic performance, all of which can contribute to higher long-term growth.

41. For the position of those opposing public investment to be coherent requires the *additional* assumption that there do not exist public investment opportunities with high returns. But, as we discussed earlier, it is widely recognized that there are many high- return investments in infrastructure, education, and research, among other things.

42. In addition, most of the examples entail countries with flexible exchange rates. Lower exchange rates generate more exports. The U.S. exchange rate is to a large extent outside of its control: if Europe's crisis worsens, for instance, the euro may decline relative to the dollar and the United States will have a harder time exporting.

43. See Arjun Jayadev and Mike Konczal, "The Boom Not the Slump: The Right Time for Austerity," Roosevelt Institute, August 23, 2010, and their forceful critique of Alberto Alesina and Silvia Ardagna, "Large

Changes in Fiscal Policy: Taxes Versus Spending," NBER Working Paper no. 15438, 2009. The IMF has come to similar conclusions. See also Olivier J. Blanchard, David Romer, Michael Spence, and Joseph E. Stiglitz, eds., *In the Wake of the Crisis: Leading Economists Reassess Economic Policy* (Cambridge: MIT Press, 2012), and in particular the article by Robert Solow, "Fiscal Policy," pp. 73–76. See also Jaime Guajardo, Daniel Leigh, and Andrea Pescatori, "Expansionary Austerity: New International Evidence," IMF working paper, July 2011.

44. See Domenico Delli Gatti, Mauro Gallegati, Bruce C. Greenwald, Alberto Russo, and Joseph E. Stiglitz, "Sectoral Imbalances and Long Run Crises," paper presented to the International Economic Association meeting, Beijing, July 2011, and forthcoming in its proceedings. For a more accessible version, see J. E. Stiglitz, "The Book of Jobs," *Vanity Fair*, January 2012, pp. 28–32, available at http://www.vanityfair.com/poli tics/2012/01/stiglitz-depression-201201 (accessed March 5, 2012).

45. See Sumner H. Slichter, "The Downturn of 1937," *Review of Economic Statistics* 20 (1938): 97–110; Kenneth D. Roose, "The Recession of 1937–38," *Journal of Political Economy* 56, no. 3 (June 1948): 239–48; and E. Cary Brown, "Fiscal Policy in the Thirties: A Reappraisal," *American Economic Review* 46, no. 5 (December 1956): 857–79.

46. As we've argued elsewhere, however, the financial sector is not fully back to health. Many of the smaller banks, responsible for so much lending to the country's small and medium-size enterprises, still face problems. Nonetheless, overall, investment outside of real estate has been largely restored to precrisis levels. Private nonresidential fixed investment as a percentage of GDP was around 10.0 percent in the second quarter of 2011, while the historical postwar average is 10.7 percent (though we note that GDP has fallen below trend). Equipment and software investment by firms in real terms was about 8.2 percent of GDP in early 2011 compared with a high of 8.4 percent in 2007 and 6.6 percent at the peak of the crisis in the fourth quarter of 2008.

47. And it affected judgments about the value of a political battle to get a larger, longer, and better-designed stimulus. A critical weakness of the stimulus was that a third of it went to household tax cuts, which had proven themselves relatively ineffective earlier (the Bush tax cuts of 2008). For a more extensive discussion of the design flaws, see J. E. Stiglitz, *Freefall* (New York: Norton, 2010).

48. As the crisis has continued, officials have become more cautious.

The Fed's announcement that it expects interest rates to be near zero at least until the end of 2014—saying, in effect, that the downturn for which its precrisis policies bear considerable culpability would last at least seven years. (The recession began in December 2007.)

49. In a period of prolonged underutilization of capacity, one is concerned not just about the immediate impact of the spending but also about the effects even two or three years down the line, when the economy is still weak. Some of what is not spent today is spent in these future years, stimulating the economy, and the knowledge that this is so may provide even more stimulus to the economy now. See P. Neary and J. E. Stiglitz, "Toward a Reconstruction of Keynesian Economics: Expectations and Constrained Equilibria," *Quarterly Journal of Economics* 98, suppl. (1983): 199–228. Moreover, one of the reasons that money doesn't get recycled—to increase GDP even more—is "leakages," to spending abroad. But when other countries (such as those in Europe) are also weak, spending abroad increases *their* income, and they reciprocate, spending more on imports, including from goods from the United States. One is, accordingly, interested in long-run *global* multipliers, not just short-run national multipliers. These multipliers are likely to be large, much larger than the 1.5 number usually used. See United Nations, "Report of the Commission of Experts of the President of the United Nations General Assembly on Reforms of the International Monetary and Financial System" (also known as the Stiglitz Commission), New York: United Nations, September 2009, published as *The Stiglitz Report* (New York: New Press, 2010). For a recent survey, see Jonathan A. Parker, "On Measuring the Effects of Fiscal Policy in Recessions," *Journal of Economic Literature* 49 no. 3 (2011): 703–18. Many of the statistical studies cited by those claiming a small multiplier are badly flawed, since they rely heavily on periods in which the economy is at or near full employment and/or where monetary authorities have taken offsetting actions—increasing interest rates. The difficulty is that periods of long and deep downturns, such as the Great Depression and the Great Recession, are relatively rare, and that impedes the use of statistical analyses.

50. There is a standard argument among conservatives against deficit spending, that the anticipation of increased tax liabilities in the future so increases savings, as workers today prepare for those future tax burdens, that aggregate demand is unaffected. The argument is called the

Barro-Ricardian equivalence theorem, after the Harvard professor Robert Barro, who discussed it in his paper "On the Determination of the Public Debt," *Journal of Political Economy* 87, no. 5 (1979): 940–71. But subsequent work, such as my paper "On the Relevance or Irrelevance of Public Financial Policy," in *The Economics of Public Debt: Proceedings of a Conference Held by the International Economic Association at Stanford, California* (London: Macmillan Press, 1988), pp. 4–76, explains that the result holds true only on very peculiar conditions, e.g., perfect capital markets and perfect altruism across generations. In fact, when Bush lowered his taxes on the rich and the deficit soared, household savings rates *fell,* moving in just the opposite direction predicted by Barro's theory.

Chapter Nine A Macroeconomic Policy and a Central Bank by and for the 1 Percent

1. Inflation hawks—monetary policymakers who seem to have an obsession with even the slightest increase in inflation—maintain that the economy sits on a precipice; even the slightest increase in inflation can set the economy down the wayward path of higher and higher inflation. There is no statistical support for this view, as the 1997 *Economic Report of the President* pointed out.
2. Critics will say that it's all well and good to point this out *after* the crisis—our understandings are always better in twenty-twenty hindsight. But the fact of the matter is that I and others who raised these concerns about the obsessive focus on inflation pointed out these risks well before the crisis.
3. This is partly because, with interest rates so low, their cost of capital is very low; partly because the high unemployment has put downward pressure on labor costs; and partly because large American firms earn much of their profits overseas, including in the emerging markets, which quickly recovered from the Great Recession and have been doing very well. Some may claim that the very wealthy suffered a great deal from the crash of the stock market—that they lost more than those at the bottom and in the middle ever hoped to have had. But the statistics given earlier on the losses in net wealth of Hispanics and African Americans (and even of the *median* white American) show how devastating the crisis was for them.

486   NOTES TO PAGES 302–303

4. See Jason Furman and Joseph E. Stiglitz, "Economic Consequences of Income Inequality," in *Income Inequality: Issues and Policy Options: A Symposium* ([Kansas City]: Federal Reserve Bank of Kansas City, 1998), pp. 221–63, available at http://www.kc.frb.org/publicat/sympos/1998/s98stiglitz.pdf (accessed March 30, 2012).

5. "In the U.S. non-farm business sector, real median hourly wages rose at an average annual rate of 0.33 per cent between 1980 and 2005, while labour productivity increased at an average annual rate of 1.73 per cent over the same period." Peter Harrison, "Median Wages and Productivity Growth in Study of Living, Canada and the United States," Center for Study of Living Standards Research Note 2009-2, July 2009. There are large cumulative effects. Looking only at the period between 1989 and 2011, while productivity (private sector plus state and local government) was up more than 60 percent, wages over the same period were up only 20 percent. See Heidi Shierholz and Lawrence Mishel, "Sustained, High Joblessness Causes Lasting Damage to Wages, Benefits, Income, and Wealth," Economic Policy Institute, August 31, 2011. Shierholz and Mishel provide a more complete description of what has happened to wages in "The Sad But True Story of Wages in America," Economic Policy Institute, Issue Brief no. 297, March 14, 2011.

6. Median hourly wages (all occupations), adjusted for inflation, were lower in 2007 than in 2001 (based on calculations from Bureau of Labor Statistics data).

7. For minimum wage history, see the U.S. Department of Labor website, http://www.dol.gov/whd/minwage/chart.htm.

8. On average, outside of recessions, when benefits are temporarily increased (often with a contentious congressional fight), only 25 percent of unemployed workers receive unemployment assistance, and their assistance replaces, on average, less than half of the lost income. (Center on Budget and Policy Priorities, "Introduction to Unemployment Insurance," April 16, 2010.) The United States provides much poorer unemployment insurance than do many other advanced industrial countries. For instance, while (outside of periods of high unemployment) the United States provides for six months unemployment insurance, only Italy and the Czech Republic provide less; France provides for 23 months, Germany 12, and Denmark 48 (from OECD Employment Outlook, 2006, p. 60). In terms of replacement rate (the fraction of normal income that unemployment insurance replaces), the United States is also low: during the first year of

an unemployment spell, France's replacement rate is 67.3 percent, Germany's, 64.9 percent, Denmark's, 72.6 percent, and the United States' only 44.9 percent (from OECD Employment Outlook, 2011, p. 40).

9. See, e.g., Gretchen Morgenson, "0.2% interest? You Bet We'll Complain," New York Times, March 4, 2012, available at http://www.nytimes.com/2012/03/04/business/low-rates-for-savers-are-reason-for-complaint-fair-game.html (accessed March 5, 2012).

10. Some economists—such as the Columbia economist Michael Woodford; see "Bernanke Needs Inflation for QE2 to Set Sail," Financial Times, October 11, 2010, available at http://www.ft.com/intl/cms/s/0/4d54e574-d57a-11df-8e86-00144feabdc0.html#axzz1oHWZWjKv (accessed March 5, 2012)—have suggested that the Fed commit itself to a maintaining inflation at a given level. With inflation of, say, 4 percent and interest rates of 0 percent, the real interest rate would be minus 4 percent. What is impeding economic recovery (in this view) is the "zero lower bound" to interest rates. I find this approach unpersuasive—putting aside the difficulty of the Fed's credibly committing itself to a high inflation rate. The analysis just presented explains why a very low real interest rate may actually reduce aggregate demand. The situation in the United States today is markedly different from that in the Great Depression, when rapidly falling prices meant that real interest rates were very high. Real interest rates are already negative, and these negative real interest rates have not elicited the hoped-for response. Those who advocate such policies (and other related policies, like nominal GDP targeting) typically put excessive focus on the role of real T-bill rates in determining the level of economic activity. Equally or more important is credit availability and the terms at which credit is made available to firms. See Bruce Greenwald and J. E. Stiglitz, Towards a New Paradigm in Monetary Economics (Cambridge: Cambridge University Press, 2003).

11. The consumption of the poor and middle is, as we have noted, often constrained by their resources, but this is not so true of those at the top, which is why increasing temporarily their capacity to consume today is not likely to have much effect on consumption levels.

12. I am indebted to Miguel Morin for his analysis of this and his insights on this issue.

13. It does involve some risk—that the long-term bond will decrease in value—but with the government systematically socializing losses, the risk is borne at least partially by taxpayers.

14. *Bloomberg* calculated more conservatively that easy access to the Federal Reserve amounted to a gift to the banks of $13 billion, *Bloomberg Markets Magazine* reports in its January 2012 issue. See Bob Ivry, Bradley Keoun, and Phil Kuntz, "Secret Fed Loans Gave Banks $13 Billion Undisclosed to Congress," available at http://mobile.bloomberg.com/news/2011-11-28/secret-fed-loans-undisclosed-to-congress-gave-banks-13-billion-in-income (accessed March 5, 2012). The claim that the government had been repaid on the money that it had given to the banks was nothing but a shell game: the Fed in effect gave the banks the money that they then passed on to the government.

15. Banks have long had a reserve requirement—a minimum proportion of liquid funds that they are required to maintain. The Federal Reserve's explanation for why, in 2008, it had chosen to pay interest on excess reserves deposited with Reserve Banks is posted on its website: "The inability to pay interest on balances held to satisfy reserve requirements essentially imposes a tax on depository institutions equal to the interest that might otherwise have been earned by investing those balances in an interest-bearing asset. Paying interest on required reserve balances effectively eliminates this tax. . . . Paying interest on excess balances should help to establish a lower bound on the federal funds rate by lessening the incentive for institutions to trade balances in the market at rates much below the rate paid on excess balances. Paying interest on excess balances will permit the Federal Reserve to provide sufficient liquidity to support financial stability while implementing the monetary policy that is appropriate in light of the System's macroeconomic objectives of maximum employment and price stability." See http://www.federalreserve.gov/monetarypolicy/ior_faqs.htm#4 (accessed March 5, 2012). The price tag for the Fed's 0.25 percent interest rate paid on the current amount of excess reserves deposited with Reserve Banks—about $1.5 trillion—is likely almost $4 billion dollars a year. See, for excess reserves amount, the website of the Federal Reserve Bank of St. Louis Fed, http://research.stlouisfed.org/fred2/series/EXCRESNS (accessed March 5, 2012).

16. Bruce Greenwald and I have argued, in *Towards a New Paradigm in Monetary Economics*, that the role of interest rates has been greatly exaggerated by central banks; equally, and in some cases more, important is the availability of credit. Paying banks on their reserves held at the central bank both raises the interest rates that banks will

charge customers and reduces the credit they make available. Through both channels, the policy has adverse consequences. But the Federal Reserve evidently shunted these concerns aside, as it focused on its more immediate business of transferring money to the banks. It might defend these actions as helping recapitalize the banks, and bank recapitalization would, it was hoped, lead eventually to more lending. But there were better ways of recapitalizing the banks.

17. Chapter 6 provides a description of the battle over perceptions in the bank bailout—did we have to do what we did in order to save the entire economy?

18. For a breakdown of where the money went, see http://projects.pro publica.org/bailout/list/index.

19. Between 2009 and February 2012, 398 went bankrupt. See http://www.fdic.gov/bank/individual/failed/banklist.html.

20. As of September 30, 2011 (the most recent data available), the FDIC's "Problem List" had 844 institutions with assets of $339 billion. See FDIC Quarterly Banking Profile and Federal Deposit Insurance Corporation, Failed Bank List, available at http://www2.fdic.gov/qbp/2011sep/qbp.pdf (accessed February 24, 2012).

21. Probably the most important deregulatory measure was the repeal in 1999, under President Clinton, of part of the Glass-Steagall Act of 1933 which separated investment banks (responsible for managing wealthy individuals' and corporations' money) and commercial banks. The repeal is also known as the Citigroup Relief Act because it legalized a merger of Citibank with securities and insurance services that had occurred in 1998. During debate in the House of Representatives, Representative John Dingell argued that the bill would lead banks to become "too big to fail," and that this would lead to a bailout by the federal government. As chairman of the Council of Economic Advisers from 1995 to 1997, I had opposed (successfully) the repeal, on those grounds, as well as because of the risk of conflicts of interests (between the role of the issuer of new securities, by an investment bank, and providing operating funds, as a commercial bank) and because of the danger that the risk-taking culture of investment banks would contaminate the rightly more conservative culture of commericial banks. All three worries proved justified. Had Greenspan opposed the repeal, it is unlikely it would have been passed. The role of the Fed chairman and the secretary of Treasury in opposing regulation of derivatives is well documented. See J. E. Stiglitz, *Free-*

fall (New York: W. W. Norton, 2010), and Stiglitz, *The Roaring Nineties* (New York: W. W. Norton, 2003), and the references cited there.

22. See, e.g., Alan Greenspan, speech at Credit Union National Association 2004 Governmental Affairs Conference, Washington, DC, February 23, 2004, though, after forcefully pointing out that those who had taken out variable-rate mortgages did much better than those who had taken out fixed-rate mortgages, he did issue some warnings that things could have turned out differently, i.e., that there was still risk.

23. Dean Baker and Travis McArthur have estimated that the difference between the interest rates at which too-big-to-fail banks can raise capital and the rate smaller banks have access to increased from 0.29 percentage points—where it had been for about seven years before the crisis—to 0.78 percentage points in a matter of months after the bailouts. This, they argue, shows that markets recognized that too-big-to-fail banks had become "official government policy," and implied "a government subsidy of $34.1 billion a year to the 18 bank holding companies with more than $100 billion in assets in the first quarter of 2009." Baker and McArthur, "The Value of the 'Too Big to Fail' Big Bank Subsidy," Center for Economic and Policy Research, September 2009, available at http://www.cepr.net/documents/publications/too-big-to-fail-2009-09.pdf (accessed March 5, 2012). In January 2010 Obama discussed the possibility of imposing a tax to offset this advantage. He didn't pursue this, in face of the opposition from the banks (and perhaps even those within the administration).

24. There is a huge literature on the subject discussed in this section. My own views are set out in a lecture in memory of one of the great economists of the twentieth century, and the (first) Nobel Prize winner in economics, Jan Tinbergen, delivered at the Central Bank of Netherlands, "Central Banking in a Democratic Society," *De Economist* 146, no. 2 (July 1998): 199–226. See also Alex Cukierman, *Central Bank Strategy, Credibility, and Independence* (Cambridge: MIT Press, 1992); and J. Furman, "Central Bank Independence, Indexing, and the Macroeconomy," unpublished 1997 manuscript.

25. See chapter 3 for more details.

26. Edward M. Gramlich not only anticipated the bubble and its breaking but also argued forcefully that something should be done to avoid the foreclosures. The Fed did nothing on either front. See his book *Subprime*

Mortgages: America's Latest Boom and Bust (Washington, DC: Urban Institute, 2007).

27. This was a position that was clearly political and consistent with his known ideological views. See chapter 8 for a discussion of the specious arguments that were put forward in defense of his position.

28. The 2010 Dodd-Frank regulatory reform bill made some improvements in governance.

29. "Remarks by Governor Ben S. Bernanke," October 2004, available at http://www.federalreserve.gov/boarddocs/speeches/2004/200410072/ default.htm.

30. An argument sometimes put forward for secrecy is that disclosing information will roil the markets, and could lead to a run against a bank that has borrowed money from the Fed. But at issue in this case was disclosure of information long after the transactions had occurred. Besides, capital markets can't exercise discipline in the absence of relevant information. Those who advocate secrecy are advocating policies that would undermine the discipline of the marketplace.

31. JPMorgan Chase benefited through the Bear Stearns bailout. In another instance of questionable governance, Stephen Friedman became chairman of the Federal Reserve Bank of New York in January 2008, while he was simultaneously a member of the board of Goldman Sachs and had a large holding in Goldman stock. He resigned in May 2009 after the controversy over the obvious conflicts of interest (including share purchases, which enabled him to make $3 million). See Joe Hagan, "Tenacious G," *New York*, July 26, 2009, available at http://nymag.com/ news/business/58094/ (accessed March 28, 2012); and Kate Kelly and Jon Hilsenrath, "New York Fed Chairman's Ties to Goldman Raise Questions," *Wall Street Journal*, May 4, 2009, p. A1.

32. See, e.g., Binyamin Applebaum and Jo Craven McGinty, "The Fed's Crisis Lending: A Billion Here, a Thousand There," *New York Times*, March 31, 2011, available at http://www.nytimes.com/2011/04/01/busi ness/economy/01fed.html (accessed March 5, 2012). From the article: "And the Fed helped to save some of the largest banks in Europe by pumping desperately needed dollars into their American subsidiaries. In fact, the biggest borrower from the Fed program was Dexia, a French-Belgian bank that frequently held more than $30 billion in outstanding loans from the program from late 2008 to early 2009."

33. The central mission of a central bank (such as the Fed) is to act as a lender of last resort for the banks within the country, that is, when no one else is willing to lend to banks that are solvent (i.e., whose assets exceed its liabilities), the Fed steps in to provide liquidity.

34. On March 27, 2007, Bernanke testified before Congress, "Although the turmoil in the subprime mortgage market has created severe financial problems for many individuals and families, the implications of these developments for the housing market as a whole are less clear. The ongoing tightening of lending standards, although an appropriate market response, will reduce somewhat the effective demand for housing, and foreclosed properties will add to the inventories of unsold homes. At this juncture, however, the impact on the broader economy and financial markets of the problems in the subprime market seems likely to be contained. In particular, mortgages to prime borrowers and fixed-rate mortgages to all classes of borrowers continue to perform well, with low rates of delinquency. We will continue to monitor this situation closely." See "Chairman Ben S. Bernanke: The Economic Outlook: Before the Joint Economic Committee, U.S. Congress," available at http://www.federal reserve.gov/newsevents/testimony/bernanke20070328a.htm (accessed February 24, 2012).

35. There are other important institutional reforms that would make for a more effective monetary policy. A fashionable doctrine in economics holds that separate institutions should be created to pursue different objectives and to control different instruments. In this view, the central bank should focus on inflation, and its instrument of choice should be the interest rate. Fiscal authorities should focus on employment, using tax and expenditure policy. Unfortunately, while in some very simple theoretical models this institutional arrangement can achieve desirable outcomes, in the real world there needs to be coordination. It is often desirable to use multiple instruments to pursue even a single objective. Bank lending is as affected by regulatory requirements (like capital adequacy standards) as by interest rates; and quantitative restrictions (e.g., down payments on housing) can be a much more effective instrument in controlling excesses than a blunt instrument like the interest rate.

36. The sense of loss of sovereignty that countries in Europe have felt is reflected in a statement made by Giulio Tremonti, Italy's finance minister at the time, privately to a group of European finance ministers. He is quoted as saying that in August his government had received two threat-

ening letters—one from a terrorist group, the other from the ECB. "The one from the ECB was worse." From Marcus Walker, Charles Forelle, and Stac Meichtry, "Deepening Crisis over Euro Pits Leader against Leader," *Wall Street Journal*, December 30, 2011.

37. An alternative explanation is that the ECB knows that the financial system lacks transparency and knows that investors know that they cannot gauge the impact of an involuntary default, which could cause credit markets to freeze, reprising the aftermath of Lehman Brothers' collapse in September 2008. The ECB should have insisted on more transparency—indeed, that should have been one of the main lessons of 2008. Regulators should not have allowed the banks to speculate as they did; if anything, they should have required that the banks buy insurance— and then insisted on restructuring in a way that ensured that the insurance pays off. The one argument that seems, at least superficially, to put the public interest first is that an involuntary restructuring might lead to financial contagion, with large eurozone economies like Italy, Spain, and even France facing a sharp, and perhaps prohibitive, rise in borrowing costs. But that raises the question of why an involuntary restructuring should lead to worse contagion than a voluntary restructuring of comparable depth. If the banking system were well regulated, with banks holding sovereigns having purchased insurance, an involuntary restructuring should perturb financial markets less. Another explanation is that by insisting on its voluntariness, the ECB may be trying to ensure that the restructuring is not deep. It might worry that if Greece gets away with a deep involuntary restructuring, others would be tempted to try it as well. Financial markets, worried about this, would immediately raise interest rates on other at-risk eurozone countries, large and small. But the riskiest countries already have been shut out of financial markets, so the possibility of a panic reaction is of limited consequence. Moreover, they would be tempted to do so only if Greece were indeed better-off restructuring than not doing so. That is true, but there's no news in that. In the end, . the restructuring did trigger a credit event, and there was no trauma to the financial markets—the ECB's concerns were proven baseless.

38. On July 15, 2011, the European Banking Authority, as part of its European bank stress tests, gave Dexia a clean bill of health (http://www.bloomberg.com/news/2011-10-13/no-1-financial-strength-ranking-spells-doom-commentary-by-jonathan-weil.html). On October 4, 2011, Dexia shares fell 22 percent. On October 10, 2011, Dexia was bailed out

(http://online.wsj.com/article/SB1000142405297020363310457662072 0705508498.html). The ECB's position was odder still. Whether a credit event had occurred was determined by a secret committee of the International Securities Dealers Association (ISDA), which might be described as a cooperative group—or a cartel—of the writers of derivatives, some of whom might have a strong financial interest in the outcome. They—or their employer—might receive or have to pay billions. One member of the committee reportedly even used her position to try to influence bondholders' cooperation in restructuring, hinting that if they didn't, the committee might still put a high bar on whether it was or was not a "default" event. The decisions of the ISDA were not appealable, either to arbitration or to the courts. It seemed curious that the ECB was apparently willing to delegate authority to a private institution, operating in secret, on what was or was not an acceptable restructuring. So much for democratic accountability.

39. The term "Chicago school" has come to refer to Milton Friedman and his disciples who believed in market fundamentalism, the idea that unfettered markets are always efficient even in the absence of government regulation. Milton Friedman taught for many years at the University of Chicago. But, of course, many economists who teach there do not subscribe to market fundamentalism—and many economists at other schools do. See chapter 3 for a longer discussion.

40. See the website of the Board of Governors of the Federal Reserve for the most up-to-date balance sheet figures, http://www.federalreserve.gov/monetarypolicy/bst_recenttrends.htm.

41. There's another theory of the Great Depression that is relevant to what has been going on more recently. Some put blame for the Great Depression on the gold standard. It impeded adjustment. Countries that left the gold standard did better. In some ways, the euro has imposed on Europe some of the same kind of rigidity that the gold standard imposed on much of the world in the 1930s. And yet, there's a sense that the gold standard didn't *cause* the Great Depression, just as the euro didn't cause the Great Recession. The origins of the disturbance to the economy lay elsewhere. And some of the benefits accruing to those countries that left the gold standard were *at the expense* of others. If they had *all* moved to a flexible exchange rate system, would that, by itself, have been sufficient to restore the global economy to prosperity? I doubt it.

42. For a discussion of these bubbles and the repeated financial crises

that are often associated with the bursting of the bubbles, see Charles Kindleberger, *Manias, Panics, and Crashes: A History of Financial Crises* (New York: Basic Books, 1978), and Kenneth Rogoff and Carmen M. Reinhardt, *This Time Is Different: Eight Centuries of Financial Folly* (Princeton: Princeton University Press, 2009).

43. Or, similarly, increasing margins in the purchase of stock (which act like a house down payment). Interestingly, in the tech bubbles of the 1990s, the possibility of increasing margin requirements was briefly discussed, but then evidently dismissed: perhaps the free marketers that dominated the Fed didn't like this kind of interference with the wonders of the market. See J. E. Stiglitz, *The Roaring Nineties: A New History of the World's Most Prosperous Decade* (New York: W. W. Norton, 2004).

44. Among the list of those who have officially adopted inflation targeting in one form or another are Israel, the Czech Republic, Poland, Brazil, Chile, Colombia, South Africa, Thailand, Korea, Mexico, Hungary, Peru, the Philippines, Slovakia, Indonesia, Romania, New Zealand, Canada, the United Kingdom, Sweden, Australia, Iceland, and Norway. The United States never fully adopted inflation targeting—as we have noted, the Federal Reserve's mandate requires that it look also at the level of unemployment and the rate of growth. But over long periods of time, its policies have been little different from those of countries that have explicitly adopted inflation targeting.

45. This list is not meant to be exhaustive. Another hypothesis is that the best way to fight inflation—regardless of its source—was to increase interest rates. There are other macroeconomic tools (fiscal policy), and even within the domain of monetary policy, there are other instruments (e.g., restraining credit availability through raising reserve requirements). It can be shown that the best way to respond to inflation depends on the source of the disturbance—what caused the bout of inflation.

46. There is another rationale for the view that a central bank should focus only on inflation. It isn't that the advocates of inflation targeting don't recognize the importance of these other issues, but rather that they believe that there should be different institutions and policy instruments for different objectives. Fiscal authorities, for instance, might want to focus on unemployment, or even on distribution. The notion that there can be a simple pairing of instruments and objectives is associated with the Nobel Prize–winning economist Tingbergen. This notion is valid in

simple linear models. However, it's known now that it's not true in general, and especially so in the context of uncertainty.

47. See data on the website of the World Bank, "Inflation, consumer prices (annual %)," available at http://data.worldbank.org/indicator/fp.cpi .totl.zg (accessed March 5, 2012).

48. Indeed, given the size of the U.S. economy, a slowdown there might conceivably have had a far bigger effect on global prices than a slowdown in any developing country, which suggests that, from a global perspective, U.S. interest rates, not those in developing countries, should have been raised.

49. For many developing countries, high oil and food prices represent a triple threat: not only do importing countries have to pay more for grain; they have to pay more to bring it to their countries and still more to deliver it to consumers who may live a long distance from ports.

50. In practice, inflation targeting is often implemented in less doctrinaire ways. Because central bankers *have* to say they are committed to fighting inflation, it has become de rigueur for them to declare that they are engaged in inflation targeting. But the better central bankers know that raising interest rates won't dampen inflation much when the inflation is "imported" and the economy is not overheated. They know, too, that they have to look after other things, like the exchange rate and financial stability. Some central bankers don't always acknowledge these nuances: they see inflation today and raise interest rates, even though the economy is slowing down and the full effect of the higher rates will be felt six to eighteen months later, when the slowdown has already occurred. To take one example, the ECB raised its interest rates in April 2011 in response to the threat of inflation from rising oil prices even though unemployment was still near 10 percent and expected to remain so. The economy later slowed, inflation did not increase, and the policy had to be reversed.

51. These issues are discussed more extensively in Stiglitz, *Freefall*; *Economic Report of the President*, 1997; and J. E. Stiglitz, "Reflections on the Natural Rate Hypothesis," *Journal of Economic Perspectives* 11, no. 1 (Winter 1997): 3–10.

52. Indeed, by some calculations, Social Security is overindexed, i.e., individuals are actually better-off when inflation increases, or at least that has been the case in the past, over extended periods of time. See the Boskin report, "Toward a More Accurate Measure of the Cost of Living," December 4, 1996, available at http://www.ssa.gov/history/reports/boskinrpt.html.

53. Countries in which there is persistent high and variable inflation typically put in clauses that provide for automatic adjustments in wages to changes in the cost of living (called COLA, cost of living adjustment).

54. See, e.g., Robert J. Shiller, *Irrational Exuberance*, 2nd ed. (Princeton: Princeton University Press, 2005. For S&P/Case-Shiller Home Price Indices see http://us.spindices.com/index-family/real-estate/sp-case-shiller (accessed December 10, 2012).

55. That requires that the deceleration of inflation from an increase in unemployment is weaker than the acceleration of inflation from a decrease in unemployment. See Stiglitz, "Reflections on the Natural Rate Hypothesis." There is a huge literature on the hypothesis that, in the long run, the relationship between the acceleration of inflation and unemployment is vertical ("the vertical Phillips curve"). See, in particular, Edmund S. Phelps, "Phillips Curves, Expectations of Inflation and Optimal Employment over Time," *Economica*, n.s., 34, no. 3 (1967): 254–81; and Milton Friedman, "The Role of Monetary Policy," *American Economic Review* 58, no. 1 (1968): 1–17.

56. See, in particular, Arjun Jayadev and Mike Konczal, "The Stagnating Labor Market," Roosevelt Institute, September 19, 2010. If the only problem in the labor market was a mismatch, then one should see wages rising in the many sectors in which there was a shortage, and given the downward rigidity of wages, average wages should be rising. One piece of evidence that is sometimes alluded to is that there has been an increase in vacancies relative to the number of unemployed. But this may have more to do with the changing job composition of those sectors of the economy that are doing well and expanding. For an excellent overview—coming down to the same policy conclusion—see Peter A. Diamond's Lecture for the Sveriges Riksbank Prize in Economic Sciences in Memory of Alfred Nobel, "Unemployment, Vacancies, Wages," *American Economic Review* 101, no. 4 (June 2011): 1045–72.

57. See Catherine Rampell, "Where the Jobs Are, the Training May Not Be," *New York Times*, March 1, 2012, available at http://www.nytimes.com/2012/03/02/business/dealbook/state-cutbacks-curb-training-in-jobs-critical-to-economy.html (accessed March 5, 2012).

58. Ben S. Bernanke, "Implications of the Financial Crisis for Economics," speech at the Conference Co-sponsored by the Center for Economic Policy Studies and the Bendheim Center for Finance, Princeton University, September 24, 2010.

Chapter Ten THE WAY FORWARD: ANOTHER WORLD IS POSSIBLE

1. See chapter 1 for a more detailed discussion of the trend.

2. This is one of the major insights of the Nobel Prize–winning economists Franco Modigliani and Merton Miller. For applications to the banking sector, see Joseph E. Stiglitz, "On the Need for Increased Capital
Requirements for Banks and Further Actions to Improve the Safety and
Soundness of America's Banking System: Testimony before the Senate
Banking Committee," August 3, 2011; A. R. Admati, P. M. DeMarzo, M.
F. Hellwig, and P. Pfleiderer, "Fallacies, Irrelevant Facts, and Myths in
the Discussion of Capital Regulation: Why Bank Equity Is Not Expensive," Stanford University Working Paper no. 86, 2010, and the references cited there.

3. The banks are now suggesting that trading derivatives on exchanges
may expose the financial system to more systemic risk, because of the risk
that undercapitalized exchanges will implode. There's an easy answer:
require the exchanges to be adequately capitalized, backed up by joint
and several liability for all those trading on the exchanges. There's no
reason that the risks of those trading in these explosive products should
be shifted to others.

4. New Zealand and the Scandinavian countries are examples of countries that have sought such alternatives with some success. See Marie
Bismark and Ron Paterson, "No-Fault Compensation in New Zealand:
Harmonizing Injury Compensation, Provider Accountability, and Patient
Safety," *Health Affairs* 25, no. 1 (2006): 278–83; and Alan M. Scar-
row, 2008, "Tort Reform: Alternative Models," *Clinical Neurosurgery* 55
(2008): 121–25.

5. The alternative minimum tax—ensuring that the rich paid at least a
certain minimum rate on their income—was not a bad idea; but the way
it was structured was flawed, because it added complexity and eventually
brought into its net not just the very wealthy but many ordinary Americans as well.

6. See the fuller discussion in chapters 2 and 3 and Thomas Piketty,
Emmanuel Saez, and Stefanie Stantcheva, "Optimal Taxation of Top
Labor Incomes: A Tale of Three Elasticities," NBER Working Paper
17616, 2011, available at http://www.nber.org/papers/w17616; and Peter
Diamond and Emmanuel Saez, "The Case for a Progressive Tax: From

Basic Research to Policy Recommendations," *Journal of Economic Perspectives* 25, no. 4 (2011): 165–90. As we noted earlier, President Obama has endorsed the "Buffett rule," the notion that the tax system, at a minimum, should be progressive, with those at the top paying at least as high a rate as other Americans.

7. Because taxes on rents are nondistortionary, taxes on income derived (at least to some extent) from rents should be higher. See, e.g., Partha Dasgupta and J. E. Stiglitz, "Differential Taxation, Public Goods, and Economic Efficiency," *Review of Economic Studies* 38, no. 2 (April 1971): 151–74. To the extent that we can target rents in our tax on higher-income individuals, there is in fact no adverse effect: the only difference is that the public will be compensated a little more for the costs that these monopolists impose on them.

8. In chapter 6 we noted a peculiar feature of our tax system: capital gains (largely) escape taxation when assets are passed on to heirs. That fact distorts behavior. Eliminating this provision (called step up of basis) would create both a fairer and a more efficient tax system. Conservatives harp on the adverse effects on small businesses and farms. As we noted earlier (chapter 6), the vast, vast majority of small businesses fall well below currently discussed thresholds for the estate tax ($5 million for a single individual or, effectively, $10 million for a married couple). In addition, there are provisions that allow the payment of the estate tax to be spread over many years, so that there will be no or minimal interruption to the conduct of the business. Additionally, the statistics show that the top 10 percent of income earners account for nearly 98 percent of all estate tax returns; the top 1 percent account for 35 percent all by themselves. See Leonard E. Burman, Katherine Lim, and Jeffrey Rohaly, "Back from the Grave: Revenue and Distributional Effects of Reforming the Federal Estate Tax," Urban Brookings Tax Policy Center, October 20, 2008, available at http://www.taxpolicycen ter.org/UploadedPDF/411777_back_grave.pdf (accessed February 28, 2012). In 2009, a year in which the exemption was lower than it is now, it is estimated that just 1.6 percent of all farms had to pay an estate tax. See Ron Durst, "Federal Tax Policies and Farm Households," *USDA Economic Information Bulletin*, no. 54, May 2009, p. 15, available at http://www.ers.usda.gov/Publications/EIB54/EIB54.pdf (accessed February 28, 2012). It has been estimated that a mere 1.3 percent of all taxable estates are small businesses or farms. See "The Estate Tax:

Myths and Realities," Center on Budget and Policy Priorities, February 23, 2009, available at http://www.cbpp.org/files/estatetaxmyths.pdf (accessed February 28, 2012).

9. For an interesting discussion, see Steven Brill, *Class Warfare: Inside the Fight to Fix America's Schools* (New York: Simon and Schuster, 2011).

10. The distinctive aspect of these is that they increase homeowner *equity*, rather than encouraging debt, the peculiar feature of current tax programs.

11. On June 28, 2012, the Supreme Court ruled in favor of the mandate—requiring all individuals to purchase insurance—but gave states greater discretion in opting out of the expanded Medicaid program that was central in extending coverage to the uninsured. At this point, it is not clear how many states will take advantage of this to deny some of their citizens access.

12. It did set up a process that, in the long run, may lead to a more efficient health care system, though it did not directly attack the two major sources of inefficiencies discussed below, or at least didn't do so as much as it could and should have.

13. In January 2013, the longer extensions of federal unemployment insurance are set to lapse, leaving some 2 million Americans without coverage.

14. See J. E. Stiglitz, *Making Globalization Work* (New York: W. W. Norton, 2006).

15. As in all areas of tax and regulatory policy, circumvention is a problem, and a key challenge for government is to outsmart such attempts by corporations.

16. See U.S. Census Bureau website, "U.S. International Trade in Goods and Services Highlights," February 10, 2012, http://www.census.gov/indicator/www/ustrade.html (accessed March 6, 2012).

17. In the 1990s, we maintained a trade deficit and full employment, even with a government surplus; but the circumstances were unusual—an investment burst fueled by a stock market bubble (the tech bubble). And it was not sustainable. In chapter 8 we explained how one could stimulate the economy even within the confines of a limited budget deficit, but the politics of what is required (under current circumstances) may make even this unachievable.

18. Part of the reason for the trade imbalances is the role of the United States as a reserve currency. Others want to hold dollars as backing for

their country and their currency. The consequences is that we are exporting T-bills (U.S. short-term bonds), rather than automobiles. Exporting T-bills, however, doesn't create jobs. In spite of global recognition of the anachronistic system—it makes no sense for the United States to play such a disproportionate role in the global monetary system in the multipolar world of the twenty-first century—the Obama administration has resisted change, partially out of worry that if the United States was not the reserve currency, it would be more difficult to borrow so cheaply. But the United States pays a high price for this exorbitant privilege. See United Nations, 2009, "Report of the Commission of Experts of the President of the United Nations General Assembly on Reforms of the International Monetary and Financial System" (also known as the Stiglitz Commission) New York: United Nations, September 2009, published as *The Stiglitz Report* (New York: New Press, 2010); and Stiglitz, *Making Globalization Work*, chap. 9.

19. Here's one suggestion proposed by Warren Buffett. For every dollar of exports, the government could issue an import "chit." Importers could import only if they had the appropriate number of chits. If importers wanted to import more than exporters succeeded in exporting, the price of chits would rise, until demand equaled supply: a market mechanism for restoring trade balance, and helping restore the U.S. economy to full employment. International trade rules are sufficiently complex that it is often difficult to ascertain what is or is not allowed. Thus, there is some debate about whether or under what circumstances this proposal is consistent with WTO rules. See Buffett, "America's Growing Trade Deficit Is Selling the Nation Out from Under Us. Here's a Way to Fix the Problem—And We Need to Do It Now," *Fortune*, October 26, 2003, available at http://www.berkshirehathaway.com/letters/grow ing.pdf (accessed March 6, 2012).

20. See chapter 8 and the references cited there.

21. Ann Harrison (UC Berkeley and NBER) and Jason Scorse (Monterey Institute of International Studies) report, similarly, that the combination of antisweatshop activism plus a minimum wage led to a more than 50 percent increase in real wages for unskilled workers in foreign plants. Interestingly, while activism had an impact on wages, it had no adverse effect on employment. "Multinationals and Anti-Sweatshop Activism" http://www.econ.ucdavis.edu/seminars/papers/146/1461.pdf.

22. Alexander J. Field, *A Great Leap Forward: 1930s Depression and U.S. Economic Growth* (New Haven: Yale University Press, 2011).

23. They are called "GSE," government-sponsored enterprises, because they were originally started by the government. They had long been turned over to the private sector—Fannie Mae in 1968—but the government took them over in the midst of the financial crisis.
24. Or in which they hold a substantial fraction, through their holdings of securities.
25. Chapter 4 defined the concept of a "public good" in the technical sense in which economists use that term—something from which everyone benefits. Because everyone benefits, whether he pays for the good or not, everyone is tempted to let others pay for the good—which is referred to as being a free rider. That's why such goods *have* to be publicly provided if they are to be provided in adequate supply.
26. Some restraints remained—such as that contributions to Super-Political Action Committees (Super-Pacs) could not be directly coordinated with the campaign committees of candidates.
27. From Walter Dean Burnham, "Democracy in Peril: The American Turnout Problem and the Path to Plutocracy," Roosevelt Institute Working Paper no. 5, December 1, 2010. Data for Australia refer to maximum poll over the period 1975 to 1996; for the United States, for the somewhat longer period 1974–2008.
28. For instance, in systems where representation in Congress (parliament) are proportional to the total vote garnered in a state. Some countries have a mix of "district" representatives (as we have) and proportional representation.
29. Adam Smith understood as much. See his *The Theory of Moral Sentiments* (1759), published in 2000 by Prometheus Books, in Amherst, NY. See also Emma Rothschild and Amartya Sen, "Adam Smith's Economics," *The Cambridge Companion to Adam Smith* (Cambridge: Cambridge University Press, 2006), pp. 319–65, especially the discussion of the commonwealth beginning on p. 347.

INDEX

Abed, Fazle Hasan, 246
Acacia Research Corporation, 254
Accenture, 457
advertising, 184, 427, 442, 450
 see also marketing
affirmative action, 353
Affordable Health Care Act (Obama-
 care), xiv
Afghanistan, 179, 220, 261, 262, 264,
 273
Africa, 29, 50
African Americans:
 discrimination against, 85, 86,
  88–89, 162, 387, 389, 393, 418,
  465, 468
 disenfranchisement of, xxii, 438, 443
 wealth of, 17, 88–89, 419, 485
agriculture:
 government subsidies in, xxx, 64, 80,
  225, 407, 415, 479
 in Great Depression, 71, 290, 292
AIG, 44, 61, 84, 225, 316–17, 468
airlines, deregulation of, 404
air traffic controllers, xxxvii, 81
Alien Torts Statute, 74–75
Ally, 473

Alperovitz, Gar, 98
alternative minimum tax, 498
American Airlines, 405
American Tobacco Company, 404
Andreessen, Marc, 405
Angelides, Phil, 471
antiglobalization movement, xli, 347
Apple, xvi, 254, 370, 457
Arab Spring, xxxvii–xxxviii, xliii, 360
Archer Daniels Midland (ADM), 64,
 407
Argentina, bank bailout in, 214
Arnall, Roland, 424
Arnault, Bernard, xxviii
Asia, 80, 197
 financial crisis in, 76, 226, 290, 447,
  448
asymmetric globalization, 347, 352
AT&T, 55, 254, 404
Atkinson, Anthony B., lv
auction theory, 62
austerity, xxvi, xxvii, xxviii, 259, 264,
 276, 288–95
Australia, 6, 17, 22, 24, 27, 169, 231,
 232, 358
autoworkers, 84

bailouts, *see* government, U.S., bank bailouts by; *individual countries*
balanced-budget multiplier, 272, 273, 479
Bangladesh, microcredit schemes in, 246–47
bankers:
    bonuses for, xxxix, xliv, 26, 98–99, 177, 212, 307, 309, 338, 406, 423, 460
    criminal prosecution of, xlv–xlvi, 88, 149, 249, 257, 471, 472
    economic influence of, liv–lv, 99–100, 300
    private incentives of, 41, 42, 109, 112, 120, 137
    risky behavior by, xxiv, xl, liv–lv, 45–46, 112, 126, 137, 214, 248, 300, 308, 309, 337, 339, 428, 489
    see also corporations; financial markets; financial sector
Bank of America, 88, 473
bankruptcy:
    corporate, xvi, xxiv, 38, 45, 399
    derivatives claims in, 61, 339
    government regulation of, 38
    personal, 12, 345, 384
    reform of, 72, 365
    student debt in, x, 72, 118, 244, 245, 332, 339, 340, 365, 411, 469–70
    see also Chapter 11; foreclosures
bankruptcy law, 242–47, 252, 253, 338, 339–40, 356
Bardeen, John, 51
Bartel, Larry, lvi
Basov, Nikolay, 401
Bear Stearns, 491
Belarus, 17
Belgium, 24, 27, 358
Berlusconi, Silvio, 443
Bernanke, Ben, 310, 315, 322, 492
Berners-Lee, Tim, 51
Bhutan, 153, 398
Bilmes, Linda, 220
Bipartisan Policy Center, 259
Bischoff, Kendra, 94
BlackBerry, 254

Blankfein, Lloyd, 155
Bloomberg, Michael, xliii
bondholders, 210–11, 300, 326, 327
bonds, municipal, xxxi, 265–66, 478
Bowles, Erskine, 259
Bowles-Simpson Deficit Reduction Commission, 259, 277–78, 480, 481
Brattain, Walter, 51
Brazil, xxx, 6–7, 63, 311
    economic growth in, 174, 381, 448
Bridgestone/Firestone, 130
British Petroleum (BP), xlviii, 124, 237, 465, 474
Buffett, Warren, xii, 97, 225, 337, 367, 424, 499, 501
"Buffett rule," 499
Burnham, Walter Dean, 163
Bush, George W., xxxi, 89, 91, 92, 108, 109–10, 122, 126, 142, 211, 221, 261, 265, 277, 285, 420, 457, 485
Bush administration, xliv, 209, 211, 214, 222
business:
    anticompetitive behavior in, 54–59, 404, 405–6
    corruption in, 221
    government partnerships with, 218
    government regulation of, 58–59
    innovations in, 44, 51, 58, 97–98, 120–21, 223–24, 400, 401
    political power of, 58–59, 62, 64, 77, 119, 124, 126, 138, 165–66, 169, 171, 357–58, 406, 407, 414, 445
    teamwork in, 141, 436
    trust in, 152–53
    see also corporations; financial sector
business, small, 76, 209, 282, 283, 302, 307, 499

California, x
California, electricity market liberalization in, 222
campaign finance, xvii, xxii, 46, 59, 165–66, 170, 203, 245, 250–51, 258, 357–58, 406, 414, 444–45, 473, 502

Canada, 6, 22, 24, 231
capital, 74, 412
    social, 153–54, 156, 157, 169
capital controls, 76, 227, 228, 347, 448
capital gains, xvi, xvii, xxxi, 89–90, 109,
    110, 143, 265, 343, 372, 380, 402,
    420, 458, 478, 499
capitalism, xvi
Cardoso, Fernando Henrique, 6
Carter, Jimmy, 89
Cayman Islands, 338
cell phones, 122, 123, 254, 344
Census Bureau, U.S., 33, 389
Central Intelligence Agency (CIA), 262
Chait, Jonathan, 23, 145–46
Chapter 11, 356, 399, 460
    see also bankruptcy
Chavez, Hugo, 49
Cheney, Richard, 126
Chicago school, 55–56, 58, 321, 404,
    494
child care, 13, 384
Chile, 176, 323
China, xxx, 24, 67, 80, 311, 350
    economic strength of, 180, 219
    inflation in, 325
Citibank, 255, 468, 489
cities, community segregation in, 94–95
Citizens United v. Federal Election Com-
    mission, xvii, 165, 170, 357, 445
civil rights, 166, 198
class warfare, 225, 279
Clayton Holdings, 472
Clinton, Bill, xxxi, 89, 109, 124, 142,
    220, 224, 420, 489
Clinton administration, 60, 62, 205,
    225, 312, 456
Coakley, Martha, 251
Coase, Ronald, 237
cognitive capture, 59–60, 125, 202, 312
cognitive framing, see framing, cognitive
Colbert, Jean-Baptiste, 40
colleges, x, 24, 392–93
    tuition and, 366
Commission on the Measurement of
    Economic Performance and Social
    Progress, lxii, 232, 388, 431, 441

Commission on Wartime Contracting in
    Iraq and Afghanistan, 220
communism, failure of, 130, 154, 197,
    204, 226, 373
competition:
    excess profits and, 43–44, 45, 53
    in globalization, 75, 177, 178
    government regulation of, xlii, 38, 39,
        44, 45, 48, 50, 55, 58–59, 72, 112,
        220, 334, 337, 338–39
    imperfect, 42, 43
    see also monopolies
confirmatory bias, 188, 190
Congress, U.S., 75, 107, 242, 276, 316,
    328, 360, 397, 404, 408
    corporate influence in, 60–61, 62,
        119, 124, 242, 357
    lobbying in, 60, 119, 231, 413
    tax legislation in, 110, 314, 475–76
    see also House of Representatives,
        U.S.; Senate, U.S.
Congressional Budget Office (CBO),
    261
Congressional Oversight Panel, 241
consumerism, 130–32, 433
consumer protection, 171, 220, 240,
    241, 247
contracts, 247, 340
Cordray, Richard, 468
corporate governance laws, 39, 47, 48,
    50, 72, 82–85, 109, 139, 338, 339
"corporate welfare," 224–26, 340–42
corporations, xlviii, 114, 125–26, 184,
    442
    deregulation in, 112, 127, 222–23
    dishonest accounting in, 109,
        137–38, 339
    dividend payments by, 110, 265
    economic influence of, liv–lv
    executive compensation in, xv, 4, 26,
        39, 50, 52, 82, 83–84, 98–99, 109,
        136, 137, 138–39, 192–93, 339,
        379, 394–96, 403, 418, 423
    government munificence toward, 50,
        60–64, 122, 124, 170, 225–26,
        236, 239, 262–64, 268, 269–70,
        278, 281, 286, 340–42

corporations (*continued*)
  idea-shaping by, 184, 189, 201, 224
  legal advantages of, 83, 165–66, 237,
    239, 253, 341, 473–74
  patent control by, 54, 253–54
  risk-taking by, xlviii, 124, 236–37, 432
  shareholder influence in, 39, 83, 84,
    169, 339, 357, 418
  taxation of, xxviii, 77, 92, 119, 143,
    178, 225, 268, 269, 277–79, 281,
    338, 341, 343, 348, 354, 379,
    421–22
  as tax shelters, 91–92, 338, 379
  see also business
Council of Economic Advisers, 124,
    138, 218, 225, 231, 420, 489
credit default swaps (CDSes), 58, 310,
    320
creditworthiness, 72, 134
Crick, Francis, 51
crime, 18–19, 87, 95, 387, 388
Cuba, 17
Cyprus, xxv

Daly, Lew, 98
debit cards, 413
debt:
  international, xxix, 173–74
  U.S., 259, 271, 272, 274–75
  see also bankruptcy; credit default
    swaps (CDSes); deficit reduction;
    foreclosures; predatory lending;
    student loans
debt ceiling, 259, 476
Declaration of Independence, 198
Deepwater Horizon disaster, 237
Defense Department, U.S., 262
defense industry, government procure-
    ment in, 50, 127, 220, 262–64,
    281, 340
deficit, U.S., 142, 144, 224, 260–64,
    314, 349, 350, 420, 432, 484
"deficit fetishism," 272
deficit reduction, 259–90, 297, 321,
    350, 477
  expenditure implications of, 116–17,
    144, 272

Right's insistence on, 271–72, 287–88
  strategies for, 264–70, 280–81,
    286–87, 295, 296
democracy, U.S., 148–82
  corruption in, 166, 179, 202, 250–51
  diminishing confidence in, xli, 151,
    160, 161–62, 164, 166, 167, 169,
    179–81, 313–18, 360
  disenfranchisement in, 162–69, 438
  globalization and, 173–81
  ideological battle over, 195, 203
  media's role in, 160–62, 170, 204,
    316, 358
  trust and, 157–58
  weakening of, 171–72, 178
  see also politics, U.S.
Democratic Party, U.S., xvii, xxii, 145,
    146, 159, 163, 443, 454
Denmark, 22–23, 229, 486–87
derivatives, xxiii, 44–45, 53, 61, 97,
    274, 308, 309, 316, 320, 337, 338,
    339, 399, 408, 489, 494, 498
developing world, xl, 20, 177, 197, 292,
    362
  financial sector's influence in,
    226–28
  inflation in, 325, 496
  labor in, 79, 80, 415, 501
Dexia, 321, 491, 493
Diamond, Peter, 407
Dingell, John, 489
Dirksen, Everett, 122
discrimination, 66, 85–89, 251, 353, 452
discriminatory equilibrium, 191
disenfranchisement, 162–64, 168–69,
    183, 443–44, 445
  backlash against, xxii
disinflation, 326, 329
"dissaving," 292
dividends, 90, 110, 265, 478
Dodd-Frank bill, 149, 171, 241, 309,
    337, 491
Donovan, Shaun, 459

earned-income tax credit, 93, 347
East Asia financial crisis, 76, 289, 447,
    448

East India Company, 54, 453
Economic Mobility Project, 22, 24
Economic Policy Institute, 24
economics:
  behavioral, 141, 186, 189, 191, 452
  collective action in, 116
  confidence in, 290
  development, 127
  discrimination theories in, 85–87
  distribution of endowments in, 38
  efficiency in, xxxix–xl, 42, 43, 44,
    70–71, 75, 78, 158, 460
  externalities in, 42, 217, 235–36,
    237–38, 321, 403
  game theory in, 55, 86
  idea-shaping in, 184, 186–203
  information asymmetries in, 42, 55,
    86, 217, 321–22
  perceptions in, 201–2, 230
  Right's view of, liii, 31–33, 55, 133,
    134, 135, 142, 144, 145, 190, 194,
    197, 202, 204, 209, 217, 369
  standard model of, lvii–lviii, 37, 41,
    55–56, 58, 66, 82, 97, 141, 158,
    184, 187, 188, 228–30, 304, 321,
    326, 334
  supply-side, 277, 281–82, 295, 354
  trade-offs in, 299, 331
  trickle-down, xvi, 8–9, 78, 193, 353
  see also financial markets
Economist, xi, xv, 371
economy, U.S.:
  alternative frameworks for, lii–liii, liv,
    110–11, 194, 330, 331
  bubbles in, xvi, 68, 106, 108–9,
    110–11, 229, 265, 323–24,
    327–28, 340, 478, 494–95
  conventional view of, liv, 7, 8, 31–32,
    33, 115, 133, 190, 228–30, 287,
    323, 335, 373
  demand in, 70, 71, 106–7, 108–12,
    113, 282, 288–89, 296, 303, 313,
    329, 354, 426
  Gini coefficient in, 28–29, 387, 395,
    396
  global influence of, 179–81
  gross domestic product in, 19, 78,
    104, 121, 123–24, 131, 228–32,
    264, 269, 273–74, 293–94, 335
  gross national product in, 228–32
  growth in, 5, 7, 8, 27, 30, 115, 125,
    146, 180, 197, 220, 223, 271,
    296–97, 330, 335, 349, 353–54,
    381, 428
  idea-shaping and, 185, 189–90, 194,
    204–24, 228–32, 278–79, 295,
    321–30
  inefficiency in, xxxix–xl, xliv, l–li, liii,
    7, 72, 104, 105, 106, 111, 112,
    113, 115–32, 134, 146, 206–7,
    259–60, 334
  inflation in, 302, 324–26
  instability in, 6, 106–15, 146, 207,
    220, 301, 308, 318, 323, 330, 340,
    428
  monopolies in, 52, 54–59
  myths in, 281–95
  politics' linkage with, xxxix–xl, l–li, lvi,
    42–43, 48, 58–59, 66, 73–74, 82,
    112, 149, 165, 169, 173, 189, 217,
    333, 359, 361, 442
  privatization in, 221–23, 284, 285
  productivity in, xix–xx, 63, 67–68, 70,
    78, 82, 84–85, 98, 113, 115–32,
    135, 142, 143, 144, 146, 156, 157,
    159, 354, 428, 486
  reform in, 335, 336–37
  saving in, 1, 16–17, 49, 88, 89, 107,
    110, 215, 292, 305, 420, 481, 484
  size of, 496
  stimulus for, 107, 264, 271–74,
    290–93, 296
  structural changes in, 67, 70, 291–
    92, 294–95, 329, 346, 356–57
  unfairness in, xxxviii–xxxiv, xxxix, xli,
    xliv, l, liii, 2–3, 8–9, 143, 146,
    159–60, 167, 168, 179, 180, 212,
    217, 218, 237, 239–40, 256, 299,
    305, 306–7, 334, 336, 442
  see also financial markets
Ecuador, 162
education, xx, xxii, 8–9, 140, 179, 200,
    201, 202
  cost of, 71, 94, 118, 344–45

education (*continued*)
    government support for, 6, 18, 94,
        105, 116, 127, 135, 144, 194, 245,
        271, 329, 334, 344, 351, 353, 354
    inequality in, xv, xliii, 24–25, 38,
        85, 86, 94, 118, 127, 135, 200,
        392–93, 410
    labor supply and, 48, 67, 69, 100
    life expectancy and, xiii, 368
    nutrition and, 128, 393
    parental circumstances' effect on,
        xxxii, 22, 24, 94, 95, 118, 135,
        367, 392–93
    poor and, xxx, 24–25, 38, 49, 94,
        118, 128
    standard of living and, xii
    states' funding of, 244, 329, 388
    see also student loans
Egypt, 173, 372
Einstein, Albert, 51
Eisenhower, Dwight, 463
elderly:
    health insurance and, xix
    population growth of, xxix, 350
    poverty among, 21, 32, 93, 285, 391
    retirement income of, xix, 221–22,
        305
    Social Security protection of, xix, xxxiv
elections, U.S., 168, 213, 315
    see also campaign finance; politics,
        U.S.; voting
emerging markets, 67, 180, 226, 292,
    485
employment, 63, 87, 94, 95, 236, 264
    globalization and, xvi
    parental circumstances' effect on, 22,
        95, 392
    restoring, xx, 278, 282, 322, 349–52,
        356, 357, 481, 501
    see also labor; unemployment
energy industry, 63
    corporate recklessness in, xlviii, 124,
        236–37, 432, 473–74
    and global warming, xlviii, 201
    lobbying by, 119, 231, 430
    rent seeking by, 50, 61–62, 124, 340,
        465

    subsidies to, 225, 236, 268, 465
Enlightenment, 37, 196
Enron, 222–23
entitlements, middle-class, 284
environment:
    costs to, 123–24, 125, 231, 236–37,
        341, 432, 473–74
    "Green GDP" accounts and, 231
    protection of, 153, 177, 222, 223,
        230, 231, 237, 271, 355
    see also global warming; resources
environmental justice movement, 230,
    393
equilibrium, discriminatory, 191
equilibrium fictions, 188, 197, 452, 454
Ericcson, 254
estate taxes, 91, 96, 110, 208–10, 343,
    458, 499
ethanol subsidy, 63–64, 226, 408
euro, x, xxvii, 275–76, 494
    crisis, xxx
Europe, xxv–xxx, 69, 132, 177, 195,
    350, 358
    declining wages in, xxviii
    economic mobility in, 22, 146, 332
    financial crisis in, 30, 173–74, 177,
        228, 274, 275–76, 289–90, 295,
        319–21, 467, 482, 492–94
    globalization's effect in, 79, 80
    inequality in, xxix, xliii, 6, 29
    inflation in, 301, 319, 324, 496
    politics in, xxviii
    unemployment in, 349, 372
European Central Bank (ECB), 174,
    228, 275, 311, 319–20, 493–94,
    496
European Commission, 268
eurozone, xxv, xxvi, xxvii
exchange rates, 350–51
extrinsic rewards, 139–40
Exxon, xlviii, 201
Exxon Valdez, 474

fairness:
    changing views of, 84, 185, 191–95,
        440–41
    economists' perceptions of, 201

importance of, xliv, 143, 146,
158–60, 169, 204, 268, 334
fairness, in income distribution, xx
fairness, in labor, 129–30, 159
Fannie Mae, 198, 356, 452, 460, 502
Federal Bureau of Investigation (FBI),
247, 471
Federal Communications Commission
(FCC), 59, 427
Federal Deposit Insurance Corporation
(FDIC), 310
Federal Reserve, monetary policies of, xi
Federal Reserve, U.S., 88, 306–11,
312–19, 321–30, 334
appointees to, 59–60, 166, 312–13,
407, 491
bank lending by, 46, 61, 305, 306–7
financial sector's favoring by, 46, 61,
305, 306–11, 314–18, 323, 331,
413, 488
monetary policies of, 106, 108,
110–11, 166, 222, 260–61, 293,
300, 304–6, 310, 313, 314, 315,
318, 321–30, 349, 481, 484, 487,
492, 495
Open Market Committee of, 315
oversight of, 314, 315
political nature of, 313–14, 315
regulatory position of, 308, 309, 310,
489, 491
Ferguson, Thomas, lv
Fields, Alex, 354
filibusters, 166, 358, 445
Financial Accounting Standards Board,
138
Financial Crisis Inquiry Commission,
see Angelides, Phil; National
Commission on the Causes of the
Financial and Economic Crisis in
the United States
financial crisis of 2008, xxvi, xxx, xxxi,
xxxix, xliv, xlvii, xlix, liv, 1–2, 3, 16,
41, 61, 76, 97, 98, 114, 190, 194,
208, 210–12, 214, 218, 219, 225,
291, 308, 319, 326, 400
causes of, xl, 41, 43, 46, 61, 113,
219–20, 323, 331

criminal prosecution for, xlv–xlvi, 88,
149, 249, 471, 472
economic situation prior to, 67, 106
see also Great Recession; subprime
crisis
financial markets:
deregulation of, xxxi–xxxii, 6, 61, 75,
101, 112–15, 127, 190, 197, 220,
222, 227–28, 300, 308–11, 312,
323, 489
distributive impact of, 217–18
equilibrium fictions in, 191, 219
failures in, xxxix–xliii, xlvii, xlviii, 7,
42, 51, 112, 134–35, 216, 302,
372, 399
globalization in, 74–76, 175,
177–78, 226–28, 347, 350–51,
413, 414
government regulation of, xxvii, xxx,
xlii, l, li, lii–liii, 35, 42, 44, 45, 46,
47–48, 50, 55, 59–60, 100, 109,
149, 171, 177–78, 190, 194, 213,
216, 223–24, 241, 309, 310, 313,
337–38, 413, 467, 491
ideological perceptions of, 193, 194,
196, 198, 204–8, 216–24, 233,
321–30, 399, 404, 452
information asymmetries in, 45–46,
138, 155, 206–8, 399, 491
international debt in, 174
legal underpinnings of, 53
price discovery in, 206
transparency in, 44–45, 309, 337,
493
see also bankers; business; economy,
U.S.; stock market
financial sector, 61, 109–10, 211–12,
213, 274, 283–84, 285–86, 483
abusive credit card practices in, xx,
46, 50, 112, 113, 120, 122–23,
149, 155, 205, 300, 308, 337, 338,
344, 400
anticompetitive behavior in, 43–45,
58–59, 309, 337, 338–39, 405–6;
see also monopolies
criminal behavior in, 248, 249, 251,
255–57, 471, 472

financial sector (*continued*)
  Federal Reserve's favoring of, 46, 61,
    305, 306–11, 314–18, 323, 331,
    413, 488
  government bailouts in, xxvi, xliv, 45,
    76, 93, 126, 194, 208–12, 214,
    215, 220, 225, 241, 248–49, 267,
    292–94, 306–7, 316, 323, 337,
    413, 458, 459
  government lending to, 46, 61, 137,
    304, 306–7
  growth of, 99–101, 301, 308–11, 339
  hidden subsidies to, 278, 279, 300,
    309, 490
  incentive pay in, 98–99, 109, 137,
    434–35
  international influence of, 226–28,
    233
  legal system's favoring of, 239–53,
    255–57
  moral deprivation in, xlvii–xlviii, liv–
    lv, 46–47, 88, 247, 252, 401
  political power of, 43, 46, 51, 60–61,
    76, 169, 171, 240–41, 242, 251,
    253, 406, 407, 413, 430
  predatory lending by, xx, xxvi, xlvii,
    46, 50, 73, 88, 113, 149, 155,
    239–41, 242–43, 247, 252–53,
    300, 308, 312, 338, 400, 424, 468
  purpose of, 78, 120, 178, 220, 352,
    400
  ratings agencies in, 240, 272, 275
  rent seeking by, 45–48, 50, 51, 208,
    338
  risky behavior by, xxvi
  securities fraud in, 255–57
  student loan practices in, 118,
    244–45, 252, 411, 469–70
  taxes on, 267–68, 269, 309, 310
  trust in, 155, 439
  undercapitalization in, 309, 321, 489
  see also bankers
Finland, 22, 24
fiscal policy, 349, 357
  see also government, U.S., macroeco-
    nomic policies of

flash trading, 207
food stamps, 93, 264, 347, 390
Forbes, 51, 52
foreclosures, xxxix, xli, xliv, 1, 12, 16, 29,
    212–13, 247–53, 340, 375, 386,
    458, 460, 468, 473, 490
  see also mortgage restructuring; sub-
    prime crisis
foreign policy, U.S., 126
"47% of Americans" quote (Romney),
    xviii, xxii
framing, cognitive, 186–88, 200, 204,
    232–33, 456
France, 22, 27, 121–22, 229, 232, 267,
    446, 486–87
Freddie Mac, 198, 356, 460
"free banking" concept, 323
free riders, xix, 357
Friedman, Milton, 55, 197, 321–22,
    323, 404, 494
Friedman, Stephen, 491
FUD, 57

G-8, 180
G-20, 180, 232
Galbraith, Jamie, 101
Galbraith, John Kenneth, 160
game theory, 55, 86
Gates, Bill, 52, 401
GE, 278, 421
Geithner, Tim, 59
General Motors, xvi
George, Henry, 266
Georgia, 240, 467
Germany, 22, 29, 267, 288, 324, 350,
    446, 486–87
gerrymandering, 166, 169, 358
Gettysburg Address, 172
Ghana, 329
GI Bill, xxxii, 6, 69
Gilded Age, xii, xxxiv
Gini coefficient, 28–29, 387, 395, 396
Glass-Steagall Act, 112–13, 489
globalization, xxiii–xxx, 73–80, 99, 100,
    196, 231, 324, 325
  asymmetric, 347, 352

competition in, xxxii, 75, 177, 178
democracy and, 173–81
drawbacks of, 75, 78, 79–80, 178,
    413
employment and, xvi
financial, 74–76, 175, 177–78,
    226–28, 347, 350–51, 413, 414
inequality and, 75, 79–80, 99, 101,
    175, 178, 181
labor and, xxxii, 69–70, 75, 77, 79,
    81, 101, 292, 347, 348, 351–52,
    413, 414
management of, xlii, 77, 80, 101,
    172, 178, 180, 181, 347–48
taxes and, 77, 79, 178, 348
technology and, xxxii
Globalization and Its Discontents (Stig-
    litz), 76, 226
global warming, xl, xlii, 180, 201, 434
see also environment
Golden Rule (Ferguson), lv
Goldman Sachs, 76, 155, 256, 317,
    448, 491
Google, 219, 254
government, U.S.:
    bank bailouts by, xxvi, xliv, 45, 60,
        76, 93, 126, 194, 208–12, 214,
        215, 220, 225, 241, 248–49, 267,
        292–93, 306–7, 316, 323, 337,
        413, 458, 459
    budget cuts in, 259, 271, 276–77,
        283–86, 287, 288–95
    budget of, 259–97
    collective action through, 103, 116,
        133, 146, 152, 157, 352–53
    ideological perceptions of, 117, 194,
        196–97, 198, 216–24, 232–33,
        321–30, 452
    inequality-supporting policies of, xvii,
        7, 35, 39, 40, 66, 72–73, 93, 95,
        96–97, 99, 101, 102, 192
    investment by, 28, 49, 101, 105, 110,
        115–17, 127, 142, 144, 194, 218,
        271–74, 288, 291–92, 329, 334,
        342, 350, 351, 353–54, 482
    litigation by, 255–56

macroeconomic policies of, 47, 78,
    80, 100, 103, 107, 127, 166, 282,
    289, 290, 296, 297, 298–331, 349,
    479, 495
market regulation by, xxxi–xxxii, xlii,
    l, li, lii–liii, 6, 35, 42–43, 44, 45,
    46, 47–48, 54–55, 59–60, 61, 75,
    100, 101, 109, 112–15, 127, 149,
    171, 177–78, 190, 213, 216, 220,
    222–24, 241, 308–11, 313, 323,
    337–38, 413, 467, 489, 491
media's relationship with, 160, 170,
    316
military spending by, 50, 127, 220,
    261–64, 271, 273, 281, 432
munificence of, 40, 50, 52, 60–64,
    122, 124, 126, 170, 216, 220,
    225–26, 236, 239, 262–64, 267,
    268, 269–70, 278, 281, 286,
    340–42
research funded by, 98, 116–17, 127,
    218, 271, 354, 428–29
size of, 117, 194, 196, 270, 276, 296,
    314, 321, 322
social spending by, 2, 7, 17, 18,
    20–21, 32, 80, 93, 96, 99, 105,
    106, 107–8, 135, 216, 261, 263,
    264, 270, 283–87, 290, 297,
    346–47, 382, 463, 481
see also politics, U.S.
government procurement, 50, 61, 127,
    220, 262, 281
Great Depression, 6, 71, 112, 196, 197,
    220, 289, 290, 292, 322, 335, 484,
    487, 494
Great Recession, xi, 63, 88, 149, 206,
    225, 244–45, 283, 284, 294
    causes of, 247, 252, 316, 350
    deficit consequences of, 259, 263–64
    effects of, 1–2, 11–21, 34, 103, 114,
        247, 299, 346, 359, 453, 484
    ideological interpretations of, 197,
        198, 201, 219
    jobless recovery from, 306, 331
    labor outcomes of, 71, 81, 156,
        302–3, 313, 385, 481, 482

Great Recession (*continued*)
  monetary policy in, 301, 322
  profit-making in, 36, 84, 137, 302
  resource waste in, 113, 302
  savings depleted by, 1, 16–17, 88
  stimulus package in, 107, 264,
    290–93, 296, 483, 484
  wage share in, 36, 71, 81, 84, 418
  worsening of, 272, 288
  see also financial crisis of 2008
Greece, xxv, 27, 178, 371
  financial crisis in, xxviii, 173–74,
    177, 228, 274–75, 290, 319–20,
    403, 493
"Green GDP" accounts, 231
Greenspan, Alan, 59, 110, 260–61, 308,
  310, 314, 323, 476, 489, 490
gross domestic product (GDP), xviii,
  92, 179, 228–32, 260, 264, 269,
  273–74, 277, 289, 293–94, 296,
  298, 335
  Spain's drop in, xxv
  see also economy, U.S., gross domes-
    tic product in
gross national product (GNP), 228–32
Güth, Werner, 158

Hacker, Jacob S., lv
Halliburton Corporation, 126, 262, 340
Hammonds, Tim, 430
Harrison, John, 136
health care, 14, 195, 279, 330
  cost of, 12, 121–22, 136, 333, 342,
    344, 346, 369, 384, 404, 449, 478,
    481
  government assistance with, 17,
    29, 38, 87, 93, 283, 346; *see also*
    Medicare
  inefficiency in, 220, 229, 286, 481,
    500
  inequality in, xiii, xiv
  Obama's reform of, xiv, 17, 204, 346
  poor and, 49
  racial discrimination in, 87, 387
health industry, 119, 121–22, 220
  see also pharmaceutical industry
Hemsley, Stephen, 52

Hewlett-Packard (HP), 254, 457
Hispanics:
  discrimination against, 85, 86, 88,
    418, 468
  wealth of, 17, 419, 485
Holder, Eric, 249
homeownership, 95, 134, 190, 197,
  214–15, 279–80, 480
Hoover, Herbert, 289
House of Representatives, U.S., 116,
  125, 168, 259
  Financial Services Committee of, 171
  see also Congress, U.S.; Senate, U.S.
housing discrimination, 88–89, 393
housing market:
  bubble in, 68, 106, 111, 229,
    239–41, 265, 291, 304, 305, 328,
    478, 490
  collapse of, 3–4, 10, 16, 111, 212,
    248, 280, 357, 375, 378, 386, 397,
    400, 460
  recovery in, 355–56
  see also foreclosures; mortgage
    restructuring; predatory lending;
    subprime crisis
housing subsidies, 93, 371
human rights, 74, 195, 196
Hungary, 27

Iceland, 228
ideas:
  democracy and, 232
  evolution of, 195–99, 200
immigration, 67, 284, 378
imprisonment, 18–19, 87, 387, 388–89
incentive pay, 98–99, 109, 134, 135–42,
  192–93, 204–5, 217, 257, 434–35,
  440–41
income redistribution, 106, 264
  criticisms of, xx, liii, 133
  government's role in, 38, 89–96, 194,
    298–99, 349
  political limitation of, 39, 96
India, 191, 246–47, 311
  Bhopal, 237
Indonesia, bank bailout in, 214
Industrial Revolution, 37, 131, 439

inequality:
  alternative models of, 102–3
  consequences of, xx–xxi, 104–47,
    157, 167–69, 184, 185, 233,
    234–58, 292
  deficit reduction and, 277–81
  determinants of, xl, 35, 38, 41–48,
    99–103, 334, 340, 346
  educational, xliii, 24–25, 38, 85, 94,
    118, 127, 135, 200, 392–93, 410
  efficiency and, 132–45, 146
  in Europe, xxix, xliii, 6, 29
  globalization's effect on, 75, 79–80,
    99, 101, 175, 178, 181
  government's role in, xvii, 7, 35, 38,
    66, 72–73, 93, 95, 96–97, 99, 101,
    102, 184, 192, 216–17, 237, 260
  and health care, xiii, xiv
  historical, 36–37, 423
  income, xxix, xxxii, 2–3, 5, 9–10,
    11–12, 27, 30, 31–34, 36, 37, 65,
    66–72, 89, 90, 96, 99–100, 101,
    106, 108, 159, 192, 223, 230, 253,
    292, 300, 302, 334, 375–77, 379,
    380, 381, 382, 383, 396–97, 418,
    423, 426, 427; see also income
    redistribution
  and instability, 6, 106–15, 146, 301
  in Japan, xxix
  justifications for, 33, 36–37, 97–98,
    102, 193, 195, 369, 434
  lifetime, 32, 133, 397
  macroeconomic factors in, xxv,
    298–331
  markets' effect on, 65–103
  perceptions of, 159, 184–86,
    191–95, 199, 200, 224, 231
  remedies for, 36, 134, 142–47, 266,
    297, 336–37, 359
  rent seeking and, 39–41, 47, 49, 96,
    133, 216, 266
  and social distance, 185, 200
  societal effects of, xlvi–xlvii, li, liii, 2,
    22–23, 24–25, 33–34, 81–82, 95,
    105, 113, 125, 130–32, 147, 416
  societal factors in, 66, 80–89, 102,
    105, 353
  in United Kingdom, xxiii
  vs. community, xxi
inflation, xix, 275, 299, 301–4, 311,
  319, 324–30, 349, 463, 478, 485,
  486, 487, 495, 496, 497
Informant, The, 408
infrastructure, 110, 116, 127, 144, 146,
  194, 271, 334, 354
innovation:
  in business, xvii, 44, 51, 58, 97–98,
    120–21, 223–24, 400, 401
  direction of, 73, 306, 339, 354–55
  patent law and, 54, 254
  scientific, 51, 97–98, 116, 125, 254
insurance industry, 220, 222, 286, 344,
  346
intellectual property, 176, 253–54, 404,
  412, 449, 474–75
  see also patents
interest rates, xi, xxiii, xxiv, xxv, xxvii, 4,
  9, 61, 90, 101, 108, 111, 137, 222,
  260, 261, 272, 294, 302, 304–5,
  306–7, 314, 324, 325, 327, 350,
  355, 481, 484, 485, 487, 488, 496
International Monetary Fund (IMF),
  76, 114–15, 173, 177, 224, 225,
  226–28, 289, 403, 447–48
Internet, 51, 56, 57, 108, 144, 218,
  219, 443, 454
interns, internships, x, 95–96
intrinsic rewards, 139–40
investment:
  globalization and, 75, 92
  private, xvi, 7, 92, 108, 110, 115,
    278, 282, 283, 288, 294, 305, 306,
    354, 426, 483
  public, xx, xxix, 28, 49, 101, 105,
    111, 115–17, 127, 142, 144, 194,
    218, 271–74, 288, 291–92, 329,
    334, 342, 350, 351, 353–54, 482
Iran, 27, 29
Iraq War, 126, 179, 220, 261–63, 264,
  432
Ireland, xxv
Ireland, financial crisis in, 228, 263,
  274, 276, 319, 321
irrigation, 153–54, 411

Israel, 17, 329
Italy, xxv, 22, 232
    financial crisis in, 173, 319, 492–93

Jamaica, 27
Japan, xxviii–xxx, 17, 24, 237, 394
"Japanese malaise," xxix
Jim Crow South, unfairness in, 162
jobs, see employment; unemployment
Jobs, Steve, 51, 401
JPMorgan Chase, 438, 473, 491
judges, 55, 250–51, 473
Justice Department, U.S., 249, 405, 406

Kerry, John, 455
Kessler, David, 453
Keynes, John Maynard, 107, 131, 132,
    189–90, 335
King, Mervyn, 310
Korea, 24, 214, 232
Krueger and Mas, 130
Krugman, Paul, 171

labor, 68–69, 191
    bargaining power of, 77, 81, 347,
        352–53; see also labor unions
    demand for, 47, 48, 67–72, 77, 79
    in developing world, 79, 81, 415, 501
    discrimination in, 85–89
    fairness in, 129–30, 159
    free mobility of, xxviii, 75, 77
    globalization's effect on, xxxii, 69–70,
        75, 77, 79, 81, 101, 292, 347,
        351–52, 413, 414
    Great Recession's effect on, 36, 71,
        81, 84, 114, 156, 290, 302–3, 313,
        481, 482
    macroeconomic policies affecting,
        100, 282, 349
    motivation of, 127, 129
    polarization of, 10–11, 70, 100, 167,
        347
    public-sector, 72, 410
    in recessions, 36, 84–85, 156
    and social capital, 156
    structural changes in, 67, 70,
        291–92, 329, 351–52, 356–57

technology's effect on, xxxii, 67–70,
    79, 99, 100, 347, 351, 355, 426
    women in, 18
    work hours and, 11, 18, 33, 369, 416
    see also employment; unemployment;
    wages
labor unions, xxxii, 47–48, 72, 81, 83,
    84, 99, 100, 352–53, 417
Latin America, 29, 49, 50, 105, 289
Latvia, austerity in, 290
Lauder, Ronald, 90
lawyers, 53, 124–26, 237, 254–55, 431
Lay, Ken, 222
legal system, U.S., 234–58
    alternative frameworks for, 235, 253
    banks' deception in, 248, 249, 251,
        252, 472
    burden of proof in, 250
    contracts in, 247
    corporate advantages in, 83, 165–66,
        237, 239, 255, 341, 473–74
    costs in, 125, 237, 253
    distributive consequences of, 238,
        242, 339, 403, 468
    economic bias in, 55
    Federal Reserve accountability in,
        315–16
    financial crisis prosecution in, xlv–
        xlvi, 88, 149, 249, 471, 472
    financial sector's favoring in, 239–53,
        255–57
    information asymmetries in, 340, 466
    political influence in, 55, 238–39,
        250–51
    property rights in, 237, 243, 247,
        248, 249
    purpose of, 125, 235–39
    reform of, 342
    rent seeking in, 53, 54, 255, 342
    and social responsibility, 152
    unfairness in, 53, 54, 125, 237,
        239–53, 254–55, 258, 466, 472,
        475
Lehman Brothers, 180, 317, 399, 493
Leme, Paulo, 448
Lenin, Vladimir, 449
Lessig, Lawrence, lvi

LG, 254
life expectancy, xiii–xiv, 17, 368,
    386–87
Lincoln, Abraham, 172
List, John, 441
lobbying, 60, 119, 231, 245, 250, 407,
    413, 414, 430
Lockheed Martin, 263
London, 177
London Interbank Offered Rate (Libor),
    xxiii–xxiv, 58
Longitude (Sobel), 136
Louisiana, 237
Lula da Silva, Luiz Inácio, 7, 174, 448
Luxembourg, 229, 358

Malaysia, 17
manufacturing:
    compensation shifts in, 82, 418
    job losses in, 67–68, 70–72, 291–92,
        357, 409
    societal impact of, 196
marginal productivity theory, 37, 41,
    97, 334
marketing, 189, 201, 203, 452–53, 455
Marlboro Man, 189, 450
Marmot, Michael, xiii
marriage, economic insecurity and, 18,
    387
Marshall, Alfred, 128
Marx, Karl, 37, 373
Massachusetts, 251
McCarty, Nolan, lvi
McDonald's, 482
media, 160–62, 168, 170, 200, 204,
    316, 340, 358, 427, 442, 443,
    454
Medicaid, xiv, 17, 286, 347, 478
Medicare, xiv, xix, 21, 61, 122, 184,
    204, 220, 263, 284, 286–87, 333,
    371, 407, 450, 461, 478, 481
Mexico, 20, 52, 80, 173, 221, 462
    bank bailout in, 214
MF Global Holdings, 399
microcredit, 246–47
Microsoft, 52, 55, 56–68, 92, 254, 255,
    404, 405, 406

middle class, xvii–xviii, 67, 147, 172,
    284
    assistance to, 36, 344
    economic insecurity of, xlvii, 15–17,
        29, 33, 128, 332–33
    globalization's effect on, 79, 80
    Great Recession's effect on, 12
    hollowing out of, 2, 11, 31, 47, 105,
        167, 383
    income of, xi–xii, 3–4, 5, 9, 10, 11,
        17, 31, 68, 70, 71–72, 79, 90, 300,
        379, 381, 383, 487
    recovery of, 36, 282
    tax deductions for, 279–80, 480
    unfair policies toward, xlv, liii
    wealth sources of, 3–4, 10, 16–17,
        114, 209
Middle East, 50
    see also Arab Spring
Mill, John Stuart, 466
monetarism, 322, 324
monetary policy, xi, xxv, 106, 108, 110–
    11, 166, 222, 260, 261, 293–94,
    300, 310, 313, 314, 315, 319,
    321–30, 481, 484, 487, 492, 495
    distributive consequences of, 304–6,
        330–31, 349
    idea-shaping in, 321–30
monopolies, xv, 39, 40, 44, 48–59, 119,
    121, 176, 266, 338–39, 343, 344,
    403, 405–6
    game theory and, 55
moral hazard, 214, 287, 320, 459, 460
Mortgage Electronic Registry System
    (MERS), 247–48, 251, 473
mortgage fraud, 248, 252, 471, 472
mortgage restructuring, 212–15, 252,
    356, 458, 459, 460
mortgages, tax deductions for, 279, 480
mortgage securities, 256
Mosaic, 405
motivation, 127, 129, 139
Motorola, 254
Mozilo, Angelo, 424
Mueller, Edward, 52
Mullainathan, Sendhil, 128
municipal bonds, xxxi, 265, 478

322 2 23.23

National Academy of Sciences, 32
National Center for Supercomputing Applications, 405
National Commission on the Causes of the Financial and Economic Crisis in the United States, 453, 454
National Economic Council, 225
negative-sum game paradigm, 41, 49
Netherlands, 24, 27
Netscape, 56–58, 405
New Deal, xxxiv, xlii, 111, 290
Newfoundland, 173
New York Times, xii, 14, 149, 257, 365
New Zealand, 24, 232
Nokia, 254
North American Free Trade Agreement, 176–77
Norway, 27, 28, 229, 276
NTP, Inc., 254
nuclear power, 236, 237

Obama, Barack, xxxviii, 447
  deficit reduction by, 259
  and ethanol subsidy, 63
  Federal Reserve nominees of, 407
  financial crisis response of, xlv, 210, 211, 458
  health care program of, 17, 204, 346
  reelection of, x, xxii
  tax position of, 499
  unemployment and, xxxv
Obama administration, xliv, 84, 213, 214, 251, 312, 356, 459, 501
Obamacare, xiv
Occupy Wall Street, xvii, xxxix–xlii, xlix–lii, 127, 145, 149, 160, 169, 438
"Of the 1%, for the 1%, by the 1%" (Stiglitz), xxxix
oil industry, 50, 54, 63, 123–24, 236–37
Olin Foundation, 55, 456
1 percent:
  capital gains and, 372
  definition of, liii
  economic framework's favoring of, xxv, li, liii, 39, 43, 77, 84, 114, 146, 164–65, 178, 216, 218, 238, 256, 299, 305, 306–7, 330, 442, 449

economic security of, xxviii, 31
globalization's benefits to, 77, 80, 178
idea-shaping by, xxv, 161, 168, 172, 183–233, 265, 295, 296, 321, 359–60
income of, xi, xxxii, 2–3, 5, 9–10, 31, 66, 90–91, 107, 269, 334, 376, 379–80, 382, 383, 402, 422, 426
inequality and, xx
legal framework's favoring of, 235, 238, 253, 258, 342
media's control by, 161, 168, 358
political power of, xv, xxxiii, xlix, 39, 84, 105, 108, 112, 126, 148, 149–50, 151, 161, 164–67, 168, 172, 173, 183, 238–39, 335, 357, 442, 445
public perception of, 25–26, 183, 193, 199, 454
reform aimed at, 36, 336–43
rent seeking by, xv, xvii, xxxiii, 40, 47, 52–53, 96
saving by, 107, 110, 280, 345
small government preference of, 117
social contract violation by, xlvi–xlvii
social contributions of, 33, 51, 97–98, 120, 334
social norms' shaping by, 66
taxation of, xxviii, xxxi–xxxii, 6, 47, 53, 77, 89–92, 95, 96, 105, 106, 108, 109–10, 142, 143, 144, 145, 173, 178, 199, 209, 260, 261, 264, 266, 268–69, 273, 274, 277, 279, 281, 282, 283, 321, 343, 345, 376, 397, 426, 437, 457, 485, 498
value change in, 360
wealth of, 2–3, 9–10, 31, 40, 47, 70, 90–91, 100, 105, 208–9, 377
see also corporations; financial sector
Open Market Committee, U.S. Federal Reserve, 315
Organization for Economic Cooperation and Development (OECD), 20, 232
Orshansky, Mollie, 389
Ostrom, Elinor, 411
overdrafts, 243, 468

Pager, Devah, 87
Papua New Guinea, 231
patents, 54, 253–54, 403, 474–75
    see also intellectual property
pension funds, 285
Personal Responsibility and Work
    Opportunity Reconciliation Act, 21
Pew Foundation, 25
pharmaceutical industry:
    government munificence toward, 50,
    61, 121, 263, 264, 281, 286, 340,
    346
    research in, 121
    see also health industry
Philippines, 27
Pierson, Paul, lv
Piketty, Thomas, lv, 143
Pinochet, Augusto, 323
polarization, 10–11
Polarized America (McCarty, Poole, and
    Rosenthal), lvi
police lineups, 186
police states, 157
politics, U.S.:
    cognitive capture in, 202
    corporate influence in, 43, 46, 51,
    58–59, 60–61, 62, 64, 76, 77, 119,
    124, 126, 138, 165–66, 169, 171,
    251, 253, 357–58, 406, 407, 413,
    414, 430, 445
    distributive consequences of, 39, 66,
    72, 299, 347, 349, 411
    economy's linkage with, xxxix–xl, l–li,
    lvi, 42, 48, 58–59, 66, 73–74, 82,
    112, 149, 165, 169, 173, 189, 217,
    333, 359, 361, 442
    idea-shaping in, xxv, 161, 172, 185,
    187, 189–90, 191–95, 200–203,
    204–5, 208–15, 219, 225, 231,
    233, 357
    legal consequences of, 238–39
    media's role in, 161, 168, 170, 200,
    204, 358
    reform of, 169–70, 335, 357–59
    regulatory capture in, 59–60,
    311–13, 317, 318, 331
    societal factors in, 80–81

unfairness in, xv, xxxviii–xxxiv, xxxix,
    xli, xlix–li, 39–40, 48, 51, 104–5,
    126–27, 143, 149–50, 151, 159,
    161, 164–67, 168–69, 171, 173,
    180, 183, 238–39, 245, 250–51,
    253, 334, 357, 358, 406, 413, 414,
    430, 442, 444–45
    voting in, 150–51, 162–64, 167, 168,
    169, 172, 358, 360, 414, 438, 443,
    444, 445–46, 450
    see also democracy, U.S.; government,
    U.S.
pollution, 236, 266–67, 269, 281
    see also environment
Poole, Keith T., lvi
poor:
    assistance to, xxx, xl, 36, 282, 343
    banks' exploitation of, xlvii, 46, 50, 73,
    88, 118, 193, 246–47, 252, 340, 468
    cognitive resources of, 129
    crime and, 18–19
    disenfranchisement of, xxii
    economic insecurity of, xlvii, 15–17,
    29, 33, 128–29
    economic mobility of, 4, 22–24, 117,
    146
    education of, xxx, 24–25, 38, 49, 94,
    118, 128
    environmental conditions of, 230, 393
    food needs of, 20, 128, 389–90
    globalization's effect on, 79–80
    health care of, 17, 38, 49, 87, 93,
    345, 449
    homeownership by, 95, 134, 190,
    197, 214–15, 279–80
    income of, xi–xii, xxxii, 5, 10, 11–12,
    17, 20, 31, 79–80, 90, 300, 379,
    380, 381, 383, 422, 487
    inflation's effect on, 326–27
    political disenfranchisement of, 160,
    164, 167, 168, 169
    and productivity, xx
    public spending's effect on, 2, 12–13,
    17, 18, 20–21, 32, 38, 80, 93, 347
    saving by, 280, 345
    segregation of, 94–95
    taxation of, xix, 92–93, 110, 273

poor (*continued*)
  unfair policies toward, xlv, liii
  unfavorable view of, xviii–xix, 32, 33,
    193, 200, 215, 287, 397–98
  wealth sources of, 3–4, 10, 16, 88,
    103, 209, 214–15
  see also United States, poverty in
Portugal, xxv, 317
  financial crisis in, 290, 319
poverty gap, 20
poverty trap, 25
predatory lending, xx, xxvi, xlvii, 46, 50,
    73, 88, 113, 149, 155, 239–41,
    242–43, 247, 252–53, 300, 308,
    312, 338, 400, 424, 468
  see also foreclosures
privatization, 52, 221–23, 284, 285,
    403, 461, 462
Progressive Era, xxxiv, xlii
Prokhorov, Aleksandr, 401
property rights, 237, 243, 247, 248,
    249, 412, 466
protectionism, 348
psychology, idea-shaping and, 184,
    186–203
public goods, *see* investment, public
public schools, 94
  tuition and, 366–67

quotas, 49

racism, 199
  see also discrimination
railroads, 40, 52
Rakoff, Judge, 256–57
ratings agencies, 240, 272, 275
Reagan, Ronald, xxxi–xxxii, 6, 81, 89,
    142, 143, 220, 277, 308
real estate bubble, *see* economy, U.S.,
    bubbles in; Spain
realpolitik, 373
Reardon, Sean, xv, 94
recession of 1991, 108
recession of 2001, 306
recession of 2012, 276
regulatory capture, 59–60, 311–13,
    317, 318, 331

Reich, Robert, 224
Renaissance, 37
Rent-a-Center, 400
rent seeking, 35, 104, 119–27, 133–34,
    144, 176, 181, 208, 220, 221, 262,
    263, 274, 285–86, 334, 336, 338,
    340, 346, 370, 418, 465
  competition in, 122
  consumer exploitation and, 122–23,
    194, 340
  defined, 39–41
  and economic growth, 49, 125
  forms of, 45–46, 48–49, 50
  inequality and, 39–41, 47, 49, 96,
    133, 216, 266
  international, xxix
  in legal system, 53, 255, 342
  monopolies and, xv, 48, 50, 52, 53–59,
    119, 121, 176, 266, 338–39, 343
  from natural resources, 49, 61–62,
    123, 340–41
  participants in, 51, 403
  remedies for, 134, 337–43
  resource waste in, 119, 120, 124, 125
  taxes on, 49, 144, 266–68, 269, 343,
    499
  wealthy and, xv, xvii, xxxiii
Republic, Lost (Lessig), lvi
Republican Party, U.S., xxxv, 81, 159,
    163, 259, 446, 450, 454
Research in Motion, 254
resources:
  in GDP calculation, 123–24, 231
  government assignment of, 38, 40,
    49, 61–62, 268, 269–70, 281, 340,
    401, 402
  preservation of, 100, 125, 354, 355,
    411
  taxes on, 49, 266
  see also environment
retention bonuses, 99
retirement:
  age for, 285
  choices about, 187–88
  saving for, 15–16, 187–88, 222, 280,
    285, 305
  see also Social Security

retirement benefits, 15–16
Right:
    economic ideas of, liii, 31–33, 55,
        133, 134, 135, 142, 144, 145, 190,
        194, 197, 202, 204, 209, 219, 266,
        271–72, 275–77, 278–79, 282,
        283–84, 287–88, 296, 343, 354,
        369, 373, 397–98, 399, 452
    legal reform agenda of, 342
RIM, 254
risk aversion, 114
risk markets, 42, 135
RMBS, 466–67
Roaring Twenties, xxxiv
robo-signing, 248, 250
Rockefeller, John D., 52, 54
Rodrik, Dani, 175
Romney, Mitt, xviii–xix, xx–xxi, 33, 143,
        370
    election loss of, xxxv
    "47% of Americans" quote by, xviii,
        xxii, 370
    social spending and, xviii–xix
Roosevelt, Franklin Delano, xxxv, 111, 290
Roosevelt, Theodore, 54
Rosenthal, Howard, lvi
Rubin, Bob, 225
rule of law erosion, 234–58
Russia, 52, 154, 250, 402
    bank bailout in, 214
    life expectancy in, xiii–xiv
    see also Soviet Union
Ryan, Paul, 145, 259, 286

Saez, Emmanuel, lv, 143
sales tax, 92
Samsung, 254
Sarkozy, Nicolas, 232
Saudi Arabia, 350
savings:
    household, 1, 16–17, 49, 88, 89, 107,
        292, 305, 420, 481, 485
    of poor, 280, 345
    retirement, 15–16, 187–88, 222,
        280, 305, 420
    of wealthy, 107, 110, 280, 345
Savings and Loan Crisis, 149, 249

Scandinavia, 219, 329, 358
scarcity, 37–38
Schmittberger, Rolf, 158
Schneiderman, Eric, 473
school lunch programs, 93, 128
schools:
    for-profit, xx, 94, 244–45, 252, 344,
        411, 469, 470
    public, 94, 366
    tuition and, 366–67
Schwarze, Bernd, 158
science, 50–51, 97–98, 116, 125, 139,
        176, 254, 330
Scotland, 232
Securities and Exchange Commission
        (SEC), 59, 138, 149, 255–57
Senate, U.S., 309
    Banking Committee of, 313, 407
    see also Congress, U.S.; House of
        Representatives, U.S.
Shafir, Eldar, 128
Shelby, Richard, 407
Sherman Anti-Trust Act, 404
Shiller, Robert, 328
Shockley, William, 51
Simpson, Alan K., 259
Singapore, 24, 176
slavery, 195–96, 464–65
Slim, Carlos, 52, 462
Smith, Adam, 41–42, 43, 132, 399,
        434, 460, 502
Sobel, Dava, 136
social capital, 153–54, 156, 157, 169
social Darwinism, 373
socialism, 204
social responsibility, 125, 140, 150–51,
        152
Social Security, xix, xxxiv, 21, 32, 93,
        220, 221, 222, 283–85, 287, 327,
        333, 347, 371, 391, 450, 481
Social Security Administration, 389
social spending, xxv, xxix, xxx
    effects of, 2, 7, 12–13, 17, 18,
        20–21, 32, 38, 80, 93, 96, 99, 105,
        135, 216, 347
    income distribution and, xxxii, 38, 96,
        99, 382

social spending (*continued*)
  Mitt Romney on, xviii–xix
  in resource-rich countries, 49
Soros, George, 190
Sotheby's, 457
South, black disenfranchisement in, 162, 465
South Africa, 29
Soviet Union, collapse of, 130, 154
  see also Russia
Spain, xxv, xxvii, xxxix, xlix, 267
  financial crisis in, xxiv–xxv, xxvii, 263, 274, 276, 319
Sprint, 55
Standard & Poor's, 240
Standard Oil Company, 52, 404
Stantcheva, Stefanie, 143
Stigler, George, 55
stimulus package, 264, 290–93, 296, 483, 484
  value of, 107
stock market, 3, 10, 15–16, 68, 206–8, 222, 305–6, 378, 398, 457, 485
stock options, 137, 138
Strauss-Kahn, Dominique, 114
student loans, x, 72, 118, 244–46, 252, 332, 339, 340, 344–45, 365, 366, 411, 429–30, 469
subprime crisis, xlvii, 2, 242, 253, 313, 317, 452, 468
  legal settlements of, 88
  profit-making in, 97
  see also foreclosures; predatory lending
subsidies, xxvi, xxx, 48, 50, 63–64, 80, 101, 123–24, 225–26, 236, 239, 267, 268, 270, 278, 371, 408, 465, 479
  to financial sector, xxvi, 278, 279, 300, 309, 490
  hidden, 48, 50, 101, 123–24, 216, 239, 267, 268, 270, 278, 279, 281, 300, 309, 340–42, 465, 490
  see also government, U.S., munificence of
Supreme Court, U.S., xiv, xxii, 165–66, 357, 404, 405, 444

Sweden, 463
  economic mobility in, 22
  financial crisis response in, 210–11, 458
  financial stability in, 276
  GDP of, 229
  inequality in, 28, 160
  labor in, 288
  tax system in, 28
Switzerland, 229

tariffs, 62–63, 77, 414
taxes:
  alternative minimum, 498
  on capital gains, xvi, xvii, xxxi, 89–90, 109, 110, 143, 265, 343, 420, 458, 478, 499
  corporate, xxviii, 77, 92, 119, 143, 178, 225, 268, 269, 277–79, 281, 338, 341, 343, 348, 354, 371, 379, 421–22
  economic growth and, 28, 105, 108, 110
  and economic stimulus, 271, 273, 276
  estate, 91, 96, 110, 208–10, 343, 458, 499
  on financial sector, 267–68, 269, 309, 310
  globalization and, 77, 79, 178, 348
  income distribution and, 38, 39, 90–91
  loopholes in, 53, 90, 91, 92, 93, 143, 264, 268, 269, 278, 341, 342–43
  market correction through, 42
  middle-class deductions in, 279–80, 480
  and national debt, 259, 476
  on natural resources, 49, 266
  on pollution, 266, 269, 281
  on poor, 92–93, 110, 273
  progressive, xvi, xxxi, xxxii, xxxiii, 6, 39, 133, 142–45, 178, 265, 273, 342–43, 479, 499
  Reagan's revision of, xxxi, 6, 89, 142, 277

regressive, 47, 92, 96, 99, 197, 260,
  268, 297, 314, 382
on rent seeking, 49, 144, 266–68,
  269, 343, 499
Right's view of, 266, 271–72
state, 92
on wealthy, xxviii, xxxi–xxxii, 6, 47,
  53, 77, 89–93, 96, 105, 106, 108,
  109–10, 142, 143, 145, 173, 178,
  199, 209, 260, 261, 264, 266,
  268–69, 273, 274, 277, 279, 281,
  282, 283, 321, 343, 345, 376, 397,
  426, 437, 457, 485, 498
Tea Party, xviii
technology:
  bubble in, 106, 108–9, 110, 111,
    265, 305, 495, 500
  economic impact of, 37–38, 99,
    100–101
  government investment in, 28, 116,
    144, 194, 218, 271, 334, 351,
    354
  idea-shaping and, 196
  labor demand and, 48, 67–70, 79,
    99, 100, 347, 351, 355, 426
  monopolies in, 52, 55, 56–58, 120
  and stock trading, 206–7
telecommunications:
  government auction of, 63
  monopolization in, 55, 121, 122, 123
  see also technology
TEPCO, 237
Thaler, Richard, 201
Thatcher, Margaret, 403
Thucydides, 37
Tingbergen, 495
T-Mobile, 55, 254
tobacco industry, xlviii, 54, 189, 201,
  450, 452–53
Tocqueville, Alexis de, 360–61
Townes, Charles, 51
Toxic Asset Relief Program (TARP),
  459
trade:
  agreements on, 175, 176–77,
    413–14, 415
  austerity and, 289

globalization of, xxxi, 76–80, 181,
  413–14, 415
imbalances in, 349–51, 501
Treasury bills, 222, 260, 272, 501
Treasury Department, U.S., 76, 307,
  316, 323, 448, 467
Tremonti, Giulio, 492
trickle-down economics, see economics,
  trickle-down
trust, 143, 151–58, 168, 169, 439
Turing, Alan, 51
Turkey, 27, 29

Uganda, 27
ultimatum game, 158
unemployment, xvi, xix, xxiv, xxvi, xl,
  xliv, 13–15, 16, 93, 111, 114, 224,
  260, 496
extent of, 1, 13–14, 19, 94, 385
macroeconomic policies affecting,
  47, 76, 78, 80, 103, 107, 289, 290,
  295, 296, 297, 298, 299, 300, 302,
  314, 325, 326–27, 328, 329, 479
in manufacturing, 67–68, 70–72,
  291–92, 356–57, 409
politcal importance of, xxxv
political importance of, 315
stimulus package's effect on, 291,
  295, 296
underreporting of, 13, 19, 372, 389
of youth, xxviii, xxxix, xlix, 15, 332
unemployment insurance, xix, xliv,
  13–14, 21, 93, 263, 264, 273,
  287, 303, 346, 371, 373, 385, 450,
  482, 486
Unequal Democracy: The Political
  Economy of the New Gilded Age
  (Bartel), lvi
Union Carbide, 237
unions, see labor unions
United Automobile Workers (UAW), 72
United Kingdom, xxiii–xxiv, 26, 162,
  267, 323
austerity in, 276, 290
economic mobility in, 22–23
financial crisis response in, 214, 460
privatization in, 221, 403, 461

United Nations Development Program
(UNDP), 27
United States:
alternative futures of, 362
average tax rate in, 90–91
battle of ideas in, 194, 197–99,
203–33
changing social patterns in, 18
class distinctions in, xlvi–xlvii, 25,
225, 373
consumption in, 16, 68, 106, 108,
111, 130–32, 229, 292, 293, 294,
306, 396–97, 481, 487
cost of living in, 464
crime in, 18–19
economic history of, 5–6, 7–8
economic mobility in, xliv–xlv, 4, 6,
22–24, 31, 117, 146, 185, 332,
334–35, 392
educational attainment in, 69
family stresses in, 12–13, 18, 33,
119, 132, 212
global influence of, xli, 172, 179–81,
195, 318, 347–48
globalization's effect in, 78, 79–80,
231
income inequality in, xxix, 2–3, 5,
9–10, 11–12, 27, 30, 31–34, 36,
38, 66–72, 89, 90, 96, 99–100,
101, 106, 108, 159, 192, 223, 230,
253, 292, 300, 302, 334, 375–77,
379–80, 381, 382, 383, 396–97,
418, 423, 426, 427
inequality cycle in, xxxix–xl, xli, xliv,
l–li, liii, 4, 22–23, 38, 96, 97, 103,
108–12, 114, 335
infant and maternal mortality in, 17,
386–87
international comparisons to, xxix,
27–29, 31, 65–66, 92, 121–22,
123, 229, 394, 463–64
labor force polarization in, 10–11, 70,
100, 167, 347
liberty in, 238
life expectancy in, xiii, 17, 386–87
lifetime inequality in, 32, 397
living standards in, xli, 17–19, 20, 30,

31, 32–33, 121, 123, 124, 229,
300, 333, 335
median income in, 27, 378, 380, 381,
383
neighborhood segregation in, 94–95
opportunity in, xliv–xlv, 3, 4, 22–25,
31, 93–96, 117–19, 134–35, 145,
146, 158, 159, 201, 332, 333, 336,
342, 344, 353, 359, 363
poverty in, 19–21, 32, 33, 47, 105,
380, 381, 389–91, 397, 422; see
also poor
value system of, xlv, xlvii–xlviii, li,
180, 234, 333, 360, 362, 373
wealth distribution in, 2–4, 8, 10,
16–17, 30, 31, 40, 47, 70, 88,
90–91, 92, 95, 100, 103, 114, 117,
134, 184–85, 209, 214, 215, 253,
345, 376–77, 485
see also economy, U.S.; government,
U.S.; politics, U.S.
Universal Declaration of Human Rights,
362, 411
uranium, 221
Uruguay Round Trade Agreement, 176
U.S. Enrichment Corporation (USEC),
221
Uzbekistan, 154

Vanity Fair, xxxix, lxiii
Venezuela, 49, 173
Verizon, 55, 254
Vietnam, 325
Volcker, Paul, 310, 400
voting, 150–51, 172, 360, 414, 445–46,
450
cost to, 150, 444
disenfranchisement in, 162–64, 167,
168, 169, 371, 438, 443
mandatory, 169, 358, 446

wages, xii, xvi, xxii, xxviii, 9, 11, 36, 41,
47, 49, 65, 66–72, 75, 76, 79, 81,
82, 84, 85, 86, 99, 100, 114, 288,
292, 295–96, 330, 370, 371, 416,
417, 426
cost of living adjustments to, 497

discrimination in, 85, 86
efficiency and, 127–30, 432–33
globalization's effect on, xxiv, 75, 77, 79, 347
Great Recession's effect on, 36, 71, 81, 84, 114, 290, 302–3, 332, 418, 486
inflation and, 326–27
minimum, 303, 380
public sector, 72, 410
societal factors in, 82, 84, 85, 86
see also incentive pay; inequality, income
Wagner Act, 81
Wallison, Peter J., 453
Wall Street Journal, 251
Walton family, 10
war, economic impact of, 126
Warren, Elizabeth, 241
Watson, James D., 51
wealth, dynamics of, 38, 345
wealth transfers, 40
welfare system, 21, 193
Wells Fargo, 88, 473
West, Cornel, xxi
Winner-Take-All Politics (Hacker and Pierson), lv

women:
discrimination against, 85, 86
income of, xii, 381, 418
in labor force, 18
life expectancy of, xiii
microcredit loans to, 246
words, 204–5
World Bank, poverty measure of, 20
World Trade Organization (WTO), 175
World War II, 128
World Wide Web Consortium, 401

Yahoo!, 254
youth:
financial sector's employment of, 120
poverty among, 21
social situation of, 18, 332, 387
unemployment among, xxviii, xxxix, xlix, 15, 332
voting by, 168, 446
see also student loans
Yunus, Muhammad, 246

zero-sum game paradigm, 41
Zuckerberg, Mark, 51